THE KID: *Ted Williams in San Diego*

Published by Rounder Books, an imprint of:

Rounder Records
1 Camp Street
Cambridge MA 02140

ISBN: 1-57940-094-9

Book design by the Ted Williams Design Group
Cover photos courtesy of May Williams

Nowlin, Bill, editor, 1945 -
The Kid: Ted Williams in San Diego

1. Ted Williams 1918-2002
2. Boston Red Sox (baseball team) - biography
3. Baseball - biography

First Edition
2004095901
796.357.092
[B]
ISBN 1-57940-094-9
Printed in Canada
9 8 7 6 5 4 3 2 1

THANKS TO:

Eric Abel

Barbara Adams

Bill Adams,
San Diego Hall
of Champions

Andy Aguinaldo

David Allen

Dee Allen

James Amidon

Ron Amidon

Ron Andreassi

Hildy Linn Angius

Todd Anton

Gabriel Arellanes

Tim Badillo

Dave Barber

Karma Barber

Tom Bast

Carlos Bauer

Leonard Bell

John Bolthouse

Ray Boone

Dan Boyle

Bob Boynton

Bob Breitbard,
San Diego Hall
of Champions

Steve Brown

Bill Caldwell

Wos Caldwell

George Calvi

Henry A. Campbell

Vic Cardell

Tom Carmody

Bob Carroll

Les Cassie

City of San Diego
Central Library

Jerry Coleman

Teresa Cordero
Contreras

Harrington "Kit"
Crissey

Frank Cushing

Cliff Dapper

Stephen Davis

Mike Delgado

Sarah V. Diaz

Bobby Doerr

Dennis Donley

Edward Donovan

Eric Enders

Ann Engle

Roger Engle

Roy Engle

Denny Fallon

Donald Fraim

David Gonzalez

Ruth Gonzalez

Alan Goodwin

Linda Goodwin

Catherine
Hanson-Tracy,
California State Library

Bob Henderson

Brian Interland

Autumn Durst Keltner

John Kerby,
San Diego Hall
of Champions

Jack Harshman

Mayer Hecht

Bob Henderson

Manuel Herrera

Terry Higgins

Jon Holcombe

Todd Hollenberg

John Holway

Mark Hull

Paul Iverson

Brian Interland

Frank Jazzo

Swede Jensen

Steve Jurgensmeyer

Joseph Kahn

Madge Kho

Al Kidd,
San Diego Hall
of Champions

David Kinney

Herm Krabbenhoft

Rosalie Larson

Kathy Larwin

Tom Larwin

Geno Lucero

Brian Luscomb

Kimberly Mack

Connie Matthews

Dave McCarthy

Lawrence McCray

Alan McCutcheon

George McDonald

Sally Caldwell
McDonell

Ron Menchine

Elizabeth Meyer

Paul Milligan

Leigh Montville

Mount Vernon Public
Library

Darren Munk

George Myatt

Frank Myers

Joe Naiman

Steve Netsky

Anna Newton

Rob Neyer

Bill Nowlin

Dell Oliver

Hank Ondler

Kathleen Osowski

Marie Palmer-Jeffery,
San Diego Hall
of Champions

John Panter, San Diego
Historical Society

Edna Pearl

Ernest Ponce

Mary Ponce

Wayne Ponce

Jim Prime

Alice Psaute

Jordan Ramin

Mary Redding

Fred O. Rodgers

David Ronquillo

Mark Rucker

Armando Ruiz

Manuel Ruiz Venzor

Scott Saftler

San Diego SABR
Baseball Research
Center

San Diego State
University Library

Santa Monica Public
Library

Amby Schindler

Morris "Moose"
Siraton

Bill Skelley

Mel Skelley

Esther Slagle

Steve Sloan,
San Diego Hall
of Champions

James D. Smith III

Alan Storton

Andy Strasberg

Maureen Surratt

Bill Swank

Ralph Thompson

Stew Thornley

Chris Travers,
San Diego
Historical Society

Bud Tuttle

Chaz Venzor

Danny Venzor

Frank Venzor

Joe Villarino

Judi Vista

G. Jay Walker

Max West

Rich Westcott

Russ White

Claudia Williams

Dan Williams Jr.

Jan Williams

Sam Williams

Ted Williams

Ted Williams
(nephew)

Robert Wilson

Dr. Howard Winet

Phil Wood

Mary Woodall,
San Diego Hall
of Champions

Wilbert Wylie

John Zant,
Santa Barbara
Press-News

THE KID:

Ted Williams in San Diego

edited by
Bill Nowlin

ROUNDER BOOKS

THE KID: TED WILLIAMS IN SAN DIEGO

Ted waiting to hit with San Diego Padres.

PREFACE

There are only a handful of people who are recognized by a nickname alone. What makes Ted Williams unique is that he was known not just by one nickname, but by many. Any casual baseball fan knows who "The Kid" was, or "The Splendid Splinter" or "Teddy Ballgame." The same goes for "Number 9" or "The Thumper" or "TSW." He also bore the handle "Terrible Ted" and any number of other names, though one he said he liked as much as any other was "A Marine."

No other athlete so dominated San Diego sports history as Williams. It really is not too surprising that the San Diego Chapter of the Society for American Baseball Research (SABR) selected Ted Williams in 1991 as the name for our Chapter. Ted approved our action and wrote us in June of that year saying, "this is indeed an honor and I am certainly happy to give consent."

San Diego and Ted Williams are closely linked. He was born here and spent his youth in San Diego. While in his adult years he lived in the northeast and in Florida, Ted came back more and more often in latter years to visit with hometown friends. In a September 1989 interview by Chapter member James D. Smith III, Williams was quoted saying that "...San Diego was the nicest little town in the world. How the hell was I to know it was the nicest town in the world? I'd never been anyplace."

For 70 years – seven decades – Williams remained a prominent name on San Diego's local scene. He first made the newspapers as a star ballplayer for San Diego's Herbert Hoover High School, which he attended from 1934 to 1937. He also made a name for himself on local sandlots, active in amateur and semi-pro leagues throughout his teen years. In 1936, he was signed to the first San Diego Padres, the Pacific Coast League team that had its maiden season that very year. Ted was signed in June, before he graduated from Hoover, and played the remainder of the season for the Padres. He played the full 1937 season for his hometown team and began to show signs of the hitting prowess that blossomed into a Hall of Fame career with the Boston Red Sox. While with the Sox, and later as a manager, sportsman, businessman and military hero, Williams was always claimed by San Diego as its own. And he welcomed that connection.

Shortly after Williams' death in July 2002, our Chapter began to craft a celebration of his life, with particular focus on his San Diego roots. Our efforts resulted in a day of tribute to Ted, which we called "A Celebration of Ted Williams." It was held on Saturday, March 29, 2003 at the San Diego Hall of Champions... a perfect venue for the event, also linking Ted with Hoover High School pal Bob Breitbard, Founder and President Emeritus of the Hall. Featured along with the symposium was a public exhibit of many rare Ted Williams items from Bob's personal collection and from Hoover's Dennis Donley, and SABR members Denny Fallon and Bill Swank, memorabilia which spanned Ted's baseball career and multi-faceted life.

The daylong program for the March 29th symposium included seven sessions which focused on his San Diego years, family, military, his baseball camp, and minor league seasons is presented in an appendix.

Coincident with the symposium, our Chapter also forged a coast-to-coast partnership with Bill Nowlin. Without his energy and many hours of research and editing, this book could never have been completed. Bill's passion went beyond the ordinary and opened up an understanding of Ted based upon numerous interviews with family members and relatives. Some of these members participated in our March event, and nephew Ted Williams provided the cover art for our program, as he has for this book.

On another page we thank all of the many others who have contributed their time and resources in varied ways to write this story of Ted's roots and affection for San Diego. Without their research efforts many of these stories would never have been written and would have likely been lost. They are stories that provide an interesting connection to his life and personality, and a link with his many San Diego friends and relatives.

Ted's final visits to San Diego were on a regular basis and mainly were hosted by Bob Breitbard. Williams was here in 2001 but hospitalized the entire time. His last public visit was in February 2000 when he appeared at the Hall of Champions for a luncheon emceed by Dick Enberg. Introducing Ted, Enberg talked about heroes. He said, "...to meet them, and know them, and be rewarded by the fact that they're even more than we dream to be. That's the ultimate test that they're even better when you meet them in person than you hope they may be." Ted was a true hero, and he was quite a man and we may never see his like again.

We hope that you enjoy reading about "The Kid from San Diego" as much we have enjoyed doing the research and writing.

Thomas F. Larwin
President
San Diego Ted Williams SABR Chapter
February 2004

PLAYING BASEBALL IN SAN DIEGO:
"THE KID"...WHEN HE WAS A KID
by Tom Larwin

SAN DIEGO IN THE 1930s

In 1918, the year in which Ted Williams was born, the city of San Diego's population was about 68,000... with another 30,000 or so in the county area around the city. Twenty years later, as he was preparing to leave San Diego for Minneapolis, the city of San Diego had grown to roughly 190,000 residents while the entire county had a population of 275,000.

Ted's teen-age years found a San Diego that had 21 theaters with a seating capacity of 24,250, 149 hotels with 8,840 rooms, and an electric street railway network of 101 miles of single track operation. Freeways were not yet discovered and the busiest traffic location was between 6th and 10th Avenues along University Avenue with 48,000 vehicles daily.

For San Diego and the country, the 1930s were a time for the Great Depression. Nineteen thirty six was only the mid-point, and the contrast with today is significant. Take a headline in the February 10, 1936 *San Diego Evening Tribune* which pointed out that the highest paid major league baseball "figure" was Joe McCarthy, manager, New York Yankees, at $35,000.

Lane Field, on the waterfront in downtown San Diego.

Other comparisons of the day were some of the prices in the ads of April 1936, like the one from the Globe Furniture Co. at 12th and Broadway for a Gibson refrigerator for $79.50, no cash down, and three years to pay. At the Thearle Music Co., 640 Broadway, one could buy a mahogany Chickering Piano for $450. Double S&H stamps were available Wednesdays at Walker's located at 59th and Broadway. A far cry from today's cigarette ads, the ad from Luckies noted that "each puff less acid, a light smoke of rich, ripe bodied tobacco." At the El Cortez Hotel, one could try a cocktail room "repast" for 65¢.

The film industry was getting rolling and big name movie stars featured in April 1936 movies at local theatres included:

"*The Prisoner of Shark Island*" at the Fox Theater, starring Warner Baxter

"*Petrified Forest*" at the Orpheum, starring Leslie Howard and Bette Davis

"*These Three*" at the Spreckels, starring Miriam Hopkins, Merle Oberon, Joel McCrea, Ann Southern and Lloyd Nolan

"*Modern Times*" at the Seville in Chula Vista, starring Charles Chaplin

An editorial in the *San Diego Evening Tribune* was titled "A Dictator's Victory," and covered the 99 percent vote in support for Adolf Hitler in Germany. Given that there was only one choice on the ballot and it could only be voted as a "yes," the editorial noted that the Nazi election was "merely a gesture, typical of a dictator."

Good news was on the horizon, too! The March 31st *San Diego Sun* had an article headlining "Sally Rand to Dance at Expo." Also, Alf Landon, Governor of Kansas was to visit San Diego on May 17th. On the sour side, Bruno Richard Hauptmann (condemned kidnapper and alleged murderer of Charles Lindbergh Jr.) was about to be executed.

By the 1930s Sam and May Williams had settled down at their home at 4121 Utah Street in the North Park neighborhood of San Diego. Between 1916 and 1923 they had lived in four different San Diego locations, and moved into their Utah Street home in 1924. While living at this location Sam Williams had a photography shop at 820 5th Avenue in downtown San Diego. May was working full-time with The Salvation Army.

Professional baseball had not arrived in San Diego when the Williams family moved into their Utah Street home. However, interest was brewing in the community. By late 1935 almost daily reports were in the local news about one minor league team or another rumored to be moving to San Diego.

Finally, in early 1936 news was confirmed that the Hollywood Pacific Coast League team was going to move to San Diego for the upcoming season. Was San Diego excited? Listen to the enthusiasm expressed in this March 1936 editorial from the *San Diego Evening Tribune*:

The Home Team Wins

Judging from the enthusiasm of the crowd that attended the opening of the Coast League season here yesterday, professional baseball is one of the attractions San Diego has been waiting for. The Padres' victory over Seattle, of course, goes a long way toward sustaining the enthusiasm, but that feature isn't as important as the fact that the team has the full support of the city.

Baseball has been called a good barometer of business conditions. Heavy attendance indicates not merely a surplus of money to be spent for amusement, but it further indicates that men and women can relax and dismiss business while enjoying the sunshine and the clean sport of the diamond. As long as baseball is popular, as long as businessmen can toss off their cares and become excited over a stolen base or a long throw from center, the solution of the more weighty problems of the day will remain in pretty safe hands.

The opening of the season is an occasion for mutual congratulations, for the excellence of Bill Lane's team is matched by the excellence of the field and the enthusiasm of those who wish him well. Every day's crowds probably will not always match that of the premiere skirmish, but Mr. Lane was given ample evidence yesterday that his efforts to put the city on the baseball map will not be single handed. The "gate" always important in the perpetuation of sports events as well as theatrical ventures, shows no indication of slumping as long as the Padres maintain even a semblance of the brilliant showing they made yesterday.

San Diego has needed professional baseball enthusiasm for a long time. The friendship, the relaxation and the keen civic interest that is aroused by a crack team of go-getters often leads to a new spirit of enthusiasm that reflects upon the community in numerous ways. The advertising value of a team of winners, whether in baseball or other ventures, cannot be measured in dollars and cents. It is one of those things that goes on and on, building up from year to year.

San Diego baseball fans, and others as well, congratulate Mr. Lane upon the team he has assembled. The city showed its enthusiasm yesterday, an enthusiasm that is bound to be reflected throughout the community. With home town support, an excellent playing field and an organization spreading the message of San Diego all up and down the coast, it is an investment that should and will bring heavy dividends to all concerned.

TED GETS HIS START

Up until this time, even without a professional team in San Diego, baseball was a very active sport in the community. Because of the year-round climate offered in San Diego, baseball could be played all 12 months of the year, and it was. The three major daily newspapers covered many of the games resulting in a rich body of baseball information from area leagues, but also from semi-pro matches and touring professional teams. As a relatively small city there was significant local news coverage of high school and youth sports, too. In much of the coverage box scores were provided.

Ted Williams, Hoover High.

As a result, there is a large amount of data available that allows one to view Ted Williams' pre-professional career, beginning in the spring of 1934, when he was turning 16, leading through January 1938, when he already had nearly two full seasons under his belt as a member of the Pacific Coast League (PCL) San Diego Padres.

During the period of 1934-1938, box scores and/or game summaries were found of 99 games involving Williams in published newspaper accounts of the day. During these years in the local city leagues and high school baseball he more often than not pitched but mostly played outfield. Several games found him at first base, and one time even at shortstop in a March 14, 1936 high school game.

Williams' high school career included three seasons, 1934-36, at Herbert Hoover High School in what was then considered to be the eastern edge of San Diego's urban area. In his first year he participated mainly as a reserve, but then became a regular for his junior and senior years. Over

Ted's three seasons at Hoover High he increasingly became recognized as the team's star player and was often mentioned in game summaries, sometimes in the headlines, and a few times in photos of him individually and with his various teams.

Hoover also was a fairly new school when Williams entered, and it quickly developed a rivalry with the older, centrally located San Diego High. Ted Steinmann, the *San Diego Union* Sports Editor at the time, noted in his October 14, 1934 column that Hoover had made "a lot of progress in the four years since the doors of the school, still 'new' as schools go, first were opened to receive students." He was particularly impressed with the "athletic plant" constructed for the new school, and he predicted that Hoover would soon rival San Diego High in sports.

Other sections of this report cover Ted's baseball years at Hoover High in some detail; here the attention is on the baseball Williams played during those same years in the various independent games, and city and county leagues. Of the 99 game accounts that were uncovered, 57 were from his play in these other leagues.

While based upon incomplete data, Ted's San Diego local and semi-pro record between 1934 and 1938 included 59 recorded games and a .349 batting average and 7 home runs. He also compiled a 10-5 pitching record and 123 strikeouts in 17 games.

BREAKING IN, JULY 1934 – FEBRUARY 1935

American Legion Junior Baseball Tournament, July – August 1934, Padre Serra Post Team

Fresh from the high school championship series in Los Angeles' Wrigley Field, most of Hoover's baseball team formed the basis for an American Legion team to represent the Padre Serra Post. The region's other team was the Fighting Bob Evans Post, made up mostly of players from the rival San Diego High team. The Fighting Bob team was also coached by the San Diego High coach, Mike Morrow. The Padre Serra team was coached by the St. Augustine School for Boys' former athletic head, Herb Corriere. The June 24, 1934 *San Diego Union* reported that the team was still welcoming "aspirants" to sign up.

By July 4th the squad had been selected by Coach Corriere and Ted Williams was listed as a pitcher, but also slated for outfield duty as one of the "team's leading hitters." Friends Les Cassie and Roy Engle were both on the team, listed as one of the shortstops and catchers, respectively.

The series began with a local showdown with the Fighting Bobs on July 10, 1934 at the Golden Hill playground, featuring a two-out-of-three format, with the winning team taking the county title and advancing to the playoffs in San Bernardino. The next day's headline told the story: "Padre Serra Legion Juniors Upset Fighting Bob, 12 to 5." Williams pitched the entire nine innings allowing 6 hits and striking out 6. He also batted fourth in the line-up and went 1-5. Engle got a third of the team's nine hits. Playing second base for the Bobs was future Hoover teammate Joe Villarino, who was shut down by Williams, going 0-for-4.

The second game was played on July 12. A new coach was with the team, Carleton Bunce, replacing Corriere because of family illness. In this game Williams was to handle center field duties.

The Bobs got off to a flying start with a 6-0 lead in the first inning before the Serra team came up to bat. Starter "Red" Watters was relieved after that inning and replaced by Tommy Johnson who held the Bobs to no runs the rest of the game. Fortunately for the Padres, as they were referred to in various accounts, this pitching was sufficient as they came back for a 7-6 victory. It was lanky Ted Williams who did the "damaging hitting" according to the *Union* article. He drove in one run in the first with a single, and in the fifth he opened the frame with a home run over the right field fence. Then in the sixth he came up with Engle on second base and singled him home with what turned out to be the winning run.

After the wins, the Padre Serra team practiced against several opponents while getting ready for the tournament finals. Corriere was still tending to family matters, so Mike Morrow took over for this game. He was successful, too, winning the first game against San Bernardino on July 23, 16-7. Williams pitched the whole game and gave up eight hits. Roy Engle helped the cause by hitting a home run.

The team returned to San Diego for the next game in the series on July 24. The Padre Serra team continued its winning ways routing the San Bernardino team, 16-3. Williams played center field and went 0-1 but scored three runs, indicating he got a fair share of the eight walks given up to the Serra team. This win gave the team the Fifth Area Championship. Next was the Fourth Area Championship, to be decided by a three-game set against the Leonard Wood Post. The first game was to be at San Diego's Golden Hill playground, with the next two, if necessary, in Los Angeles.

The *Union* hyped the championship series with a team photograph indicating that the "Fifth Area Legion Champs Seek Additional Honors." In the back row, Williams was depicted in his first published baseball photograph, one which was followed by thousands more over his career. Catcher Roy Engle was shown at bat in an inset.

The series started on August 1 and Williams lost a tight 1-0 game. The *Union*'s article started off with "in a spectacular pitching duel between two 16-year old hurlers..." For the Serra team it was Ted Williams, "lanky right-handed pitcher" who gave up seven hits and struck out five. But they were shut down with only three hits, one by Williams.

The Serra team's luck ran out in Los Angeles at Wrigley Field on August 2 when they gave up eight runs in the first inning and could not come back, losing 10-1 to the Leonard Wood Post team. This was the same Wrigley Field where the Hoover team had lost to Cathedral High on June 8, just two months back. Williams started in the outfield and came in to pitch in relief but by then it was too late.

In the six games, Ted was 5-for-12 (one game account lacked an accompanying box score), with a home run, and went 2-1 on the mound.

August 1934 – February 1935
County Leagues, San Diego Market Team

Within a few weeks after the August 2 loss in Wrigley Field Williams was playing for the San Diego Market team. In three independent games in mid- to late-August 1934 he played the outfield and went 4-for-11.

In September the San Diego County Baseball Managers' Association program started and Ted continued with the Market team. On September 16, playing right field, he went 3-for-4 with a home run and scored twice in a 6-4 win.

The Winter County League started in November and Ted remained with the San Diego Market ballclub. Most of these games he pitched and did reasonably well. On December 2, he came in to relieve and was the winning pitcher striking out 10 in an 8-7 win. He also contributed offensively, going 3-for-3 including a double and triple against Ortiz Chevrolet. The Market team was 2-2 going into mid-December when rain washed our several weeks of play. They lost 9-4 on December 23 to the Mission Stars as Williams again pitched in relief.

The new year, 1935, brought a 4-3 win against Pacific Beach on January 13, as Ted played right field and went 2-for-3, with a double. The fortunes reversed the next weekend when Winter's Bakery beat Ted and the Market nine, 11-2. Ted pitched the whole game and took the loss, striking out seven and allowing 10 hits. He went 0-for-3 this day, too.

On January 27 he came back and pitched the Market team to a 5-4 win against National City. Ted struck out six and gave up 10 hits again, but pitched well enough to keep his team in the game. Down 4-1 in the bottom of the seventh inning, they rallied and won. On February 3 he played first base against Neighborhood House, and went 1-for-3 in a losing cause, 4-3.

San Diego Market continued its losing ways on February 17 when they were outscored 7-2 by Cramer's Bakery. Batting clean-up, Williams played first base and went 1-for-4. That turned out to be his last game for the Winter League as washouts caused several games to be postponed. With incomplete statistics the records show Williams batted .318, going 7 for 22, and had a 2-2 pitching record.

February found Williams getting ready for his junior season at Hoover High. The February 10 *Union* noted that Hoover High had returning letterman and pitcher Ted Williams, along with Roy Engle as one of the catchers. The article pointed out that a promising recruit was Joe Villarino of "San Diego's noted baseball-playing family who is a candidate for the second sacker's job and is expected to have no trouble making the grade." The article reported that Coach Wofford "Wos" Caldwell had "little to rave about in the way of outfield material and was planning a shake-up with everyone getting a crack at a garden job." This was obviously a situation tailor-made for Ted Williams.

THE KID BECOMES A STAR, MAY 1935 – MARCH 1936

As Hoover's 1935 season wound up early, the May 26 *Union* promised a better campaign for Hoover High in 1936 when they would debut in the Bay League which included Long Beach, Woodrow Wilson, Compton, Inglewood, Redondo, Beverly hills, and San Pedro. The article noted that Coach Caldwell has "big Ted Williams" as a "ranking hurler."

Independent Game, May 1935, Central Team

On May 26, 1935, within days of the close of the Hoover High baseball season Ted was playing right field for the Central ballclub against local star pitcher Elmer Hill and the Cramer's Bakery team. Hill never quite made it big in the professional ranks, but was a well-known semi-pro player in San Diego in the 1920s and 1930s. Hill, with Rod Luscomb in center field for Cramer's, shut down the Central team 12-0 on three hits. Williams was 1-for-4 with the hit being a double. Rod Luscomb, Ted's mentor over the years at the North Park playground, played here against his protégé.

Local All-Star Game, June 1935, Walter Church Service Station

Next up was a local all-star affair matching the Metropolitan League high school all stars against an "aggregation" from Hoover High. It was reported in the June 3 *Union* that the game, scheduled for June 7, came about because of a dispute. "Travis Hatfield, local baseball promoter and sports goods salesman who was a pretty fair hurler in his day, and Wofford Caldwell, Hoover coach, were the participants in a mild argument which finally resulted in the game being booked." Hatfield was to coach the Metropolitan team consisting of players from the eight-team county league (players from these schools were on the squad: Sweetwater, Escondido, St. Augustine, Grossmont, Army and Navy, Oceanside, and La Jolla). The article pointed out that "lanky Ted Williams, Hoover pitching and slugging star, likely will hurl for the East San Diego team." The game also was to mark being the first night game in many months at Sports Field.

Within a few days of the game a "belated hitch" in plans caused the Walter Church Service Station team to be substituted for the Hoover all-stars. However, at least two Hoover players remained part of the Church team, including Ted Williams.

In what might have been the first time Ted Williams appeared in a commercial newspaper headline, the *San Diego Evening Tribune* game article of June 8, 1935 was headlined:

"Ted Williams Stars As Prep Nine Loses"

The article explained that Ted "had things practically his own way" striking out 14 batters and hitting two triples.

More Independent Games, June 1935, Cramer's Bakery and North Park Merchants

On June 16th, now playing for Cramer's Bakery side-by-side with Elmer Hill, Williams went 2-for-4 with a home run and a double. The game was deadlocked going into the 10th inning when Williams came to bat with two on. The June 17, 1935 article takes over: "… Williams, a free-swinging, left-handed batter, drove the ball clear out of the park to provide the winning runs" for Hill. Ted batted third while his mentor Luscomb batted behind him and played center field.

Cramer's Bakery's next opponents were the North Park Merchants on June 24, and now Ted was again playing against Cramer's, playing for North Park along with Rod Luscomb and his Hoover catcher Woody Helm. Again, Hill's team prevailed, winning 6-5. As North Park's right fielder, Ted was 1-for-1, batting clean-up in a losing cause. A week later, North Park faced Winter's Bakery and lost 2-0 on three hits; Ted got two of the three. On another diamond, Elmer Hill picked up a win for Cramer's.

American Legion Junior Baseball Tournament, July 1935, Padre Serra Post

Beginning on July 2nd the 1935 tournament in San Diego included three teams: Padre Serra, the 1934 area champion, Oceanside, and Post 6. Each team was scheduled for two games against one another. Williams, as in 1934 and with several of his Hoover teammates, was on the Padre Serra team.

Articles were repetitive in their description of Williams as "lanky." A *Union* article on July 3 went even further and indicated he was "lean" and lanky! It also mentioned that he had been suffering from a sore side and has not been doing much hurling. Padre Serra's first game was in Oceanside versus that city's team with the visitors coming away with a win, 9-3. Sure enough, it was the "lanky" Hoover right-hander on the mound, but not as the starter. He pitched 1+ innings of relief, but he proved to be "ineffective" even though he struck out three. Fortunately, an ineffective Ted Williams on the mound can still hit, and he went 2-for-4 including a triple.

Next up were the Post 6 team, made up of San Diego High players. Williams was slated to pitch against Bill Skelley. The *Union* on July 6th noted that it was their third match-up of the season and both Williams and Skelley were the star hurlers of their respective teams and whichever squad lost would have no cause for alibi as both were at full strength. The game, played on July 6th at Golden Hill, was won by Post 6, 9-7. Williams allowed seven hits and struck out 11 but was betrayed by four errors. Skelley, on the other hand, was effective and was able to stop the "slugging of such hitters as Williams..." Ted batted 0-for-2 but nevertheless got on base and scored two of his team's seven runs.

The July 10 *Union* seemingly gave some incentive to the Oceanside team when it suggested that the Padre team would hold back "lanky" right-hand star Ted Williams for the fray with Post 6 after this game. Do you suppose that teenage players read the sports pages back then?

The earliest photograph of Ted Williams in a baseball context, this photo shows Ted Williams (with a necktie, even) at he Ryan Confectionery Juniors team banquet. Amby Schindler told Bill Nowlin that Ryan ran a confectionery store a block from his home, and sponsored a team. "They played these so-called semi-pro games every Sunday, made up basically of high school graduates. Boys couldn't play on those teams if they were on the high school team, but when they graduated they had no place to go but to play these semi-pro games on Sunday, which were frequented by all the old retired men around town. The semi-pro teams were in existence long before Ted and I played on the junior team. Ryan Confectionery Juniors. We were kids, basically of junior high school age. We couldn't play on those teams when we went to high school. There were just 2 or 3 years that kids could play on those." *Interview with Amby Schindler, June 1, 2003*

The game was a run away with the Padre Serras winning 13-0 on 17 hits. Ted played left field and went 2-for-5, scoring two runs and stealing a base. On July 12, the Post 6 team beat Oceanside thus setting up a continuation of their "civil war" series with the Padres.

Down by one game, and to keep their tournament chances alive, the Padre Serra team had to win versus Post 6 on July 13 in a game scheduled for Central playground. And win they did, 10-0 with Ted Williams having a "field day." Williams allowed five hits and struck out 13, plus contributed a 2-for-3, and scored 3 runs.

The rubber match of the series was played on July 15. The Padres' chances for a championship dissipated with Post 6 scoring 6 runs in the third inning off starter Forrest Davidson. After six innings it was 9-3 and essentially over. Williams did get in for a few innings of relief but it was too late to do any good. His offensive stats for the day were 1-for-2 with a triple. For the series Williams batted .438 with seven hits and 9 runs scored. As a pitcher he was 1-1 with 29 strikeouts.

Summer City League, July 1935 – October 1935, Walter Church Service Station/Cardinals

The eight-team league got started in early July. In between American Legion matches against Post 6, the Walter Church Service Station team put Williams in right field on July 14. The Walter Church nine played Cramer's Bakery and its pitching star, Elmer Hill. Hill and company won once more, 6-4, and Williams went 1-for-4.

The July 21 match found the Church team going up against the San Diego Giants and posting a 10-1 win. Williams played right field and, homered along with friend and teammate, Rod Luscomb. The next game, on July 28, was with Winter's Bakery. This time Williams was shut down at the plate and went 0-for-4, but the Church team still prevailed, 5-1.

The next recorded game for Ted was on August 18 when they played El Cajon. This time Ted was on the mound and he won 6-2, striking out nine and allowing 11 hits. He was 1-for-3 for the game. Williams took the mound against Stratton Plasterers on August 25. He won for the second time in a row, giving up five hits in a 7-2 Church victory. On offense, he was 2-for-4 with 2 runs scored.

On September 1, Church's went up against their nemesis, Elmer Hill and Cramer's Bakery. Williams started and went five innings, leaving the mound for left field with a 1-1 tie. Both teams had six hits, but Hill struck out 15 and won 3-2. Ted was held hitless and went home with an 0-for-4 on the day. In between this game and their next one on September 8, the Church team changed their name to the Cardinals. It didn't help, as they lost 3-2 to the San Diego Giants. The Cardinals managed only four hits; right fielder Williams had a 1-for-3 day.

Going into the September 22 games the City Summer League standings showed Cramer's atop the list at 9-1 and Williams' Cardinals tied with two others for second place with a won-loss record of 6-5. On Sunday, September 22, the Cardinals upped their record to 7-5 and sole possession of second place with a win over Ocean Beach, 11-7. Williams the starting pitcher for the Cardinals; however, there was no box score to indicate his performance. In the season's last game on October 6th darkness forced a 1-1 tie in 10 innings with El Cajon. Both teams scored their lone runs in the ninth inning. Ted pitched in relief and allowed the single run in three innings. He went 2-for-4 and clubbed the tying home run in the bottom of the 9th to send the game into extra innings.

For the Summer League season Williams ended up with a .288 average and eight hits in 28 at bats, and two home runs. He also was the winning pitcher in two of the contests.

Chet Smith Benefit, October 1935, Bay City Liquor Store

On October 13, Ted played for the Bay City Liquor Store in a benefit game. No doubt, from Ted's own accounts, his mother must have been appalled to learn that he was playing for a Liquor Store given her job and commitment to The Salvation Army.

The benefit for Smith, a local player for Seattle in the PCL, was to raise some money for him after he was seriously injured in a recent auto accident. The BC team had two Coscararts on the team, Pete and Steve, plus Rod Luscomb. Unfortunately the opponents were Elmer Hill and the Cramer's Bakery group. Given credit in the local *Union* for "as sensational a brand of hurling seen here in many a day" Hill won 4-0 and struck out 12. Williams was in left and center field and went 0-for-2.

San Diego Blues Colored Team, December 1935, Cramer's Bakery

The Cramer team played the Blues in an exhibition on December 21. Ted was in left field and Hill did not pitch for the home team. He went 0 for 2 against Larry Taylor, Blues pitcher, who only parceled out four hits in the Blues' 4-1 win.

Cramer's took on the Blues again on January 18 in an exhibition with the "traveling colored club." Ted pitched the last seven innings of the game and was the winning pitcher in a 6-5 win.

Winter City League, December 1935 – March 1936, Cramer's Bakery

Elmer Hill was no longer a threat to Ted, as Williams teamed up with Hill on the Cramer's Bakery in December 1935. Playing left field and going 1-for-5 with a run scored in a 15-1 win against the San Diego Giants on December 8 must have made Ted feel good - being with a winning ballclub. New teammate Hill struck out 13 and gave up only three hits.

On December 15, Cramer's played Ted's former one-game team, the Bay City Liquor House. This time, however, Hill had lost his magic and the BC won 7-4 on seven hits. Playing left field, Ted had one of the 10 hits for Cramer's. Their next game was on December 22, a day after their loss to the St. Louis Blues, when they came up against El Cajon, the league leaders and lost 10-1. Williams played in left field and went 1-for-4 in the losing cause.

On the last day of 1935 Williams' Hoover High coach, Wofford Caldwell, appeared a prophet when he was quoted in Sports Editor Ted Steinmann's *Union* column about his players' interest in professional baseball coming to San Diego:

"I feel that organized baseball here would be a great advantage to the high schools. There are always a number of young fellows on our teams who hope to make baseball their profession, and the presence of a professional team here would give them more incentive. So, again, I say, 'We're all for it.'"

The new year's first week-end of games found Elmer Hill on the mound and Williams in left field January 5 for Cramer's going up against the Plasterers. Hill started the year with a 6-3 win and 12 strikeouts, allowing just three hits. Ted, for the year, was batting .000 after going 0-for-4!

Hill kept his win streak for the year alive, and "did one better" with a no-hit, no-run game on January 12 in beating Texas Liquor House 7-0. Ted was again left field and went 1-for-2 with a home run in the contest. The next game on January 19 followed their win against the St. Louis Blues the day before and was with league-leading El Cajon. Hill's magic touch was muted in a 3-2 loss, although he only gave up three hits. Left fielder Williams went 1-for-2.

On January 26, Cramer's played to a 12-12 tie in a game with Bay City Liquor called due to darkness after 10 innings. Hill had lost his magic touch, at least for one game, giving up all 12 runs and 15 hits while striking out 11. Williams went 3-for-5 with a double.

It was becoming increasingly clear that "lanky" was a common description for pitchers in San Diego. In the January 30, 1936, *Union* it was reported that Satchel Paige was apparently back in good graces once more with his teammates having ironed out some "difficulties." The article indicated that "the lanky, 6-foot 4-inch speedball pitcher, who startled fans with his blinding fast ones when he last showed here, is said to have had an outburst of temperament last week and deserted the Giants to play an exhibition in San Francisco."

After a week-end of rain, Cramer's suited up again on February 9 to play El Cajon and lost 4-3 as El Cajon scored once in both the eighth and ninth innings to overtake Cramer's. Pete Coscarart's single in the bottom of the ninth made a loser out of Hill and the Cramer team.

The March 1, 1936 *Union* reported that Western League batting champion Earl Brucker ended up as the Southern California circuit's leading batter at .378. Rod Luscomb had as many hits but with more at bats finished at .359. The article further gave credit to Joe Villarino who compiled the statistics as the official scorer.

Cramer's played on March 1 in an independent game versus the U.S.S. Omaha. El Cajon and Bay City Liquor were playing a contest to decide the winter league championship this day, too, which ended with Bay City winning. For Cramer's, Hill pitched a four-hitter in a game called after seven innings with the score 15-3 in the Bakery's favor. In left field, Williams batted clean-up and went 1 for 4.

In the meantime, the 1936 high school season was being kicked off. An article in the February 23, 1936 *Union* reported that Hoover's 1936 team was branded as a collection of the "most promising youngsters ever gathered together" at the school. Roy Engle was slated for the catcher position as soon as the basketball season ended. And, of course, there was returning letterman Ted Williams, "lanky" pitcher. He was still referred to as a lanky right-hander in the description below his photograph contained in the March 8 *Union*. The photo shows his pitching form and "getting over (a) fast, high one." Teammate and friend Engle was shown in a photo just below Ted's flipping off his catcher's mask. The label at the top of the two photos read "Cardinal Workhorses for Legion Title Tourney."

St. Louis Nine Offers Williams Tryout

Ted Williams, slim Herbert Hoover High pitcher, with whom local diamond fans are well acquainted, has received an offer to try out with the St. Louis Cardinals of the National league. Herb Benninghoven, managing the local Waltre Church nine as a Cardinal farm, tendered the offer and informed Williams his expenses would be taken care of should he care to make the trip east for the trial. Doubt was expressed that Ted would accept, however, since he still has one more year of high school and should he go into organized baseball he would be declared ineligible for further high school competition by the Southern California Interscholastic federation.

The Padres Beckon, June 1936

It was no secret around San Diego sports circles that Williams was sought after by professional baseball clubs. As early as August 6, 1935, the *Evening Tribune* reported with an article having a headline

"St. Louis Nine Offers Williams Tryout."

The article noted that "slim" Ted Williams, "with whom local diamond fans are well acquainted, has received an offer to try out with the St. Louis Cardinals." In August 1935 he was playing with the Walter Church team which was managed by Herb Benninghoven. The *Tribune* article indicated that team was a "Cardinal farm." Benninghoven offered Williams a trip east with his expenses taken care of but, with one more year of school left, doubts were raised in the article because Ted would be declared ineligible for further high school competition. Given what we learned later from Williams, there is a likelihood that his parents also objected.

The next public report on Williams turning pro was some 10 months later on June 1, 1936, when the *Tribune* had a small article with this headline

"San Diego Contract Offered Williams"

The article stated that "Ted Williams, who has pitched and batted Herbert Hoover High's baseball teams to many victories the last three years, will join the San Diego Padres this month, if his parents consent." Padres owner Bill Lane offered Williams a contract on May 30 and Ted said he would answer in a few days. The speculation in the article was that Williams' parents were in favor of his becoming a professional player. Several local coaches and "fans" reportedly recommended Williams to Lane. Apparently, too, Lane had his eye on the "lanky powerhouse" for some time, too.

Ted's first game as a Padre actually took place before he signed any pro contract. The Padres agreed to a benefit game with the Navy and Marine Corps Service All-Stars. Proceeds from the benefit game went to the Navy Relief Society. Bud Tuttle, son of the PCL president W. C. Tuttle, and a pitcher who had been rarely used by the Padres in their maiden season, was selected to get the call on the mound for San Diego. Manager Frank Shellenback announced that Ted Williams would be given an opportunity to display his talents in the exhibition. Grossmont High shortstop standout Bill (or Bob, according to the *Tribune*) Gray and another local player, Tom Downey, were also to be given a chance to play.

The game was played on June 22 and the Padres jumped to a 12-1 lead after seven innings in front of 4,000 fans, including some of the highest dignitaries in the Navy. As expected, once out in front with a seemingly safe margin, several young high school and sandlot players entered the game, including Williams in left field. Bud Tuttle ran out of gas, giving up 9 runs in the last two innings. In his only at bat, Williams singled in his first appearance in a professional baseball game box score, albeit an exhibition.

Within a few days another development occurred and that was the signing of local fireman Elmer Hill by the Padres. He was signed for a single game to be played on June 27 that was to include an athletic carnival mixed in with a regular baseball game. The *Union* on June 25 indicated that Hill was signed to "add novelty" to the game. Earl Keller, in his "Base Hits" column in the *Tribune* on June 26, reported that Hill was at Lane Field the day before pitching batting practice getting ready for the game.

In that day's column, Keller also said that "the way things look now Ted Williams may not get lined up with any team this year. The Padres, Yankees, and Cardinals still are dickering for him."

A day later, on June 27, both papers had the big news that Williams had signed with the Padres. The *Tribune*'s and *Union*'s headlines over short articles were as follows, respectively

"Ted Williams Signs With Padres; Will Be Used as Outfielder"

"Williams, Former Hoover Star, Signed by Padres as Outfielder"

Both newspapers also had a photo accompanying their article.

The *Union*'s article referred to Ted as "Herbert Hoover High School diamond hero and one of the best natural prospects developed in this district in some time." The *Tribune*, in their article, graduated Williams from lanky to "husky" in describing the former Herbert Hoover High right-handed pitcher.

He signed a contract on June 26 and was to be in uniform with the San Diego Padres on June 27. His hitting prowess already was noted in the article: "although Williams was a pitcher in high school, he will not be used in that capacity but will be used in the outfield in an effort to capitalize on his hitting ability." Influenced to sign with the Padres by his coach Wofford Caldwell, he was also offered contracts by the New York Yankees, St. Louis Cardinals, and the Los Angeles Angels.

Certain contract details were spelled out in the article that he will be with the Padres the remainder of the 1936 season and all of 1937. It was clear, however, that Ted was being signed to be a hitter and not a pitcher. Owner Lane expressed confidence that Williams would develop quickly and in Keller's June 27 column he already noted that Padre outfielder Cedric Durst was taking the 18-year-old outfielder "under his wing" and practicing chasing fly balls.

Ted's first official professional at-bat came in his first day as a Padre, June 27, 1936, the game that also included the carnival events. For the game there was to be "a lot of hocus-pocus and carnival spirit" mixed in.

First, there was a race between the Padres shortstop George Myatt and Sacramento's Joe Dobbins, their second baseman. Dobbins was a former track star and had been coached as a sprinter, hurdler, and all-around runner. It was billed as a 75-yard race with the winner receiving $50. A second event would have the catchers throwing balls into a barrel at second base. Finally, there was also to be a fungo hitting contest scheduled.

The *Union* on June 27 noted that "Elmer Hill, who has quite a local reputation as a hurler" was scheduled to pitch the first five innings of the game. Hill didn't get his five innings in as it turned out, with Williams getting his first professional at bat pinch hitting for him in the second inning up by a score of 3-2... and striking out. With that non-noteworthy at bat, Ted Williams' professional baseball career was launched.

And, by the way, Myatt won the race by six feet!

New Padre

TED WILLIAMS
This former Herbert Hoover High mound star finally signed a San Diego contract yesterday after much discussion with scouts of major league clubs. The Padres will use Williams in the outfield for his hitting strength. — (Tribune staff photo.)

PROFESSIONAL BASEBALL WITH THE SAN DIEGO PADRES, 1936 AND 1937

As promised by Padres Owner Bill Lane, Ted finished the 1936 season with the Padres and then played the entire 1937 season with the team. From his autobiography and researching the sports pages of the time Williams apparently played no organized baseball in either the 1936 or 1937 off-seasons. It is well-reported in various of Williams' biographies that he fished and hunted in the off-seasons, and that must have been what kept him active.

Earl Keller, of the *Evening Tribune*, in February 1938 reported that Ted had added weight "... to his lanky frame..." and did "...everything he could to strengthen himself, especially his wrists. When he wasn't hunting, he was working out at some playground. Then he went home to store away a home-cooked meal as put out by his mother, Mrs. Samuel Williams, who's cocksure her sun (sic) will make the grade in the major leagues."

Aside from the Padres in 1936 and 1937, Williams' next San Diego reported baseball appearance in the local parks came in January 1938 as he prepared to leave for Spring Training with the Boston Red Sox in Florida.

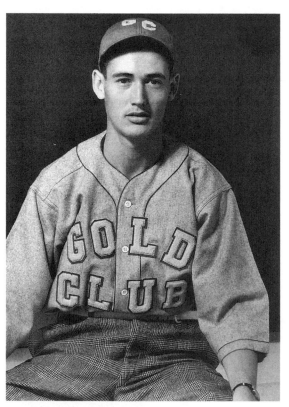

Ted Williams, Gold Club ballplayer.

TED'S LAST SEMI-PRO GAMES IN SAN DIEGO, JANUARY 1938

New Year's Day, 1938, found Ted's photo on the sports pages of both local newspapers. The one in the *Union* had the photo under the title "Major Leaguer" and he was wearing the uniform of the Gold Club which was to open a series with Farley's on January 1. He was dubbed a "San Diego Padre sensation" who was to go to the Boston Red Sox in 1938, at least according to this article. The series was to feature various major and minor league ballplayers from San Diego. But, already Williams was getting attention as "the slugging prodigy of the Padres who has been sold to the Boston Red Sox." Friend Rod Luscomb was another Gold Club outfielder, and familiar names were on both clubs like Bill Skelley, Joe, Pete and Steve Coscarart, Ernie Holman, Bill and Hal Starr, Ashley Joerndt, Herm Pillette, and Frankie Morehouse.

The Gold Club won the first contest played on New Year's Day 1938, 3-0, as Ted played left field and went 1-for-3, and scored a run. The second game of the series on January 2 went to Farley's, 10-4. Williams was in center field and went 2-for-4 with a double and a "terrific homer far over the center field fence, one of the lustiest blows in the history of the park."

The mythical city baseball championship was at stake the next week-end on January 9 between the two teams. Ted was again in center field but was held hitless as Pete Coscarart went 3-for-5 for the Farley's including a home run, as they beat the Gold Club 7-3.

Apparently the three-game series was not enough as the two teams scheduled a fourth game for January 16. This game also allowed local fans to honor Williams. Now that he was almost 20 years old, he had gone from "lanky" to "gangling" in the *Union*'s January 14 article. The *Tribune* had another slant on him. It called Williams the "gangling ex-siege gun of Hoover High." The articles indicated that many of his teammates and "admiring fans," including several merchants in the North Park district, asked permission to honor him with a "Ted Williams Day," in order to present him with several gifts as "tokens of their admiration."

This fourth match went to the Gold Club, 1-0, evening the series at two apiece. Coincidentally, Ted's big day was scripted from start to finish as he was prominent in the game with a "sensational" catch in center field and his lead-off single in the fourth inning which led to his scoring the game's only run off of Farley's "Old Folks" Pillette. However, Pillette was unable to match the no-hit performance thrown by "lanky" Tex Reichert who joined the team for the game from the U. S. Navy. In Ted's last game before heading east, he singled and scored his team's winning run and contributed in the field as well. He left town with a bit of dramatic flair.

Until his return in October 1941, this January 1938 series was Ted's last active non-exhibition appearance in his hometown. The *Tribune* noted in its January 22, 1938 edition that Ted's January 16 game was his last with the Gold Club. Apparently, the Red Sox management asked that he discontinue winter ball. So, the Gold Club's next game against the Negro All-Stars on January 23 did not include Ted in the line-up. San Diego baseball would go on without Ted Williams, but The Kid from San Diego was poised to make his mark on the national stage.

---

1) *Up until this general time there was one American Legion Post, No. 6, which was located in Balboa Park. The Padre Serra Post was a relatively new Post then, No. 370, and is no longer in existence. According to Ray Boone in an interview in early 2004, Post No. 201 (a relatively new post back then) was generally the baseball home for Hoover High while Post No. 6 was the home for San Diego High players.*

2) *So now we know that the first Padres he played for were really the Serra Padre Post in 1934 and not the Pacific Coast League Padres in 1936!*

3) *This July 1934 reference to Williams as "lanky" may have been the first public instance when he was called this. However, it became a common descriptor while he played in San Diego, and afterwards, as well. In the August 1, 1955 Sports Illustrated a caption on a photo of referred to him as "lanky Ted Williams." Even as late as February 15, 1969, an article written by Bill Jauss of the Chicago Daily News Service which appeared in The Louisville Times noted that he was "tall, lanky and lefty."*

4) *This was a local food market located at 642 12th Avenue, between Market and G Street, not far from the present location of San Diego's new Petco Park.*

5) *This bakery was located at 1955 Julian Avenue, several blocks from the location of the new ballpark in San Diego, Petco Park. Cramer's eventually became the location of the Weber Baking Co.*

6) *Hill was a fireman in San Diego and had played in various professional and semi-pro leagues beginning with Vernon in the PCL in 1920 and continuing with other teams into the late 1930s. He had stints with Beaumont/Dallas, Amarillo, Syracuse, Harrisburg, Binghamton, and Miami of the Arizona State League.*

7) *Church had several service stations, one at 915 Market and another at 734 University Avenue.*

8) *The use of the term "civil war" is not artistic license but used by the San Diego Union on July 12, 1935.*

9) *The Gold Club was a "Sporting Men's Headquarters."*

ONCE UPON A TIME IN NORTH PARK
by G. Jay Walker

THE ORIGIN OF NORTH PARK

In the summer of 1893, James Monroe Hartley purchased 40 acres of land from pioneer San Diego merchant Joseph Nash. The Hartley family got busy clearing chaparral from the mesa to plant a lemon grove. Water for the trees was always a problem but especially during times of drought, when it had to be carried in barrels from Downtown up the wagon trail that in the next century would be named Pershing Drive.

Years later, when the growing city caught up with the plot, it became bordered by University Avenue on the north, 32nd Street on the east, Ray Street on the west and Upas Street in the south. From the very beginning, Hartley had referred to the plot as Hartley's North Park. The name stuck, and decades later was used by the city of San Diego to identify its new suburb.

After Hartley died in 1904, the arid lemon grove was cleared and the land left fallow until 1911, when his oldest son, Jack Hartley, and brother-in-law, William Jay Stevens, developed the plot into residential and commercial tracts. Stevens and Hartley established themselves as North Park's first real estate firm in 1905 and in 1912 built its first multi-story commercial structure, the Stevens Building, on the northwest corner of 30th and University. The intersection became San Diego's busiest commercial center outside Downtown.

Williams family home at 4121 Utah Street, circa 1939.

Ted Williams as a toddler.

BOB BREITBARD AND TED WILLIAMS: A LIFE-LONG FRIENDSHIP

Ted's adult life, especially after leaving the game as a player in 1960, was intertwined with Bob Breitbard's. What started out in February 1934 as a casual friendship between classmates at Hoover High School evolved and developed over the 68 years which followed, until Ted passed away in 2002. Particularly in Ted's later years, the two became the closest of friends and developed a relationship where "I love you" was spoken, one to the other, without embarrassment and without the "macho" need that many athletes – indeed, most men - have to maintain a diffident posture.

What follows are first-hand summaries of conversations that Bill Nowlin and Tom Larwin had with the man who became Ted's closest friend, Bob Breitbard, on three separate occasions between June 1999 and April 2004. These conversations help us better understand Ted Williams, the Ted Williams that his closest friends knew.

Bob Breitbard

Bill Skelley and I went to the same grammar school together, McKinley. I was born in 1919, just six months behind Ted. He's August 30 of 1918 and I was April 28 of 1919. I turned 80 in April. I was born in San Diego. Just like Ted. We were both born here.

My wife passed away in November 1997 of pancreatic cancer. We'd been married 52 years. It's not easy.

There was a rivalry between San Diego High and Hoover High. They were the two major schools in San Diego. San Diego High was a bigger school and an older school, back into the 1890s or something. San Diego High was ever bigger.

Ted with Bob Breitbard.

San Diego High always had a good baseball team. They had a good coach and they had all the talent down there. Ted didn't really think he could make the ball club down there. He was only about 145 pounds. He was a string bean of a guy and he didn't think he could make the club there, but he just had the talent. He worked at it. He worked at it.

Ted had his choice, but he didn't think he could make the team at San Diego High so he went to Hoover. Hoover was started in '32 and we went there in '34.

I've known Ted since 1934. We went to Hoover High School; we both started in there in February of 1934. That was the first time I met him. When we came in, they had already started practice, but he made the team.

Had Coach Caldwell actually recruited Ted to come to Hoover?

I doubt it because there wasn't that much going on in terms of recruitment. He was a great coach and a stickler for discipline. I always liked him. He was my coach – the line coach – in football. Perry was the football coach and Wos Caldwell was the line coach. They had a short staff. The head coach Perry took care of the backfield.

[Ted and I] were in the same class and had several classes together. We got to know each other very well. He played baseball and I played football. I didn't play baseball. That was our difference.

We've been friends ever since, and we've gotten closer in the last ten or fifteen years than we were before even.

Dedication

Dedicated
To Our Friend
Mrs. Elizabeth Hamilton
To Whose
Friendship, Wisdom, and Loyalty
We Owe So Much

**Mrs. Edith Hamilton,
Hoover High typing teacher.**

We were in typing class together and I sat in front of him. He sat right behind me in typing class. This was in our senior year. Our teacher was Mrs. Hamilton. When we graduated from the school in February of '37, the principal Floyd Johnson got up and said, "Now I have two awards to present, one to Bob Breitbard and the other one to Ted Williams. These awards are for typing 32 words a minute without an error." We got typing awards. That was our claim to fame.

We had the English course together and the Social Studies course together.

The teachers loved him. This Mrs. Hamilton just broke out into smiles whenever he talked. You know how he talks. He talked then just like he talks now. I'll always remember. He would say, "Hey, teach!" to Mrs. Hamilton and she'd say, "What do you want now, Ted?" She'd come back and ask what he wanted. He'd say, "I don't understand how I can get this thing to move." You know, the carriage on the typewriter, or something.

We didn't live too far from each other, but he was playing baseball. I didn't see him that much outside of school. Really, I saw him more when he was playing professionally, playing for the Padres. I didn't see him much when he was playing for the Red Sox. Just once in a while when he would come out to the Coast, and he'd play out here. They'd play exhibition games out here. I saw him in Los Angeles a couple or three times. He was down here at an exhibition game and I took my daughters. I have pictures of that. But until he retired... when he retired, then we started seeing each other.

Look what's happened with him. Take a look at that man! He's so damned smart. He can do anything. Imagine. A man who never went to college goes out and flies jets! I sure as hell couldn't do it. The man is smart.

Was Ted seen as a jock by most of the students?

I don't think it was that way. I don't think we classified people at that time as a jock. I don't think he was known as a jock, or any of the sports guys were known as jocks. I can only remember two guys on any of the teams that smoked. We didn't think about smoking or drinking or anything. We were thinking about keeping healthy and playing football or baseball.

He never smoked. Never drank. He was a class guy. I only knew two fellows who even smoked. This guy Moose Siraton and Bill Ondler. They were the only kids I knew that smoked. Both of them baseball players. Both of them football players.

Did Ted take his studies at all seriously? He did when he went into the Navy.

I was in a couple of classes with him – I think it was English or history. We didn't have a lot of homework. They didn't have the kind of homework they have today. He liked those shop courses.

Ted didn't go to much of that [other activities] but he did go to the prom. He went to the prom with me. [The young lady Ted escorted was] Alberta Camus. Ted came to our 50th reunion. He came out to it, and she wasn't there. She was just his date for the prom. He wore a tie for the first time.

He had his own little group. He wanted to do what he wanted to do. I wouldn't call him a loner. I admired him for his tenacity and wanting to be a good baseball player. He did it at his own pace and worked hard at it. He fished with Mr. Cassie, Les's dad, and... I think he loved to fish. Hunt a little bit. But he concentrated on the baseball.

Ted was a fun guy in school. Shy, in a way. In a way. In class or anything else, hell, he was just one of the leaders. He'd always raise his hand. Asking questions. Women, he didn't care about going out with a gal. He did wear a tie to our graduation. He took out a date and we were there and we had fun, but I want to tell you he was always well respected in high school. His love

Heading to the prom, Alberta Camus and Ted Williams.

was baseball. At times, he brought his bat into the classroom. Yes, he would. He'd put it under his desk. That's true. He did carry a bat and he would put it under his desk.

Today, you couldn't do it. That's a weapon today. In those days, we didn't even lock our house. We left our cars out all night long, windows down. We wouldn't do it today. You'd lock your car. You have alarms on your door. I never had a key to our house growing up. Today they've got bars on the windows. It's a different society today.

Did some of the other students start looking up to him, after his junior year when he hit .583 and had major league scouts looking him over?

Well, everybody knew he was a damn good hitter and they knew he was a good baseball player. They knew that at San Diego High, too. He was that tall gangly guy. Good looking guy. He wasn't really interested in women then.

He played with the Padres and after that they looked at him a little more, hey, here's a guy who's a celebrity.

Ted signing autographs for the kids at the Hall of Champions, 1961.

I saw him play at Lane Field a few times. I didn't go all the time but I'd go down there. Sneak in, if I could. I'd have to get money from the folks at that time. No one had the kind of money to do a lot of that. We had a cafeteria but not many of us could afford to go to the cafeteria. Those were tough days.

You gave him his first hall of fame honor.

Oh yes, we honored him in the hall of fame. That's when we continued seeing each other. He was our second inductee into the Hall of Champions. The first one was Brick Muller who was a two time all-American at the University of California. They were the wonder team. They were undefeated for three or four straight years. Four fellows from San Diego High School – Brick Muller, Albert Sprott, Stan Barnes, and Olin Majors. Brick Muller was the first one inducted. Not only was he an All-American for a couple of years, but he won third place in the high jump in the Olympics. So he was our first choice, and Ted Williams was our second choice. We inducted him in '54, I think.

We've inducted Billy Casper, Mickey Wright, Maureen Connolly – they were still playing. We're going to induct Tony Gwynn, probably this next year. He'd be a very popular choice.

We started as the Breitbard Athletic Foundation, in '46. 53 years ago. I patterned it after the Helms Athletic Foundation. Paul Helms. Bill Schroeder was the executive director of that. Bill Schroeder was a sportswriter for the LA Times *and he quit to be the executive director of this foundation. Paul Helms was in the bakery business. They gave awards but 95% of the awards went to people around the Los Angeles area. I was coaching at Hoover High School. After I got out of college, I was only 21 and I went back and coached at Hoover High School, which we had graduated from. I spent 4 years there and then I went into business with my brothers and did, in the linen industrial supply business.*

Then in 1961, we started our Hall of Champions.

In our Hall of Champions, we honor about 42 sports. Ted likes ours better than any hall of fame that he's ever seen, because we also have an award for the disabled athlete. I want to tell you, that creates more applause than anything else you can do.

It seems that you've probably had more than anyone to do with him continuing to visit San Diego.

When we dedicated a highway after Ted here, the Ted Williams Freeway, he and John-Henry and myself and Claudia, we went down to feed the animals down in the wild animal park. We're riding around in this truck, we're feeding the animals, the giraffes were coming up and eating out of our hands. We were feeding the hippopotamus and he looks up and about 300 yards away, I would say, on the side of a hill, he said to the guide, "Isn't that an Alaskan blah-blah-blah buck?" "Sure is," said the guide. "How the hell did you know that?" "Well, hell, I saw them in Alaska."

"Gee, there's only three of them in captivity and we have one of them here." "Well, I saw them up there. Hell, that thing must weigh four hundred and forty pounds!" The guide looked at him and said, "I can't believe you. That weighs four hundred and forty-three pounds."

We'd go by and he'd tell us the name of this eucalyptus tree. "It sure is." And "I know what kind of bird that is." He knows all these things.

Right now, he watches that channel, the History Channel and Biography. He knows about history and government, and he knows the people involved. He's very, very smart but on top of it, he's a loving person and he cares about people.

I'll tell you a story. He called me about eight years ago. He says, "Bob. It's Thanksgiving Day, and Louise and I are sitting here and she's cooked a 24 pound turkey. I've been thinking about you, and I just wanted to tell you, my friend, that you're the dearest and best friend I've ever had in my life and I want you to know I love you." I'm crying my tears right now. I turned to my wife and told her what Ted had said and she started crying.

Ever since then – and I talk to him at least once a day and sometimes twice a day, every day – we end our conversations, "My dear friend, I love you, and I care about you." That's how we end our conversation. That's unusual. But he's that kind of a person.

This guy is an amazing guy in what he knows, but the big thing that people don't realize about him is his sensitivity and his caring about people and how he feels about people. They don't see that. He wouldn't turn down a kid for an autograph. He'd stay there all night long. John-Henry wouldn't let him, but this guy would do anything for kids.

I just want to impress on you the warmth that he has. He can be gruff. He sounds gruff at times, but he's got that sensitivity and caring about people. He does care about people. He cares about his friends. He cares about what happens in this world. He cares about our Marines. He cares about what happens with

Bob Breitbard with Ted at the Hall of Champions, 1963.

our Army. He cares about what happens with the President of the United States. He's very interested in everything that goes on. More and more, though, he's talking to me and he says, "Bob, we're getting older. Either you come out here..." – he wants me to come live with him. I can't do that. Hell, I'd die back there where he lives.

I want him to come out here. Out here, he's got more friends. He would be able to see more people. He gets lonesome back there. It's hard to get to his place. He just has a few people around there. If he were here, he would get to see everybody. I feel if he came out here, I'd add another 5, 6, 8 years to his life. Let me tell you: he's over-protected now, and he doesn't want that.

We talk every day, sometimes twice a day, sometimes three times a day if we feel like talking. We have a relationship and I'm proud to say, I consider him my dearest and best friend, too. It's a wonderful, wonderful feeling. I know he's sincere. He doesn't bullshit. He calls a spade a spade. If he doesn't care for you, he'll let you know but by the same token, there's very few people he doesn't like, unless they're complete jackasses. He's a true friend.

I was surprised that Yawkey didn't give Ted 2% of the club or some damn thing. Keep him there and give him a box. Jesus, what an attraction that would have been. Well, it's one of those things. Sometimes people never think of that.

–from interviews conducted by Bill Nowlin on June 10, 1999 and March 28, 2003

Bob and Ted: The Best of Friends

The story of Bob Breitbard and Ted Williams is worth telling. It shows a side of Ted Williams that appears from time-to-time during his public life, but is greatly overshadowed by the newspaper and magazine reports in the 1940s and 1950s of Ted's more volatile behavior. What Bob Breitbard was able to bring out from Williams was a side that had perhaps been inhibited by an early home life lacking some of the elements of traditional love.

With a deep affection in his voice, Breitbard told me that he believes that the best thing about their relationship was that he felt he brought love to Ted's life. To underscore his feeling, he remembered a time about 25 years ago as clear as if it were today. He said it took place in Florida at Williams' home.

As Breitbard tells the story: "I walked in the door, having just arrived from San Diego. Ted was sitting at the table. I went up to him and said 'Hi, my friend.' And I kissed him on the cheek.

"He roared back and said 'What's that for?'

"I replied that 'I just wanted to tell you that I love you.'

"Ted took the bait and responded 'Well... then I love you.'

"From then on we would always greet one another with a kiss on the cheek. For the last 20-25 years we would talk to one another one to three times a day. And we would always close with the words, 'I love you my dear friend.'

"He was the dearest friend that I ever had."

Breitbard and Williams both attended Hoover High School and started their friendship as sophomore classmates in February 1934. They graduated three years later in February 1937. They did not live that close to one another and their interests were with different sports, Bob with football and Ted with baseball.

They shared classes together and Breitbard is proud of the typing awards he and Ted each received when they graduated together in February 1937. Principal Floyd Johnson presented the two graduates with awards for typing 32 words per minute without error, which Breitbard characterizes as being a somewhat humorous award by the Principal, admitting that this wasn't too speedy!

Their friendship grew slowly following their high school years. Ted remained an east coast resident after leaving San Diego in the late 1930s. During the 1940s and 1950s, Breitbard noted that Ted would visit San Diego briefly when the Red Sox had spring exhibition games on the west coast in Los Angeles and San Francisco. But that was about it. In later years, Williams was a bit wistful that he had not come back more often.

A significant event for Williams and his relationship with San Diego took place in 1954. Williams was selected to be the second inductee into the San Diego Breitbard Hall of Fame, named after its founder, Bob Breitbard.

Ted appeared for his induction ceremony in 1954, but Breitbard is clear that they did not become the "closest of friends" until after Ted's retirement from baseball in September 1960. Williams would visit San Diego, such visits typically coinciding with the annual San Diego Hall of Fame dinner every January. When he did return, he would sometimes stay for three our four weeks with Breitbard. Breitbard, on the other hand, often visited Ted in Florida and stayed at the Williams home.

Breitbard accompanied Ted to the 1999 All-Star Game in Boston, and has fond memories of the memorable salute to Williams which preceded the game. What really touched his emotions most, though, was a visit with the children stricken with cancer being treated at the Jimmy Fund clinic in Boston.

Ted was in a wheelchair at the time and, according to Breitbard, he was wheeled down halls lined with nurses and doctors, alerted to Ted's visit. Breitbard found the experience as memorable, and more touching, than Ted's majestic entry into Fenway Park before the All-Star Game. At the game Ted received a prolonged and emotional standing ovation as he was driven around the park and then was encircled by Hall of Famers who broke ranks and left their prescribed positions on the field to come closer in welcoming the greatest of them all, Ted Williams.

But the ovation Ted received from the nurses and doctors lining the halls of the Dana-Farber Cancer Institute was not for playing baseball. It was for 50 years of trying to help youngsters and cancer researchers beat that most terrible disease. During his visit, Williams greeted stricken children as young as one or two years old, patting heads and offering words of encouragement. Breitbard noted appreciative parents with tears shining in their eyes. Ted bantered effortlessly with older children and uplifted everyone's spirits along the way.

This was the private Ted Williams who for over half a century had made a difference in the lives of so many young people... but insisted that no publicity attend his frequent private visits. This was a Ted Williams that his best friend wanted to make sure we knew about.

–from an interview conducted on April 13, 2004 by Tom Larwin

Ted Williams, age 17, snapped by the local newspaper on his way home from the playground. May Williams paid a dollar to get a copy of the photograph.

TED WILLIAMS – HOOVER HIGH, BEFORE AND AFTER
by Bill Nowlin

> *"I think I was fortunate to grow up in Southern California, where it is always warm and a boy can stretch the baseball season to his own dimensions."*
> Ted Williams, *My Turn at Bat.*[1]

ELEMENTARY SCHOOL YEARS

Ted Williams always said he was a lucky guy. He was born and raised in San Diego where one could play baseball all year long. He lived near a city playground blessed with an athletic director who took the time to work with him. He was a boy captivated by the idea of hitting a baseball; it became an obsession that gave focus to his life and drew on his formidable energy and drive.

Ted reports first being interested in baseball at around 9 years old. By fifth and sixth grade at Garfield, his elementary school, he remembered, "I'd be at school waiting when the janitor opened up. I was always the first one there so I could get into the closets and get the balls and bats and be ready for the other kids. That way I could be first up in a game we played where you could bat as long as somebody didn't catch the ball... it was worth getting to school early, because hitting was the fun."[2]

And if the janitor didn't open the closet soon enough, well, there might be other ways to get the equipment. "I'd get up at dawn, race down to the schoolhouse and climb through the window of the janitor's quarters to grab a bat and ball for a workout with chums before classes started."[3]

School was just six-tenths of a mile from the Williams home at 4121 Utah Street. At noon Ted would run home for lunch, "run all the way there and run all the way back so I could get in another fifteen minutes of ball."[4] Ted told *Sports Illustrated* that the secret to his success was all the practice he put in, adding, "Ask anybody who had anything to do with T. S. Williams and they'll tell you that he practiced more than anybody. Joe Cronin'll tell you that I hit before the games and after the games. There's never been a hitter who hit more baseballs than Williams. Hell, when I was a kid, I used to get to the schoolhouse before the janitor opened the doors. I'd get the balls and bat, and practice. Then at lunch time, I'd run home, one, two, three, four, five blocks, and grab a bunch of fried potatoes and run back to school before anybody was through eating; and I was practicing, again. Always practicing."[5]

He elaborated to Joe Cashman, saying that the only way to become a natural hitter is to hit and hit and then hit some more, hit morning, noon and night, and all year long. "That's been my system since I was knee high to a cricket. I'll grant that, starting out, I was blessed with particularly sharp eyesight and strong, supple wrists.... I also insist that, regardless of physical assets, I would never have gained a headline for hitting if I [had not] kept everlastingly at it and thought of nothing else the year round."[6]

Maybe Ted didn't always grab those potatoes. Forrest Warren, a San Diego newspaperman, talked to Ted's mother May in 1946. She told him, "When Teddy was in Garfield School, before entering junior high, he was underweight. Mrs. Alcott, a teacher, came to see me about it. 'My goodness, I give him 35 cents a day to buy his lunch. Your food is good in the cafeteria. What is the matter?'" Warren says that a visiting nurse investigated and discovered that Ted had been "giving most of his daily lunch fund to poor kids who were hungry." Ted disputed this story.[7]

And sometimes he just didn't want to take the time to eat. "Then, as now, I lived only for my next time at bat. And I'm not fooling. Why, I even objected to spending any time eating. When I'd go home to lunch, I'd grab a handful of potato chips and a glass of water, gulp them down and be off to the ball park, leaving my meal behind me on the table."[8]

Joe Villarino, who played many a game with Ted on the playground and in high school, went to Garfield grammar school, too. "Him and I used to play marbles all the time, when we were 7 or 8 years old. We'd run around with dungarees on, or knee pants with holes in them. His shoes were so split open from kneeling on the ground that you could see his toes. About third grade, we used to run to the box where they had the softballs. We used to run like the devil first thing in the morning, around 7:30. They'd have a box set out there with the bats and the balls in there. Ted and I'd run for the box first thing. We didn't wear gloves to play the softball." Villarino dates this around the mid to late 1920s. "Eight- or 9-years-old. In them days, we played ball with kids 16- or 17-years-old. They didn't have Little League or organized ball for the kids in them day. We used to get a bunch of kids up and play."[9]

Ted's class, Garfield Elementary. Ted is 7th from left, middle row.

Third grade was also more or less when Forrest Warren first recalls Ted. Warren was a neighbor who had two children in school with Ted; he was also a San Diego newspaper writer and a member of the Salvation Army Advisory Board. He dates this story to 1927:

Joe Villarino, 2004.

"'This is the year I'm gonna do it, Mom.' 9-year-old Teddy Williams said that hundreds of times to his mother in San Diego, as he would swing a stick or something that looked like a bat. Then he could say, 'I'm gonna be a Babe Ruth.'

"'Listen, Teddy,' his mother often would say, 'You ditched Sunday school yesterday; when you get to be a man, I want you to be a captain in the Salvation Army.'

"'Aw, heck, Mom, I'd ruther be a Babe Ruth.' And again he would swing anything that was handy, just so he could get quick action in his wrists.

"What was this San Diego boy thinking about? All his mother could get out of him was 'Babe Ruth' and the New York Yankees. Before he was ten, Ted seemed to have his heart set on the Yanks, perhaps because it was a catchy word and it sounded good.'"[10]

Ted remembered those days fondly: "The place, the playground, was nothing special. Balls taped together with that black electrical tape. But I loved it. I couldn't get enough of the place. We'd play baseball. We'd play softball. We'd play a game called 'Big League.' We'd play that on the playground. Hit the ball over a certain pipe - home run! That was the most fun I ever had in my life."[11]

He was relentless. He really did live to hit. "From the moment I began to play ball as a long-legged, skinny kid of six or seven, the biggest, if not only, kick I got out of the game was when I was hitting....When I wasn't sleeping or eating I was practicing swinging. If I didn't have a bat, I'd take any piece of wood, or make a bat of paper, and swing it. If I didn't have a ball to swing at, I swung at stones, marbles and even peanuts and popcorn thrown at me by my pals."[12]

Ted wrote in *Open Road* magazine, back in 1950, "From the time I was old enough to hold a bat I wanted to be a ball player. I was trying to play semi-professional ball when I was only 12 years old, still in short pants."[13]

The North Park playground was a block and a half from the Williams family home. Ted remembers the many years spent hitting at the playground, six days a week, but says, "My first game, though, would have had to be in grammar school, in the Garfield School playground." Leila Bowen, Ted's fifth grade teacher at Garfield remembered that Ted would "run out to the playground and shout 'first ups.'... My, he was a nervous boy. Bit his fingernails down to the nub. He was just an average student, but even then he loved his baseball with a passion."[14]

"Wilbert Wiley was my first boyhood pal," Ted wrote in his autobiography, *My Turn At Bat*. Wiley lived just a block away, at 4225 Utah Street. A couple of years older than Ted, Wiley held good memories of growing up with Ted: "Even in the grammar school, we had ball teams. Every day we'd go up there. Before the schoolhouse opened to take the kids in, there'd be a game of Work Up or something like that. You'd always see him in there."

Ted hung around the Wiley household a lot, even borrowing a bike and helping Wilbert do his paper route. "He'd throw papers and things like that. He and I were together a lot. He was always kind of tall for his age. He was always kind of a loud, good-natured kid. He was kind of witty, and he liked to needle people. I always liked him a lot. If he liked anybody, he'd try to do everything in the world for them."[15]

Garfield did field a team. Bill Skelley, who played against Ted throughout

Ted with Wilbert Wylie, and Ted with Wilbert's mother.

high school but was a teammate on the 1937 Padres, remembers when his fifth grade team at McKinley Elementary had a softball game against Garfield. "The big deal was, boy, are we going to be able to match these guys? Not long before that on some occasion where kids were horsing around, a pin got stuck in Ted's eyelid or something like that – not in his eye – and he was not at his best."[16] There was another time that Ted's brother Danny was fooling around, batting hazelnuts with a broomstick – and hit one into Ted's right eye. From that time forward, Ted was never fully able to see as well as before, and was forced to make adjustments. Imagine how well he could have hit, had he really been able to see![17]

Ted's eyesight was legendary, but he himself always emphasized the importance of practice, not natural vision or native ability. It was relentless practice that made him a better hitter – practice, thought, dedication and more practice. "A lot of people have as good eyesight as I have and probably better, and still they're always ready to say, 'eyesight's the reason he does it – and natural ability.' That's so easy to say and to give credit for. They never talk about the practice. Practice! Practice! Practice! Dammit, you gotta practice!"[18]

Ted got a chance to play for both Garfield and Horace Mann (his junior high school) and was a pitcher for both schools.[19] Ted remembers not being so self-confident in junior high as he became later in life. "I was forever trying to get on the junior high baseball team," he told David Pietrusza.[20] Perhaps it was just a perception problem - that the coach didn't see how solid a ballplayer Teddy Williams was. More likely, Ted was still developing as a ballplayer, and going through an awkward growth stage. His struggles to make the team at Horace Mann may have contributed to his later decision to attend San Diego's Hoover High School rather than San Diego High.

His enthusiasm for softball at Garfield aside, it was at Horace Mann, though, that Ted really got bit by the baseball bug, according to Joe Villarino. "He never got fired up until... well he started in junior high a little bit. And American Legion. He got more and more enthused, you know. But I think he was just natural, when they spanked him on the butt, he was going to be a baseball feller."[21] Ted himself always debunked the idea of him being born a natural, and credited the thousands upon thousands of batting practice swings he took, week in and week out.

Ted didn't always have the best equipment to work with, but he had the will, the determination. He committed himself to practice. In 1954, he wrote in the *Saturday Evening Post*, recounting how he'd be at grammar school waiting for the janitor, "so's I could get a bat and get in a few licks before the school bell rang. I haven't stopped practicing since. I used to hit tennis balls, old baseballs, balls made of rags - anything. I didn't think I was going to be a particularly good hitter. I just liked to do it. Then when I began playing ball in school, and people began to tell me I was a good hitter, that encouraged me a lot, and I tried harder than ever."[22]

Later in life, Ted called on an earlier memory: "I was always trying to see how I could get quicker because I heard a couple of kids at the ballpark when I was 12 years old, 13 years old, saying that kid has quick hands. I said, 'Wait until he sees me next time!' I picked up things like that, that registered with me, compliments only pushed me to improve."[23]

Villarino remembers Ted taking care of his body and already working on building up his strength. "He worked at it. He was always doing something, squeezing the tennis ball to get his fingers where he could grab ahold of a bat, where he could get his wrist movement into it. And he'd study the pitcher, he'd study the pitcher something awful."[24]

Ted might have become a tennis star, had he not stuck with baseball. "They had tennis courts," Villarino says. "We used to play against Maureen Connolly, she played in Wimbledon and all that. She just lived down the next street. Ted and I, we used to play tennis with her all the time. We had our own rackets."[25] When Ted's racket got damaged twice, though, his mother said they couldn't afford the 35 cents to have it re-strung a second time and that was the end of that.[26]

Today we are unable to learn how Ted did for the "Home of the Lions" – Garfield Elementary School. Unfortunately no school records remain at either Garfield or Horace Mann, and neither the San Diego papers nor even neighborhood papers such as the *East San Diego Press* covered the junior high ballgames. A story by Boston sportswriter Bill Cunningham, which ran early in Ted's tenure with the Red Sox, commented that Ted played on the Horace Mann team "until it disbanded."[27]

Rod Luscomb, playground director at the North Park Playground, took note of Ted's enthusiasm for baseball as early as 1929, and noticed that sometimes the lad wasn't in school when he should have been. "A couple of times I skipped my last class at school just to get there early," Ted admitted. "But Lusk got wise to that and made me cut it out."[28] Ed Linn says that Luscomb remembered Ted on the playground one day at 2 p.m., waiting for Luscomb to show up. "Where have you been? I want to play baseball," Ted remonstrated. Luscomb asked why the 10-year-old wasn't in school. "Aw, I don't care nothing about that," Ted told him. Luscomb told Ted to go back to school, then return afterward. The school day ended at 3:00, and was a number of blocks away, but at 3:00 sharp, Luscomb remembered, "here he'd come, running as fast as his legs would carry him." Lusk had to set a 3:15 start time to force the eager kid to stay in school until the final bell.[29]

Rod Luscomb, Ted wrote, was "my first real hero."[30] Luscomb was a decade older than Ted, and the youngster looked up to him. Luscomb had Ted working, early on, "doing pushups to build myself up."[31] A number of players remember Ted always squeezing tennis balls in idle moments, to strengthen his wrist and forearm muscles.

Handball is a good sport for hand-eye coordination, and Ted had a few relatives that excelled at it, one of whom (Ernesto Ponce) was tri-state champion in Texas, Arizona and New Mexico. Rod Luscomb and Ted spent hours together on the North Park court. At times, it would just be the two of them, one pitching to the other in turn, working on baseball routines. "We had the field marked off in our minds," Ted told John Underwood, "so that we'd know what was a hit and what wasn't, and we'd play regulation nine-inning games, sometimes just the two of us."[32]

High school teammate Roy Engle remembers how they used the handball court to pretend they were playing baseball: "We had a handball court where we used to go in and play baseball. If you hit the bar across there, that was a home run. And a triple and a double, and you had to catch the ball off of there. We used to play that by the hour. It gave us all the fundamentals of baseball, but we didn't have a big field, and four of us could play it, so it was very popular."[33] Kids at the playground had any number of improvised games – Over the Line, Work Up, Big League and Association - and a game with marbles called Boston.

And Ted spent hour upon hour at the playground. This was the Depression, yet the city of San Diego provided field lighting in North Park until 9:00 at night – plenty of time to get in some extra hitting. "He lived at the playground," says Engle. "I think the only reason he went to high school was to play. There was nobody else to play with, so he went to school. He made his grades so he could be eligible."[34]

Rod Luscomb.

Mel Skelley remembers his own junior high days, when Ted and brother Bill Skelley were both in high school. "Ted was a star even then; he could always hit. In fact, we made special rules when we played Over the Line because he could hit better than the rest of us. You need three on each team. We'd hit to the left field side of the diamond and we'd make Ted hit to left field because he could hit better than the rest of us. You had to hit it between second and third base and then to the left side of center field. Just pickup games. We'd play with whoever we could play with."[35] Brother Bill remembers this, too. "Ted was a left-hand hitter and he was better than all the rest of us getting it over the third base side, even though we were right-hand hitters. If you wanted to play that game, you had to hit it to left field."[36]

This experience had implications for the Boudreau Shift. Fifteen years later, in 1946, Cleveland manager Lou Boudreau was trying anything to cut down Williams' hitting, even placing three infielders on the right-hand side of the diamond to frustrate Williams' hitting to right. Yet as a kid Ted had needed to hit to left field to excel at Over the Line. He'd trained himself to hit to left. If only he'd drawn on that background, or even bunted a few times to third base, the so-called "Williams Shift" would not have been effective. And Ted knew how to bunt, as he showed in the 1946 World Series. It's not the sort of skill kids work on at the sandlot, but Ted almost certainly learned to bunt under Hoover High's Coach Wofford "Wos" Caldwell. Teammate Leonard Bell writes, "One thing Wos was big on was bunting. He drilled us on that. Every time I see a major leaguer pop up a bunt, I think, 'He should have played for Wos.'"[37]

Rod Luscomb was born July 12, 1907 – so he was 11 years older than Ted, enough to serve as something approaching a father figure to the young Ted. In 1929, Luscomb turned 22 and Ted was but 11. Having Luscomb as a mentor was essential to Ted's development as a ballplayer. He didn't get much support – if any – from his immediate family. Ted's mother May was a dedicated Salvation Army worker who was often away from home until mid-evening raising money for the cause. She was no early "soccer mom" – she only appeared at one or two of Ted's high school games. She did once give him a glove as a gift, though, a Bill Doak fielder's glove. And a shotgun. Later, when Ted was with the Padres, May Williams apparently sometimes worked the stands at Lane Field looking for donations for the Cause. Backup catcher Bill Starr told Ed Linn of the time one of the other players "asked Ted if he knew that his mother had been walking around the stands

collecting money and telling everybody Ted Williams was her son. 'Ted looked down at the floor and didn't say anything for a long time. And then he said, "I know. She embarrasses me." The whole clubhouse went absolutely silent. Everybody felt so bad for him.'"[38]

Rod Luscomb with Ted at the Hall of Champions, July 21, 1961.

Sam Williams, Ted's father, showed even less interest than May. Sam Williams "was a man who always wanted to see the other side of the hill and played but a minor role in his family's life."[39] Ted mildly objected to others who labeled his dad a "wanderer." "He was not much for sports," Ted admitted. "My father didn't take much interest until I got to the point where baseball contracts were being offered me, then he kind of liked to be in the act."[40] None of Ted's high school teammates recalls seeing his father at any of Ted's games, other than maybe once at Pomona when California Governor Merriam was present. Wilbert Wiley saw him one time, at a game Ted played in, but shook his head with sad wonderment in recollection, "Most men... if you had a kid as good as that, you'd be wanting to bust the buttons on your shirt. His mother never paid any attention to him either."[41]

Luscomb instilled in Ted some of the ambition and drive that Ted's father Sam Williams did not. "I used to spend all my time at the playground. I was 14, 15, 16. Rod Luscomb, who was about ten years older than I, was playground director. He was a baseball nut, too, and in his heart I think he wanted to be a big league player; but he used to just love to play and practice. He'd pitch to me. I'd pitch to him. I was a pitcher in those days. Rod gave me the competition I needed. He'd bear down on me and try to get me out. I'd bear down on him. He was a perfect guy to have around the playground for a kid like me."[42]

May tried to raise her two sons – Teddy and Danny – as Salvationists, but both proved intractable. Joe Hamelin reports that she had her eldest "dedicated" but it certainly didn't take. Ted stopped going to Sunday school when it began to interfere with baseball. "She was very upset when he dropped out of Sunday school," recalled May's fellow Salvationist Alice Rasmussen.[43]

Even after high school, Bill Skelley recalls, Ted's mother "didn't know which end of the bat to hold onto, I'm pretty sure." When Bill arrived in his 1929 Chrysler roadster to drive Ted to Padres games in 1937, after graduation, "She always wanted to make sure, 'Teddy, did you do this? Have you got a clean handkerchief?' and by that time he was tired of listening and out the door."[44]

Rod Luscomb wasn't the only one who took note of Ted as a young player. Amby Schindler, MVP of the 1940 Rose Bowl, was a year older than Ted and recalls playing with Ted for the Ryan Confectionery Juniors team. This was a team of 13- and 14-year-olds organized by Mel and Bill Skelley's father; they played at Golden Hill playground on Sunday afternoons. Amby caught and played center field; when Ted wasn't pitching, he played right field. It was as a pitcher, not as a hitter, that Schindler remembered Ted. "We only played on Sundays. I don't think I even owned a baseball cap. We most all of us played in tennis shoes. These were Depression years. I had two pairs of tennis shoes, and my new ones I saved to play in the game. The other ones had holes in the bottom. There was one kid that we played against who had [baseball] shoes! Nobody had uniforms."[45]

He also lacked a catcher's mask and "it used to scare the pee out of me." Schindler often caught Ted. "He was big, a little rangier than the Skelley boys and he could throw harder and faster. I remember that when he was on the pitching mound, he always appeared bigger than the other kids throwing."[46] It was as a pitcher that Ted was most known in his school days. Schindler never saw Ted play in high school or with the Padres, though, caught up as he was with his own activities in track and football.

Morris Siraton played with Ted, and remembers him from when they were both kids at Garfield at age 7 or 8, pre-Luscomb. "At North Park, it was always pick-up teams, and we played this and played that. There wasn't any coach or anything else. If we got enough guys together, we'd get a ball all taped up and a broken bat that's taped, and tried to play ball. New baseballs in those days were like gold, if you had 75 cents to buy one." A couple of years older, Siraton was on the Hoover High team during Ted's first year.[47]

There were a lot of pick-up games, and games were planned wherever and whenever possible. North Park often saw a regular Sunday afternoon game for kids, after the morning game for adults. "By the time Ted was fourteen years old he was starring in both of them," Ed Linn tells us.[48] Ted recalled his very first homer. "I remember my first home run. Came against a guy named Hunt in a Sunday game in North Park. Just a little poopy fly ball to center, but it made it over the fence. There I was, a little 15-year-old standing in against guys 25 to 30 and this guy could really throw hard. I could barely get the bat around on it, and I hit that homer… It was 280 feet, or something. Maybe 250 feet. It was just a fly ball, but it was a big thing to me."[49]

Leonard Bell, later San Diego's fire chief, was a teammate of Ted's in high school. Ted played right field. Bell played left. Bell had seen Ted play well before high school, though. He wrote, "The first time I saw Ted was at Central Playground in East San Diego. North Park Playground came down to play us. Ted was about 13-years-old – he was tall and gangly. We didn't have uniforms. No socks on the legs. We weren't into fashion in those days. He was wearing knickers and tennis shoes and playing first base."[50]

Baseballs being valuable commodities, maybe it's not surprising that Ted himself confessed to a little petty larceny, "We challenged the Navy teams off the Lexington and the Saratoga, which were tied up in San Diego harbor. We'd warm up with their balls and maybe drop a few in the trash can when nobody was looking, and go back later to get them."[51] "You couldn't say we stole them," Del Ballinger told Ed Linn, "because they knew what we were doing and they didn't care."[52]

In the 1930s, though a relatively small urban area, San Diego was "the largest hub of activity in America for the navy and marines, with bustling supply depots, hospitals, training stations, and bases."[53]

Ted loved to play anything with a bat and a ball. Bill Skelley talked with historian Bill Swank about how often they'd play Pepper. All you needed was one other person to enjoy this baseball skill game. "Ted loved Pepper and he had the bat a lot of the time. Sometimes, he just couldn't hold back and the baseball would ricochet and it was dangerous sometimes with him batting."[54]

John "Swede" Jensen, another high school teammate – who later played on the Padres for nine years – remembers clearly, "We were just in jeans and cords to go to the playground. We didn't have any uniforms. I used to go there at night maybe three or four times a week. Ted was there almost every single night. It seems to me like he used to carry a bat with him all the time. I can remember walking to school with him quite a few times, and he'd knock every flower off every bush along the way. He was very, very adamant that he would be a big league hitter someday. I hate to say this, but none of us were great students at that time. He always said, 'Don't worry about my grades. I'm going to play major league ball!'"[55]

It was in American Legion ball that Ted got his first uniform, high school rival Mel Skelley noted in a May 7, 1999 interview.

Ted wasn't always the star player. "I was always a pretty good hitter for my age bracket," he admitted to Art Turgeon. Ted was always candid, and eschewed false modesty. "But when I was 16- , 17-years-old, there were some guys much more physically developed than I was, and when they picked out a team, like American Legion, I was picked third or fourth. I wouldn't be picked first. That used to make me feel kind of bad, you know, that I wasn't picked first." This begged the question, of course: who was picked first? "There were two. A kid named Grady and a kid named Marsh. They were mature kids, strong for their age. Grady had a half-baked look from a Yankee scout, but he didn't sign him. Marsh? I don't know what the hell happened to him."[56]

Though Sam Williams was rarely around as Ted grew older, the young Teddy had a number of surrogate fathers – Les Cassie being one, and (though not quite old enough) Rod Luscomb another. A third was Johnny Lutz, who lived across the street on Utah Street. When Ted signed his first pro contract, it was on Lutz's kitchen table, not his own. This, despite the fact that Ted's parents had become involved in the negotiations and had to sign their consent for the 17-year-old to go professional.

Les Cassie, Sr. lived across the street as well, and his son Les, Jr. was just a year ahead of Ted. Ted often ate at the Cassies' house, and he knew he was always welcome there. Mr. Cassie wasn't just a surrogate father; Ted was closer to him than to his real father. The Cassies offered an alternative family but, of course, there's nothing like the real thing. When it was time for Ted to cross the country to join the Boston Red Sox for Spring Training in 1939, he asked Mr. Cassie to drive him to Sarasota. When Ted and the Red Sox made it to the World Series in 1946, it was Mr. and Mrs. Cassie he brought east, not his own parents. When Ted graduated high school, he only received one graduation present – a fountain pen from Mr. Cassie.[57]

Fishing clearly was another joy for Teddy. Les Cassie, Jr. never enjoyed it much, so Les, Sr. often took Ted fishing, surf-casting on Coronado Beach. At age 13, another neighbor took him to fish for largemouth bass. It was Ted who got hooked: "I was just carried away with the whole damn thing," he said in a 1998 interview. In fact, Dave Strege wrote, "Catching fish became addicting, and one sportfishing trip out of Point Loma in 1934 contributed heavily to his growing passion. Williams and his party caught 98 barracuda and gave them all away at the dock. People of the Depression were eager to take fresh fish home for dinner." Ted felt good about his fishing skills. "I belong at least in one (Hall of Fame), and that's fishing... If I had my life to live over again and I could take fishing or baseball, I'd take fishing and I'll tell you why: I don't think I would do as well in baseball if I had to do it over again. I know I'd have done as good in fishing."[58]

Certainly, he'd rather be fishing, or playing ball, than attending Salvation Army services. Some stories tell that Ted was ribbed by classmates his first day at Hoover, called a "sissy" for accompanying his mother to Saturday night street corner meetings, and ribbed as well in months to come because his brother Danny's name showed up on the police blotter in the San Diego papers all too frequently.[59] Gene Schoor, in *The Ted Williams Story*, confirms the ribbing. Regarding Ted and May, Schoor wrote, "For a long time, out of respect for her feelings, he refused to play ball on Sundays. 'What's the matter with you, Ted? Church is out. Everybody's playing ball. C'mon! Get your glove! We need you!' It wasn't easy to withstand the pressure of the boys batting out the ball on the sandlots. Sunday was the day for the big game."[60]

Johnny Lutz recalled one time a minister dropped by his house and asked whether or not Lutz would be coming to church that Sunday. "I told him I didn't think so, that I'd planned to go fishing, and he turned to Ted, who was sitting right over there, and said 'What about you, young man?' Ted told him, 'Reverend, with all the Salvation Army services I've been to, I've probably spent more time in church than you have.'"[61]

Ted and Danny Williams at the San Diego harbor.

Danny Williams didn't take to Salvation Army services, either, and Danny was no athlete. Short of stature, like his parents, he also lacked a strong constitution. He could never keep up with Ted, even if it was just heading out for a hike to go hunting. He did in fact get himself in a fair amount of troubles – "scrapes" as Ted phrased it. Former fire chief Leonard Bell says, "Danny Williams was kind of incorrigible. He was hitchhiking down Pershing Drive. So I picked him up and said, 'Where you going, Danny?' He said, 'I'm supposed to be in court, but the hell with it; I'm just going to ignore them.' I think he was one of the reasons Ted never came back to San Diego off season."[62]

There were many of the pleasures of boyhood. Joe Villarino reminisced, "We used to go swimming. We'd go hunting down by where the stadium [Jack Murphy Stadium] is. There used to be a swimming hole down there called Dobie Pond. In them days, there was two or three dairies down there. We'd go down there hunting rabbits. I remember one time we went down there and we were walking along and a big rattlesnake come out right in front of Ted, and Ted just got the gun and shot him. He picked it up, wrapped it around his neck and took it home.

"We just walked over. It wasn't too far. It used to be called Ferrari's dairy. We used to go there, have a lot of fun in that valley down there, Mission Valley. Texas Street, that was an old dirt road then."[63] It was the family life that was lacking, Joe continued, "They usually just left him money as far as I know. And he'd go down and buy a hamburger or something like that. She wasn't home for dinner most of the time." The word was that brother Danny developed the habit of lifting items from the home, and so the kids would be locked out of the house until one of the parents came home. All the more time on the playground for Ted, or practicing his swing in the backyard.

All told, though, Ted felt very fortunate to have grown up in San Diego, and not just because of the climate. The support of neighbors, playground officials and others all helped him develop as a ballplayer, and as a fisherman. "I think I got the chance to cultivate these interests because I lived in a small town, which San Diego was then, and in a small town, you're not as insulated. You get to know people, you know your neighbors."[64] Life wasn't perfect, but Ted made the most of it by focusing on things he enjoyed and working to get better and better at them.

Hoover High School.

"Wos" Caldwell on the Hoover High field.

ENTERING HOOVER HIGH SCHOOL, FEBRUARY 1934

Ted Williams enrolled at San Diego's Herbert Hoover High School in February 1934, after spending his middle school years at Horace Mann. He did eventually make the baseball team at Horace Mann, competing against other schools in the city, but he was not mentioned in the *Cardinal*, the official publication of Hoover High School, until a month into his tenure at Hoover. He had apparently not forged a sufficiently strong reputation at Horace Mann to have his Hoover arrival heralded in print. Ted also recalls playing on the team organized by the Junipero Serra post of the American Legion, as well as sandlot ball – sometimes playing against sailors from ships stationed in the harbor at San Diego – boats like the Lexington and the Saratoga.

Ted believed in himself, and chose Hoover as his high school with baseball in mind. He himself stated, "I felt I had a better chance to play on a team just starting out and I managed to get in." The Williams family's Utah Street home fell within the San Diego High School district, not in Hoover's. Les Cassie and other teammates and family confirm: Ted feared he might not make the team at San Diego High and felt he would have a better chance at making the varsity team if he attended the smaller Hoover High. He told Bill Liston of the *Boston Traveler*, "I didn't think I had a chance of winning a letter on the San Diego High team. So I went to Hoover instead."[65]

Cassie, Ted's boyhood friend and neighbor, has a clear memory of Ted's first day on the Hoover diamond. It's the story that has gone down in legend. "I can still see him the day he came up to Hoover for the first time. He was in junior high school getting finished with the 9th grade, which he completed in midyear. We had started baseball practice at Hoover a couple of days before the fall semester ended. It wasn't a ballpark, just a big old open space. In right field was a lunch arbor, a roof over a bunch of benches.

"He came walking up right by the shops, which were close by where we were having batting practice, and he hollered out, 'Coach, let me hit!' Coach Caldwell didn't pay much attention to him. We must have had a hundred guys there trying out for baseball. He sat there on the steps of the print shop. Finally, he said again, 'Coach, let me hit!' By this time, we'd run out of pitchers and coach Caldwell was pitching batting practice. So he said, 'All right. Get up there and hit.' The first ball went up on top of that lunch arbor, and no one had ever hit one anywhere near there. That was our introduction to Ted."

Caldwell asked, "What's your name, kid?" And he replied, "Ted Williams. I go to Horace Mann, but we get out next week. I'll be here Monday."[66]

Hoover was the newer school. It had just opened on September 2, 1930 with 900 students and Coach Wofford Caldwell had to build a baseball program from scratch. The 1932 schedule was comprised of a total of three games – against LaJolla, Point Loma and Army Navy Academy. Caldwell, born January 26, 1906, had been the phys ed director at Woodrow Wilson Junior High School for a couple of years, and then was promoted to Hoover. He died January 22, 1998. Ted never forgot his first real coach.

Donald Fraim was a year ahead of Ted in high school. He also remembered Ted as an opponent during junior high. Fraim was "manager" of Hoover's baseball team in 1936 but, of course, it was Caldwell who ran the team. What were Fraim's duties? "I had a heart condition that wouldn't let me play. The coach was good enough that he said, 'Go and keep records for me, and do the figuring.' I kept all the records. I did all the scoring and records for the averages and so forth of the different players," he explained in mid-2003. Fraim turned them in to coach Caldwell, and unfortunately no longer has copies. He and coach Caldwell actually knew each other before both came to Hoover; Fraim knew Ted in junior high, too. "I met Ted in junior high school. He was an opponent in junior high, just a good kid ballplayer. I went to Woodrow Wilson. Horace Mann, our junior high school team played against [Wilson] so we knew him there. He was not a standout, not in junior high. I don't remember him as a standout. In summer ball, he really started standing out. At the playgrounds." He recalls Ted as pitching "off and on" and playing first base occasionally, not necessarily a regular on the Horace Mann team.

The familiar story tells how Caldwell first met young Teddy Williams and Ted talked Caldwell into letting him hit a few, a week or so before he came to Hoover. But Caldwell apparently saw Williams a few times during junior high school years, Fraim reveals. Fraim also kept records for Caldwell in junior high. "Coach Caldwell was a junior high coach at Woodrow Wilson, and we both moved to Hoover at the same time. Coach Caldwell, I think, actually recruited him away from San Diego High to get him to come out to Hoover."[67]

Caldwell told this author that May Williams wanted Ted to go to Hoover, not to San Diego High.[68] Ted doesn't credit any advisor for the particular decision to attend Hoover, but Ted was only 15 years old at the time and may not have come to this decision entirely on his own. How actively Caldwell may have courted Ted, if at all (Cassie's report of Caldwell asking Ted his name makes it seem he hadn't known him) is only conjecture, but Wofford Caldwell was clearly an ambitious coach determined to build the high school's baseball program.

Contemporary press reports show that Caldwell was very active reaching out to other schools across southern California to schedule games and to position Hoover to enter different leagues. It is not unlikely that he had contact with a few playground directors such as North Park Playground's Rod Luscomb. He may also have been in touch with the athletic director at Horace Mann, despite the baseball team being disbanded. Either or both may have recommended young Teddy Williams as showing interest, dedication and fledging talent. Or the story may have developed precisely as Les Cassie recalled it.

What did Fraim recall of Ted as a high school player? "He was a cocky young fellow, but he could live up to all of his cockiness. He could do what he wanted to. There was one time we were up at Wrigley Field and one of the pro teams of the time was playing, and we were watching before we got to take the field. Babe Herman hit a ball out of the park and Ted immediately said, 'Oh, that's nothing. I could do that.' Of course, everybody started ragging him about it. We had to wait until the pro team was off of the field but, sure enough, as soon as we got the field and started practice, the first hit he got was out of the park – right in the same place Herman had hit. He was just a normal teenage kid. He was cocky, but he did live up to all of it."[69]

Teammate Del Ballinger told Ed Linn a similar story about Babe Herman, and places it in Santa Monica in the spring of 1935. In Ballinger's account, Ted wasn't quite as sure of himself, but instead was in awe of Herman, saying, "Oh, I wish I had power like that. I wish I was that big and strong." But then, Ballinger says, "Ted got up in the game and hit two balls farther than Babe Herman! I mean, seven miles farther. He hit them farther as a high school boy. I said, 'Ted, you're a doozy.' He never seemed to realize how good he was."[70]

Fraim was offered some speculation: Rod Luscomb was the playground director at North Park. Might Caldwell have called up some of the playground directors looking for players for Hoover? "Yeah, he did," Fraim replied. "Caldwell played Saturday and Sunday ball locally, you know. He got Ted on the same team he was playing on. Even though he was just a kid, he got Ted on the same team. I always understood that he actually talked Ted into coming to Hoover."[72]

Looking back some years later, San Diego High's coach Mike Morrow did feel scooped, and ascribed the decision to the proverbial "they." He remarked that Ted's home in University Heights fell within the SDHS district, "but they got him to go to Hoover."[72] Morrow's memory was faulty, though, when he asserted at the same time that his teams never lost to Hoover in the three years Ted was in high school. In fact, of the eight official games between the two, both teams had 4-4 records. They did handle Williams well enough, though – he "only" batted .370 (10 for 27) with 2 home runs and 6 runs batted in, according to "Caver Conquest," another unattributed clipping found at the Hall of Champions. As a pitcher against the rival school, Ted was 3-2 with a 5.25 ERA, striking out 28 but walking 18.

Bill Caldwell, Wos Caldwell's son, reached far back into his memory in a 2003 interview and told me, "My dad's number 1 rival was 'Turkey Neck' Mike Morrow at San Diego High School. Ted played for him during the summer, Pony League ball – they called it American Legion then. Dad saw a real talent in Ted and managed somehow, by hook or by crook – maybe a little more crook (laughs) - to get him enrolled at Hoover. How Dad was able to do it, I don't know but he was able to get Ted to go to Hoover."[73]

Playground director Luscomb was clearly a very influential figure in Ted's life, so much so that Ted singled him out for mention in the brief speech Ted gave at Cooperstown on his 1966 induction into the National Baseball Hall of Fame. Of Lusk, Ted wrote, "I tagged after Rod Luscomb almost every day of my life for six or seven years, hanging around like a puppy waiting for him to finish marking the fields or rolling the diamond."[74] Luscomb would pitch over and over and over again to Ted; if there were ever a human definition of the word "mentor" it would be Rod Luscomb, who put in long extra hours to work with young Teddy Williams. Of course, Ted also mentioned Coach Wos Caldwell.

Ted stayed in touch with both, and Coach Caldwell was able to attend the opening ceremonies for the Ted Williams Museum in 1994. Luscomb treasured the knowledge of how significant he had been in the development of his ball field protégé. Chris Cobb, writing in "Down Memory Lane with Vintage (PCL) Padres," tells us that "when Rod Luscomb lay dying in a hospital in San

Diego, a letter from Williams was taped to the wall beside his bed, describing how much his help meant to Williams. As Luscomb drifted in and out of consciousness, he would look at the letter and talk about Ted Williams. He didn't want to see anything but that letter from Ted Williams."[75]

Ted wrote in *My Turn At Bat*, "Wos Caldwell tells the story that on my first day out, as a tenth grader I guess, I hit a couple balls on the cafeteria roof and the janitor came running out and made us change diamonds."[76]

Maybe it didn't take that much to spot the raw talent Ted Williams possessed, and maybe it didn't take that much to note how driven he was. Certainly Rod Luscomb did and so did Coach Caldwell. Other players may have not caught the eye, or benefited as much from Caldwell's coaching. Leonard Bell wrote of Caldwell, "Nice guy, but if you didn't have natural ability – forget it. He was no teacher."[77] On the other hand, Caldwell is credited by some as having effectively channeled Ted's energies. "Ted's coach toned him down," says his cousin Ruth Gonzales.[78] Caldwell's daughter Sally says that Ted and Wos Caldwell kept in touch right to the end. "I know Dad loved Ted very much," she wrote me in September 2003. "They had such a special bond that lasted so many, many years. Not long before Dad died I was able to get a message to Ted that if he wanted to speak with Dad before he passed on, he needed to call as soon as he could. About a week or two before Dad passed on, Ted called him and they talked for a long time. I know it meant so much to Dad when Ted had cared to call. It was so important that he got to say goodbye.

"I personally have many memories of Ted (even a crush on him when I was 13 and the only girl at the Ted Williams Camp in Massachusetts). One I distinctly remember was back about 1966 when I was working at Sunland Training Center (a residential facility for handicapped and retarded children) here in Gainesville (my first job), we had a baseball team of boys that I helped with (I always loved baseball myself). During one of his visits to Gainesville to see Dad, I asked Ted if he would come out and give the boys pointers. He didn't think twice, he was so wonderfully gracious and the boys were absolutely ecstatic. He gave them pointers on hitting and showed them all the love and respect he would have any top little league team. He certainly rose higher on the pedestal I always had him on."[79]

When he summed up his own baseball career, Ted praised the dedication that many coaches bring to their work. "Coaches at that level... where the hours are long and there isn't much remuneration, I think they are special people, dedicated and selfless people who have a kid in the palm of their hands during the most impressionable years of his life. A lot of times they're more of an influence than the parents."[80] Of Luscomb, he said, "I wish every kid could have a coach like Rodney Luscomb."[81]

YEAR ONE AT HOOVER - THE 1934 SEASON

The first mention of baseball in the pages of the *Cardinal* during the 1933-34 school year was on the sports page of the January 26, 1934 issue. "Coach Caldwell Opens Class Baseball Season" ran the headline. An interclass tournament began three weeks earlier, right after New Years. Each of the high school's three classes – seniors, juniors and sophomores – fielded a team. There were three weeks of workouts – the first focused on pitchers and catchers, the second on infield and the third on the outfield. Then followed three weeks of games between the teams.

One of the sophomores mentioned was Sheldon Fouts, who "has shown up so well he is within an ace of being as good as [Don] Kimball." It was also noted that "Roy Engle is giving [Woodrow] Helm a hard and tiresome chase for the catcher's berth."

The article continued, "Other good prospects are: Albright, Ondler, and Beckett for first base; Grinett [actual name Ed Grimmett] and Miller, short; Jones, third base; and Gilbert outfield." There was no mention of Ted Williams. This is understandable, because Williams only arrived at Hoover the next month, as one of the "Sophomore Bs" – the new class enrolling in February 1934 and scheduled to graduate in February 1937. This staggered class schedule, with two graduating classes each year, was common practice from the time Hoover opened until into the 1940s. The "feeder schools" also followed the same convention; it wasn't as though Horace Mann students sat around from June to the following February waiting to enter high school. As library media teacher Dennis Donley of Hoover High pointed out in a 2003 e-mail to this author, "No one would want a bunch of 15-year-olds with that kind of time on their hands."

Hoover was a sizable school; there were 1,461 students enrolled as of February 1934. Classes began on February 5 and Principal Floyd A. Johnson welcomed the incoming class noting, "We are looking for you to make a very definite contribution in helping to build and maintain worthwhile conduct and standards at Herbert Hoover senior high school." Johnson could not have been aware of the contributions that Ted Williams would make in baseball, in military service and to the fight against cancer in children, as the young student's life unfolded.

A February 23 *Cardinal* story entitled "Caldwell Uncovers Baseball Prospects" might have foreshadowed the coming of the greatest hitter who ever lived, but it did not. It did note that the sophomores turned in "much better performances than expected and a number of capable performers were uncovered." Apparently, Ted Williams was not among those deemed among "capable" – unless it was just that *Cardinal* sports editor Orville Nordberg failed to observe the young 15-year-old's talent. The Sophs beat the Seniors 8-3 and downed the Juniors "to a groveling defeat." Ralph Twiss was noted as a soph hurler. Little Tommy Johnson, second baseman, cracked out three hits. Roy Engle and Bill Ondler were considered promising behind the plate and at first base, respectively. Caldwell began to book games against other schools, these games arranged directly as Hoover was in no particular league or conference at the time.

Hoover High School team, 1934. Left to right: Back row: Ted Williams, unknown, Bill Ondler, Maury "Pop" Hurst, Coach Wos Caldwell, unknown. Insets: Roy Engle, Ralph Twiss. Front row: Don Kimball, Joe Villarino, Morris "Moose" Siraton, Woody Helm, unknown, unknown.

Cards Open Ball Series With Hillers

Two highly primed baseball teams representing San Diego and Herbert Hoover high schools today were to begin their annual three-game series for the city's mythical prep school championship in City Stadium.

A second game is billed on the Hoover diamond Tuesday.

The Hillers last year won two games to one and were favored to repeat. Coach Mike Morrow's team is completely changed from the one which met the Cardinals last season.

Don Kimball, ace Hoover hurler, probably will not be used today. He is expected to be saved for the Tuesday tussle.

Lineups:
Hoover—Siraton 2b, Hurst p or lf, Williams rf, Kimball lf or p, Helm c, Ramsey cf, Ondler 1b, Grummet c, Fouts 3b.
San Diego—Chilton cf, Tallamante p, R. Rafalovich ss, Randolph ss, Moore c, Prose 1b, Marshall 2b, Galindo rf, Sevara lf.
Umpires—Gravelle and Robbins.

The next issue of the school paper was the first to mention Ted Williams. The March 9 issue (the paper was published semi-monthly) ran an article written by "A. Doubleplay" – presumably a tongue-in-cheek cousin of Abner Doubleday. Helm and Kimball were noted as mainstays of the squad. Al Roberts, Morris Siraton and Bill Ondler were considered shoo-ins. Sheldon Fouts, [Morrie] Hurst and Twiss were all expected to play and John "Red" Ramsey was considered a cinch in the outfield. Then "Doubleplay" wrote the following sentence: "Other fielders include Sam Gilbert, Harold Jensen, Ted Williams, James Jones, Ed Grimmett, and Ray Gilbert." The writer foresaw a "fine baseball team and a whole string of first rate games with opposing clubs." Ted Williams had made it to the printed page, as one of the "other fielders."

Hoover High and rival San Diego High played a series of three games against each other, splitting the first two. Few players were mentioned by name in the *Cardinal*'s game account, though the story on a junior varsity game against Escondido mentioned Twiss, Engle, both Gilberts, Tommy Johnson and several others. Leslie Cassie was listed at third base, but the story had no mention of Ted Williams. Another story indicated that coach Caldwell was far from satisfied with the team's play and might be shaking up the lineup. This may have offered an opening for the young kid from Utah Street.

The *Cardinal* had a "jokes" column and in the April 13 edition, it ran one that might be deemed apropos of Ted's starting Hoover with a blank slate. Wilbur Kitchen asserted, "I can tell you the score of this baseball game before it starts." Don Law responded, "What is it?" to which Kitchen replied, "Nothing to nothing, before it starts."

Hoover beat Sweetwater 23-2 on March 25. Only Ramsey was mentioned by name in *Cardinal* coverage. Hoover's team name was the same as the school newspaper; the baseball team was the Cardinals, a/k/a the Cards or Redbirds. The March 29 Pomona baseball tournament was kicked off with an appearance by Will Rogers, and the Cardinals topped Colton 11-2 in the first round, but were shut out 4-0 by Santa Maria in the second round. Williams did not play in either game. It was noted that there was a week or two with no baseball games scheduled, so the team had to schedule some practice games to keep sharp.

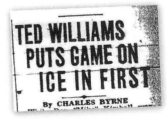

TED WILLIAMS PUTS GAME ON ICE IN FIRST

By CHARLES BYRNE

After 15 games on the season, the team had a .266 average and a .375 slugging percentage, but a poor .910 fielding percentage. Al Roberts was hitting .400, with Helm (.388) and Kimball (.351) right behind him. Kimball had led the team the year before, with Helm second and Roberts third. There was still no indication in the *Cardinal* that Williams had yet appeared in a game.

The San Diego city papers, on the other hand, had already recognized Ted Williams in print. The first reference found to the future Hall of Famer appears in the March 10, 1934 *San Diego Sun*. There, in a small bit headed "Cards Open Ball Series with Hillers" the lineups are presented for that afternoon's game. The lineups show, batting third, "Williams rf". This was to be the first game in what the *Sun* dubbed the "annual three-game series for the city's mythical prep school championship in City Stadium."

Was this Ted's first official high school appearance? As far as we can tell, it was. March 10, 1934. Hoover won that first game, as the next day's *San Diego Union* informs us. The score was 3-1 and it was a "wild 10th inning finish that brought thrills and chills to some 400 spectators." Hoover came out on top, behind the pitching of "Doleful Don" Kimball. Ted was not involved in the drama during the top of the tenth. But Hoover might never have been in extra innings – San Diego High scored once in the bottom of the 8th, and the score was tied 1-1 after nine – had it not been for Ted. The *Union*'s Charles Byrne reported that "Hoover had previously scored one run in the fifth, when Williams, an unsung sophomore outfielder, batting from the south side of the plate, tripled and scored on Kimball's single to left." Ted was 2-for-5 in the game, against Walter Tallamante. Batting .400.

Lanky mound ace for Hoover Cardinals

San Diego's "Hillers" came back and beat Hoover 11-8 in the second game, on the 13th. Ted went 1-for-3 and scored one of the runs. Again, he batted third and started in right field, but then took Ondler's place at first base after Ondler committed 2 of Hoover's 7 errors. Ted was flawless in the field.

On the 17th, San Diego High scored 15 runs to Hoover's 4, and thus took the three-game set. Ted played right field once more but, even though Tallamante was pitching again, Ted was dropped down in the order from third to fifth place. He went 0-for-3 and made an error, too.

Ted played all three games, but he was by no means cemented in the lineup. Before the March 27 game against Grossmont, the *Union* listed the Hoover squad but had Ted last on its list, as "Ted Williams, reserve outfielder."

There were better days ahead.

April 20, 1934 was a very big day indeed for Ted Williams. As a result, his name broke into print in the pages of his high school paper. The Cards defeated the leading Coast League team, Alhambra, 19-3. Pitcher John Stocking held Hoover scoreless in the first, but in the second inning Ted Williams hit a grand slam home run to center field, "a hard-hit line drive over the shortstop's head and between the outfielders."[82] "Ted Williams, sophomore outfielder, started the fireworks with a home run with bases full," reported the *Cardinal*. The *San Diego Sun* wrote, "Ted Williams started the Cardinals off on the victory road with a home run in the second canto with the bases loaded. From then on, Alhambra's pitchers seemed unable to put them where 'Waas' Caldwell's men couldn't connect." Caldwell had Ted batting seventh in the order, and one of the few times he batted in the 7 hole. (Tom Larwin's research shows Ted batted 9th in a game in November 1934, once in 8th and once in 9th in January 1935, and twice in the 7th slot during July 1935.) Ted went 2-for-2 and scored 3 runs. The Alhambra Moors walked 10 and committed seven errors. The *Alhambra Advocate* termed the loss a "farce." Perhaps a bit embarrassed, the Alhambra paper also noted that the game was a "practice affair." Ted's slam was the game-winning hit. Ted's feat earned him the sub-head in the *Union*:

"TED WILLIAMS PUTS GAME ON ICE IN FIRST."

The *Union*'s own box score and other game accounts demonstrate that the headline writer had the wrong inning. Nevertheless, it's a safe bet that the grand slam by the neophyte right fielder caught coach Caldwell's eye.

The next day, if Ted were in the mood to celebrate with a movie, he had a choice in his part of town. *Perils of Pauline* was showing at the New Ramona Theatre at 30th and University, while just a block away, the North Park Theatre offered "W. S. Van Dyke's epic *Eskimo*." It would have been surprising, though, if Ted weren't right back at the North Park playground hitting balls.

Ted may have been nuts for baseball, but one baseball-related event we can be reasonably sure Ted would have tried to avoid was the Baseball Dance scheduled for April 28 in the Hoover library after the Hoover-Covina game. The school paper advised that "each Hoover player is to bring a

Hoover team, 1935. Coach Caldwell at far right, Ted Williams, front row, far left.

girl" and that "a limited number of tickets, with name and positions of Covina players will be sold to Hoover girls." The dance was to honor the Covina team. The Covina Colts lost the game 6-2. Ted went hitless, 0-for-3. It's unlikely he attended the dance; if he did, he was probably running each at-bat through his head, trying to learn from his mistakes.

Ted had an eye for the ladies in later life, but in high school, he admitted, "I never went out with girls, never had any dates, not until I was much more mature-looking. A girl looked at me twice, I'd run the other way. You see pictures of me as a kid – gaunt. Nervous. Gee, I bit hell out of my nails, right down to the quick. Even later, when I first started signing autographs, I'd hold my head down."[83] High school teammate Leonard Bell says, "I don't remember ever seeing him with a girl."[84]

Some of the girls at Hoover may have perceived Ted as preoccupied and distant. One, the former Ruth Browning, recalled thinking he was "very arrogant, conceited." She saw him play baseball a few times, but preferred football herself. Much later in life, she met Ted in the hallways during an event in Balboa Park and they spoke. Maybe Ted had mellowed. He was, she found, "a very friendly man."[85]

With a wistful look back, Ted did have some regrets on this score. He told his cousin Manuel Herrera that when he attended his class reunion, there was a beautiful lady he had never noticed when he was going to school at Hoover High. He said, "Where was I when she was at school?" Manuel said, "I reminded him that he was hitting a baseball out at the high school baseball field!" That earned a laugh, and Ted's comment, "Baseball is only for a little while, and living is for the rest of your life."[86]

More comfortable on the diamond than the dance floor, in a home game against Pasadena on May 4, Hoover's right fielder Ted Williams "hit a two-bagger over the right field fence" off Bulldogs pitcher Schuelke. Ted went 1-for-2. Why was a ball over the fence only a double? Apparently a ground rule. The *San Diego Union* reported that "Woody Helm and Ted Williams also propelled the ball over the right field fence, but to the right of the 'barber pole,' the hits only going for doubles." Hoover won 10-3.[87] In fact, Hoover ran off a 6-game win streak beating Calexico, Escondido, and Montebello as well, carrying right into the California Interscholastic Federation (C.I.F.) championship.

The "barber pole" in right field robbed Ted of a few home runs. The right field fence was a short one, only about two hundred feet, because the team was really playing on the football field. There was a pole in right center and, Ed Linn informs us, "anything leaving the ballpark on the right-field side of the pole was only a double." Linn quotes Bud Maloney, a sportswriter for the *Union*, as a grammar school kid who watched Ted play. Maloney remembers, "I lived three blocks away, and after school I'd come down and watch the games. Ted used to hit some of the most majestic doubles I've ever seen over that short right-field fence. The ball would still be going up when it left the field and would land on a roof a block away. He used to hit under the ball even then, and it would go sky-high."[88]

Ted did not appear in the 6-3 defeat of the Calexico Bulldogs, at Hoover, on May 18 for the first round game of the C.I.F. tourney. Calexico was the Imperial Valley champion, so Hoover's win was a sweet one.

On May 25, the Escondido Cougars hosted the Cards in the semi-final round. Escondido was the best team in the Metropolitan League and Hoover was but one of the "free-lance" schools invited to the tourney. Ted didn't play in the 2-1 Hoover victory. The win should have placed Hoover in the finals, but the organizers shifted the rules and Hoover had to play yet another semi-final game, against Montebello, on June 2. The *Union* noted that, "The C.I.F. moguls get a big kick out of playing such jokes." Hoover 10, Montebello 8. Ted's only role was to draw a base on balls, pinch-hitting for Ondler in the eighth.

On June 8, the Hoover Cardinals lost to Cathedral High School of Los Angeles when Hoover star pitcher Don Kimball imploded and let in 8 runs in the bottom of the eighth. That was enough to overtake Hoover's lead, and prompted its ultimate defeat in the 1934 C.I.F. tourney.

The last mention of Ted Williams in the high school paper that season was with regard to the Montebello game. Hoover had been leading 6-4 after seven innings, but Montebello scored four times in the top of the eighth. Hurst reached first on an error and Swede Jensen sacrificed him to second. "Williams and Siraton walked, an error in handling Roberts fly tied the score 8-8." Ted's patience at the plate paid off; his was the tying run.

Ted's baseball play had made the printed page, noted by the local knights of the keyboard. The young sophomore earned himself a letter in baseball. His junior year, though, was Ted's breakout year.

Incomplete statistics for Ted Williams first year at Hoover High, compiled by Tom Larwin, are as follows:

	Pos	G	AB	R	H	2B	3B	HR	RBI	AVG
1934	OF-1B	6	18	6	6	1	1	1	unknown	.333

Ted had enrolled at Hoover in February, and hit his grand slam on April 20. The April 27 *Cardinal* gives a sense of what life was like around him that first year of high school.

The very evening of Ted's home run, a number of Quill and Scroll members attended an event at the Golden Lion Tavern.

"The Spider" as presented by the June class of 1934 was quite a success. The house was sold out three straight nights – May 3, 4 and 5 – at 25 cents a head. In addition to "The Spider" there was a Disney cartoon, a number by the orchestra, tap dance numbers and the Dunkel family trapeze act.

Henry Wilson, school custodian, commented, "I believe that this campaign for cleanliness on the school grounds is really bringing results."

Full cut dress shirts cost 79 cents at Frank's, while white sport shoes went for as low as $2.89. Hoover Drug Stores, across El Cajon Boulevard offered 17-cent specials on Rose Hair Oil Cream and Soothe Skin Talcum Powder. School activities included Pan-American Day with "dancing and music of Sunny Spain" while Hoover's string ensemble offered a performance for teachers and those interested. California Public Schools Week ranged from April 23 through the 30th, and an open house for parents was a key component. The Glee and Choral Clubs held a beach picnic, and the Student Concert Guild offered a special 15-cent student rate to a program of compositions from the 17th century to present times. A charity drive raising money

for the crippled children's pool was under way, collecting money in tiny stockings distributed throughout the school.

A dress code controversy broke out soon afterwards, related to proper dress for Hoover's female students following the summer of 1934, the dean of girls announced a bit of a relaxation in the code: "Girls are not required to wear ties with their middies and shirts." If they did elect to wear a tie, though, it had to be black. The girls had to adhere to a uniform apparel policy; the boys did not.

SUMMERTIME 1934

In the summer of 1934, and perhaps 1933 as well, Ted attended Camp Marston, a YMCA camp in Julian, California, about 60 miles east of San Diego. There he served as an assistant life guard with Bob Henderson, under a senior life guard named Art Linkletter. Henderson later became principal of a grammar school in Arizona and, in 1952, Bob wrote Ted on behalf of Jeff Kiehl, a kid at the Phoenix grammar school whose hopes for an athletic career had been dashed when he was found to have muscular dystrophy. Henderson requested, and received back, an autographed ball for the youngster. In an accompanying note, Ted wrote, "I certainly do remember Camp Marston (wish I was that young again)."

Henderson remembered Ted and the camp, when contacted early in 2003. "We went up for a couple of weeks. Ted's mother... he wasn't rich. He was a poor kid, and I was, too. Our parents didn't have the money to pay for the camp and so we worked, and one of the jobs was assistant lifeguard. Another one ran the little store where the kids could buy candy. I mainly did that. The other kids didn't work. They could go take a nap. We'd work. I think we paid five dollars or something like that, because we worked. They had about 12 cabins with about eight kids in each cabin. Ted and his brother and I were in one cabin. As I recall, they called him Buddy. Then they had a little softball league, you know. Ted's cabin would always win. I used to catch and Ted used to pitch. He was pitching at that time. We'd play every day. All the cabins would play and then you'd finally get down to the championship. Sure, he was a good hitter, too. Probably always was. He was a good pitcher, too. He was quite an athlete.

"He would lose his temper once in a while. Something happened in the baseball game, he would throw the ball in the creek and go back to the cabin. He stopped pitching. That just happened once. Maybe he just didn't feel like pitching anymore.

"I don't remember much about his brother. I remember one time we went for a long hike. There was a long row of kids, maybe 20 kids, and I stepped over a snake and Ted stepped right on him. He jumped about 20 feet in the air. There was an apple orchard right next to the camp. They warned all the campers, 'Now, don't you go over and eat those apples because they're green.' Well, Ted went anyway, and he got real sick. He got real sick. Then he wouldn't go down to headquarters to take castor oil or anything. They told him that he had a package from his mother, so he ran down to headquarters and they got him and gave him a dose of castor oil. Ted got mad and he left. Hitch-hiked back to San Diego. But then he was back in a few days."[89]

No wonder that when Linkletter mentioned Ted on his TV show many years later, he said, "There was a guy in our camp who wasn't always on his best behavior." Ted said that the only thing he remembered about the camp was that "I had a dollar for the week and it was stolen from me the first day, and the camp was down in a gully where the rain could settle." He added, "I peeled potatoes until I couldn't peel the bastards any more. Gee, I peeled potatoes all the time. I must have been there on a work scholarship."[90] When he started his own baseball camp in Lakeville, Massachusetts, he was very concerned to make sure it provided a much better experience for the campers.

Feisty already, and independent, very willing to strike out on his own – that was Ted Williams. No kids ever got in any real trouble at the camp, but later in life Henderson recalls a friend joking about Ted being a lifeguard. The friend quipped, "I hope he was doing better than .400 as a lifeguard!"

No doubt Ted got in a lot of baseball on the playgrounds that summer as well, back in San Diego. He was certainly primed for a big year, come 1935.

YEAR TWO - THE 1935 SEASON

September 28, 1934 – the very first issue of the *Cardinal* for the 1934/35 academic year announced that baseball training would begin after Christmas and that there were a number of open berths despite eight returning lettermen: Woodrow Helm and Roy Engle, catchers; Morris Siraton, second base; Morris Hurst, left field and pitcher; Ted Williams, right field; Ralph Twiss and Sheldon Fouts, pitchers; and Bill Ondler, first base. Given the season, most of the news, of course, was about football and, among the stories, one detailed the installation of new bleachers and lighting to enable night football. The bleachers offered seating for an additional 3,000 spectators. Hoover Field games could now seat 6,000 fans - a capacity rivaling many minor league baseball parks today. Baseball rarely drew even a couple of thousand (a couple of hundred was more typical.) By the early 1940s, though, there were probably many thousands who claimed to have first seen Ted Williams while he played at Hoover High.

Baseball coach Wofford Caldwell was looking forward to the new season, after such a successful 1933/34 campaign. He was looking in particular to continued improvement from Fouts on the mound. Ted Williams was not singled out by name.

In the October 12, 1934 *Cardinal*, football coach John Perry, apparently seeking a better practice regimen, decreed, "No more late dates for the football squad, no more dances and holding hands shall cease at precisely nine o'clock." As it happens, Hoover won the first five games on the gridiron schedule – without yielding a single point to any of its five opponents. Perhaps Perry's discipline was bearing fruit. It's a well-known fact that holding hands after 9 pm can be debilitating.

The shutout streak was shattered as the team lost 41-7 to Santa Barbara on Armistice Day, but all in all it was considered the best football season in the school's short history.

San Diego's climate was favorable to baseball. The annual interclass baseball tourney began on February 1, 1935, and typically the older students prevailed. On February 8, the seniors beat the juniors, and the juniors beat the sophomores – though in one of the four contests the sophomores beat the juniors. Not a single player's name was mentioned in the account of the tourney and its scores. One item of note, though, was the signing to a professional baseball contract of Don Kimball, the "three-year letterman and captain and ace moundsman" of the 1933 Cardinal team. "Deliberate Don" Kimball was signed on January 20 by Marty Krug of the Detroit Tigers and was to head for Beaumont, Texas – a class A team in the Texas League. He planned to try out for either first or third base. One can safely presume that others on Hoover's team took note of Kimball's signing. Everything we know about Ted Williams tells us that this probably helped fuel his determination to succeed at baseball.

Coach Caldwell was reported trying to organize some night baseball games.

The March 8, 1935 *Cardinal* announced that Opening Day of the season would be March 16, a home game against Santa Ana. The starting lineup envisioned Williams at first base. Before the regular season began, though, an alumni game was set for March 9. "Williams at the initial sack" was the plan here, too. Principal Johnson announced free passes to 500 dads of Hoover students, as a special favor (regular attendance was 25 cents for an adult.) Whether Ted's father Sam Williams took advantage is unknown. It seems unlikely. Ted did write in his autobiography that his father "had never seen me play too much." That changed when the scouts started sniffing around Ted a year later.

Come that time, Ted's dad began to buy him steaks. "My dad was never much of a baseball fan when I was a kid, never took much interest in it at all. I had to learn how to play from people like Rod Luscomb over at the playground, but as I started to get famous my dad would take more of an interest. I was starting to hit and get my name in the paper, and he would buy me a steak, a half-pound steak, before I played my game that day. I guess he was looking to build me up."[91]

The same issue of the school paper had photographs of Hoover's coach Caldwell, as well as "Ted Williams, pitcher" and Woody Helm, catcher. This was the first mention of Ted as a pitcher. Caldwell offered his opinion that "Helm is probably the outstanding young catcher in So. California, and Williams should develop into an excellent pitcher and very powerful hitter." The coach said he thought the varsity team was going to be the best in school history, but that "You can't win the Southern Cal. baseball championship unless you beat every strong team in Southern California." Williams was being moved around a bit and had worked out as a pitcher as well. After playing outfield the previous year, he was seen as likely "one of the principal pitchers this season."

Reflecting later in life, Caldwell said the decision to have Ted pitch was a simple one: "He pitched in high school because he had the strongest arm. He was a skinny bastard. But he could rear back and really throw that ball in there. In high school, that's all he had to do, pitch them high and hard."[92] Caldwell, meanwhile, was working with Ted on running. "What I remember is the switch Wos used to have. He was always after me to run faster, and he'd start me at home plate, let me get halfway to first base, then come after me with that switch. Usually he caught me between first base and second and was hacking at my butt the rest of the way."[93]

The Hoover team already had one pre-season game under its belt. In early March, they "showed early season power" in beating the Naval Hospital 6-5. Ted played first base, and the game account noted that "Ted Williams and McBurnie led the Hoover team in batting, each pounding out a pair of safe hits for two times at bat." The box score, however, showed Ted as 1-for-2, though scoring 2 runs. Presumably he walked once as well, perhaps displaying some of the plate discipline he became known for. His hit was a single.

Those new bleachers may have held thousands, but only 300 fans showed up for the first baseball game of the year, the game against Santa Ana on Saturday, March 16. That morning, Henry Hache, sportswriter for the *Union* noted, "Hoover's mound hope this afternoon will be Ted Williams, one of the ranking member of Coach 'Wash' Caldwell's prized mound staff. Williams promises to be one of the best hurlers ever turned out at the East San Diego high school, but up to the present time has seen most of his diamond action at first base..."

Indeed, Ted began the game at first base, with Twiss on the mound. Twiss struck out 11 and the Cards were leading 4-2 after six innings. Ted was brought in and held the Saints scoreless. The final score was 6-2. As far as we can tell, this was Williams' first "save."

Ted didn't waste any time cranking up his offense. Willie "Emperor" Jones was regarded as one of the best pitchers in southern California. The "whirlwind Negro pitcher" had shut out Brea-Olinda in his previous effort, striking out 16 opponents – including 8 in a row to end the game. The *Cardinal* columnist noted, "Coach Wofford Caldwell's team started scoring in the first inning, when Ted Williams, lanky Redbird slugger, connected with one of 'Emperor Jones" fast ones for a long home run over the Saint center fielder's head, bringing in McBurnie, Card center fielder, from second base." In the 4th inning, McBurnie came up again and was hit by a pitch by the "dusky Saint hurler." Ted was up next, batting cleanup. "Williams then took the measure of another of the Saint mound ace's deliveries and sent it over the right field fence for a double, missing the home run marker by only a few feet." Once again, he'd hit one out of the park but it only counted for two bases. Hoover had scored twice in the first on Ted's two-run homer. Now they added one in the 4th. Ted faced the Emperor one more time. In the 6th, "Williams layed into one of the 'Emperor's' fast ones and lifted it high over the right field fence for a home run."

As if going 3-for-4 with 2 home runs and a double was not good enough, Ted came in and pitched those final three innings for Hoover, striking out 5 and not allowing a run. "Between his pitching and his slugging... [Williams] was the game's outstanding star," noted the *Union*.

It may be worth noting, parenthetically, that Ted Williams and his teammates seem to have had no problem playing against teams that fielded African-American ballplayers. It just doesn't seem to have been a point of controversy. Bill Swank, San Diego baseball historian, explained, "Blacks and Whites played with and against each other all the time in San Diego. There were several Black baseball teams that played against White teams in Southern California dating back to the 1890s. San Diego High School always had Blacks on their athletic teams. Was there prejudice against Blacks and Mexicans in Southern California? Yes, but playing ball together (as teammates or opponents) was common."[94]

GAME: March 16, 1935
Hoover High Cardinals 6, Santa Ana Saints 2
Williams 3-for-4, with 2 runs scored. 2 HR, 1 2B. 3 IP, 5 K, 0 runs.

There had been two practice games the previous week, both against military teams. One, against the Marine Base nine, Hoover lost 12-11. It was a high-scoring, sloppy affair. Ted Williams played first base for the first six innings, then pitched. He was "touched for only four runs" but it sounds as though at least some of those were unearned, as the "game was played very poorly, with both teams making frequent errors." The Hoover squad made seven errors. At the plate, though, Williams was flawless: he went 5-for-5. The rest of the Hoover team combined only managed three additional hits.

Hoover also played the Naval Hospital again, and beat them once more, this time by a lopsided 17-3 score. Williams played first, and again was a perfect 5-for-5.

They also played a "strong Central Playground nine" and lost 3-0 in another practice game. If Williams played, it wasn't noted. Possibly he had not; Hoover only had two hits in the whole game against Central's Swede Smith.

GAME: March 22, 1935
Hoover High Cardinals 10, Woodrow Wilson Beachers 1

This was an away game against Long Beach. Ralph Twiss and Ted Williams combined pitching duties and held the Long Beach team to just five hits. Williams played in center, until being asked to relieve Twiss on the mound. There was no mention of Ted's offense in the Hoover newspaper, though Helm, Hurst and Engle were all noted for a multiple hit game. Ted went 1-for-3, and scored 2 runs. Ted the pitcher was credited with the win.

GAME: March 30, 1935
Hoover High Cardinals 11, Ingelwood High School 4

Winning their third straight game of the season, Ted played first and was 2-for-2 at the plate. He scored 2 runs and made one of the six Hoover errors. Twiss threw a complete game.

In between regular games, Caldwell kept his boys busy. On April 4, warming up for the game on the 6th against Covina, Hoover beat Marshall Pierson's Texaco Servicemen, 8-3.

GAME: April 6, 1935
Hoover High Cardinals 15, Covina Colts 0

Covina and Hoover both came into this game with perfect 3-0 records. Caldwell's crew dropped the Covina nine in their tracks, 15 to 0. Ralph "Crooner" Twiss spun a shutout; he let the Colts have but one hit, and struck out 13. He also knocked out a couple of hits himself, but the offensive star was "Theodore Williams, lanky Hoover first-sacker" who hit for the cycle, pounding out a home run, a triple, a double and two singles in six trips to the plate. The *Union* reported, "Ted Williams and Morris Siraton were the heroes of the Hoover 19-hit attack off Yiregoyan and Parbose." (Siraton had two doubles and three singles.)

On the 10th, the Hoover nine beat the sailors of the U.S.S. Detroit, 9-7. Ted shared pitching duties with Fouts and Twiss.

GAME: April 12, 1935
Hoover High Cardinals 10, Glendale High 5

Ted handled all the pitching in this game, striking out 16 batters and yielding but six hits. The *Cardinal* wrote: "Ted Williams, stellar Card moundsman, led the field in batting, gathering four safe hits in five times at bat." The *Union* box score showed that Ted walked two and yielded a home run to the Glendale Dynamiters' Zuniga, but reportage stated, "Ted Williams, lanky Cardinal chucker, pitched six-hit ball, fanned 16 batters and pounded out four hits in five trips plateward to grab the starting laurels."

GAME: April 13, 1935
Hoover High Cardinals 7, San Bernardino 1

Caldwell took his charges to San Berdoo, and Ralph Twiss went the distance. "Ted Williams, lanky Card flyhawk, led the batting for the day, pounding out a home run and a single in three times at bat." – The *Cardinal*. "Lanky" was clearly the word of the day, when applied to Ted.

POMONA TOURNAMENT GAMES, APRIL 1935

Hoover was undefeated in its regular season games, and was welcomed to the Pomona Invitational Diamond Tournament, sponsored by the 20-30 Club and played on five baseball diamonds in Pomona. Hoover was seeded fourth.

The "San Diego Herbies" of Herbert Hoover High won the first round, beating Whittier 4-1 in the 6-inning game on April 18. Williams started, relieved at some point by Fouts; the two combined to hold Whittier to just eight hits. All the scoring took place in the fourth inning, Hoover scoring four times while Whittier pushed across its lone run. Twiss threw a complete game in the second round, against Glendale, and it was a good one. Hoover was losing 2-1 but scored once in the top of the seventh, Engle's double driving in Siraton. In the bottom of the inning, Glendale scored once and Hoover's Redbirds took a 3-2 loss. The overall tournament winner was Long Beach Poly. Hoover's Woodrow Helm was chosen first-string catcher on the honorary nine, and awarded a gold baseball.

GAME: April 23, 1935
Hoover High Cardinals 3, San Diego High 1

A Tuesday morning away game against San Diego High was the first game of the third annual series between the two high school rivals. The *Union*'s Harry Hache hyped it as "the series of the century... a three-game baseball civil war series." He characterized Ted as "a cool customer when in action before a hostile crowd" and added, "Williams has been pounding the 'apple' like a Babe Ruth, and along with his mound ability, is looked upon as Hoover's best bet to stop the Hillers." The *Sun* saw a different side of Ted: "Ted Williams, who seems to have a lot of fun pitching for the Cardinals and who was accused of not having 'anything' on the ball but a prayer, allowed the Morrowmen only five hits..."

"Ted Williams, Card hurler, pitched a brilliant game for Hoover," the *Cardinal* reported, "allowing the Hilltoppers only five scattered hits and striking out the same number of batters. He also con-

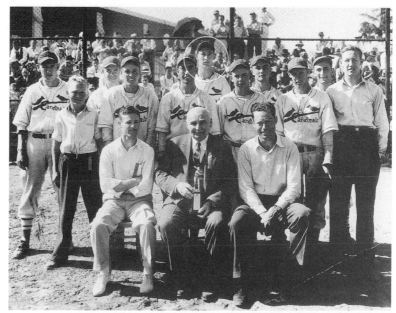

tributed to the scoring column, driving in a run in the third inning and scoring one himself in the fifth." Williams singled in the third to score Moose Siraton, who'd reached third with a triple. The run Ted scored in the fifth followed a walk; Roy Engle drove in both Johnson and Williams for the second and third Hoover runs. The only run San Diego High got off Williams was on back-to-back doubles in the fourth. Moose Siraton, by the way, was so named because he was the smallest player on the team.

Hoover team at Pomona Tournament, Ted Williams in center, rear.

GAME: April 24, 1935
San Diego High 9, Hoover High Cardinals 5

On the 24th, San Diego High beat Hoover 9-5. Ted hit a home run, in a game where he started out as the right fielder, was brought in to pitch and then, when relieved, finished the game in centerfield. Ted had relieved in the sixth, Caldwell hoping (in vain) that Ted could put the brakes on what became a 5-run inning.

GAME: April 27, 1935
Hoover High Cardinals 4, Pomona High 0

Ralph Twiss handled matters, striking out 15 and letting up just three hits to the visitors from Pomona. "Williams, Helm and Fouts led the Cards in batting, each pounding out a two-base hit" – Williams' was a scorching RBI double in the fifth, driving in Fouts from second.

GAME: April 30, 1935
Hoover High Cardinals 6, San Diego High 2

"Ted Williams, lanky Cardinal mound ace, hurled a brilliant five hit game for the Hooverites, and helped his team along in batting with a pair of scorching singles." So wrote the *Cardinal*. Williams was 2-for-3, batting in his now-customary cleanup position. This was one pitcher who didn't bat in the number 9 slot. The game was played before an estimated 2,000 spectators, the *Union* told readers, and "Lanky Ted Williams, loose-jointed Cardinal who dotes on hitting 'em where they ain't, was the hero of the engagement, pitching five-hit ball to check potent Hilltop sluggers, and clouting out a pair of sharp singles to play a big part in the run scoring."

GAME: May 11, 1935
San Diego High 14, Hoover High 11

Hoover had won all eight of its regular season games, and taken the series from San Diego High to boot. For the third year in a row, the strong Hoover team was invited to play in the Southern California C.I.F. playoffs, but they lost to San Diego High in the first round, in a wild 14-11 game, despite jumping out to a 5-0 lead in the first. Ralph Twiss gave up 2 in the second and 2 in the third, then relieved by Ted Williams, on whose watch 10 runs scored, the deathknell sounded by a 7-run eighth inning. Ted struck out 4, but walked 5. SDHS catcher Moore hit a two-run homer off Ted in the bottom of the fifth, putting the Hillers up 6-5. Williams contributed to the offense, though, with a "terrific home run" in the sixth inning, a grand slam according to the *Cardinal*. The more detailed *Union* account, though, shows it as a 3-run homer driving in Fouts and Siraton. The *Union* game account and boxscore present conflicting information as to the number of Hoover hits, but the reportage makes it clear that Ted's homer was of the 3 RBI variety.

Hoover was back on top and Ted held them scoreless in the sixth and seventh, and had two outs in the eighth, but then Ted collapsed, allowing 3 walks, 4 singles and 2 doubles for those 7 runs. Williams was 1-for-4 but scored 3 runs.

The season over, Sports Editor Lloyd Baskerville of the *Cardinal*, presented a summary under the headline "Baseball Team Leaves Impressive Record." The Cardinals won 12 out of their 15 regular season games. On the mound, Williams won four games and lost two; the star pitcher was Twiss with a 6-1 record. Fouts was 2-0. As a fielder, Ted made 16 putouts and had 18 assists, but made 2 errors - a .945 fielding percentage, which kind of left him in the middle of the pack. In hitting, though, he excelled, leading the team in home runs with seven, in runs batted in with 22, in hits with 30, and in hitting with a .588 batting average (30 hits in 51 at-bats.) The team batting average was .346, with Helm and Ballinger hitting .424 and .423 respectively. Helm, like Don Kimball, reportedly received an offer to play baseball professionally.

Morris Siraton was named honorary captain for the just-completed season. Helm and Twiss also received gold baseballs for their three years of varsity service. The *Union* noted that Ted, who "starred both at bat and afield for the Cardinals as pitcher and outfielder, paced the Cardinals at bat with the fat average of .588 for the 15 games comprising Hoover's regular schedule." The newspaper also recognized the seven home runs by "the elongated mound ace."

Having led the team in average, "the stringy Cardinal slugger" earned the right to have his name engraved on the Kelley-Todd perpetual trophy.

SUMMERTIME 1935

It was back to the North Park playground and a series of pickup games for the summertime. Ted may have helped out some at America's Exposition which San Diego hosted during the summer. Some accounts have Ted's father as active in running the Exposition, but this has so far proved impossible to confirm. (Ted's cousin Ernesto Ponce and his wife visited San Diego for their honeymoon and say that Sam Williams was in charge of the Exposition at the time.)

Though just a junior in high school, Ted had attracted the interest of major league scouts. The first interest was expressed when Ted was still just 16. Ted told author Cynthia Wilber that he'd been invited to a Cardinals tryout camp in Fullerton, California, but the day before he'd been hit on the upper leg by a pitch and bruised to the bone. "The very first thing they did was put a big number on your back," he told Wilber. "There were about five hundred kids there and I was near four hundred someplace." He certainly wasn't Number Nine yet![95]

With the injury, Ted said, "I couldn't run a lick and I didn't hit particularly well that day and of course they passed me right up."[96] "If I couldn't run fast when I was healthy, that sore leg made me look like I was anchored," he explained. "I was discouraged, I didn't hit particularly well, and they hardly gave me a look."[97] Ted says he eventually did get an offer from the Cardinals, "but they probably would have sent me to Oshkosh or Peoria or someplace, because they had a huge farm system and you could get lost."

Ted joined the occasional semi-pro team as well, and more than one. Cousin Frank Venzor had heard that men occasionally came around the Williams family house on Utah Street, trying to get Ted to play for various teams. At one point, perhaps on the playground, he was approached to play for the Texas Liquor House team, and he was excited at the prospect. Meredith "Rosey" Rose took

Baseball Team Leaves Impressive Record

Hoover varsity baseball team has just completed its successful 1935 season, and Coach Wofford Caldwell has named 12 men who will receive varsity letters for their service on the team. Lettermen are: Williams, Fouts, Twiss, hurlers; Helm, catcher; Siraton, shortstop; Engle, third-base; Johnson, second base; Ondler, first base; and Bickerton, Bennett, McBurnie, and Ballinger, outfielders.

Morry Siraton, flashy little Card shortstop, has been chosen by his teammates as honorary captain for the season just closed.

Ralph Twiss, hurler; Woody Helm catcher; and Morry Siraton, shortstop, have been awarded gold baseballs for three years of service on the varsity nine.

On their regular season games the Cardinals won 12 out of their 15 games, and went as far as the second round in the annual Southern Cal. C. I. F. diamond play offs.

Seasonal batting averages:

	G.	Ab	R	H	Rbi	Pct.
Williams, p-cf.	15	51	20	30	22	.588
Helm, c	14	59	10	25	8	.424
Ballinger, cf.	9	26	8	11	2	.423
Siraton, ss.	15	60	16	23	8	.384
Fouts, cf-p.	14	52	12	18	8	.347
McBurnie, cf.	4	9	3	3	1	.333
Engle, 3b	15	56	14	17	17	.304
Johnson, 2b	11	40	12	11	3	.275
Bennett, cf.	15	51	5	14	12	.274
Bickerton, cf.	6	15	1	4	1	.266
Ondler, 1b	11	32	3	6	6	.187
Twiss, p-cf.	12	38	2	7	3	.184
Totals		489	106	169	90	.346

Seasonal Fielding Averages

	PO	A	E	Pct.
Ballinger	9	0	0	1.000
Bickerton	4	1	0	1.000
Ondler	89	0	1	.989
Helm	111	5	4	.976
Fouts	25	3	1	.966
Williams	16	18	2	.945
Johnson	18	15	2	.943
Siraton	11	37	3	.941
Bennett	20	11	3	.912
Engle	32	14	3	.875
Twiss	2	14	3	.842
Totals	337	128	27	.926

over management of the team in mid-May, 1935, and the *Union* ran a story on the 11th indicating, "Rose has procured the services of Frankie Morehouse... Morris Hurst, Ted Williams and Woody Helm, all of Herbert Hoover High school." Rose jumped the gun with the announcement.

When he excitedly told his mother he had a chance to make good money playing baseball, she said that was fine but when she asked for the name of the team, and he told her it was the Texas Liquor House team, Ted wrote, "If I said Murder, Inc., I wouldn't have been turned down any quicker."[98]

Ted would have been paid $5 a Sunday. His mother was also opposed to him playing baseball on Sundays. May Williams was horrified; she could hardly imagine a worse scenario than her eldest son playing while wearing a shirt that promoted liquor sales at the same time she was preaching the evils of alcohol and ministering to those suffering its ill effects.

PADRE SERRAS JUNIOR CHAMPS

Paced by Ted Williams, lanky right hander who allowed but two hits, the Padre Serra baseball team yesterday won an easy 4 to 1 victory over Mountain Meadow Creamery at Golden Hill playground. With its win, the Serra nine became champion of the Junior Exposition League composed of youths under 16.

Williams also was the leading hitter of the day when he collected a single, two triples and a home run. Williams struck out 16 batters while Jewel Marsh, Mountain Meadow hurler, was not far back when he whiffed 11 men. Tony Angeles, Creamery fielder, suffered a severe cut on his mouth when he crashed into a wooden frame when trying for a long foul fly. The score:

	R.	H.	E.
Padre Serra	4	8	2
Mountain Meadow	1	2	1

Had one of the other teams in the city league – say, Qualitee Dairies – signed Ted, it would likely not have upset "Salvation May" as much. Cramer's Bakery, Ortiz Chevrolet or Henry's Coronado Ferry Market may also have represented acceptable alternatives.

"No Sunday playing, and no tie-up with demon rum," she told Teddy. They worked it out, though. "We finally compromised," he told the *Boston Evening American*'s Joe Cashman. "She relented on Sunday playing, and I yielded on the liquor connection. I got a job playing Sundays for a grocery concern at $3 per game."[99]

Box scores of the day show us that Bernard Storton was on the Liquor House team, playing third base, and so was San Diego High's Dick Tallamante. Bernard Storton's brother Alan still lives on Oregon Street, and showed Bill Swank the house two doors away hit by one of Ted's deep flies over the right field fence. Alan told Bill that Ted "always wanted to play with us at University Heights playground. We were older and Ted was just a kid then. The Tallamante boys, Frankie Morehouse, Hank Jones, Pino Sada, Tony Galasso, Travis Hatfield... they were good ballplayers. Ted was about 9, 10 or 11 and he wanted to play with us. It's kind of funny now. Ted used to come watch us play for free. Later we paid to watch him play, but we wouldn't let him play with us back then."[100]

For a kid of even 10 or 11 to be paying with kids five or six years his senior would have been remarkable, but something in Ted made him want to – and feel he could hold his own. Where for some kids, this frustration of wanting to play and being denied would have been discouraging, in Ted's case we can only surmise that it contributed to his determination and drive. Family relatives tell of how Ted wanted to play with his uncle Saul Venzor, a semi-pro player in Santa Barbara, but again Ted was turned down. One can almost hear Ted swearing to himself, "I'll show them!" The echoes were there at Spring Training with the Red Sox in 1938, when Ted was sent to Minneapolis for a year instead of being kept with the big league club and he vowed to clubhouse man Johnny Orlando, "I'll be back. Vosmik, Cramer and Chapman think I'm just a fresh young punk, don't they? Well, you can tell them I'll be back, and I'll make more money in a single year than the three of them put together!"[101]

Ted did play for the Walter Church Service Station team and the *Union* reported on a night game held on June 7, 1935. Apparently under deadline pressure, the story was filed after seven innings, with Walter Church leading the Metropolitan All-Stars 3-1. "Ted Williams, pitcher for the Church team, had dealt out only three hits in the seven innings and was the batting star with a triple and double in two chances." One wonders where Ted hit in the order, though, as we read that the Metropolitan pitcher "struck out the first seven batters to face him."

One can also surmise that the Salvation Army's May Williams would be far more pleased to read of her son on "the Church team" than had she read of him on "the Liquor team." Ted tells us in *My Turn At Bat* that Walter Church owned both a chain of service stations and the Texas Liquor House, so perhaps there was little difference in the end![102]

Tom Larwin's research shows that Ted did sneak in one game for the Bay City Liquor team in October, 1935.

These neighborhood games were never systematically covered by local papers, but box scores do pop up from time to time. Ted played right field for the North Park Merchants against Cramer's Bakery on June 23. He went 1-for-1, but since no one else played right field, he must have either walked or reached on errors the other times up. Ted scored 1 run, but the Merchants lost 6-5 in the tenth inning. Rod Luscomb was the losing pitcher.

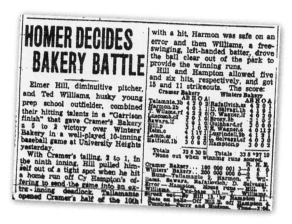

Another box score shows Ted playing left field and mentor Rod Luscomb playing center. There are two Villarinos in the same boxscore, one in right field and the other at first base. Luscomb was older, but Ted had closed the gap to where 11 years seniority no longer made a difference. Alan Storton remembers even back when Ted was younger, though, "Rod Luscomb used to pitch to Ted. He saw the potential."

On June 30, North Park lost to Winter's Bakery, the North Park team only getting two hits all day. Both hits were Ted's; he went 2-for-4.

In early July, on the 6th, Ted pitched for the Padre Junipero Serra Post American Legion junior baseball team on the Golden Hill diamond in a 2:30 game. This was a sort of proxy battle between Hoover and San Diego High; the *Union* noted, "the Padres are made up of Hoover High players while Post 6 is made up of San Diego High performers." The paper further commented, "Ted Williams of the Serra squad and Bill Skelley of the Morrowmen will take the mound to do battle for the third time this season. Both are the star hurlers of their respective teams and the squad that loses will have no cause for alibis as both are at full strength. Padre Serra is shooting at its second straight title while Post 6 will be endeavoring to gain revenge on Wos Caldwell's outfit for the drubbing received last year." Thus, this truly was a Mike Morrow vs. Wos Caldwell match-up under the names of the two American Legion teams. Ted was listed at cleanup, but as events transpired he went 0-for-2 at the plate. Despite striking out 11 and only giving up seven hits, he lost to Skelley and the Post 6 team, 8-7.

The Serras beat Oceanside 13-0 four days later. Ted played left field in that game, and went 2-for-5 with a double, scoring 2 runs. On the 13th, the Padres put Ted back on the mound and he revenged the July 6 loss, blanking Post 6 by a 10-0 score. Frank Sherwood wrote for the *Union* that "Ted Williams, Padre Serra's right handed pitching ace had a field day yesterday... Williams allowed five hits while fanning 13 batters and also collected two hits in three times at bat." They were both singles. Ted got on base otherwise, too; he scored three times.

Post 6 bounced back and beat Serra 11-4 on the 15th, Bill Skelley again dominating – though Ted touched him for a triple in 3 at-bats. Ted came in as a relief pitcher but was ineffective ("just another pitcher to the Morrowmen.") Skelley was one hot pitcher; on July 19 he pitched a perfect game to win the California Fifth Area championship in the American Legion junior baseball tournament.

While Williams continued to play for the Padre Serra post team, he was also probably picking up a little cash in a few other games. Some players could make $3 a week. Pitchers got a bit more. In a City League game on July 21, Ted was back playing for the Walter Church Service Station team, and they beat the San Diego Giants 10-1, with both Ted and Rod Luscomb hitting home runs. Even though these were city games with teams mostly made up of men and boys who were semi-pro at best, there was clearly a very high level of quality evidenced on the city's ball fields. Back on July 8, Ted had gone 0-for-4. On the 21st, the Walter Church team scored 10 times, but Ted only had the one hit (the homer) and went 1-for-4.

On August 3, the Padre Serras became champions of the Junior Exposition League (there were a confusing array of leagues, tournaments, and championships in those days) in a game "paced by Ted Williams, lanky right hander who allowed but two hits" as the team beat Mountain Meadow Creamery at the Golden Hill playground 4-1. The *Union* wrote: "Williams was also the leading hitter of the day when he collected a single, two triples and a home run." Ted struck out 16.

August 18 came and the Walter Church "Powerenes" beat El Cajon 6-2. Ted pitched, and batted third. He went 1-for-3 with 9 Ks. A week later the "Churchmen" beat the Bert Stratton Plasterers 7-2, Ted going 2-for-4 and pitching a five-hitter with five strikeouts (he yielded four walks.) One week after that, on the first of September, Walter Church lost to Cramer's Bakery 3-2. Cramer's Elmer Hill allowed just six hits, out-pitching the Powerenes' Williams and Hurst. Ted was 0-for-4 in the University Heights game. One can bet that Ted took a few extra swings in his home neighborhood that evening! The Church team changed their name to the Cardinals, but that didn't help them much; they lost their September 8 game as well. Ted may have been back at school by that time; news coverage didn't mention him.

Did Ted Williams ever have another job aside from semi-pro ball? Apparently so, according to Edward S. Bernard, manager of the Biltmore Hotel in Los Angeles. Bernard told the *Christian Science Monitor*'s Frank Waldman in 1957 that he had given teenage Ted his first job. Ted worked as elevator operator and bell boy at Bernard's U.S. Grant Hotel in San Diego. Ted had a "great pair of hands" even then, Bernard recalling that he "never dropped a room service order, never spilled ice water on hotel guests and never was impolite – not even to the occasional minor league umpires who wandered into the U.S. Grant lobby from time to time."[103]

AUTUMN 1935 / WINTER 1936

During the autumn of 1935 at Hoover, there was certainly a lot going on, but young Ted Williams seems not to have taken active part in any of the other school activities. In the yearbook, the only affiliation noted was "baseball" and his name never cropped up in the pages of the *Cardinal* for anything other than baseball. He didn't enroll in R.O.T.C., though 98 boys did. He wasn't an actor in "Ice Bound," the drama presented by students. He didn't join the accordion band. He did, by all accounts, keep his mind on baseball. He tried other sports, though.

"I went out for football," Ted told Wayne Lockwood of the *Union* in 1977. "But I wasn't much good at it. I was too skinny, got knocked around a lot. Besides, I knew that baseball was all I really wanted to do." In the early 1990s, the short-lived Ted Williams Card Company issued a "Teddy Football" card depicting Ted in his football uniform.

Though he apparently never saw court action, Ted was on the basketball team. Bruce Maxwell, Hoover's basketball coach, said that he carried Ted on the team "so we could improve his footwork. He was clumsy at first."[104] Across town, Art Linkletter – who had served at Ted's counselor at the YMCA camp Ted attended – was captain of the San Diego State College championship basketball team, which won the Southern California conference title. Ted, though tall for his era, never liked basketball. He said, "The only sport I didn't particularly like was basketball because the ball always seemed four sizes too big."[105]

Ted may have been trying to add weight with the 10-cent malted milks served at Hoover Drug Store, across the street from his high school at the corner of 45th and El Cajon Boulevard. Sandwiches and home made pies were just five cents apiece. The young Ted, later to be dubbed "The Splendid Splinter" in Boston, hated to be so skinny. Ted's aunt Sarah Diaz told her family that he sometimes locked himself in his room at home, angry and frustrated at being such a stringbean.[106]

"I was forever telling myself, you got to have bigger arms, you got to put on weight," he remembered in *My Turn At Bat*. A self-described "malted milk hound", he'd have four or five a day – with eggs – trying to put on weight.[107] Ted combined exercise and a high fat diet, he told *Sports Illustrated* in 1955, "When I was a kid, I used to do different exercises to develop my arms and chest because I was so skinny and didn't have much strength. I have to laugh now. Fifteen years ago, every night before I went to bed, I'd eat a quart of ice cream or have a big malted milk with eggs in it because they said that'd put fat on me."[108]

Coach Caldwell's son Bill remembers, "Every time Ted would hit a home run, Dad would have to buy the whole team a malted milk. Ted loved those malted milks. One year, that got expensive."[105]

Bill Caldwell had another memory from his childhood. "The North Park business people would tell the story about watching Ted as he walked along with his bat. Every business then had a bay window. Ted would stop and stand in front of a window and take a few practice swings. He'd watch his reflection. He didn't have any idea that they could see him – and he'd stop and swing and stop and swing, then he would walk along and think of something else [about his form], and he'd stop and swing again. Later when Ted became famous, these batting exercises became the talk of the North Park businessmen, each attempting to out-do the other."[110]

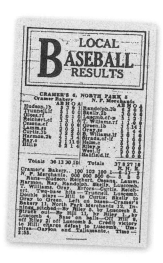

Early in 1936, the *Cardinal* ran a profile of baseball coach Wofford Caldwell. He'd attended high school in Huntington Park and Riverside, and earned seven letters in varsity sports. He attended Chapman College, UCLA and the University of Illinois, where he was tendered an offer to play baseball for the Chicago Cubs. All along, he pursued his calling as an engineer and took employment with the city engineer's office in San Diego. Though he quickly rose to become assistant engineer, he decided to become a coach and took a position at Woodrow Wilson

Hoover High Cardinals, 1936. Left to right: First row: Todd (Mgr.), Siraton, Douthit, DeLauer, Nieumiester, Bell, Oliver, Mitchell, Collins (Mgr.). Second row: Coach Caldwell, Johnson, Ballinger, Monsees, Curtis, Ondler, Villarino, Bennett, Fraim (Mgr.). Third row: Brown (Mgr.), Engle, McBurnie, Williams, Bickerton, Means, Helm, Highley (Mgr.)

Junior High before moving on to Hoover. Caldwell was also an army reserve officer. The profile concluded, "Besides sports, his favorite pastimes are fishing and hunting, and his pet dislike, unnecessary noise." The latter comment was perhaps a bit ironic is that the greatest player he would ever coach was known for his loudness. This author interviewed Wos Caldwell in 1997 and the old coach remembered meeting Ted Williams:

"I had heard how loud he was! This particular afternoon, we were out practicing baseball on the girls' side of the field, just warming up, before the season started. I could hear him and two other boys approaching, about a block away. That's how loud he was.

"When he arrived on the field, he shouted to me, 'How about taking a couple of cuts, coach?' I said, 'OK. Get your bat, and get up here and hit a couple.' He proceeded to hit two of them on top of a three-story school building. I decided right then that he was really serious about hitting, and he was.

"He was either not liked by the teachers in the school, or else they loved him. He was loud, there was no question about that. They either loved him or hated him, because he was so loud."[111]

What degree of Williams' success should be credited to Caldwell? Clearly, Ted himself was generous with his praise of his high school coach, and of Rod Luscomb. But Roy Engle wants us to keep the focus on Ted Williams himself. Engle says, "I don't want to take anything away from Wos Caldwell. He was a good high school coach. But Ted was a student. I don't know where he got his information. But he always had that bat in his hand, and he taught himself all the fundamentals that he needed to become a good baseball player."[112]

Ted had his fun, too. Dell Oliver says, "I know that he lit the trash can in the print shop on fire about once or twice a week. He was just fooling around. The teacher's name was Mr. Evans. He just loved old Ted, but Ted made him so mad when he set that trash can on fire. Inside the building. Ted, he'd leave. Then it was up to Evans to put it out. He was well-liked in high school. People looked up to him. He never smoked or drank. The thing that I really liked about him was he was one of the cleanest living boys that I associated with in high school. He had a goal set early in life about what he was going to do.

"I remember when I was in his typing class. He was a talker, you know. He was always out to have some fun no matter where he was, and he was a great personality, but because he talked so much, he disturbed the class. So the teacher had him sit right up in front, right in front of her desk, so she could control him. Otherwise, he'd have the whole class disrupted. I was sitting in the back, and one day I looked up there and Mrs. Hamilton, she was crying. I said to myself, 'Oh, man, what did Ted say to her now to make her cry?' I heard her say, 'Ted, what are you going to do with your life?' And he says, 'I'm going to be the best baseball player in the world.' Then she really began to bawl. She said, 'Ohhhh, Ted!' [animated moans]

"He did OK in school. He could have done a lot better, but he did OK in school. He was a very talented guy."[113]

Classmate Bob Breitbard recalls Mrs. Hamilton, too: "When we graduated from the school in February of '37, the principal Floyd Johnson got up and said, 'Now I have two awards to present, one to Bob Breitbard and the other one to Ted Williams. These awards are for typing 32 words a minute without an error.' We got typing awards. That was our claim to fame."[114]

The announcement that Ted had won an academic award (of sorts) seemed to surprise at least a few students. Another classmate, Elizabeth Meyer, recalls, "Everybody started to laugh. Johnson turned around – it looked so funny – and said, 'But he earned it!'"[115]

Bob Breitbard, though, says, "The teachers loved him. This Mrs. Hamilton just broke out into smiles whenever he talked. You know how he talks. He talked then just like he talks now. I'll always remember. He would say, 'Hey, teach!' to Mrs. Hamilton and she'd say, 'What do you want now, Ted?' She'd come back and ask what he wanted. He'd say, 'I don't understand how I can get this thing to move.' You know, the carriage on the typewriter, or something."[116]

Joe Villarino remembers Ted and he "used to raise Cain on Halloween. Used to grease the streetcar tracks. They'd just skid. Oh, we had a lot of fun. Then we'd steal fruit. We used to steal loquats."[117] Mel Skelley recalls a few purloined fruits as well. "It was right by the North Park playground. The people had fruit trees growing in their yard. We were hanging around the playground. We'd go up there in the evening and there wasn't much to do sometimes. We'd swipe some peaches from the trees. We filled up our pockets, but Ted wanted even more and he started stuffing them down the front of his sweater. The peach fuzz rubbed off on him and he was itching all over!"[118]

Apparently, Ted enjoyed a few hi-jinks when he joined the ranks of pro ball. Dell Oliver says, "He was doing the tricks on the old-timers like the old-timers were supposed to do with the rookies. He had a ball with them on the train. He was always the one who was short-sheeting them and putting water in their beds, doing all that kind of stuff."[119]

The off-season provided other opportunities for Ted to play baseball in San Diego. He even financed future major leaguer Ray Boone's entry into professional baseball. "In the wintertime, after the ball season was over with, we would go over to Central playground. Our coach and our playground director over there, Rod Luscomb, he was a close friend of Ted's. He used to throw batting practice to Ted and about four of us guys would shag for Ted in the outfield. Ted would give us all a quarter when we got through for the day."[120]

YEAR THREE · THE 1936 SEASON

The February 14, 1936 *Cardinal* informed readers that when Coach Caldwell announced the 1936 Hoover schedule, he had Williams penciled in as his pitcher, the only one of the eight returning lettermen designated as a pitcher. The alumni game, set for March 7, also had Ted set to pitch. "Lanky Williams will pitch the first ball in the opening game," ran a news story, "and Goo-Goo Engle will be catcher. Bill Ondler plays first base, Tommy Johnson, second base, and Ballinger, Bennett, Bickerton and McBurnie are out fielders." Third base was up for grabs.

Boys' sports editor of the *Cardinal* was Som Ching, and it was presumably he who interviewed both principal Johnson and coach Caldwell about the possibility that Hoover would transfer from the Bay League to the Coast League. Hoover had proven too strong for the other Bay League teams. Hoover would be the second smallest school in the Coast League, should the transfer be effected. Ted was evidently with the coach at the time Caldwell was interviewed. "What do you think of the chance we have against Long Beach, Muir Tech and Santa Barbara?", the interviewer asked. "I suppose we will win a championship once in seven or eight years," answered the coach. "Once in seven years nothing!" broke in Ted. "We will take them in the first year."

Herbert Hoover High School
Invites you to attend
ANNUAL DAD'S DAY
Alumni Baseball Game
Saturday, March 7
Hoover Field   2:15 P.M.

The March 7, 1936 alumni game was foreseen as the toughest game on the Hoover varsity schedule, in that half of the alumni team was reportedly playing either semi-pro or professional baseball. "Ralph Twiss, singing baseball player, will pitch for the alumni against Ted (Samuel) Williams, Dizzy Dean of Hoover's varsity club. Ted is not at all worried about Ralph's pitching, it is the rest of the team that gives him the goose pimples." Woody Helm was in San Diego playing semi-pro ball, Don Kimball was playing professional ball for the Texas League in San Diego.

The Hoover varsity was set to sport new uniforms. The school purchased fifteen new suits for the Cardinal Red Birds, made of white grade-A flannel by Rawlings. The old striped suits would be used in practice, with the new ones saved for regular games. Two Red Birds sitting on a bat with the name Cardinals written across it replaced the simple "Hoover." The field was done over during the off-season as well.

The first game of the season was set for March 21 against Covina. Covina was looking for revenge against a Hoover squad that had dominated two years in a row, but the March 13 front page *Cardinal* story predicted, "Unless something happens to his pitching arm, Ted Williams should allow Covina five hits or less. Roy Engle promises to sock any ball that they can pitch in, regardless of whether it is a fast one or a slow one." A later issue of the *Cardinal* ascribed this prediction to Ted himself.

Ted had done well against the Hoover alumni on March 7, but the alums prevailed 5-4. "Ted Williams, ace chucker, fanned 12 batters and slugged two of Don Kimball's tosses over the fence. Red Ramsey, center [fielder] of Alumni, got wise at his next time up. He climbed the fence before Ted swung his bat." Joe Villarino was valuable at third base for the Hooverites. The Cardinals held the lead until the ninth, when a walk, two hits and an error allowed the alumni to put across the winning run.

Dell Oliver, who later enjoyed a cup of coffee with the Padres himself as a pitcher, felt that pitching came easy for Ted. "He was always a starter. In high school, if you can throw the ball hard and you have a good fastball, you can get away with it. About half of those kids coming up there, they're afraid of getting hit by the ball, by a fast ball. When you get into the minors, you've got to have something else."[121]

Card Baseball Eleven To Play Covina Colts

The Galloping Covina Colts, who were runners-up in the recent Pomona Invitational Tournament, are to meet the Hoover Cardinals tomorrow on the Hoover field at 2:15.

Both Hoover and Covina are freelance teams this year, and victory will mean much for both schools.

Coach "Butter" Gorrell is bringing 16 players to town today. Billy Green, star southpaw pitcher, and Poore, catcher who turned in some nice performances in the tournament, will be the starting battery. Both of these were on the Covina football squad last year. Kimball and Helm will act as the Hoover battery.

Wilbert Wiley felt that Ted had more than just a fast ball. "I always had the feeling that Ted would have made the majors as a pitcher. The guy had good stuff. When you got up to bat, he'd throw you that breaking stuff and, I'll tell you, it did break. And he had the best, the best... he called it a palm ball. A few players still remember that; it'd come out of your hand like a knuckler. When he threw that thing, he'd give all the motions of throwing a fastball, same motions, and that thing would slip out, and if you weren't watching yourself, you'd swing when the ball was halfway there. Sometimes made guys feel kinda foolish."[122] Pitching was what Ted's uncle Saul Venzor did, for semi-pro teams in Santa Barbara. From an early age, Ted had wanted to know how to pitch.

Oliver knew, however, that "pitching wasn't really his interest. Everybody knew that. I knew it because I stayed 'til 5 or 5:30 throwing batting practice to him over at Hoover. That's all he wanted – somebody to chase the ball and somebody to pitch and have him hit! I guess I threw about as much batting practice to him in high school as anybody else. We used to go out there for about two hours after we quit practice. I liked to throw. Ted would take most of the time. I think everybody in high school knew that Ted was on his way to the majors. If anybody swung more than he did, they had to be staying up all night!"[123]

It was hitting that really consumed Ted Williams. Wiley remembered, "Pitching to that feller, if you tried to throw one by him, or break one off on him or pull the string on him, or anything else, that was a waste of time. If you had it in there, regardless of what it would be, more than likely he'd put it out of the park on you. I can't tell you why, but his balls would seem to carry. When he hit them flush, they just seemed to keep going."[124] And Ted was already known for his plate discipline. "He had, I guess, more or less a ruling to himself that if a pitch wasn't in there, he'd let it go by. He wouldn't swing at that pitch."[125]

After the March 7 game, Coach Caldwell talked to the *Cardinal* about Ted's prospects for pro ball. "Caldwell believes Ted Williams, lanky left-hand slugger, will sign with a coast club when he graduates in June, because he has keen diamond sense and is able to peg the ball at his will. Ted is being sought by the St. Louis Cardinals chain store system. Meanwhile Hoover relies on him to bring home the bacon during the sensational San Diego county annual baseball tournament starting of

Friday and Saturday, March 13 and 14." As a Hoover B, Ted was never scheduled for a June graduation, but he did bring home the bacon, signing with the San Diego Padres in late June, some eight months before graduation.

AMERICAN LEGION TOURNAMENT
MARCH 13 & 14, 1936

Win Am. Legion Diamond Tourney; Williams Stars

Hoover wallopped San Diego High School, 6 to 1, at the Stadium on Saturday to clinch the first annual San Diego American Legion Diamond Tourney Championship. The game was dominated by the spectacular mound work of Ted Williams, limber-armed hurler, who allowed the Hillers only three hits and six walks, and fanned 14 crossed-eyed hitters.

The Cardinals had a powerful offense and an impregnable defense. Coach Caldwell's men picked off three runs and a like number of hits in the first inning, and added another run in the third canto. Walter Bickerton, left fielder, George Means, first baseman, and Ed Curtis, shortstop, each had two hits to his credit, but it was Bickerton's hit that brought in the runs of the first inning.

Hank Ondler was plenty alert on second base, putting out two hitters who tried to steal second base. He and Bennett slugged two spectacular two-base hits.

Bill Skelley, who was looked upon by the Cardinals as a miracle at first, showed little or no skillfulness at bat, for he was fanned by Ted Williams everytime he was up. Ray Ortiz, Hilltop catcher, was the only lucky player who picked up a run when Joe Villarino, third baseman, let a toss from Engle get away. If the Hillers had as many as five hitters like Bareno, who caught two of the three hits got off Williams, they might have done better.

Sweetwater was the first opponent in the aforementioned tournament, sponsored by the American Legion of San Diego and Imperial Valley. A pre-tournament banquet was held at which Frank Shellenback, pitcher-manager of the San Diego Padres, and H. W. Lane, Padre owner, were to be guests of honor. Boys' sports editor Som Ching wrote in the *Cardinal,* "Ted Samuel Williams, best prep school chucker last season, is ready to fan the Sweetwater batters with reverse-curve balls." Ching clearly shared the same full confidence in Ted that Ted had in himself.

That confidence was merited, though Ted didn't pitch until the final game. Hoover won the tournament, taking the March 13 game against Sweetwater 18-0. The game mercifully was ended after five innings. Delmont "Del" Ballinger was named as starter, saving Ted for a later round game. Ballinger, later relieved by Dell Oliver, allowed but one hit. Though they scored 18 runs, it was on just seven hits – the hapless Sweetwater team made 10 errors, five of them by one player, Daum, who probably never forgot that particular Friday the 13th. Ted, playing centerfield, made the only miscue for Hoover. Again, Ted showed plate discipline. Not one hit was his, but he scored 2 runs, presumably being walked or having reached on one or two Sweetwater errors. Officially, Ted was 0-for-1.

The semi-final game was also a bit of a walkover, Hoover beating St. Augustine 14-3 (or 13-3 – the boxscore shows 14 runs, the accompanying story 13.) Coach Caldwell again sensed victory, and so held back Ted to pitch in the finals. Both Joe Villarino and Ted hit home runs. In this game, Ted played shortstop. Though proving his versatility, he also made a couple of errors. But he sure got on base, scoring 4 runs in the game – more than the whole St. Augustine nine.

"Card. Nine Defeats S. D. High 6-1 Win Am. Legion Diamond Tourney; Williams Stars" ran the headline and sub-head on the March 27 *Cardinal* sports page reporting the March 14 game. "The game was dominated by the spectacular mound work of Ted Williams, limber-armed hurler, who allowed the Hillers only three hits and six walks, and fanned 14 crossed-eyed hitters." Ted's contribution to the offense was not noted; his primary contribution to the win was ably holding Hoover's high school rivals to the lone run. *Union* readers got the news 12 days earlier, reporting "a brilliant three-hit mound performance by lanky Ted Williams." The "limber-armed right-hander, who usually shows more power at the plate than on the mound, received potent stick assistance from his mates" who scored 3 runs in the first. The sixth and final run was scored in the top of the ninth, when Hoover shortstop Ed Curtis and Ted pulled off a double steal, Curtis scoring safely.

San Diego High's run was unearned; it came in the sixth on a walk, a single and then "Jo Jo Villarino let a toss at third get away." The *Union* credits Ted with 13 strikeouts, but he wasn't his sharpest; he did walk seven. Ted was 1-for-3 and scored a run.

GAME: March 21, 1936
Hoover High Cardinals 17, Covina High Colts 0

These were the same Colts that Hoover had defeated 15-0 on April 6 in 1935. Rain threatened, but the teams got in the Saturday afternoon game. "Ted Williams, No. 1 chucker, had an easy time, subduing the invaders. When he told the *Cardinal* press that he would allow the invaders five hits or less, last week, he really meant one hit and no runs. Williams shares the batting laurels with Walt Bickerton, versatile outfielder." Walt went 4-for-5; Ted hit a homer and a double. Ted had 13 strikeouts and didn't miss a no-hitter by much. "A scratch single of R. McBride, center fielder of Covina, in the fifth frame ruined Ted's perfect day. Otherwise it would have been a no-hit and no-run game for 'Lanky'."

GAME: March 27, 1936
Hoover High Cardinals 4, Santa Monica High Vikings 0

The *Union* hadn't applied the adjective "lanky" to Ted for almost two weeks, but cranked it up once more on March 28th, describing the game the day before in a report from Santa Monica: "With Ted Williams, lanky hurler allowing but three hits and making as many himself, Herbert Hoover High School opened its Bay League campaign here with a 4 to 0 triumph over Santa Monica High. Williams included a double in his string of three hits in as many times at bat and fanned 13 opposing batters." The 1936 Hoover yearbook *Dias Cardinales* also referred back to this game as the start of the Bay League series, as did the *Santa Monica Evening Outlook* which described the defeat of Santa Monica's Vikings "at the hands of Slim Williams and his San Diego Hoover teammates." Ted was 3 for 5, struck out 11 (according to the *Evening Outlook*), walked one and committed one error.

Hoover's yearbook had a page on the baseball team and listed Williams first: "The first team is composed of Williams, Captain Engle, Means, Ondler, Curtis, Villarino, Ballinger, and Bennett." It also noted in summary, "Ted Williams has made a pronounced record this season, by allowing the Bay League only ten hits, and accounting for over sixty strikeouts."

Ted later recalled striking out 23 batters in a game against Santa Monica but, if he did, the feat somehow slipped the attention of the Hoover High paper as well as the various newspapers that constituted the San Diego press. Ted mentioned the 23-K game several times, though; it was not just a legend that sprang up in later years. When his memories were still fresh, he told *Minneapolis Star-Journal* sportswriter Dick Hackenberg about the game early in 1938. "I struck out 23 men once in a high school game... They got two hits off'n me..."[126]

This same 23-strikeout total has been repeated in books by Richard Johnson and Glenn Stout, and by David Pietrusza, but both rely on secondary sources. Someday, perhaps, it will be possible to locate and document this game. That Ted would mention it just the year after he graduated high school lends plausibility to there having been such a game, though perhaps not a regularly scheduled high school game. Forrest Warren attributes the information to Principal Floyd Johnson, who told Warren, "One of the biggest thrills I ever got was watching the Bay League championship game in which Ted Williams established a strikeout record. He was then a junior in Hoover, and was our No. 1 pitcher. The game was against Santa Monica High and Ted fanned 23 batters in addition to knocking a home run."[127]

By this time, Ted was widely recognized as a local star. Ray Boone recalls going with some friends to watch Ted play over at Hoover. Boone was five years younger than Ted, so their Hoover baseball years never overlapped. As we have seen, Ray would help shag flies on city playgrounds for Ted. And he'd go watch Ted play at Hoover High. "Every Friday, Hoover had a ballgame and my buddies, we all played together in American Legion and we were all on the same team, well, we'd ride our bikes down there if Hoover was playing a big team in their conference, and we'd watch Ted."[128]

Boone was familiar with the ground rule in right field. "Hoover, it was only about 248 down the right field line. Because it was a football field. We were playing up in the corner. On the bleachers way out, quite a ways out, there was a big line drawn diagonally down the bleachers. If you hit a ball in the bleachers to the right, it was a double. If you hit one to the left of the line, it was a home run – or if you hit one over the top of the fence, it was a homer, and he'd hit them in the eucalyptus trees out there." Boone played major league ball for 13 seasons, and ended up on the Red Sox later in 1960, just as Ted bowed out of ball himself. He remembered when he first met Ted in the big leagues. "When I first played in Fenway Park, I homered twice Friday night and homered again on Saturday. Sunday I was out by shortstop and when Ted came out to left field, when he got right alongside me: "Can't get ol' Hoover, can they?" I'll tell you something. I have never, ever, ever forgotten that day. I was scared to go to Ted and say I was from Hoover High School." But Ted knew.

Knowing that Ray was five years younger than Ted, but knowing the playground pickup games often embraced a wide range of ages, I asked him if he ever happened to have played a game with Ted in the 1930s. "Yeah, I did. I played in a game when Al Olsen pitched a no-hitter against the Hoover guys. This is American Legion. In those days, San Diego was divided on 30th Street. Everything east of 30th, you played for Post 201. Everything west of 30th, you played for Post 6. Well, I was a batboy for Ted's club. We were getting beat – I say 'we,' I mean the team is getting beat. I went in and played right field just one inning. Of course, I used to brag about that to my buddies. They challenged me one day, so I went and got my scrapbook. The only thing bad about it, they had the lineup in there, but they had my name spelled Bone. B-o-n-e. Just to tease me, they'd say, 'I don't see Boone, I see Bone.'"[129]

San Diego baseball changed dramatically on March 28th, the date of the inaugural game by the Pacific Coast League San Diego Padres. The team, which had played as the Hollywood Stars the year before, relocated to San Diego. Their league debut was on the road, and the Padres lost it 7-5 to the Los Angeles Angels at Wrigley Field in L.A. The Lane Field home opener was more successful, as the Padres beat the Seattle Indians 6-2 before an estimated 10,000 fans on March 31st. One wonders if high schooler Ted Williams attended the game. Within three months, he himself would become a Padre.

1936 POMONA TOURNAMENT

The fathers of some of the boys were an important ingredient in the team's success, in that they would pack a few players into a car and drive considerable distances to play games against teams as far away as Pasadena and the like. Traveling to Pomona was a lot of fun, recalls Caldwell's son Bill, who helped out as team batboy. "My dad hauled me around everywhere," he said. "I had a nice little uniform. One incident, and I don't know how much Ted was involved in this, but I got scolded for it. Traveling at 35 mph from San Diego to Pomona or Long Beach for the yearly Southern California Baseball Tournament was a fairly long trip for a bunch of wild, fun-loving high school baseball players. They would start early and stop somewhere around San Clemente for breakfast. Some of the players found that if you put a pat of butter on a napkin and snap it, you could get it to stick to the ceiling. Later it would drip on people, or fall onto them. The school, or Dad, had to pay a fine, to clean up the mess." [130]

Victory sometimes earned the team the treat of an ice cream or a malted milk. Ted did have a large appetite – and helped win more than his share of the victories. This could get expensive. One time in Pomona, Ted recalled, he polished off 13 ice creams and 11 bottles of pop during a doubleheader. [131]

When with the San Diego Padres his first season, later in 1936, as Ted and Bobby Doerr came back to Oakland's Leamington Hotel after a movie, Bill Lane informed Ted in a gruff voice that he was "heading the list." What list? he inquired. The overeater's list, he was told – Ted was routinely running up food bills well above the per diem provided for in the club's agreement with players. Ted griped, "I can't eat on that lousy $2 a day." [132]

The Hoover varsity won the consolation prize at the 1936 Pomona tourney. They dropped the very first match to Calexico, before coming back to win four in a row. The Calexico game was a real upset. Hoover entered the tournament with confidence, and Hoover "saved its No. 1 slab artist, Ted Williams, for a later game", explained the *San Diego Union*. Coach Caldwell's strategy backfired as Calexico crushed the Cards 11-0, facing pitchers Ed "Squirrel" Curtis and Dell Oliver. Calexico's Joe Andrade held Hoover to just four hits; Ted was 0-for-2. Ted pitched both the second and third games of the tourney, but by that time there was no shot at first place. Hoover trounced Monrovia 18-1 in the morning game, Ted starting and relieved by Ballinger. Ted started the afternoon game against Anaheim and won, 8-2, relieved by Bennett.

Lineup for the game was a typical one for Hoover that year:

Curtis, ss
Ballinger, lf
Engle, c
Williams, p
Bickerton, cf
Oliver, cf
Johnson, rf
Villarino, 3b
Ondler, 2b
Means, 1b
(Oliver came in to replace Bickerton in center.)

The Pomona Tournament was a major one, featuring 32 baseball teams. Comedian Joe E. Brown spoke at the "big feed" banquet on Thursday night. California Governor Frank Merriam tossed out the first ball in the championship match on April 11. Ted met the governor. Ted's father, a supporter of the governor, may have introduced them. Merriam had gotten Sam Williams a job as jail inspector in California, a patronage position. Ed Linn strongly suggests that it was May Williams, with her political savvy in San Diego, who probably pulled the strings in the background. Roy Engle recalled Ted meeting Merriam. Ted, with his own disarming yet innocent lack of respect for authority, reacted to being introduced to the Governor of the great State of California with two words. Engle says, "I can still see Ted going up to him and saying, 'Hi, Guv!'" [133]

Merriam had a chance to see Sam and May Williams' son star in his final start of the series, both offensively and defensively. Hoover punished South Pasadena 13-1 in the morning game, and then came back to beat Pasadena itself that afternoon. Williams' "clever hurling" held Pasadena to just five hits, as Hoover won the consolation contest on the strength of his 7-0 shutout. Ted homered twice in the morning's rout, then provided all the runs that were needed in the afternoon game with a 2-run first inning homer, scoring Roy Engle from first base. Dave Meiklejohn of the *Pomona Progress-Bulletin* wrote that, after Ted's third home run of the day, "From then on the Cardinals were never headed nor in any particular trouble, Williams hurling the entire game, allowing Pasadena five hits."

Bill Caldwell says, "Ted was very superstitious, as were most ballplayers in that time. He gave me a rabbit's foot and I was required to rub the rabbit's foot on his bat so he could hit home runs." In Pomona, this may have paid off. "There was no outfield fence and Ted hit a ball that went so far into the field of oats that they couldn't find the baseball, which held up the game a fair amount."[134]

There were a couple of other future major leaguers at Pomona as well. According to Arnold Rampersad's biography, Jackie Robinson played in the Pomona Tournament in 1935 and again in 1936 as catcher for the Muir Technical team. Rampersad writes of Robinson in 1936: "That year, he earned a place on the annual Pomona tournament all-star team, which included two other Hall of Fame players: Ted Williams... and Bob Lemon."[131] Robinson, not surprisingly, starred in the tournament. The *Pomona Progress-Bulletin* noted Robinson's speed: "Base-stealing feats of Jack 'Smoky' Robinson, catcher, supplied Muir Technical high school of Pasadena with two runs and the margin of victory in a 4 to 3 battle against Coach Ted Gorrell's Covina Colts.... Robinson stole five bases in the six-inning game, boosting his total for the tournament to six, which tops the field.... In the third inning, he stole home."[136]

Chuck Stevens, who later played first base in 211 games for the St. Louis Browns, was another future major leaguer in the tournament. He was playing for Long Beach, squared off against Robinson's team, when a baseball from another field rolled in the through the infield. "Ted Williams had hit another long one," said Stevens.[137]

Ted Williams, who in 1966 called for the National Baseball Hall of Fame to welcome black athletes into its ranks, had shared space on an all-star roster with Jackie Robinson three decades earlier.

No wonder major league scouts had their interest piqued. Williams, all told, pitched 17 innings in the tournament, striking out 21 and allowed only 3 runs and nine hits. Ted also hit four home runs, the most of anyone in the tournament. Third baseman Joe Villarino won the batting title, hitting a torrid .728 (8-for-11) but teammate Williams was second with .529 (9-for-17, including the four homers.) "The most novel occurrence of the tournament for Hoover was the situation caused by Ted Williams," *Cardinal* coverage concluded. "Teddy came to bat twice in the same inning of the Monrovia game and got two home runs."

In a May 1 column in the *Cardinal*, columnist Alan McCutcheon wrote, "T. Samuel Williams, Cardinal hurler whose habit of wafting nugs over all types of fences has been prominent." Wafting nugs? Another case of student over-writing. McCutcheon admitted as much. "The baseball was sometimes referred to as the 'nugget.' As for 'wafting,' that must have been one of those times when a 17 year old (pretty much full of himself) was just waxing eloquently."[138] Ted did in fact win a gold baseball as the home-run king.

McCutcheon served briefly as Sports Editor, and Assistant Boys' Sports Editor of the *Cardinal* in 1936. During an interview on the last day of 2002, he remembered Ted "was always with his baseball bat. When Ted came out, he kept trying to promote himself as a first baseman. They had a senior, Don Kimball, who was entrenched there and so when Wos Caldwell discovered that the kid could hit about almost as good as he said he could, why, he put him in the outfield. Right field. Then Ted promoted himself into pitching."

Hoover's Principal Floyd Johnson tells us how uncommonly informal Ted was as a high schooler. "He habitually stopped into my office for a chat. During those chats, it never occurred to me that Ted would usually slump down into his chair and put his feet up on the principal's desk. The subject would usually be either baseball or fishing, subjects I was just as interested in as Ted. And I'd be enjoying the conversation so much I'd be completely oblivious to his posture and unconventional way of talking to the school principal. This was never impudence on Ted's part. To him all folks on the school campus were the same – faculty, principal, or kids."[139]

MR. FLOYD A. JOHNSON
Principal

Hoover High School Principal Floyd Johnson.

Disarming he could be. McCutcheon recalls one Halloween when Ted was taken away by the San Diego police. "On Halloween, the most outrageous thing that anyone did in our time was you would take a bar of soap and write or draw on glass windows of homes, so people would have to scrape it or wash it off. I can recall one Halloween we were walking down El Cajon. There were a bunch of markets there – all open, and they always put the fruit and the vegetables out front. As we walked by – there were about six or eight of us, I guess – we picked some up. Tomatoes or things, to throw... I have no idea what we were going to do with them... but we no sooner had pocketed them and walked along than we were stopped by police. I'm now talking probably 1935. That was the outset of using patrol cars. Automobiles. They stopped and questioned us and everybody was very evasive, and I would say at best obsequious in bowing to the cops. Except Ted, of course. He was himself. He just talked back to them. He was a smart aleck kid. They were going to teach him a lesson. So they told all of us to take off. That they didn't want to see us again. And they put Ted in the car and took him to a substation out in East San Diego. Supposedly, they were going to call his parents. Well, that and 10 cents would get you a cup of coffee. So they took him in there and the story was that while they were waiting for some reaction there [from his parents], they got to playing pinochle, at which he was somewhat of a player of sorts, and they wound up by playing cards with him till twelve o'clock. Then they drove him home. That was rather typical.

"That was Ted. As a matter of fact, if he wanted to talk to someone, it would be totally in character for him to just walk in, plunk himself down – not ask permission or anything – and start talking. Of course, his voice and volume and so on would just boom out. He always had a John Wayne approach to life. Well, he had that from the very beginning. If he ever lacked confidence, I never saw it."

McCutcheon also recalls a time when Ted hit a home run off Grover Cleveland Alexander. "They used to have semi-pro teams – baseball – that would play on Sundays here in the public playgrounds. It seems to me the better players got five bucks or something like that. At the North Park playground where Ted hung out, there was a team. One Sunday, whoever the opposing team was, they brought in a ringer for a pitcher that day. It turned out to be Grover Cleveland Alexander! He obviously was over the hill. He obviously was a boozer – his face was red as a beet and so on. He didn't last too long. The first time he pitched to Ted, Ted hit a home run over deep center-field. Just really creamed the thing!"[140]

SCOUTED BY THE MAJOR LEAGUES

Scouts from a few major league teams had been following Ted's play. The April 17, 1936 Hoover High *Cardinal* featured a front-page story "N. Y. Yanks Offer Williams Contract." The story reads, "Hearing about Ted Williams and his brilliant pitching, William Essick, a Yankees scout, coming to San Diego several days ago, offered the Cardinal ace chucker an attractive contract to play with the New York Yankees next year. The contract guarantees Ted $150 a month, covering all travel expenses. Ted will sign the dotted line when he is graduated from Hoover High, and begin his training for the next spring.

N. Y. Yanks Offer Williams Contract

Hearing about Ted Williams and his brilliant pitching, William Essick, a Yank scout, coming to San Diego several days ago, offered the Cardinal ace chucker an attractive contract to play with the New York Yankees next year. The contract guarantees Ted $150 a month, covering all travel expenses. Ted will sign the dotted line when he is graduated from Hoover High, and begin his training for the next spring.

Although Ted is only 17 years old he pitches fast ball and has character in his make up, Essick says, which is the kind of player that the Yankees want.

Ted was voted by a staff of coaches as the best short stop of the all-star team of the American Legion tournament. He led the Cardinal Red Birds to capture the consolation at the Pomona baseball tournament, winning four straight games in a row.

Ted was beaming but modest in his reply when he was asked how he liked the contract.

"I think it is all right, if I am good enough."

Coach Wofford Caldwell and the Red Birds are eager to see Ted in the the baseball limelight before long.

"Although Ted is only 17 years old he pitches fast ball and has character in his make up, Essick says, which is the kind of player that the Yankees want.

"Ted was voted by a staff of coaches as the best short stop of the all-star team of the American Legion tournament. He led the Cardinal Red Birds to capture the consolation at the Pomona baseball tournament, winning four straight games in a row." [Actually, Williams was voted all-star right fielder. The vote was, not surprisingly, unanimous.]

"Ted was beaming but modest in his reply when he was asked how he liked the contract. 'I think it is all right, if I am good enough.' Coach Wofford Caldwell and the Red Birds are eager to see Ted in the baseball limelight before long."

The school newspaper again deemed Ted "Hoover's Dizzy Dean."

Forrest Warren says that Essick first saw Ted at an American Legion game back when Ted was 15. Warren may have enjoyed writing a good story, but as a friend of the family and a member of the Salvation Army Advisory Board, he may not have exaggerated too, too much. He wrote that on one particular Sunday, Ted had hit a ball so hard it broke a window across the street from the park. "That's what you get for breaking the Sabbath day," May Williams supposedly told her son when Teddy came home and told her he'd broken a window and would probably have to pay for it. The next day, two men showed up at the door, one in uniform. This was assistant Fire Chief Elmer Hill, along with Bill Essick. May Williams supposedly thought Hill was a policeman (one would assume from her work she would know better) and reportedly pleaded,

"Teddy didn't mean to do it; he's a good boy. I try so hard to keep him in Sunday School, but he wants to play ball all the time and talk about Babe Ruth."

"We are not officers," explained Hill. "This man with me is Essick, a Yankees scout. He saw your boy hit the ball that broke the window. Teddy is wonderful. We want to sign him." Essick said he wanted to take Teddy to Oakland for training, and later put him on the Yankees.[141]

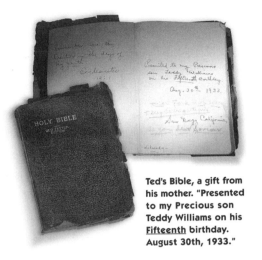

Ted's Bible, a gift from his mother. "Presented to my Precious son Teddy Williams on his Fifteenth birthday. August 30th, 1933."

Whether or not Essick's offer was truly tendered is unknown. Ted says it was, but "the story is my mother asked for a $1,000 bonus and Essick refused." It sounds as though they did make a bid for the budding slugger. The Yankees may have not pursued him as doggedly as they otherwise might have, though, if a scouting report from Yankees scout Joe Devine is any indication. Written in 1936, Devine advised his superiors, "Williams is a very slow lad, not a good outfielder now and just an average arm. There is doubt whether Williams will ever be fast enough to get by in the majors as an outfielder. His best feature now is that he shows promise as a hitter, but good pitching so far has stopped him cold."[142]

It was Marty Krug who, scouting for the Detroit Tigers, had sat with Ted's mother watching a doubleheader in Pomona and "they talked and that night she was in tears. He had told her that I had a lot of good moves, but I was so scrawny a year of professional baseball would kill me. Literally kill me."[143]

"I was still in high school when I worked out several times with the San Diego Padres. A few of the scouts saw me play my last high school game, and one of them, a top man from Detroit, was sitting with my mother. I was 6 feet 3 1/2 inches tall then and I weighed 145 pounds. When the Detroit scout saw what I looked like, he told my mother, 'If you send that boy out and have him play professional ball, it'll kill him.' Gee, my mother came home crying and everything. She was just sick. I didn't say anything because I knew I hadn't played very well that day."[144]

Meanwhile, Hoover's season continued to unfold. Apparently May Williams felt secure letting her son play for the Hoover High Cardinals.

GAME: April 17, 1936
Hoover High Cardinals 7, Compton 1

Ted threw a one-hitter. Compton's sole run came on a walk, followed by a triple by Johnson in the fourth, which gave Compton a 1-0 lead at the time. The pitcher for Compton High was cautious while facing Ted, the *Cardinal* concluded, "for he passed Ted Williams, heavy hitter, three times, and put one over on him once." The *Union* concurred: "Pitcher Jones of the visitors, working under orders apparently, purposely passed the Hoover pitcher three times in a row." The fourth time up, Ted might have been surprised to see a ball over the plate; he swung at it but was out on an infield grounder.

In this case, the walks were intentional, but there were other times not as obvious. Smart pitchers often pitched around Ted Williams, and Ted didn't chase bad pitches. "Most teams, when the score was close, Ted always got walked. There was no pitching to him when things were tough," Roy Engle explained.[145]

Right from high school days, Ted demonstrated that tremendous discipline at the plate that characterized his major league career – his 20.75% walks percentage is the highest of any player in baseball history – but it wasn't necessarily something he enjoyed. Roy Engle and Del Ballinger both recall one time that Ted got so frustrated with the intentional walks that he threw his uniform onto Coach Caldwell's desk and spouted, "All I do is walk. I'm not playing baseball to walk." Ted was truly upset. Ballinger says that when they walked Ted that way, "he'd sit there in the dugout and cry like a baby." For someone who loved to hit as much as Ted did, it had to be incredibly upsetting.[146] Caldwell calmed Ted down and convinced him not to resign from the team.

Roy Engle muses, "I often wonder what would have become of Ted if Caldwell hadn't talked him out of it." Had Ted quit baseball and gone on to some other job – in 1940 he talked with some envy of the life of a fireman – well, the world would have been different.

Even in Hoover days, Ted was seeing things other players could not. Del Ballinger remembers Ted saying that he could actually see the bat hit the ball, where Les Cassie Jr. says, "Ted told me he used to see the ball flatten against the bat."

Williams Sets New Pitching Record

Ted Williams, Cardinal pitcher, set a new record for the Bay League, fanning 20 Redondo batters at the Hoover - Redondo game on Friday, April 24. He led the Cardinal nine to a 5-2 victory over the Redondo team allowing only two runs and three hits. The Cardinals scored one run in the first inning, two runs in the third and picked up two more runs in the last inning.

Bill Ondler, who was on the bench for sometime because of an injured ankle, was active again in the right field. He scored one hit in three trips to the plate for the Cardinals. His brother Hank Ondler, also a diamond star, was dropped out of this game.

Coach Wofford Caldwell shifted Tommy Johnson from right field to second base. Ballanger led the Cardinals on a two-for-five batting average.

Colmer, Redondo pitcher, had one home run to his honor. He allowed the Cards six hits and five runs, checking the Cards from tallying for five innings.

GAME: April 24
Hoover High Cardinals 5, Redondo 2

Ted set a new Bay League record in this Friday afternoon game, striking out 19 Redondo batters (the *Cardinal* reported 20, but both the *Union* and the *Sun* agreed it was a still-impressive 19) while he allowed just 2 runs on three hits. Ted was no longer seen as just a local star but "one of the best prep diamond prospects in southern California."[147] If 19 or 20 strikeouts were deemed a Bay League record, then there could not have been an earlier 23-K game in the league, as recounted by Floyd Johnson.

Whether he'd thrown a 23 strikeout game or not, Ted Williams had drawn and held the attention of a number of major league scouts. *San Diego Union* sports editor Ted Steinmann reported on April 26 that Ted Williams "was a marked young star. His name on a contract is in big demand. The [St. Louis] Cardinal organization wants him, so do scouts for the New York Yankees. But so far school authorities have kept him from becoming embroiled in eligibility difficulties. They hope to keep him clear until his graduation."

As of the 1st, after 21 games, Ted was batting .480. He'd scored 19 runs.

GAME: May 1, 1936
Hoover High Cardinals 17, Inglewood 0

This game reportedly electrified Hoover baseball fans "like the capture of Addis Ababa." Ted pitched the first five innings, allowing just one hit while he struck out eight. Gordon Bennett came in and pitched four hitless frames, striking out seven.

GAME: May 8, 1936
Hoover High Cardinals 14, Long Beach 1

Ted threw a complete game against Long Beach a week later. "Ted Williams' twirling was sensational to the baseball fans. He struck out 13 batters, allowing only three hits and 1 run by Backtelle of Woodrow Wilson, which was undoubtedly an accident. Ted always kept the Wilson batter hitting the ball to the infield, and let the infielders pick it up." At the plate, Williams was walked twice "whether it was fear or good diamond sense... It was more or less a repetition of three-on-bases and Williams up throughout the last seven innings."

The *Sun* envisioned a game that could have turned out even better: "Ted Williams, stellar Card hurler, tossed three-hit ball and might have turned in a blank attempt except for four Hoover errors." Long Beach's Woodrow Wilson High topped Hoover in that department, though, committing seven errors. Their only run came on a couple of singles in the ninth inning. Ted struck out 13 and walked three. He was 1-for-3 at the plate, with a two-base hit. As always, the other hitters around Ted in the order had more at-bats. Engle, batting third, had six at-bats in the game, and Bickerton, batting fifth, had five. Ted earned his bases on balls and slashed one or two error-inducing drives at opposing infielders.

GAME: May 12, 1936
Hoover High Cardinals 9, Beverly Hills 1

Gordon Bennett pitched a complete game. There was no mention of Williams in the game account. This game won the Bay League championship for Hoover.

GAME: May 22, 1936
Escondido High 8, Hoover High Cardinals 3

Ted's last game for Hoover was disappointing. Perhaps he had his mind on negotiations regarding his future, watching others deal with the scouts who wanted to sign him. On the strength of its record, Hoover had won a bye in the first round. Hoover lost in a "startling upset" (*Union*) at Escondido. "Caldwell shot his big ace, Teddy Williams, at the Grape city bunch." Williams issued three free passes and struck out seven, but he couldn't hold them, and he didn't offer much in the offense department, his single being one of only five Hoover hits. Ted yielded 9 hits. Roy Engle was still a little upset 44 years later, when interviewed in the *San Diego Union*: "It seemed like their coach's brother was the umpire."[148]

San Diego Contract Offered - Williams

Ted Williams, who has pitched and batted Herbert Hoover High's baseball teams to many victories the last three years, will join the San Diego Padres this month, if his parents consent to his playing of professional baseball.

A contract was offered Williams by Bill Lane, owner of the San Diego club, Saturday and Williams said he would give him an answer within a few days. It is understood that Williams' folks are in favor of Ted becoming a professional player. Lane would not give Williams a tryout as a pitcher. He would be used in the outfield, and if he can hit, he might earn a regular berth. Several local coaches and fans recommended Williams to Lane, and the owner of the Padres has had his eye on the lanky powerhouse for some time. Lane told Williams that he would not send him out for seasoning if he signs a contract. If Williams accepts he will report to the Padres as soon as school is out. He will graduate this month.

Though Hoover was expected to win the Southern California Invitational, this loss eliminated Hoover's team. This was, apparently, Ted's only loss of the season. He finished 12-1, but it was an anti-climactic conclusion to a brilliant senior year season. When it came time to end his career as a pro, on September 28, 1960, Ted had learned how to go out with flair. As most baseball fans know, Ted Williams hit a home run in his final at bat in the major leagues.

When the All-League Team was named, "T. Samuel Williams, elongated chucker" was the pitcher, along with Colmer of Redondo. Ted's league record was 5-0 but, the *Union* noted, "he would rather boast of his home run hitting ability." Ted had 66 strikeouts in 39 innings of work. Ted appeared in 30 games, and was 33 for 82 (.402) while scoring 25 runs.[149]

MOVING ON TO PROFESSIONAL BASEBALL

On the last day of 1935, December 31, the *Union*'s Ted Steinmann had quoted Wos Caldwell as saying, "there are always a number of young fellows on our teams who hope to make baseball their profession, and the presence of a professional team here in town would give them more incentive."

Ted's days of playing high school ball were over – but he still had to finish out his senior year in high school. When school resumed after the 1936 summer break, the *Cardinal* noted that Ted Williams had played pro ball for the San Diego Padres of the Pacific Coast League. "Although Williams was a capable pitcher in high school," the paper noted, "he is now being used in the outfield in order to preserve his hitting ability." His contract required that Ted stick with the Padres through the 1937 season, but, the student paper speculated, "The prospects are bright that he will go up to the big leagues in 1938. He already has bids from the New York Yankees, St. Louis Cardinals and Los Angeles."

The one team Ted could never have envisioned signing with before early 1936 was the San Diego Padres – simply because the team did not exist before that time. The Yankees, Cardinals and (Pacific Coast League) Angels may have been contending for Ted's services for some time, but it was a dark horse that won the bidding. Ted signed with his hometown San Diego Padres on June 26, 1936. Less than six months earlier, there was no such team. Negotiations to bring a Coast League team to San Diego continued throughout much of January and February. The field was only leased in March. San Diego newspapers provided very good coverage of major league baseball in this period, and did a decent job covering PCL and even local high school ball.

Ted began to work out some with the Padres and noted that, "by now the pressure's on pretty good for me to sign with San Diego... and everybody was getting civic-minded about the Padres." Ted told David Pietrusza, "Lane got a few politicians to work on my mother."[150] Ted's mother liked the idea "because she wanted me close to home."[151] It could also be that Lane connected to May Williams another way as well. The Padres' George Myatt explained, "I used to see his mom. She was a Salvation Army woman. And Mr. Lane, the owner of the old San Diego ball team, he was a big Salvation man, so they were real good friends. She used to come to the ballpark all the time."[152]

Gene Schoor even suggests that Uncle Bill Lane (as he was known to some) offered a degree of comfort to Ted's mother. "To May Williams, the 'Uncle' carried a warm paternal quality, and it would please her very much to have Ted playing for an 'Uncle.'"[153] It's doubtful May was anywhere near that naïve, as politically savvy as she seemed to be.

When Ted did sign, it was for $150 a month. Paul Maracin adds that "as a signing bonus, pay for the entire month of June was generously included" despite the signing on the 26th. Bill Lane's interest may first have been spurred by a visit to Hoover at some point. Veteran San Diego sportswriter Earl Keller reported that one afternoon Lane was "in the Hoover High bleachers at the encouragement of his friend, umpire Bill Englen. Lane wasn't disappointed as Williams connected for two home runs and two doubles. Englen was given a job as a PCL umpire and Williams a $150-a-month contract."

As with the elusive 23-K game, research has not turned up any game when Ted hit two home runs and two doubles. That would have been a noteworthy game. There was the game against Monrovia in mid-April; Ted hit 2 homers in that game, but the game was in Pomona, and Lane couldn't have seen it from the bleachers at Hoover. There was a home game at Hoover back on March 16, 1935 when Ted hit two home runs and one double. Lane might have been at that game, even though the move from Hollywood to San Diego was still nine months or so away from being decided. If Keller's account has substance to it, perhaps Lane was there and it was the first time he had taken note of the young hitter.

Padres manager Frank Shellenback

On the other hand, Earl Keller may not have been the most reliable reporter. Ed Linn quotes Keller as claiming, "Wos Caldwell had tremendous influence over Ted. Bill Lane paid him to get Ted to sign. The sum I heard was $500."[155] Perhaps it's true that everyone has their price, but nothing anyone else has ever intimated about Caldwell suggests that he was anything other than a dedicated and honest man. Caldwell was on the Hoover faculty. He likely would have wanted Ted to stay on for his final semester and graduate high school. In this desire to keep Ted close to home, he would have had a staunch ally in May Williams. If local civic leaders were also leaning on "Salvation May" (and she was nothing if not well-connected in San Diego), for there to have been any other resolution would have been surprising. Why should Lane have had to spend that $500?

Padre player Cedric Durst's daughter Autumn Keltner always understood that her father had a role in securing Ted for the home team. Talking about Ted's mother, she says that her dad "went over to her house several times, to try to convince her that the team would not lead her son into Purgatory, as she might have called it. I think it took several visits to really convince her that everything was going to be all right."[156]

However it came about, Ted Williams was on his way. The contract was not signed in the Williams family home, but across the street on the table of Johnny Lutz, who might have been one of the first to pitch batting practice to young Teddy. In 1983, Lutz related how the 5-year-old Teddy "would drag his little bat across the street and ask Lutz to pitch to him."[157] Be it a Lutz or a Luscomb, or others on the playground or at school, those who helped Ted saw the years of his hitting and hitting and hitting begin to bear fruit.

Ted actually played with the Padres before he was signed to them. It was in an exhibition game on June 22, between the All-Navy Stars and the Padres, a benefit for the Naval Relief Society. Ted and a few other high school players came into the game, probably a play for more hometown support. "Once out in front with a seemingly safe margin," sportswriter Monroe McConnell wrote, "the Padres gave up their places to young high school players who had been working out at the park daily. Ted Williams went to left field."[158] Ted had one at-bat and singled off the Navy's Reynolds. 1-1 in his first Padres box score.[159]

The Lutz family.

Ted was thrilled and proud to become a Padre. Bill Swank talked with Frank Kerr, who in 1947 himself became a catcher with the San Diego Padres. Swank tells us, "Kerr recalled seeing a very excited Ted Williams at University Heights playground on an otherwise uneventful day in 1936. 'Ted told us that he had just signed with the Padres. He told us to come to the next game and sit in the right field bleachers. Sure enough, Ted came out wearing a uniform. He ran over to us and waved and yelled, 'Hi, gang! Look at me!'"[160]

Though thrilled, Ted was also, almost always, brimming with self-confidence. Al Olsen spent 11 years with the Padres. He was a couple of years younger than Ted, and had seen him in high school games and with the Padres. Ted always knew he could hit, and he was cocky. Olsen noticed it first in high school, but also in the pickup workouts they'd have at Navy Field, when a number of players would work out before Spring Training. "He didn't have much muscle then, but he had pretty good timing. I knew him a little bit in high school and American Legion ball. I wasn't a buddy of his or anything, but he was a topic of conversation among the rest of us. All the kids, we admired him and looked at him with a bunch of awe, and we would share stories. At high school, in the print shop, he was always a topic of conversation."[161] Olsen says, "He wasn't a great student in school. He was bored with it; he wanted to get the class over and let's go out to the ballfield! A lot of the managers he played for didn't think he was smart, because they didn't like him. He was cocky and hard to deal with, but he was a genius, no doubt about it."

Olsen was a left-hander and Ted drew on this. He'd pay lefties to throw to him, because he wanted to work on the lefty on lefty matchup. "I'd throw batting practice, and he'd wear you out."[162]

The *Cardinal* reported Ted as age 17, slightly over 6 feet tall with a weight of 165 pounds, though in *My Turn At Bat* he recalled himself as already 6'3" but only 155 pounds and believed even that was exaggerated by around seven pounds. He was supposedly "so skinny that he wore up to three pairs of socks to make his legs look more muscular."[163] Del Ballinger told Ed Linn that Ted's mother would sew the stockings together for him.

The Padres were clear that they wanted Ted for his hitting. The *Union* reported, "Although Williams was a pitcher in high school, he will not be used in that capacity but will be sent to the outfield in an effort to capitalize on his hitting ability." May Williams had a lot to say with the choice of team; signing with the Padres kept Ted at home, except for the team's road trips. The *Union* story credited Coach Caldwell: "Williams was developed by Wofford Caldwell, Herbert Hoover baseball coach, who influenced him to sign with the Padres for his best interests."[164] The Padres placed Ted under the watchful eye of sober, mature veteran player Cedric Durst, who was assigned as Ted's roommate on the road. Under the terms of the contract, Ted was not to be farmed out by the Padres at any time during the 1936 or 1937 seasons. Reports were that Ted was to stay in San Diego until age 21. If so, that undertaking was abandoned.

Bill Skelley recalls Durst as even-keeled and good-natured. "Ced Durst, he was almost too nice of a guy. I think Ced kind of tried to do things like give him some 'hitting' chewing gum. 'There's a lot of hits in this jaw breaker I'm giving you' – buoying him up when he thought Ted was getting down."[165]

As she told the author in a phone interview on May, 23, 1999, Autumn Keltner remembers, "Dad would come home and talk about this young kid who had all this talent, but his mother didn't want him to go out of town. She was very protective of him. Since dad was the oldest player on the team, he was asked to be like a father figure and also to intercede with Mrs. Williams, to say he'd watch over him and that he'd make sure he didn't get any trouble when he was out of town with the team." "I was Ted's first roommate in pro ball," Durst told Phil Collier. "He was a big, good-natured kid and full of confidence. He woke me up one morning – he was jumping on his bed, beating his chest, and he said, 'Christ, Ced, it's great to be young and full of vinegar.' I said, 'Sure, Ted, but not at six o'clock in the morning.'"[166]

Stuart N. Lake, a pre-World War I reporter for the *New York Herald*, had moved to San Diego and followed Ted's career. He credited Durst for much of Ted's development as a player. In comments made early in 1939, he noted that Ted was such a valuable natural hitter, he couldn't be wasted as a pitcher. He also allowed that Ted "knew no more about defensive play than a jack-rabbit, had the impression that all he had to do was step up and swat. Hustling in the outfield was beyond his comprehension, and as a base-runner he was more so. It was Durst who taught him to field and who had him take a course of training under a track coach to improve his getaway and to speed him up on the bases. More important, it was Cedric who gave him that smooth, effortless swing with that wrist-snap at the crucial instant of impact – almost a golfer's swing. Notice the kid. He doesn't hit the ball; he doesn't hit at it. He swings clean through it."[167]

Lefty O'Doul had told Ted early on, "Don't let anybody change your stance and your swing. Attempts will be made to, you can bet on that. Ignore them. Even if your own manager down there [in San Diego] suggests that you try this or that at the plate, pay no attention. Just go on the way you are."[168] Ted credited Durst for helping him at the plate. "I did, however, heed one bit of advice that helped me as a sticker. In those early days, the sinker ball used to baffle me... [Durst] suggested that I move up further towards the front of the batter's box against pitchers who broke the ball down. I thought of O'Doul's warnings but I couldn't see how following Durst's advice would change my style or stance. So I tried it and it worked like a charm."[169]

Ted brought his boyish ways to the Padres. Bud Tuttle, a teammate in '36 and '37, remembers Ted's entry, "It was mid-June and I was sitting in front of my Padre locker when the locker room opened and in walked a tall, lean, lanky young fellow. He stopped and looked around, then slowly closed the door. In his right hand was a battered suitcase. Frank Shellenback, our manager, stepped forward with a welcome to Ted Williams, the lamb! Right out of high school in San Diego. Shelly took him around, introducing him to all of us. Ted plumbed down on the bench next to me and said, 'When do we hit?'"[170]

Shellenback popped Ted into his first game the next day, pinch-hitting for pitcher Elmer Hill in the second inning as the Padres hosted Sacramento. He struck out. 0-for-1. Ted recalled the at-bat: "I just stood there too scared to swing while he powered three straight down the middle."[171]

Interestingly, the pitcher Ted faced in his debut at-bat was Cotton Pippen, a Sacramento righthander. In Ted's first series at Fenway Park his rookie year in the major leagues, the first two hits Williams got were both off Pippen.

Frank Haven, writing in the *San Diego Sun*, noted Ted's debut. He liked the "L word", too. "Williams, lanky ex-Herbert Hoover high youngster, fanned in his professional baseball debut." Haven went on to appraise Ted. "Signing of Ted Williams, San Diego prospect, gives the Padres excellent material to develop into major league timber, but it doesn't solve Shelly's problem."[172] The reference was to Frank Shellenback, Padres manager (who didn't hesitate to put himself into a few games as well.) Shellenback needed "seasoned and dependable" hitters – slugging first basemen or hard-hitting outfielders. Haven faulted Lane for waiting too late to make his move. All the good players had been snapped up. If true, Lane's tardiness may have given Ted more of a opportunity than he otherwise might have had.

Haven did note, in the same June 28 piece, "We think that in time Williams will be one of the Padres' best assets. The Padres were lucky to nab him from under the very noses of enthusiastic major league scouts who long have tempted the pride and joy of Hoover High."

He continued, "We were among the first in San Diego to recognize this gangling, free-swinging youth as a comer. And we're going to be among the first to praise him if he happens to prove of considerable value to the Padres in his very first season as a pro."

Shellenback was impressed with The Kid's work ethic early on. Ted would show up at Lane Field at 10 in the morning for batting practice, through some batting practice, take his regular pre-game workout and then ask for a couple of baseballs to take home with him. Was he selling the balls to make a little extra cash? "No, sir," Ted replied. "I use them for a little extra hitting practice after supper." He needed two new baseballs every night? Shellenback was skeptical. "I decided I would do a little investigating," he told writer Arthur Sampson. "So I piled into my car after supper and rode around to Williams' neighborhood. There was a playground near his home and sure enough I saw The Kid himself driving those two battered baseballs all over the field. Ted was standing close to a rock which served as a plate. One kid was pitching to him. A half dozen others were shagging his drives. The field was rough and stony. The baseballs I had given him were already showing signs of wear. The stitching was falling apart. The covers were as rough as sandpaper. Blood was trickling from Williams' hands as he gripped a chipped bat. But he kept swinging. And hitting."[173]

The image endures as a tribute to Ted's relentless pursuit of perfection – he kept hitting and hitting with his chipped bat until the blisters broke and blood trickled from his hands.

George Myatt saw a bit of that work ethic, too, and he'd seen it at Hoover before Ted joined him on the Padres. "I saw him play in parts of two or three games in high school. He was one of the first ones on the field. Came out for practice and he had three, four bats in his hands. He was awfully skinny, tall and everything. You looked at him and his feet were as long as the legs, it looked like, but when he started fooling around with those bats all you could see was rhythm, which was a sight to see... The first thing he'd do is come up out of the clubhouse dressing room and pick up a half a dozen bats or so and start swinging them.

"When he joined us in San Diego [with the Padres], he was a real brazen kid. Knew everything. All he thought about was hitting. He was playing left field. I was shortstop. He didn't play in a game for I don't know how long. Shellenback started him in a game, gave him a little experience, along in the season. He's in left field. I had been playing ball a few years then. I was kind of stationing him and the other outfielders on what the pitch was. I stationed him someplace. The pitch is made. It's a ball. That put the hitter ahead and changed the positions the outfielders should have been in to the hitter's advantage. Right after the pitch was made, I turned around to see where he was. Well, his back was toward the infield. He had his glove in his hands and acting like he was swinging the bat. He never even saw that pitch. Well, I gave him hell."[174] Myatt also added, "He wanted to swing that bat. He didn't want to be walked for anything. He wanted to swing that bat. At first he didn't walk too much, but after he got a little more experience he was walked an awful lot. Hitting, hitting, that's all he thought about in baseball was hitting. He'd come running out of the clubhouse and he'd grab a bat. He never grabbed a glove. He'd grab a bat."

Ted's second appearance for the Padres was on July 3, at Wrigley Field against the Los Angeles Angels. Ted talked his way into the game, promoting himself as a pitcher in a game the Padres were losing by 9 runs. Inserted as a pinch-hitter, he got his first hit as a pro off Angels' pitcher Glen Babler. Ted recalled it as a double while writing his autobiography. The ball was hit hard, "a rocket off the right-field screen" in the words of Yosh Kawano.[175] Ted's shot kicked off a 5-run rally, putting the Padres back in the game. Shellenback left Ted in, and let him take the mound – the third of four Padres pitchers. Next time up, another single - also off the fence. Ted went 2-for-2, both singles, and scored two runs. The Padres lost 14-9 and Ted was charged with two of the runs. On the mound, Ted faced six batters, giving up two hits and 2 runs in 1 1/3 innings. He walked one but struck out no one. Not embarrassing by any means, but the two hits were solo home runs by Steve Mesner and Wes Schulmerich. The sense was that once opposing batters began to time his fastball, Ted's effectiveness was lost.

Manager Frank Shellenback remembered it thus: "The first fellow doubled. Then there was a home run and another double. Three or four runs scored. I walked out to the mound. 'Skip,' he told me, 'as a pitcher, I'm a good outfielder.'"[176]

Ted talked a lot. He had talked a lot about his pitching as well as his batting, but now he had to perform against Pacific Coast League hitters. "Having pitched batting practice every day for almost a week, I could hardly lift my arm," he recalled. "I can still hear the swish of the line dives past my ears. The Angels wore me and themselves out as they knocked down the fences."[177]

Ted had always wanted to hit more than anything. In his third year with the Red Sox, Ted had admitted that "I took up pitching because I was an awkward, sloppy fielder and couldn't run any faster than a snail. I got to be a pretty fair sandlot pitcher, but always I derived more satisfaction from connecting for a base hit than from striking out an opposing hitter."[178]

Other than throwing a couple of innings for the Red Sox in 1940, Ted's pitching career was over. He was destined to focus on what he had always enjoyed most: hitting a baseball. He later told Jim Smith, "Here's a funny thing. There's not one hitting picture of me until I signed my first professional contract. All of them in high school were pitching. So the first was in a Padre uniform."[179]

As a bit of a footnote, Ted's battery mate was Harold Doerr, Bobby Doerr's older brother. Both Doerrs were teammates of Ted in San Diego, Hal only briefly, but Bobby for the balance of the 1936 season. A dozen years later, Bobby remembered the day Ted first walked into Lane Field and asked for a tryout as a pitcher. He told Bob Holbrook of the *Boston Globe*, "We were all standing around the batting cage watching our heavy hitters do their work when this skinny guy with his pants worn up to his knees stepped in to hit. The way he wore his pants gave him a funny appearance. But we didn't pay too much attention until he started to hit. He hit three balls right out of the park... [they] went over everything and across landed across the street. And none of the players on our team could come close to the fences." A player standing next to Doerr said, "I'll bet that kid signs with this club before the week is over." Doerr then recalls, "That week went by and so did the next one and we didn't hear anything more about him. Suddenly, he showed up and donned a uniform." School was out for the summer.[180]

The Padres had close ties to the Boston Red Sox, largely negotiated by Padres owner Bill Lane and the historically under-appreciated man in charge of Red Sox minor league operations, Billy Evans. In late March 1936, Monroe McConnell wrote in the *Union* that the Padres were due to get two pitchers and an outfielder once the Sox trimmed their roster at the end of Spring Training, part of a deal which called for the Padres to ship both Bobby Doerr and George Myatt to the Sox for the 1937 season. The deal had been consummated with Lane's Hollywood club late in 1935, before the club moved south to San Diego. On April 14, it was announced that the Sox would send pitcher Manuel Salvo to San Diego; he won his first game for San Diego, 7-2, on the 18th. Over a month later, Boston sent Long John Welch to help San Diego pitching. Welch never arrived. He refused to report. But that's another story. It got worked out and didn't affect things with Ted Williams.

Padres batboy Ralph Thompson called Ted "a very eccentric young kid. I used to go on a road trip occasionally with them, and the ballplayers would not associate with Ted on the road. They would not go to theaters or anything with him, because if the theater didn't start the movie on time, he'd get up on his feet and start hollering and raising hell. As a kid, I didn't care. He paid my way in. I was happy to go. That didn't bother me. I was very sedate, but still, his actions didn't bother me any. He was always good to me. The other players wouldn't go anywhere with him. They'd be embarrassed."[181] Bill Swank's interview with Wally Hebert confirms that "he was always tryin' to get somebody to go with him, but he'd holler and laugh and you wanted to get away from him. You could always spot old Ted in a movie house, 'cause he'd be alone."[182]

9-year-old Ralph Thompson, Padres mascot, flanked by Bill Starr and George McDonald, 1936.

Williams batted .271 for the Padres in the 1936 regular season, getting 107 at-bats in 42 games. He had eight doubles and a couple of triples, with 11 runs batted in – but didn't hit a single home run. The home run hitter on the team was a fellow named DiMaggio – Vince DiMaggio – with 19.

Ted Williams' first home run as a pro came on September 15 in the first game of the playoffs, and it was hit off one of the best pitchers in the Coast League, Willie Ludolph of the Oakland Oaks. Ludolph, a 17-year veteran, described at "the Matty of the minors" by Oakland sportswriter Ed. R. Hughes, held the Padres scoreless until the eighth and Ted's two-run homer. Writing from Emeryville, sports-writer Abe Kemp said that Williams hit "a robust clout over the right field fence." Kemp added, "Williams, a 17-year-old lad who still breathes the aroma of school books, drove the ball over the right field fence on a line. The ball was hit with such force that the outfielders never made a move."[183] The Padres lost the game, though, and the playoffs 4 games to 1. The next year Ted hit 23 home runs.

For the first time, in the playoffs, Ted got a chance to hit against both righthanders and south-paws. Beforehand, he'd been used pretty exclusively against righties. He did well, though, against two Oakland lefties and it no doubt helped him prepare for the year that followed.

Box score, Ted's first professional home run, September 15, 1936.

Bud Tuttle gives us a sense of what Ted was like while on the Padres:

"He used to get me out there early before batting practice, to pitch to him because I was left-handed. I'd pitch to him and there was a bunch of kids used to get out in right field and chase the balls. What stayed in the ballpark. He hit them clear out of the ballpark. There was a main highway right outside and several of them hit cars going by.

"We had a lot of fun, though. He just enjoyed it. He wanted to be ready. They usually threw a lot of left-handed pitchers against us because we had a lot of left-hand hitters. So he got out there and he was ready for them. Boy, he sure could hit them. He had such good eyesight. He'd tell the umpire, 'That pitch was an inch and a half outside the plate and you called it a strike.' He could tell. A lot of times, we'd go on the road and he'd say, 'Oh, my eyes are bothering me. I'd better go for a checkup.' So I'd go with him to the eye doctor. He'd check him and the doctor would say, 'You've got perfect vision.' But he was worried.

"I'd wake up in the morning and he'd be standing in front of a full-length mirror with a newspaper rolled up in front of him and he'd be swinging it like a bat. He was really something.

"I went to his house one Sunday after a ballgame. I had dinner with he and his mother, and we were about halfway through the dinner when in comes his brother through the front door and he runs right through the house and out the back door. Ted yells, 'What's going on?' and his brother wouldn't even answer. He just left. Just about two minutes later, the police showed up. They were after his brother for breaking a traffic law. They finally caught him, but poor Ted, it had him all upset. What was going on?

"When we used to go up north, we always traveled by train. Up in California, the little town on Dunsmuir up there. The train would stop there and on the platform outside, there was a woman who had a cart. She had homemade ice cream – ice cream you've never tasted before. Boy, was this the best! And everybody wanted to get there. We had no air-conditioning on the train, so we'd open the windows, and when we got there, Ted would climb out the window to be the first one there to get the ice cream. He'd usually get about a quart of ice cream for each one of us and then he'd come back in with the ice cream while everybody else was lining up their to get theirs. My favorite flavor was chocolate, his was vanilla. We looked for that time we'd come through there. Coming back, we always hit it at night and she wasn't there then. He'd go right out through that window like there was somebody shooting at him.

"Get up and have breakfast in the morning and come back to the hotel and sit in the lobby and watch people. Read newspapers and all. Go to the ballpark and then afterwards come back and have dinner. Go up to our room. There was no TV so we just went up to our room and went to bed. We'd get up real early. He liked to get up early and swing that newspaper like he had a bat in his hand. He was always swinging.

"In San Francisco, one of the biggest restaurants had a sign in the park. If you hit it, you won two free dinners. Ted hit a home run and hit the sign. I could taste that steak dinner. But, what happened? When Ted found out that he would have to wear a necktie, it was no deal! I lost my steak dinner."[184]

Tuttle did meet Ted's father on the road in Sacramento in 1937, where Sam Williams "was a friend of the governor and he had a position with the state. He'd come out to the ballpark. He was very nice. Ted was as thin as a rail then. He was proud of Ted. He was thrilled. Ted hit a home run when he was there at the Sacramento stadium and, oh, his father was just so happy and he reached clear over the fence to shake Ted's hand when he came by afterward. I only saw him about once or twice."[185]

Others tell of Ted swinging bats in hotel rooms, too. George Myatt remembered, "On the road trips in those days, we stayed in not-too-good hotels. It was in Sacramento, the Hotel Clooney if I remember right. He was in the room next to ours. An old hotel, probably not there anymore. Six o'clock or so in the morning, and this whistling wakes me up. I was rooming with Bobby Doerr. I didn't know that Ted was next door. There were doors between the rooms. Every door in the hotel had holes in drilled in it. Little old thin doors. I looked through one of the holes, and there was Ted with a newspaper rolled up, standing in front of the mirror and shadow hitting with that paper rolled up. That was his life. He come out of the clubhouse, and he didn't sit on the bench. The first thing he'd do as he walked through the dugout was grab a bat and go out. Used to do anything that had to do with a bat. Hit pepper, talk baseball. All he'd talk about was hitting, all about hitting."[186]

Through it all, Ted remained the exuberant young player who prompted so many stories. Bobby Doerr, thinking back again to that first year with the Padres, said, "He was something then. I remember him always going around swinging an imaginary bat. You know how he does. Well, one day in the lobby of a hotel in San Francisco Ted swung with an imaginary bat and fell down on the floor. It was slippery footing as the floor was marble."[187] A couple of years later, Ted and Bobby, Babe Herman and Max West were all traveling east to 1938 Spring Training with the Red Sox in Sarasota. "He kept asking Herman all kinds of questions about hitting. We were in the lounge car and you could hear the two of them all over the train. That night in the Pullman, Ted was making more imaginary swings with a pillow. A porter had to come back and tell him to quiet down as he was keeping the car awake."[188]

Doerr also saw how driven Ted was, always in a hurry – even if there was no cause for hurry. "I remember in Sacramento Eddie Mulligan was sitting next to him at the lunch counter. Ted came in and pounded on the counter, 'Get this waitress. I want this right away. Food. I've got to catch a train!' He'd eat, my gosh, bang bang bang and out, and you'd wonder where the heck is he going now?"[189] "He was always kind of an exciting kid. He was good. Not anything out of line or smart alec that way. He was just excited that he was playing ball, and the older guys kind of got a kick out of him. Chewed his fingers all the time. High strung kid."[190]

Was Ted a bit of a *naif* when he first traveled with the Padres? Perhaps so. His long-time companion Louise Kaufman told Ed Linn, "That part of *The Natural* where the kid is in the dining car, going to where he was going. That was taken from Ted Williams' life right there. That's one of his favorite stories. He says, 'My God, and here I was, on the train in a dining car. To read a menu.' Who knows how to read a menu if you never saw one? He was a child."[191] Even by the time he got to Florida for Spring Training in 1938, he came across to Red Sox clubhouse man Johnny Orlando as a real rube. Orlando wrote, "This Li'l Abner walks in. He's got a red sweater on, his shirt open at the neck, a raggedy duffle bag. His hair's on end like he was attached to an electric switch. If anyone ever wanted a picture of a raw rookie, this was the time to take the shot."[192]

Some of Ted's initial brashness was likely prompted by his discomfort in his new environment. Old friend Frank Cushing says, "Ted told me that when he first came up, he felt insecure. Not about hitting, but about other things. Manic, animated, talked a mile a minute. That animation was his way of demonstrating his insecurities, and he's the first to admit that. He always felt he was under-educated, which is nonsense because he's very well-read. That's just his personality."[193]

Monroe McConnell, *Union* sports editor, wrote in 1941 on the day Ted returned for an exhibition game at Lane Field, "Even when he wore the tag of the rawest rookie who ever wore the spangles of the game, Teddy went to the plate with absolutely no sign of tension – as 'loose as a goose,' as the players say. He took his cuts as though he meant it, and when he missed, he hung his head. But when he connected, you could count his teeth from second base. He rarely hit singles." McConnell added, "At least one of his local records still stands – he is the only player in the San Diego club's six-year history who ever got away with putting away two over-grown T-bone steaks and a platter of rolls at breakfast."[194]

Ted drew fans to Lane Field and was a popular player. Among them was Ray Boone. "I saw him play for the Padres. Oh, yes. Oh, man, there ain't no way... if we're going to go down and watch him play at Hoover, we're going to watch him play with the Padres. You didn't have to pay. You'd just wait outside the ballpark and catch foul balls and you got in the gate. Bring a ball back to the gate, and you'd get in. There were a bunch of us buddies – five or six of us. As soon as one of us got a ball and another one would come over, we'd block out guys so your next guy could get one."[195]

FINISHING UP HIGH SCHOOL

After the 1936 season, though, Ted had to go back to high school. Ted finished up his senior year by completing the final fall semester. Ted attended classes, but it's pretty certain he didn't make the October 31 dance at Mission Hill after the "big game." He may have attended "Mary's Ankle" – the play presented by students – on December 3 or 4, but probably did not. He probably didn't enter the senior class song competition. Chances are he skipped the time ditching snow at Pine Valley on January 12. He may have passed on the A.S.B. Ball on January 22, but we know he escorted Alberta Camus to the senior prom at the Casa de Mañana on January 28. It may have been his only date in high school. We also know he attended the school's Tower Day on February 2, because he signed the

Detail, *Dias Cardinales*, Hoover High School yearbook, 1937, p. 21.

book. Some seniors listed a number of school activities with their photograph in the yearbook. The "Williams, Ted" photograph in *Dias Cardinales* has but one word under his name: "Baseball."

Ted Williams graduated on February 3, 1937 in ceremonies in the State College Gymnasium which began at 8 p.m.

Ted graduated first in his class in batting average, runs batted in and home runs. Academically, he himself recalled, "I wasn't a good student. In fact I was a lousy student. The best grades I got at

Hoover High were in history, and the reason was I liked it. I always took subjects I wouldn't have a lot of homework in." Actually, aside from physical education, his best subjects were social studies, typing and, from time to time, one of the shop classes.

Ted's choice of shop was deliberate. "In school, I wasn't much of a student – a little below the other kids. I never pushed myself at all. I always took subjects that I wouldn't have much homework in because I wanted more time for hitting. I took shop and things like that. I'm just lucky I didn't get my hands cut off. I wasn't very good at shop.[196]

One of Ted's teachers once told the youngster, "Ted, you have promise. We just haven't brought it out yet."[197]

Al Olsen, a fellow Padre who also spent some time in the Red Sox system, said, "He probably felt he was dumb because he hadn't gone on to college. He related intelligence to how much education he had, which wasn't true in his part. He was bright as hell. When he went to Sears, he made analyses on different kinds of sporting equipment – fishing poles and things like that. All those college boys didn't know what he was talking about half the time, at least that's what I heard."[198]

TED'S ACADEMIC RECORD

Ted Williams' academic record reflects his final four years, 9th grade at Horace Mann and 10th, 11th and 12th grades at Hoover High School.

Ted's academic record, Horace Mann and Hoover High.

In the section of his record labeled "Mental Tests", the notation "No record" appears. It would have been interesting to know the results of any IQ test, because those who knew him best were always deeply impressed with his native intelligence and intellectual curiosity.

His name was officially listed as Ted S. Williams (not Theodore, and not Teddy) and Mr. S. S. Williams was listed as Parent or Guardian.

The record notes that he was "prominent on baseball team" and it also says "gold baseball".

Graduation was on February 5, 1937. There is a handwritten comment on the top of the report which seems to read "Non college" – indicating that he was not on track for college.

At Horace Mann:	1st semester June 1933	2nd semester Feb 1934
	2.0 GPA	1.2 GPA
	English D	English D
	Jr. Business Fr. D	Jr. Business Fr. F
	Metal B	Metal D
	Social Science B	Soc. Sci. C
	Spanish D	P.E. C
	Phys Ed B	

At Hoover:	1st semester June 1934	2nd semester Feb 1935
	2.0 GPA	1.8 GPA
	English D	English D
	Com. Geog. C	Bus. Prin. D
	Phys. Sci. D	Bus. Prin. D
	Struc. Art C	Art C
	P.E. A	P.E.

	1st semester June 1935	2nd semester Jan 1936
	2.4 GPA	1.8 GPA
	English D	English C
	U.S. Hist. C	U.S. Hist. C
	Print Shop B	Print Shop D
	Life Draw C	Wood Shop C
	P.E. A	P.E. C

	1st semester June 1936	2nd semester Feb 1937
	2.8 GPA	1.667 GPA
	Typing B	Adver. D
	Citizen. C	Typing C
	Print Shop C	Com. Law D
	Wood Shop B	Print Shop D
	P.E. A	Wood Shop B
		P.E. C

Why did he only get a "C" in P.E. both the Jan 1936 and Feb 1937 semesters? In the Spring semesters, he got an A each year – perhaps reflecting his stellar performance on the school baseball team. In the final two Fall semesters, he got just an average grade, the C, though he'd done well in the fall of 1934-35.

There was only one failing grade, though there are a few D's scattered here and there. His print shop grades went from B to D to C, and then back to D. By far his best semester was the one ending in the June of 1936, despite that being the semester he was being pursued by baseball scouts to sign a pro contract. His success at typing helped, as did his improvement in Wood Shop.

All in all, Ted's record fits the profile we've long understood – he was never fully engaged with academics. His mind was on baseball and he rarely applied himself in the classroom. He graduated, though, with a respectable overall GPA at Hoover High School of 2.06, just a touch above a straight C average. The physical education grades clearly made a big difference.

Ted may have under-achieved, but he did graduate, and he applied his considerable native intelligence to becoming the best baseball player he possibly could become.

Having signed with the Padres pretty much eliminated any thought Ted might have given to continuing education. In the spring of 1939, he told Alyce Healy, a student at Arlington [Mass.] High School, that he'd received a scholarship to attend college but chose professional baseball instead. "I wish now I had gone to college," he told Healy.[199] The scholarship Ted mentioned may have been offered by the University of Southern California. A Bob Coyne sports cartoon in the *Boston Post* reads, in part, "passed up a scholarship at U.S.C. for a major league career."[200] Talking a bit about his high school past, he said he pitched, played first base, and the field. "I really think I am a great pitcher," he said, "but, after all, most ball players think they can pitch, and most pitchers think they can hit. My teammate 'Lefty' Grove, takes pride in his hitting."[201]

Ted also told Healy that he'd seen Babe Ruth play in an exhibition game against the PCL Los Angeles Angels and that, before the game, Ruth had tossed about 20 baseballs into the grandstand, "and you should have seen us kids scramble for them. I, being lucky, got one."[202]

Ted may have been telling her what he thought would look best in print in a high school paper. It's hard to imagine The Kid as rookie sitting in the bleachers at Fenway Park, regretting not being a college student. His interest in baseball simply overrode everything else. This was the kid who Hoover teammate Del Ballinger recalled raising his hand in class to go to the bathroom, and being excused from the classroom. "He wouldn't go to the bathroom, though. He'd climb out the window and run out to the field."[203] That was before Rod Luscomb caught on and called Ted to task.

HIGH SCHOOL GRADUATION

Reverend Carnez gave the invocation. Bob Breitbard, president, spoke for the class. Leland D. Stanford was the speaker of the evening. Music was supplied by the Hoover orchestra and singing by the Choral and Glee Club. Perhaps they sang "Farewell to Hoover" by student James McCoy or Joe Liggins' "Sing to Hoover." In any event, the *Cardinal* informed readers that "The honored guests of the evening were the members of the Board of Education." Now that must have been a treat for the graduating seniors!

In later life, Bob Breitbard became perhaps Ted's closest and dearest friend. The two Hoover grads traded a couple of phone calls a day for Ted's last few years, and Bob came east to spend weeks at a time at Ted's home. In the early 1950s, Bob Breitbard founded the Breitbard Athletic Foundation and selected his old classmate as the first man inducted into what became the San Diego Hall of Champions – years before Ted Williams was inducted into baseball's Hall of Fame.

Breitbard played football at Hoover, which earned him the nickname "helmet head" from Hoover's greatest baseball alumnus.

Ted wasn't eligible to play in Hoover's 1937 baseball season, but some 65 boys went out for baseball in the springtime. The *Cardinal* averred, "The pitching staff is somewhat unorganized without Ted Williams, but the material present this season looks good."

Tom Boyle, sports editor of *the Cardinal*, wrote, "Now that the cup annually given to the best baseball player every year has been given to Ted Williams permanently, it seems that some new trophy will probably be begun for this year. There will be plenty of competition for such a trophy with about 60 eager baseball players turning out." The actual trophy cup awarded Ted is today in the care of Ted's nephew, who also goes by the name Ted Williams. The cup reads:

> BATTING CHAMPION
> TED WILLIAMS
> 1935 - .583
> 1936 - .403

These figures disagree with those cited in Ted's autobiography, where he says that he batted .583 and .406 for the two years.[204] If Ted truly made 30 hits in 51 at-bats, then the average was the .588 printed in both the *Cardinal* and the *San Diego Union* at the end of the 1935 season. It's hard to figure out what combination of hits and at-bats would produce a .586 average.

Looking ahead, as the spring 1937 baseball schedule was announced, the *Cardinal* comments, "The baseball team's three largest replacements this year are going to be the positions that Ted Williams, Gordon Bennett and George Means left. Hoover's baseball enthusiasts know the hard job it is to fill those boys' shoes."

Ted's baseball trophy from Hoover High, 1935 and 1936.

Coach Caldwell added to the list the names of Joe Villarino ("the best third baseman ever developed at Hoover," in the coach's words) and Hank Ondler. Of Ted, the coach's quick quip was, "Played as well as he talked, loud."

Ted himself was interviewed, and asked the question, "What is your advice to a sophomore going out for baseball?" Ted Williams, Hoover's greatest claim to baseball fame, trotted another fifty yards before he replied, the reporter wrote. The balance of the article reads as follows:

"Well, I can't say much that hasn't been said in every training book ever put out. The main thing is to play baseball. I didn't play much before I came up here, then Coach Caldwell began putting me in these Sunday ball games all over the city."

Here a raucous voice shouted, "The strikeout kid."

"Rugged. That's me," he yelled back and he continued. "I'd like to tell the sophomores how to be a good player, but I haven't found out myself yet."

"How many games have you played?"

"I could tell you, but I might be twenty-five off. Coach Caldwell would know."

Coach Caldwell did know. He told the *Cardinal* that Williams had played in eighty-five high school games. The paper wrote, "Since his first year as an outfielder and subsequent two years as a pitcher, he has been a letter man. Last year he won both the All-Bay Pitcher and the best hitter in the Pomona tournament. He was elected captain of the team in 1936 instead of Engle, as reported in the annual. The State College Varsity fell twice under his heavy hand. In 1936 he won 12 high school games and lost 1. In those 13 games he struck out 133 batters and allowed only 17 runs to slip by. His batting average is .418. To quote Coach Caldwell, 'It will be a long, long time before anybody here beats that record.'"[205]

Life continued at Hoover in Ted's final months before graduation. The girls' dress code struggle advanced. They were fighting a double standard, as the boys had no dress code. The next issue of the *Cardinal*, the one following Ted's graduation, reported that "relaxed uniform regulations permit girls of city high schools to wear white shirts as well as middies. Midnight blue wool or white wash skirts are still required. Blouses may be worn with senior sweaters. White ones are preferred." Letters to the editor complained about students barging into the cafeteria ahead of teachers, and "'cute' auto acrobatics" in Hoover's parking lot.

Grooming of the boys was an issue, too, particularly to the girls. "What about it, boys?" wrote "Female" in a letter to the editor printed in October 1936. "This being a year for campaigns, why not a tie campaign? I'm so tired of seeing untidy looking boys. It's a relief to see one dressed really neatly. The girls are neat-appearing in their uniforms, but some of these boys!"

Anyone who knew Ted would realize that "Female" had not endeared herself to Ted Williams. Neckties? No, thanks!

Another letter, this one by "Very Disgusted Female," concurred: "What would you boys do if the girls didn't use makeup? Would the boys like to see all the girls looking like hags? Boys make me sick, they complain of the girls' makeup, and then they go with the girls that use a lot... Anyway... it's better than going around as sloppy and unkempt as most of the Hoover boys do." – *Very Disgusted Female*

All of the available photographs show Ted as neatly dressed – or in his baseball uniform. There is no question, though, that he had become a bit of a character at the school. In January 1937, the "Senior Soundings" column posed and answered an inquiry. "Question: What does Ted Williams do with all that lunch he buys every noon? Answer: He eats it, believe it or not."

Verbal "bouquets" were offered in the pages of the paper to selected class members. "Ted Williams for home runs" read Ted's entry. The class prophecy whimsically foresaw Ted as "Tiddly-winks champion."

There were others at Hoover who hoped to make it in baseball, but did not. Classmate Leonard Douthit was on the team, a second-stringer who mostly played centerfield. Douthit had aspirations; he told the yearbook staff he planned to be a "professional baseball player." He had the dream, but perhaps lacked the talent. "I didn't get to play too much," he admitted in a 2003 interview. How was it to have Ted Williams as a teammate? "Everybody liked him. He got along with everybody real good. He got along with his teammates pretty well." Ted wasn't moody? "I think that all developed in the big leagues. I wasn't with him socially or anything. Just on the team. He was enthused about the game, that's for sure. He took it seriously. He did his fair share of pitching. He was pretty good."

Caldwell was a really good coach, Douthit recalls. Did Douthit understand how great a player Ted was going to be? "No. Not really." With an after-school job, and the need to work after high school, Douthit never saw Williams play as a Padre. "He came back from a school reunion when he was through playing, and we did see him that one time."[206]

Ted did indeed return to Hoover High for his 50th reunion, held at the La Jolla Country Club. There Fire Chief Bell noted that Ted looked tan and fit. He approached his old teammate and "I told him he should look good, since all he had ever done was fish or play baseball."[207]

SIGNING WITH THE RED SOX

Ted Williams became the property of the Boston Red Sox in December 1937, and left for spring training in Florida only a matter of weeks later. He rarely returned to San Diego. Major league scouts had been hovering around the high school star even before he signed with the Padres back in early '36. By the time he'd completed two seasons with the Padres, he was a hot commodity.

Earlier reports on Williams were mixed. Other scouts had a head start, though the reports were not uniform. Marty Krug of the Detroit Tigers had been following Ted's progress but, as we have read, Krug was worried about Teddy's splintery physique. "If you let this boy play baseball now," he warned May Williams, "it will kill him." Krug said he wouldn't sign Ted unless his parents built him up: "The kid is nothing but arms and legs now. He'd collapse if he tried to play regularly for a month. He needs to add at least 30 pounds to his skinny frame before he'll be ready for a pro trial."[208]

That prescription almost did Ted in. "My father never forgot those words," he said. "When I finally signed with San Diego, Dad insisted that I eat a steak, weighing at least a pound and a half, every day before I went to the ball park, so as I'd have the strength to play nine innings if called on. I was silly enough to do it. I was too young to realize that I couldn't have made a bigger blunder. I was aware that I didn't have as much life and pep as formerly, but it was a long time before I got wise to the fact that it was those heavy week-day meals that were making me logey."[209]

Former Hoover Star Bought By Red Sox

Ted Williams, former Hoover baseball star, was recently sold to the Boston Red Sox, American League team.

Ted who has played only two years in the minor league with the San Diego Padres, is likely to prove to be a sensation in the big league if he gets the chance. Only 19, Ted plays in the outfield and bats left-handed. He batted .291 for the Padres last season, but has a powerful swing. Knocking more than 21 home runs, Williams ended up in third place in home runs hit in the Coast League for the season.

When Ted teams up with the Red Sox in the spring he will meet many famous players. Most notable among these is Jimmy Foxx, home run hitting first baseman, and Lefty Grove, one of the big league's really great pitchers.

Ted played three years of varsity baseball for Hoover and pitched and batted the Cardinals to many a victory and championship.

The St. Louis Cardinals' Herb Benninghoven had given Ted a few workouts with a Cardinals team in Fullerton, California, and remained interested.

There were even a couple of Yankees scouts in on the action. Bill Essick could have signed Ted before he signed with the Padres. Essick was introduced to Ted by Elmer Hill, who played with Ted on the Cramer's Bakery team. The New York scout made the Williams family a firm offer in 1936, but they demurred, preferring to wait until Ted graduated high school the following year. Sam Williams kept talking to Essick, though, who upped his offer after seeing Ted play in Pomona (at the first semi-pro game Hill took Essick to, Hill actually pitched for the other team and struck Ted out three times). It seemed to Hill that Essick and Sam Williams were getting closer to a deal, but then learned that the Padres' Lane and May Williams had worked out their own deal, and Ted's father assented. "Bill Lane and Frank Shellenback... must have gotten to May Williams the very night I spoke to Sam. I don't know for sure what the deal was, but it was rumored that Mr. Williams was offered a couple of hundred dollars on the spot and grabbed it."[210]

Ted said, though, that he declined the Yankees offer because he'd been told that he'd have to start one of their Class B farm teams and "I couldn't see that. It wasn't that I thought I was a big leaguer. I knew I wasn't. But I felt I was good enough to start in Class A or Double A and I didn't want to leave California if I could help it, unless I was given a chance to join a club in the majors."[211]

When it came crunch time, after Ted had graduated and completed his second year with San Diego, there were a number of teams angling for the opportunity to pry the budding ballplayer loose from Bill Lane and the Padres. In the end, Ted Williams was signed for the Boston Red Sox by General Manager Eddie Collins.

When Collins first spotted Ted Williams, it was – Arthur Sampson writes – on the very day that Chick Shiver quit the Padres, which would make it the last day of August 1936, though Sampson dates it as "mid-August" and says that it was in Seattle that Collins saw Williams play. Michael Seidel is more precise: Collins saw Ted collect three hits and knock in two runs on August 9 during a doubleheader against Portland. Ed Linn confirms the August 9 weekend in Portland as key. Collins was on a scouting trip, giving another look at Bobby Doerr and George Myatt before their options ran out. He had taken out options on both earlier on, but this time noticed Williams taking batting practice. The Padres and the Red Sox had a working agreement between their clubs, and Collins exercised the option on Doerr while declining that on Myatt. "In the meantime, I want you to tell me about that left-handed hitting outfielder you got."[212] Ted tells us, "[Lane] didn't even know who in the hell he was talking about! I wasn't playing then, I'd only been up that one time. He said, 'Well, who do you mean?' and Collins answered, 'That tall, thin, skinny left-hander.' Finally, he decided it was me and he told Collins, 'Hell, he hasn't even played yet. He's just a kid out of high school. He's only seventeen. Give him a few years.'"[213]

Collins himself said it was in Portland, but he says it was a pinch-hit performance in the seventh inning of a game. "The announcer yelled, 'Williams hitting for San Diego." I looked down on the field and nearly broke out laughing when I got a peek at the gawky bean-pole who was striding toward the plate. But I didn't laugh when I saw him swing at the ball and line a double over the first sacker's head.

"There was nothing remarkable about the hit. There certainly was nothing impressive about the appearance of the hitter. But there was something about the way he tied into that ball which all but knocked me out of my seat.

"It was as though a shock of electricity had just passed through my body. In that fleeting moment, as he swung at that ball, I became so convinced that here was one of the most natural hitters in baseball history, I'd have staked my life on it."[214]

Collins was a lifetime .333 hitter, soon to become a Hall of Famer (he was inducted in 1939.) He'd seen The Kid take but one at bat.

"I tried to tell myself a little later that I must be mistaken… but my judgment wouldn't listen to that argument. So I decided to have another peek at the kid in action… I stayed with the San Diego club through that series in Portland. I moved with it down to San Francisco and then into Los Angeles. But I saw no more of my find. He didn't get into another game."[215]

Consulting the research done into the Padres' 1936 season by Dan Boyle, Tom Larwin and Frank Myers, however, one can't locate any such date. There doesn't seem to have been any game – in Portland or otherwise – when Ted pinch-hit a double. He only hit 9 doubles for the Padres in 1936, and they're all accounted for. Collins' memory doesn't appear to match the historical record. Ted did play in Portland on a weekend in August, and he went 3-for-7 with two doubles and two RBI in the August 9 doubleheader. That could well have impressed Collins. He impressed Monroe McConnell, who wrote, "Young Ted Williams… has been delivering like a veteran and Padres fans will probably see more of him."[216] One way or another, though, Ted Williams had made an impression on Eddie Collins.

When the Padres owner turned up in L.A., Collins surprised Lane by asking him on the spot for an option on Ted Williams. Lane agreed, apparently without any particular compensation. Interestingly, the players who were most affected by Collins' scrutiny from the stands were Bobby Doerr and George Myatt. Referring to a game on August 8, the *Union* reported that Doerr had committed four errors and Myatt two. For fans wondering why both fielders had fumbled so badly, the paper explained, "That was the night they learned Collins was in the stands for the first time…" Collins was also looking at Padres pitchers Wally Hebert, Howard Craghead and Dick Ward.[217]

The way Arthur Sampson tells the story, after they'd concluded their business, Lane asked Collins if there were any other players that interested him. "There's one lad I might take an option on. That tall, skinny kid who has been trying to play the outfield." Lane was surprised. "Not that Williams boy! Don't be silly. That boy is several years away from being a big league ball player." Collins says that Lane replied, "He's just a child, only a couple of months out of high school. He couldn't be more crude." He said that Ted was a pitcher, really, who had just joined them from Hoover and that the only reason he was playing outfield was Shiver's sudden departure. Collins persisted, "I like the way he swings a bat. I don't care about the particulars. If you'll give me an option on that boy, I'll buy it right now."

Lane didn't ask for a thing, but he made a promise. "You don't need to buy any option on a rookie so far away from the big leagues. But if you're really serious about him, I'll promise you that Williams will never be sold to a big league club until you've had a chance to buy him." Collins was satisfied: "I don't need any written agreement with you."[218]

All this on the basis of that one at-bat. Collins later said, "Listen, if your Aunt Emma had been in the stands that Saturday night out there in Portland, she'd have realized as quickly as I did that the rookie pinch-hitter, who went to bat in the seventh inning, couldn't miss being a big league great within a few years. He was just a natural."[219]

Ironically, Ted was only in those August games in Portland because of a combination of circumstances that saw the Padres traveling on that particular road trip with only three regular outfielders. When Durst aggravated a muscle pull, Williams was put in. Collins had already noticed Ted's swing during batting practice; now he had the chance to see him in game situations. The 9th was a Sunday. On Friday, Collins was in San Diego meeting with Lane.

Eddie Collins, Babe Ruth, Ted Williams at war benefit game, 1943, Boston.

The following December, 1937, at the winter meetings in Chicago, Collins was ready to do the deal. In the meantime, though, scouts from as many as a dozen different big league teams had had their eyes on Ted during the 1937 season. Collins kept in touch with Lane, telephoning him twice during the season. "Don't worry about Williams," Lane told Collins. "I promised you nobody else would get him until you had a chance to bid for him. And I don't forget my promises. Don't you bother to come out here for that. When the time comes I'll let you know. The kid may not be ready yet. Wait until we see how he finishes the season."[220]

Others in baseball were after Ted, including Bill Terry for the Giants and Casey Stengel for the Boston Braves. Terry, though, reportedly concluded, "The kid is too high-strung for New York."[221] Stengel enlisted Shellenback with a tempting offer of a number of players, and Shellenback reportedly urged Lane to listen to Stengel. "When word trickled around the lobby of the Palmer House that the skinny kid at San Diego might be sold, the bidding for him became serious from all sides," wrote Sampson.[222] Lane held firm, though, telling each club that he had promised matching rights to a certain club and that he felt honor bound to hold to his promise. There was time pressure on Collins, though. The Red Sox did have to commit to their end of the deal. And suddenly Yawkey balked. He'd decided to invest in building a farm system rather than buying players from other teams. Collins had to argue for Williams, while telling Yawkey that he fully supported the commitment to the farm system. "But this happens to be the one time in 100 that we should break our rule," he argued.[223] It wasn't an easy argument, but Cronin apparently chimed in his support and though the discussion dragged on, in the end Yawkey yielded. And not a moment too soon. Lane had been waiting without word, and he was about to pull the trigger on a pending offer.[224]

Collins, "rushing down to the lobby to find Lane happened to step out of the elevator just as Lane had given up waiting and was on his way upstairs to negotiate with one of the other clubs."[225] Lane had told Shellenback that he'd waited long enough and that his conscience was clear: "Let's go." Collins let Lane know that he was ready to deal, and it took only ten minutes to work out the cash part of the deal. Agreeing on which players would go, as the other part of the agreement, took a bit longer but was wrapped up the very next day. "Lane gave the Red Sox a midnight deadline on Ted and they made the deal about fifteen minutes to twelve," Shellenback told Ed Rumill years later.[226]

Ted wasn't pleased when he found out he was supposed to go to Boston. Lane pocketed maybe $35,000 and also got two major leaguers, Dom D'Allessandro and Al Niemiec, and a couple of minor leaguers Griffith and Harris. Ted learned about the deal second-hand. "I read about that for the first time in the paper too and I was sick. The Red Sox didn't mean a thing to me. A fifth-, sixth-place club, the farthest from San Diego I could go. I sure wasn't a Boston fan."[227] But Collins made a strong and positive impression on Ted.

When Collins returned to San Diego in December 1937, Ted now had two seasons with the Padres under his belt and was looking like a legitimate prospect. Collins came by the Utah Street house to visit, and Ted recalls what an "awfully nice, kindly man" Collins was. The Williams family was a poor family, and when Collins paid a visit, Ted remembers, "the only decent chair we had was an old mohair thing that had a big hole you could see the springs through. We covered the hole with a five-cent towel and that's where Collins sat."[228] Both Ted's mother and father were there for the negotiations, and they were looking for a $1,000 signing bonus. The Red Sox were offering a two-year deal worth $7,500, and Ted became uncomfortable with the talk about money. "My father began pressing him a little bit and I left the room. That kind of thing always embarrassed me, any kind of hang-up over money."[229] Collins didn't have the authority to spend that much, without checking with Tom Yawkey. He'd already been spending a lot. Ted's understanding was that Collins again made a convincing case to Yawkey and is pretty sure his parents got the money. Ted later told the *Boston Traveler*, "Maybe the upholstery made the difference."[230]

Some sources have said that Ted's parents got as much as $2,500. Ted himself, testifying in 1958 before the United States Senate Subcommittee of Antitrust and Monopoly, was asked if he had gotten part of the purchase price as a bonus. "No, I didn't. I didn't make provision for that when I signed up. In fact, I signed up with the San Diego club at $150 a month. And when the Red Sox did buy my contact from San Diego, I tried to get a bonus. We were very poor, and I tried to get a bonus, and later did get a little bit of a bonus from the club as I signed a Red Sox contract."[231] Ted was asked who acted for him in the negotiations, given that he was a minor. "Well, my mother. I mean, I didn't do anything without the advice of my high-school coach, who I was very close to, and my mother, of course, had to be with me when I signed the contract, my dad, and I think that is the way they generally work."[232]

In the end, it was Bill Lane's integrity that prevented other scouts from snapping up Ted during 1937 and particularly at the Winter Meetings. He'd made a promise to Collins and he was true to his word. Arthur Daley of *The New York Times* wrote a 1943 column about Brooklyn Dodgers scout Ted McGrew, reporting that McGrew had seen an outfielder in San Diego in 1937 "who positively enraptured him." I want him, he told Bill Lane. "But he's only batting .204," answered Lane. "I don't care. If I can get him, I want him." Lane then told him that the Red Sox had an option on the outfielder. "That string-bean kid had the stamp of greatness on him then," McGrew told Daley. "It was Ted Williams."[233]

Seidel says that it wasn't over yet. Even after the deal was done, the Dodgers' Larry MacPhail tried to obtain Williams from Collins with a special visit to Boston. *The Sporting News* reported the deal but noted that the young player displayed "uncertainty in fielding flies, and a tendency to get caught off base."[234]

That did happen – Ted said that his most embarrassing moment in baseball was a day in which he was picked off base twice in the same game.

Collins never claimed much credit for the signing. In 1939, he told Hy Hurwitz, "Your Aunt Susan could have picked Teddy out of 1,000 players."[235] The aunt's name may have changed, but the sentiment was the same. Collins put it another way to Arthur Sampson: "It was like looking out onto a pasture where there are eight red cows grazing along with one black cow. You can't help noticing the one black cow. It's the same way in baseball. You only had to watch Williams swing once to know that he was a standout prospect."[236]

For his part, Williams always deeply respected Eddie Collins. Jim Stygles, a fellow Marine Corps veteran, visited Ted in his home in Perrine, Florida. He was impressed above all else by one thing. "He had a living room you could play catch in, and he had a large room with all his fishing gear - and he had one picture in it. That one picture was the guy who signed him up. Eddie Collins. Eddie Collins' picture was the only one he had in the house."[237]

Assessed as a whole, could there have been a better deal than to have signed Ted Williams for a pittance, and to have him put up Hall of Fame numbers from 1939 through the 1960 season? If The Kid from San Diego was not the "greatest hitter who ever lived," there weren't more than one or two others who could lay legitimate claim to the honor.

1938

Ted played baseball in San Diego right up until January 16, 1938, a very few weeks before setting out to Sarasota for Spring Training with the Red Sox.[238] In fact, on the 16th, the *Los Angeles Times* still believed that Ted would play one more season with the Padres and so, according to Bob Ray's column, did Frank Shellenback. Ray notes that Ted had already been purchased by Boston, but was going to get one more season of experience in the Coast League. Interestingly, Shellenback commented on Ted's fielding, "While everyone sings Williams' praises as a slugger, a lot of folks are over-looking what a brilliant outfielder he is. I saw him make some of the most sensational catches I've ever seen last year. He covers acres of territory with that long, awkward stride of his, and his throwing compares with Joe DiMaggio's."[239] Either the decision to send Ted to Sarasota was made shortly afterward, or neither Shellenback nor Ray was privy to the decision having been taken.

Ted was talented, but Boston's *Christian Science Monitor* simply listed him as one of the prospects who might earn a spot as backup outfielder. "Granting that Joe Vosmik, Cramer and Ben Chapman will be the Red Sox outfield... Gaffke is thrown into the battle for a reserve garden berth. In competition with him will be Lindsey Deal and Leo Nonnenkamp of Little Rock, Ted Williams of San Diego and Bob Daughters of Rocky Mount."[240]

Ted Williams didn't make the big league team that first year, but instead was assigned to the Minneapolis Millers in the American Association. That was the Red Sox organization's top farm club. The idea was for Ted to develop a little more maturity so he would be better prepared for the majors come 1939. It was probably a very good idea. Ted won the Triple Crown in the American Association, leading the league in average, home runs and runs batted in. He also was voted "The Screwball King of the American Association" by sportswriters who covered that circuit. In Ted's first Spring Training camp, ballplayer Doc Cramer had opined, "Theodore S. The S is for Screwball."[241] The very first day he joined the Millers, Ed Linn was told, Ted arrived at the train station, borrowed a bicycle from a Western Union messenger and rode all around the station, emitting screams as he rode, frightening women and little children.[242] Some reporters dubbed him Peter Pan. He was young and enjoying himself, but when it was time to hit, he produced.

To follow Ted Williams to Minneapolis, see Jim Smith's article, "The Kid Leaves Home: Ted Williams and the 1938 Minneapolis Millers", in this book.

LATER BASEBALL IN SAN DIEGO

There were other times that Ted visited San Diego, but not all that many. The 1941 barnstorming games detailed elsewhere in this volume represent the first such visit to make the news. Joe Naiman's article portrays a 1959 visit for a couple of Red Sox Spring Training games. The last time Ted stepped into a San Diego batter's box, bat in hand, took place where – in some senses – it all began, on the Hoover High School diamond in November 1977. See Bill Nowlin's article, "Ted's Last Home Run in San Diego." Just as he did in the major leagues, it seems that Ted Williams hit a home run his last time up at the plate in his hometown.

Special thanks to Dennis Donley for invaluable assistance with Hoover High School newspapers and other documents.

NOTES

All interviews cited were conducted by author Bill Nowlin, except as noted. Throughout the text, references from the *Hoover High Cardinal* have not been footnoted, but can easily be tracked by date. Likewise, specific game commentary from the San Diego newspapers have often not been footnoted if the date and newspaper are clear in the text itself.

1) *Ted Williams with John Underwood,* My Turn At Bat *(NY: Fireside, 1988), p. 17*

2) *Ibid., p. 20*

3) *Joe Cashman, "Constant Practice From Childhood Made Williams Hitter He Is Today,"* Boston Evening American, *July 14, 1941*

4) *Williams,* My Turn At Bat, *op. cit., p. 20*

5) *Joan Flynn Dreyspool, "Subject: Ted Williams",* Sports Illustrated, *August 1, 1955. Leonard Bell wrote, "Ted had natural ability and worked and worked and worked. He was obsessed. He had very little family life. Baseball was it!" to which Bell then added, "I hit about .200 – if I could have spent some time with Lefty O'Doul...? .300 or better?" Letter to author from Leonard Bell, October 21, 2003.*

6) *Cashman, op. cit., July 14, 1941*

7) *Forrest Warren,* Boston Globe, *September 8, 1946*

8) *Cashman, "Cards' Scout Makes First Offer But Williams Feared Chain Gang,"* Boston Evening American, *July 15, 2004*

9) *Interview with Ernest (Joe) Villarino, May 9, 1997*

10) *Forrest Warren,* Boston Globe, *op. cit.*

11) *Ted Williams with David Pietruza,* My Life in Pictures, *(NY: Total Sports Publishing, 2001), p. 16*

12) *Cashman, op cit., July 14, 1941*

13) *"Ted Williams Tells Us What Makes A Good Hitter,"* Open Road, *May 1950*

14) *Ed Linn,* Hitter *(NY: Harcourt, Brace and Company, 1993), p. 35 - citing a* San Diego Tribune *article I have not located. Ted's quote is from* My Turn At Bat.

15) *Interview with Wilbert Wiley, May 7, 1997*

16) *Interview with Bill Skelley, May 31, 1999*

17) My Turn At Bat, *p 93. Adjustments could make a difference. In 1941, when Ted hit .406, he'd hurt his right foot early in Spring Training, chipping a bone in the ankle. He favored the ankle all year, and some felt that he held back on his swing just that fraction of a second more, thereby giving himself that little bit more of a look at the pitch.*

18) *Dreyspool,* Sports Illustrated, *op. cit. Williams got even more carried away in an interview for Amazon.com's Jeff Silverman in 1998. "I'll tell you what I tell the kids: practice, practice, practice, practice, practice, practice, practice, practice, practice, practice. Then I give them a few good exercises: pepper, pepper, pepper, pepper, pepper, pepper, pepper. Get a bat. Swing it a hundred times a day. And you try to make it quick, with a slight upswing. Little things like that I practice, practice, practice, practice." Interview located on Amazon website, March 26, 1998.*

19) Arthur Mann article in Liberty, *March 9, 1940*

20) Williams with Pietrusza, My Life in Pictures, *op. cit., p. 16*

21) Interview with Joe Villarino, May 7, 1997

22) Ted Williams, "My Last Year in Baseball," Saturday Evening Post, *April 10, 1954*

23) Williams with Pietrusza, My Life in Pictures, *op. cit., p. 16*

24) Interview with Joe Villarino, May 7, 1997

25) Ibidem

26) My Turn At Bat, *op. cit., p. 18*

27) Undated clipping found in the San Diego Hall of Champions archive.

28) My Turn At Bat, *op. cit., p. 24*

29) Linn and also Phil Collier in the San Diego Union, *October 16, 1960. Collier's article offers more comments by Luscomb on how he and Ted worked together on the handball court and the ball field.*

30) My Turn At Bat, *op. cit., p. 22*

31) Ibid., p. 25

32) Ibid., p. 23

33) Interview with Roy Engle, May 8, 1997

34) Ibidem

35) Interview with Mel Skelley, May 7, 1999

36) Interview with Bill Skelley, May 31, 1999

37) Letter to author from Leonard Bell, October 21, 2003

38) Linn, Hitter, *op. cit., p. 73. An unattributed January 10, 1962 newspaper column by David Conlon found in Hall of Fame archives has Ted telling Conlon that he often "cooked his own breakfast and sped off to the schoolhouse" to grab the bat. That way, Ted said, "I was certain I would be first up to hit." At times, then, May Williams was already out saving souls before breakfast, and Ted and Danny left on their own.*

39) Oscar Fraley, "Ted Williams, Heel or Hero," Man's Magazine, *August 1956*

40) My Turn At Bat, *op. cit., p. 31*

41) Interview with Wilbert Wiley, May 7, 1997

42) Dreyspool, Sports Illustrated, *op. cit.*

43) Joe Hamelin, San Diego Union, *July 7, 1980*

44) Interview with Bill Skelley, May 31, 1999

45) Interview with Ambrose Schindler, June 1, 2003

46) Ibidem

47) Interview with Morris Siraton, May 14, 1997

48) Linn, Hitter, *op. cit., p. 30*

49) San Diego Union-Tribune, July 7, 1988 and undated 1992 article.

50) Letters to author from Leonard Bell, September and October 2003. Bell also recalled one time at North Park when Ted "borrowed a Ryan 'bottle bat' from me and never gave it back. So at a dinner he gave 20 years later, I asked him where my bat was. He said he broke the S.O.B."

51) My Turn At Bat, *op. cit., p. 21*

52) Ballinger quotation found among Ed Linn personal notes, made available to author by his daughter Hildy Linn Angius.

53) Seidel, Ted Williams: A Baseball Life, *p. 1. Seidel says the high school ballplayers "earned their spurs" in pickup games against Navy teams.*

54) Interview of Bill Skelley by Bill Swank, January 30, 1995.

55) Interview with John Jensen, May 8, 1999

56) Art Turgeon, Providence Sunday Journal Magazine, *April 7, 1985*

57) My Turn At Bat, *op. cit., p. 28*

58) Dave Strege, "Ted Williams was proficient with more than just a baseball bat," KRT Newspapers, July 11, 2002

59) Steve Corey, "Why Ted Williams Plays It Cool," Uncensored, August 1961

60) Gene Schoor, The Ted Williams Story *(NY: Julian Messner, 1954), p. 20*

61) San Diego Union, July 7, 1980

62) Letter to author from Leonard Bell, September 19, 2003

63) Interview with Joe Villarino, May 9, 1997

64) My Turn At Bat, op. cit., p. 26

65) Boston Traveler, March 14, 1959

66) Interview with Les Cassie, Jr., April 27, 1997

67) Interview with Donald Fraim, June 6, 2003

68) Interview with Wofford Caldwell, April 24, 1997

69) Interview with Donald Fraim, June 6, 2003

70) Linn, Hitter, op. cit., p. 40

71) Interview with Donald Fraim, June 6, 2003

72) Undated newspaper clipping in San Diego Hall of Champions files.

73) Interview with Bill Caldwell, September 2, 2003. Leonard Bell is of the opinion that Caldwell neither recruited Ted for Hoover nor later influenced him to sign with the Padres. Correspondence from Leonard Bell, October 21, 2003.

74) My Turn At Bat, op. cit., p. 24

75) Society for American Baseball Research, A History of San Diego Baseball, *1993*

76) My Turn At Bat, op. cit., p. 34

77) Letter to author from Leonard Bell, September 19, 2003

78) Interview with Ruth Gonzalez, February 28, 2003

79) Correspondence to author from Sally Caldwell McDonell, September 5, 2003. Ted had hired both Caldwell and old Hoover teammate Roy Engle to work summers at the Ted Williams Camp in Lakeville, Massachusetts.

80) My Turn At Bat, op. cit., p. 23

81) Williams with Pietrusza, My Life in Pictures, p. 16

82) San Diego Union, April 21, 1934

83) My Turn At Bat, op. cit., p. 33

84) Letter from Leonard Bell, September 19, 2003

85) Interview with Ruth B. Couvrette, February 9, 2004

86) E-mail to author from Manuel Herrera, May 18, 2000

87) The Cardinal reported the score as 11-3, but the San Diego papers had it as 10-3. Where there have been different data presented in the Hoover school paper and in the San Diego dailies, we have used the numbers provided by the professionals, though there are occasions when the writers for the San Diego dailies wrote accounts which differed from the box scores in their own papers.

88) Linn, Hitter, op. cit., pp. 39, 40

89) Interview with Bob Henderson, January 15, 2003

90) My Turn At Bat, op. cit., p. 30

91) Williams with Pietrusza, My Life in Pictures, op. cit., p. 15

92) Interview with Wofford Caldwell, April 24, 1997

93) My Turn At Bat, op. cit., p. 34

94) Communication to author from Bill Swank, January 23, 2004. The Pacific Coast League was first integrated in 1948. See Bill Swank's interviews with Jack Ritchey and others in Bill Swank, Echoes from Lane Field *(Paducah KY: Turner Publishing, 1997).*

95) Cynthia Wilber, For the Love of the Game, *(NY: William Morrow, 1992), p. 27*

96) *Ibidem*

97) My Turn At Bat, *op. cit., p. 37*

98) *Ibid., p. 36*

99) *Joe Cashman, "Constant Practice....", Boston Evening American, July 14, 1941*

100) *Interview of Alan Storton by Bill Swank, 2003.*

101) *Quoted in Linn, Hitter, op. cit., p. 82*

102) My Turn At Bat, *op. cit., p. 35*

103) *"Frank Waldman, "Frankly Speaking," The Christian Science Monitor, September 11, 1957.*
Whatever he might have felt about sportswriters, Ted always respected umpires, as any number of umpires commented in later years. He was never thrown out of a major league game.

104) *Undated, unattributed clipping from San Diego Hall of Champions files.*

105) My Turn At Bat, *op. cit., p. 18*

106) *Interviews with Dee Allen, Rozie Larson and Frank Venzor, March 2, 2003*

107) My Turn At Bat, *op. cit., p. 20*

108) *Dreyspool, Sports Illustrated, op. cit.*

109) *Interview with Bill Caldwell, September 2, 2003*

110) *Ibidem*

111) *Interview with Wofford Caldwell, April 24, 1997*

112) *Interview with Roy Engle, May 8, 1997*

113) *Interview with Dell Oliver, May 16, 1999*

114) *Interview with Bob Breitbard, June 10, 1999*

115) *Interview with Elizabeth Meyer, December 3, 1999*

116) *Interview with Bob Breitbard, June 10, 1999*

117) *Interview with Joe Villarino, May 9, 1997*

118) *Interview with Mel Skelley, May 7, 1999*

119) *Interview with Dell Oliver, May 16, 1999*

120) *Interview with Ray Boone, January 19, 2004*

121) *Interview with Dell Oliver, May 16, 1999*

122) *Interview with Wilbert Wiley, May 7, 1997*

123) *Interview with Dell Oliver, May 16, 1999*

124) *Interview with Wilbert Wiley, May 7, 1997*

125) *Ibidem*

126) Minneapolis Star-Journal, *May 10, 1938*

127) *Forrest Warren, op. cit. This would appear to be the same game reported in the Union and cited above, the March 27 game where Hoover faced Santa Monica in the Bay League series, and in which Ted struck out 13 (or 11, according to the Santa Monica Evening Outlook) and hit a double and two singles. Santa Monica High did have a school paper, but the archives are packed away during some kind of construction project and will be inaccessible for a couple of years to come. It's hard to know what to make of the reputed 23 strikeouts.*

128) *Interview with Ray Boone, January 19, 2004*

129) *Ibidem*

130) *Interview with Bill Caldwell, September 2, 2003*

131) My Turn At Bat, *op. cit., p. 36. Imagine just the starting nine all matching Ted's appetite. That would be 117 ice creams and 99 bottles of pop. Maybe that's where the song about 99 bottles of pop on the wall had its origin.*

132) *Ed Linn interview of Bobby Doerr, in Linn papers. When Ted signed with San Diego, he told Cynthia Wilber, "That was when I started to eat like I never ate before, because the team had a little account, and I could eat whatever I wanted. Then I started to put on some weight, maybe five, seven, eight pounds a year. Three or four years of that and you know I was a bit bigger size and stronger." Wilber, op. cit., p. 38.*

133) *Interview with Roy Engle, May 8, 1997*

134) *Interview with Bill Caldwell, September 2, 2003*

135) *Arnold Rampersad,* Jackie Robinson *(NY: Ballantine Books, 1997), p. 37*

136) Pomona Progress-Bulletin, *April 10, 1936*

137) Boston Herald, *May 10, 1993*

138) *Letter to author from Alan McCutcheon, March 14, 2003*

139) *Arthur Sampson,* Ted Williams *(NY: A. S. Barnes & Company, 1950), p. 161. Sampson may have borrowed the story from Forrest Warren, who wrote a virtually identical account a few years before Sampson's book, in which he told how he had visited Johnson to get first-hand information about Ted's high school days. Forrest Warren, op. cit.]*

140) *Interview with Alan McCutcheon, December 31, 2002*

141) *Forrest Warren, op. cit. There is at least some collapsing of time here; while Essick may have first seen Ted in 1934, the reported offer was made a couple of years later.*

142) *Jim Prime and Bill Nowlin,* Ted Williams: The Pursuit of Perfection *(Champaign, IL: Sports Publishing, Inc., 2002), p. 13 Regarding this Yankees scout's report, Ted belatedly offered this retort to David Pietrusza, more than 60 years later: "Well bleep, I'm 15 or 16 for chrissake and smart pitching will get me out? They ain't got smart pitching down here." Williams with Pietrusza,* My Life in Pictures, *op. cit., p. 19.*

143) My Turn At Bat, *op. cit., p. 36*

144) *Dreyspool,* Sports Illustrated, *op. cit.*

145) *Interview with Roy Engle, May 8, 1997*

146) San Diego Union, *July 6, 1980*

147) San Diego Union, *April 25, 1936*

148) San Diego Union, *July 8, 1980*

149) San Diego Union, *May 31, 1936*

150) *Williams with Pietrusza,* My Life in Pictures, *op. cit., p. 20*

151) My Turn At Bat, *op. cit., p. 39*

152) *Interview with George Myatt, July 7, 1997*

153) *Gene Schoor,* The Ted Williams Story, *op. cit., p. 32*

154) *"Baseball Gold", January 1985, reprinted in* A History of San Diego Baseball, *created by the Ted Williams Chapter of the Society for American Baseball Research, 1993.*

155) *Earl Keller comment found in Ed Linn papers.*

156) *Interview with Autumn Durst Keltner, May 23, 1999*

157) *Linn,* Hitter, *op. cit., p. 35*

158) San Diego Union, *June 23, 1936*

159) *Dan Boyle, Tom Larwin, Frank Myers,* The First Padres, *unpublished manuscript, September 2002. See also Seidel,* Ted Williams: A Baseball Life *(Chicago: Contemporary Books, 1991), p. 13.*

160) *Bill Swank, "Echoes from Lane Field" newsletter, December 1999*

161) *Al Olsen, interviewed by Ed Linn, Linn's personal notes.*

162) *Ibidem*

163) *Chris Cobbs, "Down Memory Lane with Vintage (PCL) Padres" in* A History of San Diego Baseball, *created by the Ted Williams Chapter of the Society for American Baseball Research, 1993*

164) San Diego Union, *June 27, 1936*

165) *Interview with Bill Skelley, May 31, 1999*

166) San Diego Union, *October 17, 1960*

167) *Stuart N, Lake, "More Praise for Ted Williams Rolls In From Pacific Coast,"* The Christian Science Monitor, *April 11, 1939*

168) *Cashman, "O'Doul First to Spot Williams as 'Natural'",* Boston Evening American, *July 16, 1941*

169) *Ibidem*

170) *Interview with Bud Tuttle, May 17, 1999*

171) My Turn At Bat, *op. cit., p. 62*

172) San Diego Sun, *June 28, 1936*

173) *Sampson*, Ted Williams, *op. cit., p. 28*

174) *Interview by Ed Linn, in Linn papers, and interview with author, July 7, 1997*

175) *Linn*, Hitter, *op. cit., p. 57*

176) San Diego Union, *March 8, 1959. The home run was hit by Wes Schulmerich. Ted told Ed Linn, "I shook Hal Doerr off and threw a fast ball, and Schulmerich hit it a mile." Ed Linn personal notes.*

177) *Cashman*, Boston Evening American, *op. cit., July 16, 1941*

178) *Ibid., July 14, 1941*

179) *Swank*, Echoes from Lane Field, *op. cit., p. 25*

180) Boston Globe, *August 13, 1948*

181) *Interview with Ralph Thompson, March 30, 2000*

182) *Swank*, Echoes from Lane Field, *op. cit., p. 16*

183) *Unattributed clipping from Bobby Doerr scrapbook. Williams had recently turned 18, but may have already begun telling people that he was born in October. See the discussion of Ted Williams and his treatment of his birthday in the chapter "Ted Williams' Family Roots" later in this book.*

184) *Interview with Bud Tuttle, May 17, 1999*

185) *Ibidem*

186) *Ray Boone interview by Ed Linn, in Linn papers.*

187) Boston Globe, *August 13, 1948*

188) *Ibidem*

189) *Bobby Doerr interview by Ed Linn, in Linn papers.*

190) *Ibidem*

191) *Louise Kaufman interview by Ed Linn, in Linn papers.*

192) *Leigh Montville quotes from the* Boston American; *see Leigh Montville,* Ted Williams *(NY: Doubleday, 2004), p. 43.*

193) *Frank Cushing interview by Ed Linn, in Linn papers.*

194) San Diego Union, *October 5, 1941*

195) *Interview with Ray Boone, January 19, 2004*

196) *Dreyspool*, Sports Illustrated, *op. cit.*

197) *Ted told this to San Diego sportswriter Jack Murphy, according to Leonard Bell. Letter from Bell to author, September 19, 2003.*

198) *Al Olsen interview by Ed Linn, in Linn papers. Olsen presents an interesting tangent. For some years, he was listed in* The Baseball Encyclopedia *as having made a brief appearance in major league ball, for the Boston Red Sox on May 16, 1943. This was an error. The player who debuted that day was Leon Culberson. Olsen never made the majors. For more on this, see Clifford S. Kachline's "Phantom Ballplayers" in the second edition of* Total Baseball.

199) *Alyce Healy, "Sand-Lot Artist Rises to Fame",* The Chronicle, *student newsletter of Arlington High School, June 9, 1939.*

200) Boston Post, *March 19, 1938*

201) *Healy,* The Chronicle, *op. cit.*

202) *Ibidem*

203) *Linn*, Hitter, *op. cit., p. 31*

204) My Turn At Bat, *p. 35*

205) Hoover High Cardinal, *February 13, 1937*

206) *Interview with Leonard Douthit, June 9, 2003*

207) *Letter from Leonard Bell to author, September 19, 2003*

208) *Cashman*, Boston Evening American, *op. cit., July 15, 1941*

209) *Ibidem*

210) Letter from Elmer Hill to Ernest Lannigan, March 5, 1957 from the National Baseball Hall of Fame Library, as reported by Michael Seidel, Ted Williams: A Baseball Life, *op. cit., p. 12.*

211) Cashman, Boston Evening American, *op. cit., July 15, 1941*

212) My Turn At Bat, *p. 43*

213) Wilber, For the Love of the Game, *op. cit., p. 38 and Williams,* My Turn At Bat, *op. cit., pp. 43, 44.*

214) Cashman, July 13, 1941

215) Ibidem

216) San Diego Union, *August 11, 1936. Williams played two full games in that doubleheader, substituting because of injuries to the regulars. Perhaps Collins just simply confused the two when he said Ted was pinch-hitting. In the same series of articles by Joe Cashman, Ted himself said that Shellenback "began using me as a pinch-hitter. That's how Eddie Collins happened to see me one night in Portland."* Boston American, *July 16, 1941. It had been five years, and it's not hard to excuse anyone for less than perfect recall under the circumstances. No one could truly have expected the raw youngster to become as overshadowing a star as he became.*

217) San Diego Union, *August 11 & 14, 1936*

218) Sampson, Ted Williams, *op. cit., pp. 9, 10. The "crude" quotation comes from Joe Cashman's article "One Hit – One Job Rise of 'Kid',"* Boston Sunday Advertiser, *July 13, 1941.*

219) Cashman, ibidem

220) Ibid., p. 13

221) According to Heinie Groh, as reported by Michael Seidel, Ted Williams: A Baseball Life, *op. cit., p. 26.*

222) Sampson, Ted Williams, *op. cit., p. 15. Joe Cashman devotes an entire article to the possibility that the Boston Braves could have come up with Williams, had Lane not held true to his promise to Collins. "Williams Might Have Been a Brave, If Collins Hadn't Put in Red Sox Bid,"* Boston Evening American, *July 17, 1941. Cashman quotes Collins as saying that the amount the Red Sox paid to get Ted Williams was "ridiculously small, considering what we received. I know Ted didn't get as much as we gave Lane for Bobby Doerr, and Dom DiMaggio cost us far more than Teddy and Bobby together. We just happened, as I've said before, to have the good fortune to be dealing with a man as fair and square as Lane. Because he had made me a promise, he was willing to take less from us than he was being offered by other clubs."*

223) Ibid., p. 17

224) Cronin's support is mentioned in Seidel, Ted Williams: A Baseball Life, *op. cit., p. 25.*

225) Sampson, Ted Williams, *op. cit., p. 18*

226) Ed Rumill, "Stengel Tells Story Of Deals That Didn't Click," The Christian Science Monitor, *August 11, 1958. Stengel told Rumill he'd seen Ted in 1936, and that he had prevailed upon Braves' owner Bob Quinn to sign him up. At the 1937 winter meetings, they went for it, and the Braves offered a total of five players who were National League regulars for Ted Williams, but Lane's promise to Collins held.*

227) My Turn At Bat, *op. cit., p. 43*

228) Ibid., p. 44

229) Ibidem

230) Boston Traveler, *February 6, 1957*

231) Testimony of Ted Williams before the United States Senate Subcommittee on Antitrust and Monopoly, July 9, 1958.

232) Ibidem

233) Arthur Daley, "About A Good Scout," The New York Times, *March 27, 1943*

234) Seidel, Ted Williams: A Baseball Life, *op. cit., p. 27*

235) Boston Globe, *July 22, 1939*

236) Sampson, Ted Williams, *op. cit., p. 18*

237) Interview with Jim Stygles, April 6, 2004

238) See Tom Larwin's article on Ted's last games, "Playing Baseball in San Diego: 'The Kid'...When He Was a Kid", elsewhere in this book.

239) Bob Ray, "Ted Williams Next Coast Loop Sensation," The Los Angeles Times, *January 16, 1938*

240) "Sporting Around the Hub," The Christian Science Monitor, *February 15, 1938*

241) Notation found in Ed Linn's personal notes

242) Notation found in Ed Linn's personal notes

TED WILLIAMS GAME SUMMARIES, 1934-1938:
HIGH SCHOOL, AMERICAN LEGION, AND AREA LEAGUES

	Date	Team	Pos.	Batted	Batting						Pitching					
					AB	R	H	2B	3B	HR	IP	W-L	R	H	BB	K
High School	3/10/34	Hoover	RF	3	5	1	2	0	1	0	0		0	0	0	0
	3/13/34	Hoover	RF/1B	3	3	1	1	0	0	0	0		0	0	0	0
	3/17/34	Hoover	RF	5	3	0	0	0	0	0	0		0	0	0	0
Pomona Baseball Tournament	3/29/34	Hoover	DNP													
	3/29/34	Hoover	DNP													
	4/20/34	Hoover	RF	7	2	3	2	0	0	1	0		0	0	0	0
	4/28/34	Hoover	RF	7	3	0	0	0	0	0	0		0	0	0	0
	5/4/34	Hoover	RF	did not start	2	1	1	1	0	0	0		0	0	0	0
	5/18/34	Hoover	DNP													
	5/25/34	Hoover	DNP													
	6/2/34	Hoover	PH/RF	0	0	0	0	0	0	0	0		0	0	0	0
	6/8/34	Hoover	DNP													
American Legion	7/10/34	Padre Serra 370	P	4	5	0	1	0	0	0	9	W	5	6	6	6
	7/12/34	Padre Serra 370	CF	4	3	1	3	0	0	1	0		0	0	0	0
	7/23/34	Padre Serra 370	P									W	7	8		
	7/25/34	Padre Serra 370	CF	4	1	3	0	0	0	0	0		0	0	0	0
	8/1/34	Padre Serra 370	P	4	3	0	1	0	0	0	9	L	1	7	0	5
	8/2/34	Padre Serra 370	OF/P													
Independent	8/12/34	San Diego Market	RF	3	4	0	1	0	0	0	0		0	0	0	0
	8/19/34	San Diego Market	RF	3	4	1	2	0	1	0	0		0	0	0	0
	8/26/34	San Diego Market	CF	9	3	0	1	0	0	0	0		0	0	0	0
San Diego County Managers Association	9/16/34	San Diego Market	RF	3	4	2	3	0	0	1	0		0	0	0	0
	9/23/34	San Diego Market	RF	4	4	0	0	0	0	0	0		0	0	0	0
	9/30/34	San Diego Market	CF/P	4	5	2	2	0	0	0	1	L	1	0	0	0
	10/28/34	San Diego Market	P													
County Winter League	11/4/34	San Diego Market	P	9	4	0	0	0	0	0	9	L	12	7	3	3
	12/2/34	San Diego Market	RF/P	6	3	0	3	1	1	0		W			3	10
	12/23/34	San Diego Market	P													
	1/13/35	San Diego Market	RF	4	3	1	2	1	0	0	0		0	0	0	0
	1/20/35	San Diego Market	P	8	3	0	0	0	0	0	9	L	11	10	2	7
	1/27/35	San Diego Market	P	9	2	1	0	0	0	0	9	W	4	10	2	6
	2/3/35	San Diego Market	1B	4	3	0	1	0	0	0	0		0	0	0	0
	2/17/35	San Diego Market	1B	4	4	0	1	0	0	0	0		0	0	0	0
High School	2/22/35	Hoover	P								9	W	1	3		
	3/6/35	Hoover	P													
	3/12/35	Hoover	1B		5		5									
	3/13/35	Hoover	P													
	3/14/35	Hoover	1B													
	3/16/35	Hoover	1B/P		4	2	2	1		2						
	3/20/35	Hoover	P													
	3/23/35	Hoover	CF/P	4	3	2	1					W			5	5
	3/26/35	Hoover	P													
	3/30/35	Hoover	1B	4	2	2	2									
	4/6/35	Hoover	1B		5		5	1	1	1						
	4/10/35	Hoover	P													
	4/12/35	Hoover	P	4	5	2	4				9	W	5	6	2	16
	4/13/35	Hoover			2	1	2			1						
Pomona Diamond Baseball Tournament	4/18/35	Hoover	P													
	4/19/35	Hoover														

	Date	Team	Pos.	Batted	Batting						Pitching					
					AB	R	H	2B	3B	HR	IP	W-L	R	H	BB	K
High School	4/23/35	Hoover	P		3	1	1				7	W	1	6	3	5
	4/25/35	Hoover	RF/P/CF	4	3	1	2	0	1	1	5	L	9	9	1	4
	4/27/35	Hoover							1							
	4/30/35	Hoover	P	4	3	0	2	0	0	0	9	W	2	5	2	2
	5/3/35	Hoover			3	1	2			1						
	5/7/35	Hoover														
	5/11/35	Hoover	RF/P	4	4	3	1	0	0	1	5	L			5	6
Independent	5/26/35	Central	RF	4	4	0	1	1	0	0	0		0	0	0	0
	6/7/35	Walter Church	P		2		2	0	2		7	W	1	3		14
	6/16/35	Cramer's Bakery	RF	3	4	1	2	1	0	1	0		0	0	0	0
	6/23/35	North Park Merchants	RF	4	1	1	1	0	0	0	0		0	0	0	0
	6/30/35	North Park	RF	3	4	0	2	0	0	0	0		0	0	0	0
American Legion	7/3/35	Padre Serra 370	3B/P/LF	4	4	1	2	0	1		1.1		3			3
	7/6/35	Padre Serra 370	P	4	2	2	0	0	0	0	9	L	9	7	3	11
	7/10/35	Padre Serra 370	LF	4	5	2	2	1	0	0	0		0	0	0	0
	7/13/35	Padre Serra 370	P	4	3	3	2	0	0	0	9	W	0	5	4	13
	7/15/35	Padre Serra 370	LF/P	4	2	1	1	0	1	0	2.2			3		2
Summer City League	7/14/35	Walter Church	RF	3	4	0	1	0	0	0	0		0	0	0	0
	7/21/35	Walter Church	RF	3	2	1	1	0	0	1	0		0	0	0	0
	7/28/35	Walter Church	RF	3	4	0	0	0	0	0	0		0	0	0	0
	8/18/35	Walter Church	P	3	3	0	1	0	0	0	9	W	2	11	5	9
	8/25/35	Walter Church	P	3	4	2	2	0	0	0	9	W	2	5	4	5
	9/1/35	Walter Church	P/LF	3	4	0	0	0	0	0	5		1		2	5
	9/8/35	Cardinals (frmrly Church)	RF	3	3	0	1	0	0	0	0		0	0	0	0
	9/22/35	Cardinals	P/													
	10/6/35	Cardinals	RF/P	5	4	1	2	0	0	1	3		1		1	3
Independent	10/13/35	Bay City Liquor	CF/LF	5	2	0	0	0	0	0	0		0	0	0	0
	12/21/35	Cramer's Bakery	LF	6	2	0	0	0	0	0	0		0	0	0	0
	1/18/36	Cramer's Bakery	LF, P	6	3	1	1	0	0	0	7	W	4		2	5
	3/1/36	Cramer's Bakery	LF	4	4	2	1	0	0	0	0		0	0	0	0
Winter League	12/8/35	Cramer's Bakery	LF	6	5	1	1	0	0	0	0		0	0	0	0
	12/15/35	Cramer's Bakery	LF	6	4	0	1	0	0	0	0		0	0	0	0
	12/22/35	Cramer's Bakery	LF	6	4	0	1	0	0	0	0		0	0	0	0
	1/5/36	Cramer's Bakery	LF	6	4	0	0	0	0	0	0		0	0	0	0
	1/12/36	Cramer's Bakery	LF	6	2	1	1	0	0	1	0		0	0	0	0
	1/19/36	Cramer's Bakery	LF	6	2	0	1	0	0	0	0		0	0	0	0
	1/26/36	Cramer's Bakery	RF	6	5	0	3	1	0	0	0		0	0	0	0
	2/9/36	Cramer's Bakery	RF	5	4	1	0	0	0	0	0		0	0	0	0
High School	3/3/36	Hoover	P									W		1		8
	3/7/36	Hoover	P		2	2	2			2		L	5	8		12
1st Annual American Legion Interscholastic Tourney	3/13/36	Hoover	CF	4	1	2	0	0	0	0	0		0	0	0	0
	3/14/36	Hoover	SS	4	2	4	2	0	0	1	0		0	0	0	0
	3/14/36	Hoover	P	4	3	1	1	0	0	0	9	W	1	3	7	13
High School	3/21/36	Hoover	P		2	1	2	1	0	1	9	W	0	1		13
	3/27/36	Hoover	P		3	3	1				9	W	0	3	1	13

	Date	Team	Pos.	Batted	Batting						Pitching					
					AB	R	H	2B	3B	HR	IP	W-L	R	H	BB	K
Pomona Baseball Tournament	4/9/36	Hoover			2		0									
	4/10/36	Hoover	P									W				
	4/10/36	Hoover	P									W				
	4/11/36	Hoover														
	4/11/36	Hoover	P													
Tournament Totals*										4	19		3	9		21
High School	4/14/36	Hoover	P													
	4/17/36	Hoover	P		1		0				9	W	1	1		
	4/24/36	Hoover	P								9	W	2	3		19
	5/1/36	Hoover	P								5	W	0	1		8
	5/8/36	Hoover	P	4							9	W	1	3		13
	5/12/36	Hoover														
	5/22/36	Hoover	P								9	L	8	9	3	7
1936 High School Totals*					82	25	33				39	5-0***				66
Exhibition	6/22/36	Padres Exhibition	LF	1	1	0	1	0	0	0	0		0	0	0	0
Independent	1/1/38	Gold Club	LF	3	3	1	1	1	0	0	0		0	0	0	0
	1/2/38	Gold Club	CF	3	4	1	2	1	0	1	0		0	0	0	0
	1/9/38	Gold Club	CF	3	3	0	0	0	0	0	0		0	0	0	0
	1/16/38	Gold Club	CF	3	4	1	1	0	0	0	0		0	0	0	0

Totals

	BA	AB	R	H	2B	3B	HR	IP	W-L	R	H	BB	K
1934 Totals	.377	61	15	23	2	3	3	28	3-3	26	28	12	24
1935 Totals	.444	133	33	59	7	6	10	116.3	10-4	52	83	41	116
1936 Totals	.439	41	15	18	3	0	5	75	11-2	22	33	13	111
1938 Totals	.286	14	3	4	2	0	1	0	0-0	0	0	0	0
1934-38 Totals	.418	249	66	104	14	9	19	219.3	24-9	100	144	66	251
1934-38 Totals**							23	238.3		103	153	66	272

*tournament summary published in article dated 4/14/36, *San Diego Union*

**high school record for 30 games published in article dated 5/31/36 in *San Diego Union*

***cited as Bay League record in 5/31/36 article; loss indicated was in non-league game

****includes the reported Pomona Tournament totals

Notes:

1. DNP - did not play

2. zeroes in game summaries are shown where substantiated

3. if runs were not reported independently, then they were added if there were home runs cited

TED WILLIAMS POSITION SUMMARIES, 1934-1938:
HIGH SCHOOL, AMERICAN LEGION, AND AREA LEAGUES

Season	Team	League	Defensive Position Played										Batting Order Position									
			P	C	1B	2B	3B	SS	LF	CF	RF	OF	1	2	3	4	5	6	7	8	9	PH
3/34 - 6/34	Hoover Cardinals	High School			1						7				2		1		2			1
7/34 - 8/34	Padre Serra 370	American Legion	4							2		1				4						
8/34	San Diego Market	Independent/ Miscellaneous								1	2				2						1	
9/34 - 10/34	San Diego Market	County Baseball Managers Association	2							1	2				1	2						
11/34 - 2/35	San Diego Market	Winter County League	5		2						2					3		1		1	2	
3/35 - 5/35	Hoover Cardinals	High School	14		5					2	2					6						
5/35 - 6/35	Central	Independent/ Miscellaneous									1					1						
	Walter Church	Independent/ Miscellaneous	1																			
	Cramer's Bakery	Independent/ Miscellaneous									1				1							
	North Park Merchants	Independent/ Miscellaneous									2				1	1						
7/35	Padre Serra 370	American Legion	4				1		3							5						
7/35 - 10/35	Walter Church/Cardinals	Summer City League	5						1		5				7		1					
10/35	Bay City Liquor Store	Independent/ Miscellaneous							1	1							1					
12/35 -3/36	Cramer's Bakery	Independent/ Miscellaneous	1						3							1		2				
12/35 - 1/36	Cramer's Bakery	Winter City League							6		2						1	7				
3/36 - 6/36	Hoover Cardinals	High School	14					1		1						4						
6/36	San Diego Padres	Pacific Coast League Exhibition							1													
1/38	Gold Club	Winter League							1	3						4						
Totals			50	0	8	0	1	1	16	11	26	1	0	0	18	27	4	10	2	1	3	1
			44%	0%	7%	0%	1%	1%	14%	10%	23%	1%	0%	0%	27%	41%	6%	15%	3%	2%	5%	2%

Note: Does not add up to 100% due to rounding

Of his game appearances he pitched in 44% and played outfield in 48%

Note: Does not add up to 100% due to rounding

He batted clean-up 41% of the games started and in the 3rd, 4th or 5th spot in 74% of his starts

Unique Achievements:

First game - March 10, 1934

First hit - March 10, 1934

First home run - April 20, 1934

First pitching performance - July 10, 1934

First win as pitcher - July 10, 1934

First five-hit game (as batter) - March 12, 1935

First multi-homer game (as batter) - March 16, 1935

First cycle - April 6, 1935

Pitched first shutout - July 13, 1935

Received three intentional walks - April 17, 1936

Struck out 19 - April 24, 1936

Hit in 60 of 79 games where box score reported (76%)

NEWS COVERAGE OF TED WILLIAMS WHILE IN HIGH SCHOOL, AND JANUARY 1938 SERIES

Date	Source	Notes	Noteworthy Events
3/10/34	*San Diego Union*	Ted Williams mentioned in tentative lineup in RF and batting 3rd for opening game of "city bowl" with San Diego High.	FIRST NEWSPAPER MENTION OF WILLIAMS
3/11/34	*San Diego Union*	Hoover beat SD High 3-1 in 10 innings for "first game of their mythical city championship series." "Hoover.. .scored one run in the fifth when Williams, an unsung sophomore outfielder, batting from the south side of the plate tripled and scored on Kimball's single to left."	FIRST RECORDED BOX SCORE WITH WILLIAMS IN LINEUP
3/14/34	*San Diego Union*	Hoover lost to SD High 11-8. Under fielding, Williams was listed as back-end on a double play.	
3/18/34	*San Diego Union*	Hoover lost to SD High 15-4. Williams had an error.	
4/21/34	*San Diego Union*	Column headline: "Ted Williams Puts Game on Ice in First." "Ted Williams, sophomore outfielder, practically put the game on ice for the Cardinals in the first inning (sic, it was really the 2nd inning) when he cleaned the loaded bases with a home run drive to center field. It was a hard hit line drive over the shortstop's head and between the outfielders." Hoover won 19-3 vs. Alhambra.	FIRST NEWSPAPER REPORT WITH WILLIAMS NAME IN HEADLINE; FIRST REPORT OF HR
4/29/34	*San Diego Union*	Williams mentioned in the article that he grounded out in one situation.	
5/5/34	*San Diego Union*	Hoover beat Pasadena 10-3, "...Ted Williams also propelled the ball over the right field fence, but to the right of the "barber pole," the hits going only for doubles."	
5/13/34	*San Diego Union*	Ted Williams in large Hoover team photograph (Cardinals shirts) "Herbert Hoover Nine Points for Southland Championship"	FIRST RECORDED NEWSPAPER PHOTO OF WILLIAMS AS PART OF 1934 HOOVER TEAM SHOT
5/31/34	*San Diego Union*	Article indicates that, in preparation for the game with Montebello, Caldwell "intends to try two other changes in the lineup, sending Ted Williams to first in place of…"	
6/3/34	*San Diego Union*	Noted in the article was that Williams walked as pinch hitter in 8th; won 10-8 against Montebello at Hoover HS	
6/8/34	*San Diego Union*	Williams listed as a "reserve" making the trip to LA Wrigley Field for Southern California Interscholastic Baseball Championship	
7/4/34	*San Diego Union*	Article indicates only 2 OFs on Serra team and that other OF post will be filled by one of the 3 pitchers including Ted Williams who "rank(s) among the team's leading hitters."	
7/10/34	*San Diego Union*	Williams mentioned in article in the lineup for the game the next day as starting pitcher and batting 4th in the order	
7/11/34	*San Diego Union*	Beat Fighting Bob 12-5 at Golden Hill playground; "Although off to a shaky start Ted Williams, Herbert Hoover High school sophomore, settled down and pitched the Padre Serra nine to an easy victory. He allowed one run in the opening inning and three in the third, then gave only one run in the remaining six innings. He pitched a six-hit game."	FIRST WIN AS PITCHER
7/12/34	*San Diego Union*	"With rest of the lineup remaining intact except that Ted Williams, pitcher who won the opening game, probably will be in centerfield to make use of his hitting ability." He is listed as batting 8th in the order.	
7/13/34	*San Diego Union*	Beat Fighting Bob 7-6 at Golden Hill; "...and lanky Ted Williams, who did the damaging hitting." "...Ted Williams' single drove in Aguirre for one run in the first…" "In the fifth Williams opened with a home run over the right field fence…"	
7/14/34	*San Diego Union*	Williams and Engle noted as battery for the Padre Serras for upcoming game	
7/17/34	*San Diego Union*	(Coach) Corriere plans to start Ted Williams on the mound...	
7/24/34	*San Diego Union*	not mentioned in the accompanying article, Williams pitched the entire game as was shown on the line score for the game	
7/25/34	*San Diego Union*	"…with Ted Williams, winner of Monday's game, stationed in center field."	
7/26/34	*San Diego Union*	Williams only listed in box score but scored three runs in a 16-3 victory	
8/1/34	*San Diego Union*	Article notes that the Padre Serra team hopes to get off to a good start "... behind Ted Williams. No. 1 pitcher Williams, who also is one of the leading hitters of the club, has won two games in as many starts."	TEAM PHOTO OF PADRE SERRA TEAM WITH WILLIAMS
8/2/34	*San Diego Union*	Lost to Leonard Wood Post 1-0. "Ted Williams, Padre Serra's lanky right-handed pitcher, and his Leonard Wood mound rival, Mangold, stole the show in yesterday's conflict. They pitched like a pair of veterans instead of two previous games, pitched his best game of all yesterday, but ran into the misfortune of having his own team shut out. The Herbert Hoover sophomore retired the first 12 batters to face him, but Meyers, Leonard Wood first baseman, greeted him at the start of the fifth with a single to center."	

8/3/34	*San Diego Union*	lost to Leonard Wood Post 10-1; Williams pitched in relief… Los Angeles scored 8 in the first and it is unknown from the article when he came into the game.
9/17/34	*San Diego Union*	S. D. Market won 6-4 against Mission Stars; noted that "Williams led the hitters with three blows, including a home run." at University Heights Playground.
9/24/34	*San Diego Union*	Lost to National City 5-1 (record 0-4) at National City; Williams pitched the 10th and gave up the winning run
10/14/34	*San Diego Union*	Steinmann's column touted new facilities at Hoover. Herbert Hoover High school demonstrated that as it opened its new athletic plant, lighted and equipped for night games, before a fine crowd of enthusiastic community supporters and students. A lot of progress in the four years since the doors of the school, still "new" as schools go, first were opened to receive students." Now listed at 1,400 students. "... it has a turf field, lights for night games and when more bleachers are added it will be as good a plant as required, certainly on a par with the average high school field anywhere. As Hoover comes along it will provide a fine, natural rivalry between this institution and San Diego High."
10/30/34	*San Diego Union*	Article has line score as Market beat Pacific Beach 5-4; appears Williams pitched some in the game.
2/10/35	*San Diego Union*	Letterman Ted Williams mentioned as a "pitcher" for Hoover Cardinals; Joe Villarino is a "promising recruit" and of San Diego's noted baseball family
2/23/35	*San Diego Union*	In a Hoover inter-class game "Ted Williams went the distance and limited the regulars to three blows in the nine innings."
3/8/35	*Hoover High Cardinal*	Early reviews of the 1935 team noted "Ted Williams, outfielder last year, who will be one of the principal pitchers this year…" Coach Wofford Caldwell said "…Williams should develop into an excellent pitcher and very powerful hitter…"
3/10/35	*San Diego Union*	Coach Caldwell indicated that he had many "chuckers" playing the infield and outfield, and that Ted Williams would start at 1B. He also noted that Williams five who made up their mound staff.
3/13/35	*San Diego Union*	In a win over Naval Hospital "…Ted Williams, first sacker, paced the Cardinals with five hits in as many times up."
3/14/35	*San Diego Union*	The Marines won 12-11 and lit up starting pitcher Morris Hurst and "… Ted Williams, who relieved him, went along in fairly even fashion as his mates managed to draw up on fairly even terms with the Marines."
3/15/35	*San Diego Union*	Article noted that in upcoming game with Santa Ana "Ted Williams, who holds down first base when not drawing flinging duties, is slated to oppose Jones on the mound for Hoover." "Williams is one of Coach "Wash" Caldwell's brightest prospects, and although not rated the team's No. 1 mound artist, is said to be a real comer."
3/16/35	*San Diego Union*	"Hoover's mound hopes this afternoon will be Ted Williams, one of the ranking members of Coach 'Wash' Caldwell's prized mound staff. Williams promises to develop on of the best hurlers ever turned out at the East San Diego school, but up to the present time has seen most of his diamond time at first base. " Later on in the article Williams is named as one of Hoover's three "leaders in the bat department."
3/17/35	*San Diego Union*	"Plastering out two home runs and a double in four times up, Ted Williams, who doubles between first base and the pitcher's mound, yesterday led Herbert Hoover High's baseball team to a 6 to 2 victory over Santa Ana…" "…Williams moved over to the mound and between his pitching and slugging, the latter was the game's outstanding star."
4/7/35	*San Diego Union*	Hoover 15, Covina 0; "Ted Williams and Morris Siraton were the heroes of the Hoover 19-hit attack…" Williams had five hits including a home run.
4/10/35	*San Diego Union*	Hoover beat the USS Detroit 9-7; Hoover team photograph under title "Carry Hopes of Hoover for Diamond Championship"
4/13/35	*San Diego Union*	Hoover 10, Glendale 5, at Hoover; "Ted Williams, lanky Cardinal chucker, pitched six-hit ball; fanned 16 batters and pounded out four hits in five trips plateward to grab the starring laurels."
4/14/35	*San Diego Union*	Hoover 7, San Bernardino 1; "Williams, with a homer and a single…led the batting"
4/23/35	*San Diego Union*	Article mentions "Ted Williams a cool customer when in action before a hostile crowd, is slated to pitch for Hoover. Williams has been pounding the "apple" like a Babe Ruth, and along with his mound ability, is looked upon as Hoover's best bet to stop the Hillers."
4/26/35	*San Diego Union*	San Diego 9, Hoover 5; Ted Williams had a HR but was "slugged from the mound." "Ted Williams, who had been the winning hurler Tuesday, then stepped into the box, and the Hillers greeted him like a long lost cousin, picking up two more runs before the session ended."

NEWSPAPER PHOTO OF WILLIAMS AS PART OF 1935 HOOVER TEAM

PITCHED A COMPLETE GAME VICTORY, STRIKING OUT 16, AND WENT 4 FOR 5.

5/1/35	*San Diego Union, San Diego Sun*	A big deal in San Diego at the time with the "city title" on the line, 2,500 fans watched Hoover beat San Diego High, 6-2; at Hoover. (Union) "Lanky Ted Williams, loose-jointed Cardinal who dotes on hitting 'em where they ain't, was the hero of the engagement, pitching five-hit ball to check potent Hilltop sluggers, and clouting our a pair of sharp singles to play a big part in the run scoring." (Sun) Sub-head: "Williams Hurls Red Birds to Triumph; Rally in 5th Decisive." The article mentions "gangling Ted Williams of Hoover had only one man left to put out when San Diego manufactured a run on singles... " "Williams again proved capable on the mound for the Cards, he struck out a pair, walked the same number and only three times had the ball hit out of the infield as Ondler's 17 put outs will attest."	WILLIAMS AS PITCHER LAUDED IN SUB-HEADLINE
5/4/35	*San Diego Union*	Beat LaJolla 13-3 at LaJolla: "Ted Williams, Hoover's elongated slugging star, pounded out two hits in three trips to the plate, one of them a home run."	
5/9/35	*San Diego Union*	In preparation for a game with San Diego High "lanky Ted Williams, who won two of the series games and was losing hurler in the other, is likely to start for Hoover again…"	
5/12/35	*San Diego Union, San Diego Sun* (5/13)	San Diego 14, Hoover 11; (Union) Played before "2,000 rabid fans... Ted Williams, lanky Cardinal slugging and hurling star who had been called upon to take over the mound chores after Ralph Twiss, then surprise starter, faltered the third frame, put his club back in front in such a way that it seemed almost impossible for the Hillers to catch up..." Further, related to his hitting, "... the lanky Cardinal found one of Randolph's offerings much to his liking and drove it even farther down the line in right to chase in the two runners ahead of him." He hit a three-run home run in the 6th inning for a 10-7 lead that held up until the bottom of the 8th when SD High scored 7 runs.	
5/26/35	*San Diego Union*	For 1936 "Coach Wofford Caldwell will have big Ted Williams"... as one of his "ranking hurlers."	
5/27/35	*San Diego Union*	Lost 12-0 to Cramer's Bakery at University Heights; "Ted Williams' double was the only extra base hit off (Elmer) Hill.	
6/4/35	*San Diego Union*	Article indicates that Walter Church took Hoover's place in the Metropolitan League All-Stars, including "star battery" combination of Ted Williams and Woody Helm.	
6/7/35	*San Diego Union*	"Ted Williams, lanky Herbert Hoover High school pitching and batting star, has been selected to appear on the mound…"	
6/8/35	*San Diego Union, San Diego Evening Tribune*	"Ted Williams, hurler for Herbert Hoover High, had things practically his own way" striking out 14 batters and hitting two three-base. hits, vs Metropolitan All Stars at Sports Field. Ted Williams "lanky Herbert Hoover High School pitching and batting star for Church, "Ted Williams Stars As Prep Nine Loses"	
6/17/35	*San Diego Union*	Ted Williams "husky," young prep school OF 5-2 win over Winter's Bakery 10 innings at University Heights; Ted Williams "free swinging" left handed batter drove ball clear out	
7/3/35	*San Diego Union*	"Ted Williams, lean and lanky pitcher from Hoover, probably will start the contest for Padre Serra although he has been suffering from a sore side and has not been doing much hurling."	
7/4/35	*San Diego Union*	"...Ted Williams, lanky Hoover right-hander, proved ineffective" but won 9-3 at Oceanside	
7/6/35	*San Diego Union*	"Ted Williams of the Serra squad and Bill Skelley of the Morrowmen will take the mound to do battle for the third time this season. Both are the star hurlers of their respective teams and the squad that loses will have no cause for alibis as both are at full strength."	
7/7/35	*San Diego Union*	"Ted Williams hurled 7-hit ball and fanned 11 only to see his mates commit 4 miscues;" Bill Skelley was effective in pinches and stopped slugging of Ted Williams; lost to Post 6 9-7 at Golden Hill	
7/10/35	*San Diego Union*	"Wes Caldwell, Padre Serra coach will call on Delmont Ballinger… in order to save Ted Williams, lanky right-hand star for the fray with Post 6 Saturday."	
7/14/35	*San Diego Union*	Beat Post 6 10-0 at Central; "Ted Williams, Padre Serra's right handed pitching ace, had a field day yesterday…Williams allowed five hits while fanning 13 batters and also collected two hits in three times at bat." He was the "big star of the day."	
7/16/35	*San Diego Union*	Ted Williams pitched in relief against the Post 6 team and he "… proved to be just another pitcher to the Morrowmen…"	
8/6/35	*San Diego Evening*	Article headline read "St. Louis Nine Offers Williams Tryout." "Ted Williams, slim Herbert Hoover High pitcher, with whom local diamond fans are well acquainted, has received an offer to try out with the St. Louis Cardinals of the National League. Herb Benninghoven, managing the local Walter Church nine as a Cardinal farm tendered the offer and informed Williams his expenses would be taken care of should he care to make the trip east for the trial. Doubt was expressed that Ted would accept, however, since he still has one more year of high school and should he go into organized baseball he would be declared ineligible for further high school competition by the Southern California Interscholastic federation."	FIRST MENTION OF PROFESSIONAL BASEBALL INTEREST IN WILLIAMS

8/19/35	*San Diego Union*	Won 6-2 vs. El Cajon; Ted Williams scattered 11 hits in the win.	
8/26/35	*San Diego Union*	Won 7-2 "…the Plasterers, held to five hits by Pitcher Williams…"	
9/1/35	*San Diego Union*	Lost 3-2 before 3,000 fans at University Heights playground; tied 1-1 when starting pitcher Ted Williams was relieved vs. Cramer's Bakery.	
10/6/35	*San Diego Union*	Williams hit HR in last of 9th to tie game, 1-1…which is how it ended after 10 innings.	HOME RUN IN LAST OF 9TH SENDS GAME TO EXTRA INNINGS
2/23/36	*San Diego Union*	Article indicates "returning lettermen are Ted Williams, lanky pitcher…"	
3/4/36	*San Diego Union*	Intrasquad game, and "the Lefties with Ted Williams hurling one-hit ball, downed the Right Handers, won 4-0. Williams fanned eight batters."	
3/7/36	*San Diego Union*	For the forthcoming American Legion tournament Coach Wofford Caldwell "…probably will start lanky Ted Williams against the Alumni."	
3/8/36	*San Diego Union*	Photo of Ted Williams pitching in striped uniform with title "Cardinal Workhorses for Legion Title Tourney." Caption says "Ted Williams, lanky right-hander shown at the top getting over fast, high one, and Catcher Roy Engle are expected to be the workhorses of Herbert Hoover High's varsity baseball team when it goes into action Friday and Saturday in the first annual American Legion Invitational tourney. Williams is expected to have more than his share of the mound work, with Engle slated to divide the backstopping work with his catching teammate, Joe Helm."	RARE PHOTO OF WILLIAMS PITCHING
3/8/36	*San Diego Union*	Article on game with the Hoover Alumni which noted that "…Ted Williams pitching winning ball, but the alumni managed to touch the lanky righthander for a pair of blows which were converted into runs when his teammates tossed in a pair of costly runs. Williams fanned 12 batters and had a field day at bat catching hold of a pair of Don Kimball's tosses for home runs."	
3/14/36	*San Diego Union*	Game report in article noted "Rising to the heights behind a brilliant three-hit mound performance by lanky Ted Williams, Herbert Hoover High yesterday defeated its arch rival, San Diego High, 6 to 1, in the first annual American Legion Invitational Interscholastic Baseball championship… Williams, limber-armed right-hander who usually shows more power at the plate than on the mound, received potent stick assistance from his mates…" "Williams fanned 13 men, but partially nullified his efforts by issuing seven free passes to first."	
3/19/36	*San Diego Union*	Ted Williams announced as a unanimous choice for the all-star tourney team for the RF position and with a batting average for the tournament of .500.	
3/21/36	*San Diego Union*	"Ted Williams, lanky Hoover star who doubles as an outfielder and pitcher, will forget his "pasture" chores today in favor of the pitching assignment."	
3/22/36	*San Diego Union*	Beat Covina 17-0. "Lanky Ted Williams, ace Cardinal chucker, went the entire distance and just missed chalking up a no-hit, no-run game, a scratch single in the fifth frame by center fielder R. McBride depriving the Hoover chucker of a perfect game. Williams had an easy time subduing the invading Colts, fanning 13 batters to mow them down in machine-like order. Williams shared batting laurels in the fray with Walt Bickerton, versatile outfielder… Williams pounded out a homer and a double." The AB and R nos. are minimum since no way to confirm how many times he batted and runs scored from the narrative account.	
3/27/36	*San Diego Union*	"Ted Williams, Hoover's No. 1 hurler and one of their best hitters on the roster, will be counted upon to silence the bats of the northerners and also to lead the Cardinal attack."	
3/28/36	*San Diego Evening Tribune, San Diego Sun, San Diego Union*	Hoover beats Santa Monica, "Ted Williams, hurler for the victors, permitted but three hits." (*Sun*) "Ted Williams set down the (Santa Monica) squad with three scattered hits and led his team with three for three." (*Union*) Sub headline "Ted Williams Hurls Hoover to League Win." Article continues "with Ted Williams, lanky hurler allowing but his string of three hits in as many times at bat and fanned 13 opposing batters." (*Evening Tribune*)	SUBHEAD LAUDING WILLIAMS' PITCHING
4/13/36	*San Diego Union*	Photo of Ted Williams swinging under banner "They'll Be Calling Him Bambino." Caption says "The 'Babe Ruth' of the Herbert Hoover High school team, Ted Williams, pictured above, got three home runs as he pitched the Cardinals to the consolation title in the 20-30 club championship tournament at Pomona Saturday. One of the heaviest hitters in southland prep circles (undecipherable) startled the railbirds with his flinging in the semi-finals and finals."	PHOTO OF WILLIAMS AT BAT
4/14/36	*San Diego Union*	Ted Williams was lauded by his coach and teammates for his "iron man" performance. The article continued "Williams, regarded as the city's finest diamond prospect, hurled a total of 19 innings, struck out 21 batters and allowed only nine hits and three runs. At the same time he managed to collect four home runs himself, getting two in the same inning on one occasion."	WILLIAMS RECEIVES IRON MAN SALUTE

4/17/36	*San Diego Union*	Beat Compton 7-1 at Hoover; Ted Williams walked intentionally three times; headlines read "Ted Williams Hurls Hoover to League Win." Article began "The devastating bat that has made Ted Williams one of the most dangerous prep school hitters of the year was silenced, but his throwing arm was just as good as ever as he pitched Herbert Hoover High to a 7 to 1 victory over Compton in a Bay League game yesterday on the Cardinal diamond. Williams, exhibiting too much speed and deception for the visitors, was in command all the way and the best Compton could do was pick out one hit... Williams, who has featured just about hitting every Hoover contest with his hard hitting didn't have a chance to demonstrate his prowess at the platter." Williams was purposely passed three times in a row.	SUB HEADLINE CREDITS WILLIAMS FOR HURLING
4/25/36	*San Diego Union*	Hoover 5, Redondo 2 at Redondo; The headline read "Williams Hurls Cards to Victory, Fans 19 Men." The article continued "Ted Williams more firmly established himself as one of the best prep diamond prospects in southern California when he established a new Bay league record in pitching Herbert Hoover High of San Diego to a 5 to 2 victory over Redondo here today. The lanky San Diego youth fanned 19 Redondo batters to break the mark which had stood since 1924..."	SUB HEADLINE THAT WILLIAMS HURLS CARDS TO VICTORY
4/26/36	*San Diego Union*	Steinmann article indicated Ted Williams is in "big demand. The Cardinal organization wants him, so do scouts for the New York Yankees." "Ted Williams, Hoover High's star pitcher, is another marked youngster. His name on a contract is in big demand. The Cardinal organization wants him, so do scouts for the New York Yankees. But so far school authorities have kept him from becoming embroiled in eligibility difficulties."	BIG LEAGUES REPORTED INTERESTED IN WILLIAMS
5/2/36	*San Diego Union*	Playing against Inglewood "Ted Williams and Gordon Bennett twirled for Hoover and kept the home team in check...Williams allowed but one hit in five innings."	
5/9/36	*San Diego Union*	"With Ted Williams, ace hurler of the Hoover staff, allowing but three hits while his mated pounded out 14 safe blows…"	
5/23/36	*San Diego Union*	"…Ted Williams, losing moundsman, was knocked for nine…" hits.	
5/31/36	*San Diego Union*	Making the All-Bay circuit squad, "T. Samuel Williams, elongated chucker who was unbeaten in five loop starts and would rather boast of his home run hitting ability…"	
6/1/36	*San Diego Evening Tribune*	Article headline read "San Diego Contract Offered Williams." "Ted Williams, who has pitched and batted Herbert Hoover High's baseball teams to many victories the last three years, will join the San Diego Padres this month, is his parents consent to his playing of professional baseball. A contract was offered Williams by Bill Lane, owner of the San Diego club, Saturday and Williams said he would give him an answer within a few days. It is understood that Williams' folks are in favor of Ted becoming a professional player. Lane would not give Williams a tryout as a pitcher. He would be used in the outfield, and if he can hit, he might earn a regular berth. Several local coaches and fans recommended Williams to Lane, and the owner of the Padres has had his eye on the lanky powerhouse for some time. Lane told Williams that he would not send him out for seasoning if he signs a contract. If Williams accepts he will report to the Padres as soon as school is out. He will graduate this month."	ARTICLE HEADLINE THAT SAN DIEGO CONTRACT OFFERED TO WILLIAMS
6/22/36	*San Diego Union, San Diego Evening Tribune*	Preparing for a benefit encounter, Padre manager Frank Shellenback "... indicated yesterday that Ted Williams, the Herbert Hoover High school athlete who several clubs have been trying to nab... will be given an opportunity to display their talents." (*Evening Tribune*) Shellenback "...will insert Bob Gray and Ted Williams, and Tom Downey, local boys who have been working out with the Padres in the lineup early in the game in order to give his sluggers a day's rest..." (*Union*)	PLAYS FIRST GAME FOR SAN DIEGO PADRES–BENEFIT GAME
6/23/36	*San Diego Union*	Ted Williams got into the line up with the Padres having "...a seemingly safe margin…" He played left field and went 1 for 1.	
6/26/36	*San Diego Evening Tribune*	Earl Keller writes that "The way things look now Ted Williams may not get lined up with any team this year. The Padres, Yankees, and Cardinals still are dickeringwith him."	ARTICLE HEADLINE ABOUT WILLIAMS SIGNING
		Photo accompanies an article, the headlines indicate that "Williams, Former Hoover star, signed by Padres as Outfielder." "Ted Williams, Herbert Hoover High school diamond hero and one of the best natural prospects developed in this district in some time, signed a contract with the San Diego Padres, yesterday and will be in uniform with the Coast Club this year. Although Williams was a pitcher in high school, he will not be used in that capacity but will be back to the outfield in an effort to capitalize on his hitting ability. Williams also was offered contracts by the New York Yankees, St. Louis Cardinals, and the Los Angeles Angels, but turned down all other offers in favor of the one from H. W. Lane, Padre owner. Williams is 17 years old, slightly over six feet in height, and weighs 165 pounds. Williams worked out with the Padres yesterday and was under the watchful eye of Syd Durst, veteran Padres centerfielder, who will give him the benefit of the experience."	

6/27/36	*San Diego Union*	Under the terms of his contract, Williams will be kept with the Padres for the reminder of the season and all of next without being farmed out. By that time, he is expected to develop to a point where he will be of first string caliber. In the meantime, he will be given a chance to show what he can do under fire whenever the opportunity presents itself. Williams was developed by Wofford Caldwell, Herbert Hoover baseball coach, who influenced him to sign with the Padres for his best interests."	PHOTO AND ARTICLE HEADLINE ABOUT WILLIAMS SIGNING
		Photo showing Ted's mug shot with a description as "New Padre." "If Ted Williams, who joined the Padres yesterday, listens to Durst's advice, he is sure to get somewhere. Ced if taking the 18 year old outfielder under his wing and yesterday he gave himself lesson No. 1 on how to chase flies." Article headlines "Ted Williams signs with Padres; will be used as Outfielder. Ted Williams, husky former Herbert Hoover High right-handed pitcher today was signed to a contract by H. W. Lane, owner of the San Diego Padres. Williams lined up with the local team in the Pacific Coast league in preference to joining the New York Yankees, St. Louis Cardinals, or the Los Angeles Angels all who were angling for his contract.	
6/27/36	San Diego Evening Tribune	Lane, in announcing the signing, said Williams would be put to work immediately and would not be used on his mound staff because of his heavy hitting. Instead he is to be shifted to the outfield. Lane expressed confidence the youngster would develop quickly, since he handles himself naturally. Williams probably will understudy Van Wirthman in left field. The terms of the Williams' contract call for him to stay with the Padres the remainder of this season and all of next and not be farmed out."	
6/28/36	*San Diego Union*	Gets an at bat in his first professional game as a San Diego Padre and strikes out.	FIRST PROFESSIONAL GAME
12/31/37	*San Diego Evening Tribune*	"Ted Williams Plays with Gold Club Nine"	
1/1/38	*San Diego Union*	Photo of Ted Williams with title "Major Leaguer." Caption reads "when the new Gold Club baseball team opens a series with Farley's this afternoon at 2 at Monroe field. Ted Williams, above, San Diego Padre sensation who goes to the Boston Red Sox in 1938, will be holding down an outfield position." The article goes on "Also in the new uniform of the Gold Club will be Ted Williams, the slugging prodigy of the Padres who has been sold to the Boston Red Sox."	PHOTO IN GOLD CLUB UNIFORM
1/2/38	*San Diego Union*	The Gold Club won 3-0 against Farley's as Williams had a double in the first "through Bill Starr's legs" and eventually scored the 2nd run of the game.	
1/3/38	*San Diego Union*	Farley's won this contest, 10-4. Ted Williams knotted score at 2-all "...when Williams poled a terrific homer far over the center field fence, one of the lustiest blows in the history of the park."	
1/9/38	*San Diego Union*	Farley's and Gold Club are getting ready to play for the "City Ball Title." " In Gold Club uniforms will be such stars as Ted Williams, the Padre rookie ace who recently was purchased by the Boston Red Sox..."	
1/10/38	*San Diego Union*	Farley's won the third game of the series, 7-1. Williams' only mention is for getting an intentional walk.	
1/14/38	*San Diego Union*	Article headline reads "Diamond Fans Honor Ted Williams." "Ted Williams, the gangling former Herbert Hoover High school athlete who goes up to the Boston Red Sox this spring, will be honored at Monroe field Sunday when the Gold Club and Farley's baseball teams clash for the fourth time in their winter series. In preparing for his major league debut, Williams, who broke in with the San Diego Padres, has been holding down an outfield job for the Gold Club. Many of his followers, including several merchants in the North Park district, asked permission to honor him with a "Ted Williams day..."	HEADLINE MENTIONS HONORING TED WILLIAMS
1/15/38	San Diego Evening Tribune	"It will be Ted Williams' day, and the angling ex-siege gun of Hoover high will be the recipient of gifts from admiring fans and merchants."	NEWS RE TED WILLIAMS DAY
1/16/38	*San Diego Union*	"It will be "Ted Williams day" with the young Gold Club outfielder who goes up to Boston Red Sox this spring being honored by his team mates and the fans. Some of his admirers asked that a day be set aside for him so they could present him with gifts as tokens of their appreciation."	
1/17/38	*San Diego Union*	The Gold Club won 1-0 against Farley's with the aid of "successive singles by Williams...rang the gong." He scored the only run, and their pitcher Tex Reichert, pitched a no hitter." The article mentions that Reichert received excellent support from a "sensational" catch by Williams.	

Left to right: Ted Williams, Eddie Collins and Bill Lane outside the Padres'
Lane Field offices, February 15, 1938.

Ted with the Padres, April 5, 1937.

THE SPLENDID SPLINTER'S PCL DEBUT: "WHO IS THIS KID?"
by Dan Boyle

> *"We were just a little hamburger town. Things really picked up when the Padres got here..."*
> Earl Keller, in Bill Swank's *Echoes from Lane Field,* p. 30

With the conclusion of the Hoover High baseball season in late May 1936, Ted Williams and his family considered his baseball options. As May turned to June, a report tucked at the bottom of the last page in the sports section of the *San Diego Union* confirmed that Bill Lane had offered a contract for the remainder of the 1936 season to Ted Williams.[1] Lane's rivals were said to include the St. Louis Cardinals, who offered to send the prospect to a Class B team, and the New York Yankees.

Negotiations proceeded privately without media scrutiny. The next mention of Williams in the *Union* appeared when the Service All-Stars (comprised of Navy and Marine Corps players) met the Padres in a benefit game for the Navy Relief Society on a Monday off-day. Manager Frank Shellenback announced that Ted Williams would be given an opportunity to display his talents in the exhibition.[2]

CAPABLE RECEIVER

Bobby Doerr with the Padres.

On June 22 the Padres jumped to a 12-1 lead after seven innings in front of 4,000 fans, including some very high-ranking Navy dignitaries. Several young high school and sandlot players then entered the game, including Williams in left field, Bill Gray from Grossmont High at shortstop, Benny Simpson in center field, and Tom Downey at third base. Williams singled and scored a run in his only at-bat. It was his first appearance in a San Diego Padres box score, albeit an exhibition game.

Bobby Doerr remembers the first time he saw Ted Williams:

> I saw Ted Williams come in for a tryout in June. Shellenback was pitching batting practice and he said, "Let the kid get in and hit a few." The older players around the cage didn't like this too well, as he would take up their time. Ted hit about seven or eight balls, and I think about two or three were out of the park. So everyone started to say, "Who is this kid?" One of 'em said, "This kid will be signed before the week is out."[3]

The unidentified player was prophetic. Sports fans opening the *San Diego Union* on June 27, 1936 found this sports page headline: "Williams, Former Hoover Star, Signed by Padres as Outfielder." Ted Steinmann's bylined story read:

> Ted Williams, Herbert Hoover High School diamond hero and one of the best natural prospects developed in this district in some time, signed a contract with the San Diego Padres yesterday and will be in uniform with the Coast League club today. Although Williams was a pitcher in high school, he will not be used in that capacity but will be sent to the outfield in an effort to capitalize on his hitting ability.
>
> Williams also was offered contracts by the New York Yankees, St. Louis Cardinals, and the Los Angeles Angels, but turned down all other offers in favor of the one from H. W. Lane, Padre owner.
>
> Williams is 17 years old, slightly over six feet in height, and weighs 165 pounds.
>
> Williams worked out with the Padres yesterday and was under the watchful eye of Syd Durst, veteran Padre centerfielder, who will give him the benefit of his experience.

Under the terms of his contract, Williams will be kept with the Padres for the remainder of the season and all of next without being farmed out. By that time, he is expected to develop to a point where he will be of first string caliber. In the meantime, he will be given a chance to show what he can do under fire whenever the opportunity presents itself.

Williams was developed by Wofford Caldwell, Herbert Hoover baseball coach, who influenced him to sign with the Padres for his best interests.[4]

Boxscore showing Ted's first professional at-bat.

Williams had not yet graduated from high school when he debuted with the Padres. He returned to Hoover High after the 1936 season and graduated early in 1937.[5]

As it happened, the last place Sacramento Solons were the visiting team in San Diego when Ted joined the Padres, and when a last place team comes to town, fans can always count on interesting and unusual promotions at the ballpark. The Padres promoted a foot race, throwing contest, and a race around the bases. It could only help to give a local boy the opportunity to appear in the game for the Padres. Ted Williams made his official professional debut as a pinch-hitter in the second inning of the game on that day, Saturday, June 27. He was retired by Sacramento pitcher Henry Pippen. As Ted recalled, "I took three strikes right down the middle. Didn't even swing."[6]

In an unusual move that continued the spirit of the June 27 pre-game festivities, the Padres signed veteran pitcher Elmer Hill and started him against Sacramento.[7] Hill had had a modestly successful PCL career, but had only pitched in local semi-pro games in 1936 while serving as captain of the firehouse in North Park near the Williams residence. He gave up two runs in the first two innings, and in his only game with the Padres all year he earned the distinction of being the first pitcher to be pinch hit for by Ted Williams. This distinction may not have been accidental. Hill later claimed that he played a significant role in persuading Williams to sign with the Padres. His status as a former PCL star and a civic leader in the North Park neighborhood lends plausibility to this claim, as does the Padres' willingness to sign him for one last PCL appearance, possibly as a way of thanking him for helping to sign Williams.

For Ted Williams, it was an inauspicious debut, to say the least. An ordinary Padres fan may not have even realized that Williams was officially part of the team, since the local papers concentrated on the pre-game festivities in their reports and made no mention of his professional debut.

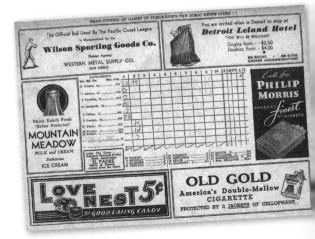

1936 Padres scorecard showing Williams in the lineup.

Ted Williams in June, 1936

Date	Vs.	Pos	AB	R	H	2B	3B	HR	RBI	SB	Avg*
June 27	Sacramento	PH	1	0	0						.000

* Cumulative Average as of this game

On July 3 versus Los Angeles, Williams was the third of four Padre pitchers in a 14-9 loss. He gave up two hits, a walk, and two runs (both earned) in 1 1/3 innings, his first professional appearance as a pitcher (he would subsequently appear on the mound with Boston in 1940 for two innings). But on the bright side, Ted Williams collected his first two hits in pro ball.[8]

Ted Williams in July 1936

Date	Vs.	Pos	AB	R	H	2B	3B	HR	RBI	SB	Avg*
July 3	Los Angeles	P, LF	2	2	2						.667
July 4-1	Los Angeles	PH	1	0	0	1					.500
July 4-2	Los Angeles	LF	4	1	1				1		.375
July 5-1	Los Angeles	LF	3	0	0						.273
July 5-2	Los Angeles	LF	3	0	0						.214
July 15	Seattle	PH	1	0	0						.200
July 17	Portland	PH	1	0	0						.188
July 22	SF Missions	PH	1	0	0						.176
July 24	SF Missions	PR	0	1	0						.176
Jul 26-1	SF Missions	LF	3	0	1						.200
July 30	Los Angeles	PH	1	0	0						.190
			11	20	4	4	1	0	0	1	0	.200
Season			12	21	4	4	1	0	0	1	0	.190

Date	Vs.		IP	H	R	ER	SO	BB	W	L	ERA
July 3	Los Angeles		1.1	2	2	2	0	1	0	0	13.50

* Cumulative Average as of this game

1937 San Diego Padres team. Front row: Ernie Holman, Hal Patchett, Manny Salvo, Bill Lane (owner), George McDonald, Jimmy Reese, George Myatt; **second row:** Cedric Durst, Wally "Preacher" Hebert, Herm "Old Folks" Pillette, Dick Ward, Eddie Mulligan, Bill Star; **third row:** Frank Shellenback (manager), George Detore, Les Cook (trainer), Gene "Bud" Tuttle, Howard Craghead, Bill Skelley; **back row:** Jim "Tiny" Chaplin, Rupert "Tommy" Thompson, John "Junk" Walters, Joe Berkowitz, Ted Williams, Marion "Pat" Tobin.

Ted appeared in back-to-back doubleheaders in Los Angeles on July 4 and 5, but the acquisition of power-hitting outfielder Ivey "Chick" Shiver in early July made it clear that Williams was not expected to play a key role on the ballclub in 1936. It was Ted's turn at bat only 20 times in July. He got a chance to play in early August, starting seven games between August 7 and 12 when Syd Durst suffered a groin injury and backup outfielder Vance Wirthman was also nursing injuries. The *San Diego Union* reported: "Young Ted Williams... has been delivering like a veteran and Padre fans probably will see more of him."[9] Once Durst returned, though, Shellenback continued to hold Williams out of the lineup more times than not. Ted didn't seem to mind. In a letter home to F. B. Naylor, Williams said he was learning a lot about baseball and adding weight at the request of Lane and Shellenback.[10]

August was the most successful month to date for the Padres. A 21-12 mark separated them from the middle of the pack and elevated San Diego into the thick of a very tight pennant race. Williams saw more action in August, appearing in 12 games and rapping seven hits in 25 trips (.280) with two doubles and three RBIs. Shellenback still appeared reluctant to insert the rookie into the lineup on a regular basis in what had become a pennant race. When the 40-year old Durst was injured again during the Oakland series, Shellenback selected Vance Wirthman as the substitute outfielder. As best we can tell, there was no doubt regarding Williams' ability, but only a desire to bring him along slowly.

The month ended with a benefit exhibition game sponsored by the Rotary club on Monday August 31 against local semi-pro all stars. Ted Williams was the hitting star, with a home run, a double, and two singles.

Ted Williams in August 1936

Date	Vs.	Pos	AB	R	H	2B	3B	HR	RBI	SB	*Avg
Aug 7-1	Portland	LF	0	0	0						.190
Aug 7-2	Portland	LF	4	1	1				1		.200
Aug 8-1	Portland	LF	3	1	2						.250
Aug 8-2	Portland	LF	3	0	0						.226
Aug 9-1	Portland	LF	4	0	2	1			2		.257
Aug 9-2	Portland	LF	3	1	1	1					.263
Aug 11	SF Missions	LF	3	0	0						.244
Aug 12	SF Missions	LF	4	0	0						.222
Aug 16-1	SF Missions	PH	1	0	1						.239
Aug 16-2	SG Missions	RF	1	0	0						.234
Aug 19	Sacramento	PH	1	0	0						.229
Aug 23-1	Sacramento	PH	1	0	0						.224
Aug 28	Oakland	PR	0	0	0						.224
Totals for August		13	28	3	7	2			3		.250
Season		25	49	7	11	3	0	0	4	0	.224

Cumulative Average as of this game

On September 1, with two weeks left in the season, the team and its fans were stunned by the sudden departure of Chick Shiver. Georgia College had offered Shiver the position of head coach of its football team if he would join them immediately. He took them up on the offer and left town on the evening train on his way to Georgia.[11] The turn of events took the Padre front office completely by surprise. Bill Lane suspended Shiver indefinitely, but several players felt that it was Shiver's intention to retire from baseball and so the suspension meant little.

The loss of Shiver, who was red-hot through most of August, seemingly was a knock-down blow to a team that had fought back to within two games of first place. To make up for Shiver's abrupt departure Manager Frank Shellenback made the decision to replace him in the lineup with Ted Williams. Through July and August, Shellenback and the Padres had essentially allowed "The Kid" to get his feet wet in professional baseball. With the pennant on the line, though he had Vance Wirthman available (Wirthman had filled in for Durst throughout the crucial Oakland series), Shellenback determined that Williams was ready. It was Williams who would start in left field in every remaining game.

With the luxury of hindsight (and knowing how baseball history turned out), it is tempting to read more into this startling development. What if Shellenback had decided that Williams was ready, possibly confirmed by the exhibition performance on the previous day, and what if he had communicated his plans to Shiver or Shiver had read the writing on the wall?

Ted Williams, #19 with the San Diego Padres.

In the context of 1936, this speculation makes no sense. If Shellenback really had this in mind, he certainly would have played Williams over Wirthman against Oakland. Moreover, Shiver had found his batting and power stroke after a slow start, and had pounded the pitching staffs of the top teams in the PCL through the month of August.

There was no conceivable scenario in which Shellenback would have replaced his top slugger with an untested rookie, no matter how much raw talent the rookie had. The much more logical option has Shiver concluding that his chances of getting back to the major leagues at his age were not high and that a college football coaching opportunity would open up a career beyond baseball. Shiver would indeed coach college and high school football in Georgia through the 1940s before going into the insurance business.[12]

As Shiver's train wound east, Ted Williams found himself with his first starting job in professional baseball, and the Padres prepared to try to close the gap in the PCL standings between San Diego and Portland. Williams' debut as a regular, on September 1 against Sacramento, received considerable attention:

After seeing young Ted Williams cover his left field sector like a blanket and smack out a double and triple in three times up, most of the fans were willing to join in on the chorus of the sad little ditty, "We're plenty glad you're gone, you rascal you!"...Young Williams, who definitely was on the spot, made good on every fielding opportunity, two of his catches being hard enough to satisfy the most exacting test.[13]

In his first week as a regular, "young Williams" hit .346 with five extra base hits (leading the team) and six RBIs. Williams also improved the outfield defense (Shiver was not known for his glove), and stole two bases to boot. To those familiar with Ted's later reputation as an indifferent outfielder, this description from the first game of the Sunday doubleheader on Labor Day weekend is an eye-opener:

Williams Has Field Day

Ted Williams, Padre rookie outfielder, has a field day all his own in the opening contest and was pretty much a thorn in the side of the Solons all afternoon. In the third inning he made a one-hand stab to take Frank Doljack's long fly and in the eighth he reached over the left field fence to catch a well pasted drive by Peters that would have gone for a home run had it eluded him. To top matters off, he made two more sensational catches in the ninth...[14]

Williams batted .305, with six doubles, two triples, and seven RBIs over the final two weeks of the season, raising his season average to .271. He hit in the eighth spot in the batting order through September 9, then batted third for the remainder of the season and in the first two games of the playoffs.

Ted Williams in September 1936

Date	Vs.	Pos	AB	R	H	2B	3B	HR	RBI	SB	Avg*
Sep 1	Sacramento	LF	3	1	2	1	1		2		.250
Sep 2	Sacramento	LF	3	0	0						.236
Sep 3	Sacramento	LF	3	0	0						.224
Sep 4	Sacramento	LF	3	1	2				2		.245
Sep 5	Sacramento	LF	3	0	1	1					.250
Sep 6-1	Sacramento	LF	4	2	1	1			2		.250
Sep 6-2	Sacramento	LF	1	0	1					1	.262
Sep 7-1	Sacramento	LF	3	1	1	1					.265
Sep 7-2	Sacramento	LF	3	1	1					1	.268
Sep 9-1	SF Seals	LF	3	0	0						.257
Sep 9-2	SF Seals	LF	3	1	1	1					.260
Sep 10	SF Seals	LF	4	1	1						.259
Sep 11	SF Seals	LF	5	0	1						.256
Sep 12-1	SF Seals	LF	4	0	0						.244
Sep 12-2	SF Seals	LF	5	1	3		1		1		.263
Sep 13-1	SF Seals	LF	4	1	2						.272
Sep 13-2	SF Seals	LF	4	1	1	1					.271
Totals for September		17	58	11	18	6	2	0	7	2	.310
Season		42	107	18	29	9	2	0	11	2	.271

* Cumulative Average as of this game

The Padres took on the Oakland Oaks in the first round of the 1936 playoffs. Williams provided virtually the only highlight of the first game on September 15 with his first professional home run off Wee Willie Ludolph, one of the best pitchers in the PCL in 1936, in the eighth inning.[15] The shot over the right field fence with a man on base brought the Padres to within 3 runs, but they did no further damage. The Oaks won the game, and took the best-of-seven series in five games. Williams hit only .176, but tied for the team lead with three RBI along with his home run. After batting third in the first two games, he hit seventh in Game 3 and sixth in Games 4 and 5.

Ted Williams in 1936 PCL Playoffs, First Round

Date	Vs.	Pos	AB	R	H	2B	3B	HR	RBI	SB	*Avg
Sep 15	Oakland	LF	3	1	1	1			2		.333
Sep 16	Oakland	LF	4	0	0						.143
Sep 19	Oakland	LF	3	1	0						.100
Sep 20	Oakland	LF	3	1	0				1		.077
Sep 21	Oakland	LF	4	1	2						.176
Totals for Playoff		5	17	4	3	0	0	1	3	0	.176

* Cumulative Average as of this game

Ted Williams returned to San Diego in 1937 before moving on to Minneapolis in 1938 and to Fenway Park in 1939. He later recalled his time in San Diego fondly:

> There was no particular pressure on me playing in San Diego. I didn't know what pressure was. I was nervous – not because I was born there, but because it was a whole new experience playing before crowds, professional baseball. San Diego was the nicest little town in the world. How the hell was I to know it was the nicest town in the world? I'd never been anyplace.[16]

1) San Diego Union, *June 2, 1936.*

2) San Diego Union, *June 22, 1936.*

3) *Bill Swank,* Echoes from Lane Field:
A History of the San Diego Padres, *1936-1957*
(Paducah KY: Turner Publishing Company, 1997), p. 15.

4) *Steinmann,* San Diego Union, *June 27, 1936.*

5) *Swank, op. cit., p. 25.*
Confirmed by Joe Villarino, high school teammate,
at Society for American Baseball Research
San Diego chapter presentation, January 2001.

6) *Swank, op. cit., p. 25.*

7) *McConnell,* San Diego Union, *June 28, 1936.*
Thanks to Carlos Bauer for additional details of
Hill's PCL career and his 1936 activities.

8) San Diego Union, *July 4, 1936.*

9) *McConnell,* San Diego Union, *August 11, 1936.*

10) *Steinmann,* San Diego Union, *August 20, 1936.*

11) San Diego Union, *September 1, 1936.*

12) *Swank, op. cit., p. 23.*

13) *McConnell,* San Diego Union, *September 2, 1936.*

14) *McConnell,* San Diego Union, *September 7, 1936.*

15) *McConnell,* San Diego Union, *September 16, 1936.*

16) *Swank, op. cit., p. 25.*

Still in high school, young Ted Williams with the Padres at Lane Field, 1936.

Showing plate discipline, Williams takes a pitch.

TED WILLIAMS, EARL KELLER AND THE 1937 SAN DIEGO PADRES
by Bill Swank

On March 29, 2003, the Ted Williams Society for American Baseball Research chapter, in cooperation with the San Diego Hall of Champions, co-hosted a tribute to the chapter's namesake - Ted Williams. Ted and Hall of Champions founder Bob Breitbard were Hoover High School classmates and lifelong friends. One of Breitbard's prize possessions is an autographed bat that Ted used when he was the last man to hit over .400, with the Boston Red Sox in 1941.

The Hall of Champions has an impressive permanent Ted Williams exhibit. For the March 2003 event, numerous other photos, books, albums, scrapbooks and assorted memorabilia were on display. The event featured panel discussions with friends, family members, teammates and many who admired Ted Williams.

My presentation was to be about the 1937 Pacific Coast League Champion San Diego Padres. Since Ted and local sportswriter Earl Keller of the *San Diego Evening Tribune* had a special relationship, my initial narrow approach was to record every word the writer wrote about the promising young ballplayer that season. During my research, the scope widened to include the daily progress of the team. Every Padres box score is included in my full report. It seemed important to also create a daily log of Ted's batting statistics. In the process, this seemingly straightforward project turned into a complicated, time-consuming, contradictory obsession with some surprising conclusions and questions.

Most journeys begin with a question. We have expectations about what will be learned along the way. My goal was to gain insight about Ted Williams through the eyes of Earl Keller. As a young man, I heard my elders complain about the quality of San Diego newspapers. We should not judge the past by today's standards. If Ted Williams were playing today, he'd still be a helluva hitter, but journalism in San Diego has come a long, long way since 1937.

As an aside, I had a former colleague who was a history professor. One day, in frustration, preceded by a profanity, I told him, "This isn't history. This is baseball. It has to be accurate!"

It really is not the purpose of this paper to comment on Keller's writing style, which has variously been described as uninspired, repetitious, and pedantic. (After all, the same could be said about my style.) Although Earl was critical of the accuracy of statistics that were produced by others, I experienced great frustration when our numbers did not conform. This became so difficult that I stopped transcribing his words and completed Ted's batting average for the year. In the end, my numbers matched those in the 1938 Spalding *Official Base Ball Guide*.

Earl Keller and Ted Williams, in San Diego.

Gene "Bud" Tuttle, son of Pacific Coast League president W. C. Tuttle, was a relief pitcher for the 1936 and 1937 Padres. He also helped Earl with the team's statistics. Gene is now 89 years old and we correspond regularly. I have teased him about the discrepancies. Was it Keller or Tuttle who inflated their friend's batting average as the season progressed?

The *Evening Tribune* did not have a Sunday edition. Box scores from Saturday games simply did not appear in the *Evening Tribune*. The line score would be given above the box scores for the Sunday doubleheader in the Monday paper. Frequently the box score of the second game of the Sunday doubleheader would not be printed in the *Evening Tribune*. Night game box scores were often missing in the *Tribune*. They would also be omitted in the *Union*, yet could be found in the *Los Angeles Times* or even the *San Francisco Chronicle*. Does it make sense that a score for a night game at Lane Field would appear in a Los Angeles paper, but not in either of San Diego's two major newspapers? Additionally, Earl Keller did not travel with the team. *Evening Tribune* coverage of road games came from the news wire services.

Curiously, Earl did not write about the Padres from Friday, July 23, 1937 to Monday, August 30, 1937. At first this did not appear unusual because San Diego was on the road until August 9th. *Evening Tribune* Sports Editor Tom Akers covered the team during a brief home stand from August 10th through August 15th, so an assumption could be made that Earl was on vacation. The Padres returned to the rails and, predictably, the accounts of the out-of-town games were provided by the Associated Press. But where was Earl Keller when the Padres came home on August 24? Mysteriously, he did not report on the team again until August 30. For our purposes, we will never know what Earl might have thought or written regarding the prolonged slump that Ted experienced from July 25th through August 15th, when "The Kid" batted only .147 (11-75). Keller was on the Padres beat when Williams started hitting again. Ted exploded with a .356 batting average (48-135) and he slugged 10 home runs in the final 38 games of the season.

Evening Tribune coverage of the playoff-bound San Diego Padres was so underwhelming that six of the final nine box scores used in this report had to come from the *Los Angeles Times* (though part of the reason was the poor quality of *San Diego Union* microfilm.) The *Tribune* published unofficial batting averages for the 1937 season and credited Ted Williams with a .300 average on the basis of 132 hits in 454 at-bats. When is the last time you questioned the long division of a batting average in a newspaper? 132 hits divided by 454 at-bats equals .290749, which rounds off to a .291 batting average. It is NOT a .300 batting average!

> Even in his second year with the Padres, Ted Williams was still very much a kid.
>
> Early in 1937, the Padres were visiting the Seattle Rainiers and Ted Williams was on the bench. The visiting batboy was Dick Rasmussen, a high schooler from Tacoma who later in life ended up as a comedian with the Ice Follies. Ted met Rasmussen while dressing in the clubhouse before the game, and noticed that the batboy had a package with him. "What do you have in that package?" Ted asked. "Oh, a couple of pipes and some soap that makes great big bubbles."
>
> As Murray Kramer tells the story, "Somewhere along the third inning, sitting on the bench started to irk Williams and he called Rasmussen over. 'Say, kid, go in and get that package and we'll have a little fun.' In went Dick and brought the package to the bench. He and Ted retired to the further corner where the water pail was standing.
>
> They soaped it up and started to blow bubbles. At first, nobody paid attention to them but as the huge bubbles started wafting off onto the playing field, the crowd, the players and the umpires started to look around for the phenomenon.
>
> Suddenly, Williams and Rasmusseun were spotted blowing pipe bubbles and oblivious to everything else.
>
> The umpire had no sense of humor - he threw both of them off the field."
>
> *Boston Record-American,*
> *February 19, 1948*

The *Evening Tribune* articles about the first three games in the opening round of the Shaughnessy Playoffs with Sacramento were perfunctory news wire copy from the Associated Press. The only apparent reason Earl Keller wrote about the fourth game was because it was played in San Diego. He covered the first three games of the championship series contested at Lane Field, but the article about the championship game in Portland, won by the Padres, was written by the Associated Press without subsequent follow-up by the *Evening Tribune*.

Although Ted hit .333 in the playoffs, the true batting star was Rupert Thompson. Wally Hebert, "Tiny" Chaplin, Dick Ward and Manny Salvo combined to throw eight consecutive complete games to win the PCL Championship. The *Tribune* ran a pennant with player portraits.

When Ted was sold to the Boston Red Sox on December 8, 1937, Earl Keller did not write the story for the *Evening Tribune*. The first time he wrote anything about Williams after the championship was a short article in January 1938 about a winter league game. Ted was mentioned briefly in some of Keller's stories about the outlook for the Padres in the upcoming 1938 season.

Williams became a holdout in February 1938 when his family demanded a $5,000 bonus to sign with the Red Sox. Earl wrote the subdued story as though sports editor Tom Akers were looking over his shoulder. Akers sided with Padres owner Bill Lane in the dispute.

As anticipated, Earl did not write anything critical about Ted. Did this give "The Kid" a false sense of security about the role of sportswriters? The San Diego press, in general, and specifically Earl Keller, had praise for the budding hometown star. Everything changed when Ted Williams moved on to Boston. Did Ted have unrealistic expectations about sportswriters based on his friendship with Earl Keller? Did Tom Akers object to Earl Keller's cheerleading? Did Earl want to write more about Ted Williams than he did? We'll never know...

GAME-BY-GAME SUMMARY

The PCL Padres played a 178-game season in 1937, a full 24 games more than either of the major leagues with their 154-game seasons (in terms of games actually played, the New York Giants played 152 games that year and the Washington Senators played 158 games; the other teams were ranged in between.) The following table presents the number of the game (1 to 178), the date on which the game was played, along with Ted Williams' individual game performance, and his cumulative totals and average after each game's record was integrated into the year total to date.

1. Apr 03 0-for-1 0-1 .000	26. Apr 28 0-for-2 11-42 .262	51. May 23 did not play
2. Apr 04 did not play in first game	27. Apr 29 1-for-4 12-46 .261	52. May 23 did not play
3. Apr 04 0-for-1 0-2 .000	28. Apr 30 1-for-4 13-50 .260	53. May 25 did not play
4. Apr 06 did not play	29. May 01 did not play	54. May 26 did not play
5. Apr 07 0-for-2 0-4 .000	30. May 02 did not play	55. May 27 did not play
6. Apr 08 did not play	31. May 02 did not play	56. May 28 0-for-1 21-93 .226
7. Apr 09 0-for-1 0-1 .000	32. May 04 1-for-4 14-54 .259	57. May 29 did not play
8. Apr 10 did not play	33. May 05 did not play	58. May 30 did not play
9. Apr 11 1-for-4 1-9 .111	34. May 06 0-for-2 14-56 .250	59. May 30 did not play
10. Apr 11 1-for-3 2-12 .167	35. May 07 1-for-4 15-60 .250	60. May 31 did not play
11. Apr 13 0-for-0 2-12 .167	36. May 08 1-for-4 16-64 .250	61. May 31 did not play
12. Apr 14 did not play	37. May 09 0-for-3 16-67 .239	62. Jun 01 did not play
13. Apr 15 1-for-1 3-13 .231	38. May 09 1-for-2 17-69 .246	63. Jun 02 1-for-1 22-94 .234
14. Apr 16 0-for-3 3-16 .188	39. May 11 did not play	64. Jun 03 0-for-1 22-95 .232
15. Apr 17 did not play	40. May 12 did not play	65. Jun 04 did not play
16. Apr 18 1-for-4 4-20 .200	41. May 13 0-for-4 17-73 .233	66. Jun 05 1-for-1 23-96 .240
17. Apr 18 did not play in second game	42. May 14 0-for-3 17-76 .224	67. Jun 06 3-for-5 26-101 .257
18. Apr 20 did not play	43. May 15 1-for-4 18-80 .225	68. Jun 06 2-for-3 28-104 .269
19. Apr 21 did not play	44. May 16 1-for-5 19-85 .224	69. Jun 08 0-for-4 28-108 .259
20. Apr 22 did not play	45. May 16 1-for-3 20-88 .227	70. Jun 09 0-for-0 28-108 .259
21. Apr 23 1-for-5 5-25 .200	46. May 18 did not play	71. Jun 10 did not play
22. Apr 24 1-for-4 6-29 .207	47. May 19 did not play	72. Jun 11 did not play
23. Apr 25 1-for-4 7-33 .212	48. May 20 0-for-1 20-89 .225	73. Jun 12 did not play
24. Apr 25 1-for-3 8-36 .222	49. May 21 1-for-3 21-92 .228	74. Jun 13 did not play
25. Apr 27 3-for-4 11-40 .275	50. May 22 did not play	75. Jun 13 did not play

March 31, 1936 Lane Field Padres ticket stub from first Padres game.

76. Jun 15 0-for-1 28-109 .257
77. Jun 16 1-for-2 29-111 .261
78. Jun 17 did not play
79. Jun 18 1-for-1 30-112 .268
80. Jun 19 0-for-4 30-116 .259
81. Jun 20 1-for-5 31-121 .256
82. Jun 20 did not play
83. Jun 22 1-for-3 32.124 .258
84. Jun 23 1-for-3 33-127 .260
85. Jun 24 2-for-4 35-131 .267
86. Jun 25 2-for-4 37-135 .274
87. Jun 26 2-for-4 39-139 .281
88. Jun 27 1-for-4 40-143 .280
89. Jun 27 2-for-3 42-146 .288
90. Jun 29 0-for-4 42-150 .280
91. Jun 30 2-for-3 44-153 .288
92. Jul 01 1-for-3 45-156 .288
93. Jul 02 4-for-5 49-161 .304
94. Jul 03 1-for-4 50-165 .303
95. Jul 04 1-for-3 51-168 .304
96. Jul 04 0-for-2 51.170 .300
97. Jul 05 1-for-4 52.174 .299
98. Jul 05 1-for-3 53-177 .298
99. Jul 06 0-for-3 53-180 .294
100. Jul 07 2-for-4 55-184 .299
101. Jul 08 0-for-2 55-186 .296
102. Jul 09 1-for-3 56-189 .296
103. Jul 10 3-for-5 59-194 .304
104. Jul 11 2-for-4 61-198 .308
105. Jul 11 0-for-4 61-202 .302
106. Jul 13 2-for-3 63-205 .307
107. Jul 14 2-for-2 65-207 .314
108. Jul 15 0-for-3 65-210 .310
109. Jul 16 1-for-4 66-214 .308
110. Jul 17 1-for-2 67-216 .310
111. Jul 18 0-for-4 67-220 .305
112. Jul 18 1-for-2 68-222 .306
113. Jul 20 0-for-4 67-220 .301
114. Jul 21 1-for-3 69-226 .301
115. Jul 22 1-for-3 70-232 .302

116. Jul 23 0-for-3 70-235 .298
117. Jul 24 2-for-5 72-240 .300
118. Jul 25 0-for-3 72-243 .296
119. Jul 25 0-for-2 72-245 .294
120. Jul 27 0-for-4 72-249 .289
121. Jul 28 1-for-5 73-254 .287
122. Jul 29 0-for-3 73-257 .284
123. Jul 30 1-for-4 74-261 .284
124. Jul 31 0-for-4 74-265 .279
125. Aug 01 1-for-4 75-269 .279
126. Aug 01 did not play in second game
127. Aug 03 2-for-5 77-274 .281
128. Aug 04 0-for-4 77-278 .277
129. Aug 05 0-for-4 77-282 .273
130. Aug 06 1-for-5 78-287 .272
131. Aug 07 2-for-4 80-291 .275
132. Aug 08 2-for-5 82-296 .277
133. Aug 08 1-for-1 83-297 .279
134. Aug 10 0-for-4 83-301 .275
135. Aug 11 0-for-3 83-311 .267
136. Aug 12 0-for-4 83-308 .269
137. Aug 13 did not play
138. Aug 14 0-for-3 83-311 .267
139. Aug 15 0-for-4 83-315 .263
140. Aug 15 0-for-0 83-315 .263
141. Aug 17 1-for-4 84-319 .263
142. Aug 18 2-for-4 86-323 .266
143. Aug 19 0-for-1 86-324 .265
144. Aug 20 2-for-2 88-326 .265
145. Aug 21 3-for-4 91-330 .276
146. Aug 22 2-for-4 93-334 .278
147. Aug 22 2-for-3 95-337 .282
148. Aug 24 1-for-4 96-341 .282
149. Aug 25 1-for-3 97-344 .282
150. Aug 26 1-for-2 98-346 .283
151. Aug 27 1-for-4 99-350 .283
152. Aug 28 2-for-3 101-353 .286
153. Aug 29 0-for-4 101-357 .283
154. Aug 29 1-for-4 102-361 .283
155. Aug 31 2-for-4 104-365 .285

156. Sep 01 2-for-3 106-368 .288
157. Sep 02 0-for-2 106-370 .286
158. Sep 03 2-for-6 108-376 .287
159. Sep 04 1-for-5 109-381 .286
160. Sep 04 0-for-3 109-384 .284
161. Sep 05 1-for-5 110-389 .283
162. Sep 06 3-for-4 113-393 .288
163. Sep 06 2-for-4 115-397 .290
164. Sep 07 1-for-4 116-401 .289
165. Sep 08 3-for-4 119-405 .294
166. Sep 09 3-for-5 122-410 .298
167. Sep 09 0-for-4 122-414 .295
168. Sep 10 1-for-5 123-419 .294
169. Sep 11 1-for-4 124-423 .293
170. Sep 12 1-for-4 125-427 .293
171. Sep 12 2-for-3 127-430 .295
172. Sep 14 1-for-4 128-434 .295
173. Sep 15 0-for-4 128-438 .292
174. Sep 16 0-for-2 128-440 .291
175. Sep 17 0-for-2 128-442 .290
176. Sep 18 0-for-4 128-446 .287
177. Sep 19 3-for-4 131-450 .291
178. Sep 19 1-for-4 132-454 .291

Ted hit 23 home runs and drove in 98 runs.

Playoff Series with Sacramento
1. Sep 21 4-for-5 4-5 .800
2. Sep 22 0-for-3 4-8 .500
3. Sep 23 0-for-5 4-13 .308
4. Sep 25 2-for-4 6-17 .353

Championship Series with Portland
1. Sep 28 0-4 6-21 .286
2. Sep 29 3-4 9-25 .360
3. Sep 30 1-4 10-29 .349
4. Oct 03 1-4 11-33 .333

Ted hit 1 home run and drove in 3 runs.

1937 Padres line-up, all lined up. Williams is third from the left, Durst sixth from the left.

COAST MANAGERS SEE EARLY MAJOR LEAGUE CAREER FOR SAN DIEGO BOY

"If you want to make a little extra money to put in the old sock, bet it on young Teddy Williams to be taken as the outstanding major league prospect after this year's Pacific Coast league baseball race is finished. Coast diamond experts predict this 18-year-old San Diego boy will follow the footsteps of Joe DiMaggio, Bobby Doerr and Joe Marty and wind up with some major loop club within two years. There wasn't a manager who didn't say Williams had the makings of a great slugger after they saw him in action the later part of the 1936 season. Lefty O'Doul, manager of the Seals, who has been around enough to know a natural ballplayer when he sees one, said Williams will be in the majors by 1938, or he misses his guess. 'He's a natural,' said Dutch Ruether, ex-pilot of Seattle. "'Wee Willie' Ludolph, the Coast's leading chucker in 1936, was the pitcher who learned to respect this

lanky kid before the season was history. Williams collected a couple of hard hits off Ludolph at Lane Field, and 'Wee Willie' didn't think anything of them. But when Williams hit one of the longest home runs ever seen in the Oakland park off him later, Ludolph said that boy must have something on the ball. 'Wee Willie' passed Williams twice before that game was over rather than let him connect again and break up the ball game.

"Williams will be heavier and in better condition than ever when the 1937 season rolls around. From his mother we learn he has put on more than five pounds since the 1936 season ended. 'Teddy is drinking more milk and putting on weight steadily,' said Mrs. Williams. 'Every night after he comes home from school he gets a bat and practices swinging for 30 or 40 minutes. The boy really is confident of making good and we all are sure he will go places.'

"Harry Williams, secretary of the Coast League, is another diamond critic who has words of praise for the youngster. 'He reminds me of Cy Williams, former Portland slugger,' says W. C. Tuttle's right hand man. 'I knew Ted was a natural born ball player the minute I saw him.'

Swinging on the sidelines.

"Despite all of the praise that is being tossed his way, Williams is not becoming 'cocky' in any way. The youth appreciates all of the kind words and says he will be in there giving his best." *(Keller,* Evening Tribune, *January 7, 1937)*

"It is likely Teddy Williams also will receive a contract with an increase in salary. He expects it and he's going to be a disappointed (indistinguishable on microfilm) in his first year in organized ball in 1936. Williams proved he is of Class AA caliber." *(Keller,* Evening Tribune, *January 25, 1937)*

"Ted Williams who will be holding down a regular job with the San Diego Padres this season will graduate from Herbert Hoover High tomorrow. The 18-year-old flyhawk has kept in excellent condition during the winter months and is anxious to begin Spring Training. Williams will be entering his second year of professional baseball. He made his debut with the Padres last July and made a big hit with the fans and in the 'enemy camps.'" *(Keller, ET, February 2, 1937)*

"At commencement exercises of the Hoover High school graduating class in the State college gym last night, Bob Breitbard, class president spoke for his class. Among the Herbert Hoover High honors students who graduated last night was Ted Williams, young San Diego Padres outfielder. The 18-year-old flyhawk received honors in baseball and typing. A gold baseball and two trophies went to Williams for his outstanding performance on the diamond for the Cardinals. He was the only boy to get honors in typing." *(Keller,* ET, *February 4, 1937)*

San Diego won the Southern California Winter Leagues Championship in a three game series with the Philadelphia Royal Colored Giants. Hal Doerr, older brother of former Padres second baseman Bobby Doerr, hit a home run with two teammates aboard in the bottom of the ninth inning for a come-from-behind victory over the Royal Giants in the deciding game. Ted Williams was a pinch hit out for Herm 'Old Folks' Pillette in the fifth inning. Since he had been a student, this was his only appearance with the San Diego team during the winter season. *(ET, February 2, 1937)*

"From Los Angeles comes the report Outfielder Van Wirthman wants to quit baseball because he has a good job, but no announcement has been made by the Padres' office. That would leave the Padres with only four experienced flyhawks, Thompson, Patchett, Cedric Durst and Ted Williams..."

"Shellenback will make no decision as to what fields Thompson, Patchett and Williams will play until he sees what kind of throwing arms the new men have. Durst may be utility outfielder, or he may be in the lineup regularly if he is hitting better than one of the other outfielders." *(Keller,* ET, *February 27, 1937)*

Detail, early Padres scorecard.

(Spring Training began on March 1, 1937 at Navy Field in San Diego.)

"Also missing was outfielder Van Wirthman, a holdover from last year's team. Wirthman is quitting baseball to work on a roofing company in Los Angeles. This leaves the Padres with only four regular flyhawks, Ted Williams, Durst, Patchett and Thompson." *(Keller, ET, Mar. 2, 1937)*

"In the outfield will be Ted Williams, left; Cedric Durst, center, and Rupert Thompson, right. Hal Patchett, new flyhawk from Tulsa, will not get in the game because he needs a week or more to get in shape. He is due here today or tomorrow.

"In batting practice, Thompson, Detore, McDonald, Holman and Williams socked out some exceptionally long drives. Thompson hit one ball that nearly landed aboard The Star of India anchored in the bay off right field." *(Keller, ET, Mar. 4, 1937)*

"Ted Williams thinks manager Frank Shellenback is about the swellest guy in the world. 'Shelly sure helps me,' says Ted. 'I have learned much from him since I joined the Padres and if I go places in baseball, I will have him to thank." *(Keller, ET, Mar. 5, 1937)*

(The Padres defeated the San Diego All-Stars, 3-0, in an exhibition game.) "Detore was forced at second by Ted Williams who scampered to the hot corner on a one-base knock to center field by George McDonald. Williams spiked the plate when Reichert heaved one over Catcher Cesena's head." *(Keller, ET, March 8, 1937)*

Playing left field for the Regulars in a four-inning scrimmage, Williams went 0-for-2 and scored a run as the Regulars thumped the Rookies, 10-1. The rookies could manage but two hits off the old spitballer, Padre skipper Frank Shellenback. *(ET, March 12, 1937)*

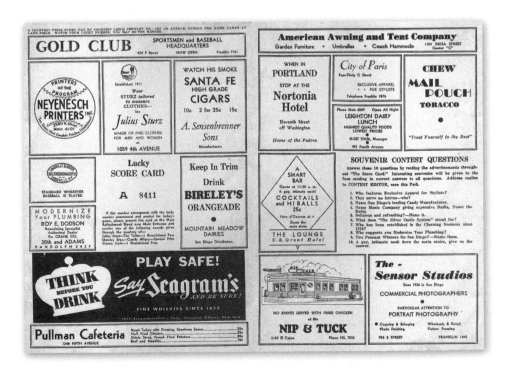

"A fan writes in to get the birthdays of the San Diego regulars. Here is the list: Frank Shellenback, Dec. 16; Ernie Holman, Dec. 17; Ted Williams, Oct. 30 (Ted's birthday was – apparently – August 30); Howard Craghead, May 25; George McDonald, April 12; Bud Tuttle, March 15; Hugh McMullen, Dec. 16; Jimmy Reese, Oct. 1; Jim Chaplin, still holding out, July 13; Cedric Durst, August 23; Tommy Thompson, May 19; George Myatt, June 14; Wally Hebert, August 21; George Detore, Nov. 11; Hal Patchett, May 10; Bill Starr, Feb. 16." (correct birthdate – Feb. 26. Apparently this information was provided by the Padres.) *(Keller, ET, March 13, 1937)*

(Editor's note: the question of Ted Williams' birthday is a complicated one, with at least three possible dates suggesting themselves. See further discussion in another article in this volume.)

WILLIAMS CRACKS OUT FOUR HITS AS PADRES TRIM PORTLAND, 12-1

"Ted Williams will be chasing flies in the major leagues in 1938, if he hits the ball on the nose during the coming Pacific Coast League race as he did in yesterday's exhibition game between San Diego and Portland at Lane Field. The 18-year-old Padre outfielder went to the plate five times and on four occasions he hit safely to personally lead San Diego to a 12-1 win over the 1936 Coast champions.

"Williams went to the plate for the first time in the second inning with Ernie Holman on second base and none away, and singled into deep right field to score Holman. Holman again was on base when Ted went to bat in the third inning. This time Williams connected with one of Hank McDonald's fast balls and drove the pill far to right. The ball hit the telephone pole and bounced back on the playing field, but Williams touched all the bases.

"If the ball hadn't hit the pole, it would have landed on top the Santa Fe freight building. On his third trip to the plate in the fourth, Williams flied to deep center field for his fourth single to score another runner in the eighth." *(Keller, ET, March 15, 1937)*

(Photo headline and caption) Gets 4 Hits "All this 18-year-old San Diego Padre outfielder did yesterday in the exhibition game with Portland was hit a home run, three singles and drive in four runs. Pacific Coast league pitchers will have a tough time getting Ted out this season if he continues to hit the ball as he did yesterday." *(ET, March 15, 1937)*

"Shelly had the flyhawks display their throwing arms for the first time and the San Diego manager went to the shower with a broad smile on his face. Left Fielder Ted Williams, Center Field Hal Patchett and Right Fielder Rupert Thompson showed powerful arms in throwing several 'strikes' to the plate from the deep pastures... Ted Williams certainly can throw strikes to the plate from left field." *(Keller, ET, March 18, 1937)*

"Ted Williams kept the ball rolling by singling to right to score Thompson and Guy Pickerell went to the showers in favor of Ray Lucas. Ernie Holman got a one-base swat to center and Detore trotted home. Williams scored on George McDonald's infield hit." *(Keller, ET, March 19, 1937)*

"Earl Keller, who writes baseball for this newspaper, is pretty high on Ted Williams, the local kid who seems sure to hold down a regular outfield berth with the Padres. But Keller is not alone in that. Even Frank Shellenback, veteran pilot for the club, says Williams is a 'natural' and predicts a bright future for him. The boy tries all the time and praise hasn't swelled his bean in the least. The fans and the players all like him and that's a good sign, too." *(Sports Editor Tom Akers, ET, March 19, 1937)*

WILLIAMS SETTING PADRE BAT PACE

"Local baseball fans who are betting Ted Williams hits better than .300 in the Pacific Coast league this year are going to make themselves a pot of money if the 18-year-old flyhawk continues to hit as he has in the two exhibition contests played to date. In the two tilts he has been to the platter nine times, and hit safely on five occasions for an average of .556. Williams also is setting the pace in runs batted in with five to his credit. Jimmy Reese is second in this column with four.

"Catcher Bill Starr has a better bat average than Williams, but he has played in only one game. Starr has two for three for a .667 average." *(Keller, ET, March 20, 1937)*

"Have you noticed how the outfielders step backwards when Ted Williams comes to the plate? Yes sir, that kid is making a name for himself. If you want him to hit a home run every time he comes to bat, just yell, 'Come on, Lamb!' How that does burn him up." *(Keller, ET, March 20, 1937)*

{Photo headline and caption} Ted Goes Up For One. "Spearing high drives with one hand is a specialty with this 18-year-old San Diego Padre outfielder. In the above photo, he is shown leaping high in the air to get a fly ball. Besides turning in many brilliant catches, Williams has been hitting the ball to all corners of the park." *(ET, March 25, 1937)*

TEN PADRES BAT ABOVE .300 MARK

"Ten members of the San Diego Pacific Coast league baseball club are hitting .300 or better for exhibition games played to date. Catcher Bill Starr, with five hits in nine times up, is setting the pace with a .556 average.

Williams posing, catching the ball, March 1937.

"The actual leader, however, is Ted Williams, who has seven safeties to his credit in 18 chances. This gives him a mark of .389." *(Keller, ET, March 30, 1937)*

"Outfielder Ted Williams has a slight charley horse, but he will be in the starting lineup at Wrigley Field. (Williams did not play in a game against San Diego State College.)

"Teddy Williams will be in the Padres' starting lineup at Los Angeles on Saturday. The young outfielder has been on the sidelines with a charley horse the last few days, but he will be ready to go on Saturday." *(Keller, ET, March 31, 1937)*

"Ted Williams, who has been suffering from a charley horse, will be in the lineup for San Diego tomorrow. Shellenback held him out of last night's tilt to allow the soreness to leave his leg." (Williams made an out pinch-hitting for Manny Salvo in the sixth inning.) *(Keller, ET, April 2, 1937)*

Taking aim at opposing pitching, *San Diego Sun*, April 4, 1937. Left to right: Jimmy Reese, George McDonald, Ernie Holman, Ted Williams, George Detore, Rupert Thompson, Hal Patchett, George Myatt.

San Diego Padres Spring Training record: (6-3) San Diego Padres 3, San Diego All-Stars 0; Padres 12, Portland 1; Padres 8, Seattle 5; Seattle 3, Padres 2; Padres 6, Seattle 5; Padres 4, State College 2; Padres 12, San Diego High School 2; Pittsburgh 7, Padres 3; Pittsburgh 10, Padres 2. *(ET, April 3, 1937)*

GAME 1. In a repeat of 1936, the Padres again dropped their first game of the season at Wrigley Field to the Los Angeles Angels, 9-7. Ted Williams batted for starter Tiny Chaplin in the eighth inning and recorded an out. *(San Diego Union, April 4, 1937)* 1 AB, 0 H, 0 HR, .000

GAMES 2 and 3. San Diego split with the Angels (6-2, 0-6) to close a short three game series as Coast League teams eased into their routine schedule of daily games with doubleheaders on Sunday. Mondays were off days to accommodate travel. The team headed home to meet the San Francisco Mission Reds on Tuesday in the local season opener at Lane Field. Ted did not play in the first game. In game two, he replaced Cedric Durst in left field and made an out in his only at-bat. *(ET, April 5, 1937)* 2 AB, 0 H, 0 HR, .000

The above-mentioned photo may have eventually been used in an advertisement for the Don Lee auto dealership. The first time Ted Williams appears in an *Evening Tribune* advertisement is in a full two-page spread titled, "Do You Know Our Padres?" Player portraits are included with small ads for San Diego merchants as part of the "1937 home opener" feature. A serious Ted Williams is shown beside an advertisement for Baranov's, Fifth Avenue at Broadway. "We know it will be tough to beat you PADRES AND IT'S TOUGH TO BEAT BARANOV'S for Real Satisfaction when Buying Jewelry. Jewelry and Radios can always be had at Baranov's on Easy Credit Terms... NO DOWN PAYMENT"

Johnny "Junk" Walters, a lumpy veteran whose baggy uniform resembled a sack of Idaho spuds, appears in a Shulack & Mason Custom Tailors advertisement beside Ted. "If You Think Tailored Clothes Don't Make a Person Just Try Walking Around the Ballpark Without Any On. Tailored Clothes for Ladies and Gentlemen As Low as $39.50." Could Shulack & Mason really give old Junk the tailored look so popular back in the 1930s? I don't think so. *(ET, April 5, 1937)* This spread also appeared the following morning under the headline, "Opening Game Today." *(San Diego Union, April 6, 1937)*

"The Padres' regular lineup was to be on the diamond for the opener with Ted Williams in left field. Williams has been on the sidelines for several days because of a charley horse." *(Keller, ET, April 6, 1937)*

GAME 4. As indicated above, Ted Williams was listed in the starting lineup in the paper on the sixth. He even rated a subhead: "Williams Ready To Play." Apparently, he remained a bit sub-par, so Ced Durst filled in at left instead. The Padres beat the Missions, 3-2, behind the 4-hit pitching of Tiny Chaplin.

Bill Lane's new 1937 Cadillac V8 at Lane Field: (left to right) Hal Patchett, Bill Starr, Frank Shellenback, George Myatt, Ted Williams, George Steff (salesman for Don Lee Cadillac-LaSalle Olds) and Bill Lane. (Note the roof rafters.) *(ET, April 3, 1937)*

GAME 5. San Diego scored two runs on a double by Jimmy Reese in the bottom of the 13th to beat the San Francisco Missions, 4-3. Cedric Durst started in left field and moved to center field after Junk Walters pinch hit for Hal Patchett in the eighth inning. Ted Williams entered the game and was hitless in two at bats. *(ET, April 8, 1937)* 4 AB, 0 H, 0 HR, .000

GAME 6. The Padres took the third straight game from the Missions, 4-1. Wally Hebert picked up the victory. Ted did not play. *(ET, April 9, 1937)*

GAME 7. The Missions mauled the Padres, 15-1. Ted registered a put-out in left field and went 0-for-1 as a late inning replacement. *(ET, April 10, 1937)* 5 AB, 0 H, 0 HR, .000

GAME 8. Tiny Chaplin improved his record to 2-1 in the young season. The Padres beat the Missions, 6-1. Williams did not play. *(San Diego Union, April 11, 1937)*

GAMES 9 and 10. San Diego swept the Missions, 3-2 and 4-0, to move into second place in the PCL. Ted was 1-for-4 in the first game and 1-for-3 in the second. Hal Patchett and Ted Williams each hit two-run homers in the nightcap. *(ET, April 12, 1937)* 12 AB, 2 H, 1 HR, .167

"Center Fielder Hal Patchett sewed up the contest for the Padres in the fifth by parking one of Stuart Bolen's fastballs over the right-center field fence with Salvo on second base, and Ted Williams made the win even more convincing by duplicating Patchett's feat in the sixth with Cedric Durst on the keystone bag." *(Keller, ET, April 12, 1937)*

George McDonald leads PCL in hitting (.455, 33 AB, 15 H); Rupert Thompson second (.429, 35 AB, 15 H); Ted Williams (.167, 12 AB, 2 H, 1 HR). *(ET, April 13, 1937)*

GAME 11. Williams made one put-out in left field, but did not get a chance to bat in a 5-4, 16-inning thriller over the Oaks in the East Bay city. *(ET, April 14, 1937)*

GAME 12. San Diego Captures Fifth in Row; Ward Goes to Hill Today. Ted did not play in a 4-1 victory over Oakland as Tiny Chaplin won his third straight. *(ET, April 15, 1937)*

Lane Field from the air.

GAME 13. "The Padres picked up their third run in the eighth. Singles by Thompson, Ted Williams (batting for Holman), and before turning the trick. With two out and runners on second and third, Pinch Hitter Junk Walters popped out weakly to first base. Walters batted for Jimmy Reese, who never should have been taken out. Reese is the greatest money hitter in the Coast league." (San Diego lost 4-3. Ted was 1-for-1.) *(Keller, ET, April 16, 1937)* 13 AB, 3 H, 1 HR, .231

GAME 14. Ted went 0-for-3 and registered an assist as the Padres lost to Oakland, 7 to 2. *(ET, April 17, 1937)* 16 AB, 3 H, 1 HR, .188

GAME 15. Oakland prevailed again, 10-8. Ted did not play. *(San Diego Union, April 18, 1937)*

GAMES 16 and 17. The Padres swept their doubleheader with the Oaks, 2-1 and 8-5. Williams drove in a run with a single in the first inning of the first game. He was hitless in his other three plate appearances and did not play in the second game. San Diego's record improved to 11-6. *(ET, April 19, 1937)* 20 AB, 4 H, 1 HR, .200

The *Evening Tribune* posted the batting averages for the past week, but not for the season. This would be equivalent to a current "Who's Hot" feature in modern newspapers. Batting average lists appeared infrequently in 1937. *(ET, April 20, 1937)*

"If Ted Williams doesn't stop growing, the Southern Pacific will have to build a special berth for him. Ted has to tie himself into knots to get into a berth." *(Keller, ET, April 21, 1937)*

GAME 18. Dick Ward "sinker balled" the Sacramento Solons, 5-1. Ted Williams did not play. *(ET, April 21, 1937)*

GAME 19. Despite a 5-2 loss to Sacramento, San Diego retained first place in the PCL. Ted did not play. *(ET, April 22, 1937)*

GAME 20. Unable to deliver in the clutch, the Padres again lost, 6-3, to the Solons. For the fourth consecutive game, Williams did not play. *(ET, April 23, 1937)*

"The Padres skipper said this morning he intended to juggle his batting order for this afternoon's fourth contest in hopes of finding more scoring punch. Cedric Durst probably will ride the bench in favor of young Ted Williams." *(Keller, ET, April 23, 1937)*

GAME 21. San Diego Regains Lead By Taking 9-8 Slugfest. Inserted in the starting lineup, Ted Williams responded with a single hit in five at bats and knocked in one of the Padres 9 runs. *(ET, April 24, 1937)* 25 AB, 5 H, 1 HR, .200

"After Joe Berkowitz grounded out, Tommy Thompson walked and Ted Williams singled Patchett home and Klinger took a walk to the showers. McDonald greeted George Murray with a double, driving in Thompson and Williams with the sixth and seventh markers of the inning.

One of the highlights of the game was the 400-foot drive hit by young Ted Williams in the fourth inning. The ball would have been over the fence in many parks, but Adams took it in after a long run in deep center field." *(Keller, ET, April 24, 1937)*

GAME 22. Ted doubled in a run in four at-bats as the Padres defeated Sacramento, 10-4. *(San Diego Union, April 25, 1937)* 29 AB, 6 H, 1 HR, .207

"San Diego came near equalizing a Coast League record for doubles in one inning Saturday. In the seventh inning, the Padres hit five two baggers in addition to a single and a home run for seven tallies. Holman, Reese, Berkowitz, Detore and Williams hit for two bases in the frame. The Coast record for doubles in an inning is believed to be seven." *(Keller, ET, April 26, 1937)*

GAMES 23 and 24. The Padres and Solons split their Sunday doubleheader. The Sacs took the opener, 5-4, and Howard Craghead spun a 2-0 shutout in the 7-inning nightcap. Williams was 1-for-4 and 1-for-3. *(ET, April 26, 1937)* 36 AB, 8 H, 1 HR, .222)

"Detore's double, singles by Ernie Holman and Ted Williams, and pitcher Tom Seat's error produced two more San Diego tallies in the fourth. Williams' single bounced off Seat's left shin and the injury was so painful he was forced to leave the game. With Williams on third and only one out, neither Reese nor Chaplin were able to hit the offerings of George Murray out of the infield." *(Keller, ET, April 26, 1937)*

GAME 25. Padres Stretch Lead With 18 To 3 Triumph, McDonald, Williams Star At Bat; Salvo, Rego to Hurl Today. This was Ted's breakout game in the young season. One of his three hits in four times at bat was the home run that would appear on Padres programs from 1947 through 1954 and again in 1956. The *Evening Tribune* photo caption reads: "Williams pounds out second homer of season as Padres win. Cameraman Charles Grable snapped this photo just as young Ted Williams, San Diego Padre outfielder, connected for his second home run of the 1937 season at Lane Field yesterday. The round-trip swat came in the second inning with one on. Williams batted in five runs and was one of the heroes of the Padres 18 to 3 victory over Oakland in the series opener." *(ET, April 28, 1937)* 40 AB, 11 H, 2 HR, .275

"Before the 'track meet' ended, the skipper of the Padres found out Wally Hebert is in shape, George McDonald has developed a home run punch and Ted Williams really can do things with a bat. Hebert, McDonald and Williams were the heroes of the San Diego triumph, which put the Padres farther out in front in the Pacific Coast league ball race.

Between them, McDonald and Williams drove in eight runs, with the latter setting the pace with five tallied batted in. They also accounted for seven of the 17 hits Sam Diego made in the bat orgy. Each smacked out his second home run of the season with a runner on base...Williams batted in two runs in this inning with a single.

Williams and McDonald hit their home runs in the second, McDonald's coming first with Detore, who had singled in Thompson from second, on base. Ernie Holman drew a pass, then Williams lined one over the right center field fence.

Patchett doubled with the sacks loaded in the fifth to give San Diego three more runs. McDonald, Holman and Williams were on base at the time. In the seventh, Hebert collected his first hit of the season, a double to right center, to score Williams and Reese." *(Keller, ET, April 28, 1937)*

GAME 26. The Padres beat Oakland, 4-2. Ted was 0-2. *(ET, April 29, 1937)* 42 AB, 11 H, 2 HR, .262

"San Diego tied the game in its half of the second. George McDonald singled, and the bases were all occupied when Ernie Holman and Ted Williams received free tickets to first. Reese grounded to First Baseman Fern Bell and McDonald was forced at the plate on a close play.

Salvo, who was a fence buster as an outfielder in sandlot baseball, cracked a single to center, scoring Holman. Williams stopped at third, but when Reese overran second, Shellenback told Williams to go home. The lanky 18-year-old outfielder was out by a city block." *(Keller, ET, April 29, 1937)*

GAME 27. Ward Driven To Showers; Bonham Best. Oakland knocked Dick Ward off the mound with five runs in the seventh inning en route to an 8-4 triumph over the Padres. Ted was 1-for-4. The team's record was 17-10. *(ET, April 30, 1937)* 46 AB, 12 H, 2 HR, .261

"When outfielders Ted Williams and Hal Patchett couldn't decide who would take Bill Baker's fly, the ball dropped for a single, Hitchcock scoring. Fern Bell flied to Williams for the second out and Williams made a perfect throw to the plate to double Judnich.

"Bonham whiffed George Detore and George McDonald, the first two Padres up in the second, but walked Ernie Holman. Williams then landed on one of his fast slants and slammed it to right for two bases, putting Holman across the platter.

"A local fan predicts the Padres will get $50,000 from a major league club for Ted Williams within the next few years." *(Keller, ET, April 30, 1937)*

GAME 28. "Oakland's winning runs came in the sixth. Koy, first up, drove a liner into left. Williams came in fast and dove for the ball, but he missed and the pellet got past him, rolling to the fence and allowing Koy to make it a round trip.

Williams kept the pot boiling by getting a base knock into center to put Holman on the hot corner." *(Keller, ET, May 1, 1937)* 50 AB, 13 H, 2 HR, .260

GAME 29. With Howard Craghead pitching, San Diego defeated Oakland, 6-1. Ted Williams did not play. *(San Diego Union, May 2, 1937)*

GAMES 30 and 31. The Padres' win streak reached four games as the team swept a 4-2 and 5-0 Sunday doubleheader to close the series at Oakland. Williams did not play in either game. *(ET, May 3, 1937)*

"If Ted Williams, 18-year-old outfielder with the San Diego Padres, is to make the grade in the diamond sport, he has one thing to learn. Ted must get it in his head that fielding is just as important as hitting. The young flyhawk believes all he has to do is get up to the plate and hit the ball, but that's where he is wrong. The veterans on the Padres team are trying to convince Ted of this fact, and the sooner they do, the quicker the youth will make good. 'You must hustle in the field just as much as you do at the plate to get anywhere in baseball,' Ted has been told by the Padres vets." *(Keller, ET, May 4, 1937)*

Ted Williams pounds out second homer of the season, April 27, 1937.

Ted takes a warm-up swing.

GAME 32. San Francisco came back with a pair of runs in the bottom of the ninth inning to claim a 4-3 victory at Seals Stadium. Ted went 1-for-4. "Then came the ninth and the Padres again unknotted the tie when George McDonald, leading hitter of the Coast League, singled. He went to third on Ted Williams' right field single and scored while Jimmy Reese was being thrown out at first." *(Keller, ET, May 5, 1937)* 54 AB, 14 H, 2 HR, .259

GAME 33. San Diego beat San Francisco, 7-2. Williams did not play. *(ET, May 6, 1937)*

GAME 34. The Seals defeated the Padres, 8-4. Ted was 0-for-2 after replacing Rupert Thompson in right field. *(ET, May 7, 1937)* 56 AB, 14 H, 2 HR, 2.50

GAME 35. San Francisco pounded Manny Salvo and San Diego, 10-2. Ted had one of the three Padres hits in his four at-bats. He also had one of the four Padres errors. *(ET, May 8, 1937)* 60 AB, 15 H, 2 HR, .250

GAME 36. Wally Hebert blanked the Seals, 7-0. Ted Williams again went 1-for-4. *(San Diego Union, May 9, 1937)* 64 AB, 16 H, 2 HR, .250

GAMES 37 and 38. The Padres dropped the Sunday doubleheader to San Francisco, 12-6 and 8-2, and slipped to fourth place in PCL standings, 3 1/2 games behind Sacramento. Ted was 0-for-3 in the opener and 1 for 2 as a late innings replacement in right field for Rupert Thompson in the nightcap. *(ET, May 10, 1937)* 69 AB, 17 H, 2 HR, .246

GAME 39. Ted was held out of an 8-7 loss to Sacramento. *(ET, May 12, 1937)*

GAME 40. The Solons' Tony Freitas out-dueled Dick Ward and the Padres, 3-2. Williams did not play. *(ET, May 13, 1937)*

GAME 41. Ted was hitless in four at bats as Tiny Chaplin crafted a 5-0 shutout in Sacramento. *(ET, May 14, 1937)* 73 AB, 17 H, 2 HR, .233

GAME 42. The Solons came from behind to beat San Diego, 4-3. Williams went 0-for-3. *(ET, May 15, 1937)* 76 AB, 17 H, 2 HR, .224

GAME 43. The Padres scored 5 runs in the ninth to defeat Sacramento, 6-3. Ted contributed two runs batted in with a single. He was 1-for-4 on the day. *(San Diego Union, May 16, 1937)* 80 AB, 18 H, 2 HR, .225

GAMES 44 and 45. San Diego and Sacramento split the getaway doubleheader with identical 4-1 scores. The Padres won the first contest. Ted Williams was 1-for-5. He hit a double in three at-bats in the second game. *(ET, May 17, 1937)* 88 AB, 20 H, 2 HR, .227

GAME 46. The Padres returned home and pounded Seattle, 7-2. Ted did not play. "(Current Seattle and former Padres pitcher Berlyn) Horne hated to leave the San Diego club... Says he never met a sweller bunch of fellows in his life." *(Keller, ET, May 19, 1937)*

GAME 47. Ted was again out of action as the Padres' Manny Salvo shutout Seattle, 5-0. *(ET, May 20, 1937)*

GAME 48. Kewpie Dick Barrett duplicated Salvo's performance. The Padres were on the losing end of a 5-0 score. Ted made an out pinch-hitting for Tiny Chaplin in the ninth inning. *(ET, May 21, 1937)* 89 AB, 20 H, 2 HR, .225

GAME 49. The Padres scored twice in the eighth to tie and once in the ninth to beat Seattle, 5-4. Ted was 1-for-3. According to the box score, this is a game in which Bill Starr pinch-hit in a bunt situation for Ted Williams. Earl Keller did not mention this in his article. "An error by Left Fielder Ted Williams gave the Indians their first counter in the first frame... After going down in order in the first, San Diego touched Thomas for the tying tallies in the second. Detore and Williams singled. The former scored when Second Baseman Fred Muller, who was charged with three misplays, let Durst's grounder get away. Williams countered when Berkowitz hit into a double play...Unofficially, Seattle's third run wasn't earned. With one out and Muller on second and Dick Gyselman on first, Strange hit a high fly into left. The ball dropped between Williams and Berkowitz, Muller scoring." *(Keller, ET, May 22, 1937 and Los Angeles Times, May 22, 1937)* 92 AB, 21 H, 2 HR, .228

GAME 50. The Padres pounded Seattle, 12-4. Ted did not play. *(San Diego Union, May 23, 1937)*

GAMES 51 and 52. San Diego won the Sunday doubleheader, 10-3 and 1-0. Williams did not play in either game. *(ET, May 24, 1937 and Los Angeles Times, May 24, 1937)*

GAME 53. The series moved to Seattle where the Padres won again, 7-1. Williams did not play. *(ET, May 26, 1937)*

GAME 54. Tiny Chaplin shutout the Indians, 5-0. Ted did not play. *(ET, May 27, 1937)*

GAME 55. San Diego took the ninth of its first ten games with Seattle, 6-4. Ted continued to ride the bench. *(ET, May 28, 1937)*

GAME 56. Seattle prevailed, 6-2. Ted made an out pinch-hitting for Manuel Salvo in the ninth inning. *(ET, May 29, 1937)* 93 AB, 21 H, 2 HR, .226

GAME 57. After surrendering a second inning home run to George Detore, Kewpie Dick and the Indians came back to beat San Diego, 2-1. Ted did not play. *(San Diego Union, May 30, 1937)*

GAMES 58 and 59. The Padres dropped a twin bill to Seattle, 11-1 and 3-2. Ted Williams did not play. *(ET, May 31, 1937)*

GAMES 60 and 61. San Diego and Seattle split a Memorial Day doubleheader with the Padres taking the opener, 7-5. Frank Shellenback was on the mound and seemingly in control when the Indians erupted with four hits and two runs in the final inning of the nightcap to claim a 3-2 victory. Was Ted in the doghouse? We know he wasn't in the lineup. *(ET, June 1, 1937)*

GAME 62. The San Diego Padres clubbed Hobo Carson and the Portland Beavers, 8-2. Ted did not play. *(ET, June 2, 1937)*

GAME 63. San Diego lost 4-3 to Portland in ten innings. Ted Williams collected a ninth inning pinch-hit single for Manny Salvo. Did Shelley hold Ted out of 13 games following the young outfielder's apparent defensive lapses on May 21 to teach Ted a lesson? *(ET, June 3, 1937)* 94 AB, 22 H, 2 HR, .234

GAME 64. Ad Liska and the Beavers beat the Padres, 6-2. Ted made an out as a pinch-hitter for Howard Craghead. *(ET, June 4, 1937)* 95 AB, 22 H, 2 HR, .232

GAME 65. There was a fire in the Vaughn Street ballpark as Portland burned San Diego, 8-4. Bill Starr was a pinch-hitter. Ted remained on the bench. *(ET, June 5, 1937)*

GAME 66. The Beavers came from behind to defeat San Diego, 8-7. Ted got a pinch-hit single. *(Los Angeles Times, June 6, 1937)* 96 AB, 23 H, 2 HR, .240

GAMES 67 and 68. Ted singled five times in a doubleheader sweep in Portland on June 6. Batting fifth, Ted went 3-for-5, with 2 RBI in the first game. Ted batted in the six-hole in game two, and went 2-for-3, again knocking in 2 runs. The Padres won handily, 12-1 and 8-5. Seven Beavers errors didn't help matters for the home team, though the tone was set when the Padres' Patchett hit the first pitch of the first game for a home run. *(Oregon Daily Journal, June 7, 1937)* 104 AB, 28 H, 2 HR, .269

GAME 69. Williams went 0-for-4 as the Padres lost the home opener of the San Francisco series, 5-1. *(ET, June 9, 1937)* 108 AB, 28 H, 2 HR, .259

GAME 70. The Seals beat the Padres, 6-4. "Ballou passed Ted Williams who batfed (sic) for Chaplin, but made Hal Patchett force Williams at second for the third out. Ballou was credited with the victory, his fourth of the year." Williams officially was 0-0. *(Keller, ET, June 10, 1937)*

GAME 71. San Diego beat league-leading San Francisco and the great Sad Sam Gibson, 3-2. Williams did not play. *(ET, June 11, 1937)*

GAME 72. The Padres again humbled Lefty O'Doul's Seals, 13-6. The team collected 17 hits, but Williams was not in the lineup. *(ET, June 12, 1937)*

GAME 73. The San Diego hit parade continued, with 20 safeties off Seals pitcher Ed Stutz in a 14-6 victory. Ted did not play. One can almost hear Ted, "Put me in, coach; I'm ready to play." *(Los Angeles Times, June 13, 1937)*

GAMES 74 and 75. The Padres swept the Sunday doubleheader with San Francisco, 8-1 and 1-0. Williams did not play. *(ET, June 14, 1937)*

Frank Shellenback used his rookies in a charity game against the San Diego Prep All-Stars at Lane Field. Gene Tuttle was the winning pitcher for the Padres. "The hardest blow collected off Gonzales was a home run by Ted Williams. With (Ed) Stewart on base after doubling, Williams kissed one of Gonzales' fast ones on the hose in the third and drove it to deep center field for four bases. The ball must have carried 400 feet." (The All-Stars' pitcher was Joe Gonzales, on option from the Boston Red Sox.) *(Keller, ET, June 14, 1937)*

GAME 76. The Angels stopped San Diego's five game win streak, 4-1. Williams made an out as a pinch-hitter for Wally Hebert. *(ET, June 16, 1937)* 109 AB, 28 H, 2 HR, .257

GAME 77. LA beat the Padres, 10-2. Ted hit a single in two at-bats after replacing Cedric Durst in left field. *(ET, June 17, 1937)* 111 AB, 29 H, 2 HR, .261

GAME 78. The Angels took the third straight from San Diego, 4-2. Ted did not play. *(ET, June 18, 1937)*

GAME 79. 14,000 fans watched the Angels win a wild game from the Padres, 10-8. Williams drove in a pair of runs with a pinch-hit double, batting for Joe Berkowitz in the fifth inning. *(ET, June 19, 1937)* 112 AB, 30 H, 2 HR, .268

GAME 80. "Ted Williams sparkled in left field, making two brilliant catches on line drives by Mesner and Russell in the ninth... Statz backed up against the center field bleacher screen to pull down Williams' long drive in the first inning." Ted took the collar in four at-bats, but the Padres beat the Angels, 5-1. *(Los Angeles Times, June 20, 1937)* 116 AB, 30 H, 2 HR, .259

GAMES 81 and 82. San Diego took both ends of the Sunday doubleheader with Los Angeles, 11-4 and 3-2 in eight innings in the second game. Ted Williams hit a home run in five at-bats in the first contest, but did not play in the second. *(ET, June 21, 1937)* 121 AB, 31 H, 3 HR, .256

GAME 83. Williams Wins for Padres, Homer Gives San Diegans Close Game. "A booming home run from the bat of 18-year-old Ted Williams brought big Jim Chaplin his 11th mound victory of the season and the Padres to a 3 to 2 triumph over Portland in the first game of the series at Lane Field yesterday.

Williams dealt the knockout punch to Pitcher Bill Posedel of the Beavers in the eighth inning with George McDonald on first base and the Padres trailing, 2 to 1. Posedel tried to breeze a fast one by Williams, but the youth smacked it right on the kisser, and the ball went zooming over second, rolling almost to the fence in deep center field. The Beavers made their mistake when they played Williams for a dead right field hitter. His swat would have been a single if Center Fielder Nino Bongiovanni had been playing in the right spot.

Reese and Williams earned big hands in the ninth with great plays. When Tresh smacked a sizzler through Chaplin's legs, Reese dashed behind second, scooped up the pellet, and fired it to first in time to nab the runner. Williams went all the way back to the left field fence to take Pinch Hitter Bill Sweeney's long drive with one hand and on the run." Williams was 1-for-3. *(Keller, ET, June 24, 1937)* 124 AB, 32 H, 4 HR, .258

GAME 84. Hebert Wins, 3-2, as Thompson Homers. "San Diego's first run came in the second when Ted Williams doubled and came in on a single by Bill Starr." Ted was 1-for-3. *(Keller, ET, June 24, 1937)* 127 AB, 33 H, 4 HR, .260

GAME 85. "The Padres sank Portland's submarine chucker, Ad Liska, at Lane Field last night and scored their sixth victory in a row by a 13 to 7 count as 5000 paying customers looked on.

Every Padre came through with at least one hit. Tommy Thompson, whose batting average remained at .381 when he collected 2-for-5, and Ted Williams were the bat stars. Both sent four runs across the platter.

Thompson's double with the bases loaded in the fifth cooked Liska's goose. Williams drove in the fifth and sixth runs of the inning with a single. In the seventh, Williams teed off on one of Shealy's fast balls and swatted it over the right center field fence.

George Detore tripled and came in when Williams flied to right in the fourth." Ted had two hits in four at-bats. *(Keller,* ET, *June 25, 1937)* 131 AB, 35 H, 5 HR, .267

GAME 86. "San Diego's sixth run was a smashing homer by young Ted Williams. Leading off in the third, he caught one of Carson's 'express balls' squarely and sent it far over the center fielder's head. The pellet landed in the dirt by the center field fence, 470 feet from home. It was by far the longest drive ever hit in San Diego." Ted went 2-for-4 as the Padres beat Portland, 6-1. *(Keller,* ET, *June 26, 1937)* 135 AB, 37 H, 6 HR, .274

GAME 87. San Diego won an 11-9 pitchers' duel over Portland. Williams was 2-for-4. *(Los Angeles Times, June 27, 1937)* 139 AB, 39 H, 6 HR, .281

GAMES 88 and 89. Williams Hammers Out Five Circuit Smashes in Series; Angels Next. The Padres split with Portland. The Beavers took the first game, 3-2, and San Diego came back with a 6-2 victory in the second game. Ted Williams hit a home run in each game. He was 1-for-4 in the opener and 2-for-3 in the nightcap.

"The batting star of yesterday's twin bill was 18-year-old Ted Williams of the Padres. He put the Padres ahead, 2 to 1 in the seventh inning of the first encounter by smacking a long home run over the right field fence, and in the night cap, he hit another homer and a double to drive in four runs. Williams' record for the week shows he hit five home runs, drove in 14 runs and batted .440.

For the second time in the series, Ad Liska was beaten by San Diego in the second contest. Williams' bat spelled defeat for the submarine ball pitcher. He drove in the first run with a double, and the last three with a long home run in the fifth. Detore and McDonald were on base when Williams connected." *(Keller,* ET, *June 28, 1937)* 146 AB, 42 H, 8 HR, .288

Base Hits. "Ted Williams, 18-year-old San Diego Padre outfielder, is the talk of the town today. The former Herbert Hoover High pitcher was the batting star of last week's Padre-Portland series despite the fact that Tommy Thompson out hit him. Five times during the week, Williams smacked home runs, and on six other occasions he hit safely to drive in 14 runs, seven more than Thompson batted in. Williams' mark for the week was .440, as compared to Thompson's .481.

Three of Williamss (sic) circuit blows last week went out of the park and two were hit inside the field. Yesterday he became the first Coast leaguer to hit two round-trip swats in one day at Lane Field when he connected in the first and second tilts. His total for the season is eight. Williams swings so easily when he takes a cut at the ball that one wouldn't believe he could hit the ball out of the park, but his perfect wrist action gives him the 'old sock.'" *(Keller,* ET, *June 28, 1937)* Williams 142 AB, 42 H, 8 HR, 40 RBI, Pct. .296 (The fact that the *Evening Tribune*'s statistics do not always match game account totals was noted above.)

GAME 90. The Angels beat the Padres, 6-3. Ted was 0-for-4. *(ET, June 30, 1937)*

GAME 91. Howard Craghead and his San Diego teammates shut down the Halos, 4-0. Ted drove in two runs with a double. He had two hits in three at-bats. *(ET, July 1, 1937)* 153 AB, 44 H, 8 HR, .288

GAME 92. Los Angeles took the Padres, 6-4. Ted Williams went 1-for-3. *(ET, July 2, 1937)* 156 AB, 45 H, 8 HR, .288

GAME 93. Ted Williams hits a home run, a double and two singles in five at-bats to pace the Padres in an 11-2 victory over the Angels. *(ET, July 3, 1937)* 161 AB, 49 H, 9 HR, .304

"There now are six regulars hitting better than .300. Ted Williams joined Thompson, Detore, Jimmy Reese, George McDonald and Hall (sic) Patchett in that group this week. Williams has batted in 46 runs with 49 hits." *(Keller, ET, July 3, 1947)*

Williams 45 G, 157 AB, 49 H, 9 HR, 46 RBI, .312; Fielding: 52 PO, 1 A, 3 E, .946 *(ET, July 3, 1937)*

GAME 94. Ted went 1-for-4 as the Padres defeated LA, 5-4. *(San Diego Union, July 4, 1937)* 165 AB, 50 H, 9 HR, .303

GAMES 95 and 96. San Diego won the 4th of July doubleheader with the Angels, 2-1 in the nine inning game and 12-1 in the seven inning nightcap. Williams was 1-for-1 in the opener and 0-for-2 in the second. "Ted Williams won the first game for the Padres when he doubled in the winning run in the sixth." *(Keller, ET, July 5, 1937)* 170 AB, 51 H, 9 HR, .300

GAMES 97 and 98. The Padres split a Monday doubleheader with Los Angeles at Lane Field. They won 5-0 and lost 3-5. Ted was 1-for-4 and 1-for-3. *(ET, July 6, 1937)* 177 AB, 53 H, 9 HR, .299

GAME 99. The San Francisco Missions squeezed past San Diego, 5-4. Williams was hitless in three at-bats. *(ET, July 7, 1937)* 180 AB, 53 H, 9 HR, .294

GAME 100. The Padres beat the Mission Reds, 5-1. Ted went 2-for-4. *(ET, July 8, 1937)* 184 AB, 55 H, 9 HR, .299

GAME 101. San Diego topped the Missions, 7-2. Williams was hitless in two at-bats. *(ET, July 9, 1937)* 186 AB, 55 H, 9 HR, .296

GAME 102. It was deja-vu, 7-2, in San Francisco as the Padres again prevailed over the Missions. Ted went 1-for-3. *(ET, July 10, 1937)* 189 AB, 56 H, 9 HR, .296

GAME 103. Ted was 3-for-5 and the Padres lost, 9-7, to the Missions. *(Los Angeles Times, July 11, 1937)* 194 AB, 59 H, 9 HR, .304

GAMES 104 and 105. George Detore and Dick Ward were injured during a doubleheader split with the Missions. San Diego lost the first game, 10-2, but won the nightcap, 5-2. Williams was 2-for-4 in a losing cause and 0-for-4 in the victory. *(ET, July 12, 1937)* 202 AB, 61 H, 9 HR, .302

GAME 106. Padres Win, 8-3, Gain On Leaders, Williams Smashes 2 Homers. "Howard Craghead chalked up his 12th triumph of the season and Ted Williams accounted for a new Lane Field record by hitting two home runs as the San Diego Padres trounced the Missions, 8 to 3, in the series opener on the lower Broadway diamond yesterday. In winning, the Padres gained ground on the Sacramento and Seal clubs, as they both dropped games. San Diego is now only two percentage points out of second place.

"Williams hit his first homer in the second, starting a 5-run rally, and the second came with a runner on in the fifth. They were homers Nos. 10 and 11 for Williams. A circuit clout for George Myatt climaxed the 5-run rally, two being on the bags at the time. Walter Beck was the victim." Williams was 2-for-3. *(Keller, ET, July 14, 1937)* 205 AB, 63 H, 11 HR, .307

GAME 107. San Diego held on to an 8-6 victory over the Missions. Ted was a perfect 2 for 2. "When George McDonald grounded out to the pitcher, it looked like as if Babich would get out of the tough spot, but he made the mistake of tossing a pitch that Ted Williams liked. Ted singled into left to score both runners.

"Singles by Jimmy Reese, Patchett, Thompson and Williams, a triple by George McDonald and walks to Myatt and Salvo did the damage." *(Keller, ET, July 15, 1937)* 207 AB, 65 H, 11 HR, .314

GAME 108. Wally Hebert limited the Missions to three hits as the Padre southpaw shutout the cellar dwellers, 3-0. Ted was 0-for-3. *(ET, July 16, 1937)* 210 AB, 65 H, 11 HR, .310

GAME 109. Fourth Straight Win Puts Padres in Circuit Lead. San Diego beat the Missions, 8-3 and Ted Williams had one hit in four at bats. "A walk to Tommy Thompson, Ted Williams' single and Jimmy Reese's base hit produced San Dieog's (sic) fifth run in the same inning." *(Keller, ET, July 17, 1937)* 214 AB, 66 H, 11 HR, .308

Ted Williams, lf 61 G, 207 AB, 66 H, 20 R, 37 RBI, .319. Fielding: 73 PO, 1 A, 4 E, .949 *(ET, July 17, 1937)* (Sharp readers may note that the July 3 *Tribune* had credited Williams with 46 RBI two full weeks earlier, and had credited him with 40 RBI on June 28. Since July 3, we've seen at least 2 RBI in the July 14th paper and another 2 in the paper of the 15th, on top of his RBI on the Fourth of July.)

GAME 110. The Padres slipped past the Mission Reds, 5-4. Ted Williams had a single in two at-bats. *(Los Angeles Times, July 18, 1937)* 216 AB, 67 H, 11 HR, .310

GAMES 111 and 112. San Diego and the Missions split the Sunday doubleheader. The Padres blew the first game when the Reds scored 8 runs in the ninth inning to claim a 9-6 victory. Wally Hebert got his second shutout of the week, 1-0, in the 7-inning game. Ted was 0-for-4 in the opener and 1-for-2 in the nightcap. *(ET, July 19, 1937)* 222 AB, 68 H, 11 HR, .306

GAME 113. Jim Chaplin Hits Homer, Blanks Foes. Tiny Chaplin shutout Seattle, 4-0, for his 16th victory. Ted was 0-for-4. *(ET, July 21, 1937)* 226 AB, 68 H, 11 HR, .301

GAME 114. Indians Are Beaten, 5 To 1, By Craghead. "Howard Craghead pitched yesterday's triumph, his 14th win of the year and his eighth in a row. Craghead had young Ted Williams to thank for his win, for it was his home run in the sixth inning that broke up a pitching duel between Craghead and Bill Thomas.

"For the next four and a half frames, the big crowd saw a slab battle. In the sixth, Thompson, who had just made one of the greatest catches ever seen at Lane Field, doubled. McDonald's single moved him to third. Williams leaned on the next pitch, driving the ball deep over the right-center field wall." Ted was 1-for-3. *(Keller, ET, July 22, 1937)* 229 AB, 69 H, 12 HR, .301

GAME 115. Gonzales Is 3 To 2 Victim; Honor Myatt. "McDonald singled and Ted Williams doubled him to third. Barrett was yanked and Pickrel came in. Reese greeted him with a single that scored McDonald, but Williams was held at third, where he died." Ted had one hit in three at bats. *(Keller, ET, July 23, 1937)* 232 AB, 70 H, 12 HR, .302

GAME 116. The Padres lost, 5-1, to the Oaks in Oakland and Ted Williams went 0-for-3. Salvo struck out 13 in a losing cause. *(ET, July 24, 1937)* 235 AB, 70 H, 12 HR, .298

GAME 117. Jim Chaplin hit an apparent home run that Milt Steengrafe ruled foul. The Padres surrounded the umpire and almost caused a riot. San Diego won, 8-6 and Ted Williams was 2-for-5. *(Los Angeles Times, July 25, 1937)* 240 AB, 72 H, 12 HR, .300

GAMES 118 and 119. "San Diego's Padres, whose hometown fans are hard on umpires and visiting ball players, found fans at the Oakland ball park equally as enthusiastic yesterday. Oakland won both games, 2 to 1 and 6 to 1, to make it three out of four for the series." – Associated Press. Williams was 0-for-3 and 0-for-2. *(ET, July 26, 1937)* 245 AB, 72 H, 12 HR, .294

GAME 120. Padres Go 10 Heats to Conquer Seattle, Score 6-5 Victory in First Game. Williams went 0-for-4. *(ET, July 28, 1937)* 249 AB, 72 H, 12 HR, .289

GAME 121. Ted Williams was 1-for-5 as Jim Chaplin and the Padres scalped the Seattle Indians. Chaplin also hit a home run. *(ET, July 29, 1937)* 254 AB, 73 H, 12 HR, .287

GAME 122. San Diego beat Seattle, 4-1. Ted was 0-for-3. *(ET, July 30, 1937)* 257 AB, 73 H, 12 H, .284

GAME 123. Despite a 6-1 defeat in Seattle, the Padres saw their league lead increase to 3-1/2 games over Sacramento. Williams had a single in four at-bats. *(ET, July 31, 1937)* 261 AB, 74 H, 12 HR, .284

GAME 124. Ted went 0-for-4 and the Padres lost to the Indians, 7 to 3. *(San Diego Union, August 1, 1937)* 265 AB, 74 H, 12 HR, .279

GAMES 125 and 126. San Diego split with Seattle. The Padres were white-washing, 5-0, in the first game, but roared back to claim the second contest, 9-2. Ted went 1-for-4 in the opener, but did not play in the short game. *(ET, August 2, 1937)* 260 AB, 75 H, 12 HR, .279

GAME 127. San Diego blasted the Beavers, 11-3, in Portland. Ted had a home run and single in five at-bats. *(ET, August 4, 1937)* 274 AB, 77 H, 13 HR, .281

GAME 128. Portland beat the Padres, 3-2, and Ted was hitless in four at-bats. *(ET, August 5, 1937)* 278 AB, 77 H, 13 HR, .277

GAME 129. The Padres got 16 hits and defeated Portland, 5-1. Ted Williams did not contribute any hits in his four at-bats. *(ET, August 6, 1937)* 282 AB, 77 H, 13 HR, .273

GAME 130. Pitcher Tiny Chaplin's solid single to left knocked in Ted Williams in the 12th inning as San Diego edged Portland, 4-3. Ted had singled a couple of batters ahead of Chaplin and was 1-for-5 on the night. *(ET, August 7, 1937)* 287 AB, 78 H, 13 HR, .272

GAME 131. Ad Liska and the Portland Beavers shut out the league-leading Padres. Ted was 2-for-4. *(San Diego Union, August 8, 1937)* 291 AB, 80 H, 13 HR, .275

GAMES 132 and 133. Sports Editor Tom Akers wondered which PCL team would "grab the gonfalon for the season." The Padres needed 17 innings to drown the Beavers, 6-5, in the first game of the Sunday doubleheader, but only required seven stanzas to take the nightcap, 4-1. Ted was 2-for-5 and 1-for-1. *(ET, August 9, 1937)* 297 AB, 83 H, 13 HR, .279

GAME 134. Tiny Chaplin and the Padres beat Oakland, 4-3, in ten innings at Lane Field. Ted was 0-for-4. *(ET, Aug 11, 1937)* 301 AB, 83 H, 13 HR, .275

GAME 135. San Diego's league-leading margin was cut to 2 1/2 games as they lost, 4-2, to Oakland. Williams was 0-for-3. *(ET, August 12, 1937)* 304 AB, 83 H, 13 HR, .273

GAME 136. Poison Oaks Beat Padres Under Stars. Ted Williams was 0-for-4 and Oakland left town as a 4-2 winner. *(ET, August 13, 1937)* 308 AB, 83 H, 13 HR, .269

GAME 137. Tony Freitas pitched the Solons to a 3-1 victory to cut San Diego's league lead to a game. Williams did not play. *(ET, August 14, 1937)*

GAME 138. Tiny Chaplin stopped the Padres' skid and halted Sacramento, 9-2. Williams was 0-for-3. *(Los Angeles Times, August 15, 1937)* 311 AB, 83 H, 13 HR, .267

GAMES 139 and 140. San Diego and Sacramento split their Sunday doubleheader in an abbreviated four game series at Lane Field. The Padres won the first game, 3-2, but Tony Freitas came back to blank San Diego, 5-0, in the nightcap. Ted Williams suffered through his sixth consecutive hitless game and saw his batting average drop to .263. He was 0-for-4 in the first game and 0-for-0 in the second. *(Los Angeles Times, August 16, 1937)* 315 AB, 83 H, 13 HR, .263

GAME 141. Ted broke out of his slump with a double in four at-bats as the Padres beat the Solons, 6-1, in Sacramento. *(ET, August 18, 1937)* 319 AB, 84 H, 13 HR, .263

GAME 142. Sacramento defeated San Diego, 7-5. Williams had two hits including a double in four at-bats. *(ET, August 19, 1937)* 323 AB, 86 H, 13 HR, .266

GAME 143. Umpire Powell Lands in Jail, Solons Protest Fray As Salvo Wins 14th, 8-0; Sacramento Fans Heave Pop Bottles. Umpire Jack Powell was arrested by three Sacramento police officers for intoxication after irate Solon bleacher fans, angered by Powell's calls, tossed bottles and seat cushions at the arbiter. Later that evening, Padre Jimmy Reese posted the $10 bail required to free the embattled umpire from the slammer. Ted Williams' 0-for-1 seemed almost incidental to the arrest. *(ET, August 20 1937)* 324 AB, 86 H,13 HR, .265

GAME 144. Williams' Homer Wins For Padres, Kid Fielder Smashes One In Eleventh. Ted Williams hit a pinch two run double in the ninth inning to tie the score at 6-6. His solo shot won the game. The kid was a hero. *(ET, August 21, 1937)* 326 AB, 88 H, 14 HR, .270

Jack Powell forfeited bail. PCL President W. C. Tuttle ordered the umpire suspended pending an investigation. "There appears to have been little doubt that Umpire Powell was intoxicated." The league president also confirmed that Sacramento had not protested the game. *(ET, August 21, 1937)*

GAME 145. Ted was hot. He went 3-for-4, but the Padres lost to Sacramento, 4-2. *(San Diego Union, August 22, 1937)* 330 AB, 91 H, 14 HR. 276

GAMES 146 and 147. The Solons cut the Padres' lead to a half-game as they swept the Sunday doubleheader, 8-5 and 2-1. Williams was 2-for-4 in the first game and 2-for-3 in the finale. *(Evening Tribune and Los Angeles Times, August 23, 1937)* 337 AB, 95 H, 14 HR, .282

GAME 148. Ted Williams hit a bases-empty home run in the ninth inning to spoil "Sailor Bill" Posedel's shutout as the Padres lost, 2-1, to the Portland Beavers in the series opener at Lane Field. Ted was 1-for-4 in the game. *(ET, August 25, 1937)* 341 AB, 96 H, 15 HR, .282

GAME 149. The Padres could only manage three hits off Portland's Ad Liska. One of the San Diego safeties was a single by Ted Williams. *Tribune* Sports Editor Tom Akers wrote that the submariner was given a wide strike zone by Umpire Morgan. The Beavers won, 3 to 1. Ted was 1-for-3. *(ET, August 26, 1937)* 344 AB, 97 H, 15 HR, .282

GAME 150. Padres Slump Streak Ends; Salvo Stars, Blanks Foes Under 'Arcs'. Manny Salvo, San Diego's big Italian fastballer shut out Portland, 1-0. Ted Williams had one hit in two at-bats. *(ET, August 27, 1937)* 346 AB, 98 H, 15 HR, .283

GAME 151. The Beavers bounced the Padres, 8-4. Ted hit a home run in four at-bats. *(ET, August 28, 1937)* 350 AB, 99 H, 16 HR, .283

GAME 152. Ted's 17th home run of the season was the margin of victory as Wally Hebert lost his shutout in the ninth. The Padres beat Portland, 3-2. Ted also had a single in three at-bats. *(Los Angeles Times, August 29, 1937)* 353 AB, 101 H, 17 HR, .286

GAMES 153 and 154. San Diego, Beaver '9' Split Pair. Earl Keller was finally back writing about the Padres. Portland took the first game, 3-1, and San Diego captured the nightcap, 10-1, in seven innings. Ted was 0-for-4 in the first game and he hit a double in four at-bats during the rout. Why was the box score for the second game in the *Evening Tribune* while there was only a lone score for the first game? The box score had to be found in the *L.A. Times*! *(Evening Tribune and Los Angeles Times, August 30, 1937)* 361 AB, 102 H, 17 HR, .283

GAME 155. Williams Hits Homer; Padres Win. "Ted Williams' big bat boomed out home run No. 18 of the season in the eighth inning at Lane Field yesterday to give San Diego's Padres a 4 to 2 win over the San Francisco Seals in the series opener and hand Jim Chaplin his 22nd triumph. Williams' homer, which barely missed hitting a man perched in a tree on the other side of the right field fence, broke up a pitching duel between Chaplin and Frank Lamanske.

"Williams also batted in the Padres' first run and scored the second in the first frame. After two were out, Thompson walked and Ted doubled him in. George Detore hit a one-base blow to send Williams cantering across the home platter." Williams had two hits in four at-bats. *(Keller, ET, September 1, 1937)* 365 AB, 104 H, 18 HR, .285.

Base Hits. "Lefty O'Doul, skipper of the San Francisco Seals, surely would like to have Ted Williams, San Diego flyhawk, under his wing for the next year. Williams has drawn more praise from O'Doul than from any other manager in the Pacific Coast League, and every time Lefty sees or gets the chance to give the kid a helpful pointer he does. 'That kid is the best prospect his circuit has seen since Joe DiMaggio,' says O'Doul. 'He has the makings of a great player and, if handled right, he will go places. I would like to be his teacher.'" *(Keller, ET, September 1, 1937)*

August 30 was – pretty certainly – Ted's 19th birthday; if so, hitting a game-winning homer for the home crowd had to be a real thrill. Reading some of the comments in the next day's papers offered the chance for Ted to savor the memory once again.

GAME 156. Two Homers By Williams. "The Padres again combined timely hitting with effective pitching to dump the Seals yesterday at Lane Field by a score of 10 to 5. Ted Williams, George Myatt and Joe Berkowitz provided the timely hitting and Wally Hebert turned in the good hurling. All Williams did was smack two home runs – his 19th and 20th – to drive in three runs and make 'Sad Sam' Gibson, the league's No. 1, all the 'sadder.'

"Williams' first round trip of the contest came in the second inning with Myatt on base. It was a line smash over the air mail sign in right field. First up in the fifth, Williams landed on a slow ball and sent it soaring over the right field wall. It was the second time this season that Williams had hit two circuit blows in one game.

"Three hits and a walk gave the Padres two runs in the seventh. Durst's infield hit scored Thompson and George McDonald singled in Williams who had walked." Ted was 2-for-3. *(Keller, ET, September 2, 1937)* 368 AB, 106 H, 20 HR, .288

GAME 157. The Padres were back on top of the PCL as San Diego swept San Francisco in a short three game set at Lane Field. Manny Salvo hung zeros on the board for manager Frank Shellenback to blank the Seals, 4-0. Williams was 0-for-2. The teams would travel north for six more games in San Francisco.

"Hal Patchett had struck out to start the Padres' half of the frame. George Myatt single sharply to left and stole second. Tommy Thompson walked and Williams was hit in the back, loading the sacks. Then George Detore was passed, Myatt strolling in with the first run. Singles by George McDonald and Joe Berkowitz after two were out sent Thompson and Williams home." *(Keller, ET, September 3, 1937)* 370 AB, 106 H, 20 HR, .286

GAME 158. The Padres dropped a wild 16-15 game at Seals Stadium. Down by 9 in the ninth, San Diego rallied to tie the score. O'Doul brought Win Ballou in from the bullpen to stop the bleeding. (With a nine run cushion, one wonders if the bat boy had to go across the street to find "Old Pard" at the Double Play saloon.) Ballou earned the victory when the Seals got a run in the bottom of the ninth. Ted Williams had two hits in six at-bats. *(Evening Tribune and San Francisco Chronicle, September 4, 1937)* 376 AB, 108 H, 20 HR, .287

GAMES 159 and 160. San Francisco dumped the Padres twice, 4-3 and 2-1. Ted was 1-for-5 and 0-for-3. *(Los Angeles Times, September 5, 1937)* 384 AB, 109 H, 20 HR, .284

GAME 161. 10,000 kids, guests of manager Lefty O'Doul, watched the Seals beat San Diego, 6-4, in San Francisco. Ted Williams was 1-for-5. The reeling Padres fell 2 1/2 games behind the league-leading Solons. *(ET, September 6, 1937)* 389 AB, 110 H, 20 HR, .283

GAMES 162 and 163. The Seals made it six in a row over San Diego as they swept a Labor Day doubleheader, 11-2, and 2-1. Ted Williams went 3-for-4 in the first and 2-for-4 in the nightcap. One of Ted's hits was a triple. *(Los Angeles Times, September 7, 1937)* 397 AB, 115 H, 20 HR, .290

GAME 164. The Padres lost their seventh straight as Los Angeles took the series opener, 7-2, in San Diego. Williams was 1-for-4. "Ted Williams' infield out and Berkowitz's single scored Detore to end the rally." *(Keller, ET, September 8, 1937)* 401 AB, 116 H, 20 HR, .289

GAME 165. Chaplin Wins 23rd Game; Padre Slump Ends With 5-1 Triumph; Two Games Today. "Durst whiffed, but George Detore came through with a double to score both runners, and Ted Williams' single tallied Detore and spoiled the afternoon for Flowers. Lieber came in.

"Everything went well for Lieber until Thompson kissed a fastball on the nose in the fifth and put it over the right field fence. Williams, first up in the sixth, duplicated the feat to end the day's scoring." Ted was 3-for-4. *(Keller, ET, September 9, 1937)* 405 AB, 119 H, 21 HR, .294

GAMES 166 and 167. Padres Drop 2 Tilts; Tied With Seals. The Angels collected 32 hits and a pair of victories in an unusual Thursday twin bill with the Padres at Lane Field, 11-7 and 9-2. Ted was 3-for-5 with a double in the opener and 0-for-4 in the night game. *(Evening Tribune and Los Angeles Times, September 10, 1937)* 414 AB, 122 H, 21 HR, .295

GAME 168. The Padres nipped the Angels, 4-3. Ted Williams had one hit in five at-bats. "Goerge Myatt, who is hitting like the Myatt of old again, singled over third, and two infield outs put him on third, from where he tallied when Ted Williams drove a terrific single into right." *(Keller, ET, September 11, 1937)* 419 AB, 123 H, 21 HR, .294

Base Hits. "Official figures from William McGee, Pacific Coast League statistician, show Tommy Thompson, right fielder, still is leading the Padres at bat with a mark of .337. Leo Moriarty, who figures averages for the news services, is wrong on many of the averages according to McGee's figures, which are official. Moriarty had George Detore leading Thompson in his figures this week, but Detore is second with a mark of .333." *(Keller, ET, September 11, 1937)*

GAME 169. Wally Hebert Shuts Out Seraphs, 5-0. Ted Williams had a single in four at-bats. *(Los Angeles Times, September 12, 1937)* 423 AB, 124 H, 21 HR, .293

GAMES 170 and 171. Padres Divide Series With Angels, Ward Hurls 8-3 Win as San Diego Gains Even Break in Two Contests; Local Club Takes 59 Home Games. After losing the opener 5-2, the Padres came back to take the nightcap in the final home doubleheader. Ted Williams was 1-for-4 in the first game and 2-for-3 in the second. "Ted Williams cracked out home run No. 22 of the season in the second inning (of the first game. In the second game) William (sic) singled in one run and George McDonald also singled to send in two more." *(Keller, Evening Tribune and Los Angeles Times, September 13, 1937)* 430 AB, 127 H, 22 HR, .295

GAME 172. The Missions beat San Diego, 3-2 in 11 innings in San Francisco. Ted was 1-for-4. *(ET, September 15, 1937)* 434 AB, 128 H, 22 HR, .295

GAME 173. Ted Williams was hitless in four at-bats and the Mission Reds again beat the San Diego Padres, 6-3. *(Los Angeles Times, September 16, 1937)* 438 AB, 128 H, 22 HR, .292

GAME 174. The Missions made it three in a row over faltering San Diego, 4-3. Ted was 0-for-2. *(ET, September 17, 1937)* 440 AB, 128 H, 22 HR, .291

GAME 175. Hebert Takes Mound Duel From Mission Hurler, 4-2. Ted went 0-for-2 again. *(ET, September 18, 1937)* 442 AB, 128 H, 22 HR, .290

GAME 176. Padres take Mound Duel; Salvo Beats Nitcholas as San Diego Wins From Missions, 2 to 1. Ted Williams went 0-for-4. *(Los Angeles Times, September 19, 1937)* 446 AB, 128 H, 22 HR, .287

GAMES 177 and 178. Padres Lose Twice to Reds: Lowly Missions Club Ball to Topple San Diego, 5-2, 5-4. Ted Williams had three hits in four at-bats in the first game and 1-for-4 in the nightcap. In his last game, Ted Williams' last hit as a Coast Leaguer in regular season play was a home run. *(Los Angeles Times, September 20, 1937)* 454 AB, 132 H, 23 HR, .291

POOL LEADS COAST BATTERS FOR YEAR

"According to unofficial figures, Harlan Pool, of Seattle, led the Pacific Coast league in hitting during the 1937 season, which closed yesterday. His unofficial average for the year was .336, two points better than George Detore, San Diego catcher.

"During the year, Pool collected 153 hits in 458 times up, while Detore his safely 145 times in 434 trips. Two points behind Detore was Marvin Gudat, Los Angeles outfielder, with 206 hits in 621 trips. *(Evening Tribune, September 20, 1937)*

(As a matter of fact, if the person who compiled the above unofficial statistics had done his math just one more time, he would have realized that George Detore actually had the higher batting average: Detore .33410; Pool .33406.)

Coast Sluggers In Close Finish; Padre Is Leader. The following day, the AP list of unofficial batting statistics appeared which correctly computer the Detore and Pool averages. Ted Williams was shown to finish the year with a .300 batting average based on 132 hits in 454 at-bats. (132 divided by 454 equals .291.) The official statistics in the 1938 *Spalding Official Base Ball Guide* agree that Ted had 132 hits in 454 at-bats. His batting average was .291 and he hit 23 home runs.

THE PLAYOFFS

Playoff Game 1. Jim Chaplin Hurls 6-4 Padre Win; Williams Gets 4 Hits as Sacs Fall In Opener. Ted had a triple, a double and two singles in five at-bats. Chaplin pitched a complete game. *(Evening Tribune, September 22, 1937)* 5 AB, 4 H, 0 HR, .800

Playoff Game 2. San Diego Again Sinks Solons; Salvo Holds Sacramento To 4 Blows. Ted was 0-for-3. Salvo pitched a complete game. *(Evening Tribune, September 23, 1937)* 8 AB, 4 H, 0 HR, .500

Playoff Game 3. Beavers, Padres Need Only One Game To Clinch Place in Finals. Williams went 0-for-5, but San Diego won, 6-1. Rupert Thompson hit a home run and Ward pitched a complete game. *(Evening Tribune, September 24, 1937)* 13 AB, 4 H, 0 HR, .308

Playoff Game 4. Wally Hebert To Hurl First Game Against Portland '9'; Solons Tamed by Jim Chaplin, Out of Flag Race. "Ted Williams had put the Padres out in front in the fourth by hitting one of Tony Freitas' curve balls over the right field wall." Williams was 2-for-4. Chaplin pitched a complete game. *(Keller, Evening Tribune, September 27, 1937)* 17 AB, 6 H, 1 HR, .353

PADRES BEGIN TITLE SERIES AS FAVORITES

"The many followers of young Ted Williams, Padre outfielder, look for the youth to break up at least two games in this series with home runs and lead the Padres to the pennant. Williams has hit Portland pitching with great consistency in the past and it's going to be hard stopping him now. Tommy Thompson is another Padre who relishes Portland pitching."
(Keller, Evening Tribune, *September 28, 1937)*

Championship Game 1. Two Homers By Flyhawk Decide Game. Which flyhawk? Rupert "Tommy" Thompson accounted for every Padre run in a 10-inning, 4-3, conquest of Portland at Lane Field. His three run shot gave San Diego a 3-1 lead in the bottom of the third inning. The game was later decided by his solo shot in the tenth. Williams was 0-4. Wally Hebert pitched a complete game. *(Keller,* Evening Tribune, *September 29, 1937)* 21 AB, 6 H, 1 HR, .286

Championship Game 2. Ward Hurls San Diego to 2nd Win. San Diego won 3-1. "Ted Williams was the batting hero. Bill Posedel silenced the big bat of Tommy Thompson, but Williams cracked out three singles in four times up and batted in the winning tallies... Williams again touched Posedel for a single and Patchett walked home... Ted Williams and Tommy Thompson who hit Portland pitching with ease in 1937 season play, have both been the batting stars of the games to date. Tommy won the opener with two homers and Williams dealt the damaging blows yesterday. He collected three singles and batted in the second and third runs." Ward pitched a complete game. *(Keller,* Evening Tribune, *September 30, 1937)* 25 AB, 9 H, 1 HR, .360

Championship Game 3. Beavers Are Beaten 5 To 1 Under Stars. Thompson hit another home run and Ted was 1-for-3. Salvo pitched a complete game. *(*Evening Tribune, *October 1, 1937)* 29 AB, 10 H, 1 HR, .349

Championship Game 4. Padres Take Title; San Diego '9' Takes Eight Tilts In Row. Rupert Thompson hit his fifth home run of the playoffs as the Padres swept the Beavers n Portland, 6 to 4. Ted had one hit in four at-bats. Hebert pitched a complete game. Incredibly, the Tribune article about the game was written by the Associated Press. Ted Williams went 1-for-4. *(*Evening Tribune, *October 4, 1937)* 33 AB, 11 H, 1 HR, .333

Ted Williams Bought By Red Sox; San Diego Figures In Ball Deal. "Go on, you're kidding me," Williams told the *Tribune* yesterday after he had been informed that the Red Sox had bought him. "Boy, this is the happiest day of my life. If the Red Sox give me a chance, I'll make good. I'm going to keep myself in fine shape this winter so I will be able to impress my new bosses in Spring Training." *(Paul Mickelson,* Evening Tribune, *December 8, 1937)*

Padres Obtain Five New Ball Players. "Lane said he had three other players in addition to the two who will come here from the boston (sic) Red Sox in the Ted Williams deal... Lane denied that the Yankees had offered $35,000 for Williams." *(Keller,* Evening Tribune, *December 13, 1937)*

Farley's Defeat Gold Club, 10-4, to Break Even. "Ted Williams had knotted the count at 2-all for the Clubmen in the fourth by hitting one of the longest homers ever seen at Monroe Field." *(Keller,* Evening Tribune, *January 3, 1938)*

"(Al) Niemiec and (Dominic) Dallessandro came to the Padres from the Boston Red Sox in the Ted Williams deal." *(Keller,* Evening Tribune, *January 4, 1938)*

"Niemiec and Dallessandro came to the Padres in the Ted Williams deal and Griffiths' (sic) was purchased from Little Rock." *(Keller,* Evening Tribune, *February 1, 1938)*

TED WILLIAMS STILL ON OUTSIDE, LOOKING IN

"Unless Bill Lane, owner of the San Diego Padres, sends Mr. and Mrs. S. S. Williams a check for $5,000, Ted Williams who helped bring a pennant to this baseball mad town in 1937, will not play for the Boston Red Sox this year.

"Eddie Collins, general manager of the Red Sox, was told so much by Mrs. Williams yesterday. Collins made a special trip here from Los Angeles to attempt to get Williams in line for the 1938 season but he departed without a signed contract.

"'The next move is up to the Williams family,' Collins told the newspapermen. 'The Red Sox are stymied. The 'war' really is between Mr. Lane and the Williams, and there isn't a thing the Red Sox can do.'

"'I hate to think that Williams' career might be ruined because of money. The lad has a brilliant future and, in my opinion, he's "one in a million." He has all the chance in the world to become a great player and I know he will. I have done all I can and I feel everything will turn out okay.'

"Both Lane and Collins say Williams has been treated exceptionally well. 'He's getting a break that many youths would like to get,' they said.

"Williams' 1938 contract calls for a salary of $3000. Collins even went so far as to offer Williams a 2-year contract, calling for a $1500 raise in 1939. Even if Williams didn't impress Manager Joe Cronin in Spring Training, he would be carried with the Red Sox club all season.

"If Williams' name is not on a contract by opening day of the 1938 American league race, he will be place on the suspended list and his case will be sent to Judge K. M. Landis, high commissioner of baseball.

"The Williams family faces a slim chance of getting $5000 from Lane as part of the sales price which the Red Sox paid him for Williams. Lane declared Ted has been treated squarely and he has intimated he will NOT give Williams a penny of the sales price.

"Williams is supposed to depart for the Red Sox training camp in Florida next week, but the way matters look now, he'll not be leaving. There is absolutely no chance of Williams signing until Lane comes through with a check, Mrs. Williams told baseball scribes.

"Lane is not bound by any contract to give Williams any of the sales price. Mrs. Williams says Lane made a verbal promise to give Ted a check if and when he sold him, but the Padres owner denies this.

"Mrs. Williams also says Lane did not fulfil (sic) his promise to send Ted to college. Lane asked young Williams in front of newspapermen yesterday if he hadn't offered to keep his promise to send him through college.

'Yes, you did, Mr. Lane,' Williams answeredf (sic), 'but I told you I had enough of school and I wanted to hunt.'

"A baseball rule prohibits players or managers from getting a cut of the sales price, Lane informed the newspaper writers.

"Many fans here are of the opinion the Williams family should forget the $5000 and send in the signed contract. It's not every day a 19-year-old boy gets a chance such has (sic) been handed Ted's way.

"Collins wasn't too wrapped up in the Williams case to talk about the Red Sox chances in the American league race this year. 'Boston will have a young, hustling club that should finish in the first division, or I miss my guess,' the man who handles Tom Yawkey's millions said.

"Asked if Bobby Doerr, former San Diego player, had a chance of playing regularly this year, Collins said Doerr would be given every chance to make good. The ball chief was high on the lad.

"When the question, 'Do you think the Red Sox can beat the Yankees this year?' was fired at him, Collins said, 'I wish I could answer that truthfully, but I can't. Anything is liable to happen, and you can bet the Red Sox will be in there giving it their best.'" *(Earl Keller,* Evening Tribune, *February 16, 1938)*

WILLIAMS LEAVES FOR FLORIDA NEXT WEEK

Evening Tribune Sports Editor Tom Akers wrote two columns following the impasse story. In the first, he paraphrased Keller's article and suggested that Ted should sign. Two days later, Williams was reported bound for Florida. According to Akers, Collins compromised and gave a $2500 bonus. *(Evening Tribune, February 17 & 19, 1938)*

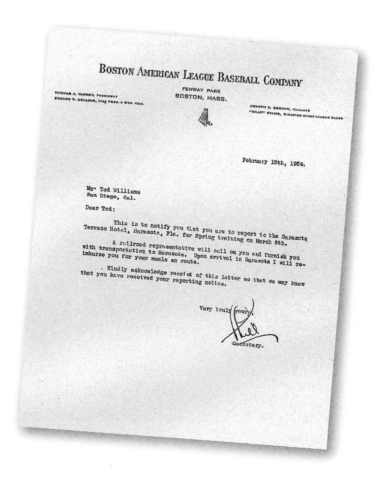

Williams, happy with the Millers, 1938

THE KID LEAVES HOME:
TED WILLIAMS AND THE 1938 MINNEAPOLIS MILLERS
by James D. Smith III

The day after Ted Williams' passing on July 5, 2002, the *Minneapolis Star Tribune* front page picked up an article by Bob Hohler of the *Boston Globe*. It included the following: "Ted Williams, the graceful and strong-willed athlete who was recognized as the greatest baseball hitter who ever lived, died Friday at 83... His professional baseball career began in 1938 with a season as a member of the minor league Minneapolis Millers, but he moved up to the Red Sox in 1939 and was an instant success..."

Those familiar with the great slugger's story will readily recall that he turned pro in 1936, signed out of San Diego's Hoover High School by "Hardrock" Bill Lane, owner of the new, home-town San Diego Padres (PCL). In my September 24, 1989 interview with Ted, found in Bill Swank's fine book, *Echoes from Lane Field* (1997), he called San Diego "the nicest little town in the world". And one can only imagine the choice words he would offer in response to yet another sports writer's blunder.

The front page gaffe, however, raises an interesting point. In the baseball literature, several accounts of Ted's professional career have understandably focused on issues of "How did he start?" and "Where did he star?" That framing of the story makes his 1938 season with the Minneapolis Millers only a parenthesis in an exciting "coast to coast" move. The purpose of this paper is to take a closer look at that remarkable year, outlining some reasons why Ted himself (in print and to this writer) felt that seasoning in Minnesota played a vital role in his professional and personal development.

How did he end up spending the 1938 season with the Millers? Williams' own foundational account (referenced throughout this essay) is given in his autobiography, *My Turn at Bat* (1969). It narrates Red Sox general manager Eddie Collins' visit to San Diego as part of his December, 1937 purchase from the Padres for a reported $35,000 (plus Dom Dallesandro and Al Niemiec, later Spencer Harris. Some accounts place the figure at $25,000.) Some time earlier, Collins had been present to look at Bobby Doerr and George Myatt, on whom the Sox had options. Advising Lane of his club's picking up

Ted's APBA membership card, 1937.

Doerr only, he noticed the skinny, left-handed outfielder Williams in batting practice, and the old Hall of Famer wisely secured an option on his contact. Later, during Collins' off-season visit to the Williams home, he cemented the deal with Ted's parents, May and Sam.

When Spring Training of 1938 arrived, the teenager borrowed $200 to make the Florida trip. Doerr, who had enjoyed a strong rookie year with the Sox in '37, used ham radio operators in Los Angeles to ask Ted to meet him en route for the cross-country adventure, as floods had impaired Southern California train travel and communications. Finally connecting in Indio, and driving east with Babe Herman and Max West, they were ten days late arriving in Sarasota. As Williams recalled, "I lasted about a week... I thought they were all wonderful, all the guys, and to them I was probably as cocky a kid as they'd ever seen."

In March, prior to a Sox exhibition trip to Tampa, manager Joe Cronin made the anticipated decision to send "The Kid" to Daytona Beach, where the Red Sox' Minneapolis farm team was training. The teenager's farewell words to clubhouse man Johnny Orlando have been variously quoted: "Tell 'em I'll be back, and make more money than all three of them (Cramer, Vosmik and Chapman) put together."

Though initially upset by his reassignment, Williams (in his autobiography) later summed up his 1938 experience with the Millers: "I have so many good memories of that year with Minneapolis." Here are several of the reasons:

1) He enjoyed his first breakthrough season. Following a solid 1937 campaign with the Padres, the Splinter's American Association marks are striking:

AVG	G	AB	R	H	2B	3B	HR	RB1	TB	BB	SO	SLG	OBP	SB	POS	RECOG
.366	148	528	130	193	30	9	43	142	370	114	75	.701	.451	6	rf	All Star

On Opening Day, the newcomer tallied a home run, two singles and four runs batted in. In Ted's words, "I hit well, really up to standard for the first time in professional ball." He was elected to the AA All-Star team, with teammate LeRoy "Bud" Parmelee (a pitcher, who went 17-13), on his way to winning the league's first Triple Crown. At a high level of competition, his personal dreams and self-promotion were now being matched by his production.

Radio station giveaway premium, 1938 Minneapolis Millers team.

2) He was tutored by Rogers Hornsby. The Rajah ("Get a good ball to hit") had concluded his Hall of Fame (.358) playing career, and was traveling. In 1938 he coached for a time in Baltimore (IL) and, beginning in July, managed the Chattanooga (SA) team to season's end. But while in Spring Training (and even during the season), he was drawn to where the action was – and that included personal time with a promising student. "I liked Hornsby because he talked to me, a kid of nineteen, and boy I picked his brains for everything I could. We'd talk hitting... Every day I'd stay out after practice with Hornsby and maybe one or two others who wanted extra hitting."

3) He was managed by Donie Bush. To this day, longtime Twin Cities baseball fans draw from a rich oral tradition to describe their relationship. The favorite exchange is that between Bush and longtime Millers owner Mike ("Williams is my meal ticket") Kelly. Driven to the edge by Ted's antics and temperament (slapping his rump and yelling "Hi Ho Silver" chasing fly balls, furiously putting his fist through a bloodied water cooler, swinging imaginary bats in the outfield, errors of mind and mitt), Bush essentially said, "It's Williams or me," to which Kelly replied, "Gee, we'd miss you, Donie." Reflecting back on the experience, Ted recalled, "I had a wonderful manager, who put up with me... a lovable little tiger" – and, like his Padres mentor Frank Shellenback, a dedicated, veteran baseball man.

At least once in the early going when Williams threatened to leave the team, Bush's realistic review of the options gave him a new resolve. "Donie Bush got so he could get to me with a little psychology."

4) He entered a great baseball tradition. Unlike San Diego, Minneapolis' experience with first-rate minor league ball went back a half-century. As chronicled in Stew Thornley's *On to Nicollet* (1988), the "Millers" formed as the grain mill city's first professional team, members of the Northwestern League, in 1884. That same year, across the river, St. Paul fielded an entry in the ill-fated Union Association. The area is represented in the 1880's "Old Judge" baseball card series. Each Minnesota spring, fans with knowledge often matching their enthusiasm would gather at the ballpark, and some great sluggers were part of the folklore: Perry Werden, Gavvy Cravath (San Diego's own), Nick Cullop, Joe Hauser, Buzz Arlett, et al. Ted many times reflected on his awareness of that tradition, and his place in it. I was personally touched when one of our conversations brought up "Unser Choe," and he wanted the old slugger's phone number in Sheboygan to call him up and express appreciation. Wearing the red "M" was a sign of distinction.

Ted swinging as a Miller.

5) He played at Nicollet Park. "I was always jawing with somebody in that little park in Minneapolis. Not only the fans, but the guy in the scoreboard, which was right behind me in right field." Phil Lowry's *Green Cathedrals* (1986) records some vital statistics: 279 feet down the right field line and 328 feet to right center, with a 30 foot wooden fence. Ted's left-handed pull hitting – a natural groove encouraged by Lane Field's sea breezes – was perfected and richly rewarded at cozy Nicollet. The inviting target was no longer Pacific Highway but Nicollet Avenue. Of Ted's 43 home runs, 24 came at home. Despite the team's disappointing 78-74 record, the support was enthusiastic: "The town was mine, and I loved it".

6) He discovered a lighter bat. In the hot and humid Midwest summertime, traveling and playing games each day, and on base almost half the time (he called it "swing and sweat" baseball), the slender Williams began to wear out. One muggy August night in Columbus, he picked up one of teammate Stan Spence's bats: "What a toothpick, lightest bat in the rack. It had a bigger barrel than mine, but was lighter by two ounces at least... Real pumpkin wood, but it felt good in my hands. It made me feel strong." Ted thought over the discovery, and used lighter bats later in the year – sometimes down to 31 ounces. Thereafter, he would swing the heavier wooden models earlier in the season while feeling strong, then lighten up as the season progressed. Hillerich and Bradsby received their special instructions.

7) He enjoyed a friendly press. Richard Ben Cramer, in his *Ted Williams: The Seasons of the Kid* (1991), summarized that memorable 1938 season. "In Minneapolis, he'd led the league in everything: average, home runs, runs batted in, runs scored, screwball stunts and ink consumed." A longtime friend of mine, and Minnesota baseball fan, Lee Johnson provided me his childhood scrapbook for informal study. In it, press clippings hail "the Millers' youthful home run slugger" congratulating teammates, frames of his swing as "Ted follows through perfectly," Williams pictured giving an exclusive interview to a giggling "Little Betty Samuelson, the girl reporter" on a caring visit to Glen Lake Sanitarium, and #19 (a carry-over from Padre days) crushing one in a packed ballpark with the caption, "Ted Tees Off." While his ears inevitably would pick up a single leather-lung in the crowd, the public imagination was captured by the teenager. Williams, a lifelong friend of San Diego sports writer Earl Keller, continued healthy relations with the press until his contentious Boston reception: "Before this, I was willing to believe a writer was my friend until he proved otherwise."

Ted and Doris Soule, back from hunting.

8) He found a taste of home in Minnesota. Williams carried memories of his 1938 season with him to the big leagues, and after his rookie year with the Red Sox, the southern California boy chose to spend the winter of 1939-40 in Minnesota. "It had always been a struggle at home (in San Diego), the tension, my father and mother never really together, my brother always in some kind of scrape." So Ted took a $5 room at the King Cole Hotel in downtown Minneapolis, traveled west to hunt mallards, north to fish for walleyes at Lake Mille Lacs, out to the city park rinks to learn ice skating, and enjoyed the heated hotel pool as well. "A lot of things I did by myself. I went to the movies a lot." He also began courting the daughter of a hunting guide from Princeton, Minnesota, Doris Soule, who a few years later (during World War II duty), would become his wife.

9) He left behind a legacy. When Williams joined the Red Sox to stay in 1939, at camp in Sarasota with Millers teammates Spencer and Jim Tabor, he left behind a lasting cadre of fans. Five players hit over 20 home runs for Minneapolis that year, but none rivaled Ted in the popular imagination. Bush resigned to become manager and part owner of the Louisville Colonels. My good friend and long time Millers fan, Alvin Anderson, remembers with fondness the 1930s "when we cheered while Ted and Joe Hauser rattled a lot of fences." The dean of Minnesota sport writers today is the *Star Tribune*'s Sid Hartman, who first met Williams while a teenager selling papers at Nicollet Park: "He bought a new car while he was here and once took me for a ride on Wayzata Boulevard. We must have been going 100 miles per hour... The only Millers' player who compared to Williams was Willie Mays... (Ted) was a great story teller and a great friend and an unbelievable character."

The last word here belongs to Hall of Famer Bobby Doerr who, in a recent (3/19/03) conversation with me, reflected on his longtime friend. "Ted really enjoyed that year in Minnesota, and went back many times. He liked the outdoors – hunting birds (especially in the wintertime), all that water to fish, and so on. Of course he met Doris there, too. There was a big difference in Ted between San Diego in 1936 and Minneapolis after '38. Some of it was just physically 'filling out'... but the experiences he gained and baseball knowledge he picked up had a big effect. He always remembered: 'Get a good pitch to hit.' You hear so much about that ballpark in Minneapolis, but when Ted got ahold of one it really didn't matter where the fence was. Off the field, he did some really nice things in Boston, too – but so many of those people were looking for a different story... He was a great ballplayer, but also a wonderful person just to be with. We all miss him a lot."

TED WILLIAMS (#19) WITH THE 1938 MINNEAPOLIS MILLERS
by Stew Thornley

Ted Williams was sent to the Minneapolis Millers by the Red Sox out of Spring Training on March 20, 1938. Dick Hackenberg, writing in the *Star* a few days later, declared, "Williams is tickled to death to be with the Millers, especially so be under the tutelage of Donie Bush, talks a blue streak, wants to know all about Minneapolis and Minnesota, when the duck hunting season opens, the fishing', would like to get his hands on the guy that started this 'second DiMaggio business.'"
[Minneapolis Star, March 24, 1938]

Though Williams hit just .276 for the Millers in Spring Training, and went hitless for his first three games once the season opened, he broke out with a bang in Louisville. Rogers Hornsby was the team's Spring Training hitting instructor and "Rajah" impressed on Ted the phrase that became his watchword: "Get a good pitch to hit."

Ted wanted to take another shot at pitching, but Donie Bush kept him off the mound, and tried to keep his mind on the game. There were several instances in which Ted failed to run out a ball, booted a ball in the field, lost a fly ball in the sun, etc. He did keep his mind on hitting, though, and Ted was one of just two unanimous picks for the American Association All-Star Game. Roy Parmelee was the only other Miller chosen.

	AB	R	H	RBI	
April					
16, at Indianapolis	5	0	0	0	
17	4	0	0	0	
18	3	0	0	1	
19, at Louisville	1	2	1	1	Williams walks 5 times, tying A.A. mark
20	5	1	2	2	double
21	4	2	3	2	Ted hits not one, but TWO inside-the-park home runs*
22, at Columbus	5	1	1	1	double
23	6	0	1	0	
24	5	0	2	1	
25, at Toledo	5	1	1	0	double
26	5	1	1	1	HR (#3)
27	4	0	2	0	double
29 Louisville	4	3	3	3	HR (4) long HR to right; lands on roof of building across Nicollet Avenue
30	3	0	1	0	

	AB	R	H	RBI	
May					
1	6	2	3	6	two doubles, two HRs (5 & 6)
3 rain					
4 rain					
5 rain					
6 rain					
7 rain					
8 rain					
8 rain					
9 rain					
10, Columbus	2	1	0	0	
11	4	1	2	1	HR (7)
12, St. Paul	4	2	1	1	HR (8)
13, at St. Paul	2	2	1	1	
14, St. Paul	4	2	1	0	
15, at St. Paul	4	1	1	0	
17, rain					
18, rain					
19, rain					
20, Kansas City	3	0	1	1	triple
21	4	1	2	0	
22	4	3	2	3	HR (9) 2-run HR in bottom of 11th for 10-9 win
22	2	1	1	0	
23, at Milwaukee	3	1	1	1	HR (10)
24	3	0	0	0	
25	2	0	1	2	double
26, at Kansas City	3	1	1	1	HR (11)
27	4	0	0		
28 did not play / stiff neck					
29 did not play / stiff neck					
30 did not play / stiff neck (in first game)					
30, at St. Paul	3	1	2	1	HR (12) on top of Coliseum roof

	AB	R	H	RBI	
June					
1, at Toledo	5	2	2	1	HR (13), triple
2	4	1	1	1	
3, at Columbus	4	0	1	1	
4	3	3	2	4	two HRs (14 & 15)
5, at Louisville	2	1	1	0	
5	4	0	2	2	double in 9th drives in winning run
6	2	0	1	0	
7, at Indianapolis	5	1	2	5	HR (16) as of June 7, Ted had homered in every park in the American Association
8	5	1	1	0	
9	4	1	1	1	triple
11, St. Paul	4	1	1	0	double
12, at St. Paul	4	1	2	1	HR (17), double
13, Toledo	3	2	1	0	double
14, Columbus	4	0	1	0	
15 rain, wet grounds					
16, Columbus	3	1	3	0	double
17, Toledo	3	2	2	2	double
17	5	3	3	3	two HRs (18 & 19)

	AB	R	H	RBI	
June					
18	4	1	1	3	
19, Indianapolis	4	1	1	1	HR (21), hitting streak extended to 21 games
19	2	1	1	0	
20	4	0	0	0	
20	3	1	2	1	HR (22)
21, Louisville	2	1	1	0	
22	3	1	1	0	
23, at Kansas City	4	1	2	3	triple
24	3	2	1	1	triple
25, at Milwaukee	4	0	0	0	
26	4	0	2	0	
27, Kansas City	5	0	1	0	
28	1	1	1	0	
29, Milwaukee	5	1	2	3	double
29	4	1	1	0	
30	4	1	2	1	double

	AB	R	H	RBI	
July					
1, at St. Paul	2	1	1	0	
2	3	1	1	2	
3, St. Paul	3	1	0	0	
4, at St. Paul	4	0	0	0	
4, St. Paul rain					
6, at Louisville	4	1	1	1	triple
7	4	0	1	0	
8, at Indianapolis	5	0	1	0	
9	5	0	1	1	double
10, at Toledo	3	2	2	3	HR (23), double
10	5	1	1	0	
11	4	1	1	1	triple
12, at Columbus	4	1	2	2	two doubles
13	5	2	3	4	grand slam HR (24), double
14 ****	4	0	1	0	** American Association All Star Game **
15, St. Paul	3	0	0	2	
16, Louisville	4	0	3	0	
17	4	1	1	1	HR (25)
17	3	0	1	0	
18, Indianapolis	5	2	2	1	HR (26)
19	4	1	1	1	HR (27)
20	3	0	0	0	
20	3	1	1	0	
21, Toledo	2	0	1	0	
22	5	1	2	1	HR (28)
22	3	1	2	0	double
23	3	0	2	2	
24, Columbus	3	1	1	3	HR (29)
24	3	1	3	2	
25	4	1	2	1	
26, Milwaukee	4	0	2	0	
27	3	1	1	0	
28	4	3	2	2	HR (30)
28	4	1	1	1	HR (31)

	AB	R	H	RBI	
29, Kansas City	2	0	1	0	double
30 rain					
31, at St. Paul	5	0	1	0	

	AB	R	H	RBI	
August					
1, St. Paul	5	2	2	2	HR (32)
2, at St. Paul	4	0	2	0	
3, at Milwaukee	2	1	2	4	double, beaned in 5th, taken out of game
4 did not play					
5 rain					
6, at Kansas City	4	1	2	4	HR (33), double
7	4	0	1	0	
7	3	1	2	2	HR (34)
8	4	1	1	4	HR (35) grand slam
9, St. Paul	5	0	1	2	
10, at St. Paul	3	0	1	0	
11, at Toledo	3	2	1	0	
12	4	0	2	0	
13	5	2	3	0	double
14, at Columbus	4	2	3	0	double
14	3	0	0	0	
15	3	1	0	0	
16, at Columbus	4	1	2	1	HR (36)
17 rain					
18, at Louisville	4	1	2	1	HR (37)
18	4	1	1	3	HR (38)
19	4	0	1	0	
20, at Indianapolis	4	1	1	0	
21	3	1	1	1	
21	3	0	1	0	
22, Louisville	3	0	1	2	triple
23	4	0	1	0	
24	3	1	2	1	HR (29)
25, Indianapolis	3	1	1	0	double
26	4	1	2	0	double
26	3	2	2	4	HR (40), double
27, Toledo	2	2	2	5	HB (41) home run cleared buildings on Nicollet Avenue and landed in alley between Nicollet and 1st Avenue
28	1	2	0	0	
28	3	0	1	1	
29, Columbus	2	1	1	0	
30	4	2	3	2	
30	1	1	0	0	
31, at Kansas City	3	1	1	0	

	AB	R	H	RBI	
September					
1	3	0	0	0	
2, at Milwaukee	4	1	2	0	
2	2	1	1	0	
3	4	0	0	0	
4, St. Paul	4	1	1	0	double
5, St. Paul	4	0	2	0	double
5, at St. Paul	4	0	1	0	
6 rain					
7, Kansas City	3	1	0	0	
7	4	1	1	0	
8 rain					
8 rain					
9 rain					
10, Milwaukee	4	0	1	1	
10	3	2	2	2	HR (42)
11	4	1	4	4	HR (43)
11	2	0	1	0	

G	AB	R	H	2B	3B	HR	RBI	TB	AVG.
148	528	130	193	30	9	43	142	370	.366

won American Association Triple Crown, also leading the league in runs and total bases

* In an article for the *Minneapolis Journal*, George Barton estimated the two home runs to have traveled 470 and 512 feet, the latter having rolled right to the base of the 512' sign on the fence in dead center field.

All data compiled by Stew Thornley.

A SELECTION OF SPORTSWRITING COVERING TED'S 1938 SEASON
by Bill Nowlin

March 1938, Ted Williams to Joe McGlone of the *Providence Bulletin*: "Don't be surprised if you see me back with the Sox before next July... I'll rattle those fences in the American Association."

Writing about Bill Lane's prospects for the 1938 San Diego Padres: Bill is determined to go after another big gate in 1938. He kept the majority of his popular players – though he did peddle Ted Williams, 19-year-old idol of the San Diego fans, for $25,000 and the draft speared Rupert Thompson, who led the league in hitting until a late–season slump shrunk his average like a woolen sock.

Incidentally, in connection with Ted Williams, there was some grumbling by Spider Baum, secretary of the San Diego team, and others, when the Red Sox sent Ted to Minneapolis for seasoning. They thought he should have been left with his mammy club, a la Lefty Gomez, Lyn Lary, Joe DiMaggio and some of the other boys the Yanks allowed to stick in San Francisco after purchasing them from the Seals. Teammates and other Coast league players, however, say that it will be good for Williams to be in another league, because of the pampering resulting from the fact he's a San Diego kid and that his adoring relatives were a very appreciable element in his rooting section.
J. G. Taylor Spink, "Three and One – Looking them Over with J. G. Taylor Spink," The Sporting News, *March 31, 1938.*

unidentified San Diego newspaper clipping: Williams was a great kid player in our loop, but he didn't find favor in the eyes of the *Boston Post*'s Bill Cunningham, who observed: "The axe dropped on the voluble Californian, Ted Williams, who silently packed his bag and took the bus across state to join in with Minneapolis in its Daytona Beach camp. 'Sent to the minors for more seasoning' is the official term used, and it's right in his case. A tall, gawky kid, but 19 years of age, really just out of high school and coming from the Coast with a reputation as a slugger, he couldn't even pound the batting practice pitching here and, according to the Cronin-Pennock-Daley-Duffy board of strategy, he likewise needs some polishing in his fielding.

"If things work the way the Sox are hoping, he'll wise up beautifully through a season in the west and return here next year a powerful outfielder. They seem to think he's just cocky enough and just gabby enough to make a great and colorful outfielder, possibly of the Babe Herman type. Me? I don't like the way he stands at the plate. He bends his front knee inward and moves his foot just before he takes his swing. That's exactly what I do before I drive a golf ball, and, knowing what happens to the golf balls that I drive, I don't believe this kid will ever hit half a Singer midget's weight in a bathing suit."

Paced by the slugging of Ted Williams and Jim Galvin, and the strong-armed pitching of Bud Parmelee, the Millers opened the 1938 season in auspicious fashion at Nicollet park Friday afternoon by smothering the Louisville Colonels under a 14 to 4 score...

[Fans] saw Ted Williams, the 19-year-old sensation from the Pacific coast, wallop a tremendous home run that reminded them of the circuit smashes Joe Hauser used to pole during the years he wore a Minneapolis uniform and became the king of home run hitters in organized baseball by belting 69 in 1933. They also saw the youngster get two singles in two previous times at bat, walk once, drive in four runs and score three times himself...

The fans almost lost sight of the ball as it sailed through the air and landed on the roof of a building on the far side of Nicollet avenue.

George A. Barton, *"Williams, Galvin, Parmelee Shine in the Nicollet Opener,"* Minneapolis Tribune

Guess who's been nominated "the screwball king of the American Association."
Our own Ted Williams! This dubious honor has been conferred on the San Diego youngster now with Minneapolis, by sports writers throughout the A.A. circuit.

Ted, you'll remember, supposedly was farmed out to the Millers by the Red Sox because he called the manager, Joe Cronin, a "grandstander."

Ed Prell, sports editor of the Scripps-Howard *Toledo News Bee*, queried Donie Bush, Minneapolis manager, on the matter and Donie answered: "I never heard of it if he did. He's really a good kid, but he's awfully childish. I think he'll get over it. The main fault I find with the kid is that he's not really ready half the time at the plate."

Prell also reported an incident that occurred in a Minneapolis-Toledo game a few hours after Prell's talk with Bush. Teddy was perched on second base. He had just knocked the boards loose on the right field wall for a double. Manager Bush was coaching at third.

"If it's a ground ball to third or short, stay on second," Bush yelled at the youngster. "Say, you pay attention to the hitter and I'll do the running,' Williams cracked back.

"Why, you fresh busher so and so," Donie exploded.

Screwball or not, Williams has impressed many an old baseball head since he went East. Rogers Hornsby... said of him, "He'll be the sensation of the major leagues in three years."

Ted still has his old habit of fidgeting, both at the plate and afield, I understand. When he first broke in with the Padres, I remember, he used to hold dummy batting practice in left field during a ball-game. A gangling, loose-limbed fellow with a nonchalant air, who appears as if he's a bit bored with the proceedings, Williams naturally gives one the screwball impression. He is a bit of the natural clown, built as long as he can shatter those fences, he can do a lot of things and get away with them.

The boy, I think, has that intangible something the writing boys always refer to as color. He'll do all right by himself. *Frank Haven,* San Diego Sun, *May 5, 1938*

There was not a fan in the park who did not form an immediate attachment to gangling Ted. He is as loose as red flannels on a clothes line but as beautifully coordinated as a fine watch when he tenses for action. He is six feet and several inches of athlete and the same number of feet and inches in likeable boyishness. His is positively splashed with class, up to that rare point where he looks good making mistakes.

You see a lot of players you THINK will make the big league grade. You accord them a good chance; but once in a long while you have one quick glance of a natural and you KNOW he will make it, and not as just an average big leaguer, but as a star. That would be Ted Williams. He's a dead mortal cinch. *Dick Cullum,* Minneapolis Journal, *April 30, 1938*

They've christened him the "screwball king" – they also say he's a cocky kid... The former Herbert Hoover High school star has been voted the most popular player on the Minneapolis team. *photo caption from* Minneapolis Journal

What price glory? Telephone jangling from morn till night, feminine admirers seeking his favor; fan mail, invitations, adulations; center of attention at luncheon clubs...

Nineteen years old... current craze of Miller fandom's fanfare... the baseball world anxious to make him its shining star of 1939... of 1940...

All because of a nervous stance at the plate... a flick of the wrists... a lightning swing of a lightweight stick... a towering arc described by a baseball as it leaves the park.

And Ted Williams wants to pitch!

That telephone... Now Ted refuses to answer it... The job is Catcher Jim Galvin's, who shares a Sheridan hotel room with the San Diego kid... No, Ted ain't in!... And he don't want no dates!...

And across the room sits Ted, trying to drown out the phone calls with a radio going full blast. It's been going full blast since 7 a.m. – Ted's rising time. He turns in every night between 9:30 and 10 p.m...

"I wanna pitch... I struck our 23 men once in a high school game... They got two hits off'n me..."

Pitcher Belve Bean: "I knew an outfielder who thought he could pitch... They put him in there and they got 10 runs off'n him before they could get him outa there..."

"Well, nobody'll get 10 runs off'n me, I'll guarantee you that..."
Dick Hackenberg, Minneapolis Star, *May 10, 1938*

In a recent Minneapolis contest here he spent the final inning afield standing by the right field foul line, chatting with fellow players in the Millers' bull pen. This is in his own peculiar style of fun. Last Sunday when leaving the Red Bird stadium two taxicabs were awaiting a load. Williams had the two drivers sound their horns. Pointing to one driver, he said, "I'll take your cab. Your horn is the loudest." *R. E. Hooey,* Columbus Journal, *ca. May 11, 1938*

"An Open Letter to Ted Williams, Promising Young Minneapolis Right Fielder" [written in the aftermath of Ted being booed by men and women alike in the ninth inning of a home game against the Columbus Redbirds, a game Columbus won 21-9.] Minneapolis writer Halsey Hall wrote, "He had it coming. Seized with one of those inexplicable attacks of nonchalance and lack of hustle, Williams gave one of the strangest displays any baseball player ever gave. In the first inning he did not have his sun glasses on and missed a simple fly ball that led to three runs. Bush went out to right field and handed him Browne's glasses, plainly criticizing him. From that point on, it is a good thing Billy Evans of the Red Sox was not in the stands, or Ted's graduation to the majors might be postponed indefinitely. He did not hustle to pick up ground singles or throw them back to the infield. He laughed and kidded with the Columbus bench when the Kels were 13 runs to the rear... We trust, for his sake (he's a good kid) that he can shovel away these fits of lackadaisical play which seize him now and then. He is too grand a prospect to be cruified by his own foolishness.

Ted, you have been of tremendous value to the Minneapolis Millers this year, both as a box office drawing card and as well as a hitter and all around ball player. You're only a boy of 19 years. You have a fine future ahead of you, possibly reaching heights you never dreamed of after you signed a contract with the San Diego ball club when just out of high school.

But of late something has come over you. We aren't sure what it is, but it appears to be indifference. Your attitude isn't any secret. All of the fans have noticed it. This was particularly true yesterday when you were booed in your last time at bat.

In Saturday's game, a ball was hit in your direction (right in front of you), but something else was on your mind. You never even saw it, and Spence had to come all the way over from center to take it on the dead run. It was so close to you that it almost hit you.

In the pathetic exhibition the Millers put on against Columbus yesterday, you were guilty of many acts that should never be committed by a youngster with as much ability as you have and with the bright future that lies ahead of you. First, you lost a ball in the field that you would have caught easily if you had been wearing your glasses. It was a costly misplay as it led to three runs. Donie Bush actually left the bench and went to you to discipline you for your uncalled-for action. You got mad as a result. You sulked openly even to the point where you failed to run out a fly ball when you were on first base.

As much as the Minneapolis fans admire you, they resented your tactics yesterday. They showed it to you in your last appearance at the plate. That should have proved to you that you were at fault.

We have seen few young ball players in recent years who have such a wonderful chance to achieve greatness. However, you can spoil it all if you don't change your tactics immediately. As a rule, no one loves to play the game more than you. Very few professional ball players have more genuine enthusiasm for baseball. Everyone is for you. But like your manager, they can't stand to see you become temperamental. Public opinion and sentiment are invaluable to you and to your career.

So take a tip and get yourself straightened out before you're sorry. You can't act the way you have lately and advance in your profession. HOW ABOUT TURNING OVER A NEW LEAF RIGHT AWAY? *Charles Johnson, "The Lowdown on Sports,"* Minneapolis Star

Ted Williams can "take it."

In other words, the Millers' sensational youngster has seen the error of his ways and had quickly turned over a new leaf. To us, that means he has the qualities of which great stars are made.

By telephone and through the mail we have received considerable criticism (and considerable favorable comment, too) for our open letter to Ted Williams for his sulking and apparent indifference at Nicollet Park over a period of three days.

But Ted's attention had to be called to the error of his ways only once and he set about to do something about it. As a result, he once again is the hustling, enthusiastic young ball player that he was before his lapse of a week ago... it was in our anxiety to see Ted Williams make the most of his natural ability and escape the pitfalls that so many of them do not avoid that we took the young man to task for his conduct...You can't go wrong on any youngster with outstanding athletic talents if he absorbs the lessons that contact with the public teach him and doesn't make the same mistake again. *Charles Johnson, "The Lowdown on Sports,"* Minneapolis Star

Williams continues to dazzle with his right field play. His throw on Silvestri's hit averted a score and made it only a base-filling single. *unidentified clipping*

Game of June 18: Williams turned on his power. The ball cleared the right-center fence at the 328 foot mark and landed on the back of a building on the other side of Nicollet avenue, sailing a good 400 feet. It was No. 20 of the year for Ted, and kept his consecutive hitting mark at 19 straight games. The Millers were leading 2-0 when Ted came up, 5-0 afterwards, and his homer meant the ball game for Toledo fell two short...

Dick Durrell, founding publisher of *People* magazine, told Peter Golenbock: "The Millers would have problems with the merchants on the street across from the ballpark, Minken's department store, the President Café. The balls Ted hit would frequently go into their windows, and the team had to pay for them." *Golenbock, Fenway, p. 120*

"Ted Williams' Two Homers Break A. A. Distance Mark" The two home runs Ted Williams, 19-year-old San Diego youth hit for Minneapolis last week in Columbus have been recognized as the longest clouts in American Association history, it was learned here today. Teddy's first clout measured 425 feet from homeplate. The other, a terrific smash almost directly into center field, traveled a distance of 500 feet. Both homers came off Jack Tising, Columbus hurler, who had little trouble with Minneapolis otherwise that day. *unidentified clipping*

That Williams is one of those fellows "who can't miss" is due almost entirely to Donie Bush, the old major leaguer... The boy was too raw for the Red Sox' immediate use, so he was sent to Minneapolis. There were days and weeks when Donie Bush thought his old pal, [Billy] Evans, had sent him a candidate for the psychopathic ward... During the spring exhibition games, Williams almost caused Bush to have apoplexy... Minneapolis opened the season in Indianapolis and Williams was horse-collared in 12 times at bat. Overnight, the kid changed. He became serious, started to ask questions and "bear down," as players say.

Minneapolis moved on to Louisville. "I won't monkey with Williams any longer," snarled the fiery Bush. "Either he does or he doesn't in this series." In the next game, Ted hit a single and double. Minneapolis lost the following game and its only runs were two homers by Williams. One hit the centerfield gate, the other just missed it and for the first time one player has his two homers inside the Colonels' park. Next Williams belted a homer in Toledo, and from that day he has not gone more than five games without a hit and once he had a run of batting safely in 21 consecutive contests. Before the season was two months old, Williams had hit a home run in every Association park...

Williams not only is a great hitter; his fielding is sensational, he is very fast and he has a marvelous arm. There's nothing in baseball the kid cannot do well, now that he had decided to do it. *Francis J. Powers, Chicago Daily News, ca. June 20, 1938*

San Diego's favorite son, 19-year-old Teddy Williams, is the big noise of the American Association these days with a capital "N"! Latest Association figures show Teddy, Minneapolis flyhawk, to top the league in four departments – batting, home runs, runs batted in, and total bases... In home runs, Williams with 22, is 10 ahead of his nearest rivals...

Williams not only has been Minneapolis' mainstay in the Association race, but also he's been a life-saver at the gate. Although they've had their hands full fighting for a first-division berth, the Millers are second in attendance, due largely to the fact that Minneapolis fans turn out in droves just to see Teddy perform.

Because of his prowess at the plate, Teddy now is being walked frequently. In addition to drawing bases on balls, Young Williams is being brushed off frequently, the Association pitchers being that scared of him. He was hit twice in one game recently...

When with the Padres, Williams was used in left field. At Minneapolis, he's been used almost exclusively in right field, another indication that the Red Sox are grooming him for use in the immediate future in the Red Sox outer garden...

Williams' stickwork isn't all that had made him the prize minor leaguer of the year. He has polished his seemingly awkward, gangling fielding style to the point of near perfection, coming with "impossible" stops and catches, as well as bullet-like throws from the outfield.
Frank Haven, San Diego Sun, *ca. June 23, 1938*

Ted Williams has lived up to everything said about him... Williams has made such wonderful progress under the able handling of Donie Bush that he will be ripe for the big show in 1939. Williams came into the association with a reputation for being one of the best natural hitters developed in the Pacific Coast league sine Joe DiMaggio went from San Francisco to the Yankees three years ago. He was regarded as a weak fielder, but those who have watched the youngster, among them veteran managers, players, scouts and critics, were surprised by his ability as a flyhawk. Ted had proved to all and sundry that he is an excellent judge of fly balls, breaks fast when the ball is hit and gets under it without any faulty maneuvering, and is gifted with a pair of sure hands.

The youngster also is fast afoot, owns a strong and accurate throwing arm, and to date, has made few, if any mistakes, in throwing the ball to the right base with runners on the paths...
George Barton's Sportographs, Minneapolis Tribune

PHOTO CAPTION: Exclusive! Little Betty Samuelson, the girl reporter, sits at her toy typewriter and gets the lowdown from Ted Williams, the Millers' young hitting star, on a recent visit of Miller players to Glen Lake sanatorium. The Millers will try their hand at diamond ball at The Parade the night of July 18, against the state championship Jerseys in the annual game staged by the *Star*, proceeds from which go to the Children's hospital at the sanatorium.

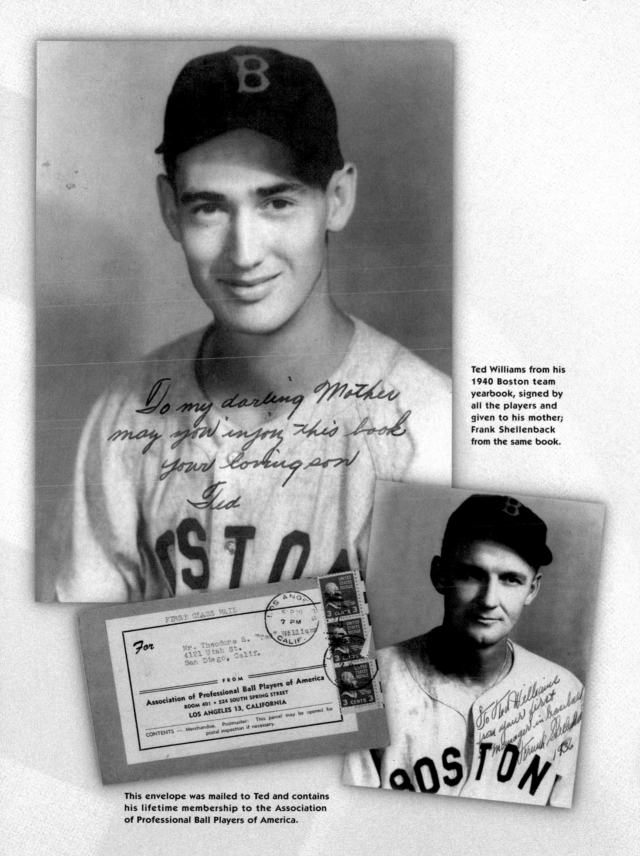

Ted Williams from his 1940 Boston team yearbook, signed by all the players and given to his mother; Frank Shellenback from the same book.

This envelope was mailed to Ted and contains his lifetime membership to the Association of Professional Ball Players of America.

Wos Caldwell, coach of Hoover High's
Cardinals during Ted's playing days.

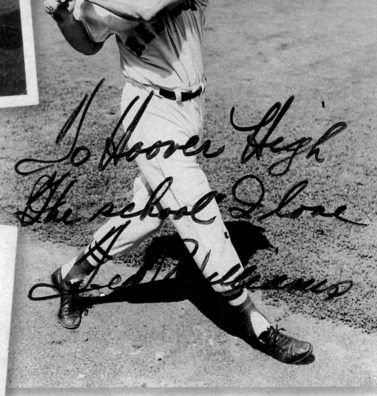

A signed photograph from Ted shows his love for his school.

Ted Williams and fellow Cardinal
teammate Hank Ondler.

An early Padres' program features owner Bill Lane, manager Frank Shellenback and players Cedric Durst and Ted Williams on the back.

A young Padre under the girders at Lane Field.

Ted's first professional baseball players membership card, 1937.

Ted Williams in a series of photographs from batting practice for an exhibition game at Lane Field, October 5, 1941.

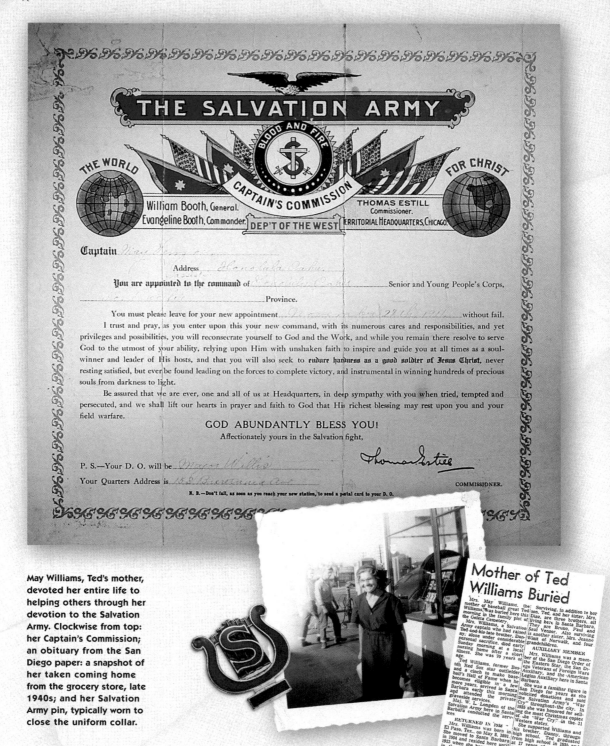

May Williams, Ted's mother, devoted her entire life to helping others through her devotion to the Salvation Army. Clockwise from top: her Captain's Commission; an obituary from the San Diego paper: a snapshot of her taken coming home from the grocery store, late 1940s; and her Salvation Army pin, typically worn to close the uniform collar.

Samuel Williams, Ted's father, held a wide variety of positions throughout his life: a member of the United States Cavalry, streetcar conductor, Deputy Sheriff, State of California Inspector of Prisons, and photographer. Although he had many colorful tales of other exploits, these are known to be true.

Clockwise from above: Samuel Williams as a young man; his badge as Investigator for the District Attorney of San Diego; his business card from the photo studio in Walnut Creek, California; and a portrait as the State Prison Inspector for the State of California.

Williams Photograph Studio
1523 MAIN STREET
WALNUT CREEK, CALIFORNIA

BRANCH PHONES
CONCORD 8266
LAFAYETTE 2153

TELEPHONE
WALNUT CREEK 2502

SAM WILLIAMS
INVESTIGATOR
DISTRICT ATTORNEY
SAN DIEGO
CALIF.

Clockwise from top left:

Ted's mother May with her mother, Natalia Venzor.

Catarina Hernandez (Natalia's mother) and one of her many grandchildren.

Bruno Venzor, one of Ted's uncles.

Natalia Venzor and her brothers Santiago and Rayo Hernandez.

Another of Ted's uncles, Paul Venzor.

Clockwise from top left:

Ted gives his support to another baseball player in the family, his cousin, Paul Herrera.

Ted visits his aunt Sarah in Santa Barbara, and family members gather for a feast at a local restaurant. Left to right: Cara Lucero, Dee Allen, Ted Williams, Ron Lucero, Hope Lucero, Henrietta Venzor, Jody Lucero, Sarah Diaz, Geno Lucero, Jeremy Lucero.

The Venzor family homestead at 1008 Chino Street, Santa Barbara as it looks today.

Danny Williams and his wife Jean; his last business card.

Another family gathering; Catarina Hernandez, center, clockwise from left: Natalia Venzor, Lupe Venzor (Pete's wife), Henrietta Venzor (Saul's wife) and their daughter, a young Dee Allen.

Lifelong friends, from left to right: Roy Engle, Bob Brietbard, Wilbert Wylie, Ted Williams, Joe Villarino and Les Cassie, Jr., July 6, 1991. At right: Hoover High School also chose to rename their field for Ted.

HOOVERS
TED
WILLIAMS FIELD
PEPSI
1 2 3 4 5 6 7 8 9 10 Total
Home Visitor

Joe Villarino, Ted's friend and high school teammate, still playing baseball and swinging strong in 2004.

The old North Park Playground, one block from his childhood home was renamed "Ted Williams Field" in Ted's honor in 1991. At right: 4121 Utah Street as it looks today.

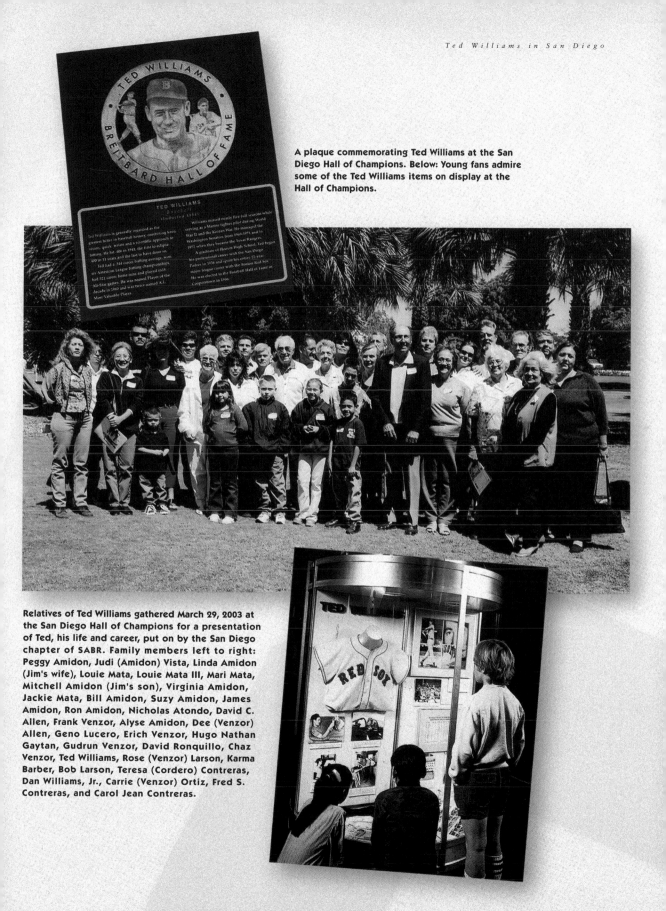

A plaque commemorating Ted Williams at the San Diego Hall of Champions. Below: Young fans admire some of the Ted Williams items on display at the Hall of Champions.

TED WILLIAMS
Baseball
(Inducted 1953)

Ted Williams is generally regarded as the greatest hitter in baseball history, combining keen vision, quick wrists and a scientific approach to hitting. He hit .406 in 1941, the first to eclipse .400 in 11 years and the last to have done so. Ted had a .344 career batting average, won six American League batting championships, had 521 career home runs and played in 18 All-Star games. He was named Player of the decade in 1960 and was twice named A.L. Most Valuable Player.

Williams missed nearly five full seasons while serving as a Marine fighter pilot during World War II and the Korean War. He managed the Washington Senators from 1969-1971 and in 1972 when they became the Texas Rangers.

A graduate of Hoover High School, Ted began his professional career with the San Diego Padres in 1936 and spent his entire 22-year major league career with the Boston Red Sox. He was elected to the Baseball Hall of Fame in Cooperstown in 1966.

Relatives of Ted Williams gathered March 29, 2003 at the San Diego Hall of Champions for a presentation of Ted, his life and career, put on by the San Diego chapter of SABR. Family members left to right: Peggy Amidon, Judi (Amidon) Vista, Linda Amidon (Jim's wife), Louie Mata, Louie Mata III, Mari Mata, Mitchell Amidon (Jim's son), Virginia Amidon, Jackie Mata, Bill Amidon, Suzy Amidon, James Amidon, Ron Amidon, Nicholas Atondo, David C. Allen, Frank Venzor, Alyse Amidon, Dee (Venzor) Allen, Geno Lucero, Erich Venzor, Hugo Nathan Gaytan, Gudrun Venzor, David Ronquillo, Chaz Venzor, Ted Williams, Rose (Venzor) Larson, Karma Barber, Bob Larson, Teresa (Cordero) Contreras, Dan Williams, Jr., Carrie (Venzor) Ortiz, Fred S. Contreras, and Carol Jean Contreras.

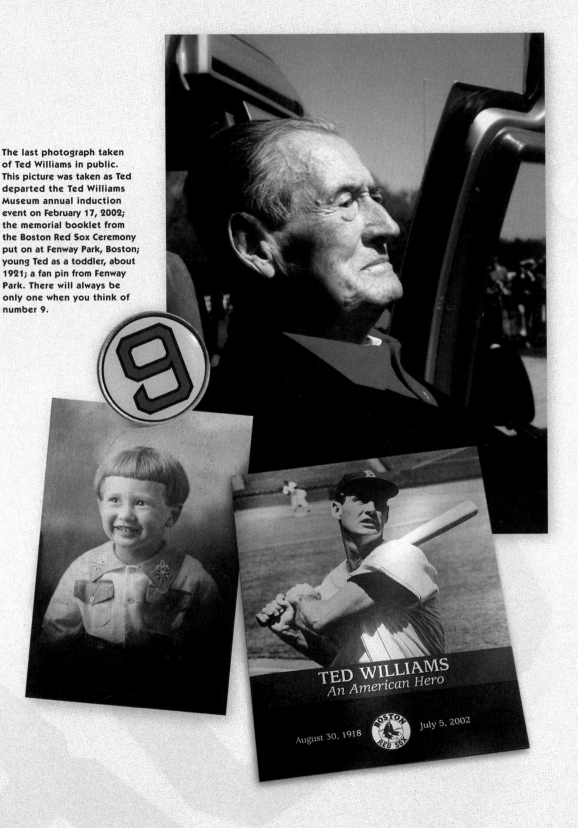

The last photograph taken of Ted Williams in public. This picture was taken as Ted departed the Ted Williams Museum annual induction event on February 17, 2002; the memorial booklet from the Boston Red Sox Ceremony put on at Fenway Park, Boston; young Ted as a toddler, about 1921; a fan pin from Fenway Park. There will always be only one when you think of number 9.

9

TED WILLIAMS
An American Hero

August 30, 1918   July 5, 2002

BOSTON RED SOX

Ted Williams and LeRoy Parmelee of Minneapolis have been voted to the American Association All-Star team. And Mr. Williams is one of only two men who received a unanimous count of eight votes from sportswriters of the American Association. The other player so honored is Pitcher Vance Page of Indianapolis. More than 35 individual writers voted, the ballots of each city being tossed into a consensus from that city. So a score of eight was perfect, landing on the shoulders of Messrs. Williams and Page.

Ted Williams with Roy Parmelee, the Millers' contribution to the 1938 All-Star Game.

Theodore Francis (sic) Williams, the Millers' punch-laden problem child, got a home run off a right hander and another one off a left hander as the Kels broke even with Milwaukee in a nocturnal double header at Nicollet park last night. [Of his 31 homers], Ted has hit only six off left handers... The uncanny thing about those other 25 wallops, however, is that Ted has banged them off 20 different hurlers. He has no "cousins," he plays no favorites... Count in the left handers now, and you have the amazing news that Ted's 31 home runs have been hit off 26 different moundsmen.

And if you can stand another knockout drop of information, only six of Williams' homers have been hit at night. [The Millers had played 66 day games and 31 night games at this point in the season.] *Dick Hackenberg,* Minneapolis Star, *ca. July 29, 1938*

After passing Spence, the lead-off man, Zuber hit Ted Williams, the league's home run king, back of the head with a "high hard one." Williams was knocked out and after being revived was removed to the clubhouse, where Dr. William J. McCarthy worked on him. Fortunately, the pitch hit Williams a glancing blow, according to Dr. Murphy, who gave Ted permission to resume play Thursday night.

Before he was knocked out, Williams drove in the first four runs off Zuber and thus became the first batsman in the A.A. to pass the century mark in the RBI department. His total now is 102.

Schoolboy Ted put his club in the lead in the first inning when his double to left center scored Andy Cohen... *Sam Levy, "Miller's Star Knocked Out", August 4, 1938*

Ted Williams, the most talked of rookie in the minor leagues, is here with Minneapolis for four games... The name "Peter Pan" was hung on him when he reported to the Millers' training camp at Daytona Beach, Fla. He became the problem child of Donie Bush from the moment he reported. Mentally, he was off-center. Physically, he was "too thin." Morally, he was clean as a whistle, a perfectly clean-minded sophomore.

The words "off-center" are used to denote that he was in an uncertain frame of mind. He didn't know what he wanted to do. Half the time he wanted to pitch, the other half was divided between wanting to drive in runs and wanting to go home, back to San Diego on the sunny slope, for it was his first trip away and the kid was homesick.

Gracious, what a popoff. He popped off on anything and everything, belittled the American association, bragged up the Pacific Coast league from whence he came, talked of pitching like a Walter Johnson, engaged in many an argument with Pat Malone as Pat tried to impress on the boy what a chance he had.

"You have a chance to be Babe Ruth's successor, you sap," yelled Pat at him across the locker room one day. "With your youth and that natural swing and all-around ability, you may make a million dollars in baseball. And you talk about going home. I wish I was in your shoes."

Peter Pan drove Donie Bush to the verge of distraction with his antics. He would be picking up a blade of grass when a ball was hit to right field. He would stand at the plate looking at Donie coaching at third, while the hurler was winding up. "Come on, Ted, be ready," Bush must have yelled 10,000 times.

The players liked him, except when they were on him. Twice, in exhibition games, he did not run out hits because he thought they were foul, was retired at first base as a result. And how they rode him. "Come to life, you big busher. Do they do that in the Coast league?" and sundry sizzling remarks went his way and the players meant them. Why? Well, because every man realized that this kid for whom the Red Sox paid $25,000 and two good ball players, Spencer Harris and Al Niemic, was to be the bellwether of the team. He was their mainstay. If he flopped, they flopped.
unidentified Kansas City Journal-Post *clipping*

Williams received six bases on balls in the first two games of the Toledo set over the weekend, five of them intentional. They hike Ted's total to 12 in his last seven contests and his season's total to something like, 120, official figures not being available until the campaign's close. *[seems to refer to Aug 27 and 28 games vs. Toledo]*

Williams' forty-first homer of the season was a mighty wallop, the ball clearing the buildings on the far side of Nicollet avenue, the pellet finally landing in an alley between Nicollet and First avenues. Ted's circuit smash topped off a five-run outburst in the third inning. Williams plated two of his buddies with a single in the first inning, thereby driving in five tallies.
"George A. Barton, Kels Thump Hens, 15-11, in Bat Spree," Minneapolis Tribune

Maybe the Boston Red Sox master minds don't think so now. But before the 1939 season rolls around, they'll discover they'll have to find a spot in the regular lineup for one Ted Williams, who is leading the American Association in almost every offensive department.

When Boston bought this sensational youngster from San Diego last winter, Billy Evans, chief scout, was of the opinion that Ted would need at least two years of seasoning in double A company before he would be ready for the majors.

Minneapolis players, Manager Bush and seven other pilots in the loop can vouch for Williams' outstanding hitting ability and furnish plenty of proof that Boston will have to insert Ted in its outfield next spring even with Cramer, Vosmik, Chapman and Nonnenkamp hanging around.

It looked like most ridiculous baseball, but over the weekend Manager Fred Haney of Toledo tipped his mitt on how much he likes Williams as a hitter. Fred ordered his pitchers to pass the kid every time he came to bat with a runner on the scoring bases. *Charles Johnson, "The Lowdown on Sports,"* Minneapolis Star

If you like Ted Williams' rhythm at the plate you ought to see him in front of a radio... Ted's a nut on swing bands, rates Benny Goodman tops, but can't dance a lick, says he'll learn this winter... Ted likes Minneapolis so well he's entertaining the idea of getting a job here for the off-season... Williams... received a birthday cake celebrating his twentieth birthday from his mother, Aug. 30, although baseball records say he won't be 20 until Oct. 30... Think what power Ted'll get in back of those homers when he fills out that wiry frame of his. *unidentified clipping*

If you've liked Ted Williams, Miller outfielder, you'll really love the guy now. Ted bumped into a little 10-year-old infantile paralysis victim the other day. In fact, they were introduced at an oil station. Ted discovered that the young lad was an ardent baseball fan, so the two of them visited for more than a half hour. Two days later the youngster, as the biggest surprise in his life, received a brand new baseball on which were the autographs of every player on the squad plus the signature of Donie Bush - a gift from Ted Williams. And right now there isn't a happier kid in town. Too bad more of us don't think of little turns like that. *Cedric Adams, "In This Corner,"* Minneapolis Star, *September 17, 1938*

The promised land beckons – but Ted Williams wants nothing to do with it, for another year at least. Prospective hitter of 50 home runs, league leader in hitting, in runs batted in, in total bases, in runs scored, the Millers' sensational young outfielder is a cinch to be recalled by his owners, the Boston Red Sox, when the American Association campaign comes to a close.

But Ted doesn't want to "go up," not just yet.

"I want to stay right here in Minneapolis with the Millers, for another year at least," he says. "I'm not ready for the major leagues. Another year under Donie Bush will do me a lot of good. I'm young yet. I figure that if a fellow gets to the majors when he's 21 or 22, that's time enough. He's got a better chance of sticking if he takes his time getting there. I don't want to be rushed. I've got plenty to learn and I've learned plenty under Donie this year. Maybe one more year and I'll be ready. *unidentified clipping*

An unprecedented situation – a tie between two players for first place – cropped up in the selection for the most valuable player in the American Association this year, and, as a result, the distinction is shared by Whitlow John Wyatt, pitcher of Milwaukee, and Aloysius Frank (Ollie) Bejma, second baseman of St. Paul. Both earned a total of 52 points in the votes of the committee for *The Sporting News*, with Ted Williams, outfielder of Minneapolis, a close runner-up, with 47 points, the trio dominating the choices... The two, together with Williams, will be in the majors next year, the outfielder having been recalled by the Boston Red Sox and the other pair going back for renewed chances, Wyatt with Brooklyn and Bejma with the White Sox...

The highest ranking of Bejma and the third-place finish of Williams may prove a surprise, but the second baseman, transferred from the St. Louis Browns, proved a spark-plug with St. Paul in helping them win the pennant... *Edgar G. Brands, "Two Tied for Most Valuable Honors in A.A.,"* The Sporting News, *September 29, 1938*

Hot Stove league talk around Boston would indicate that the Red Sox are thinking of making room for Ted Williams, former Padre outfielder, who played last year for Minneapolis on option. The talk is that Ben Chapman might be used for trading material this winter. Young Ted isn't too anxious to go up. Would just as soon spend another season at Minneapolis. They say there is a feminine reason... *unidentified clipping*

"Williams and Tabor In Line to Fill Berths of Chapman and Higgins"

...in right field, with the understanding that the job is his, unless he proves he cannot handle it, will be the phenomenal youthful slugging marvel, Ted Williams, late of the Pacific Coast League and American Association. "We'll be gambling, but at least, we'll be gambling with two of the finest young players in the country," Cronin added, with a smile...

Ted Williams has been so sensational as a batter in his two years in O.B. – 1938 at Minneapolis and 1937 at San Diego in the Coast League – that it is the unanimous opinion of all who have seen him and played with or against him, that he cannot miss as a big leaguer.

A left-handed hitter, Williams is a lanky 20-year-old, standing six feet three inches tall. He is a distance clouter and can hit to left and center, as well as to right. Ted probably will be a better fielder as he gets older and loses some of his kiddish mannerisms. He has a great arm, and though he is not fast getting down to first base, he can get up speed in the outfield to reach fly balls....

Williams will join the Sox with a reputation of being colorful. He needs stricter handling than he has received, but if he hits in the big leagues as he did in the minors, his trivial shortcomings will go unnoticed. *Jack Malaney,* Boston Post, *writing in* The Sporting News, *February 2, 1939*

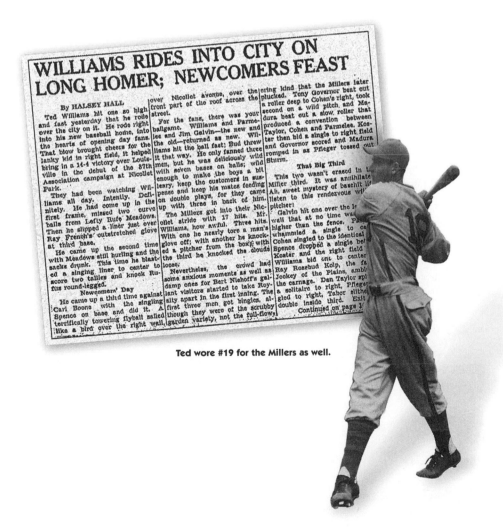

WILLIAMS RIDES INTO CITY ON LONG HOMER; NEWCOMERS FEAST

By HALSEY HALL

Ted Williams hit one so high and fast yesterday that he rode over the city on it. He rode right into his new baseball home, into the hearts of opening day fans. That blow brought cheers for the lanky kid in right field, it helped bring in a 14-4 victory over Louisville in the debut of the 37th Association campaign at Nicollet Park.

They had been watching Williams all day. Intently. Definitely. He had come up in the first frame, missed two curve balls from Lefty Rufe Meadows. Then he slipped a liner just over Ray French's outstretched glove at third base.

He came up the second time with Meadows still hurling and the sacks drunk. This time he blasted a singing liner to center to score two tallies and knock Rufus round-legged.

Newcomers' Day

He came up a third time against Carl Boone with the singling Spence on base and did it. A terrifically towering flyball sailed like a bird over the right wall, over Nicollet avenue, over the front part of the roof across the street.

For the fans, there was your ballgame. Williams and Parmelee and Jim Galvin—the new and the old—returned as new. Williams hit the ball fast; Bud threw it that way. He only fanned three men, but he was deliciously wild with seven bases on balls; wild enough to make the boys a bit leary, keep the customers in suspense and keep his mates feeding on double plays, for they came up with three in back of him.

The Millers got into their Nicollet stride with 17 hits. Mr. Williams, how awful. Three hits. With one he nearly tore a man's glove off; with another he knocked a pitcher from the box; with the third he knocked the clouds loose;

Nevertheless, the crowd had some anxious moments as well as damp ones for Bert Niehoff's gallant visitors started to take Royalty apart in the first inning. The first three men got bingles, although they were of the scrubby garden variety, not the full-flowy

ering kind that the Millers later plucked. Tony Governor beat out a roller deep to Cohen's right, took second on a wild pitch, and Madura beat out a slow roller that produced a convention between Taylor, Cohen and Parmelee. Koster then bid a single to right field and Governor scored and Madura romped in as Pfleger tossed out Sturm.

That Big Third

This two wasn't erased in the Miller third. It was annihilated. Ah, sweet mystery of baseht life, listen to this rendezvous with pitcher!

Galvin hit one over the left wall that at no time was higher than the fence. Pfleger whammied a single to center. Cohen singled to the identical spot. Spence dropped a single between Koster and the right field. Williams bid one to center. Ray Rosebud Kolp, the famous Jockey of the Plains, ambled the carnage. Dan Taylor split a solitaire to right, Pfleger gled to right, Tabor slithered double inside third. Exit Kolp.

Continued on page 1

Ted wore #19 for the Millers as well.

Ted Williams, 1941.

TED'S BASEBALL RETURN TO SAN DIEGO IN 1941
by Tom Larwin

Less than a week after finishing his legendary season hitting .406 for the Boston Red Sox, Ted Williams returned to his home town for a special two-game series. Billed as "exhibitions," the games in San Diego were part of a post-season California tour for a number of major league players.

In Philadelphia on Sunday, September 28 in a season-ending doubleheader, Williams went 6-for-8 to finish the season at .406. With a few days off, he was on his way to San Diego for two exhibition games on October 4 and 7.

The *San Diego Union* was already reporting Williams' arrival in its October 1 edition with a small headline that said "Fans Plan Greeting For Ted Williams Friday." The article noted that "local baseball fans, gloating over Ted Williams' efforts in winning the American league batting championship with a .406 average and also becoming the major league home run king, are planning a welcoming party when he returns here Friday night."

SAN DIEGO TURNS OUT TO WELCOME TED

You don't think San Diego was proud of their local hero? The next day the newspaper reported that a "welcome parade" for Ted Williams was set for Friday, October 3. "A parade through the center of town when he gets off the plane will be the reception accorded Ted Williams by North Park and city officials." The article further noted that he "will be given the most enthusiastic welcome any individual athlete has ever received here." The parade began at Lindbergh Field, the local airport, at 3:50 p.m. when Williams and Red Sox teammate Jimmie Foxx arrived and then proceeded to the civic center for a welcome ceremony.

Ted Williams and Jimmie Foxx at Lindbergh Field, San Diego.

The parade turned out "thousands" of San Diegans to greet Williams, and included former Hoover High School mates. The *San Diego Union*'s article indicated that while his booming bat has made Williams an "international figure," he is the "same old Ted, unchanged and unspoiled by his successes." The reports noted that Williams seemed to be more embarrassed than pleased by the demonstration in his honor. But he and Foxx made "short talk" at the ceremony and then were whisked away to University Heights playground where a program was held in his honor.

Foxx paid tribute to Williams by saying "you will find that Ted still wears the same size hat despite his success. The only thing that's bigger is the bat he waves in front of opposing pitchers."

HOME RUN HITTING PRE-GAME SHOW

Prior to the October 4 contest, Williams and Foxx put on a display of their hitting talents. Both "swatsmiths" consented to show their skills at "clouting." Williams, it was reported in the *San Diego Union*, played "Santa Claus to the kids on Pacific Highway" where he "rained baseballs over the Lane Field fence in a convincing demonstration of batting power." He hit four "towering balls over the right field fence and bombarded the boards with a succession of wallops which would have been good for from one to three bases." Foxx, on the other hand, was unable to knock any out of the park but "rapped the ball sharply to all fields."

A sequence of five color slides featuring Williams during this hitting contest was captured by amateur photographer Heber Epperson. The *San Diego Union-Tribune* in a December 17, 1999 article reported that Charles Strada was the batting practice pitcher that day. Strada, who later played for the Los Angeles PCL team, said he "threw inside to both Williams and Foxx, so they could have their home runs."

Bill Swank, author of *Echoes from Lane Field*, speculated that because Epperson was a good friend of Padres' manager Cedric Durst, he was allowed on the field to take photos at relatively close range during batting practice. Allowing photographers on the playing field near the batting area was a common practice at the time.

Swank tells the story about how Russell Keltner discovered the slides in October 1999, some 58 years after they were taken. Apparently the old slides, with film taped between small pieces of glass, remained in an old wooden cigar box for years. Durst's daughter, Autumn Keltner, had been the administrator for the Epperson estate. The box was discovered when Autumn asked her son to look for Halloween decorations that were stored in the basement of his parent's home. Curiosity led to the box that contained numerous slides and fortunately Autumn took the time to examine all of them. Her good fortune paid dividends when she found the ones of Williams in the five images which, taken together, provide an action sequence of his beautiful swing... in color. These are the first action color pictures of Ted Williams.

THE SATURDAY, OCTOBER 4 GAME

For the first game on October 4, the rosters for the two teams were filled with a combination of all-stars from the major leagues and from the Pacific Coast League (PCL). Heralded along with Williams was Jimmie Foxx who it was reported "agreed to play every position on the club throughout the game."

Along with Foxx and Williams, Cedric Durst was the manager of their team, called Kent Parker's All-Stars. Durst appeared to be an easy choice for manager having just managed the local Padres to 101 wins in the 1941. Some position players were from the San Diego Padres PCL club while came from other minor league teams. From San Diego, George Detore agreed to play third base. Mel Skelley was at shortstop and had completed the year with Tacoma of the Western League, and Salt Lake of the Pioneer League. Padres' first baseman, George McDonald, held down that position for Parker's and was on his way to a long minor league career that included 11 seasons with San Diego. Hal Patchett and Swede Jensen took the outfield, and Bill Thomas pitched. From Connie Mack's Philadelphia Athletics, a coach at the time, Earl Brucker, the "Iron Duke" would be behind the plate.

For the other club, Joe Pirrone's All-Stars, Jesse Flores, called by reporters the "Los Angeles Mexican"and "Big Mexican," was to be on the mound and Cliff Dapper, his battery mate. Flores was born in Guadalajara and pitched for the Los Angeles PCL club where he won 12 games in 1941. He eventually became a 21-game winner for the Padres in 1949 and spent seven seasons in the major leagues winning going 44-59. Catcher Dapper played with Hollywood in 1941 appearing in 125 games and hitting .277. His minor league career ended in 1957 after seven seasons of being player-manager with several teams. St. Paul (American Association) player-manager Red Kress was recruited to play an infield position. Kress ended his major league career in 1946 with a .286 average and 1,454 hits. Vince DiMaggio was reportedly lined up to play, too, but he did not. Others that were filling up the Pirrone roster were Peanuts Lowrey, an outfielder with Los Angeles who in 1941 finished up a strong season with 203 hits and a .311 batting average. He eventually spent 13 seasons in the National League beginning in 1942 and lasting through 1955. Infielder Eddie Mayo, also with Los Angeles in 1941 was on the Pirrone team, and eventually played in the American League with several teams between 1943 and 1948. Shortstop Nanny Fernandez of the San Francisco Seals led the PCL in hits (231), doubles (46), triples (16), and RBI (129) in 1941. He eventually played four seasons with Boston and Pittsburgh of the National League. Pitcher Fred Gay was a southpaw with the Hollywood Stars. Al Unser was enlisted to catch for Parker's team. He had played with Beaumont of the Texas League in 1941 and batted .310. He had a short major league career in the middle of a lengthy minor league career from 1933 until the late 1950s.

Programs for the two October 1941 exhibition games.

As to the game itself news articles estimated that 4,000 fans attended. Fans got to see what they hoped to see – both Foxx and Williams hit home runs. Foxx batting in the first knocked in George McDonald with a home run to left field. In the third, Williams had his second chance, and he hit one over the right field fence, making the score, 3-0. That was enough as Parker's San Diego team ended up winning 5-1.

Foxx didn't follow through with the promise to play all positions, but he did start at third base and ended up pitching two innings and "mowed down" all six batters he faced with one strikeout. [Foxx did pitch in ten major league games during his career, but nine were in the war year of 1945 for the Philadelphia Phillies; 1945 was also his last year in the majors.]

THE TUESDAY, OCTOBER 7 GAME

With a few days' rest Williams and Foxx were ready for Philadelphia's Eastern Colored Giants. The Giants were rated as one of the outstanding Negro teams in the country and the *San Diego Union* indicated that the team "will present a lineup of stars who might have made the grade in the majors had there been no color line."

Chet Brewer, who had a long career in the Negro Leagues and played with Philadelphia and Kansas City in 1941, was slated to pitch, and was hailed as the "equal of Satchel Paige," with Bib Mackey to catch. The pre-game hype quoted Mackey as saying that "the two Boston stars would be lucky to get the ball out of the infield, let alone out of the park." Well, we will never know, because neither Brewer pitched, nor Mackey caught. Instead, the hurler for the "Negro '9'" was Nathan "Nate" Moreland, a "speed ball pitcher." Moreland had a relatively long career in the Negro Leagues and in 1941 played with Tampico of the Mexican League and went 16-12. Someone by the name of Irvin did catch and whether that was Monte Irvin is unknown... probably not given that records show he never caught during any of his stints in the Negro or Major Leagues.

For the San Diego team, a new pitcher was added for the game, "bespecled" (sic) Wayne "Fish" Osborne, from the Hollywood PCL club where he went 12-12 in 1941. Osborne had a 13-year PCL career with several clubs. The other change was to bring in Ballinger to catch and Unser to play third as Jimmie Foxx moved to his normal position at first base.

Williams was held hitless in the game but was on base with three walks and scored two runs. In the first inning he and Mel Skelley scored on a double by George Detore to pull the San Diego team ahead 2-0. Then in the third Jimmie Foxx came up with Williams on first and he "rammed a liner into the left field stands, 375 feet" away to put the home team up 4-1.

Perhaps the most exciting part of the game was the performance by pitcher Nick Carter for the Giants who came on in relief of Moreland in the seventh inning. He fanned Mel Skelley, Hal Patchett, and Dell Oliver in the seventh, and then struck out Williams, Detore, and Swede Jensen in the eighth.

After these two games, it was on to Los Angeles for the two Boston stars in their coast barnstorming tour; however, San Diego fans got their money's worth, with both Foxx and Williams living up to their advance billing. A significant and related sidelight of the short October 1941 visit to San Diego were the five color slides taken of Ted Williams at bat, and their inadvertent and fortunate discovery some 58 years later.

Saturday, October 4, 1941

	AB	H	O	A		AB	H	O	A
Pirrone's					**Parker's**				
Lowrey, cf	4	1	1	0	Patchett, cf	4	0	2	0
Mayo, 3b	4	0	1	0	McDonald, 1b	4	1	10	2
Barton, 1b	4	1	5	0	Williams, lf	4	1	2	0
Fernandez, ss	2	1	2	2	Foxx, 3b, p	4	2	3	3
Kress, 2b	3	1	3	3	Brucker, c	2	0	1	0
Reich, lf	3	0	4	0	Detore, 2b	4	1	1	3
Gay, rf	3	0	3	0	Jensen, rf	4	1	1	0
Dapper, c	2	0	3	0	Skelley, ss	4	2	3	2
Flores, p	1	0	0	0	Thomas, p, 3b	3	0	1	1
Tost, p*	0	0	0	0	Unser, c	2	0	3	0
Partee, c	1	0	2	0					
Total	27	4	24	5	**Total**	35	8	27	11

* Batted for Flores in the 5th

	1	2	3	4	5	6	7	8	9		R	H	E
Pirrone's	0	0	0	1	0	0	0	0	0		1	4	3
Parker's	2	0	1	1	1	0	0	0	X		5	8	0

Runs–Barton, McDonald 2, Williams, Foxx, Detore. Errors–Lowrey, Barton, Gay. Winning pitcher–Thomas. Losing pitcher–Flores.
Runs responsible for–Flores 1, Tost 1, Thomas 1. Bases on balls–Thomas 1. Struck out–By Thomas 3, Flores 1, Tost 1, Foxx 1.
Three-base hits–Skelley, McDonald. Home runs–Foxx, Williams, Barton. Runs batted in–Foxx 3, Williams, Barton, Skelley.
Double plays–Foxx to Detore to McDonald, McDonald to Skelley to McDonald. Left on base–Pirrone's 2, Parker's 6. Time–1:45.
Umpires–Fournier and Gottberg.

Tuesday, October 7, 1941

	AB	H	O	A		AB	H	O	A
Giants					**All-Stars**				
Wade, cf	5	2	2	0	Skelley, ss	3	0	2	5
Mathews, rf	5	0	0	0	Patchett, cf	4	1	5	0
Hughes, 2b	4	2	2	2	Williams, lf	1	0	1	0
McGinnts, lf	4	0	0	0	Foxx, 1b	3	1	8	0
Flannoy, 3b	4	2	0	0	Detore, 2b	4	1	4	2
Davis, 1b	5	1	6	0	Jensen, rf	4	1	2	0
Sergio, ss	4	1	2	4	Unser, 3b	3	1	0	1
Irvin, c	4	0	11	0	Ballinger, c	2	0	5	0
Moreland, p	3	1	1	3	Osborne, p	2	0	0	1
Carter, p	0	0	0	0	Oliver, p	1	0	0	3
Nubio*	1	0	0	0					
Total	39	9	24	9	**Total**	27	5	27	12

* Batted for Carter in the 9th

	1	2	3	4	5	6	7	8	9		R	H	E
Giants	0	1	0	1	0	0	0	0	1		3	9	0
All-Stars	2	0	2	0	0	0	0	0	X		4	5	3

Runs–Flannoy, Nubio, Skelley, Williams 2, Foxx. Errors–Skelley, Detore, Oliver. Winning pitcher–Osborne.
Losing pitcher–Moreland. Hits–Off Osborne 6, Oliver 3, Moreland 5. Runs responsible for–Osborne 1, Oliver 1, Moreland 4.
Bases on balls–Off Osborne 1, Oliver 1, Moreland 4, Carter 1. Hit by pitcher–Ballinger by Moreland.
Struck out–By Osborne 3, Oliver 2, Moreland 5, Carter 6. Left on bases–Giants 13, San Diego 5.
Two-base hits–Detore. Home run–Foxx. Runs batted in–Detore 2, Foxx 2, Irvin, Hughes.
Double plays–Sergio to Hughes to Davis, Hughes to Sergio to Davis. Time–2:10.
Umpires–Serrano and Teachout.

AN ITEM OF NOTE REGARDING THESE 1941 GAMES
by Bill Nowlin

> I remember one time I was sitting at the dressing room down at the field. We were going to play an exhibition game with Ted Williams, and Jimmie Foxx, Pepper Martin and some of those other guys. They come around on a tour and they came to San Diego... This was in 1941, and I was sitting back there getting dressed and you had to come under the stands and go through the trainer's room before you got into the dressing room. I could hear old Ted down there under the stands talking and he was a-hollering; he was excited about being there. I thought, oh, he won't remember me. So he comes through there and he looked down at me. He said, "Hey, Ollie! Are you still trying to get somebody out? You've got the hardest job in the world!" *Dell Oliver, interview with Bill Nowlin, May 16, 1999*

When San Diego hosted these two games in 1941, just a few months after Ted was on top of the world with his .406 average, one is struck by what today we might call the multiculturalism of the teams. Playing for Pirrone's were a couple of Hispanic players. Nanny Fernandez played shortstop. He was a month and a half younger than Ted, and made the majors the following year, appearing in 145 games with the Boston Braves (hitting .255.) Baseball Library.com informs us that the "dark, stocky Fernandez was of Castilian descent, his parents having left Spain for California shortly before his birth. He drove in 55 runs his first season but was not the same after losing three prime years to military service."

Pitching for Pirrone was Jesse Flores, who also debuted in '42. He was a few years older than Ted, born in 1914 in Guadalajara, Mexico. Jesse's parents arrived in California when he was 8, and he worked with the family picking fruit in La Habra. He told Cynthia Wilber that his mother never did learn English. "She never went to a ball game, but she went to church a lot," he said. His father, though, went to almost every game as Jesse began to make it in semi-pro ball. From 1943 through 1947, he pitched for the Philadelphia Athletics and faced Williams several times in the latter two years. He pitched Philly's home opener in 1943 and lost a two-hitter to Tex Hughson, 1-0. Next time out, he held the opposition to a single run again, beating Early Wynn and the Senators 2-1, going deep into extra innings. "I beat him in the sixteenth," Flores said. Over seven seasons, Flores posted a 3.18 ERA. He became a scout and was selected "Scout of the Year" in the West in 1985 by the Scout of the Year Foundation.

Flores reports suffering discrimination in La Habra, but never in baseball. He spoke fluent English and did not appear "dark" like Fernandez. It was his name that did him in: "I tried to buy a house... and when I went over to close the deal, they saw my name was Flores and they said no deal. Ted Williams, half-Mexican himself, was aware that he himself might have suffered discrimination had he not borne the surname Williams. The ethnicity of some of the other players may have been mixed as well; from surnames alone it is impossible to know.

The October 7 game was one of evident differences – the Giants were billed as a "colored" team. Ted, Jimmie Foxx and others obviously didn't let them that keep them off the field.

When Ted was center stage at Cooperstown in 1966, being inducted into the National Baseball Hall of Fame, he took the occasion to speak out for the great Negro League players who had never had the chance to play ball in the majors before Jackie Robinson and Larry Doby broke the "color line" in their respective leagues. Perhaps this is not surprising, given Williams' experience in southern California where he'd played with – or against – players from many backgrounds, such as Santa Ana's "Emperor" Jones, described in print as a "whirlwind Negro pitcher."

Bill Swank, on the 1941 Heber Epperson photographs

October is a month when surprises hide in dark places. Russell Keltner was visiting his mother, Autumn (Durst) Keltner, who asked him to bring some Halloween decorations up from the basement of the family home. While looking for plastic pumpkins and cardboard skeletons, Russell came across an old wooden cigar box that contained strange color film slides taped between small pieces of glass.

Initially the slides confused Autumn. Then she recognized Heber and Helen Epperson on vacation in Idaho. Autumn had been the executor of Helen's estate. Anyone who has ever had to endure a slide show of in-laws on a summer trip to the lake would know she should have immediately closed the cover of this box. But because the Eppersons were such good friends of her folks, Cedric and Brownie Durst, Autumn was hopeful that she might find some shots of her parents among the contents. She removed more slides and was amazed to discover Ted Williams at Lane Field.

In 1936, while still a student at Herbert Hoover High School, Ted Williams signed a contract with the Pacific Coast League San Diego Padres. Ted's mother, May, was concerned about her young son going on the road with a professional baseball team. The worried woman was assured by team owner Bill Lane that Ted would get along fine since he would room with Cedric Durst, a respected and responsible veteran outfielder who had played on the 1927 Yankees. When she met Durst, Mrs. Williams knew her boy would be in good hands. And Cedric Durst knew Ted Williams was a good kid.

Aunt Alice Williams and mother May V. Williams outside Lane Field, October 1941.

But what was Ted Williams doing in San Diego in a Boston Red Sox uniform?

Autumn looked in her baseball books and scrapbooks. She located an interview with Dell Oliver that made reference to a local exhibition game in which the former schoolmates had played. She found a program for a game that was played on October 5, 1941 at Lane Field between Pirrone's All-Stars and the San Diego All-Stars. Promoter Kent Parker had added Ted and Jimmie Foxx to the Padre roster. The Pirrone team was comprised of major leaguers and Coast League ballplayers from the Los Angeles area. Such exhibitions were easy money for the players, who had to find employment in the off-season.

Parker's All-Stars beat the Los Angeles team, 5-1. Jimmie Foxx hit a home run in the first inning with Padres first baseman George McDonald aboard. Ted had a solo shot off Jess Flores in the third inning. Foxx and Mel Skelley each collected two base hits for San Diego. Legendary minor league pitcher Bill Thomas got the victory and Jimmie Foxx took the mound to shut down the Pirrones in the last two innings.

During batting practice before the game, Williams and Foxx played an early version of Home Run Derby for the fans. Ted put four balls over the right field fence that bounced off the Pacific Highway. Foxx could only find the distance for one blow into the faraway wooden bleachers in left field.

Because Heber Epperson was a good friend of Cedric Durst, who had become the Padres manager, it is speculated that he was allowed to film batting practice at close range. In those days, players were allowed to leave their gloves in the grass and professional photographers were permitted on the field

during games. The cameramen would station themselves within a few feet of home plate in order to record the action. Rarely did the ball ever hit a photographer or a discarded glove.

Baseball fans know that on September 28, 1941, Ted Williams went 6-for-8 in the final doubleheader of the season against Connie Mack's Athletics. This performance raised his average to .406 after it had dropped below the .400 mark the previous day in Philadelphia. How many recall that exactly one week later, Ted Williams was back in San Diego to play before 4,000 home town fans in his Red Sox uniform? Some locals still remember being in the stands for the game and now there are photographs to preserve this moment in San Diego history. Although the five Epperson slides were taken on different swings, when arranged together, they capture the famous Williams swing in a rare color sequence at Lane Field. One wonders what Russell will find in the Keltner basement next Halloween?

1941 Lane Field exhibition photograph by Heber Epperson.

Alice Williams, Ted Williams, May V. Williams at Lindbergh Field, San Diego, October 3, 1941.

Ted Williams, arriving from Phoenix at San Diego's Lindbergh Field, March 12, 1959.

TED WILLIAMS' LAST HOMECOMING – 1959
by Joe B. Naiman

"San Diego is the only city where [Ted Williams] has never been able to hit .300." So wrote *Boston Globe* sportswriter Harold Kaese on March 13, 1959, as Ted and the Red Sox were about to open a three-game Spring Training exhibition series in Ted's hometown of San Diego. With the Pacific Coast League Padres, Ted had batted .271 in 1936, and raised his average .291 in 1937 - but he hadn't cracked .300. He managed .3 in Minneapolis the following year, and then posted a lifetime .344 average in 19 seasons with the Boston Red Sox.

The Red Sox, who had trained in Sarasota, Florida from 1946 through 1958, moved their Spring Training site to Scottsdale, Arizona, beginning with the 1959 exhibition season. In so doing they joined the San Francisco Giants, the Chicago Cubs, and the Cleveland Indians in the

**Left to right: Les Cassie, Jr., Ted Williams, Roy Engle at Westgate Park
for the Red Sox / Indians exhibition game, March 13, 1959.**

Ted relaxing back in the El Cortez Hotel, San Diego, March 12, 1959.

Cactus League. The Sox moved back to Florida – to Winter Haven this time – in 1966.

In 1959, the San Diego Padres were still in the Pacific Coast League and served as the Class AAA farm team of the Indians. The Red Sox had their own San Diego connection. Ted Williams was born and raised in San Diego and began his professional career with the Padres in the 1930s. Williams was coming off back-to-back American League batting titles in 1957 (.388) and 1958 (.328) – unprecedented accomplishments for a man who turned 39 in '57 and 40 in 1958.

The inclusion of the Red Sox in the Cactus League permitted a three-game exhibition series with the Indians in San Diego in 1959. The Sox were hoping to draw well, and the *Boston Herald*'s Bill Cunningham acknowledged that "the future of the Red Sox in Scottsdale may depend on the size of the crowd that greets them in California." *[March 13, 1959 Boston Herald]* Cunningham said that it was clear in conversations with Joe Cronin that the move to Scottsdale was "strictly a search for bigger gates at Spring Training, and Mr. Cronin expected to find them in California, certain, and Texas, possibly." Three California regular season major league franchises had begun operation on the West Coast just the year before, 1958.

It would be a homecoming of sorts for the 40-year-old Teddy Ballgame, who had last played baseball in San Diego during a previous exhibition there in October 1941. That visit came during a barnstorming tour hard on the heels of his spectacular .406 1941 season.

Ted checked into Room 358 at the El Cortez Hotel. "Three fifty eight, huh?" Williams reportedly asked the bellhop. "Well, I hope that's what I hit this year."

Ted arrived a day early and told the *San Diego Union*'s Jerry Magee that he'd heard from some old high school pals. "I've got two or three letters in my bag right now, from fellows I played with who want me to come out and see their sons in the Little League." Union, *March 13, 1959*

The Spring Training series with the Indians was held at Westgate Park on March 13-15. In addition to Williams, the Red Sox featured 1958 American League Most Valuable Player Jackie Jensen, who had signed a contract for $40,000, and a clause allowing him to travel separately from the team if the Red Sox traveled by air. The Indians figured to draw well in San Diego – the Tribe featured fourteen former PCL Padres on their 45-man roster.

The first game was played before a crowd of 7,538 on Friday, March 13, after an 8 p.m. start. Cleveland was the home team and they started well, scoring one run in each of the first three innings off Dick Sisler, including a home run in the third by Rocky Colavito. Sisler left after three, having yielded 3 runs on six hits.

Indians starter Gary Bell got himself in trouble, walking the first two Red Sox batters, but then Williams tapped the ball back to the mound and was easily retired. Bell then struck out Vic Wertz and Jensen to close out the first inning. The score was 3-0 Indians after three, with defense playing

Ted with young fans, Westgate Park, March 13, 1959.

a role as Minnie Minoso made a running backhanded catch of a drive hit by Pete Runnels in the top of the third.

The Sox were without a hit when Williams led off in the fourth. He dribbled to Doby at first. Wertz doubled to deep left down the line, though, and Jensen tripled to right center field. Gene Stephens supplied a single to short center, scoring Jensen from third. Score 3-2 Tribe.

Cleveland scored twice against Tom Borland in the bottom of the fifth to regain the three-run lead, on the strength of two bases on balls, a single, a hit batsman and an infield roller. But, this being Spring Training, Bell, who had limited Williams to two weak infield rollers in two plate appearances, was replaced by John Briggs in the fifth inning.

Briggs got through that frame, but in the Red Sox sixth he walked Williams to lead off, and walked Dick Gernert behind Ted. The Splendid Splinter was taken out of the game in favor of pinch-runner Jim Busby, who scored on Jensen's single. Billy Martin committed an error trying to go for the double play and Frank Malzone reached first, while Gernert crossed the plate. A two-run home run over the right field fence by Gene Stephens capped a four-run inning which put the Red Sox ahead, 6-5.

Boston added two more runs in the seventh, Briggs walking Pumpsie Green, beaning Busby and walking Gernert. Fortunately, Busby – hitting in Ted's place, was wearing a helmet – something Williams would never do. Ted Lepcio's single drove in two, completing the offensive part of the 8-5 Red Sox victory. This brought the Red Sox record in Spring Training to 6-0. Tom Borland gave up two runs on two hits and got the win in the first Westgate Park game while Leo Kiely earned a save for the Red Sox with three scoreless innings. Briggs was assigned the loss. He would only pitch 12-plus innings for Cleveland that year. Borland didn't make the bigs until 1960, and had only a very brief major league career. Pumpsie Green's appearance was his first in a major league uniform, and manager Mike Higgins – not known for his graciousness or racial tolerance - had put Pumpsie in at short in place of Don Buddin since Pumpsie's wife had come down from Oakland to watch the game.

Cleveland had out hit the Red Sox in the series opener, tallying nine base hits against seven for the Sox. Ted himself was held hitless, but had walked and the runner who took his place had scored. He'd had a little more in mind. Bill Liston of the *Boston Traveler* wrote that he'd been "determined to treat his home-town fans to at least a couple of homers." Liston told readers that equipment manager Johnny Orlando had been told to leave the 36 ounce bats behind and to pack a couple of 33 ounce and a couple of 31 ounce bats. Ted normally started the season with a heavier bat, then progressively adopt lighter bats as the months passed. "But, Kid," Orlando was said to have asked, "You don't start using 31-ounce bats until the middle of the season. What goes?" "Listen, I'm going back to my home-town and I want to make sure I hit a couple of home runs for the home folks. I'll be able to get around quicker with those lighter bats." The writer said that Williams "had the bounce and vigor of a teen-ager" before Friday night's game. He did hit a couple of batting practice home runs over the wall in right field. He then signed autographs "for a horde of youngsters." Most of the day before Ted visited with friends, including ten former Hoover High teammates.

The Saturday game on March 14 once again saw the Indians out hit the Sox, seven to six, but once again fall short on runs as Boston bounced back from an initial deficit. The *Boston Herald* reported that the Kid from San Diego had stayed out partying with friends until 5 a.m. He'd been "hosting a late supper gathering of 50 San Diego friends at his home-coming party. Not forgetting a 7:30 a.m. breakfast date with seven Little Leaguers, T.W. was up bright and cheerful at 7 o'clock." Herald, *March 16*

This time the Red Sox were the home team before the Saturday night crowd of 6,159. Cleveland scored twice in the top of the first off Tom Brewer, but the Red Sox came back with one in the bottom of the inning despite Al Cicotte retiring Williams on a fly to center field. Williams then tied the game in the third, doubling off the 380-foot outfield sign, which scored Pete Runnels. It was Ted's first hit of the spring, described by Bob Holbrook in the *Boston Globe* as "a long double to right center... that drove in a run and delighted the Williams rooters in his home town." A story in the *Boston Traveler* reported that the ball "missed by only a couple of inches of going over the screen in right center."

Despite it being the seventh game of the spring for the Sox, it was indeed Ted's first hit. He'd had a rough spring, pinching a nerve in his neck while still at home in the Florida Keys. Playing two night games in what proved to be damp and cool conditions didn't help, and before too long Ted was in traction in a Boston hospital. Of course, he couldn't anticipate that in mid-March and he'd wanted to shine in his first professional appearance in San Diego since 1937.

The score remained at two apiece until the bottom of the sixth. With Runnels on first, Williams hit a roller wide of the base, and pitcher Cal McLish crossed the bag without a toss from Vic Power. Williams reached on the error, putting runners on first and second. Runnels later scored on Jensen's sacrifice fly to give the Red Sox the lead.

In the seventh inning the Indians brought in Hal Woodenshick, who had won ten games in a row for the Padres in 1958 before a midseason callup to the majors. In one-third of an inning Woodenshick allowed a hit, walked three batters, and hit a batter – giving the Red Sox three more runs.

Cleveland scored twice in the eighth, but the Red Sox held on to give Willard Nixon the victory in his first pitching outing since July. The 6-4 win was Boston's seventh straight Spring victory.

The two Westgate night games were followed by a 1:30 p.m. Sunday start on March 15, and the afternoon crowd of 8,882 brought total attendance to 22,579 for the series; the Red Sox had reportedly only drawn 7,000 in all twelve home games in Sarasota the previous year. The Indians won this one, 5-4, prompting a *Boston Globe* headline, "Home City Jinxes Ted As Sox Lose."

The Globe story began, "Ted Williams still is in the grip of a batting jinx as a professional ball player in his native city of San Diego. Williams today was held hitless by southpaws Herb Score and Don Ferrarese of the Indians and wound up his three-game series here with a total of one hit in seven trips to the plate." It was the first defeat of the season for Boston. The newspaper added that Williams "was stopped in a barnstorming tour here in 1941 and again this weekend."

Indians pitcher Herb Score, who won two games in 1958, was still trying to recover from the effects of being hit in the face with a line drive in 1957. Score started strongly by striking out Don Buddin, Williams, and Jensen in the first inning, catching the Splendid Splinter looking on a curveball after a 1-2 count.

Score held Boston to one hit in two full innings, although the Red Sox scored a run in the top of the third when Buddin singled and Runnels walked. Buddin stole third and Williams hit a soft sacrifice fly to Piersall in center. The Indians tied the game in the bottom of the third on Woody Held's home run to left, off Ike Delock. The two teams traded runs in the fifth, and in the bottom of the sixth Cleveland scored twice to take a 4-2 lead.

The Indians received a break in the seventh; Williams walked and rookie Gary Geiger came in to pinch-run. Wertz doubled for the Red Sox, but Geiger failed to touch third base as he streaked home and umpire Art Runge called him out. Marty Keough then doubled to put Boston within one.

In the top of the ninth Geiger singled to right center, Keough walked, and (after Gernert forced Geiger at second) Malzone singled Gernert home for the tying run. Busby hit into an inning-ending double play. But in the bottom of the ninth Jimmy Piersall, who had been with the Red Sox the previous year, drew a walk off Murray Wall. On a hit-and-run Jim Bolger's single sent Piersall to third base, leading to an intentional walk of Colavito.

Pinch-hitter Hal Naragon popped up for the first out, and then Power hit what looked like a double play ball, but shortstop Pumpsie Green's error brought home Piersall for the winning run. Dick Stigman received the win for the Indians, who improved their record to 3-5.

Green would start the 1959 season in the minors, but on July 21 he made his debut for the Red Sox, becoming the first black player on the last Major League team to integrate.

Ted Williams was 0-for-2 on the day. His day was not fruitless, however. In the third inning, Ted hit a sacrifice fly off Ferrarese, knocking in Don Buddin. Ted also walked, so two of his four at-bats were productive ones. In all, The Kid had one hit in seven official at-bats, but he batted in two runs during the three games. Joe Cashman, writing in Boston's *Daily Record*, summarized the three games generously, indicating that "while he had only one hit, a booming double, he hit several other balls well." (Boston Daily Record, *March 17, 1959*)

Ted's hopes to hit a few homers for the home-town fans fell short. He started all three game, but going just 1-for-7 left him hitting .143 for the weekend matchup.

1959 was not a good season for the man once called "The Kid." He hit a dismal .254 - not much higher than the afore-mentioned Buddin's .241. It was his only sub-.300 season, almost 100 points behind the lifetime .349 average he sported through the 1958 campaign. Williams reportedly refused the 1960 contract tendered him by the Red Sox, tearing it up and demanding a 30% paycut since he'd under-performed. He felt he hadn't earned his salary. In 1960, he bounced back substantially, batting .316, but clearly his best days were behind him and it was time to retire.

It wasn't a good season for the Red Sox, either. They'd placed third in 1958, though 13 games behind the league-leading Yankees, and a game and a half ahead of the Indians. In 1959, the Sox finished fifth, 19 games out, while the Indians were just 5 games behind the first-place White Sox.

The two teams were each entitled to 37 1/2% of the gate receipts, so each team took home about $18,000 for the three games. As a result of the success of the series Red Sox general manager Bucky Harris and Indians GM Frank Lane agreed to play another series in San Diego in 1960.

Higgins gave everyone the day off on Monday. The Red Sox team flew back to Scottsdale on Sunday evening. Jensen, though, took a late afternoon train back to Arizona, while Ted stayed around for an extra day "to renew a few old friendships."

The 1960 Red Sox played in Scottsdale, Phoenix, Mesa, Las Vegas, Tucson and even New Orleans – but the San Diego rematch never eventuated. 1960 was Williams' last year as a ballplayer, so the 1959 series stood as the last games he ever played in San Diego.

It was not until 1961 that the Red Sox returned to Westgate, but by that time Ted had homered in his last at-bat in the major leagues and retired from baseball.

Bill Nowlin contributed to this research.

SAN DIEGO STAY SPURS STIFF NECK SEASON
by Tom Larwin

In 1959 Ted got off to a slow start due to a pinched nerve in his neck incurred during Spring Training. He was out for the first month-plus of the season – and when he got into the lineup he had 21 at bats without a base hit, then got two, and went on for another 16 without a hit. As it turned out, the likely cause for this early season slump was from spring games played in San Diego. In a 1959 story for *Sport* magazine, Ed Linn offered information related to the events that led to Ted's sore neck. Excerpts from that story are below.

Joe Naiman has told us about these three games that were against the Cleveland Indians as part of a March 1959 Spring Training exhibition series held in San Diego's Westgate Park.

THE LAST SUMMER OF #9 AND #6 [1]

"Williams, of course, has always disliked the spring-training exhibition games, so much so that it has been his custom in recent years to duck them all under the pretext that he was suffering from some minor ailment or another. Because of this, the first stories about the pinched nerve in his shoulder (originally diagnosed as a cold) were taken with a grain of salt.

"The irony of it all is that if Ted had kept to his usual program, he would not have been injured at all. He had come to camp in unusually good shape because he had strong misgivings about his ability to work up a sweat in the thin air of Scottsdale, Arizona, the Red Sox' new training site. He quickly discovered that his information could not have been more incorrect. After a couple of weeks, he was in the best shape he had been in for years. In mid-March, the Red Sox and Indians were to play a three-game series in San Diego, Ted's home town. Since Williams had not been in San Diego for 16 years,[2] sheer nostalgia led him to play. He arrived a day early, did some advance publicity work, and had a great time renewing acquaintances with old friends and schoolmates. Although the first two nights were cool and damp, he played five and seven innings. In the final game, on a warm Sunday afternoon, he played seven more.

"Ted was given permission to remain in San Diego, but before the Indians left, Frank Lane asked him, as a special favor, to try to make one of the upcoming games at Cleveland's own training camp at Tucson. Ted, who is fond of Lane, promised that he would. Although his neck was already beginning to stiffen up on him, he drove 150 miles over the desert, suited up, came to the back of the batting cage, and tried to swing a couple of bats. The neck hurt so bad that he didn't even try to step into the cage. "I'm going to have to back out on you, Frank," he told Lane. "I just can't swing.""

"'I know you didn't drive 150 miles to back out of anything,' Lane told him. 'I'm grateful to you for making the try.'"

Linn wrote that Williams was "…shipped up to Boston at the end of March… fitted with a thick collar and told that he would probably miss the opener. He missed much more than that. It was another month before he finally got out of the collar, and another ten days before he got into a game." The competitiveness of Williams comes through, however, as Linn continued with the story…"it was expected that he would work his way into the lineup slowly – as he always had in the past – but Ted surprised everybody by going into the starting lineup as soon as the club came back to Boston. His muscles were still sore, his hands were still blistered and he bore little resemblance to the old Ted Williams."

As it turned out his performance not only suffered during this early part of the season but it adversely affected his batting average for the entire year. As Linn noted, Williams "…had foregone the slower, surer route because he felt he was in such terrible condition that only steady, hard, competitive play could bring him around. It was a mistake."

Linn concluded with this quote from Williams: 'I didn't expect to do real good,' Ted says, 'but I never thought I'd be that bad.'"

1) Ed Linn, Sport, September 1959, excerpts from pp. 71-72.

2) So, this would have made Ted's last trip to San Diego in 1943, which we know is wrong.
   He attended his induction into the Breitbard Hall of Champions [now the San Diego Hall of Champions] in 1954.

Ted checking rod and reel at the Coronado Yacht Club, July 21, 1961.

ANOTHER VISIT, ANOTHER SPORT
by Bill Nowlin

Ted Williams didn't make that many visits to San Diego, so it was big news when he came to town in July 1961, less than a year after he'd retired from big league ball. It was on July 21, and The Splinter weighed 230 at the time.

He arrived at the Coronado Yacht Club to launch a fishing contest, and the perfectionist in him immediately picked up something wrong with the equipment he'd been provided. "This isn't right," he told Lowell "Monty" Montgomery, manager of the sporting goods department at the Sears store on Cleveland Avenue. Ted was scheduled to give a casting demonstration in the Sears parking lot later that night, and another one the following afternoon. "This reel'll have to be re-wound. A big fish hits this and the line'll dig in."

Ted had his own rod and reel company at the time of this visit. The Sears reel was re-wound for Ted, and word of his concern for quality may have reached some of the higher-ups in the company. Some years later, Ted had his own signature line of sporting goods at Sears – and was reputed to have personally tested every piece of equipment before he would allow them to put his name on it.

On July 22, he went fishing for albacore with Angelo Alessio of Coronado. Rolla Williams, the outdoor writer for the *San Diego Union* (and no relative), could hardly get Ted to talk about fishing. Instead he wanted to talk about Mantle and Maris and the heavy home run totals they were beginning to build up as the season got deep into July. He did answer one question about fishing.

"What do you get from fishing that you were never able to get from baseball?"

"Solitude," he grinned, "Seriously, fishing has always meant a lot to me. I've always tried to learn as much about it as possible and to do it as well as I can. It's like baseball, you get about as much out of it as you put into it." *"Ted Brings Diamond Questions To Gaff"*, San Diego Union, *July 22, 1961*

Ted relaxing in his hotel room, March 12, 1959.

TED'S LAST HOME RUN IN SAN DIEGO
by Bill Nowlin

"The count 1 and 1 to Williams. Everybody quiet now here at Fenway Park, after they gave him a standing ovation of two minutes, knowing that this is probably his last time at bat.

One out, nobody on, last of the eighth inning. Jack Fisher into his windup. Here's the pitch. Williams swings. And there's a long drive to deep right! That ball is going... and it is gone! A home run for Ted Williams in his last time at bat in the major leagues." *Curt Gowdy, Red Sox broadcaster, September 28, 1960.*

Every baseball fan with any sense of history knows that Ted Williams hit a home run in his last time at bat in major league ball, at Boston's Fenway Park during the final home game of the 1960 season.

Less known is the fact that Ted Williams also hit a home run in his last at-bat on the field at Hoover High. It was not when Ted was in his final year as a student at Hoover. In that game, he didn't fare too well, going 1-for-5 with a single earlier in the game. His last home run at Hoover came when Ted was 59 years old and back at his old high school to film a video with pitcher Tom Seaver.

It was November 1977. Ted had turned 59 in August, and Rotfeld Video had scheduled a shoot with Tom Seaver hosting a segment in the Greatest Sports Legends series featuring Ted Williams. The 22-minute video was shot in San Diego, and included a visit by star pitcher Seaver, who'd just completed his eleventh year in major league ball, along with native Ted Williams. Most of the video was shot on the baseball diamond at Ted's alma mater, Hoover High School.

The November 17, 1977 *Los Angeles Times* ran a story on Ted's return to San Diego and reported when the shoot was complete and the cameras were being packed away (too bad this wasn't caught on tape), Ted "stepped into the batter's box to take a few swings against one of the Hoover High kids." Who was that kid? "It looked like the same old swing," *Times* staff writer Charles Maher

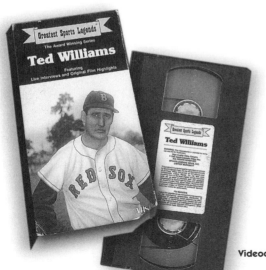

wrote, "replayed at about three-quarters speed. On about the third or fourth pitch there was a sharp crack. The ball flew toward right field, cleared the high fence there and landed in a street, maybe 350 feet from home plate. That ended a rather prolonged slump. Ted Williams hadn't hit a home run at Hoover High in 40 years."

Yes, who was the pitcher – the kid who threw The Kid that ball? I reached out to librarian Dennis Donley of Hoover High, who for many years has been the point person at Hoover for inquiries about Ted Williams. In the latter half of 2003, Dennis searched school records and gave me a list of some of the baseball players

Videocassette of the Greatest Sports Legends show.

who'd been on the Hoover High Cardinals that year. I mailed letters out to several of them, and got a call back from Alan Goodwin. He was calling from Broken Arrow, Oklahoma. He was the pitcher who'd served up Ted's last home run at Hoover.

He hadn't wanted to. Like any competitive ballplayer, he wanted to strike out the great hitter – even if he was no longer in his prime. Like Ted, Alan lived in another district and had to get special permission to attend Hoover, which by the 1970s was highly regarded for its baseball program. Like Ted, Alan and the Hoover team went to the C.I.F. playoffs. In fact, they went all three years while Alan was there.

A starting pitcher his junior and senior years under coach Bob Warner, Alan doubled as catcher. Whenever he wasn't pitching, he was the receiver. He'd started playing baseball at 7 years of age in San Diego and was a catcher all the way up until about age 14 when he mixed in a little shortstop but

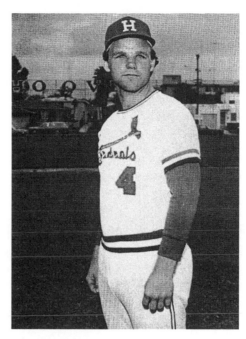

Alan Goodwin, Hoover High pitcher.

then became a pitcher as well. He bats right and throws right, and had hopes of a pro career until blowing out his knee catching. Since high school, he's had 11 operations on his knees.

Several ballplayers from Hoover in Goodwin's years went on to the pros. "Michael Davis went into the Oakland Athletics program right out of high school. He was a senior when I was a sophomore. Craig Daniels went to the minor leagues. There's been several. If I hadn't hurt my knee, I would have tried to see how far I could go. I was going to go semi-pro – I did play some semi-pro ball after high school, but my knees just wouldn't let me catch the whole nine innings. I had a good bat and everything."

It was during Alan's senior year that Ted Williams returned to Hoover to tape the program. The boys on the baseball team knew about it well in advance, and all had to sign release forms.

It was during the season for winter ball. Hoover played year round and getting players out for the occasion to provide a little background flavor during the taping was no problem. There was no ceremony welcoming Ted, no presentation or remarks - just the business of making the video tape, largely a conversation between Tom Seaver as host and his guest Ted Williams.

"My dad was there," Alan remembers with a laugh. His dad Harold worked at Hoover High as a locker room attendant. Working there, he would never let strangers enter the school. "He got in trouble for not letting Tom Seaver into the men's bathroom. He didn't know who he was! Then the baseball coach said, 'Harold, that's Tom Seaver.' 'I don't care. Nobody gets in here!' Then he realized who it was, after it kind of dawned on him, and he said, 'Oh, my God.'"

Some of the footage has Seaver lobbing a few pitches to Ted, while Ted was at the plate. Ted was making a few points, but didn't swing his bat in earnest. Goodwin was the catcher while Seaver was pitching to Ted. He had no idea what was going to happen next. It was exciting enough taking pitches from a star major leaguer, a three-time Cy Young Award winner with the Mets. Looking forward to the day, though, "I was more excited about meeting Ted Williams. That's all you heard about when we were growing up. He was the greatest hitter of all times and he was from San Diego. That's all that everybody talked about."

After five or six hours, with a break for lunch, the taping was done, and the crew was breaking down the equipment, Ted called out to Alan Goodwin: "Hey, let me step in and let me hit a few off of you. You need to get up there and throw to me." He threw four pitches to Ted.

"The first three, he took one and then swung at two, and he looked at me and said, 'I got you zeroed in now, kid.' I was going to blow it by him! (laughs) Who wouldn't? Being Ted Williams, one of the greatest hitters ever. It's like, 'All right. He's not going to get this by me,' not after he said that. I think it was inside, belt-high. He hit the next pitch over the apartment complex over the right field fence. 450, 500 feet.

"That was the next pitch – boom! Too much power to him, man – it was just right down [his power alley]. It went on top of the apartment complex and then we don't know where it went.

"That was it. He said something to the effect of, 'I can't do better than that.' He said, 'Thanks.' I went up and shook his hand. He signed autographs for several people. My dad's got it somewhere. He gave me the bat that he used, also, and my dad has... we moved three times after high school and he doesn't remember where it's at. He brought his own. We were all aluminum by then. He brought his own wooden bat. Actually, he brought two of them. He kept one and he gave me the other one."

Had Ted been timing his pitches? "That's the way it sounded, when he said what he said."

But as far as you could tell, he was swinging at them and just not hitting them? Did you think you'd gotten one past him at that point? "I believe I was thinking that, yes."

Ted was 59 years old at this point. He might not have been working on his swing like he used to. "Oh, he had no problem with that swing! It was the talk of the town there for a while, how Ted Williams just blasted me over the wall. How he had me zeroed in. People compared it to Babe Ruth pointing his finger, you know."

Alan never had contact with Ted later in life, but he's got a memory to last himself a lifetime.

"We talked about it for a long time. Just to have had the opportunity to meet him and actually watch him swing the bat. Tom Seaver being there, too. A lot of people talked about him."

Did you consider it an honor to have Ted Williams hit a home run off you? "I sure do. I think we as the group that were there were honored just to be on the same field he was standing on. It was a neat feeling."

Did Ted's ball really travel 450 to 500 feet? It sure may have seemed that way to the young pitcher. But Ted's longest drive ever in Boston's Fenway Park was measured at 502 feet. If he'd hit the ball that far when he was within a year of turning 60, that would have been a tremendous clout. As a matter of fact, it was quite a clout but maybe a bit shy of the mark.

There's nothing like doing a little bit of original field research, so I asked Dennis Donley of Hoover High if he would go out and look at the field (the field is positioned the same now as it was in 1977, and still is named "Ted Williams Field.") Ted's 1977 "home run" was hit out of the park – and over 47th Street. It also, according to Goodwin, landed on top of – or over – the apartment complex on the other side of 47th Street. I asked Dennis how far away was that from Hoover's home plate, and how high was the complex?

The distance to the right field fence is quite a respectable 320 feet. The sign indicating the distance was removed a few years back. The apartment complex is named Pacific Pines and it is a two-story building, "but the front has a peak to it that goes up another half-story, as if the top floor apartments have open-beam ceilings," Dennis reported. "We figure 400 feet max to the apartment building roof. The building does extend back another 100 or so feet from the street, however."

Apparently, Ted DID have Alan Goodwin zeroed in! And it was a home run for Ted Williams in his last time at bat in San Diego.

IN THE NEWS

Fittingly, it was back where it all began, on the ball field at Hoover High School. Writing in the *Los Angeles Times*, Charles Maher said the film crew was pretty much done with the shoot and they "were starting to load up the cameras when Williams stepped into the batter's box to take a few swings against one of the Hoover High kids. It looked like the same old swing, replayed at about three-quarters speed. On about the third or fourth swing, there was a sharp crack. The ball flew toward right field, cleared the high fence there and landed in a street, maybe 350 feet from home plate. That ended a rather prolonged slump. Ted Williams hadn't hit a home run at Hoover High in 40 years." Los Angeles Times, *November 17, 1977*

Like watching a baseball game, and calling on a second camera angle to give us another replay, we can turn to Joe Hamelin of the *San Diego Union* who also told us that Ted grabbed a bat and took some pitches from a Hoover High player. "One line drive followed another until, inevitably, the Hoover High moundsman fed him a fast ball up and in – and Williams drove it into the bright blue afternoon sky, high over the 307-foot sign atop Hoover's 12-foot fence, high over 46th [sic] Street, up against a house on the other side, nearly 400 feet away. A woman emerged, ready to strangle "the kid" who'd done the deed." San Diego Union, *July 6, 1980*

Ted Williams Field, the old North Park Playground.

TED WILLIAMS FIELD
by G. Jay Walker

"We lived in a little $4,000 house on Utah Street. The North Park playground was a block and a half from my house. It had lights and we could play until nine at night. I was there all the time... The playground director was my first hero. When they inducted me into the Hall of Fame, he was one of the people on my mind, one of the people who made it possible. I tagged after him almost every day of my life for the next six or seven years, hanging around like a puppy waiting for him to finish marking off the baseball field. I was so eager to play, and hitting a home run off him in those makeshift games was as big a thrill for me as hitting one in a regular game. For those next seven years, I don't suppose I missed a day at the North Park playground." *Ted Williams in* My Turn At Bat

According to my best calculations, it's approximately 2,850 miles as the crow flies from home plate at San Diego's North Park playground to home plate at Fenway Park. Drive your old Mustang and we're talking 3,000 miles plus. Literally and figuratively it represents the long road Ted Williams traveled from being a lanky, skinny kid in what was then small-city San Diego to his Hall of Fame career in the Hub.

Your reporter has also traveled the same road in his life – only in reverse. A native New Englander, I almost made it to home plate at Fenway the same age as Ted. Unable to hit a good curveball (come to think of it, good fastballs gave me problems, too), I had to settle for staring at the Fenway light towers from my Boston University dormitory room by winter and cheering from the bleacher seats by summer.

And while I never planned or even thought about it, those weird and unexpected twists and turns that life takes now find me, nearly 20 years later, with a wife and two kids living a few blocks west of home plate at the North Park playground.

When my son got so he could throw those rolled-up socks around the living room pretty well, we decided it was time to hit the big time with a real ball and glove. And where else to go but the North Park playground. Now understand Southern California is not New England, meaning tradition is not our forte. Advertisements saying things like "proudly serving San Diegans for over 8 years" don't leave us with bemused smirks. And if you ever want to get something named after yourself, your best bet is to be a 16th century explorer or an 18th century missionary. So it didn't seem all that unusual to the California way of life that the playground would have nothing indicating that Ted Williams had learned to play ball here. And the only ones who seemed to be aware that Ted had grown up here were the old timers and the small remnant of snow-fearing Red Sox fans. Still, throwing that ball around with my young son, one could almost see the footprints in the sand and imagine the skinny kid working at developing that perfect swing, swatting line drives in to the fading sunset. Sure –why not? Was there really anything to keep this from being called Ted Williams Field? I mean, it was our neighborhood field and we were now the neighborhood.

A proposal to name the field Ted Williams Field was put before the North Park Recreation Council in mid-1990. The proposal passed and began to move its way up the Parks and Recreation bureaucracy in mid-1990. By early 1991 the proposal was before the City Council where it received final approval. The Parks and Recreation staff members working at the North Park playground had been supportive of the idea all along, and when final approval was given they decided to make the ball-field dedication the highlight of the North Park Family Day on July 6, 1991.

It was intended to be just a little neighborhood thing, but in the two weeks before the dedication, other parts of the city began talking about it. *San Diego Union* TV critic Don Freeman abandoned the world of show business for a day to devote his entire column to previewing the event. It was confirmed that the *Union*'s leading sports columnist, Barry Lorge, would be covering the event. And the City Council had managed to contact Ted and extend a formal invitation to attend. Unfortunately he already had plans for that weekend with an old fighter pilot buddy named George Bush at the All-Star Game in Toronto, but the word was that he would be forwarding a letter.

The big day arrived. After introductory remarks by the proposal's originators and City Councilman John Hartley, it was time for the three guest speakers. First up was Wilbert Wiley, probably Ted's closest friend during most of his years at the playground. Ted relates in *My Turn At Bat* how he and Wilbert would call out what type of pitch they were going to throw to each other. One day Ted told Wilbert to just throw whatever he wanted without first announcing it. He relates how pleased he was that he was still able to hit the ball so well, and describes it as one of those key days in his life that you can always remember. Next came former American League umpire Ed Runge. A born storyteller, he managed, between jokes, to tell how Ted was the greatest that he ever saw. Finally came Bob Breitbard, Ted's high school friend and now director of the Hall of Champions (basically a San Diego all-sports Hall of Fame.) Bob brought along a number of items from the Hall of Champions collection including the bat Ted used for a good part of the 1941 season when he hit .406. Then he said that Ted's letter had arrived by express mail, and read it to the crowd:

> "I'm sorry I'm not there with you today, because there is no place on earth besides Fenway Park, that I remember more than the North Park playground. I spent the first 18 years of my life there only a block and a half from my house."

Ted spends a few paragraphs reminiscing about some of the people and events of San Diego baseball at that time. He then concludes:

> "I sincerely want to thank everyone who had anything to do with those days. I can't think of a nicer or more everlasting memory than to have played in that playground as a kid, and then, nearly 60 years later, to have the same playground named after me."

The signs proclaiming Ted Williams Field were hung up around the diamond with a plaque to follow. The *San Diego Union* carried Barry Lorge's column of the event on the front page of the Sunday sports section the next day.

Besides the satisfaction of seeing the park named for Ted, the events surrounding the ball park dedication provided me with a few answers to things I had wondered about. First, the impression is given in some quarters that Ted Williams was happy to leave San Diego and never turned back once he left. The truth is that Ted has maintained friendships with a number of boyhood friends over the years and has visited San Diego off and on throughout his adult life, the most recent being the 50th reunion of his high school graduation.

Second, I had wondered if there was any indication when Ted was a boy that he would turn into the great player that he was; any indication that he was to be the anointed one. While obviously a good player, apparently nothing stood out that marked Ted above the other good players around the neighborhoods at that time. As one old friend put it, "He was good all right, but it wasn't until about 15 that he started shooting ahead of the rest of us. After that, there was just no stopping him."

Then there was Ted's sayonara song to the North Park playground. It was the winter of 1938, the last winter Ted would spend in San Diego. He had just finished a strong year in Minneapolis, and would soon be leaving for Spring Training. Within a year he would be a household name. But for now he was hanging out with his buddies in his last few months of relative anonymity, hunting, fishing and playing some baseball. In one makeshift game at the playground that winter (for all I know, possibly the last game he ever played there), Ted lit into a pitch and said to his mates "keep an eye on that one." The ball went over the backstop on deep center field and into Oregon Street. The backstop is about 400 feet from home plate (392 feet by my tape measure), and 15 feet high. It was the type of poke that would not be unusual for Ted in the future, but for then it was the final affirmation that all those hours of practice in the playground had paid off as he was about to embark on his big league career.

You may feel you're the greatest Red Sox fan around, but can you really say you've done it all until you make the pilgrimage to San Diego, go to the North Park playground, stand at home plate at Ted Williams Field, stare intently west into right field and the setting California sun and let these words echo through your mind:

> "I wanted to be the greatest hitter who ever lived. A man has to have goals – for a day, for a lifetime – and that was mine, to have people say, 'There goes Ted Williams, the greatest hitter who ever lived.' Certainly nobody ever worked harder at it. It was the center of my heart, hitting a baseball. They used to say I lived for the next turn at bat, and that's the way it was. I feel in my heart that nobody in this game ever devoted more concentration in the batter's box than me, a guy who practiced until the blisters bled and loved doing it." *My Turn At Bat, pp. 7, 8*

The North Park playground is about 3 miles northeast of downtown San Diego at 4044 Idaho Street.
If you get to North Park, just look for the big green water tower. Ted Williams Field is one block directly to the south.

Game in progress, Ted Williams Field.

Ted signing baseball during a visit to Ted Williams Field.

TED'S LAST VISITS TO SAN DIEGO
by Tom Larwin

Williams' last visit to San Diego was for about four months in 2001, but he remained hospitalized the entire time in Sharp Hospital, while recovering from an operation performed in New York City. Friend Bob Breitbard had hopes that the medical experts of one of the country's leading medical institutions would be able to do more for Williams, and that coming home to San Diego would prove salutary. Unfortunately, despite the best attention and care, Williams was never able to fully recover.

His last two public appearances in San Diego had been in 1998 and 2000.

On February 7, 1998 he had been guest of honor at Larry Lucchino's house in La Jolla. Lucchino, now President of the Boston Red Sox, had then served as President of the San Diego Padres. Guests included Padres players Tony Gwynn and Steve Finley, former player and manager and longtime San Diego radio-television announcer Jerry Coleman (who also served his country as a Marine Corps pilot like Ted) plus legendary television sports broadcaster Dick Enberg. Inside the house there were informal conversations between Ted, and Gwynn and Finley... about hitting, naturally.

A panel session was held later that evening outside the house in a tented facility. Moderated by Jerry Coleman, Williams and Gwynn held court in a panel question and answer session for the ages. Two players representing 14 batting titles! Ironically, both wore #19 on their San Diego uniforms.

For over an hour Williams showed his quick wit hadn't lessened over the years, and certainly his voice still boomed. And, as Tony noted several times during the session, it was difficult to get a word in edge-wise. Ted was in his element and you could tell he enjoyed being the center of attention. They went back and forth about Ted's advice to Tony when they had met several years earlier: "Major league history is made on the ball inside." He chided Tony on his lightweight bat and chuckled as he referred to it as a "drug store model." While never a big home run hitter, nonetheless, Gwynn's two big home run years were, coincidentally, 1997 and 1998. Tony gave Ted the credit for his newly acquired power and said that he wanted to "tip his hat" to Ted Williams.

Left to right: Roy Engle, Bob Breitbard, Wilbert Wiley, Ted Williams, Joe Villarino, Les Cassie, Jr., July 6, 1991.

The stories went on: Ted's strong desire to see Shoeless Joe Jackson have his day in the Hall of Fame "court." How, as a youngster in 1932, he read about Mel Ott. And how, when he was 15 years old, he had gone to see Satchel Paige pitch on a barnstorming team coming through San Diego. Judge Landis, Jackie Robinson, Eddie Collins, and Joe DiMaggio all were cited in one or more of his recollections.

Williams returned to San Diego in 2000 when he visited Bob Breitbard and made a public appearance at a luncheon held at Breitbard's San Diego Hall of Champions on February 7, 2000. Williams was in a wheelchair but the voice was the same energetic and booming voice of earlier times. Following a few other speakers, including Alan Trammell, then a coach with the San Diego Padres, Ted talked to the luncheon crowd for about ten minutes.

He expressed his good fortune to have grown up in San Diego where there were two or three baseball fields within three or four blocks of where the Williams family lived on Utah Street. He talked about his friend Bob Breitbard and noted, "I taught him how to type... and I always give him credit... he taught me how to hit!"

Afterwards Ted held court, but this time it was a little different than the 1998 panel. The venue was Breitbard's office in the Hall of Champions. Seated around Williams were Padres players Phil Nevin and Trevor Hoffman, Manager Bruce Bochy, Coach Rob Picciolo. Jerry Coleman and Dick Enberg also were there for a while. It was another Ted Williams hitting seminar, perhaps his last... complete with pointed questions. He was a maestro and everyone was rapt in attention. Talking pitching with Hoffman, and hitting with Nevin and Picciolo, and managing with Bochy. He touched on it all.

This was a memorable visit for those lucky enough to be in Breitbard's office that afternoon... not only for what Ted said, but memorable because it also turned out to be his last public appearance in San Diego. And, as you would expect, the main subject was hitting.

Other photographs from Ted's visit July 6, 1991.

SAN DIEGO SITES RELATED TO TED WILLIAMS

Here are some sites that are related to Ted Williams and his association with his hometown, San Diego:

RESIDENCE, AT BIRTH (1918) AND THROUGH 1920 He lived at 933 13th Street; his father, Samuel, worked as a photographer in downtown San Diego at 725 Broadway, Room 32.

RESIDENCE, 1921-1923 He lived at 1140 4th Avenue; his father worked at 961 4th Avenue.

RESIDENCE, 1924-1939 His home was at 4121 Utah Street; his father worked at 820 5th Avenue. Ted's residence changed to the east coast after joining the Boston Red Sox in 1939.

ELEMENTARY SCHOOL Garfield Grammar School is at 4460 Idaho Street.

MIDDLE SCHOOL Horace Mann Junior High School was at 4200 Park Boulevard (subsequently moved).

HIGH SCHOOL Herbert Hoover High School, is at 4474 El Cajon Boulevard. The baseball field on the campus's eastern side has a large sign on the outfield fence in honor of Ted Williams. This current field is east of where it existed in 1934-1936 when Williams played at Hoover.

NORTH PARK PLAYGROUND Between El Cajon Boulevard and University Avenue (bounded by Idaho and Oregon Streets, and Howard and Polk Avenues – this is where he played his youth baseball. There are signs at the field today which commemorate the playground in Ted Williams' honor.

"TED WILLIAMS PARKWAY" (also designated as State Route 56) is also named in his honor. It is an east-west highway in north San Diego that bears no geographic relation to anything baseball, but was named after Ted in 1992.

THE SITE OF LANE FIELD The ballpark in downtown San Diego where Ted Williams played in 1936 and 1937 for the Pacific Coast League Padres. An historical marker commemorating the site contributed by the San Diego Ted Williams Chapter of the Society for American Baseball Research (SABR) is located at the northwest corner of Broadway and Pacific Highway.

SAN DIEGO BREITBARD HALL OF CHAMPIONS Chock-full of historical baseball memorabilia related to San Diego, including a number of important Williams items, is located in Balboa Park, just northeast of downtown San Diego.

Ted, May and Danny Williams, about 1921.

TED WILLIAMS' FAMILY ROOTS
by Bill Nowlin

The news that Ted Williams had Hispanic blood – that he was really the first Latino inducted into the National Baseball Hall of Fame – takes a lot of people by surprise. I've had a couple of articles published on the subject, and they elicited quite a surprised response. Of course, his family knew it all along. They just never made much fuss about it, and neither did he.

Ted's maternal grandparents emigrated to the United States from Mexico. A couple of sentences in Ted's autobiography *My Turn At Bat* caught my attention, but there didn't seem to be a lot to go on. Ted had written, "Her maiden name was Venzer, she was part Mexican and part French, and that's fate for you; if I had had my mother's name, there is no doubt I would have run into problems in those days, the prejudices people had in Southern California." Ted wrote that on page 28, and that was about all he ever had to say about his Hispanic heritage.

It may have been a heritage he never wanted known, because of those very prejudices.

I wanted to pursue this further, though, so back in 1997 when I was working on my first book about Ted Williams, I did a nationwide web search on the name Venzer. There were five people listed. I called them up. They didn't know anything about having Ted Williams as a relative. There was no thread for me to follow. So I gave up. I made reference to Ted's Hispanic heritage, saying "Ted's mother May Venzer Williams, originally from El Paso, gave Ted his Mexican blood."
That was about it.

I asked some of his childhood friends about it when I visited with several of them in April of 1997. Joe Villarino had played ball with Ted in San Diego, as far back as the third grade at Garfield Elementary School. Joe's father, he told me, came from Mexico. Asked about Ted's mother May, Villarino said, "His mother was Mexican. I'm a Mexican – my dad was Mexican and my mother Spanish. Once in a while somebody will ask me about Ted's mother, and if she was Mexican. They didn't believe it, because Ted, you know, he had no signs of being a Mexican at all."[1] I had never doubted it, since Ted had said so in *My Turn At Bat*, but it was good to confirm that Ted did have an Hispanic heritage. I kept hoping to learn more.

A THREAD TO FOLLOW

My first book on Ted was one I co-authored with Jim Prime. It was published by Masters Press and named *Ted Williams: A Tribute*. The book came out in November, 1997, a little late in the year to get good distribution – but out it came. Nearly a year and a half later, Jim received an e-mail out of the blue from Manuel Herrera, informing Jim that he was Ted Williams' cousin. We'd received a few notes we'd had to treat with skepticism, but Jim passed this right on to me, knowing of my interest in this aspect of the Ted Williams story. I wrote Mr. Herrera that I was responding to the note he'd sent Jim and asked him for more information about himself, and asked if I could call him and do an interview. He replied positively, and sent me his phone number.

On May 29, 1999 I phoned him and we talked for a full hour. Manuel filled me in on a lot of history on Ted's mother's side of the family – and even told me that Ted's mother's sister, his Aunt Sarah Diaz, was still living at age 94 in Santa Barbara. It was maybe seven or eight minutes into the interview before he used the name Venzor. Venzor? Venz-oar? As I transcribed the tape later, I kept hearing him say "Venzor" – not "Venzer", which I'd always been pronouncing "Venz-air." Part Mexican and part French, Ted had written. Either way, that would be the way it was pronounced. But this was clearly "Venz-oar" – with the accent on the second syllable. I pulled out a copy of Ted's birth certificate, which was reproduced on page 2 of Dick Johnson and Glenn Stout's 1991 book *Ted Williams: A Portrait in Words and Pictures*. There it was, clear as anything: Venzor. Yet in the text right on the very next page, the authors use the name "Venzer." Why wouldn't they? After all, that's the way Ted spelled it in his own autobiography.

Who would think that Ted would misspell his own mother's maiden name? Of course, the truth is he might not have done anything of the sort. First of all, the autobiography was written by Ted Williams with John Underwood. John spent a LOT of time with Ted and ended up collaborating on three books with him – *My Turn At Bat*, *The Science of Hitting* and *Fishing the Big Three*. He is a talented professional writer who came to know Ted Williams well, and helped produce some excellent work. Both *My Turn At Bat* and *The Science of Hitting* are classics, and have been in print from one of the world's largest publishing houses for over 30 years. That doesn't happen with many books. But it would have been John Underwood who did all the actual writing, all the typing and probably the final proofreading. My guess is that he heard the way Ted pronounced his mother's name, and Ted probably pronounced it in his Southern California way, not with the intonation a Spanish-speaker would have used. When I had an opportunity to talk with Ted himself over dinner at his home, he indeed pronounced the family name "Venz-urr" – with the accent on the first syllable. Underwood probably heard that and, quite reasonably, wrote Venzer. And Ted never spotted it, if and when he proofread the manuscript.

In late 2002, I wrote John Underwood and asked him if he thought this might have been what happened. He wrote back, "Regarding the family name, I'd say – without really knowing, you understand – that your take on it is correct."[2]

Interestingly, Ed Linn took *My Turn At Bat* as gospel and even declared in his biography *Hitter* that the birth certificate had misspelled her name as Venzor.[3]

However it came to be, from 1969 when *My Turn At Bat* first was printed, anyone wanting to research Ted's family history would have read his mother's name as Venzer and accepted that as correct. If anyone noticed the discrepancy between the birth certificate and the autobiography, they would have been likely to figure that Ted's spelling was correct and that the clerk who completed the birth certificate had erred. After all, it was Ted's autobiography. And clerks do make errors.

Manuel Herrera.

After I finished interviewing Manuel Herrera, and as I transcribed the cassette tape from our phone conversation, I realized the depth of information he had revealed and I was astounded. None of what he told me was in any of the many books about Ted Williams. Manuel was, and remains, an energetic fount of information. He'd never written this all down, but he had soaked up and retained a full family history in his head.

RESEARCHING THE FAMILY

At this point, I did two things. First of all, I telephoned Sarah Diaz. She was 94. I didn't waste any time. I phoned her within a day or two. She was articulate and had a wonderful memory, and we talked for a full hour. She was a Venzor herself. May Venzor's younger sister. In our talk, she came across as a wonderful woman of the West and I thoroughly enjoyed our conversation. Everything Manuel had told me jibed with what Aunt Sarah recounted. And there were many family members they'd both mentioned. Off and on over the next three years, I contacted a number of family members

Arnold Diaz, Ted and his aunt Sarah, Santa Barabara.

and filled in my knowledge as best I could. When I did a web search on Venzor, there were a lot of them. There were 37 listings in California. I knew May Venzor had been born in El Paso; there were 114 listings in Texas. The main outlines of the Venzor family history presented here came from Aunt Sarah and Ted's cousin Manuel Herrera. In speaking with numerous other relatives since, the information they provided has only been augmented and elaborated, never contradicted.

Ernesto Ponce, handball player.

Nearly a year later, in 2000, I learned that one of Ted's uncles was still living, in El Paso. I'm a member of the Society for American Baseball Research (SABR) and SABR offers a very active online chat list for its members. At some point in April 2000, the subject of Ted Williams' Mexican ancestry came up. Eric Enders, a researcher at the Hall of Fame in Cooperstown, had written in about the subject, so I dropped Eric a note and we traded a few e-mails. Eric comes from El Paso himself, and recalled a local newspaper column about Ted's uncle living there. This was fascinating, because Ted Williams' birth certificate said that May Venzor Williams had been born in El Paso. An uncle in El Paso made perfect sense, and seemed to offer new vistas.

Eric was able to locate the article for me, written by Ray Sanchez of the *El Paso Herald-Post*, and it supplied the uncle's name: Ernesto Ponce. Well, there was no Ernesto Ponce listed, but I tried entering "Ernest" and struck paydirt. I called him up and conducted another telephone interview. This gave me more information, but it was a more difficult conversation – not as fluid as I would have liked. I figured if I'd have the opportunity to meet him in person, I could probably learn a lot more.

Eulalia and Fedrico Ponce.

Since I'd never been to El Paso (but always loved the Marty Robbins song), I decided to visit. My wife comes from Laredo, another Texas border community. It could be interesting to visit El Paso. Besides, how many people in the last year of the twentieth century were ever going to get the chance to visit Ted Williams' uncle? Ted himself was 82 at the time.

The year before, 1999, I had hoped to visit Sarah Diaz in Santa Barbara. I booked my flights for later in June and made my arrangements. Manuel Herrera suggested a number of people in town I should seek out. At the last minute, though, Sarah got cold feet and requested that I not come. Ted had always been very private about his family, and while she had been very forthcoming over the telephone, perhaps the prospect of my coming to visit left her feeling a bit of trepidation – understandably so. After all, Ted might not like her to be divulging all this information, and the family had never been ones to publicize their famous relation. I tried to reassure her, and also spoke with Dee Allen, her niece who lived nearby, but in vain. I was disappointed, but naturally respected her decision.

Sarah Diaz died on November 3, 1999. I never met Aunt Sarah, which I truly regret, but I did make my way to El Paso, in Texas, on Election Day 2000 – the election it seemed would never end. Weeks later, they were still counting and recounting ballots in Florida. I'd voted absentee.

The day after the election, I visited the Ponces – Ernie and his wife Mary, and we had a good chance to talk. I'd also been in touch with another relative in the area, Kathleen Osowski. She is Manuel Herrera's sister and though she only lived a few miles away from the Ponces had never met them. I visited her at her real estate office, and Kathleen and I drove up the mountain together for the visit and had a chance to meet Ted's uncle and aunt that morning. Ernie was wearing a New York Mets cap, and I gave him a bit of a hard time about that, but both Mary and Ernie told me of their honeymoon to San Diego in the 1930s and told me more about the family and their own stories. Later in the day, after I spent a couple of hours in Juarez across the border, I enjoyed dinner with Kathleen and her husband.

Ernest Ponce, it turns out, served on the El Paso City Council from 1951 to 1957, the first Hispanic council member in the city's history. There was once a time that he played against John Wayne in a handball tournament in Hollywood. John Wayne asked him, "You really play to win, don't you?" "Yes, sir. I'm going to hit the ball where you're not," was the reply.[4]

Eric Enders and I coincidentally both met in Toronto a few months later, on our way to Cuba where we spent a week on a Cubaball tour, taking in five Cuban baseball games and doing some research there. Two different hotels – the Sevilla and the Nacional – had photographs of Ted Williams in their lobbies. I was also able to find three different photos of Ted in Cuba from street vendors or private collectors. Pre-Castro, Ted had thought about retiring to the Varadero area on Cuba's north coast. But that's another story.[5]

Throughout all of this, I kept in touch with Manuel. We have traded a few hundred e-mails. He is an amazing repository of family knowledge. He has an encyclopedic mind and a good memory for story after story after story. Family clearly means a lot to him and he seems to have absorbed and remembered a wealth of information. He can spin out stories and genealogies like the honored *griots* of western Africa, who rely on their prodigious memories to pass the stories of their clans and the lore of their villages down from generation to generation. Every family should have a keeper of tradition like Manuel Herrera.

So what is the story? Enough of the introduction.

TED'S RETICENCE ABOUT HIS FAMILY

Ted wrote little about his family. And he didn't like prying newspapermen. When he first arrived in Boston, he was the talk of the town. He was a fresh, enthusiastic kid full of vim and vigor and an overflowing love of playing the game of baseball. This was the youngster who would wake up his veteran San Diego Padres roommate Cedric Durst at 6:00 in the morning, practicing his batting swing in the hotel room, with a rolled-up newspaper, crowing, "Christ, Ced, it's great to be young and full of vinegar!"

This was The Kid who would be in a reverie in right field (he played right field his first year with Boston) swinging at imagined pitches, while he was supposed to be setting himself defensively for the opposing batter. This was the lanky colt most baseball fans have seen in the old film clip (and most have seen it a dozen or more times) who, in his third year in the majors, was still so unaffected he truly leapt around the bases, galloping and bouncing and clapping his hands after hitting the home run to win the 1941 All-Star Game for his fellow American Leaguers.

Ted struggles with a Mexican outfit during a Texas Rangers game.

But The Kid had grown wary. After his honeymoon season in 1939, when he set a rookie record for runs batted in (145) which has never been topped, reporters wanted more stories about Teddy Williams. Ted had already made one enemy in the press, by declining an interview with one of the deans – Bill Cunningham – because Cunningham was intoxicated. Ted's mother May was a soldier in the Salvation Army, staunchly opposed to drink, and Ted himself shunned alcohol for many years. He didn't have much patience for drunks. When Cunningham approached Ted in a Florida hotel lobby, he was obviously inebriated. Red Sox pitcher Elden Auker told me, "Ted looked up at him and said, 'I'm sorry, Mr. Cunningham, I don't give interviews to sportswriters that are drinking.' And boy, you could have... this just embarrassed Cunningham terribly. In front of all of us... Cunningham spent the rest of his sportswriting days trying to hurt Ted and I think the rest of them kind of copied what he'd done."[6]

Young Danny Williams, on the Salvation Army drum.

Boston was a highly competitive newspaper town, with many editors vying for stories to sell papers and many reporters eager to please. One or two enterprising reporters made their way to Ted's home in San Diego and started asking questions. Where was Ted? He wasn't in San Diego. They learned he was in Minnesota, visiting a girl he'd met there and enjoying some hunting and some fishing. The young woman was Doris Soule, whom Ted later married. Her father was a hunting guide. With no Ted, they started asking questions of his mother: why didn't Ted come home to see you? How much money did he send home?

These days, with all the supermarket tabloids and with any number of television programs tapping the same vein, these questions would almost be expected. Par for the course. In those days, they were really beyond the pale. Many of the writers partook of the same temptations offered the ballplayers, and the personal lives of players were pretty much off-limits. Ted resented this prying, this intrusion into his family life. Ed Linn suggests that a Harold Kaese column in the *Boston Transcript* in May, 1940, was perhaps the last straw. Ted wasn't hitting well. This always upset him. Kaese quoted manager Cronin and a couple of Ted's teammates as critical of The Kid's lackadaisical fielding, and accused Ted of "extreme selfishness, egoism and lack of courage," adding (Kaese supposedly tried to retract this latter part prior to publication), "Whatever it is, it probably traces to his upbringing. Can you imagine a kid, a nice kid with a nimble brain not visiting his father and mother all of last winter."[7]

This sort of thing turned Ted against newspaper writers for the rest of his life. He had some vicious things to say about some of the writers, and it was only well after he'd finished his career that he reached some guarded accommodation with the "knights of the keyboard." Needless to say, many of the writers struck back and took out their resentments one way or another – denying Williams a vote for MVP, creating columns condemning his approach to the game, and the like.

Another player might shrug off stories nosing into his relationship with his family. The ferocity of Ted's reaction to these stories, though, betrayed his conflicted feelings about family. Bluntly, Ted was embarrassed and even ashamed of his family, so it infuriated him when writers started turning over rocks to see what they might uncover. He became enraged, because he was ashamed, and he couldn't just let it go.

One of the reasons *My Turn At Bat* is such a remarkable book is that John Underwood was able to get Ted to be so honest about his feelings. It was one of the first sports biographies where a player was willing to open up and admit to personal vulnerabilities. To Underwood, Ted talked about his family as candidly as a writer could hope. He wrote that his father had served in the Army and perhaps in combat. "Whenever anybody wrote about my dad they seemed to delight in calling him a 'wanderer' or a 'deserter of the family,' but that's a lot of bull. He stuck it out with my mother for twenty years, and finally he packed up, and I'd probably have done the same." Some say that Ted in effect did do the same; he rarely made visits home, even in his mother's declining years. "My mother was a wonderful woman in many ways," he continued, "but, gee, I wouldn't have wanted to be married to a woman like that. Always gone. The house dirty all the time... She was religious to the point of being domineering, and so narrow-minded... My mother had a lot of traits that made me cringe." Still, despite all that, "My dad and I were never close. I was always closer to my mother, always feeling I had to do right by her, always feeling she was alone, and knowing for years afterward how hard she had worked with nothing to show for it. I loved my dad, it wasn't that I didn't love him. But he didn't push very hard. He was just satisfied to let things go as they were."[8]

Ted Williams was forthright and honest. He admitted his own shortcomings, and laid bare a lot of the disappointment he felt about his own childhood and his own family. He told of being closer to other fathers in the neighborhood than to his own father. He told how humiliated he felt when his mother continually dragged him to Salvation Army events, making him march with the band. He let us know about his younger brother Danny, who always seemed to be getting into trouble.

Some of his classmates ribbed him about his mother and he had flushed with shame. He didn't have a happy home. His family was deteriorating around him by the mid to late 1930s. His parents' marriage had effectively dissolved and his brother was becoming more difficult, hanging out with "an altogether different bunch," and always in "some kind of scrape." He knew that Rod Luscomb had taken a loaded revolver off of Danny one time. Ted, though, had his girlfriend in Princeton, Minnesota. He had fashioned a new life for himself in professional baseball; the players were his peers. He really didn't have sufficient reason to want to go home. And so, being Ted Williams and becoming more and more accustomed to doing things his own way, he did not.

Years later, in 1992, he visited the Utah Street house with his son John-Henry. The current owner, Terry Higgins, gladly admitted them, but could sense Ted's reluctance. Higgins said, "This house, Ted don't like it. You could see it brought back a lot of bad memories. All he wanted to do was get out... This house, Ted don't like it at all."[9]

Samuel S. Williams.

TED'S FATHER, SAMUEL STUART WILLIAMS - A NEW YORK YANKEE

Ted's father struck out on his own, too, at an early age. Not a lot is known about Ted's father. He's a very difficult guy to research. Ted had relatively little to say about his dad in *My Turn At Bat*, and the impression he conveyed didn't come across all that well, though on a closer reading some of what Ted had to say was not unkind. "I loved my dad," he wrote. "It wasn't that I didn't love him. But he didn't push very hard. He was just satisfied to let things go as they were." No one ever said that about Ted Williams.

When was Samuel Stuart Williams born, and what was his family like? A researcher wanting to learn more probably starts with the famous Ted Williams birth certificate.

It offers his father's name as Samuel S. Williams, a place of birth (Ardsley NY) and the fact that Samuel Williams was 32 years of age at his last birthday. Ted was born at the Sunshine Maternity Home on August 30, 1918. Or maybe August 20. His birthday was always celebrated on the 30th, but the more likely date may be the 20th. The typed data on Ted's birth certificate provides the date as August 20, 1918. At some later time, the "20" was crossed out and replaced with a hand-written "30." Dr. J. M. Steade was the physician; whoever prepared the form dated it August 21. It was filed September 4, 1918 with the Bureau of Vital Statistics of the California State Board of Health.

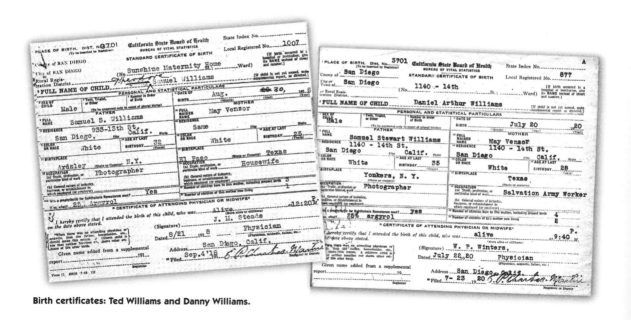

Birth certificates: Ted Williams and Danny Williams.

The *San Diego Evening Tribune* in 1937 listed his birth date as October 30, but it seems that Ted just made that date up. Biographer Michael Seidel's explanation: "he just didn't relish the distraction during the season." Harold Kaese of the *Boston Globe* says that Ted told him, way back in his rookie year 1939, that he was born at the end of August, but moved his birth date back two months, "because I didn't want to celebrate my birthday during the playing season." Ted was, if nothing else, determined to learn everything he could about baseball, and to avoid anything that might prove distracting – such as people making a fuss about his birthday during the season. As Kaese concluded, "He thought of everything, even when he was a kid."[10] Whether Ted's birthday was the 20th or 30th may remain uncertain; the date of filing of the birth certificate and The Kid's admission to Kaese should both effectively rule out the October date. For what it's worth, Ted's official high school record bears the date of 8/30/18. So do his military records, both those he completed during World War II and those when he was recalled to service for the Korean War.

What about Ted's father, and his birth, though? None of the books on Ted Williams offered much of any information. Teddy's birth certificate provided the only clue – that he was said to be 32 when Teddy was born. If Samuel Williams was born, say, in April, and was 32 years or age in 1918, then he himself would have been born in 1886. If he'd been born sometime after August 20 or 30, then perhaps he'd been born in 1885.

Maybe a search of birth records in Ardsley, New York would provide the answers. The first problem encountered, though, loomed large: there was no Ardsley, New York, in the 1880s. George Calvi, Ardsley Village Manager, wrote me, "Ardsley was not an incorporated village prior to 1896." Well, OK, the Ted Williams birth certificate was from 1918, and Ardsley existed by that time. Sam Williams might still have had family there, and even though he himself was born in – perhaps – Dobbs Ferry or Yonkers or another community, the rest of his family might in 1918 have lived in the newly-named Ardsley, and he may therefore have chosen the current name rather than the name the community had been known by in the days when he'd been born.

Tapping the network of researchers which SABR offers, I came in contact with Frank Jazzo, who lives in the area. I told Frank what I had to go on, and he researched local town records for a Samuel Williams, born around this time period. Frank is the Town Historian of Tarrytown, New York, and Frank found a record of a Samuel Williams' birth, writing me of the find on the man's actual birthday. "Happy Birthday, Sam Williams," Frank wrote me on June 8, 2002. "Happy Birthday, Samuel Williams, born June 8, 1886, in Tarrytown, N.Y., 5th child of John Williams & Josephine DeRevre Williams." Frank's research showed that Samuel was actually born in Glenville, a section of the Town of Greenburgh, with a Tarrytown post office address (things are complicated in this part of New York state.)

Wow! I was sure he'd found it. It all fit, even to the point of a sister named Florence, who I figured might have been Ted's Aunt Effie. More on her later. Where could I take this information? With this additional bit of data, there were more avenues I could explore. Williams is such a common name that it presents the problem of an overwhelming number of possibilities. DeRevre, though – that's an unusual name. I did a web search and found a book on management by Marc Van DeRevre. I thought it sounded like kind of a Belgian name, and a business associate of mine in The Netherlands agreed. But Mr. Van DeRevre never wrote back. Not that much to go on, really. I was so sure that we had found the right guy, though, that I sent off a note to Ted's son John-Henry Williams, letting him know of his grandfather's birthday. I didn't get a reply from him, either.

Ted Williams died less than a month after Frank Jazzo's note. There was no funeral service held, but a celebration of Ted's life was held on July 22, 2002 at Fenway Park in Boston. Ted's two nephews – his brother Danny's two sons, Sam Williams and Ted Williams, both attended and I had the opportunity to visit with them at their hotel on July 21 and then on the field and in the park the day of the event itself.

May Williams with her grandchildren, Ted and Sam Williams, at Sarah's house in Santa Barbara, 1958.

I had been looking for them for years – asking everyone I could if they knew how to locate them. Ted Williams Family Enterprises was of no assistance; I'm not sure how hard they tried. I even went so far as to do an Internet search for everyone in the entire country named Theodore Williams and Samuel Williams and phoned every one of the California listings, back in 2000, but turned up nothing. I seemed to have hit a dead end. I'd heard that one of them played guitar and that one had gone to Cal Poly at San Luis Obispo. There was a classical guitarist named Ted Williams, but it wasn't the right man. The Cal Poly alumni office was unable to help. Then suddenly, an article by Joseph Kahn in the *Boston Globe* mentioned that both nephews were coming to the Fenway event. Apparently they had contacted the Red Sox, who put them in touch with Club Historian Dick Bresciani. Dick let the *Globe* know, and Joe mentioned them in print. I contacted Joe and he told me how to reach nephew Ted, so I telephoned and spoke in turn to both Ted and Sam, and we met up at their hotel in Boston once they arrived.

When we met, I gave them each one a copy of my book (*Ted Williams: The Pursuit of Perfection*, which I co-authored with Jim Prime and which had been released eight days before Ted died.) The book was a revised and expanded version of our earlier *Ted Williams: A Tribute*. I met Sam and Ted again (and Ted's son Noah) the next morning at the Fenway Park event and we walked around the field. I was able to introduce them in person to Dick Bresciani and also to Leigh Montville, who had begun work on a biography of Ted for Doubleday about six months before Ted died. For sons of the brother (Daniel Arthur Williams), the brother who bore the burden of a bad reputation in all the books on Ted Williams, they both seemed very nice guys. And they were both frank in their memories of their father, readily admitting there was much about him they did not know. Had he spent time behind bars? Had he been discharged from the Army for going AWOL to see his wife? They weren't sure, but they'd heard stories. They didn't dismiss the possibilities, nor were they defensive. Both were aware that aunts and family in Texas knew more about Danny Williams, but the family diverted even their questions on the subject.

Their own memories of their father were of a hard-working man, who seemed to move house often for reasons unknown – they wondered, was he dodging creditors? – until he got sick with cancer, wasted away and died when both were relatively young. Ted paid for his brother's cancer treatment, including air flights for treatment with specialists. Danny was, as I understand it, conflicted. He needed the financial assistance but, we can appreciate, resented his dependency. When Danny died during Ted's last season as a major league ballplayer, his two sons were both less than 10 years old. Ironically, uncle Ted had for years been the leading celebrity raising funds to fight cancer in children for Boston's Jimmy Fund. It was at Children's Hospital in Boston that the first breakthroughs in the treatment of leukemia were achieved. Ted had been actively helping raise money to fight leukemia since the late 1940s. Unfortunately, Ted's own son John-Henry Williams would let it be known in October 2003, at age 35, that he himself had been stricken with acute myelogenous leukemia. Despite a bone marrow transplant from his sister Claudia, John-Henry died of the disease on March 6, 2004.

The relationship between Ted and Danny was not uniformly unfriendly, though, as one might have assumed from what has been written. Danny's son Ted remembers many phone calls between the two, and that they were much closer and more loving toward each other than an outside reader ever would have guessed.

Ted promised Danny and his wife Jean that he would ensure their boys could have something he never had: a college education. Sam became a musician and traveled up and down the West Coast as a guitarist and folksinger; he never took Uncle Ted up on the offer. But John Theodore "Ted" Williams did. He's the one who went to college, and became a graphic designer with his own firm in the Bay Area. Sam Williams became... of all things, a sportswriter! Sam works for the *Lassen County Times* in Susanville, California.

Given the negative image that Ted's son John-Henry built up over the years, it may seem ironic that the sons of the "bad seed" grew up humble, unassuming and decent men. Talking with them and learning about family from their perspective was a pleasure. They seemed as curious as I was to learn more about their famous uncle and his family background.

SOME DOCUMENTATION ON SAMUEL WILLIAMS

After he returned back home to Oakland, California, Ted (the nephew) mailed me copies of grandfather Samuel Williams' military papers. Those provided their own bits of information.

Among other documents Ted has is a copy of his father Danny's birth certificate. On Danny's birth certificate, Samuel Williams' birthplace is listed as Yonkers, NY. In 1918, he told them it was Ardsley but in 1920 he said it was Yonkers. Was he trying to confuse later historians? Sam now stated his age as 35; given Danny's birth date of July 20, 1920, this suggests that Sam was born in 1885.

I was later able to obtain copies of Samuel S. Williams' Social Security application and his death certificate. The former one, he completed. The latter was, inevitably, completed for him. His Social Security application was made on March 1, 1940. He was still married to May at the time, but he had already left the family home and was living in the Navarra Hotel at 402 Stockton Street in San Francisco. On the form, he gives his parents' names as Nicholas Williams and Elizabeth Miller. He declared his birth date as April 5, 1895. Not 1885. Had he missed the right year by a decade? Though a photographer by trade, who had run his own studio in downtown San Diego, he had no employer at the time of application. He still had a little trouble with ages. Under "age at last birthday" he seems to have written 45, then changed it to 46, then crossed it all out and entered "44."

After his divorce from May, Sam married Minnie Mae Dickson, who had worked with him as his assistant.

From his obituary, I learned the name of the funeral home which had arranged Samuel Williams' burial; it still operates under a somewhat different name today as Hull's Walnut Creek Chapel, but Mark Hull – son of the man who ran it in 1952 – graciously faxed me a copy of the funeral record. It's a family firm dating back to 1892, I learned during a personal visit in November 2002. I thought it was an odd touch that a rack outside the director's office featured color post cards of the facility. Be that as it may, office manager Bob Carroll didn't hesitate to supply me with a copy of Minnie Williams' funeral record. Ted Williams (nephew) and I both visited the graves of his paternal grandparents Samuel and Minnie Williams at Colma.

Information for Samuel's record was supplied by the informant, his widow, Minnie. There it states that he was born April 5, 1883 – though the "3" has been written in over a typed number which looks like an "8." Age (last birthday) reads, clearly, "69" but the final digit is altered as well from another number – obviously a lesser one. If he was 69 when he died on November 16, 1952, and only 44 when he applied for his Social Security card in 1940, somehow he gained 25 years between two years which most people would consider 12 years apart. The death certificate, interestingly, also states "yes" in response to the question, "Was deceased ever in U. S. armed forces?" but then adds the comment, "No war." Assuming that this was not an early manifestation of the anti-war sentiment characteristic of the Bay Area in the late 1960s, it seems to reflect that his widow did not know about his military service, or was intending to inform us that her husband had not served in a declared war. Or something else.

A visit to the Westchester County archives and the Clerk's Office of the Town of Greenburgh, New York, revealed that many nineteenth century births were not noted at all in contemporary records. Apparently birth registration was voluntary and many families simply didn't bother.

Samuel Williams death certificate.

Might there have been other relatives of Samuel Williams, whose descendants would have a family Bible or other genealogy? There might be. But I haven't found them yet. Complicating research into Sam Williams' upbringing is that he was said to have run away from home, or at least – as Ted Williams wrote – "run off and joined the Army."[11]

The varying dates given for Sam Williams' birth might reflect a desire to portray himself as older at one stage in his life – perhaps to obtain employment or to enlist in the Army – and younger at another point, for whatever reason. According to his military discharge papers, Sam Williams was a shipbuilder at the time of his enlistment and was 21 7/12 years old on December 6, 1904, the date of his enlistment at Yonkers, NY. He was 5 feet 5 3/4 inches tall (almost a foot shorter than his son Ted grew to be) and had dark brown hair with blue eyes, and a fair complexion. If he was 21 (and 7/12) in 1904, then he would have been born around June in 1883. This would match the year on his death certificate, and – more or less – the April 5, 1883 date cited there.

He may have lied about his age, of course, and Ted wrote that "he had run off and joined the Army when he was sixteen and was in the Phillippines (sic) with the Fourteenth Cavalry during the Spanish-American war." The actual Army records are almost certainly correct as to his date of enlistment. If he were 16 in 1904 – though claiming he was 21 – then he would probably have been born in 1888. It would not be at all surprising if he were actually 18 7/12 – instead of three years older, though since 18 was presumably old enough to enlist anyhow, I'm not sure what the point would have been of adding three years. He was probably 21. And he probably was born in 1883 and neither 1895 nor 1886, nor 1885, or so I figured.

The least likely date given for Sam Williams' birth was June 23, 1891. That's the date Ted Williams gave when completing his Officer Data Sheet for the Marine Corps in 1952. If Ted had believed his father was born in 1891, then he would have to have believed the possibility that his father had served in the Philippines when he was 6 years old! Sam would have turned 7 on June 23, 1898 – just 8 days before the famous Battle of San Juan Hill of the Spanish-American War.

Later, I learned that the San Diego city census of January 1920 showed Samuel and May Williams living at 933 13th Street, with their son Theodore, aged 1 year, 4 1/2 months. Samuel, the census reported, was 34 and his wife was 27. This would now suggest he was born in 1886. Of course, an 1886 birthdate would have meant he was only 11 or 12 during the Spanish-American War (April - June 1898.) The 1920 census also lends further credence to Ted's birth date being an August one. The same census data states that both of May Williams' parents were born in Mexico and both had Spanish as their native language.

May, Ted and Samuel's sister Alice at 4121 Utah Street, San Diego, probably 1941.

Nephew Ted Williams, though, beginning to ask a few more questions via the Internet, was sent information pursuant to his post on a genealogy forum. The 1900 census of Yonkers, New York stated that Samuel had been born in April 1887, to Nicholas Williams (born October 1862), a barber born in New York, to parents who were themselves both New York born. Nicholas was listed as head of the household. His wife was Maggie, born in February 1873 in England, to parents both born in England as well. Maggie was just 14 years older than Samuel, who was apparently not her son. She came to the United States in 1892, the census informs us. It also reports that she had been married for 10 years, though only in the US for eight. This might indicate that Nicholas Williams had traveled to England, married Maggie, and then brought her back to the United States a couple of years later. Maggie Williams did bear three children, according to the census, all daughters: Veasey, born in October 1893, Alice, born in March 1895, and Effie, born in January 1899. The family home at 46 Sawmill River Road also housed a boarder, a tailor from Pennsylvania named Charles Nickum (it appears.) Charles was born in June 1878. The spelling of Veasey is but a guess, too, based on the handwritten census records. It looks like it says Veacey, but while SABR genealogist Peter Morris finds no trace of the name Veacey in that era, the name Veasey shows up rarely but occasionally.[12]

Based on all the information available, it appears reasonable to believe that Samuel Stuart Williams was born in April 1887. His mother probably was the Elizabeth Miller he listed on his Social Security application. Even enlisting the assistance of more experienced genealogy researchers, I've yet been able to uncover more.

A young Samuel Williams (standing)
with an unknown army friend.

SAM WILLIAMS, UNITED STATES CAVALRY

If an April 1887 date is correct, Sam Williams was 17 1/2 when he enlisted – the age would fit more with the notion that he'd "run off and joined the Army" than would an age 21 enlistment. The notion that Sam Williams served in the Spanish-American War, though, doesn't hold water. Sam Williams had shown his family photographs of him in uniform and said that he had served with Teddy Roosevelt's old unit. Ted Williams admitted a certain skepticism about claims his father made, and admitted that he wasn't sure this was really true. It was. In a way. Sam Williams never went charging up San Juan Hill with the Rough Riders. That event occurred in 1898. Whatever might have been the dates of his birth, he wouldn't really have been old enough to be leading the charge, or even trailing along behind. But as far as we know he hadn't exactly said that he was with the Rough Riders. He said he was with Teddy Roosevelt's unit. That's a different thing. We have seen that he first enlisted at the end of 1904 – years after the Spanish-American War had been concluded.

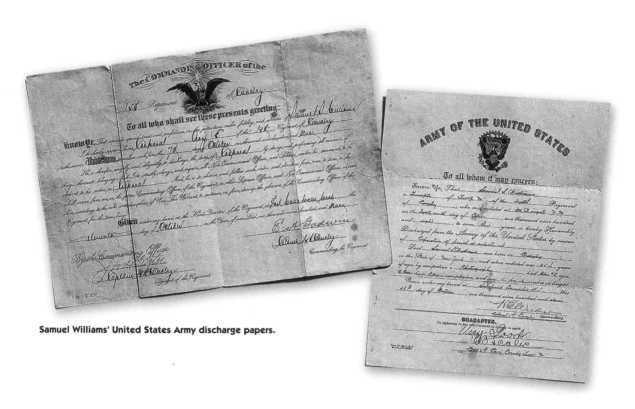

Samuel Williams' United States Army discharge papers.

Sam Williams did admire Teddy Roosevelt, though. It is likely no coincidence that his first born son was given the name "Teddy" – though you never knew what explanation Ted might come up with. In the spring of 1939, he told Harold Kaese of the *Boston Transcript*, "My dad used to be a photographer, until a couple of years ago, when he became a State Inspector of Jails. His best friend was a photographer, too, and when I was born he just naturally called me Ted, that's all."[13]

Ted Williams' original birth certificate reflects the given name "Teddy" – perhaps his birth name was not actually Theodore Samuel Williams. The document says he was born as Teddy Samuel Williams. Johnson and Stout say the name "Theodore" came later, a creation of The Splendid Splinter himself. In *My Turn At Bat*, Ted writes, "The birth certificates (sic) reads 'Teddy Samuel Williams.' I never did like that 'Teddy,' so I always signed my name 'Theodore.'"

As we've seen, the census taker in 1920 also listed the Williams son as "Theodore." By all reports, his mother always called him "Teddy." The census taker may been told that the boy was named "Teddy" but taken the liberty to assume that the youngster was truly named "Theodore" and not "Teddy." Let us revisit this a bit later.

In *My Turn at Bat*, Ted astonishes us, though, by adding, "The 'Samuel' was for my mother's brother, who was killed the last day of World War I."

It never crossed his mind (or John Underwood's) that the "Samuel" might have derived from his father's name? As it happens, May Williams had a brother who was indeed killed at the very end of the First World War. Her brother was named Daniel, and it was Ted's brother who was named after Daniel Venzor.

The United States military records which nephew Ted Williams copied for me provide evidence that Sam Williams was on solid ground when he told Ted that he had served in the military. Samuel S. Williams signed up for a three-year term in the Army of the United States on Dec. 6, 1904 at Yonkers, NY. He was assigned to Troop E of the 14th Cavalry and within just five weeks found himself in the Philippine Islands, arriving there on Jan. 27, 1905. Based at Camp Overton, Mindanao, he was part of the Third Sulu Expedition to Jolo, P.I., serving under Major General Leonard D. Wood from April 22 to May 16, 1905. It was here that he saw combat duty on three occasions.

The Teddy Roosevelt connection presumably comes from Sam Williams having served under General Wood. Wood, later in life the Army Chief of Staff, was commander of the 1st Volunteer Cavalry (the "Rough Riders") during the Spanish-American War. His second in command was Theodore Roosevelt. Wood later served as Military Governor of Cuba from 1900-02 and then served in a number of positions, including commander of the Philippines Division.

The Roosevelt connection was thus not necessarily far-fetched. No doubt all the men under Wood's command were well aware that Teddy Roosevelt – who became President of the United States in September 1901 – had served with Wood. There was maybe a little elasticity in the telling, but Samuel Williams did serve in what was at the very least an analogous unit and he did see combat.

The three engagements noted on his military record were all part of the 3rd Sulu Expedition and all took place on the island of Jolo. The first engagement was on May 1 at Maimbung Market on the southern tip of Jolo. Two days later there was another skirmish or engagement at Ipil and then on May 4, he also took part in fighting at Pala's Cotta. He was eventually transferred back Stateside, leaving the Philippines on Oct. 20, 1905 and arriving in San Francisco on Nov. 23, 1905. It remains unclear what he did for the next two years, until his honorable discharge on Dec. 5, 1907, but the discharge papers were signed by a colonel who commanded the Coast Artillery Corps at the Presidio in San Francisco, so it would appear that he may have spent at least the latter period of time serving in San Francisco.

Trumpeter Williams, like all troopers assigned special skills (for instance, cooks, farriers, or trumpeters), also held regular Army rankings, in his case probably private first class. Other than extra pay for a detail such as playing at a funeral, he shared in all aspects the duties of other troopers – daily horse exercise, stable police, kitchen police, etc., and was considered a regular army cavalry trooper, carrying rifle, side-arm and (during parade formation) a saber on his saddle. [Thanks to Emil Rohracker of the 14th Cavalry Association for this information.] He was promoted to corporal from trumpeter on October 7, 1907 and he also qualified as a sharpshooter in 1907. He held the rank of corporal at the time of his discharge. The promotion form was signed at Fort Walla Walla, Washington on October 11, 1907, effective the 7th.

Sam Williams was not injured, according to his papers, but as trumpeter he was more likely in the front ranks of any skirmish than in the rear. Attempts to learn more of his actual service from the 14th Cavalry Association have so far proven fruitless. With the passage of time, the likelihood that we will learn substantially more seems slim.

The Sulu Expedition was part of the prolonged battle of the U. S. armed forces against the Moro insurgents. The Moro Insurrection in some respects resembled the war in Vietnam. In both conflicts, the United States became embroiled in battle against an Asian populace which was waging a guerrilla-style war to repel foreign troops. General Leonard Wood was the military governor of the Moro Province from 1903 to 1906. U. S. Army estimates of the number of Filipinos killed in the Moro wars are in the tens of thousands while U.S. fatalities in the 1898-1920 period range from 4,000 to as high as ten times that many. Some have said that as many as 3 million Filipinos may have been killed.[14] A webpage prepared by the National Infantry Museum at Fort Benning describes the Moro Wars in this fashion: "The Moros are Muslim tribespeople who inhabit central and western Mindanao, the second largest island in the Philippines. They have lived there for centuries, quite apart from the rest of the Filipino people, most of whom are Christians. The Spanish, who ruled the islands until 1898 when they were driven out by Americans, had let them follow their age-old way of life and did not try to convert them, but the Americans felt differently. They wanted them to become assimilated, but the Moros resisted with sporadic outbreaks beginning in 1901. In 1903, they attacked American troops stationed near Lake Lanos in the interior of Mindanao. On the nearby island of Jolo in 1906, some 600 rebellious Moros who had taken refuge inside the crater of a large volcano (Mt. Dajo) were killed by U.S. troops under General Leonard Wood (1860-1927). This raised a cry of indignation from the American public. Fighting ceased in 1914 and the Moros continued to practice their religion and traditions in peace." In fact, fighting never entirely ended and there is still an active Moro National Liberation Front active in armed insurrection at the start of the 21st century.

On discharge, it was noted that Corporal Williams' character was "excellent" and that "no objection to his reenlistment is known to exist." His horsemanship was "good." Ted recalled, "I've got pictures of him: a little guy, posing behind a horse that was lying down, getting ready to shoot over the horse, and another of him at attention, standing real straight with a bugle slapped against his side."[15] The photographs probably were among those destroyed when Hurricane Donna devastated Ted's home in the Keys in September 1960. Samuel Williams' discharge papers further note that he had performed "service honest and faithful" and was entitled to a travel allowance. His travel destination remains unknown.

The next fact I was able to determine is that he somehow wound up at Fort Wingate, New Mexico on October 29, 1908. What he did in the intervening ten months is unclear, but at the time of this second enlistment, he declared his occupation as "photographer." Whether this is a skill he learned while in the 14th Cavalry or seconded, if such he was, to the Coast Artillery Corps, is unclear. He also may have taken up the trade after discharge, but perhaps failed to make a go of it and chose to re-up for duty again; that would be pure speculation. He joined Troop M of the 5th Cavalry Regiment for another three years. For some reason, he enlisted as a trumpeter again. And he was 25 years, 6 months old, which fits his earlier declaration. He'd either grown 1/4 inch or the measurement was slightly different; he was listed as 5'6" on re-enlistment. He still had blue eyes and dark brown hair, and several scars were noted on various parts of his body, for identification purposes.

When he enlisted this second time, he provided his residence as 27 School Street, Yonkers, N. Y. When he had enlisted the first time, he indicated that he himself lived at 26 Park Avenue, Yonkers, though his father lived on Neppihan Avenue, Yonkers. If he had run away from home, he was at least willing to have his father notified in case of emergency. He also signed up right in his hometown, in the enlistment office at 45 Warburton Avenue – not the act of someone covering his tracks. Nonetheless, it may be that once Sam left home, he chose not to return.

This time, his marksmanship rating is hard to determine. A deep crease created by a fold in the papers renders the rating impossible to read. His horsemanship, however, had improved to "excellent." His character was noted as "very good." There is no reason to think this was a downgrade of the previous "excellent" rating. Chances are it simply reflected a differing subjective judgment from the commanding officer. There was "no unauthorized absence of record" and again he had performed "service honest and faithful."

During this term, most notably, he had been transferred from Ft. Wingate to the Hawaiian Islands, arriving January 13, 1909 and apparently serving the full tour of duty there until October 28, 1911 when he was given his discharge papers at the Schofield Barracks by the colonel commanding the 5th Regiment. He was entitled to travel pay, but the form made it clear that he was "not entitled to transportation to U.S. unless claimed within 30 days of discharge." Perhaps they were concerned that he might enjoy it in Hawaii enough to want to stay. More likely, it was simply Army policy. He may well never have used his allowance; while in Hawaii, Sam Williams met and fell in love with a soldier from another army – May Venzor of the Salvation Army.

In an interesting footnote of sorts, some of Ted's relatives in Santa Barbara reported meeting a baggage handler who worked the trains in California and claimed that Ted had a Filipino half brother – who perhaps even lived in southern California. This well could have been, had Samuel Williams sired a son in The Philippines. Leigh Montville followed up on this lead, and dropped me an e-mail: "I tracked the guy down, all excited, and he said he had heard it from his aunt. He checked with her and said it was all bogus, that his aunt is 91 and suffers dementia... Ah, well..."

There have been other leads as well, some of which remain uncertain. Tom Carmody, who I "met" on a genealogy site, told me of a retired nun in her 80's named Joan Williams. She apparently contacted the Ted Williams Museum and offered to do calligraphy work for the display cases, but it never happened. Tom's mother, Cecilia Williams Carmody is, he says, Ted's first cousin once removed. There is a lot of detail Tom has assembled which makes sense, and a lot that doesn't "compute." Ongoing research may lead to further information.

MAY VENZOR OF THE SALVATION ARMY

May Venzor was serious about dedicating her life to service in the Salvation Army. She was active in the Army from age 12 or 13 and, on her 17th birthday, Corps Cadet May Venzor was given a Bible "by her comrades in the Santa Barbara Corps" on May 8, 1909. 1909? Ted's birth certificate says that she was 25 when Ted was born. This would mean she was born in 1893, or possibly late 1892. If she had been born in 1893, then her 17th birthday would have been 1910. Her obituary, and her gravestone, both show her as having been born in 1891. Yet another confusion of dates! You can't be born in 1891 and be 25 years

May's bible: how many souls did it save?

old when giving birth in 1918. The inscription in the Bible is clearly May 8, 1909, and this would support an 1891 birth date. Ted's birth certificate seems to be misleading. One of those it may have misled was Ted himself. He believed his mother had been born on May 8, 1893, according to information he filed with the Marine Corps in 1952. This is the same form on which Ted had his father

May Williams, young Salvationist.

born in 1891, though, so should perhaps be discounted. Official California death records have May born in 1891 and her sister Mary being born on April 18, 1893; it's extremely unlikely that May was born about three weeks after her sister. Of course, Mary's stated birthdate could have been wrong as well, yet May was well aware of her sister's tragic murder (described below) and might have been expected to have commented had the records of the day gotten the year of her sister's birth wrong.

On August 26th, 1909, May Venzor entered the training college in Chicago, located at 116 S. Ashland Avenue. Salvation Army National Archive files today indicate that she entered the Salvation Army's Training Home in Chicago "out of the Petaluma, Calif. corps at the age of 19. Her career sheet indicates that she played the guitar, piano, and cornet."[16] A May 8, 1891 birthdate would mean she was 18, not 19, at the time she entered the Training Home.

She graduated January 12, 1911, and was appointed a Lieutenant in the Salvation Army. The diploma also constituted an order to travel, which read in part, "You are appointed to assist in the command of Honolulu Oahu, Senior and Junior Corps, So. Pacific Province, and you must please leave for your new appointment on January 20, 1911, without fail."

In Honolulu, she served under D. O. Major Willis. The address of her quarters was at 153 Bieretania [sic] Avenue. On November 27, 1911, when she was promoted to Probationary Captain, she moved from one command to another in Hawaii, and began working with the Senior and Young People's Corps. On January 12, 1912, in effect the first anniversary of her Hawaiian service, she became a full Captain in the Army.

May Venzor in her class at the Chicago Salvation Army Training College.

After Sam Williams was discharged from the United States Army in October, 1911, he may well have stayed on Oahu and forfeited his right to paid transportation to the U.S. He'd met May Venzor.

How May became a Salvationist is unclear. Manuel Herrera told me, "May loved to go to church when she was a young girl, and she picked the Salvation Army when she was about twelve or thirteen. She used to go down to the street corner and sing praises of Jesus. Songs. Somebody would come over and say, 'Mr. Venzor, your daughter is down there singing with those Salvation Army nuts again.' He'd go get her and bring her home. Where do you think she was at the next weekend? Back down there." Perhaps the liveliness of Salvation Army revival meetings of the day appealed to young May.[17] The *Boston Globe* reported that she first joined the Salvation Army on July 4, 1907.[18]

There is no question that May became a dedicated Salvationist and one of the hardest workers they had. She also knew how to work with the system, as the many photographs of her with such public figures as the mayor of San Diego illustrate.

Yet May seems to have both risen and fallen in the ranks, for one reason or another. After nearly 33 years of service, on March 8, 1944, she held the rank of Envoy and was appointed both Publication Sergeant and Visiting Sergeant of the San Diego Citadel. Starting as a lieutenant in 1911, thirty-three years later, she was just becoming a sergeant? Part of the reason was her marriage.

May Venzor and Samuel S. Williams were married on May 13, 1913 in Santa Barbara, California. The wedding was officiated by Staff-Captain Howard Clifford at the Corps Hall. "The marriage marks the end of her service as an officer," explained Kimberly Mack, an historian with The Salvation Army Museum of the West, because "until very recently officers could only marry officers. To marry a non-officer meant giving up one's rank. Which is not to say she was no longer a soldier or a Salvationist, but rather she gave up working as a pastor."[19]

One can understand that May Venzor gave up quite a lot in marrying Sam Williams. She surrendered her status as an officer in her beloved Salvation Army.

It might not have worked out that way. Sarah Diaz reports that Sam Williams had planned to enter the Salvation Army and make a career, but after training in Honolulu he had a change of heart and left the ranks. Apparently, it was not the right fit. Sarah told me that Sam had run away from home. He was, she said, "a very nice person. He always used to tell us kids that he was a Yankee, from New York. When they fell in love in Honolulu, he had to come to Santa Barbara to ask for her hand."[20]

When the couple was married, younger sister Sarah Diaz served as the flower girl at their wedding. The Williamses moved to Los Angeles and Sam first found work as a streetcar conductor. It was probably a relatively short stint. They stayed with the Ponce family as they got settled in.

A postcard sent from Hawaii by May to her parents, 1911: note the Spanish.

May's Salvation Army Captain's Commission, 1911.

Drawing on the craft he had noted on re-enlistment at Fort Wingate, Williams worked as a photographer at the Mitchel [sic] Studio in Los Angeles in 1913 and 1914.

Sometime in 1914, Sam and May moved further south, to San Diego, and Sam began work at the Velour Studio at 820 5th Street in downtown San Diego. Here, Ed Linn says, he "eked out a living of sorts." Ted said his father worked "taking passport pictures and snapshots of sailors and their girls, and he wouldn't get home until nine, ten o'clock."[21] The information that Sam Williams had served as a streetcar conductor came from his sister-in-law Sarah Diaz.

In these happier days, Sam Williams taught May how to color photographs, working to add color to black and white photographs.

I was prepared to try dialing M-2819, the telephone number listed in his 1923 Petition for Degrees to the S. W. Hackett Lodge of Masonic Order in San Diego – but, 80 years later, that number didn't seem to contain enough digits. In the petition, he gave his date of birth as April 5, 1885. I'll forego further comment. Williams was elected a Freemason on December 11, 1923 and stayed a Mason throughout his life. On death in 1952, the Alamo Lodge of Walnut Creek paid $10.35 for a floral piece at his November 20, 1952 funeral service. This we know because the Walnut Creek lodge sought reimbursement from the Hackett Lodge.

We will return to more on May Venzor later.

SAM WILLIAMS AND HIS SISTERS

Even if Sam had run away from home, this may not have reflected as much a sense of enmity as a desire to seek adventure and find his place in the world. He did, at least in later years, maintain contact with his three sisters. I found a bit of information about one of those sisters early in 2001. In *My Turn At Bat*, Ted wrote about his uncle, a fireman in Mount Vernon, New York. It was a pretty well-known story, how Ted – frustrated at one point in the 1940 season – popped off to sportswriters about how maybe he'd just give up the whole thing, quit baseball and go and become a fireman like his uncle. Ted's comment, "Nuts to this baseball. I'd sooner be a fireman," received national play. It also prompted opposing players and fans on the road to start blowing sirens, ringing bells and showing up at ballparks in big fireman's hats. So, who was this uncle? Would there be an opportunity to track another branch of the family tree?

Ted gave his uncle's name as John Smith. Wonderful. That seemed like about as difficult a name to trace as any I could imagine. There are indeed people named John Smith, though. I went to Mount Vernon and checked the public library. By looking through fire department files in the city records, I was fairly readily able to locate a John Charles Smith and he was listed as married to Effie Williams, surely Samuel's sister. I was even able to come up with a photograph of the fire-fighter. After leaving the library, I drove by the apartment where he and Effie lived for many years and where Ted had visited.

Later, I phoned the current Mount Vernon fire chief and was rather efficiently directed to Edward Donovan, retired to New Hampshire but who had served on Engine 6 with Ted's uncle. John Smith was known in the firehouse as "Beanie" Smith. Donovan remembered well when Ted came to visit and told a colorful anecdote about the young Ted swinging the long fire broom as though it were an elongated baseball bat. "He used to pick up a broom on the back of the fire engine and swing it a little bit," Donovan explained. John Smith drove Engine 6. "That was a great big fire engine. He was good at it... getting the water on. It was an Ahrens-Fox, a great big fire engine. He was the only one who could really handle it. Six. That was the engine company I was on with him. His wife was Effie. She was a Williams. Her brother was the one who worked in photography. That made Ted Williams her nephew. His [Beanie's] badge number was 31. My badge number was 62. I used to say to him, 'You're half of me.'"

John Smith developed bursitis at a relatively young age. "He couldn't drive or wrap up hose on the street," Donovan said, so he took disability and retired. John and Effie moved to Florida. The couple had no children, Donovan told me, and if there's any name more difficult to research than Williams, it is probably John Smith.

Donovan was impressed with Ted's interest in his family. He told me that Ted kept in fairly close touch with his aunt. "I'll tell you one thing about Ted Williams," he said. "When I worked with his uncle, he used to call up and ask how his aunt was. I never forgot that. He made a phone call no matter where he was. Chicago or Detroit, he'd call the firehouse and ask for John C. Smith, and ask how was Aunt Effie doing. I thought that was a nice thing. I don't know if there was a problem with his Aunt Effie but no matter where he was, he'd call up and ask his uncle, 'How's she doing?' I thought that was wonderful, really. You know how busy they are. He called religiously."[23]

So, one of Ted's aunts on his father's side was Effie W. Smith. I learned that Ted's dad had two other sisters by asking the man himself. When I had dinner with Ted on April 28, 2000, I took the opportunity to ask him a few questions about his family. Primarily, I was asking for confirmation of information I'd gathered regarding his mother's side of the family, wanting to learn more about his Uncle Saul Venzor and the role Saul may have had in shaping Teddy's attitude towards baseball.

He didn't offer much about his father's side of the family, except to let me know, "My dad had three sisters. Little bitty gals. Around 5 feet, all of them. He was the only boy. He ran away from home and joined the Cavalry. They got there and they found out when he was in the Cavalry that he was only 16 or something." He didn't mention his sisters by name, and I didn't have the opportunity to follow up because the conversation soon switched to his friends Bob Breitbard and Bobby Knight.

John C. Smith, fireman and Ted's uncle.

Ask Ted a question about his family background and you'd soon find him on another topic, maybe talking about a fish he'd once battled. This is a man who was much more at ease talking about salmon on the Miramichi than about his own family. It had never been a comfortable topic.

There was Effie, yes. Another aunt was actually remarkably easy to find – after all, her photograph appears in more than one of the books written about Ted. I didn't put it together, though, until Ted had mentioned that he had three aunts on that side of the family. A couple of years later, I saw a photograph with Effie, Alice and Mae. Was this Mae, or was this May? The photograph is one which nephew Ted Williams owns; he sent a scan of it to me by e-mail. It depicted what I took to be two of Ted's aunts – Effie and Alice – along with Ted's mother. But on closer inspection, the "Mae" in the photograph's caption was not May Venzor Williams at all. We concluded that this was another May – the third aunt. Another possibility is that it was Minnie Mae Williams, Sam's second wife, but she seems to have been known as Minnie, not Mae. As we have seen, the third aunt's name might have been Veasey and not Mae – though perhaps Veasey enjoyed a nickname. It's also possible that the Mae in the photograph was simply a friend and not a relative at all.

Attempts to learn more about any of the sisters have so far borne no fruit. Perhaps the sisters did not, either – the general consensus in the family seems to be that none of the three had children. Hopefully, though, someone reading this book will recall their great-aunt Alice, or Mae, or even Veasey, and be in contact.

Ted Williams and his aunt Alice, left with "Mae", center, and his aunt Effie, right. The woman listed as "Mae" is possibly his third aunt, Veasey (who may have gone by the nickname Mae).

SAM WILLIAMS AND HIS WORK

Sam Williams worked at a number of jobs. As far as we can tell, he never returned to shipbuilding, but certainly he pursued photography throughout his life – and his grandson Ted Williams has also found work as a talented photographer and graphic artist. Sam was also politically connected in some fashion. It's not clear how that began, but Governor Frank Merriam of California was a patron later on.

Samuel Williams.

Samuel Williams was also a United States Marshal. Or at least a deputy United States Marshal. On October 12, 1931, A. C. Sittel, a United States Marshal working for the Department of Justice in the Southern District of California, appointed Samuel S. Williams a salaried Deputy U. S. Marshal in place of J. K. Wilson who had resigned effective close of business the day before.

"Mr. Williams was born April 5, 1886," Sittel's letter to the Attorney General in Washington read, "his address is 4121 Utah Street, San Diego, California, his occupation is Professional Photographer; his salary is $1440.00 per annum." His official residence was to remain in San Diego, and "his duties are to be the serving of process and any such work as I might direct." A copy of the Deputy U.S. Marshal's Oath of Office was attached.

Charles P. Sisson, Assistant Attorney General, wrote back to Marshal Sittel confirming the appointment and his authority to appoint Williams as a Deputy Marshal, grade Caf-2, at the indicated salary.

Merriam served as governor from 1934 to 1939. In 1934, Williams was appointed inspector of prisons for the state of California, Linn writes.[24] During the latter years of his regime, Sam Williams was Chief Jail Inspector of the State of California, until the position lost its funding in 1939 around the time Merriam left office.[25]

Ed Linn speculated that May Williams might have helped her husband link up with the governor. Sam Williams already had his appointment as U. S. Marshal, though, three years before the governor assumed his office. However it came about, the connections seemed to have been significant. When the Bay Bridge spanning San Francisco Bay was opened, Sam Williams was sent an elaborate invitation to the ceremony. He apparently also served for a while as a Sheriff in San Diego.

Sam may have been a bit of a "wanderer" and may have been absent from home a fair amount, but he left some good memories behind with some members of the family. Teresa Cordero Contreras recalls, "Samuel used to drive to Santa Barbara. He loved my dad, and him and my dad used to talk and talk and talk. He gave us a ride in his police car and he even let us push the button for the siren. Aunt May would come over and she'd go to Grandma's. My mother never went a day without going to see my grandma. Every day she'd go see her."[26]

When the marriage between Sam and May fell apart, Sam finally gave up on making a go of it in San Diego and traveled north (apparently with his secretary – Minnie Mae Dickson.) May's sister Sarah told me, "He falls in love with the woman that was supposed to be his secretary. I just happened to run across a little slip where she [May] gets a divorce from Samuel. It just broke her heart because she didn't believe in that. She couldn't imagine anyone, you know: a divorce. She was just heartbroken, but there was nothing she could do. She even went up there and tried to make up with him, with Samuel. No, he had this woman so there was nothing she could do."[27]

At least for a while, Sam seemed to operate out of Sacramento, with an office at 616 K Street. Per at least one extant report to the Governor, Samuel S. Williams served as "Chief Inspector of Jails, State of California." He also seems to have set up a photo studio in San Francisco, at one point.[28] The Walnut Creek studio was named the Williams Photograph Studio and it was located at 1523 Main Street. That address now houses an independent coffee shop of some sort. The telephone number was Walnut Creek 2502 and, intriguingly, his stationery listed "branch phones" Concord 8266 and Lafayette 2153. Did he really have three offices? From what little we know, it seems unlikely. The Williams family household was an exceptionally modest one, according to people who visited May Williams at home, and we do know that Sam Williams had difficulties in business. There are inferences that he may have had trouble with alcohol. Ed Linn writes that, after World War II, Ted received letters from his father "asking for money – like say, six thousand dollars – to open a new photography shop, and then asking for more money after he had blown the six grand on something else."[29]

When Samuel Williams died on November 16, 1952, it was only after a long illness and a prolonged stay in a convalescent home. Ted was in training with the Marines, and apparently at Cherry Point NC at the time of his father's passing. Though he could certainly have received leave for the funeral of a parent, there is no indication that Ted interrupted his military service to travel to the Bay Area for the ceremony. We can only guess at his reasons. He may have felt that there had been so little contact for so long, and what contact there was may have just seemed like a series of requests for money. Ted wasn't happy about being back in the Marines, either, training for combat at age 34. He may well have just hunkered down and brooded for a couple of days, then got back on with the matters at hand.

INTERLUDE: SAM AND MAY WILLIAMS - STANDING ON PRINCIPLE

Sam Williams

Sam Williams comes across as a bit of a colorless character about whom rather little is known. We do know that he served two stretches in the United States Cavalry and saw combat in the Philippine Islands. He'd been posted in the State of Washington, in New Mexico and in San Francisco. He'd certainly been places and done things. Stationed in the Territory of Hawaii, he met and courted May Venzor, a striking woman whose parents had come to the U.S. from Mexico. He traveled to Santa Barbara to ask for her hand in marriage. His new mother-in-law spoke very little English. We can certainly give Sam Williams credit for breaking the mold a little, and for a degree of adventurousness.

Maybe it wore him out. Ted felt that his father lacked drive. Drive is something May Williams lacked not. Sam may have retreated into a shell, finding himself confronted with a wife that their son Ted later wrote was "religious to the point of being domineering, and so narrow-minded."[30]

Sam Williams may have been a bit retiring, and not often around, but he did have a profession as a photographer. He also served in law enforcement for much of the 1930s, as an employee of the United States Department of Justice, Deputy United States Marshal of the Southern District of California.

Less than four months after his appointment, we find that Sam participated in a February 1932 raid on illegal alcohol imports from Mexico. Prohibition was still in effect and the Justice Department and San Diego police joined forces to raid some smugglers and confiscate their wares.

Sam Williams stuck with law enforcement into the late 1930s, and in early 1937 was named the State of California's jail inspector. It was a temporary appointment, paying $180 a month. (We can recall that his son Ted had signed with the San Diego Padres baseball team in June 1936 for $150 per month.) The appointment was made pending civil service examinations in April 1937. Williams "won a top position in civil service ratings and became the permanent inspector in October, 1937."[31]

In the course of his work, Williams attended the American Prison Association's 68th annual congress in St. Paul, Minnesota in October 1938. His son had just completed his Triple Crown season for

Left to right: Samuel Williams, Chief H. H. Scott, Arthur A. Jones, with confiscated contraband, February 1, 1932.

the American Association Minneapolis Millers ball team, the season having ended just three weeks before Sam Williams came to town. Ted was in the area, barnstorming in Minnesota and North Dakota, but it's unknown whether father and son met at the time.

Chief Jail Inspector Samuel S. Williams submitted a report on October 14, 1938 to Governor Merriam and the members of the State Social Welfare Board. The four-page report detailed his October 2-7 visit to the APA Congress. He was there as a representative of the California State Social Welfare Board and the State Department of Social Welfare. During the Congress, he took out membership in the APA and participated in the formation of the affiliate National Jail Association. The meeting brought together hundreds of interested parties, from federal officers, wardens, sheriffs, jail inspectors and chiefs of police to welfare workers, church officials, the governors of many states and... Salvation Army officials. Accompanying Mr. Williams were the warden of the U. S. Penitentiary at Alcatraz and the Superintendent of the California Institution for Women at Tehachapi.

While in St. Paul, Williams was given a tour of the Ramsey County Jail by the sheriff of Ramsey County, former heavyweight champion of the world Tommy Gibbons. "A fine and efficient sheriff," was Williams' assessment. One might suspect that the starring season Ted Williams had just completed cropped up in conversation with Sheriff Gibbons or St. Paul Police Chief Clinton A. Hackett.

Williams also met Director James V. Bennett of the Bureau of Prisons, Washington, D.C. and presented his executive assistant with a report he had conveyed for Sheriff Biscailuz of Los Angeles County.

A wide array of topics was addressed at the Congress, and Mr. Williams reports attending 17 meetings. He said he was asked many questions about jail inspection procedures in California, and that many looked favorably on the "watchful eye" method employed in California. It was, all in all, the reasonably typical, and well-organized report of a competent government official.

Inspired by his participation in the proceedings, Samuel Williams concluded that he would work "with renewed and refreshed efforts for the improvement of the jails in California, and for more and more progress in reclaiming for useful lives the offenders against our laws."

Though there is always work to be done, Williams expressed, "From what I learned California is keeping pace with the best jail program at the present time, in line with the foremost states, New Jersey and Virginia."[32]

At least for a period of time, Sam Williams was part of the law enforcement establishment. He lost his position the following year. On July 12, 1939, the Fresno newspaper reported, "California's only jail inspector, Sam Williams, a former deputy United States marshal from San Diego, today found himself out of a job."[33]

There had been a mix-up involving the state legislature, the attorney general's office, the department of social welfare and other bodies. The news report stated that the elimination of his job was because the 1937 legislature had "failed to include the statute providing for a state jail inspector." Williams had been operating on a temporary appointment since early 1937, while the omission was rectified. He took the civil service examinations in April 1937 and was named permanent inspector in October 1937, and all seemed well until the 1939 legislature met.

Senator Ray W. Hays of Fresno was a member of the senate's governmental efficiency committee, which killed the bill making provision for an inspector of jails in California. His argument was that the position would be duplicative of existing services that could be provided by the various counties. County health departments and other agencies had "ample authority to make jail inspections." Whether they ever did, or did not, might be another matter. The *Fresno Bee & Republican* informed us that Williams, "while acting as state jail inspector, made several inspections of the many times condemned Fresno County Jail, his last in connection with a grand jury inspection and has made repeated recommendations for correction of the crowded conditions in the jail."

Reading between the lines, it may not be a coincidence that the senator from Fresno on the committee was the one who killed the bill authorizing the position of state jail inspector. It seems safe to conclude that, at least to some degree, Sam Williams' efforts to fulfill the mandate of his position came up against political opposition in Fresno and resulted in him losing his job.

Sam Williams next turns up in San Francisco, resuming his profession as a photographer, later moving to Walnut Creek where he and his second wife ran a photographic studio until his death. It wasn't an easy existence. There were times he turned to his son for financial assistance. One newspaper report said he had been "semi-indigent."

Sam Williams died at the San Ramon Rest Home on November 16, 1952. His son Ted already held four batting titles and was in the Marine Corps receiving his final training as a jet pilot. His second wife survived him by 25 years. Perhaps the most fulfilling period of Samuel Williams' life was in 1938-1939. He had moved to northern California and felt he was doing good work for the State. He may have at least taken some degree of solace, and even pride, at having lost his position only because he was pursuing his profession so diligently.

May Williams

May Williams was willing to stand up for principle, too, even at personal cost. We have seen that May Venzor married Sam Williams, though it cost her officer status within the Salvation Army. Marrying outside officers' ranks caused her to be "busted" down to a private in the service.

May's dedication to the cause was remarkable. She didn't hesitate to go into barrooms or Mexican jails, to pursue collections or to right a wrong. Alice Psaute, a younger friend and fellow Salvationist, remembers going to the Coliseum in downtown San Diego. "That's where they had fights. They called them prize fights. Boxing matches. It was so smoky in there it was hard to find your way around in the place. May was there. She sold our magazine and went into bars and took collection. She would go tavern collecting."[34] Ted had written, "She would campaign right down into the seamiest sections of San Diego, and across the border into Tijuana, going into jails to minister to people and even into the red light districts if she thought she could get a contribution."[35]

Manuel Herrera offered a bit more insight into May's character. "She never argued. May was a very innocent type person. Naive, kind of, and yet when they gave her a direction of something to do, boy, she was going to do it. There was no two ways about it. She was very direct with the Lord. There was nothing going to stop her, and she loved to be around men. She loved to entertain men, to catch their attention. She didn't care where she was at. I used to worry about her as a kid. I guess I was about 12 or 13 and we'd go down and see her. We slept on the floor, which was no

May Williams (standing with guitar and glasses) with the Salvation Army Band, Tijuana, Mexico.
"I got permission to go to Tijuana, Mexico to hold open air meetings".

problem. She had a little home down there on Utah Street. We'd take her downtown and leave her there. I say, 'Mom, is she all right?' And Mom would say, 'Oh yes, this is her job. Seven days a week.' I'd say, 'Where are you going, Aunt May?' and she'd say, 'I'm going to see the Devil.' She'd take her Bible and her Salvation Army *War Cry* and she'd head right for the Marines in the bar. There was no stopping that woman. She was really well known in San Diego."[36]

It didn't bother her to go out in the street and praise the Lord, Manuel wrote. "She was the Angel of Tijuana. Do you know why she was named that? Here's what happened. I asked her. I went down and I said, 'Aunt May, can I see you?' She said, 'Come on in' – she was laying in bed. My mother had told me the same story and I got the same answer. Here's what May told me. I said, 'How did you become the Angel of Tijuana?' She says, 'Well, I used to go down to Tijuana to help the unfortunate people and I was walking by the jail. Some kids were yelling to me, 'Hey, lady. Hey, lady, can you help me?' and I looked up and I said, 'What's wrong?' 'They put us in jail. These people put us in jail.' She says, 'Did you do anything bad?' They said, 'No.' She says, 'Are you Christian people?' 'Yes.' 'I'll get you out of here.'

"So she went inside the jail and wanted to speak to the commandant. They're all wondering what this little old lady is coming in there for. They're looking at her and she was saying, 'I would like to talk to the commandant. I have something to say.' She went up to him, and she says, 'In the name of God, Jesus Christ, those American children are not to be in there.'

"They went back and forth. He explained her this and she told him – in the Bible – she started pointing out Scripture to him. He took her down there and they showed him where they were at. She says, 'The rats wouldn't even live in there.' It was filthy. It was beyond reproach. And they opened the door and he says, 'Open the door and let's let them out.' He did. He opened the darned door and she took the kids home. They were probably 13 or 14. They were American kids. I don't know what transpired, but after that, when people found out about what she did, somebody tagged her the 'Angel of Tijuana.'"[37]

The "Salvation lassie" set records for selling *War Cry*, the publication of the Salvation Army. In time, according to clippings from Salvation Army publications, May sold well over 100,000 copies of the magazine.

San Diego Mayor Harley Knox and May Williams, with copies of the *War Cry*.

By the time she was in San Diego, though, she'd lost the officer status she'd earned coming out of the training college. In February 1934, May Williams was "publications sergeant" and also "in charge of the county jail meeting conducted in the women's side." Back in 1913, when she married, she had given up her officer's rank. A captain at the beginning of 1912, she was reduced in rank as a result of her marriage in 1913.

She was still but a sergeant by 1934. She "married out," as the saying went – married a non-officer. She knew in advance what the consequences were, but she married for love. Perhaps she felt secure in her sense of mission and realized that the calling was more important than the rank. She could still do good work as a soldier.

Alice Psaute says, "We're getting more progressive, after one hundred or some years. In those days, they were very strict. And if they thought you had an interest in a person of the opposite sex, they'd automatically station you as far apart as possible, so we had some bad marriages that happened because of things like that."[38]

Sam Williams proved a lost cause, however, and no doubt May learned this early on. Her sons, though, were another matter. She could still raise them in the Army. Teddy was "dedicated," but the lure of baseball proved too powerful. He used to attend Sunday school, no doubt reading *The Young Soldier*, the Army's Sunday school publication of the era. Alma Parton was his teacher. But when he started playing baseball, he stopped going to Sunday school. Sunday was the big day for baseball on the playgrounds. "I guess the dedication didn't take," Ted wrote. "The thing was I had to go so damn often. I just hated it."[39]

We also know how mortified Ted was at the ribbing he received from schoolmates, who would tease him about being dragged along with his mother when she was on the street with the Salvation Army band. Ted was embarrassed that his mother was "Always gone. The house dirty all the time." He said he was "embarrassed about my home, embarrassed that I never had quite as good clothes as some of the kids, embarrassed that my mother was out in the middle of the damn street all the time."[40] Ted told Bobby Doerr that when his mother brought him along with the Army band, "I used to try to get behind the big bass drum so that I could hide."[41]

Ted may also, in time, have come to blame the Army for taking his mother away from the family. His parents drifted apart, but it wasn't as though one or the other of them stayed at home with Ted and his younger brother Danny. They were both out working in the evenings. While this freed up Ted to spend more time hitting baseballs, Danny had no such compelling drive. And Ted noticed May spent more time at 830 8th Avenue, Corps headquarters, than at home at 4121 Utah Street.

Alice Psaute acknowledged, "I think maybe he felt that if his mother wasn't spending all her time down there, maybe his brother would have turned out a little better." As Alice points out, "That was not the Salvation Army's fault. It was probably her fault. After you go there a long time, you get very dedicated and you go every day whether you're supposed to or not." If you truly believe you're doing the work of the Lord, then the idea of a day off can seem, to the True Believer, almost like sacrilege.

It seems safe to say that Ted did fault the Army for its impact on his family. He put it so bluntly and succinctly in *My Turn At Bat* that on a quick read, one could overlook five words about family, and the depth of sentiment and resentment revealed therein. Consider the second of these two sentences: "My mother was strictly Salvation Army. As a result, strictly non-family."[42]

Ted's friend Frank Cushing was willing to give May the benefit of the doubt. "She neglected her own sons. What I think was that she was so sure in her own mind that she meant only the best that she couldn't see what she was doing to them."[43] Ted filled the void with his baseball, and his fishing, and he was fortunate to find a number of other families who treated him as their own son. Danny was not so lucky, and he acted out in response. He rebelled against rules and expectations, falling in with a bad crowd, but his wayward ways may have been built right into him. A few years after Danny died of leukemia at age 39, Ted wrote of his younger brother, "Some guys have absolutely no respect for authority, and Danny was one of them."[44]

On August 21, 1932, Evangeline Booth, the Commander of The Salvation Army in America, and the daughter of founder General William Booth, appeared at the Hollywood Bowl. This was an important event. While there is no record that May Williams took her sons – Teddy almost 14 and Danny just recently 12 – to L.A., there's a very good chance that she did. She was a loyal soldier in the Army of the Lord.

There came a time, however, when May Williams stood up to the Army leadership. It was in February, 1936. She had attained the rank of envoy and already earned perhaps a more meaningful status – May Williams was already known as the "Angel of Tijuana" to the readers of the *San Diego Sun* and throughout the city. When she protested a new Salvation Army policy regarding the treatment of transient indigents, she was stripped of her rank by Major J. L. Kelso and reduced to the rank of private.

A dramatically-told story in the pages of the *Sun* illustrates the effect this new policy had:

> On the door of the Salvation Army headquarters at 830 Eighth Ave., is a crude sign. It reads: "Indigent men applying for relief, come back at 9 p.m. Applications received at no other time."
>
> A man in shabby clothes went back a few minutes before 9 p.m. A small sedan was parked near the front of the door. It contained two men.
>
> The man in the shabby clothes hesitated, and while he waited, a second poorly dressed individual shuffled up to the Army headquarters and stepped inside for his evening meal.

The men in the parked auto remained sitting.

It must have been a slim meal, for he remained inside only three minutes. Then he wandered off down the street, stopping momentarily to glance down into a gutter in search of a cigaret butt.

He had hardly passed out of sight when four youths, cold, hungry and obviously tired, stepped up to the Army door. They didn't have a chance to enter.

The two men who had been sitting in the darkened auto in front of the headquarters, clambered out and accosted the youths. A few words passed, and then the youths were directed to "climb in – you're going to the police station."

Maj. Kelso stood in the doorway as the youths were driven away. He didn't see the other figure, however, the man who first had approached the Army headquarters in search of a warm meal.

The man had melted away into the shadows after seeing what had befallen the four youths.

Maj. Kelso stood in the doorway for more than a half hour – but no more hungry men came for aid. The word must have gone out that it was "unhealthy" to go there for food any more.[45]

Envoy May Williams objected to what she termed the creation of a "trap." Homeless men were told to arrive at 9 p.m. but police prowl cars awaited them, "backed up to the curb ready to take the applicants to central station for examination." The men were reportedly "required to pass police fingerprint examinations and were subjected to 'third degree' tests." When she spoke up, Kelso stripped her of her rank.

Private Williams' demotion sparked supportive protest from the Mayor of San Diego, Percy J. Benbough. May was, the *San Diego Union* reported, "lovingly known throughout the city as the 'Salvation Army lassie'" and was "well known all over San Diego." The mayor announced that he was sending a letter to the commanding officer of the Salvation Army in Los Angeles and that it would be signed "by a number of prominent citizens who have expressed surprise at the army's action in dismissing Mrs. Williams, a beloved member of our community. We will ask that a full investigation be made on this matter. Mrs. Williams has endeared herself to the entire community, and we should like to know why the local command has summarily dismissed her." The mayor's language was blistering. "You might as well have the police cars come to church services evenings and compel those who attend to submit themselves to police surveillance. Unfortunates who attend the Salvation Army services and later apply for aid have found that the police are on hand to 'shake them down.' Any habitual criminal, of course, would not apply to the Salvation Army for aid. I understand that Mrs. Williams was dismissed because she objected to this practice."[46]

An editorial in the *Sun* allowed that the internal affairs of the Salvation Army are its own business, but noted that "to thousands of San Diegans, rich and poor, Mrs. Williams IS the Salvation Army. The jingle of her tambourine is welcome music in most of the restaurants and dine-dance places of San Diego and Tijuana. Her kindly smile and her quiet helpfulness are known to untold thousands who have lived here." The paper urged looking into the conditions May Williams had decried. "Is the city, through the police department, over-stepping its authority by herding homeless transients into the city jail for no reason at all except that they are transients and homeless? If that is the case then the alliance between the city and the Salvation Army's shelter must be terminated." The *Sun* urged that the Salvation Army not make a mistake which will "mar" its "splendid reputation."[47]

Ted's nephew Ted Williams has done some family research, too, and he is the one who first talked with Alice Psaute. May survived the controversy, of course, but it helped that her winning ways had impressed city figures in high places. "Only pressure from the mayor got her reinstated, if not at full rank. 'I won't give the Salvation Army another dime or eat another donut without May Williams.'" The mayor threatening not to eat those Salvation Army donuts may have made the difference.[48]

Anita Rasmussen, a year behind Ted at Hoover High and a young Salvationist, was "assigned May's downtown 'beat'" and she told the *Union*'s Joe Hamelin that May's demotion really cost the cause. "She knew all the people in all the right places, and a lot of people in the wrong places, too. She had access to the major, the chief of police, business leaders... and she would go into the red light district, there was white slavery in those days, and minister there as well... I remember asking the head of the gas and electric company for a donation, and his telling me, 'the day they reassign May Williams, that's the day I'll support the Salvation Army again."[49]

Psaute remembered the brouhaha nearly 70 years afterward. "She protested something I would have protested, too. It was the Census Board – it sounds sort of like the Senseless Board – that was the board that is sort of in charge of who could be a soldier and if they have to do any disciplining. My mother was on that board, but she was still very good friends with May. It didn't affect their friendship at all."[50]

The discipline also did not shake May's faith. First a captain, then a sergeant, now a private, she continued to sell *War Cry* and hold outdoor gatherings. Like Ted, she may have been a little loud at times. "She had a good open-air voice," Psaute remembers. The scrapbook that Psaute's mother kept contains a few clippings from later years as well. In May 1943, May Williams was named to head the Christmas Kettle Campaign – in charge of the traditional Salvation Army kettles we still see today at Christmas time. The funds collected were to aid 900 underprivileged San Diego families.

In December 1949, the *San Diego Union* informed readers that May Williams had assumed the responsibility of selling 18,000 copies of the special Christmas issue of *War Cry*. Though 1949 was the year Ted came in second to George Kell for the American League batting title by .0001557, his mother may well have won the title for selling the largest number of publications in the country. A clipping from a Salvation Army newsletter reads that she "at one time held the record for *War Cry* selling in the entire United States."[51]

May Williams was blessed to have such faith. She never lost her faith, and in that she was blessed as well.

MINNIE MAE WILLIAMS, SAM WILLIAMS' SECOND WIFE
(March 2, 1897 - October 9, 1977)

Minnie Mae Williams (note that middle name) was born March 2, 1897 in Oakville, Iowa to Joseph Henry Dickson and Effie Emma Johnston (note that first name) on March 2, 1895. She first arrived in California in 1937, give or take a few months.

Sam Williams and Minnie moved north to San Francisco, living at 328 West Portal, but moved to Oakland (based on his membership in the Scottish Rite based in Oakland), and by 1947 to Walnut Creek, where they lived on Hillgrade Avenue. Samuel Williams was a Freemason, and belonged to the S.W. Hackett Lodge #574, the Oakland Scottish Rite and to the 14th Calvary Association in Santa Monica, CA.

Minnie had been Sam's secretary at one point. It's unclear when they actually married. In 1942, she worked at Tidewater Associated Oil in the city. She was apparently a photographer herself, since on her funeral record (according to information supplied by her sister, Mrs. Lou Alexander of Fort Worth, Texas) she was a photographer and had been one for 20 years.

Does this mean she had taken it up five years after Sam died? She outlived him by 25 years. It's hard to know. She was listed as self-employed. How successful she was is also unknown; she is not listed in the Yellow Pages or Contra Costa County telephone directories in those years. She had moved to another home on Danville Boulevard, and died after a stay in the San Marco Convalescent Hospital, at age 82 on October 9, 1977.

Minnie Williams was a member of the Christian Science church, and worshiped at First Church of Christ Scientist in Walnut Creek. Interestingly, Sam Williams had first married a Salvationist and then a Christian Scientist. Attempts to locate others in Minnie Dickson Williams' family have so far proved fruitless. Minnie herself is remembered by a few in Walnut Creek, including a boy to whom she gave a Ted Williams signed baseball, one she had had around the house.

Larry Frank was about thirteen and he had a 1959 Fleer baseball card of Ted Williams. His mother Mickie used to take Minnie home after church. When Minnie found out that Larry had this card, she asked to borrow the card to photograph it as a memento. When Larry came by her house to pick it up, she noted his passion for baseball and gave him a baseball, telling him "This is my last autographed ball." As he got a bit older, Frank pitched briefly for Arizona State. More than 25 years later, Larry Frank is assistant baseball coach at a high school in St. Louis and for the past seven years has thrown batting practice for the St. Louis Cardinals before home games. "It inspires me to look at that baseball," he says.[52]

Her death certificate lists her as having been a self-employed photographer for twenty years, which would suggest that she took it up five years after Sam Williams died. Her sister Mrs. Lou Alexander of Fort Worth, Texas, no longer lives at the address provided. Brother Dwight Dickson no longer lives in Sedalia, Missouri, either.

When Samuel Williams applied for his Social Security card on March 1, 1940, he indicated that he was still married to May Venzor, and that his parents' names were Nickolas (sic) Williams and Elizabeth Miller. Most accounts say that May and Sam divorced in 1939, despite a last appeal by May to work things out. In any event, by the time Minnie Mae applied for hers, in October 1942, she and Sam Williams were married.

Enough on Ted's stepmother, though. He seems to have had some contact with her, but certainly it was not much. It is noteworthy that he had maintained contact for at least 20 years after his father had died.

Let's go back and look at Ted's mother in a bit more detail.

MAY VENZOR WILLIAMS

Who was May Venzor that Samuel Williams married?

Ted's birth certificate does suggest that she was born in El Paso in 1893, but it could be that she was actually born in San Diego. San Diego, Texas, that is. Sarah Diaz had told Manuel Herrera that her older sister May was indeed born in San Diego, Texas. He questioned this, naturally, but she reaffirmed it. He'd never heard of San Diego, Texas before. It's not the sort of name anyone would come up with on their own, a small town of 1,500 people at the time, the county seat of Duval County. The County Clerk of San Diego, TX, however, shows no births at all registered with the surname Venzor. (There is no record of her birth in El Paso, either.) Her gravestone in the Goleta California cemetery indicates that she was born in 1891. The California Death Index reports her birth as May 8, 1891 and death on August 27, 1961. We will assume the 1891 date, in part because we do know that her sister Mary was born in April 1893.

May and her son Ted, during a World War II visit.

Sarah was quite adamant on the geography, though, Manuel wrote me. "Sarah told me that May Venzor was born in San Diego, Texas. I said, 'No, Mom, you mean San Diego, California!' She looked at me like I was lost and said, 'If you look on the map, you will see a San Diego, Texas, just to the left of Corpus Christi.' So, I pull out our trusty map and sure enough I find San Diego, Texas right on highway 44 and near highway 359. Yeah, the old gal was correct! I am 150 percent [certain] that Aunt May was born in San Diego, Texas."[53]

May's parents emigrated to the United States from Mexico late in the 19th century. Ted's maternal grandparents were Natalia Hernandez and Pablo Venzor. The family was Basque in origin and had settled around El Parral (Hidalgo del Parral) near the border of Durango in the state of Chihuahua, Mexico.

The United States of Mexico, like the United States of America, is very much a nation of immigrants. Though Mexican by nationality, Sarah Diaz was concerned to present the family as Basque ("Basco"), not as Mexican. Racial, ethnic and class differentiation is seemingly of concern in every culture and many people will try to draw distinctions which portray them as superior in some fashion to those around them. In Mexico, those who claim pure European ancestry have long held themselves to be superior to the "Indios" – the indigenous people. One infers that Sarah didn't want to be seen as a lowly "Mexican" but to accord herself and her family the more prestigious European background. It's as though the family just passed through Mexico on its way from the Pyrenees to the United States – and that may well have been true. "We have no Mexican heritage in our family," she told me, "although my father and mother were in Mexico. We are Basque." Admitting that there is no written history to document the family history, she also wanted to let me know early on that, "I have an uncle who was the administrator to the governor of the state of Chihuahua."

As Sarah understands matters, and here she does admit the possibility of some indigenous blood in the family, the Basques came to Mexico "during the war when the English sent Maximilian to try to take over Mexico. So the French came, and they were the Basques from the Pyrenees between France and Spain. When they came to war, naturally they were looking for young girls. These girls, they were pregnant from the soldiers and from the Basques. When the war was over, they took off and went back home and left the girls with the child. These children that were born, they didn't have a name to say, 'He was my father' or 'My name was So-and-so.' We have no way of knowing the real history."

Sarah said that her uncle, who served as this administrator in Chihuahua, told her that he had fallen in love with one of her mother's sisters and they'd married. Sarah's mother was Natalia Venzor (1869-1954), born a Hernandez. Natalia's mother – Ted Williams' great-grandmother – was Catarina R. Hernandez (1837-1931). Sarah described her as "very fair. Blue eyes, blonde. In our family, we go back to where we're very fair, light-complected and with blond hair." Catarina Hernandez was a Rubio.

Left to right: Natalia H. Venzor, May Venzor, Catarina R. Hernandez with baby Chester Amidon, Sarah's son, 1926.

Archduke Ferdinand Maximilian set sail from Europe for Mexico in April, 1864, where he became – at least briefly – the Emperor of Mexico. Other hopefuls from France and Spain may have come with him, or around the same time. It could well have been that the Venzors and the others in the family had only arrived in Mexico some 24 years before Natalia Hernandez married Pablo Venzor.

It could also have been much earlier. The Center for Basque Studies of the University of Nevada in Reno notes in a report from a 1994 conference in Jalapa on the Basques in Mexico, "From 1795 to 1810 in Valladolid, Michoacan, there were more than two hundred Basques involved in the church, government, commerce, ranching, mines, and sugar factories." The report details many other communities throughout Mexico where Basques were noted.

A tangent:
ERNESTO PONCE AND HIS SISTERS CONSUELA AND RUTH

Though Sarah could not recall the name of her uncle the administrator during our interview, my later visit with Ernesto Ponce in El Paso made it clear that the uncle was Federico Ponce, who came from Valle de Allende, Chihuahua. Ponce was an administrator on the staff of Don Luis Terrazas, the "cattle baron of the world" who operated out of the governor's place in Chihuahua, Chihuahua. Federico Ponce was related to the Hernandezes through marriage; he married Eulalia Hernandez, one of Natalia's sisters. Natalia (and Eulalia) had other siblings: a sister named Micaela (nicknamed May) and another named Eduviges and brothers Manuel, Rayo, Cristofal and Santiago.

Rayo Hernandez (August 12, 1874 - January 8, 1968) was quite a character. He and Manuel Hernandez lived in Santa Barbara. Cristofal Hernandez lived in Los Angeles and Santiago Hernandez in Bellflower. Rayo was a big man who managed ranches in the Goleta area. He told Sarah Diaz that "Pancho Villa wanted him to ride with his band of warriors. He came to Santa Barbara with two pearl handle 45's and his Stetson hat."

Manuel Herrera, named after Rayo's brother Manuel, continues, "He [Rayo] was different than the rest of the brothers, he was very manly and proud. He always wore that Stetson hat and was very powerful in his manner. He lived to be about 99 years old and was very alert before he died. I used to offer him a ride when he was waiting for a bus, but he usually refused because he wanted to look at the girl who rode the bus too. He was a very positive man and had a build like a stud horse."[54]

Ted almost certainly knew many of the Hernandez family, since quite a few of them lived in and around Santa Barbara and would have attended family gatherings, especially when May and family would visit from San Diego. Santiago Hernandez,

Rayo Hernandez with his second wife, Lupe.

in fact, worked on Santa Barbara's Spaulding Ranch, according to Ernie Ponce's wife Mary (born Maria Mercedes Serrano.) Further reinforcing the Basque connection, Mary mentioned that her mother's name was Llaguno, and that both of her parents were Basque.[55] Eulalia Ponce, born in Mexico, lived in downtown Los Angeles near USC on Santa Barbara Street. Manuel Herrera knew her, and tells of her sad end, mugged going to the bank. "She was attacked while near a bus stop and was in a coma for several days then passed away. The thief took only $5 and also took her life." She died of a blood clot on January 3, 1971 at age 91. Her husband Federico had died of a heart attack at 78.[56]

Ernest Ponce knew the Hernandez family in El Parral. "El Parral, in Chihuahua, was where my mother and father met. It's a little town. My mother used to tell us that there were no schools in

Juana H. Molina with her sister, Natalia H. Venzor.

those days. The parents would let their children work for people who were educated – they would babysit and take care of their children, so that they could be taught and learn to read and write."

Natalia Hernandez, before she married Pablo Venzor, "didn't like living out like that" and consequently did not learn how to write, though she did learn to read. "She could interpret the American paper," Sarah told me. "In later years, she could understand every word, but she wasn't able to speak [English] and she wasn't able to write. We finally taught her how to write her name."

Federico Ponce, though, was highly regarded by Don Luis Terrazas. Impressed with the young man, Don Luis sent him to North Adams, Massachusetts (a Bliss Business College was located there at the time) where he studied accounting. On his return, he reportedly became chief accountant to the cattle baron. Years later, Ted Williams would make the trek to Boston as well, to pursue another profession.

One thing neither Ernest nor Mary Ponce thought to mention during my visit was that Ernest also had two living sisters. Two aunts of Ted's – Consuela and Ruth. I only found this out over two years later. Mary had mentioned that she had some photographs tucked away in a box from their honeymoon to Santa Barbara and San Diego – where they stayed with Sam Williams for a week. (May was away, and they didn't recall why but they never met her – perhaps she was on a Salvation Army retreat?) Every six months or so, I called Mary but she was often not feeling well and I wasn't able to motivate her to seek them out. Finally on almost the second anniversary of my visit, I realized (in going over my notes) that they had a son and a daughter living in El Paso still. So I phoned Wayne Ponce to see if perhaps he could help his mother locate the photographs, were she still willing to share them. I had to leave a voice mail for him the first time I called, but when I called back maybe 10 days later, he'd spoken with his mother and urged me to call her so she could give me the names, address and telephone numbers of her two sisters-in-law who both lived in the Los Angeles area.

I called a few days later. But I was on the road – visiting Ted Williams in Oakland – and had not brought the phone cord that connects my handheld cassette recorder with the phone. This was around 7 a.m. on November 22, 2002. Should I change my flight plans and head to Los Angeles instead of home to Boston? After all, one of the sisters was 92 and the other was no spring chicken.

I did not change my plans, but once home again I did telephone Connie Matthews (born Consuela Ponce) on November 26 and talked with her at length, following up with more questions on December 10. The next time I was in Los Angeles, in February 2003, I had the pleasure of meeting Ruth Gonzales at her home in Norwalk. They were not aunts of Ted, they both explained. They were first cousins to May Venzor, and cousins to Ted.

The Ponces' mother was Eulalia Hernandez and her sister was May Venzor's mother. [The more common Basque spelling is Eulali.] In my understanding of genealogy, this means that Ernesto Ponce was really Ted Williams' second cousin, not his uncle. But perhaps we are splitting hairs. In many cultures, including the Hispanic culture along the US-Mexican border, the terms *tio* (uncle) and *tia* (aunt) are used as much honorifically and as a mark of familial respect than their precise genealogical definition might suggest. In this sense, as a somewhat older close relative, Ernesto Ponce was Ted's *tio*, his "uncle" – even if he was really his cousin.

Connie was eight years older than Ted, but remembered several visits to San Diego in the 1920s. She confirmed everything that Ernest had told me, but also told me something that I hadn't learned before – May Venzor's given first name was Micaela. May was a nickname. Connie told me, "Now his mother, May, she was my first cousin. May was really Micaela, but you know everybody called her May. Micaela was her real name." It seemed as though it was a name that ran in the family, since Micaela was also the name of one of Natalia's sisters. Thus, May was named after her Aunt Micaela or Mikaela. Mikaela is a reasonably common Basque name.

Connie shared a couple of nice memories of Ted Williams as a carefree kid: "When Ted was little... he must have been 7 or 8 years old, we were there in San Diego. We were there for about a week, my sister Carmen and I forget whether it was Ernest or Fred who drove. We were coming to Santa Barbara and we stopped in San Diego on Utah Street - I remember where they lived on Utah Street. Micaela was always with her hat. I still remember she wore a Salvation Army hat and sold that *War Cry*, that paper. She'd go out to stand in town, selling the paper – that *War Cry* paper – and I remember Ted – Danny was younger – they'd wrestle like crazy. Sam, her husband, had the photo shop, but the kids, we'd take them to the beach. They were on vacation."

"I remember Ted [another] time that we visited in San Diego. He must have been about 10 or 12 years old and we took him to the beach, you know. After he grew up and became famous, he really went to the East Coast.

"Ted would run after me with crabs. He'd pick them up with his hand from the shallow water there at the beach and chase the heck out of me, after me with a crab. I was just terrified with those animals. But he was a nice kid. That's all I remember. He was just a regular kid and so was Danny."[57]

The Williams family was perhaps a happier family in those days. Connie remembers more: "Actually, Micaela, we saw her then but I didn't pay too much attention. She was very nice. We had real nice dinners. I remember she had a real nice German maid in San Diego when we visited, and that woman when we come back from the beach or wherever, we would run all over, she baked the best fish – I'll never forget – and the best salads. Especially grated – I'll never forget the grated carrot salads that she made. It was a German maid that she had."

Perhaps before the Depression hit, the young family was better off and could afford the services of a maid or housekeeper.

I asked: was that Natalia, or was it Micaela? "It was Micaela. She was working, so she hired this German maid while we were there. Maybe she was there before we came. The two kids were real nice. They were regular kids, you know. Just like kids. They were always running here or running there. Sam was too busy. I never did visit his shop.

"We had a girl that we'd take over and this girl had some kind of a tic in her eye. She would wink, automatically wink. I guess it was some kind of a problem she had with her eye. She was just a friend of Carmen and Carmen had invited her over one time there when we were visiting May. Sam, I remember at the dinner table, says, 'Hey, Rose, quit winking at me. I'm a married man, you know!' He was very outgoing. I liked him. He was very nice to us all the time we were there."[58]

Mary Ponce also remembers Sam as a good host. She told me, "When we got married in 1936, we went on our honeymoon to California to visit all the relatives because they were all the way from San Diego to Santa Barbara. We stayed at Sam Williams' home. May was a Salvation Army captain and she never was at home. We stayed with Sam for two weeks on Utah Street. We stayed there and Sam would get up every morning and cook a wonderful breakfast. He cooked everything – hot cakes, waffles, scrambled eggs, fried eggs, turnovers, muffins, biscuits. He was a marvelous cook. He cooked for us all the time we were there. Sam was a lovely man. He was so nice to us."[59]

I came across several people who had favorable impressions of Sam Williams. We may not have a rich picture of him today, but he apparently had his charm and was no doubt more than the one-dimensional person we sometimes find depicted in the books on Ted Williams, where he just comes across as remote, pretty uninterested in his son's baseball playing, and as a father away from home a lot.

There was some visiting back and forth between El Paso and Santa Barbara. Connie's sister Ruth Gonzalez remembers Maria Cordero (May's sister Mary Venzor) coming to visit El Paso at one point, but she also recalls that when her mother and father visited the Williams home in San Diego, "nobody was ever home." Two other Ponce siblings, Fred and Ruth's twin sister Elvira, visited Santa Barbara in 1939 and from that visit we have a photograph which includes May and Danny Williams on the beach. One of Ruth's memories of the Williams boys was not the best – but we're talking five-year-olds here. Ruth, born like Ted in 1918, still recalls visiting Santa Barbara in 1923. Both Ted and Danny set on her and Elvira and started roughhousing and choking them. At that moment, they wanted nothing more than to get away from Ted Williams and his little brother Danny.

Left to right: Rose (a friend), Elvira Ponce, Helen Hansen (Danny's first wife), May, and Danny Williams. Mission Beach, San Diego, 1939.

Ted's brother Danny suffers from some of the same uni-dimensionality. Before we dig into Danny a little more, though, let's try to learn more about mother May's family background. That is, more or less, where I started this deeper quest into Ted's Hispanic heritage.

PABLO & NATALIA VENZOR, TED'S GRANDPARENTS

Pablo Venzor (1868 - November 29, 1920)

Natalia H. Venzor (December 1, 1869 - January 2, 1954)

As we have learned, the family emigrated from Mexico to the United States. We don't know how long the Venzors and Hernandezes had lived in Mexico, but it wasn't a place they felt they could stay. A settled life in Mexico seemed impossible, as the winds of change were beginning to blow across the northern states of Mexico.

Pablo Venzor learned a trade, Sarah explained. "When they married, my father – golly, my mother was just a young woman. My father was very well trained. He had a good trade. He was a bricklayer and a stone mason." Pablo and Natalia married in 1888. "My father used to tell my mother, 'Now remember, three eights' – trying to explain to her the numbers." Natalia and Pablo Venzor had one child in Mexico – Pedro (Pete) Venzor was born the year after they were married, in 1889.

Maybe Pancho Villa wanted Rayo Hernandez to ride with him, but Villa posed a threat in the minds of others. "When Pancho Villa was going wild in Mexico, taking over the towns and what have you, the Mexican people called him a 'Robin Hood' because he used to take from the rich and give to the poor," Sarah Diaz said. Many others fled northern Mexico, and crossed the border.

As political troubles began to brew in Mexico, though, the young couple decided to joined what was becoming an exodus north to Texas. The Venzors left much

Pablo Venzor with children, left to right: Pete, May, Mary, Maria (an orphan), and Daniel, El Paso 1903.

earlier than the Ponces. In fact, Ernest was born on the floor of the governor's palace in Chihuahua on July 25, 1913. "Right there on the floor," says Ernie's wife Mary. "As soon as she [Ernesto's mother] could walk, they fled. They kept on, hiding in the sage and all the bushes and stuff until they got to the border. He was four months old when they crossed the border. It took four months to get from Chihuahua city to Juarez, to cross the border. In those times, everybody crossed the border."[60]

The path to the north from Chihuahua was typically through Juarez, and then across the Rio Grande to El Paso. May Venzor was born in El Paso in 1891, it seems – though if the San Diego, Texas story is correct, it may be that the family passed through El Paso but then continued on to the valley in south Texas in search of work. One way or another, they did pass through El Paso, and ultimately made their way west to Santa Barbara, California, arriving, according to a notation on the back of a family photograph, on June 24, 1907. There is a suggestion that there may have been a couple of uncles who had already settled in California. I didn't get a chance to follow up fully with Sarah Diaz to learn more about what might have prompted the continued migration. No one I've asked since seems to know, but it wouldn't have been atypical for some family members to have followed other relatives who may have settled in Santa Barbara and then let the family in Texas know that they found better prospects on the West Coast.

There were a lot of uncles in the Hernandez family. "My grandma [Catarina] had 14 children. Fourteen children. When she married my grandfather, her first pregnancy she had twins, but one died at birth. After that, she had 13. The last pregnancy, she had twins again. One of them passed away. I didn't know some of my uncles. They stayed in Texas."[61] But some had gone ahead to California and Pablo Venzor, with his growing family, followed.

What the family did in El Paso from, more or less, 1890 to 1907 is unclear. We do know that some of the family had achieved a degree of prosperity in El Paso. David Ronquillo, a lawyer in San Diego (all references to San Diego will be to the city in California unless otherwise noted) today, and a relative of Ted's (his mother Lilia Molina and Ted's mother were first cousins) had a grandfather who was a relatively well-to-do dairyman in El Paso. He also had the water rights for Fort Bliss, Texas, which provided another good source of revenue.

Ronquillo's *abuelo* was convinced to come to California by a relative, a Señor Calderon who was a pastor. In their case, it was a later migration, sometime in the 1920s. "We're told that he sends green grass blades back to my grandfather to convince him that he should come west. So finally he convinces him that he should come west. I guess it's a caravan of Model T's that they drive out here. All six kids remaining with the family, plus their belongings.

"So they come all the way out, and they have a big tent meeting in Chino. It's during that tent meeting that all seven children are called to the ministry. All the women are called to be missionaries, and the two men are called to be pastors. One man, Federico, was my uncle. Geno's grandfather. He follows his calling to the ministry."[62] David introduces another element here, that of the strain of evangelism in the larger family. There were many in the family who felt called in one way or another.

Geno Lucero is another relative of Ted's, a musician. His Aunt Mary and David's mother Lilia both became missionary companions in Nogales, Mexico, and it's David's understanding that they spent three or four years working there. David adds, "They were all very involved with the Free Methodist Church. My mother was a missionary with May and worked with her in San Diego. She wasn't in the Salvation Army. I'm not sure how May got in the Salvation Army. That was never explained to me, but I do know that Geno's grandfather – my Uncle Fred – he was in the Free Methodist Church, and I do know that he and May Williams developed together an orphanage in Tecate, Mexico."

Perhaps typically Basque, the family was very independent. Natalia Venzor was a Baptist and devoted to the Mexican Baptist Church in Santa Barbara. Santa Barbara at the time was "99 percent Catholic" and the Venzors were in the minority. Some of the children were "put down" by some of the Catholic kids as a result. Some of that independence may have served them well, and strengthened the faith of those who truly believed.[63]

Geno added, "My grandfather [Federico Hernandez Molina] and Ted's mom were very, very close, because my grandfather was a pastor. His name was Fred. He was a Hernandez. He had a church in San Diego, about the time I was born and after. 1949. He used to help May with a lot of stuff because she was always helping the poor people, especially down in Baja. Tijuana and stuff. And so my grandfather, in church, would collect stuff for her, for the Salvation Army. It was a Free Methodist church. So it was basically pretty close to the Salvation Army's doctrine."[64] Geno's aunt Esther Slagle confirms the working relationship, and then introduces yet another unexpected twist: "There's a big discussion in the family between Basque [background] and Russian. In our side of the family, there's a lot of talk about there being a Russian colony in Mexico. My aunt used to say that the men wore big tall boots and white smocks, and that they had big long beards. They must have spoken a different language, living in the middle of Mexico. I guess as time went on... my one aunt thought it was Russian. I have a cousin who went to Russia and she brought back all these pictures and it was like looking in a mirror. That would be the Hernandez side. I understand that Rubio is from Portugal, which would make me think more Basque. They say it's a Portuguese name."[65]

Some of the professions the men followed are ones that one might associate with a Basque background. There were shepherds and stonemasons, and dairymen. "Santa Barbara was a cow town," remembers Connie Matthews. "Before Santa Barbara changed, before these guys built all the beautiful hotels and all that. It was nothing but a little old town. Manuel [Hernandez] had a dairy called the Sisters Dairy, because there were eight sisters and five brothers. They all ran the dairy and would deliver the milk in a little old wagon with a little horse. In the 1930s, can you imagine? The beach was wide open and it was never like Santa Barbara is today."[66]

On the way to Goleta, Pablo and Natalia Venzor with Paul, Bruno and Jeanne.

Mr. Venzor apparently used to take the family out to the country and ride in the old wagon for a visit. "Well, on one trip," Manuel Herrera wrote me, "the weather got very foggy as it often does on the coast and they unknowingly got lost. The horse stopped and wouldn't go a step farther and Mr. Venzor was getting upset because of his stubborn horse that was pulling the old wagon and would not budge an inch. So the old man got out and took a look. Hell, they were at the edge of a cliff and if the horse took three more steps, over they would go into the gully. The old horse had some common sense. A smart horse, huh? I heard that story every time we looked at the old wagon picture that was taken in 1920 at Santa Barbara."[67]

Manuel, in the same e-mail told another story. "You will like this story. Grandmother Natalia went down to visit May in San Diego and the kids [Teddy and Danny] were still little. Well, the boys had a dog and they used to fight over the poor pet. If one had the dog, then the other one wanted it in his room. Soon they were in the middle of the living room fighting over the poor dog with not a stitch of clothing on. Natalia was embarrassed and didn't know what to do; they were mad and paid no attention to her requests. They both wanted that dog and nothing was going to stop them, not even their grandmother Natalia."[68]

Ruth Gonzales describes her: "Tia Natalia was a sweet lady. She had golden honey brown hair. She would buy rolling papers and roll her own cigarettes. She would crumble cigars and smoke that." And she remembers when Natalia came through El Paso with her sister Eduviges on their way to Europe, where Natalia was headed to visit her son Daniel's gravesite.[69]

Pablo Venzor was able to put his talents as a stonemason to good effect. "He built a lot of buildings and bridges in Montecito – that's a very restrictive area of our very famous Santa Barbara." Manuel tells about coming home from the cemetery, visiting his grave with Sarah Diaz. "We would go into Montecito and drive along the main road and there would be a sudden stop by a bridge. Mom would show us the bridges he built in that area. I guess she was sentimental and wanted to share her father's works. Beautifully made of sandstone, a local rock, and granite shipped in from other parts of the state. There was an arch on both sides, really strong looking with abutments at both ends. I told her that the bridge had weathered many storms and that it must have been built correctly. Yes, was her remark, my father built that bridge and many more of the old ones here in Montecito and Santa Barbara. The sandstone bridges are a work of art."[70]

Sarah added her memories: "My uncles were all very well trained in a trade. They were bricklayers and stonemasons and they did a lot of work here. Then they started dairies here in Santa Barbara. They were good milkers. And good sheep-herders, but they'd have to go to the island. At that time, they had a lot of sheep there. My father was a sheep-herder. He used to go to Santa Cruz Island here in Santa Barbara, in our channel, and he used to shear sheep. He used to have to do it by hand."[71]

Natalia and Pablo had nine children who reached maturity. Two others died in childbirth. The offspring they raised, and their children and their children's children are an incredibly colorful and challenging family, ranging from working cowboys to shepherds and stevedores, to cement truck drivers and beauty shop operators, and to baseball stars and evangelists.

One area they never really got involved in was politics, though Ted Williams made several campaign appearances and recorded messages of support for Republican candidates, even including a local candidate for sheriff in Massachusetts in the 1990s. Ted was a lifelong Republican, following in his father's footsteps – Sam Williams was at least somewhat friendly with Governor Frank Merriam of California, as we have seen.

After arriving in the United States, Pablo Venzor started off as a Democrat, but one day in El Paso became a Republican. He found himself at a Republican rally and, according to family lore, you could get yourself a free beer by signing onto the Republican rolls. Pablo had more than one beer, but only signed up once.

Ted Williams never truly knew his grandfather, who died around the time Teddy was 2-years-old, but family lore says that when he came to visit, he liked his grandfather so much that he wanted to sleep in the same bed with him. They had a hard time convincing Teddy it wouldn't be right, but he insisted until he finally gave in to his mother.

In the early days of the film industry, Santa Barbara was a bit of a Hollywood outpost. In the first decade of the twentieth century, the city had developed good rail and road connections to other

communities up and down the California coast. A number of westerns and other films were shot at the old Flying A Studio which was right downtown on West Mission Street between Fifth and Chapala. The American Film Manufacturing Company set up shop in Santa Barbara in July 1912, establishing themselves on the site of an old ostrich farm. The studio, known as the Flying A, was one of the largest studios in the country. Before too long, the studio had even organized a company baseball team as part of the Motion Picture League, which "consisted of teams from different studios in Southern California who played each other as well as local community teams."[72] Until the devastating June 1925 earthquake hit Santa Barbara, the studio was quite an active one.

Sarah Diaz told me of an aunt and an uncle of her mother's. "They were all fair, blue-eyed. You wouldn't think they had any Spanish blood or Mexican blood or whatever in them. They came to Santa Barbara; they used to come and visit us and right away they'd get a job in the moving pictures. That was when the Flying A was right here in Santa Barbara, with Mary Pickford and Mary Miles Mander and William Russell. All those movie stars. We used to go watch them make pictures."[73]

Natalia Hernandez Venzor.

Manuel Herrera told me that his grandfather Pablo Venzor picked up a little extra cash from time to time, serving as an extra in films, but he was cast as a peon every single time and eventually he became angry about the stereotyping, quit on the spot one day and simply refused future roles.

Pablo's health began to fail, and his son Daniel was taking care of the family until he was called off to service in World War I. Pablo Venzor died in 1920. The family never knew exactly what he died from, but after Pablo was gone, Natalia never remarried. She said she didn't want anyone else telling her children what to do, so she remained single for the rest of her life and took pride in her decision.

"I have no idea when Pablo was born, but Natalia died in 1954 and she was about 84 years old. She should have been born about 1869 or 1870. She suffered from a heart attack and had trouble breathing as well. The last time she was taken to the hospital, she stated in Spanish, "I know I will never return to my home." She had tears in her eyes and we all were crying, I remember that sad day as if it were yesterday! She never came home, she passed away in January of 1954. A sad day in my life."[74]

She bore a lot, but she held the family together as best she could. When Natalia Venzor died, the family lost its center.

Manuel describes Natalia as "the silent ruler of the home" and he notes that her children, several of whom struggled with alcoholism, "had the common decency to not be abusive in her presence. Since she was a proud woman, I could often sense the hurt on her brow with the drinking and unhappiness." No one in the family would ever curse around Natalia. She was particularly proud of May and Sarah. Her daughter Mary was also involved in charitable works and when son Bruno informed Natalia that Mary had been killed by her son-in-law, she is said to have fallen to the floor and wept, and continued to do so for days.

Natalia was the matriarch, and she held to the old values. Her brothers Rayo and Federico would come to visit, but when they did, they would always announce themselves and ask for the lady of the house – their sister. "As a child I was taught to honor my peers and to listen and be respectful. Rayo, Federico, May, Pete and a few others [impressed me favorably.] Rayo was a giant of a man and when he spoke you listened. The man could do just about anything because he was a rancher in Mexico, as [was] Pete. Heck, those guys could butcher a cow, goat, lamb or what was to your liking to grace the table. I had the best cheese at Rayo's place. He was a real rancher and knew his skills well and the same with Pete. I learned from the older people and, yes, I did respect them just as I did Pete, who was as hardworking a man as I ever knew."[75]

Ted's grandmother would have been shocked to hear Ted Williams express himself, the way he sometimes did. Ted was a master of profanity, and he certainly didn't pick up that way of speaking from his mother or grandmother. No matter how bad off some of her children became with drink, they were never offensive in her presence. She was aware of some of the dysfunctionality around her, though. "Since she was a proud woman, I could often sense the hurt on her brow with the drinking and unhappiness was brought by her sons and one daughter."[76]

"As for Ted and his cussing, I think it came from the guys whom he played with in his young days. He was always playing with older guys and in semi-professional leagues and he must have gotten it from the game of baseball at a young age. He was very much impressed with the old guys, but his Mom never cussed but one time that I knew the gal. My brother Paul teased her and wouldn't stop and she was very upset, he was provoking her and I told Paul to stop, but he continued and she told him off, I didn't blame her at all. My brother was upsetting the old gal and she wasn't well. I finally got him to stop because I was worried that May would have a heart attack. May was not one to cuss and she was not a gossip column like the rest of the family."[77]

Natalia was a mother or grandmother figure to a number of non-family members as well. Manuel remembers something he witnessed as a 6-year-old boy. He relates how a Superior Court judge named Atwell Westwick, senior judge of Santa Barbara, pulled up to Natalia Venzor's house in a police car. The judge asked if he could come in the house and, when inside, asked if he could sit down. Natalia said, "Sure, you're a guest here." She says, "Atwell, did you have the siren going when you came up the street?" He says, "Yes, I did" and she says, "Don't do that. It disturbs the neighbors." This was a man she knew well. It turns out that she had babysat him years earlier.

Manuel shook his head in wonderment. "Here's a man that I later found out put people to death, put them in prison for life – if you're wrong, he's going to punish you – and he's over here apologizing for using the siren. She said, 'Atwell, have you been drinking?' and he says, 'Yes.' 'Would you please put your bottle on the table and refrain from continuing?' He said, 'My wife, and you know her, she's divorcing me, and I came here to reminisce and to be consoled.' She said, 'You're always welcome here.' He got on his hands and knees and cried in her lap, for about five minutes. The way he talked Spanish – he had learned it from her. 'Well, we all go through some hard times; we all have some bad things' and she patted him like a little kid. Rubbed his back. The same thing as she used to do to me. He's crying and I said, 'Man, this guy really loves this woman to come over here and talk to her.'"

Judge Westwick had a home in Rattlesnake Canyon, behind the old mission. Manuel, Sarah, and Natalia all took him back home. On top of the mountain, it was a house like Manuel had never seen before. He saw lights through the fog and said, "Grandma, look, we're in Heaven. Those are angels." Natalia said, "No, *mi'ijo*. That's fog and those are the lamps from the streets." Westwick loved her so much, Manuel said, that "when he had his hardest time, he came to her and just cried."[78]

In some way or other, there were a number of people who Natalia had looked after. Manuel Herrera told me that Natalia had "raised Percy Heckendorff, a very well known lawyer in the area." Heckendorff apparently helped Ted's brother Danny get out of a very serious scrape later in life. It was a case Ted never knew about, Manuel says, and it was never conclusive. Manuel heard Sarah Diaz tell the story several times. "It seems Danny had come up to visit the family from San Diego. He had given a young girl (18 or 19) a ride. We guessed that he met her on the way to Santa Barbara. The next day the police came to the door of the old 1008 Chino Street house and asked to see Danny. They asked if he had picked up a young girl and they described her appearance. Danny agreed that he had and then the police told him that he was charged with rape. The young girl said Danny Williams had raped her, so he was taken away to jail to be charged and arraigned by the local judge.

Heckendorff had been a great friend to the family and now he was hired to clear this matter up. Mrs. Venzor had to mortgage the 1008 Chino Street house so they could get enough money to afford the lawyer and incidental costs. "Well, old Percy was a sharp character. He did some investigating and found a loophole in the security of the evidence. The office where the evidence was stored or secured was not locked and this fact was presented to the judge during the trial. Percy brought the unlocked door issue up to the judge and he said, 'the evidence was not secured, so case dismissed.' Danny was released and the mortgage was returned to Mrs. Natalia Venzor."[79]

Danny Williams in his car with his first wife, Helen Hansen.

Natalia Venzor did have the chance to see her grandson Ted play in major league baseball, albeit it an exhibition game. Manuel accompanied Natalia to the game. "I remember the only game I saw Ted and the Sox play, at Wrigley Field in Los Angeles. My Natalia was at the game, too! She saw Ted park one out and she winked at me when the ball had gone over the fence."[80] Natalia H. Venzor died early in January, 1954.

Ted attended his grandmother Natalia's funeral and made an impression on his cousin Kathleen, one of Manuel Herrera's sisters. Kathleen told me, "I remember seeing him at the wake, then going to my Aunt Sarah's house on Chino Street in Santa Barbara for a family gathering, where I decided to sit on the sofa beside him and introduce myself. He was very attentive, asked me how we were related, said he was pleased to meet me (which made my head really swell with pride.) I found him to be quite the opposite of what I had heard about him (which was that he could be extremely rude and obnoxious to people.) Actually, he was pleasant, beautifully dressed (style has always been a barometer with me), very slender and had a definite presence about him. I really liked him. Of course I mentioned that I really loved baseball (which I didn't, but thought mentioning such would gain me some points) and he said to call him for tickets whenever I was in the area and wanted to see a game. I almost asked him for his autograph, but didn't think the timing was right (being my great grandmother's funeral and all)."[81]

Manuel talks about his grandmother Natalia with the deepest respect. She was, Manuel says, "the silent backbone of the family... the quiet hero and leader of the family."

Let us return once again to learn more about May Venzor.

May Venzor Williams (May 8, 1891 - August 27, 1961)

May, who may well have been named after Micaela Hernandez, married Samuel Williams, as we know. She gave birth to four children, though the first two died at birth. Her two surviving children were both boys: Teddy Samuel Williams and Daniel Arthur Williams. Teddy was born on August 30, 1918 – or was he? Again, the birth certificate seemingly raises more questions than it answers. The name and the date on Ted's birth certificate have been changed. Let's revisit his birth certificate once more, this time in some detail. As mentioned before, note also the dating of the physician's certificate: 8/21.

Adding to the confusion is the fact that there are two or more birth certificates. One is typed and that has been reprinted in a couple of books, such as page 2 of Dick Johnson and Glenn Stout's book. There is also a handwritten one; it raises still more questions. A handwritten certificate was perhaps completed first, from information supplied by one or both parents, and then a typed copy was completed for filing purposes. The birth date on the typed one was clearly originally entered as August 20 but has been over-written to read August 30. Yet it was still dated as signed by the physician Steade on August 21.

There are actually two different handwritten certificates, and an affidavit filed by Mrs. Samuel S. Williams. The child's name on what seems to be the original handwritten certificate was Teddy Samuel Williams. It shows the date of birth as August 20. A copy supplied by the Assessor/Recorder/County Clerk of the County of San Diego in September 2004 bears a rubber stamp indicating that the certificate was amended on June 9, 1920.

May Williams with baby Ted.

The county clerk's office also produced an affidavit "for correction of a record" dated May 27, 1920. The affiant was Mrs. Samuel S. Williams and she filed the document which states: The child's name should be given as "Theodore Samuel Williams," and the date of birth as "August 30, 1918." The May 27 date shows us that the affidavit was filed just shy of eight weeks before Ted's brother Danny was born. Why the pregnant May Williams moved to correct Ted's birth certificate at this time is unknown. The original certificate was stamped "Amended" on June 9, 1920.

At this point – apparently – a new and official handwritten certificate was created. This one produces the "full name of child" as "Theodore Samuel Williams" but whoever was completing the form seems to have at first forgotten to also change the date from 20 to 30, then compensated for his or her error by over-writing the 20 and making it into a 30. The certificate of the attending physician, though, was not corrected and still reads as 8/21. It was not Ted himself who changed his name; it was clearly his mother who did so when he was less than two years old. But even her attempt to correct the record was botched, leaving later researchers still scratching their heads.

In any event, Ted's birthday was always celebrated on August 30. We've seen that his high school record bears the August 30 date, and May's own handwritten notes to herself sometimes included notes such as "Aug 30 My Teddy 1918". An unidentified clipping from a 1938 Minneapolis newspaper found in the Les Cassie scrapbook at Hoover High reads, "If you like Ted Williams' rhythm at the plate you ought to see him in front of a radio... Ted's a nut on swing bands, rates Benny Goodman tops, but can't dance a lick, says he'll learn this winter... Ted likes Minneapolis so well he's entertaining the idea of getting a job here for the off-season... Williams... received a birthday cake celebrating his twentieth birthday from his mother, Aug. 30, although baseball records say he won't be 20 until Oct. 30... Think what power Ted'll get in back of those homers when he fills out that wiry frame of his."

Ted's official military record also cites August 30 as his birthdate.

I'm guessing that the parents told the clerk filling out the form that the newborn's name was Teddy Samuel, yet s/he took it upon her/himself to "correct" this to read Theodore. When it came time for the typed copy, though, the parents had clarified that they really did mean it to be "Teddy."

Ted was known as Teddy, and even close friends like Dom DiMaggio called him that to Ted's dying day. In school days, though, at least for a while, he was called "T. Samuel" and that got into print at least once in the *Hoover High Cardinal*. The official high school file has his name recorded as Ted S. Williams.

Ted's handwritten birth certificate.

Then there is Theodore Francis Williams. Somehow, someone in Minneapolis seems to have gotten the notion that Ted's middle name was Francis. During 1938, when Ted spent the season playing for the Minneapolis Millers, any number of articles appeared in the local papers dubbing him "Theodore Francis Williams." The middle name stuck for a while in 1939, and occasionally appeared in some of the Boston papers as well. Ted's 1940 Play Ball baseball card issued by Gum, Inc., shows his name as Theodore Francis Williams. Someone figured it out before too long, though. The 1941 Play Ball card had him as Theodore Samuel Williams, and so he remained ever after. It took a little longer to correct his birthdate, at least when it came to baseball cards. The October 30 date was perpetuated from card to card, year to year. The first baseball card to reflect the August 30 birthdate was Ted's Topps card in 1956, his third year with Topps.

Early on with Boston, in the spring of 1938 and again in '39, "The Kid" had another nickname: his teammates and others called him "California."

How do we know that there were two earlier children before Teddy was born? The birth certificate asks "Number of children born to this mother, including present birth." The number "3" was entered. That was question #19. Question 20 asks, "Number of children of this mother still living" and there the completed form reads "1" – Ted. So Ted actually had two older siblings, who had died in childbirth or infancy? That was the conclusion one would draw. I asked Ted himself about this and he said he hadn't known that. Sarah Diaz had, though. She told Manuel Herrera this on several occasions. Both were pregnancies that preceded Teddy. Manuel's supposition is that "May kept on working when she should have taken care of herself during her pregnancy."

Another intriguing item: May believed she was doing God's work, but was she really so innocent that she believed herself to have conceived immaculately? I asked Manuel Herrera if he'd ever heard that May might have suffered the loss of two children before Ted was born. "Yes," he wrote me back. "Since you brought that up, it is correct. Mom told me about the loss Aunt May suffered – a child or two at birth. It did occur but, as tradition was in the old days, people never spoke about loss of a child, or loss by sickness of a child at a young age. Aunt May always professed that she had no idea how she got with child and that only the doctor was the one who informed her of the up-and-coming birth of Teddy. She stated, 'In God's name, I have no idea as to how I came with birth?' I always just smiled at her innocent statement! Who was I to doubt her word?"[82]

May was often considered somewhat of a "santa" – a saint. But immaculate conception would be going too far.

She did do some wonderful things for people. One family she knew, related to the Rubio family, moved to Los Angeles. May and this family would visit each other, and on one visit she noticed that their daughter, the little girl, had crossed eyes. She told the mother that she was going to take this little girl out. She didn't say what she had in mind. May took the little girl to an eye doctor who worked on her and then May brought her back home, with her face bandaged. "There's blood coming out of the bandages," Manuel told me. "They're all bloody. There's other fluids coming out of the child's eyes. 'Oh my God, May! What have you done? In the name of God, what have you done to our child?' 'Everything's fine.' 'No! Get out of here! We're upset. We can't handle this. This is not right.' May said, 'Take the bandages off in a week.' 'May, look at the blood! Something's wrong!'

"They took the bandages off in a week. The little girl's eyes were all right. The next time May came over, they got on their knees and apologized to her. I'll tell you, though, May never asked for praise. May never... she always had another job to do. 'Who's next?' was the name of her life, and nothing was going to stop her."[83]

May suffered at the end of her life, but she bore the awareness of her decline with faith and dignity. Sometime in 1954 or '55, "she was in a bus and had an accident. The bus stopped quickly and she was jerked forward. From then on, her back began giving her problems and she began to lean over. That began a real degeneration of her body. It really caused a lot of pain. She was bent over forward. But, you know, in her last years – she spent a year and nine months with us (staying at 1008 Chino Street with Sarah and Arnold Diaz) – that woman never complained. She knew she was dying. She never said a bad thing, never gave up her love for Jesus Christ and what she believed in."[84]

May Williams with Sarah Adams.

Over the years, before she was relocated to Santa Barbara, the house in Utah Street had begun to become more and more cluttered. Ted Williams, the nephew, recalls stacks and stacks of old newspapers piled up around the house, and papers everywhere, many of which were covered with May's jottings – short prayers or expressions of love for her boys.

Ted was kept abreast of her condition, but never visited in his mother's last two years. "He phoned and left messages for her," Manuel remembers. "He didn't come at all. I thought he might, but he didn't. I think it bothered him to see his mother so bad off. He couldn't handle it." Like many people,

Baby Danny Williams.

Ted was conflicted in his feelings about his mother. In his autobiography, he wrote that he was closer to his mother than to his father, but at the same time, her behavior rankled and he found her hard to take. "The last statement I got from Teddy about his mother was, 'My father should have gotten the Medal of Honor for putting up with that s.o.b.', then he slammed his coffee cup on the dining room table and madly walked out the dining room."[85]

Manuel admired the way May dealt with her final days. "This woman was so bad off that she used to put Absorbine, Jr. on herself, and five blankets to keep warm. She had hardening of the arteries and she had several mini-strokes. I'll tell you what, when it came time to go to church, boy, she'd get brand-spanking dressed up. I have never seen a person so committed and so strong-willed about her convictions. It amazed me. To this day, when I get upset and something bothers me, I think about May.

"People would come around and they all loved to be around her. She had an aura of love for what she believed in. She didn't care about the jealousy and everything. I asked her, I said, 'You know, people are jealous of you.' She said, 'In the Bible, it says that people will test you but the Lord will protect you.' She didn't let them bother her. It was never a problem for her. Me? Everything, hell, bothers me."[86]

As a side note, Danny's birth certificate lists his mother's occupation as Salvation Army worker; Ted's listed her as housewife. The work had perhaps become more of a vocation by the time Danny was born, two years later.

May Venzor Williams was a very special woman. When one first reads of Ted and Danny sitting at home at 9:30 or 10 at night, waiting for their mother or father to come back home, one wants to reproach May for not being a good mother. Our historic culture tends to exempt Sam Williams a bit, but only if one subscribes to the double standard that sees the wife as the homemaker.

The two boys turned out very differently, and many would feel that Ted made the most of the opportunity – befriending other families, but primarily devoting himself to the pursuit of the science and art of hitting a baseball – while Danny suffered the consequences of a breaking home and a "double A personality" older brother. Did baseball benefit because May was a bad mother?

Frank Cushing doesn't think so. He believed that "even if his mother was sitting home all day long, he still would have been down at North Park playground having Rod Luscomb throw baseballs at him 12 hours a day. There were some people who feel she was neglectful, but it wouldn't have made any difference. Ted would have been down at the playground from sunup to sundown. He was totally preoccupied with hitting a baseball. I've never seen anyone with the dogged drive to become the best. It's not just an ego thing. It's a drive."[87]

Of course, there's the question of the chicken and the egg in all of this. "The one thing his mother did show him was total commitment. That commitment took over as far as hitting."[88]

If Ted's mother was merely "sitting home all day long," would Ted have been as driven? We can never know.

She was, if nothing else, committed.

Some of the criticism she received rubbed friends the wrong way. One of Ted's Hoover High teammates, Del Ballinger, reacted, "She wasn't out doing bad. She was out doing good. I loved her." "We all did," chimed in Cushing. "May was a wonderful woman. Her calling was that strong religious thing, and she collected money and was extremely good to poor people; it's really hard to knock May Williams."[89]

This was also a woman of courage. It took "guts" to preach in the red light district of San Diego, Manuel Herrera said. "I can remember her telling me as I questioned her while we stood in front of the El Cortez Hotel, 'Manuel, I am taking the word of God to the depths of Sin' and she was pointing to the bars where the Marines and Navy guys were having a few drinks. So much damn guts! Few people have the nerve to serve the Lord like my Aunt May."[90] No evangelist has it easy, confronting people in public places when they would often prefer to be left alone. Ridicule would often result, but Manuel quotes the Bible as saying, "A great many will mock you, but stay fast with the Lord." Chances are he heard that from May Williams.

San Diego writer Barry Lorge heard how May would "trade on her son's name" to raise a little extra for the cause. A bank teller named Mel Powers told Lorge that she'd come into the bank and convince "everyone to put whatever coins they could into her tambourine... She would then canvass the bars along University Avenue, telling patrons, 'I'm Ted Williams' mother. Empty your pockets.'"[91] Not everyone knew the name Ted Williams. An amusing story told to Don Freeman of the *Union* is worth recounting. "One day Mother came home from a downtown shopping trip and told Pop that a very nice lady had been seated next to her on the bus. Mother said that this lady wore 'some kind of a Salvation Army uniform.' So, my mother related, they began to chat. As Mother recalled the moment, this woman suddenly, for no reason that Mother could figure out, said to her, 'My son is Ted Williams!' Hearing this, Mother smiled and said, 'That's nice. My sons' names are James and Charles and Hughie Lyons.' I don't think Pop ever stopped laughing at that one."[92] She sometimes went too far. Joe Villarino recalls that Ted's mother "used to ride the old streetcars and get people cornered on the Salvation Army deal. They'd say, 'Let's go! Off the car!' Ted didn't like that too well."[93]

May didn't let food get in the way of her service. She was the Mother Teresa of San Diego and often skipped meals because of her determination and dedication to the Cause. When she did sit down to eat with the family, there was sometimes quite a pause between seating and eating. "May could pray a supper prayer like no one I have ever met. You could expect a 20 minute prayer and Mom [Sarah] would tell her, 'May, please. Let's eat. We need to eat!' That cut things short, maybe only another 10 minutes. My blood sugar level would drop like crazy, but May never missed a beat with her prayers."[94]

She was dedicated even by Salvation Army standards. She aged early from giving of herself to others, but she left no stone unturned. "There aren't any like her left in the Old Army," wrote Manuel Herrera, "and that is why I don't attend any more. She was a Tough Act to follow, and so is The Kid. My Aunt Sarah told me that grandmother Natalia would ask May to stop and eat, because she was working so hard, and she was neglecting herself."[95]

As she aged, she suffered a form of dementia, and reportedly even began simply taking things out of retail stores without remembering to pay for them. Ted was embarrassed, and arranged to have her moved to 1008 Chino Street in Santa Barbara, to live with Sarah and Arnold Diaz.[96] Her grandson Sam believes the move to Santa Barbara was also intended to shield her from some of the sickness that his father (and her son) Danny was suffering in the house on Utah Street. When she arrived, she had only two pieces of luggage. Ted had sold or given away everything else, or had it sent to the dump. She had so little, but "with all she had to deal with, she always spoke very positively about the Army and the Lord. Never negative, but so ill. She was a go-getter and she did all she could for the ole Army. That's why she died so darn young and looked so damn old. The Salvation Army took advantage of her ability to get the job done at all cost. I felt bad for her, but she loved the Lord with not one ounce of regret in her heart."[97]

"When Aunt May came to live with us, she was frail. The Salvation Army was her love and her work. She never lost faith even in despair, her love for Christ was like the Blood and Fire of the old Salvation Army. Many people thought she was crazy. Yeah, with Christ and not drugs or drinking."[98]

There were good memories, though. May could enjoy herself. She was very musical. She had a piano in the living room at Utah Street. She played cornet, guitar and banjo. And, of course, she had "many, many tambourines. We loved playing with those. They made a lot of noise," remembers her nephew Ted. Manuel had his own memories. "She'd play the piano for us. We'd play rock and roll music and she'd say, 'Oh, no. We're going to play hymns.' That's the way she was."

This was the middle to late 50s. She wasn't a big Elvis fan, then? "No. No way. More William Booth. He was the founder. General Kitching, she went to training college with him in Hawaii. He became the commander of the Salvation Army. She'd call him. He was a personal friend. Well, the Army didn't like that – the majors and corporals, they didn't like May going over their heads."

Entertainment was also a feature of her pitch on the street and in visits to bars or other targets. "She would do magic tricks first. Take a cornet with her. And then the next thing, she'd be telling about the Lord. She'd get your attention, capture you and then she'd... She would do a disappearing act with a quarter and she could roll it on her fingers and get your attention with that and then ask you what hand it was in. She would hide it and you'd have to figure out what hand she had it in. She'd laugh at you, 'ah ha ha' – it was fun. That's the way she'd get your attention, and then she'd play a little violin or something. It was always a big thing when May came."[99]

Sarah and May, sister musicians with a cause.

When she got preaching, though, she must have been something. Let's allow Manuel to provide a flavor of what it might have been like. "May was a soldier in the Salvation Army and her battle was to enlighten the people around her about the Lord and the wages of Sin – to bring Salvation, so a sinner can repent and prepare to be a Christian. Since May was a simple-type person who took her orders very seriously, she always worked from early morning to late at night and often forgot to eat a decent meal. Her thoughts were to bring people closer to the Lord, because someday you will meet the King of Kings.

"When I was 10 years old I was told no more selling papers on Sunday. The Salvation Army Sunday School was waiting for me at the corner of Chapala and Haley. May told me often that there is no prejudice because, 'If you prick the surface of our skin, we all have red blood no matter what our color is.' I can hear her telling me that right now as I write. When he was inducted into the Baseball Hall of Fame, Ted talked about prejudice and how the game of baseball must open the doors to minorities and allow others to play the great game of baseball, because he had the insight to realize that baseball would some day be played all over the world. Now you see players from poverty-stricken countries in the big leagues. I guess Mom's teachings just might have rubbed off on the Kid from North Park playground.

"May was so directed that others even in the Army were jealous of her. She could easily raise money for the church and had friends in prominent places who would always have time for May Williams. Ted is a real product of his upbringing and even if he did not have an eight to five mom, The Kid from San Diego still got a baptism about the word 'giving' and helping the 'the poor souls and unfortunates!'

"When I asked May if she was embarrassed about singing on the street corner, she said that, 'I am proud to sing praises to the Lord.' As I walked out of her room, I was beginning to realize what this little Christian woman was all about and how she felt so needed.

"When May came to retire and stay at our home, she was just a shadow of herself, but mention the words 'Blood and the Fire' and the Woman of The Year in San Diego would raise her hand up to Jesus and say 'Amen!'"[100]

And she was really in a state of peace with herself and her world. Her grandson Ted provides a wonderful appreciation of May from his own childhood. "In that side bedroom at Utah Street, that bedroom that was Dan and Ted's, that's where they used to put me to take my naps. There was a little twin bed in there. It was a tiny room and it had these kind of paper curtains that came down on the roll, with a cotton ring at the bottom on a string. I never wanted to take a nap, so I lay there just looking at the light. I always noticed that the curtains would blow in the wind and sail out. It was very peaceful and the light would come through – the light was very beautiful in that room, before they built the big apartment house next door.

"I guess I always admired May for her religious beliefs, just that she was so driven by it. She so believed and she was so strong. It was always in her conversation. She wasn't preachy, but she always included the Lord in everything that she said. Her life, and what she wanted out of life, and how people should live. It wasn't, 'You're doing wrong.' It was really just from joy.

"I think she was blessed. She was blissed out with the Lord. I used to lie there sometimes trying to go to sleep, in this dreamlike state, and I imagined this angel coming into the room and touching me, and making me blessed like May was. It was such a beautiful thing. It really was. She was beautiful in this way. It wasn't fire and damnation. It was just love and beauty, and support.

"She'd glow. She radiated. Her eyes sparkled. She was very special."[101]

One son turned out to be a Hall of Fame baseball player, a decorated Marine Corps jet fighter-bomber pilot and a world class sport fisherman – and a leading fundraiser for the fight against cancer in children. The other proved to be a bit of a tough customer and a hard-luck case; he died relatively young, leaving behind a widow and two – it turns out, three – children. We can only speculate how the other two children of Samuel and May Williams – be they male or female – might have developed, had they lived.

May died nearly a year and a half after her youngest son, Danny, succumbed to leukemia. Of course, she knew he was seriously ill and undergoing treatment. That awareness may have contributed in part to her own enervation; she may have suffered a nervous breakdown of some sort. Mercifully, though, she may never have known of Danny's death, since she had been relocated to Santa Barbara before his passing. It is the understanding of both Danny's sons Sam and Ted that she was never informed of the loss.[102]

THE OTHER VENZORS / MAY'S BROTHERS AND SISTERS

Pedro Venzor (January 31, 1889 - June 8, 1958)

Pedro [Pete] was the oldest, born in Chihuahua in 1889. He was the cowboy. Pete Venzor and his wife Lupe [Guadalupe Huerta, December 12, 1899 – October 20, 1970] had no children. They "married too late," Connie Matthews explained. Pete became foreman at the Tecolote Ranch in Santa Barbara. Owned by the Spaulding family, and also called the Spaulding Ranch, this was quite a large ranch with a great stable. Like his Uncle Rayo Hernandez, who had been a rancher in Mexico, Pete was skilled at the trade. As foreman, he was "the brains of the outfit" and Lupe was the cook, not only for the Spauldings but for the ranch workers as well. At one time or another, at least six of Pete's siblings worked on the ranch. The only two who did not were May and brother Daniel.

Pedro was known as Pedro to close family members, but to most everybody else, he was Pete Venzor. When he was younger, he showed some skill with a game of ball. Sarah talked about Pete's skills at handball. "My oldest brother learned how to play, because here in Santa Barbara we had a lot of Basques. They were all in business. They all had liquor stores. They used to play handball. Not racquetball. Handball. My father used to make the balls for them. They'd start with a little rubber thing inside and he'd wind the twine around it. Then he'd cut the skins and he'd sew them like a baseball, but they were for handball. Not with a racquet, no. Handball.[103]

"The game of handball is a Basque game," Manuel chimed in later. "They take great pride in being the best in the world. The original ball was as hard as a rock and was tough on the hands. My friend was a national champion and he had great respect for the old ball that is no longer used in the game of today. The hand and eye coordination of the Basque is said to be exceptional. They are a very confident people, and their manner and attitude were also of a loner nature. Sound familiar to you?"[104]

Pete apparently had the opportunity to go on the road playing handball. "One priest – I don't remember his name – came to my mother and asked permission, could he take Pete around the world, to different countries, just as a handball player, just to show his ability and to show how

Pete Venzor, sister May, mother Natalia and wife Lupe at 4121 Utah Street.

well he could do. He was perfect." Sarah said that Natalia wouldn't give her permission to let the priest take Pete on tour. Pete was too young. "He was a great one and could not be beat," added Manuel. "He ruled the court."[105]

Ted's uncles were avid participants in sports. Three played baseball and one played handball. Young Teddy Williams spent portions of his summer time with cousins and uncles on the Tecolote Ranch. Even when not at the ranch, Ted got in time to play ball with Saul, Paul and Bruno at 1008 Chino Street, and one or more of May's brothers would visit San Diego from time to time.

Pete was an expert shot with a rifle, and was considered to have unusually good vision. He served in World War I. After receiving his training as a soldier, he was sent to France to fight and was scheduled to be advanced to the front when the Armistice was signed and he was returned to Santa Barbara. As we shall see, his brother Daniel was not as fortunate.

Pete's vision served him well on the ranch. It was said that he could post a fence line straight as an arrow without the use of a transit. One senses a bit of a connection to Ted Williams here. Ted had uncommonly good eyesight as well, and he had a very precise sense of distance and alignment – stories abound regarding his ability to estimate distances (and weights) with astonishing accuracy.

For example, there is the story of how Ted, upon returning to baseball after being away for most of two seasons while flying combat missions in Korea, immediately declared that home plate at Fenway Park was not properly situated. The season was more than half over, and not a single other player had complained. They thought Ted was kidding, but he insisted and when measurements were taken, Ted was proven right. Home plate was 1/4 inch out of proper alignment.

Another trait of Pete's that Ted embraced was his insistence on punctuality. Ted Williams was always on time, and he expected others to be on time as well. Pete's sister Sarah, when she worked as a housekeeper at the Tecolote Ranch, recalls that when Pete brought her to town, "you had better be at that certain place for a ride back home. He wouldn't wait, and would simply leave you behind." Manuel Herrera said Pete Venzor "was a kind person and he was stern and meant what he said." If you weren't there on time, you just didn't get your ride back to the ranch. This was not impatience, but just an insistence on the respect implicit in punctuality.

Manuel respected Pedro Venzor. "Pedro was a patient person and a thinker. He was confident but not a bragging type of person. He knew his talents and could rely on them when needed. He did drink, but he never got out of control and was a quiet man. I liked the guy. He was always kind to me and would invite me to stay at the Tecolote Ranch and enjoy a wonderful homemade meal that his wife made, my Aunt Lupe. Boy, could she cook some great Mexican food! I ate to my heart's content, usually with the work crew near the creek where the picnic tables were set up. If you took time to look up during the evening meal, you could see the deer up the creek in the canyon, drinking water." Of all the various aunts and uncles in the Venzor clan, Manuel felt he was treated best by Pedro and Lupe. "Maybe it was because they had no children," he reflected, "or because they liked my love of the ranch and my wanting to stay with them there."[106]

"I don't think Ted could beat Pedro in handball, because no one ever did! He was confident but not a bragging type of person. He knew his talents and could rely on them when needed. When my son was born, I took him over to the west side of Santa Barbara to visit Aunt Lupe. She was alone then; Pedro had died of throat cancer. She was very happy to see me and got to hold my son in her arms. She cried and we talked of old times at the ranch. I will never forget that wonderful day![107]

The ranch, like Chino Street, was a focal point for the family. Sarah worked as a cleaning lady for Mr. Spaulding. "It seems that the whole Venzor family worked at the Tecolote Ranch. I know that Pete, Lupe, Aunt Sarah, Jeanne, Saul, Paul, and Bruno all were employed at the ranch at one time or another. It was Paul who loved the ranch, but Pete was the brains of the outfit. Lupe was the cook and also cooked for the hired help at the ranch, Mom was the cleaning lady for Mr. Spaulding, he had a big home on the hill to the right of the ranch as you face the entrance."[108]

Sarah had already confirmed this. "We all worked out there at Tecolote Ranch. That was run by Mr. Spaulding. He was married to a very rich girl. She had more money than he did. They had one daughter, Deborah. They had a beautiful ranch. My oldest brother Pete had a very good eye. He'd be the one to take care of the Mexican help that used to go and work there, because he had a large avocado [grove] up against the hill. He was right close against the ocean, too. Mr. Spaulding had oil wells there along the coast, right across the street... the freeway went right through his property. That's where the Japs attacked Tecolote Ranch, in Goleta."[109]

Perhaps May Venzor learned how to be comfortable around governors and other political figures, because of some familiarity with them at the ranch.

"There were some special barbecues at the Tecolote Ranch, where Ted spent time running around. [There was] lots of room to run and chase cattle, or pick walnuts like I did. Mr. Spaulding hosted the Commanders' Barbecue for the California Highway Patrol and the Governor. Chill Wills, Will Rogers, Bud McSpadden, Dick Carr, Monty Montana and other notables from Hollywood came, and cowboys and screen and political people from the state capitol. Uncle Pete ran the program and did something that people do not do any more – he cooked a cow, underground. It's not done now, because it's too much work. Pete knew how and I was told that's the best way to cook beef; the meat falls right off the bone. Lupe Venzor could make the best tamales and menudo, along with a mole poblano that made me come to the ranch just to enjoy her homemade dishes. Her job was to cook for the ranch hands, but I would stand by her when she began serving and I always got invited for her special meal. My mouth still remembers that wonderful food." [110]

Pedro Venzor used to smoke Bull Durham tobacco and apparently it got him in the end. He died of cancer of the throat at the Sawtell Veterans Hospital in West Los Angeles. He is buried at the Santa Barbara Cemetery, as is his father.

Pete had some talent at music, as well.

"The picture of Pete with his guitar, Saul, Paul and Natalia was taken next door at 1006 Chino Street at Bruno's place in the back yard. The palm tree is to the right of the group and the picnic tables were under the slat swing that is directly behind them. I helped Bruno build the gazebo. This was about 1954 in Santa Barbara, CA. Uncle Pete gave his guitar to Arnold just before he passed away. Every time I drove by the place I remembered Uncle Pete. Pete often brought his guitar to play music with Arnold R. Diaz. They played my favorite, "Zacatecas." It is the National Anthem of Mexico. I first heard it played by Uncle Pete at the Tecolote Ranch at the age of maybe 4 or 5. I liked Uncle Pete to play the song for me and in later years that old song brought back some fond memories of the ranch and Uncle Pete and Aunt Lupe and her cooking. I was next to Mom when she took this picture."
Manuel Herrera

Mary and May Venzor, Santa Barbara.

Mary Venzor Cordero
(April 18, 1893 - October 7, 1943)

The oldest girl in the family was born Maria Venzor. Ted's Aunt Mary came to a tragic end, but not before bearing a "baker's dozen" – thirteen children – one of whom (Anita) was Manuel Herrera's mother. She married Albert Cordero, who worked as a trucker. Teresa Cordero Contreras was the youngest of the brood and she recalls, "Albert, my father, he had a trucking outfit. Local. Through Santa Barbara County and Los Angeles. He had seven trucks. He struggled through the Depression; then the war came and it took away three of my brothers, took them away from the trucking business. So we had to take over – the girls. We did all we could, but my dad lost a lot during that time."

It was the effort to save the firm that may have contributed to the murder/suicide which took Mary Venzor's life and robbed Manuel Herrera of his mother as well. "We were working in the fruit up north," Teresa Contreras continues. "Up north in Fairfield, picking plums, peaches, everything we could – because we had to help my dad, for the trucks that he had. He had to pay the State Board of Equalization for everything, and he had to keep the house up. My brothers had gone off to war. There was no one else, so us girls had to help. My sister Annie [Anita] had to move down from Stockton to Fairfield to work a little bit. She could make you laugh. She had a sense of humor. She was silly. She made us all laugh.

"My dad stayed back in Santa Barbara, and we went up north to work with the fruit. He used to haul away anything that was sacked or baled. He'd haul grains, alfalfa, hay, barley, beans. Ted knew my dad. I think he was kind of close to my dad, and my mom – more than he was to my Aunt Jeanne or Uncle Paul."[111]

In a later interview, Ted's cousin Teresa added, "My dad was a cowboy, you know. His father was a rancher. He was born in Las Cruces, California, right on the ranch. He used to haul for different ranches out there. He did that until he got married. I know he used to deliver milk, too. That's how he met my mom. Delivering milk and cheese. She was living in Santa Barbara; they were on Montecito Street at that time." Albert then got into the trucking business full-time.[112]

Annie Cordero – Teresa's sister – had married Salvador Herrera, who may have misunderstood his wife's departure to help save the family firm. Anita and Sal Herrera had six children: Mary [Redding], Salvador [Sal, Jr.], Kathleen [Osowski], Paul, and twins Manuel and Natalie. There was a seventh child, Carmen, but she passed away as a baby. These were difficult times and Salvador Herrera was out of work. Mary Redding says, "My dad spoke very little English, and we did not speak Spanish. On both sides, Spanish was spoken by the adults but not by the children."[113]

The work with fruit evokes the image of migrant workers and perhaps, within the state of California, that is what they were at this particular point in time. "We didn't pick apricots, but we cut them in half. Put them on trays. We picked peaches. We cut peaches also. We picked pears. We picked plums. We picked grapes." Apparently, Anita and her mother Mary went back to Anita's home together. "She told my mom, 'We've got to get some more clothes for the kids.' Well, Mr. Herrera took it wrong, I guess. I don't know what it was. We didn't get word until the next morning what had happened."[114] On a Sunday in October 1943, at 505 South Wilson Way in Stockton, Sal Herrera shot his wife, his mother-in-law, and then took his own life.

"He used an old-fashioned gun from Mexico," Teresa reports. "He used to drink a lot. Wine. I guess it was just depression, because he wasn't working. Only God knows why. She was everybody's favorite [Anita]. It was always so nice to have her around. When she died, I was 13. As soon as my mom passed on, my dad brought us home. And there was no more fruit."[115]

The Corderos were native Californians, Teresa explained, and they trace the lineage back to 1765, when "the first forefather arrived here in 1765 with Father Serra as one of the leatherjackets with the Patrol Army. My forefather was a corporal. They came from Spain. They arrived in Mexico City. He married in Baja to a Mexican woman, and they came up here to California. His son married an Indian here, the princess of the Chumash Indian tribe. He was here when they were building the missions. That was in the 1780s or 1790s." So there's even a bit of royalty in the greater Ted Williams family!

Sal Herrera and Annie C. Herrera with children Mary, Salvador Jr., and Kathleen, summer, 1941.

Albert Cordero couldn't handle all of the young Herreras as well as his own children, so they were distributed out among other relatives. Albert took in Mary Herrera. Kathleen and Paul went to live with John Cordero. Sal, Jr. was taken in by Rayo Hernandez. Manuel and Natalie went to live with Natalia Venzor, and when she died, they lived with Sarah and Arnold Diaz.

Most of the children suffered not only the initial trauma but other difficulties as well, within the homes they were placed. Mary was faced with a grandfather prepared to abuse her, and in the seventh grade – as soon as she could – she took employment as a mother's helper with another family. When she turned 18, that job ran out and she went to live with her aunt Jeanne Venzor Winet.

The Herrera family was fully fractured. The children weren't in close touch with each other at all. Manuel and his twin sister Natalie went to the center of the Venzor family, though, and spent over 10 years with Natalia Venzor at 1008 Chino Street before she passed away, then continued living at Chino Street with Sarah and Arnold. This location positioned Manuel well to soak up some of the family lore.

Manuel tells the tale of when he later met his brother Paul after a long separation. "I don't think you know how important a baseball field was in my young life," Manuel wrote me. "The game for me was always fun and I was interested in finding out how good I could play the game of baseball. Since Ted Williams was a great player and my oldest brother [Sal Herrera] played professional baseball for over eight years, I felt I had some talent for the game. Little did I know that baseball had more to offer than the game.

"In the Santa Barbara city recreational program, we had a midget league during the 50s which consisted of kids in the 9- to 12-year-old age bracket. Well, I was selected to play for the Kiwanis Club and my first game was to be at Santa Barbara Junior High School. We were playing the Lions team and I was looking forward to the game. Gosh, I was only 9-years-old and the coach put me out in right field where I wouldn't make a mistake by dropping a fly ball or whatever might go wrong!

"I don't think I hit the ball at all while at bat, but while sitting on the bench waiting for my turn at bat, a voice came to my ears. Someone called my name out. Sure enough, it was my uncle, John Cordero. I had seen him only maybe two or three times but I recognized him quickly. He told me, 'Your brother Paul is the second baseman on the other team; he is your older brother.' I was shocked to say the least. I had heard that I had a brother, but as a kid who knows when you will ever meet the person or it might not be true, who knows?

"An idea flashed in my mind. I was going to stop the second baseman and tell him he was my brother. I did just that and I said, 'Hey, Paul I'm your brother Manuel.' He just looked at me and laughed as he said, 'Way to go, brother' as he ran into the dugout.

"Yeah, it was a pretty emotional game and meeting my brother was bigger than the game of baseball, but the American pastime brought us together for the first time in our young lives. What a special event!"[116]

Ted Williams knew Annie Cordero. They liked each other and were good friends as cousins. "She could really run," recalls Manuel. "Ted liked her, because she could hit a baseball." She was a bit of a tomboy. With a dad for a trucker, the girls as well as the boys learned how to drive. Ted taught her how to hit a baseball and the two of them sometimes rode around Santa Barbara together in a car, even driving up on the sidewalk for fun. "Ted loved that!" Teresa was a lot younger, born in 1929. She remembers Ted visiting the small house her family had at 1716 Chino Street. "He had to stoop under the eaves to get in. He lifted me up and said, 'Now you can touch the ceiling!' I remember that."[117]

In general, though, Manuel says that the Venzors and Corderos were not that close. "My grandfather [Albert] was a very hard working man. He would unload a freight car of, say, potatoes, and load it onto one of his trucks and haul it up north, usually to Atascadero or Paso Robles. I remember him bringing kindling for the old wooden stove we used at the house at 1008 Chino Street. He would unload the kindling and afterwards come in and have a morning cup of coffee. He would always show grateful respect to his mother-in-law Natalia. I liked his manners and sincere ways." Manuel blames the failure of the trucking business on Albert's "no-account sons [who] ran it into the ground before their father died of a heart attack." Manuel's middle name is Albert, after his grandfather. Manuel's twin sister Natalie was named after Natalia Hernandez Venzor, and her middle name is Jean, for Aunt Jeanne Venzor.

Losing both Mary and Annie was a big loss, and to have lost them in such a shocking way was devastating to the family. Pete was "kind" but Mary had a really big heart, like her sisters May and Sarah. "Mary and May were the true givers in the old family," Manuel wrote me. "Mary, my grandmother was very much like Natalia. She would go all over town helping friends and neighbors. My Uncle Arnold said, 'Mary would give you her soul.' She loved horses and had a stallion on the ranch; one time it almost killed her, trampling her, but she came out of it. Though Natalia and her oldest daughters May and Mary had such big hearts, and Sarah as well – though to a lesser degree – "the rest of the family stood alone and never were close. Time and events took a large toll on the Venzor family."[118]

While Ted was still living, Manuel wrote me, "May spent 50 years in the Salvation Army and I really think Teddy resents the fact that the ole Army kept her from developing a family home and normal life style. She was a simple person and was so darn loyal to her cause! Mary, my grandmother, was cut from the same mold and she would drive around Santa Barbara helping the needy and poor families, while her kids tore up the house! They called her a 'santa' or in English a saint. Natalia was just like Mary, then May, but the rest were not even close to the older girls."[119]

Mary's daughter Teresa remembers her mother being active, "even with the hoboes. We lived about six blocks from the train tracks. They would come around and knock on our back door, and my mother would give them coffee and things that they could take. She would collect things and give them. She was a very loving person, just a thoughtful person."[120]

Manuel contrasts Mary with others in the family. "The family members were loners and very cold hearted. They often never conversed with each other or didn't take the time to. Mary and May were the true givers in the old family, then Sarah but not to the liking of her older sisters. The rest of the family stood alone and never were close, time and events took a large toll on the manners of the Venzor family. Most of the siblings are of the same nature; they don't know how to show one bit of love or family relationship. I really don't know why, but that has been the trend for many years. They stood alone!

"My father murdered my mother Annie and he destroyed my grandmother. He did commit suicide and left six kids to face unhappy homes and alcoholic families. There is something about not feeling a part of a family and that was always present in my heart and soul."[121]

Being farmed out to families produced some uneven results and some unhappy results. Mary Herrera spent those seven years as a mother's helper. "I finished school while I worked for Commander George and Mrs. Collins, who lived in Montecito and was a mother's helper for her and her three children – Ann, Winslow, Gina. There was never any love shown to me, I knew my place and stayed there. I was more or less the housekeeper and cleanup crew. Never ever remember any one in the family giving me a hug or any affection."[122]

Manuel sometimes wished he'd been raised in an orphanage, instead of where he was taken in. He wrote me, "You should have been there to live the experiences that my sister and I had to put up with! I feel robbed of trust and the family image I wanted. The abusive people who wanted me to be their son. When the responsibilities came, you couldn't find one family member to support your effort. I had plenty of criticism and negative input from Sarah alone, not to bring up Arnold and the drinking and abuse he offered his wife. Arnold did his own thing at the expense of the family and yet when he was home, he wanted everything right and proper. I liked Pop as a friend, but he was not a father figure and his lifestyle came first.

"I really think that being in an orphanage might have been a more positive way of life to me. Ted is easily fooled, and the fact that he didn't even call or write his mother hurts me for a person who did more for humanity than he could ever offer!"[123]

Daniel Venzor, sister May (left) and mother Natalia with a grandchild.

Daniel Venzor
(May 30, 1895 - November 11, 1918)

The first Venzor of his generation to die was Daniel. He never had a chance to realize himself in life, since he died in combat during the First World War. Sadly, his death came after the war was over. Serving in France, he dodged one bullet right near the end of the war, and lived to write home about it. That was his last letter home.

Daniel Venzor is listed as having been killed on November 11, 1918 – the very date the Armistice was signed. The reality, though, was that he was killed sometime in the four or five days after the war was officially over. After signing the peace accords, communication was late in reaching the front lines due to the more limited methods of communication available at the time, and when word finally did arrive, many German troops did not believe it and so continued on fighting. When Daniel was killed, Ted Williams was about 10 or 11 weeks old.

An allotment provided by the United States government and paid out over several years was sufficient to finance the 1920 purchase of the house and property at 1008 Chino Street for Daniel's mother and father, and that home became the center family life, despite Pablo Venzor's death that same year.

That house at 1008 Chino Street remained that center, even after Natalia Venzor passed on. Sarah and Arnold lived there, with Manuel and Natalie Herrera. Bruno Venzor and his wife Marian lived at 1006 Chino Street while Paul and Tillie Venzor were at 1002 Chino. "We were one big happy family there in three homes," said Paul's son Frank.[124]

Natalia chose not to have Daniel's body returned home to America, because she thought that might further disturb his remains, so he is buried in France, in Flanders Field. A dozen or so years after the war, Natalia was offered a trip to France to visit the gravesite, and she accepted. May Williams accompanied her mother as far as El Paso, Connie Matthews remembers. Natalia joined with other Gold Star mothers – mothers who had lost a child in the war – and took a train to New York and then a ship to England. She made her way to France and was able to visit Daniel's grave at the American military cemetery. A photographer noticed her praying at his grave, and he captured the image. It became a fairly well-known photograph and has reportedly been exhibited at the National Gallery of Art in Washington and elsewhere.

Manuel says, "When my precious Natalia returned from Europe, she viewed the Statue of Liberty and cried, for she was home again on hallowed ground. She well knew the meaning of freedom and the price her son paid for that gift. She had left Mexico because of the revolution and the killings that were occurring at that time and America was her salvation from war."[125] Ironically, 30 years later, war took her son.

Ironically as well, Manuel and Natalie Herrera – the twins – were both born on November 11. It was never a purely enjoyable day for them. On their sixth birthday, Manuel remembers, "My sister and I usually had a cake for our birthday. Mine was chocolate and my sister's was always a white cake. I can't even remember getting a gift, but that is not important. I was really looking forward to the big day and the cake. That evening after supper we gathered around the table and the 'Happy Birthday' song was sung to me and my sister, The candles were blown out and of course on went the lights. I looked at my great-grandmother and tears were streaming down from her eyes and I knew the loss of her son Daniel was in her heart. My birthday didn't matter any longer. I just wanted to be near my precious Natalia and comfort her as she so often did me, so I went to her and put my arms around her and hugged her. I knew nothing had to be said. She needed me more than I needed the cake. She gave me a home and most of all some love and I had the chance to give it back. It was never the same after I lost my Natalia."[126]

Daniel Venzor.

"Mom [Sarah] was so hurt and in pain about her brother. She knew he almost made it through the war, but fate dealt a blow that scarred the family forever. From what I know about Daniel, he was more like Pete Venzor in manner and ways. I was told that Daniel was also a very honest person and kinda long and lean in structure. Daniel was so close to making it home, Mom always had that same fear about me being in the Vietnam War with my last days. Yes, she was a worry-wart, but I can understand why, with the devastating lost of her brother in France. It was the tough experiences in life that brought those traits to be a worrisome way in her heart and of course they never did go away!"[127]

Natalia Venzor at Daniel's grave, France.

Pete Venzor saw duty in France as well. Trained in the United States, he shipped out to France and was due to be sent to the front. Spared by the signing of the Armistice, he was demobilized and returned home to Santa Barbara and the ranch.

Daniel had escaped one close call. He wrote in a letter to his mother that he was almost hit in the head by a bullet. That time, he was spared. The second time Death came calling, he succumbed, killed in action right at the very conclusion of the first World War – tragically, as explained above, some days after peace was officially declared.

Of course, Ted's brother Danny was named after Daniel Venzor. So was Bruno's son Danny. There was also a Danny Cordero as well, Ted's cousin, a son of Mary Venzor and Albert Cordero. Daniel Cordero unfortunately died early, too, falling out of a truck his father was driving, as did Danny Williams, dying at age 39 from leukemia.

Natalia Venzor was honored ever afterward in Santa Barbara as a Gold Star mother. Ruth Gonzales recalls that "during the Spanish fiestas, she would ride with another lady in little horse-drawn carriages with the Mayor of Santa Barbara. The other lady died and then it was just her."[128]

Saul C. Venzor
(November 2, 1903 - August 15, 1963)

"The old guy had street smarts and was always on me to repeat my ABC's and this was to be done while my hands were at my side and I stood at attention and I finished with a "YES SIR!" Then it was checkers or Chinese checkers, take your choice – but a 12-inch ruler was at his side if you made a mistake, and little me was often struck on the hand. The old guy never let up on me, and I was often asked, "Do you want the persuader?" and I replied a loud, "No!" I wanted to make sure Uncle Saul heard me!"[129]

"Saul could just look at you and put the fear of God in you," remembers Manuel, not that fondly. "He often made me close the back door 10 times because I slammed it so hard. I was so afraid of the man that I did what he demanded right on the spot. He was not a kind person by any means and he always threatened us kids with the 'persuader.' Hell, I had no idea what a damn persuader was but it must not have been a good thing! He always vowed to use the persuader on us, but we never saw it."[130]

Saul Venzor made a strong impression on everyone around him. He certainly left a strong impression on Manuel Herrera, and so did his "persuader." It's not hard to see how Saul had an important influence on Ted Williams and helped forge some of the drive and determination that characterized Ted's approach to baseball.

He was a longshoreman, and worked with the famous Gang 1 crew that worked in Port Hueneme or in San Pedro, the L. A. port of entry. "The gang he worked for was noted for getting the job well done. They loaded the holds of many a freighter headed to foreign ports during the Second World War and the Korean conflict. Gang 1 was respected and singled out for their work."[131]

Saul was active locally, and managed one of the area baseball teams, the Santa Barbara Merchants. He was the first real baseball player in the Venzor family. Saul Venzor's obituary says that he "is credited with giving famed ballplayer Ted Williams his first baseball lessons" and adds that "Williams, his nephew, was quoted by friends here that Mr. Venzor was his first instructor."[132]

Ted's Aunt Sarah recalled times Ted came to visit in Santa Barbara. "Ted played with my brother Saul. We made them play out in the field. We had a big garden and we have a long driveway. They'd get out there on the driveway and throw the ball to each other. That's how Ted learned a lot, too, from my brother, about throwing. It's odd how he throws right and hits left. When Ted would come, the first thing they would do is get out there in that field and pitch to each other, throw the ball to each other, and bat to each other. My mother was left-handed, too, and boy, she didn't miss us when she threw rocks at us, trying to get our attention, you know." Sarah's nephew Danny Venzor remembers Natalia's arm, too. "She just spoke Spanish, and she's the one who took care of all the grandkids, because – you know, being poor, all the parents worked. We're all playing ball in the driveway and we had to go up there and get the ball in her garden. There's all these boxes of oranges and lemons. She'd yell at us in Spanish, and we'd run. She threw left-handed. She could hit you running, and hit you in the back. She'd wing it from the porch. We'd be taking off and she could wing a lemon or an orange from the porch and she could nail you. And she was old. She could whip a lemon up there and hit you with it."[133]

Uncle Saul was tough on Ted, and Ted may have learned a few other traits from Saul as a result. Manuel reports stories he learned growing up in the family, "The old guy really had the tools and Teddy would literally beg Saul to teach him how to pitch a baseball. Ted was eager and Saul knew the kid wanted to play baseball more than anything in the world. Saul told Teddy, "Not yet, you're not ready to pitch. I will tell you when I will teach you how to pitch a ball."

One time when Ted was visiting, Saul's wife Henrietta told Manny the story at Saul's daughter's house – Dee Allen's house. She said, "Saul wouldn't give in to Ted and made him wait and plead to learn how to pitch." Manny says he looked at Ted and Ted had a big grin on his face, animated by the memories.[134]

Saul was stubborn and aggressive and talented. Manny says, "No one could beat the guy, and he hated to lose. Saul gave Ted more than just pitching lessons. He used a no-lose attitude to build Ted's confidence and [demonstrate] how to think and win. Not just get the ball over the plate, but to think with your head and always be aggressive." Ted's determination to show his Uncle Saul what he could do has to have played into the single-minded drive which made Ted such a good ballplayer. "Ted had seen him pitch in different games. He would plead, 'Uncle Saul, can I pitch now?' Saul says, 'Aw, you're not ready, kid. Come on back. Come by tomorrow. Come back in another week. Maybe you're not hungry enough.' 'Oh, please, Uncle Saul! I want to be a pitcher. I want to learn how to throw a pitch. I want to learn how to pitch.' He'd tell Ted, 'Oh, maybe another day. Not today.' 'Oh, come on, Uncle Saul! Please!' He'd beg him all day. Ted would throw his glove down and walk out of the room."[135]

UPBMI Baseball Team, Santa Barbara. Left to right, standing: Isaias Castillo, Sam Robinero, Poncho Osuna, Saul Venzor, Gene Lillard, Marion Hill. Seated: Fred Cuevas, Manuel Mendoza, Julius Sesma, Duke Dally, Albert Castillo, Esque Escobar, Eddie Cuevas, Henry Becerra, Ginger Romero.

Frank Venzor, one of Ted's cousins, confirms Saul's role in molding a young Ted Williams, determined to prove he could be good. "Saul was the one who started this baseball stuff. He was one of the oldest brothers. He was the one who got Ted into baseball. Even before he picked up a ball, before he knew what a glove was. We had a slanted driveway on Chino Street. It looked like a pitcher's mound. Everybody was a pitcher, particularly Saul. They used to put Ted up there. 'Get up there. See if you can hit this,' they would yell at him. They weren't nice to him. They were not nice to him. Ever. They used to tease him. He'd be out there bawling and crying. I get this information from my Aunt Sarah. She said, 'Boy, those guys used to get up there and tease Ted. They'd get him out there on the driveway and he'd be crying. 'Get closer! Get up there! See if you can hit this!' My uncle could throw! He could throw 19 different pitches. This is where Ted began to recognize them. My aunt used to stick her head out the window and say, 'Saul! Leave the kid alone!'"[136]

Teasing or taunting a younger cousin could be discouraging or, if you share a family trait of toughness, independence and stubborn resolve, it can hone a commitment to succeed. Ted's own mother demonstrated single-minded and unswerving dedication in her calling as a Salvationist. It's not surprising that her eldest son picked up many of the same traits and put his own twist on it. "He was determined to be the best baseball player," observed Rosalie Larson, the daughter of May's brother Paul, "and she was determined to be the best captain in the Salvation Army."[137]

Saul Venzor was apparently quite a legend in Santa Barbara. "Ted reminds me a lot of Saul," Manuel Herrera wrote. "Ted is very independent and knows what he liked best – hitting a baseball. Saul was a great pitcher and was very respected as a baseball player here in Santa Barbara. Everyone knew he could pitch and he finally got a chance to show his stuff against the barn-storming major leaguers. He pitched a great game and struck out ole Babe Ruth and a bunch the other so-called heroes of the diamond! The game was played in Santa Barbara about 1935 and I know a few people who remember the game. They were more impressed with Saul Venzor than the major league all-stars.[138]

Frank Venzor recounts another story he heard. "Uncle Saul pitched a 19-inning, 1-0 ball game in the minors against the Los Angeles, the Metro... the railroad company. My dad told me he wouldn't quit. He wouldn't give up. He just pitched the 19 innings all by himself, and they won 1-0. They used to play at Cabrillo Field. They were called the Goleta Merchants. Ted used to send them equipment and balls and gloves."[139]

John Zant's article in the *Santa Barbara News-Press* stated that Saul "was a pitcher who could really bring the heat. He dominated the semi-pro games in Santa Barbara. 'He had a great arm,' said Tim Badillo, 91, who knew all the ballplayers in town. 'I brought Satchel Paige up here to throw in some games. Saul didn't quite have that good an arm, but he could throw the ball.' Saul has been credited with stoking Williams' interest in baseball when his nephew visited Santa Barbara. Apparently, Saul had some of Satchel Paige's gamesmanship."[140]

One of the games Ted saw Saul pitch is recounted in a story Saul's son-in-law David Allen tells. David is married to Saul's daughter Dee, who was for years an active local softball player herself. David relates a story Ted told at a family reunion: "He said that Saul was pitching at a semi-pro game, and he walked the bases loaded with nobody out. Then he asked the umpire for a time-out, and he went over to the opposing bench. He said, 'I'm betting that you guys don't score. Who wants to take me up on it?' He collected all these bets, and he went out and struck out the next batter. Then, he either struck out two more or got a double play, Ted didn't remember. But he won the bet."[141] Dee confirmed that Ted was at that game, and watched it first-hand. It had to have made a real impression on young Teddy Williams.[142]

According to his obituary in the *News-Press*, Zant notes, "Saul Venzor turned down an offer to play in the Coast League with Lefty O'Doul."[143]

Could Saul have made it in pro ball? Maybe. But love got in the way. Saul was enamored of Henrietta Osuna and wanted to marry, but when he was offered a deal, there were a couple of other beaus seeking her favors. Saul was afraid to leave, Henrietta told Manuel Herrera. She also confirmed Saul's role in helping mold Ted. "She and Saul often trekked down to San Diego to visit May and the boys. She and I conversed about the trips to San Diego and how Teddy would beg Saul to teach him how to pitch a baseball. Saul would tell Ted, 'Not yet, kid. You're not ready to pitch. Just wait, your time will come' and his Uncle Saul made him wait and wait. He taught Ted the basic pitches – fastball, curve and slider. Saul and Ted got along very well; since everything was all baseball, they had a lot in common."

The marriage ended in divorce, though. "It was the bottle or the family. Saul wanted the family, but he couldn't stop drinking and he lost everything and his family as well. As a young man Saul was very strict and he only told you one time if you made a mistake! When I knew him for almost 11 years he was just a shadow of himself and the wine took its toll on him. He was a cold person when I knew him and made my life very unhappy too."[144]

Dee Allen, Saul's daughter, playing baseball in Santa Barbara.

It's tragic that the marriage did not work out. Frank Venzor called Henrietta "the kindest, gentlest, most noble person that walked the face of the earth. Her family owned a tortilla shop or tamale shop and one of them was located in Texas. Macaroni, corn tortillas, and they used to feed people if they were hungry, that didn't have anything. They ended up putting up a shop in Santa Barbara on the east side of town.[145] When the breakup occurred, Saul moved into 1008 Chino Street and there he stayed for about 10 years. Finally, it became unbearable and he had to be asked to move out.

"I saw Uncle Saul sitting on a bus bench many times. Heck, I used to be the runner for his dollar. It was like this: the phone would ring and it was Saul. He wanted a buck to win some money. One dollar; that was all he needed to make some big bucks. He was hustling a game of snooker at the Golden Lion pool hall on State Street, playing his favorite game. Saul was the best player around at one time, relentless in his game. I heard if you got the guy mad, when he didn't get his money, the next thing you knew – bam! – he would drop you and knock you down. The word was Uncle Saul was fast, lighting fast with his mitts and not to be messed with – and no one could beat him at snooker. He was injured on the job and was disabled, and he was so good no one would play him, so he traveled all over the coast to hustle a buck. He often left town and traveled from San Diego to Portland. He won big time, but the wine bottle never left."[146]

One of the reasons he traveled out of town is because the other players around San Diego caught on. Saul was just too good. Bruno often tagged along. About 5'8" or 5'9", he didn't look much like Saul, who was long and lean and about 6'3". Dee told me, "Bruno was my father's shill. My dad got to be so good that nobody in Santa Barbara would play with him. So Bruno and him would go like to Santa Maria or some of these other outlying places. My dad always made sure he lost one or two before he cleaned up."[147]

"Saul could have done anything he wanted," Manuel wrote, "but the wine took him over. He was lightning fast with his hands and could drop a guy over an argument as quick as a cat. He was very agile and loved to play thinking games. Snooker was his game and he won the city tournaments every time he entered the event. He was smart and quick to learn and he had a reputation. But Saul got old and his drinking got worse, till he hated life and made everyone miserable. He wore black frisco jeans and a white longshoreman's cap with a white or blue shirt all the time. When he hurt his leg as a longshoreman, it was over for him.

"Saul was built lean like Ted and he was about 6' 3" but still lean as he grew older. He was very positive about what he knew and was always thinking. All the cops knew him and they would often stop and bid him a hello. I was the one who took the smokes and hard candy when he was in the county jail. I hated that job, but my Mom made me do it. I still have nightmares when I dream about the place. It scared me to walk on the stone cold floor and no light and very dark to boot! I was only 5 or 6 years old but I have woken up many a time in a cold sweat over that experience. I always gave the brown bag to the guard, usually a big guy with a dark uniform and a cold looking appearance!"

Saul had a strong hand in forming Ted as a determined ballplayer. "I really do think Saul had a lot to do with building Ted's attitude toward the game of baseball," Manuel wrote. "I could see he was quick minded, a thinker and not happy just to do things, anything. It had to be done right and no mistakes. He played life like that to the hilt. He had an obsession to do it right and understand what you were doing, you know, why and it had to be right. I always had to say my ABC's in front of him and boy I could leave only after I did it right. I think Saul was trying to prove his worth, but the drinking caused conflicts and his age and bad leg caught up to him. I know near the end he tried to stop drinking, and he did for maybe nine months. It was just too late for him. He once told me Ted was a hell of a baseball player and he started thinking and just smiled at me, as he said, 'Ted, he was just a kid.' And he looked right in my eyes. I could see he was proud of the help [he gave and the] association he had with his nephew. He would never get soft. He wasn't one to look for a pat on the back. That wasn't Saul's style. He lived to win and never looked back.

"One evening I entered a restaurant and Charles Venzor [Saul's son] was at the counter eating. We acknowledged each other and got to talking and Uncle Saul came up. I asked Charles, 'Did you really know your father?' He looked at me and said, 'No, you lived with him and probably knew him better than I did.' I then realized that I did know old Saul pretty darn well. He was a loner and hard to deal with, you didn't make mistakes – and no losing, either! That was not his manner and I am sure it rubbed off on Ted. Hell, they played baseball all the time and that is all they talked about. They did have a lot in common and built a great relationship together."[148]

The last time Ted and Saul met was at May Williams' funeral in 1961. Ted had come to town and rented the entire top floor at the Santa Barbara Inn, so he wouldn't be bothered. Only the aunts and uncles were permitted to attend the funeral itself. The rest of the family waited at 1008 Chino Street. There was, of course, a reason for this: there was "a ton of reporters" at the entrance to the funeral home, and one of them was so bold as to ask his Aunt Sarah, "Did Ted cry at the wake?"[149]

Danny Venzor told John Zant, "He was staying at the Santa Barbara Inn under a fictitious name. I remember he got mad when a stranger showed up on the second floor. He rented every room on the floor so nobody would bother him. When we got there, he was standing in his undershirt at this big bay window overlooking East Beach. He could see his reflection in the window. He was swinging an imaginary bat, just to relax."[150]

Ted made his way from the hotel to Chino Street, where most of the relatives awaited him. "A white Ford pulled down the driveway and a big good-looking guy made his way out," Manuel Herrera remembers clearly. "I walked outside to greet the Slugger. He was dressed for travel and the family came out of the old house and visited him. Bruno and Marian Venzor were there, along with Mom and Pop. Natalie and I were introduced to him by Mom. Everything was baseball to him, even his vocabulary, too. He called Saul 'Old-Timer' and wanted to know how he was doing. Saul acknowledged his welcome and smiled. He told Ted, 'You did pretty good for yourself, kid, in the big leagues.' Ted, with a twinkle in his eyes, said, 'Yeah, old-timer, I guess I did all right, Saul, thanks.' Uncle Saul was like the old professor with his prime student and you could see the gleam on his face when he said, 'I see that you learned how to hit the curve ball, and you did pretty good, huh?' Now Ted was looking right at Saul as if to say, thanks for all you did for me. Teddy had a big grin on his face, focused right at Saul.

"It was like the old teacher and the student measuring his success of the seasons of the past. I was standing between Saul and Ted. I can't tell you the emotion that was in each man's eyes and the look they showed that day. I could feel it in the air and on their faces. It was a moment to behold. I lived with Saul for 11 or 12 years and knew him like the back of my hand. There was a time to stay away from him and a time to do as he said. He was a tough old guy but that one day he was human, after all that was said and done. He sure wasted a good life, sorry to say."[151]

"Saul asked Ted a few questions, and this is the one question I remember. He said, 'Ted, a ball can only go four different ways – in, out, up or down. What is a palm ball, a sinker and a screw ball?' Ted was very happy with the question and said, 'Saul, that is a great question. They are only curve balls thrown a bit differently, but the announcers make something more of it. Hell, they can't tell what the damn pitch is from way up there in the announcer's box! A real good question, old timer.'"[152]

Ted really wanted to do something for Saul, to help him get around. Sarah said Saul couldn't handle a car, so Ted asked, "What about a bike?" With the bad leg, though, that wouldn't work either. Ted probably sent some money from time to time. Saul passed away a couple of years later, a loner, and was put to rest beside his mother and his sister May on a quiet hillside in Goleta, California. Chaz Venzor tells how Ted always asked after his Aunt Sarah, too. "Two or three years ago, while Sarah was still living – she's the last of the Venzors – Ted would always call up, call Dee and say, 'You make sure you let me know if there's anything she needs.'"[153]

This author asked Ted about Saul Venzor in April 2000. "Saul was a damn good athlete," Ted answered. "He was my mother's brother. He had a little bottle problem; he couldn't handle things. He was a pretty good baseball player. Santa Barbara. I don't know any other relatives that had that much ability."

Sarah Venzor Diaz
(February 10, 1905 - November 3, 1999)

Sarah was born in 1905 in Santa Barbara in an adobe-style house with a dirt floor. When Sarah's birth certificate was filled out, her name was left off. Apparently, the Venzors wanted a girl named Sarah; it was understood that two previous stillborn children had been intended to bear the name. Perhaps they'd been reluctant to fill in the name on the certificate. Many years later, she had to add her own name "Sarah Venzor." This Sarah stuck, and lived to be 94 years old.

She told me about her life and the family background. The one time I interviewed Sarah, it was at length. As far as I know, I'm the only writer to have interviewed her – Ted Williams' aunt – and she had a lot to say. Some might find her comments a bit rambling, but there was a real charm to her way of speaking and I fortunately just let her talk. A portion of her commentary is provided here, and it touches on several points, many of which she went into in more depth after I asked follow-up questions. Let me provide a bit of what she had to say, at some length. As we saw above, her father was a shepherd and there were a number of dairymen, stonemasons and bricklayers among her uncles.

Sarah Venzor with sister May, both Salvationists.

"To cross the border, you had to have so much money to come into the United States in those days. When my brother was just about a year old, my father decided to come to California, to cross the border to Texas – El Paso – and then to come to California. My uncles... my grandma had 14 children. Fourteen children. When she married my grandfather, her first pregnancy she had twins, but one died at birth. After that, she had 13. The last pregnancy, she had twins again. One of them passed away. I didn't know some of my uncles. They stayed in Texas."

After May and Sam Williams moved to San Diego, Sarah took the opportunity to visit and stay for a prolonged period. "I took care of Ted," she told me. "I was going to high school and I was about 17. I should have graduated when I was 18, the following year. Santa Barbara was a small, Spanish town, and I thought, well, I wanted to go to San Diego and take care of Ted and Danny, his brother.

"I am 13 years older than Ted. I'm 94 years old, and he's 80 right now. Oh, Ted is a wonderful person! Oh my gosh, you talk to Ted and he looks you straight in the eye. He knows whether you're telling the truth or not. He can always tell. A wonderful person. He's been wonderful to me. I love Ted. And Danny.

"I went to San Diego and I took care of Teddy and Danny. Coming from a small school to go to a big school like in San Diego – San Diego is beautiful – I was interested in the Salvation Army. I was interested in becoming an officer, too, like May. May was very devoted. Spreckels, you know, the sugar manufacturer, he's the one who gave May that home at 4121 Utah." [The wealthy businessman effectively donated the house to May Williams in support of her devoted efforts for the Salvation Army.]

Sarah talked about Danny, and how he never could measure up to Ted, so he acted out his frustrations in a number of stunts or through delinquency. We will look more at Danny Williams later on. After he got married, though, he would visit Sarah and the family in Santa Barbara. "He used to come and visit us, Danny. And his two boys. He called his two boys Ted and Sam. Ted put them through college and one of them learned to play the guitar beautiful. He was auditioning in L.A. He came by and he had a girl. He said that was his wife. When Danny passed away, his wife remarried right away. She married a chiropractor, but I don't know his name. Just up north some place. Her name was Jean. They moved some place up north."[154]

Jean did indeed marry a chiropractor named Dave Barber. He lived in Fresno and, interestingly, also ran a folk music coffeehouse there in the very early 1960s called The Renaissance. Danny's son Sam was inspired by the music around him. "A lot of times the different people who were playing there would end up at our house." Sam remembers his grandmother May playing piano and guitar. "I don't know that I ever remember her playing trumpet, although I know that she did. Cornet. I play cornet also. And she sang, too. I'm not a great singer, but I sang some. I made my living at it for 10 years. A singer-songwriter. I started out playing in a band. Whatever was in the Top Ten, playing bars. A lot of colleges. From Port Angeles, Washington down through California. Pretty much up and down the coast. Mostly solo. Occasionally some duos and trios. Sometimes I would be forced to work regular jobs. Some of everything. Restaurants. Bar tending. A couple of summers, tomato harvesting here. When I turned 30, I pretty much decided it was time to give it up."[155]

May's sister continued, "Sam was a photographer there in San Diego, but he wasn't much of a businessman; I don't know. She had to get out and sell the *War Cry*. She used to get just so much for every *War Cry* that she sold, but she was the world's champion *War Cry* seller."[156]

"Ted was about four-years-old. Danny was just a baby. I met this fellow, so I stayed in San Diego. I started selling *War Crys* and helping May. I quit high school. I couldn't cope with such a big school. Every time I'd go to a different class, I'd get lost. I wouldn't know where I was. As long as I could, I stuck it out but I couldn't take it. I was failing in my classes. I couldn't find my class and the kids were rushing around, rushing you here and there and bumping into you and everything with your books, and I didn't know where my locker was... oh heavens! I just quit. And then I started selling *War Crys* and helping my sister and taking care of Teddy and Danny.

"I was the flower girl at May's wedding, when she married Sam Williams. I was just a little girl. When they were married here in Santa Barbara, I was her flower girl. May was born in 1891. My mother has nine children. Two passed away when they were born. There was Pete and May and Mary and Daniel – that's the one who was in World War I; he lies in Flanders Field in France. [He died when he was] 23 years old. He was the one who was taking care of us, supporting us because my father was beginning to fail them, his health. Daniel was the one who was helping us. Then my brother Saul was born in 1903. He was a ballplayer, too. He played for the Pacific League in those days. He was a good hitter, too. The first time he went to bat, he played the Foresters and other leagues here in the South Pacific, but then he was interested in a girl and he didn't want to leave town so he just forgot baseball. He turned to pool."

May was twelve years older than her younger sister Sarah, and Sarah looked up to May. Wanting to follow May's example, Sarah also joined the Salvation Army.

"I've had a wonderful, interesting life myself. I went to the Salvation Army Training College when I went to San Diego. I met a fellow who was in the Navy. He was from Michigan, Big Rapids, Michigan. Chester Amidon. And I had a son. Now I have eight grandchildren and sixteen great-grandchildren, and now I have three great-great-grandchildren. I've had a very interesting life. But being in the Salvation Army... I was a home girl. I couldn't be away from my mother, and I had my little boy. We had to travel. Salvation Army people send you. You don't go where you want to go. They send you wherever they want you to go, where they think you'll be fitted for the city and for the work that we do in the Salvation Army. We were sent to Santa Ana and then to Pomona, and then we were sent to Salt Lake City and that's where my son was born. Well, that was too far away from home. Then from there, I came on a visit to Santa Barbara. Oh heavens, I didn't want to go back, but I had to. After my vacation here, I went back to Salt Lake. From there, we were sent to Thermopolis, Wyoming and then I just couldn't take it any more. I came home."

She and Chester Amidon separated. "I remarried after I don't know how many years. My husband [Arnold Diaz] was a musician. He had a mariachi band. He was an immigrant from Mexico. His father was wounded in the war in Mexico. In the operation, he passed away. He gave his boy, my husband Arnold, to his brother. So his uncle raised him, and then they crossed the border way up in Matagorda. They went to Texas and then in 1917, Arnold joined the army, the military army, because there was a war in 1918. He was sent to France. He didn't go to fight. They put him in the medical corps. They had their band in the army, and they used to go and entertain in the camps. Wherever there was a camp, they'd go and entertain them with their music, so he never got to see any... but he saw a lot in France. A lot of French girls. Then he came to Santa Barbara. That was in 1921 or 22, I guess. I met him just from across the street. We used to talk to each other. Then I left for San Diego, and I didn't come home for about four or five years. I came back to get married to Amidon. He had gotten married [Arnold] and he had two children. That was in 1923 and then I got married here. My son was born in 1925. I left the Salvation Army because I couldn't take the traveling around. I was too far from home when I went to Salt Lake and Thermopolis, and my mother here with my brothers and my sisters. So I came home.

"My brothers bought a home for my mother here in Santa Barbara. I've lived in this home for 77 years. Ted would come up and visit when he could. That's when he would play ball with my brothers. The one that played ball with the Pacific League here, that was Saul. He was two years older than I was. When Ted would come, the first thing they would do is get out there in the field and pitch to each other, throw the ball to each other, and bat to each other. Out in the field. We always had a garden. We were poor. We always had a garden, though, and raised chickens. We grew vegetables and fruit trees. We always had plenty to eat. As I look back now, I can see I've been through I don't know how many depressions. That was terrible.

When we used to go visit in San Diego, he [Ted] was just a young boy. My brother had a Model T Ford or a Model A Ford, and we used to go to San Diego. Right away, Ted would want to drive the car and go and hunt. He loved to hunt. He loved to fish. My father, too. My father was a good fisherman. And my brothers all used to go out here on the wharf in Santa Barbara and fish. And my father."

Salvation Army group: Sarah standing, far right, May to her left.

"I'm still a Salvationist, but I don't get out very much because I have no way of going. I have to have someone take me. I still am a Salvationist. I'm a good Christian. I try. I try very much. Ted, of course, that rubbed off on him. He's very generous. He saw to that little Jimmy Fund. I never forget that, how he'd go out every year and raise money to support little children that were poor and had no way of getting treated. He loved his children. That's one thing about Ted. He loves people. Of course, he was a little cocky. I have a picture where, finally, they said, Ted takes off his hat to this audience when he played ball. I don't have a real picture. I have it from the newspaper. I live here alone.

"I don't remember if I ever talked with May about Ted's work with the Jimmy Fund, but she knew. She called him 'Precious.' Everybody was 'Precious' to May. She was a very devoted Christian woman. That little rascal of Danny. He would do anything to attract attention. That was in him. I think he was envious that Ted could do everything. Everything was Ted. Everything Danny did was wrong. He was a little scoundrel. May could never say a bad word, you know, a cuss word. All she'd call him, if she talked to my mother or talking about Danny, 'He's a scoundrel. He's a rascal,' she'd call him. But never a real bad word.

"She was very proud of Ted. They used to call her up and tell her, 'May, turn on your TV. Ted's on playing ball.' Oh, and then she'd start praying, to have him make a home run. I did, too, when I used to see him play. We used to see him play at the games here in L.A. One time my sister and I went to the back gate and we told one of the ballplayers there to call Ted. We were new at going to ballgames. We used to go and see my older brother Saul play, too, here when the Foresters would come or when they'd play here at the ball field in Santa Barbara. But in L.A., a big game, we went to the gate and we told one ballplayer, 'Would you please call Ted Williams? Tell him his two aunts are here to see him.' Oh my gosh, one ballplayer says, 'Oh, no! Not me!' Everybody used to go and call him. They'd say they were related and that they were friends or they were relations, and they wanted to talk to Ted. When Ted would go [to see who was calling on him], it wasn't [a relative at all]. It was somebody looking for money or asking for help – it wasn't true. After that he told them – the other ballplayers – he told them, 'Never call me.' They knew. They wouldn't, because he'd get mad. Well, that was kind of rude to have people go and say you were related just to get to talk to him and then find out that they're just looking for a handout.

Sarah and Carmen Ponce, cousins.

"May didn't follow baseball really, because she was too busy trying to make a living. But she was interested. When she'd know he was on TV, there she was, just rooting for him. 'Lord, help him to make a home run!'"[157]

Ruth Gonzalez says that when Ted first started playing with the San Diego Padres, May mailed newspaper writeups to the Ponce family in El Paso. San Diego newspaperman Forrest Warren, a neighborhood friend and a member of the Salvation Army Advisory Board, said that as Ted started breaking major baseball records May herself "became an ardent baseball enthusiast." Warren seems to be the only one who reported this kind of transformation, but he did document one touching moment during the 1946 All-Star Game. "I called her on the telephone to ask, 'Are you tuned in, May? Teddy is playing.' 'Yes, I'm sitting by my radio, praying for Teddy to get one good hit.' While we were talking there came more than an answer to a mother's prayer. It was his first home run. 'Thank God, my prayer was answered,' and she hung up the receiver."[158]

"[Ted] took care of May [by sending money.] I took care of my sister when she had her sickness. She came here to live with me. She spent her last few years with me. Everybody was 'Precious' to her. She'd go out – our neighbors all had children and she'd go out with the guitar and sing to them. Salvation Army songs."

Sarah knew that Ted had suffered a couple of strokes and was having a rough time of it. It made her weep to think of him incapacitated, but Ted was on the phone asking what he could do for her.

"Ted, poor thing, I remember his birthday, so I always send him a card. Sometimes maybe on Christmas, but mostly on his birthday. I talked to Ted. He talks good, bless his heart, but all I did was cry. I just feel for him, being as sick as he is. He's talked to my doctor. He's very much interested in trying to see what he can do for me. He's really been wonderful.

"You tell Ted you talked to me, his Aunt Sarah. Bless his heart. Thank you for calling me. I hope you can understand how I feel. I wish they had this in writing. I don't know why they always bring up his Mexican heritage. I know that a lot of writers don't like him. He's a wonderful person. Of course, he was cocky. He wouldn't put his hat off his head to his people, and then he finally did. But he meant well. He loved his children. He still loved, but they couldn't understand why he was never home. But then he had to have a rest! He had to get away from that work that he was doing, I mean with baseball."[159]

Sarah Diaz watched Ted's last game on television. Manuel Herrera, referring to Sarah as "Mom", remembers the day with clarity: "It was September and fall was in the air and the game was on television. I had just finished eating breakfast and I was sitting in the living room watching the TV, the Boston Red Sox and the Baltimore Orioles. The announcer was Curt Gowdy, the voice of the Sox. I called Mom to the front room to watch the game; needless to say the Red Sox were and still are her team! Well, Curt Gowdy was really giving Ted the big attention before the game, and he said "Retirement." Mom said, "Wait till he gets up to the plate." She still had her kitchen apron on. Well, Ted came up and gave one a ride in the fifth against Jack Fisher the right-handed pitcher. Curt Gowdy said, "A cold damp day kept it from going out." In the eighth he got hold of one. I looked at Mom and she had her eyes closed; she was praying for a homer. I couldn't believe it, he drove it out of Fenway like a shot. The next thing I knew, she was crying and said, "Atta boy, Ted! I was praying for him" – and he did it with a bang. Mom said, "I told you he would hit it out." I told Mom, "He didn't tip his hat. Just like a stubborn Venzor, hits one out and no hat tip." She was so happy that her nephew finished with a bang. I was crying just as she was. It was a special day at the little house redwood house at 1008 Chino Street."[160]

Aaron Paul Venzor
(June 22, 1907 - August 2, 1980)

Paul Venzor was the whole thing wrapped up in one: a cowboy, baseball player and longshoreman.

The Venzors had to work hard to make ends meet. Sarah Diaz told Manuel that Pete, Daniel, Paul and Saul all slept in the same bed as she did. "We all slept in the same bed, Manuel, and each one of us down the line would say, 'Good night, Mom, I love you' when we went to bed."[161]

Paul married Tillie Andrade and they had three children: Rosalie Larson, Frank Venzor and Carolyn O'Grady. Paul became a Catholic in marriage, one of the few Catholics in the family. Teresa Cordero Contreras was baptized Catholic, and attended Mass at 8 a.m. – but then walked down the street and attended Protestant Sunday school with her mother Mary at 9:30 at the Calvary Baptist Church.[162]

Initially, Paul was hired by his older brother Pete and worked on the Tecolote Ranch in Goleta for many years. Paul's son Frank says, "We're a bunch of cowboys. We really are a bunch of cowboys from the ranch. Spaulding was involved with Gene Autry, the singing cowboy. My dad used to take me to Tex Ritter. My dad broke horses. He was actually a cowhand, a cowboy. He worked on the ranch for maybe 10 years. After that, he went to be a longshoreman. A stevedore."[163]

Rozie Larson characterizes her father as a "quiet and passive person." Paul and Tillie lived at the Tecolote Ranch, and Paul "had a great love for horses. He helped groom the horses and helped the trainers at the ranch. The Spauldings would have big rodeos, and famous dignitaries from all over California would attend. Will Rogers was a frequent visitor. I remember my father saying that he got to ride Will's horse, which was a thrill for him. Ted and his brother Dan were frequent visitors, too."

Paul Venzor and Tillie Andrade Venzor.

Paul particularly loved to take part in the fiestas, working with horses from the Spaulding stable. "During our annual Santa Barbara Fiesta parades, Dad would drive a team of horses hauling the Fiesta dancers, or he would ride the Palomino horses in their silver splendor."

"We lived at the ranch for several years before moving back to Santa Barbara. The family ran into hard times. During the Depression, my father was able to find employment as a golf caddy at the San Ysidro Ranch. (Guests didn't have golf carts back then.) When Bing Crosby golfed at the ranch, my dad would caddy for him and other celebrities who were guests at San Ysidro.

"During World War II, he was employed at Port Hueneme as a longshoreman, becoming a foreman. He worked during and after the war, until his injury. He was on a ship loading big steel pillars, which broke loose and crushed his ankle."[164]

Even after the Depression, war, and the debilitating injury, Paul enjoyed a good rapport with horses. "My dad had a way with horses," Rozie wrote me. "He could calm the wildest horses. My sister and I had rented horses from a nearby stable, and one of the horses got spooked. We were having a heck of a time. Being we were close to home, we stopped to have our dad help us with this unruly horse. Dad got on the horse, did four steps back, and a couple of circles. The horse gave a couple of kicks, but he calmed the horse down and walked the horse down the block. It didn't give us any more trouble, but of course, we returned to the stables A.S.A.P."[165]

Paul was one of the ballplayers in the family, along with Saul and Bruno, and played on teams in Santa Barbara.

Without the ability to work, Paul became tormented by the scourge of alcoholism. It cost him his marriage, and more. Manuel Herrera minces no words in talking of his Uncle Paul. "Paul Venzor was such a wino that he didn't need to be embalmed when they buried the bum; he was so pickled that he stunk! He was what they termed 'rum dumb' and the drink got him. He once drank rubbing alcohol and had to have his stomach pumped. He turned out to be the worst of the lot and still lived longer than his brothers!"

Manuel added, "Mom [Sarah] was the silent leader of the Venzor family. When Saul and Paul lost their marriages, they fell apart and the kids really suffered. With their drinking problems, Saul and Paul, she took the time to put her brothers in a state mental hospital to dry out. If it wasn't for Mom, her brothers would have died in the streets of Santa Barbara, California. That is how really bad off her brothers were! Bruno cared less and Jean was just as bad with the drink 'til she became a Christian again."[166]

"Mom [Sarah] truly loved her family and she stood by them so darn often, and was always a force in their personal lives. When their own families gave up on her brothers, she took her cross and still marched on and never once changed her mind. I remember when Saul wanted to quit the wine, Mom took him down to Camarillo State Hospital so he could get help and 'dry out' of his addiction. It didn't help at all. The poor man was at it again as soon after he came home! Heck, we pulled Paul Venzor out of a little apartment in Watts down in the L.A. area. I will never forget Mom knocking on the apartment door and then she opening it and seeing her brother in bed going through the DT's. Mom hurried into the room and helped Paul as I looked on. He was in bad shape. She asked Paul if he wanted help and he acknowledged yes, so we got him into Camarillo State hospital as well. Paul became what people call, 'rum dumb' – he lost his sense of thinking or as we say today 'fried his brains' with wine. I think he lived to be about 70 years of age, but I still can't believe he stayed alive so long with all the abuse he dealt to himself.[167]

Growing up in the family, there would often be one adventure or another. Paul's son Frank remembers, "My dad took me to the air show at Goleta and we watched this guy jump out of an airplane, a paratrooper. They loved to fly airplanes. Goddamn, they used to love to fly airplanes! My uncle and my cousins, they rented an airplane. My cousin Sooky [Joe Moreno, Jeanne Venzor's son] had a pilot's license. He was a fighter, a scrapper. A biker. He was short, a good-looking guy, called the 'Mexican Marlon Brando.' It was around the beginning of the Korean War, they rented an airplane and they all piled in. Sooky was in charge and he was driving it and, man, they were diving at the house, over the hill at Chino Street. It was me and Manuel and Natalie. We were watching them and I could see who it was, the airplane came so low to the ground. They were all nuts."[168]

Social Security records have him listed as Aaron Venzor, and so does the California birth index, but his gravestone has him as Paul Aaron Venzor. His daughter Rozie informs me that his first name was indeed the Biblical name Aaron. Paul Venzor covered a lot of ground in his life, as his gravestone inscription reminds us. It reads, "A cowboy, baseball player, golfer, longshoreman, grandpa and our dad." It's a fair bet that a good portion of the men in America would love an inscription along those lines.

Bruno Venzor
(October 6, 1909 - June 23, 1974)

Bruno was perhaps the uncle Ted was closest to, the youngest brother among the Venzors. Less intimidating than his brother Saul the taskmaster (and not the ballplayer Saul was, either), Bruno nonetheless loved the game and played when he could. Manuel saw him pitch once in an old-timers game at Cabrillo Park in Santa Barbara. "Bruno threw a knuckleball with little effectiveness and his fast ball was even worse, but he laughed all the time on the mound 'til Saul – who was the first baseman – got fed up with his pitching and pulled him out of the game. Saul always wanted to win and Bruno always was ready to laugh at any given opportunity."[169] Saul may have inspired Ted more, and helped provide the drive and determination necessary to become a great ballplayer, but it sounds like Ted and Bruno enjoyed each other more.

Bruno Venzor on *Some Tub*.

Bruno Venzor.

One thing they shared was a love of fishing. Both Saul and Bruno fished, but Saul was exceptionally strict. Bruno was a little more happy-go-lucky by contrast, and he had his own small boat. "The man could drink a case of beer and fish like all get-out and he knew the current in the channel like a salt captain." Manuel recalls a time when there were four kids out on a boat with Bruno and the fog rolled in. He asked the kids if they knew how to get back to the dock. "We all pointed in different directions and he laughed at us. He said, 'Look at the current, you dummies; that alone will tell you the way home.' Shucks, we didn't have a clue as to what was happening.

"Uncle Bruno would show up at Stearns Wharf while me and my buddies were fishing. Bruno would put on a show with a bamboo pole and snag hooks; he caught his fish with no bait just five plain hooks and 3 or 4 shiners at a time. Soon a crowd showed up and he would have a ball with all the attention, and he would ask me if I wanted to go fishing on his boat, *Some Tub*. I said, yeah, and off to Naples Point we went where he knew the fishing grounds. It was usually sea bass or sheephead but my Dad's favorite was red snapper and that was easy to catch. He liked halibut and so did I. After fishing, he stopped at the Cliff Room for a cold one. My cousin said he would toss his catch on the bar so everyone could see, a real character. He told me he taught Ted how to drive after he hit the home run in the PCL Championship. They were headed for quail hunting out in the Borrego Mountains and Bruno taught him how to drive on the way out after the game."[170]

Bruno may have also taught Ted the curve ball. Dee Allen says that Saul refused to show Ted the curve when Ted was around ten. It could ruin his arm, Saul told him – a good point. Bruno showed Ted a few tips, though. Ted may also have helped Saul earn a little bit of money on the side during informal ball games, collecting wagers from opposing players and from spectators.[171]

Happy-go-lucky that Bruno may have been at times, and despite sharing neighboring houses on Chino Street, Manuel says of his uncles, "There were a cold lot and Bruno was always mad and upset about everything. They were not the close and kind family my aunt told me they had been." He recalls one time when he and Uncle Paul had worked all day on Bruno's retaining wall between his property at 1006 Chino and the adjoining ones. Paul lived at 1002 Chino Street. When Bruno came home, he ripped the wall down and told Paul to stay on his side and leave his work alone.[172]

Bruno's wife Marian (Romero) cleaned houses, and Bruno drove a cement mixer. Though he worked some on the ranch, and worked in construction, his primary job was transporting cement for Southern Pacific Milling and another Santa Barbara company.

He loved to dress up western style in a white cowboy hat and western pants and boots, and parade with the Elks Club. Bruno also played snare drum for the Elks drum and bugle corps. Bruno's wife Marian termed it the "Drunk Corps" since the group often repaired to quench their post-parade thirst. Bruno was dubbed the "Sheriff of Chino Street" by Sarah's husband Arnold Diaz, and he loved the moniker.

He was very proud of his nephew Ted Williams and called him a "top notcher" at baseball. Bruno named his own son after his older brother Daniel, who was killed in the first World War. He wanted Danny to become a baseball star like Ted Williams, but it just wasn't to be.

Danny Venzor remembered, "My dad played baseball. My Uncle Saul – he was Dee's dad – he was very much in baseball, and he was offered a contract when he was real young to play for Seattle, and he turned it down for some unknown reason. I remember when Ted was managing the Senators, when they were playing out here, playing the Angels. He would come up there and get tickets for my son David – who just passed away in February – my dad would pick up my son. He must have been 10 or 11 years old and they would go down to where Ted was staying, at the Royal Hotel or one of the hotels down there. I remember my son saying, 'Ted just can't sit down!' He made him nervous. Walking over to the TV, changing channels, sitting down and getting up, looking out the window... I said, 'Well, David, you've got to realize he's the manager of a major league baseball team and he's got all these things on his mind. The pitchers, the baseball club, his lineup and all that.' I explained that. 'Well, he can't sit down.' Bruno spoke to Ted like an uncle asking something of a nephew, 'I want to sit in the dugout!'" Danny explains, "My dad always talked to Ted like that – to tell him what he wanted him to do. Ted replied, 'No, Bruno. I can't. I can't do that.' Ted got them good box seats, right next to the visitors' dugout."[173]

B. P. O. E. 613 Elks Drum and Bugle Corps, Santa Barbara.

"When his mother died, he stayed at the Santa Barbara Inn. He only wanted to see my dad and, before the funeral, to take him out to the cemetery. So we went over there in the morning. He had just gotten out of the shower. He was exercising. He had a bat, you know, and he kind of used the bat to exercise. He'd take a couple of swings. He'd see his reflection in the window overlooking the beach. Then he orders breakfast for the three of us. He was under a fictitious name, because he didn't want anybody bugging him.

"At the get-together, at the barbecue it was very interesting. He had some very good memory of games, and ballplayers and different incidents. I asked him about Eddie Mathews. I played ball with Eddie in high school, in Santa Barbara. Eddie made the big leagues for Milwaukee. Yeah, he knew Eddie. He said Eddie was going to be a Hall of Famer – which he turned out to be. He was really interesting to talk to.

"At one point in time, I wanted to be a ballplayer. When I got out of the service, I had to go to Korea. That kind of halted that. I didn't see him, but he was there. I was in the 981st, the Army, a National Guard artillery battalion. We went to Japan and then went to Korea. When I got out I went to City College and I played semi-pro. I never got exposure. It's all in the timing. I was always active in sports all my life. Probably with Ted as a cousin, it made me want to go into baseball."[174]

Bruno loved baseball but wasn't a star player. He was fast and played infield, and even after Saul couldn't play any more, Bruno kept on, playing with industrial league, semi-pro teams. For his part, Danny Venzor played on the same team as his Santa Barbara High School mate Eddie Mathews, and went to the championship. A couple of years earlier, Saul had called Ted and said he was going to start a semi-pro team and needed some equipment. Shortly thereafter, some large cardboard cartons arrived and there were bats from every member of the Boston Red Sox – Doerr, Pesky and so forth, and four Ted Williams bats. Bruno kept the gloves, baseballs and bats under Danny's bed at his home at 1006 Chino Street. Danny asked Saul for one of the bats, and was told, "You can pick out any bat except a Ted Williams bat." He took a Bobby Doerr model, but Bruno told him, "Don't ever use it. You can put it up on the wall in your room." In 1949, Santa Barbara was up against San Diego for the C.I.F. championship, the same tournament Ted Williams had starred in 13 years earlier. The game was scheduled for Lane Field, and Danny snuck the bat down. It must have had some major league hits in it, because the first time up, Danny hit a ball about 400 feet to right center that bounced up against the wall, just missing going out. Danny got a triple out of it. Mathews hit one out later in the game, but Santa Barbara lost that one."

Bruno worked hard to mold Danny into a ballplayer. "All the time! Jeezus! My dad just hammered, hammered, hammered into me. At Chino Street, it's kind of an asphalt street and it rolled down. I'd come home from practice. He's got his bat and a ball. He'd say, 'Get the glove.' We'd be about 30 feet away. Pepper. He'd bang them. He'd bang them. And if missed the goddamn ball, the goddamn ball would run all the way down the end of the street, and he'd say, 'Run! Run! Run!' I'd get the ball, and 'Run! Run! Run!' back, you know. Then just to get a rest, I'd throw the ball right at his goddamn head. We had a bank in the back, a hill at the end of the street. I'd throw the ball right at his head, just to give me a rest.

"My dad, since we were in grammar school, junior high and especially Eddie's dad, my dad and him would always go to the games, even though we're down at Ventura, or Oxnard or up north. We're talking like a 50-mile radius or something like that, and they would drive together and they would critique. They were pretty close, and they both drank. They would take a jug up there, sit in the car watching the game and take some nips out of there."

Danny enjoyed the Breakfast of Champions, too. Ted had signed an endorsement contract with Wheaties, and received more samples than he could eat, so he had huge cartons of the individual serving sizes sent to his relatives in Santa Barbara. "I remember as kids, we used to get like 1000 little boxes of Wheaties. The whole family grew up - the kids all grew up - with Wheaties coming out of our ears."[175]

Danny was good, but ended up being shipped off to Korea for two years, and that interruption hurt. He was back from Korea before his famous uncle arrived there. Many years later, Danny visited Fort Pendleton to play golf with a friend who had re-upped and eventually become a full bird colonel. He went in the mess hall, and there were all these 8 foot by 10 foot photographs of honored Marines. General after general – and Lee Trevino and Ted Williams.

Bruno may have thought he knew a little more about baseball than maybe he did. Manuel told a story about Bruno and himself visiting Ted at a ballgame.

"If you wanted to know Ted, you had better search him out. He had a different lifestyle than us folks. I took it upon myself to head down to Anaheim and see if I could locate Ted at the game that evening. My wife and I enjoyed the game and then I had a brainstorm, why not give a note to the usher telling him that his cousin was a spectator and would like to see Ted after the game. It was a big chance, but what the hell? I really had nothing to lose – or did I? The usher was very kind and suggested that I wait for Ted at the rear of the stadium where the bus was waiting to take the Rangers to LAX.

"Old Ted got the message and he wanted to know, 'Where in hell is my so-and-so cousin, and who in the hell is my cousin?' I said, 'I am over here, Ted.' Then he recognized me and I introduced him to my wife and I had to answer all his family questions. It took some quick thinking to remember all the people he wanted to know about, mostly Saul, Bruno, Sarah, and Jeanne or Jeannie as he called her. He promised to call and keep in touch, and I told him the family would be coming to see his team play. He gave me a number and it was for tickets for the whole family. They were box seats, right behind the Rangers dugout on the first base side.

"The family got all my news and they were amazed about the invitation, so we planned a trip to enjoy a game and see the hero of the family. It was Mom [Sarah] and Arnold, Bruno, Jeanne and me. Just the five of us. Mom drove and I must tell you she didn't drive over 55 miles an hour in her whole life. I was getting nervous because I thought we would never make it by game time. It turns out we got there very early. Mom had the wrong start time by two hours. So I suggested we drive to the front of the stadium, get the start time and ask when the gates were to open up.

"Just then, the Rangers charter bus is heading right toward us, heading in to the stadium, and I tell Mom. Uncle Bruno yells, 'Block the bus! The bus, get right in front of the damn thing, Sarah!' Mom followed her brother's orders, the loyal Venzor that she was. Bruno got out of the car from the back seat, and guess who was in the front seat of the bus cursing to no end? And he was motioning to head for the stadium and get the hell out of the way. I was laughing. Bruno jumped back into his seat and we drove to the stadium parking lot and picked up our 'call waiting tickets' at the window for friends and family.

"I had a chance to talk with Nellie Fox. He was a coach for Ted. Mom asked Nellie if he could get Ted to come over and see his Aunt Sarah, but Nellie said, 'Lady, nobody bothers Ted when he is taking infield with the team.' Nellie was not going to get in Dutch with Ted. It was an unwritten rule; you don't bother Ted when he is working with the team.

"We did have a chance to see Ted before the game, but the fans were very rude. Mom and Jeannie were first, then Bruno and Arnold and myself. It was a beautiful day for a game and Ted had to tell the fans, 'Please let me visit with my family, then I will sign your autographs, just please wait.' It worked for a while, but then more fans showed up. Old Ted was more popular than the players on his team! No joke!

"Then Pop [Arnold] had an idea for Ted. While they were talking, he was signing autographs, Arnold suggested that Ted get a stamp with his name on it and use that instead of signing his name so damn much. Hell, there was no need to sign your name that often, Ted! Ted told him that he tried that idea and the first two autograph seekers looked at Ted after he stamped his name on their programs. They wanted to know why Ted couldn't write his name, did he break his arm or just what happened, where was he hurting? The kids ripped up the programs right in front of Ted and walked away mad. Ted told Arnold, 'You have to hand-sign your name, no way around it!' Now it is a very big business!

"Uncle Bruno had told me that he coached the local Elks service team to a championship and if Ted needed help he would be right there. He knew from experience that a manager needed all the help he could get and since he was Ted's uncle, who better to volunteer some good ole Venzor help? After all, he won the Santa Barbara Junior League Championship out of 18 teams. I began to get nervous. Uncle Bruno still wanted to send an ear full of advice to Ted. I tried to talk him out of it, saying that Nellie Fox and John Roseboro knew a little about the game, and that Ted had 17 years experience of major league baseball under his belt. After five beers and three bags of peanuts, though, Uncle Bruno was ready to give the Thumper some badly needed advice.

"Uncle Bruno told Ted, 'I had a Championship Junior League Baseball Team in Santa Barbara, and I want to tell you how you [Ted] should run your team.' I told Bruno to please not say those words, but he insisted and Ted gave him some choice words in return! Ted told Bruno, 'You see that seat I got you? Take your ass and put the damn thing back there!' I laughed as Uncle Bruno headed back to his seat. He felt Ted just didn't understand what he needed to know. My words were, 'Uncle Bruno, please let it die!'

"After the game I was given orders to follow the Rangers charter bus to the airport for their flight. I suggested no, but Uncle Bruno had too many beers and was not making a wise decision, this event I tried to talk him out of! Between him needing a bathroom and the charter, oh boy! Well, we made it to the parking area and there was Ted with the owner discussing the game, Uncle Bruno got out of my car and a long arm came out of Ted's side and Ted yelled, 'Bruno, get in that car and go the hell home.' That was my final visit to the Big A and the Texas Rangers with Uncle Bruno. He embarrassed the hell out of me."[176]

Bruno was a favorite of Ted's, though, despite it all, and when he wanted to call Santa Barbara, he always called on Bruno's phone and not Sarah's. "He never got the number right for some reason," Manuel recalls.[177]

One of Ted's last visits to San Diego was in 1992. He stopped by Santa Barbara for a family barbeque. Danny Venzor said, "The last time he was here was after the time when his mom died. He was here with his son John-Henry, when they had the All-Star Game down there in San Diego. He was honored down there. They had some of his old cronies. They had the ceremonies and they named the freeway or something after him. He stopped by here on his way down to San Diego and we had a big family barbecue and get-together."[178]

Jeanne Venzor Winet
(June 26, 1912 - Feb. 4, 1986)

Jeanne was the youngest child. Aunt Jeanne, or Jennie as Ted called her, was a full 19 years younger than her big sister May Venzor Williams. She was just six years older than her nephew Ted. Joe Villarino told Leigh Montville that his older brother was even going to marry Jeanne at one point.[179]

She married Joseph Moreno, and they had two children – Alberta (Abby) Moreno and her brother Joseph (Sooky) Moreno, Joe Jr. The nickname Sooky was given by his Aunt Sarah, taken from a comic strip character in the local newspaper. "He was short for a male," Manuel Herrera said, "and had a complex with that stigma. He was quick to fight, but always suffered a lot and made a fool out of himself as well. He was a character and liked the bar action, if you know what I mean. Remember that Jeanne was a Venzor and she married about two or three times, but Alberta was her only girl and Joe (Sooky) was her only real son. Her second marriage was to a Jewish man named Maurice Winet."[180]

Venzor women, left to right: Jeanne, Natalia, Mary and Sarah.

Most of what I know about Jeanne Venzor comes from an interview with Dr. Howard Winet, a professor of orthopedic surgery in the biomedical engineering department at UCLA He works in biomaterials, in tissue engineering. He is also Jeanne's stepson.

"My father's name was Maurice, and he was Jeanne's second husband. She was number four of my father's five wives. I was 12 or 13 and I'm now 65, so it was around 1950. When they got divorced, I was away at college. I think it was the early 60s when the divorce took place.

"She had a daughter and a son. Abby and Joe. Everybody called him Sooky. Joe didn't talk much about his father. There was also an adopted daughter – Mary – who was the Catholic of the family, and she was around the age of Abby so it was almost like they were twin sisters."[181] Mary the adopted girl, "the Catholic of the family," was Mary Redding, one of Manuel Herrera's sisters.

"Sooky was older. He was a bit of a Romeo – actually, he was a gang member. I got a real education. When I came out here, I didn't know anything. I was really a bumpkin. I was from the West Side of Chicago, so I wasn't totally innocent, but Joe was the source of... In fact, the first Spanish I learned was all cuss words, and I learned them from Joe.

"It was the gang that came after the Pachucos. The Pachucos were born in World War II and a little bit after. There was this transition and the Pachucos no longer dominated and there was a whole bunch of other gangs. It was almost like a Balkanization of the gang culture, if you will.

"Sooky was in Camarillo. He was in detention. I think the story was he pulled a knife on a cop. He was stealing something from a grocery store. This was after he came back from the Air Force. They were stationed in Greenland, but after he came home from that he got into the gangs. I don't have a clear memory of the whole story now. Prison, yes. We had to go up and get him out of Camarillo.

"We lived in Bellflower, California. For part of the marriage, I lived in Santa Barbara, and for a couple of months I lived on the little farm where Arnold and Sarah were, a little farm up on Chino Street.

"Jeanne was a beauty operator. She always spelled it Jeanne. I never knew her by any other name. Nor can I remember any document with 'Jean' on it. And poor writing was no excuse. She had excellent handwriting.

"Winet is a derived name. My Uncle Bob changed his name during World War II, and my father followed him. My father's reason was the reason of many people of Eastern European extraction – there was prejudice in the military service. People changed their names so that they wouldn't be identified with the group that they thought was being discriminated against. It was Winetski, and they just knocked off the "ski."

"We moved from Chino Street to State Street in Santa Barbara, right on State Street. You could hear the traffic and everything. And we lived right in the beauty parlor. We were in the back and Jeanne had her shop in the front.

"My father was a medic in the Pacific during the war, but there still was an aircraft industry after the war making aircraft for the burgeoning public – civil aircraft development. The airlines were starting to boom and they needed planes. He worked for Douglas. He worked for Hughes. He was a quality control engineer in the aircraft industry. Not a real engineer like a college graduate type engineer, but in those days, you got a lot of on the job training.

"We moved on to Bellflower from there. She had a shop there, too, but it wasn't in the house. We had a separate house, on Lorelei Street. She had others who worked in the shop.

"I do know that the sum of my musical training, which was minimal, resulted from her beauty activities. There were some customers who couldn't pay. One was a piano teacher and as a result I ended up getting piano lessons. This was a few piano lessons just to pay off the bill. As you can imagine, I am not going to be challenging Rubenstein. That happened in Santa Barbara.

"Then there was this other bill that was paid off with steel guitar lessons. So I learned a little bit of steel guitar.

"She didn't speak Spanish in the house to us. I do not know how to speak Spanish. My father could not speak Spanish and he was not about to allow me to learn to speak Spanish. If Jeanne got mad at him and said something to him in Spanish, he didn't want me to be the one who understood it.

"After the war, he found there were good prospects in California and he got into the aircraft industry and then he sent for me. I was raised by his parents. He sent for me and I came out and then became part of the family [with Jeanne.] I was the kid of the family. The others were older than me.

"I was definitely the kid, and they kind of dragged me around. They had to sort of babysit me. I was a teenager but I was young enough that I was not supposed to be left alone. I got to know a little bit of the culture. When the parents were gone, they'd have their friends over. They would play Spin the Bottle and I don't know what's going on. I saw couples going off to other rooms but I only had the vaguest idea what was going on."[182]

[Did you really see much of the Mexican side of the family?] "At our house in Bellflower, Sarah refried beans and the whole bit. Out on the back porch, Arnold would come out with his violin and we'd have a little mariachi. I loved that, and I still do love mariachi. I'm very much into Latin music; I took that away with me.

"Of course, I love all kinds of music. My father was a cantor. The one sort of bone that he threw to Spanish was that he and Jeanne had a song – a Spanish song – which I have not been able to locate, and I believe it was called 'El Borrachito' – The Drunkard. The Little Drunkard. He used to sing it all the time. Jeanne would play the piano and he would sing it. That seemed to me the most unifying thing in their relationship. That was all. Of course, he sung it very well, but I think that unless it was translated on the song sheet, he wouldn't really know what he was singing."

[Did he know that it was about drink?] "Yes. He definitely had to, because that was one of her problems. She used to be laid out on the couch. At night I'd go to bed and there she was, just snoring away. Sometimes she wasn't even lying down. She'd just be there in the chair, and she's gone – for the night. That was it.

"If you abused your body and you live a long time, it might be logical to think you could have lived a lot longer. I never saw Sarah drink. Jeanne talked about May, talked about her. Not a whole lot. I kind of remember the day that she informed me, 'You know, you've got a cousin... Ted Williams is your cousin.' I said, 'Really?' because I was a little bit of a baseball fan. I have to tell you, though, that I'm an Angels fan!

"She told me about it one day and I said 'Really?' and she started telling me about the family, and the dysfunctionality of the family and May's problems with her relationship with Ted. This was fascinating. I was still kind of a kid, but having a father that had already been divorced three times, this wasn't totally new stuff for me, so I could identify a little bit."

[What do you think she meant when you talked about May's problems with Ted?] "It was so long ago, and this wasn't the most important thing in my life, and it's hazy in my memory but my impression was that there were problems in the family. Relationship problems. Some sort of conflict. They lived in San Diego, so it was not like we could go visiting. I know I never met Ted. I might have met May in Santa Barbara, but I can't remember. There were a lot of people there. I remember Bruno.

"I sort of got the feeling that May was so deep into her religion that that may have made her distant from her children. That's what the problem was that I referred to. This impressed me as a young person.

"I was raised ultra-Orthodox in Chicago. Typical big city type thing, because in the ghettoes of the big cities is where you get the concentration of the most fundamental orthodoxy. Typical Russian-type Jew. Straight Orthodox. The Germans tended to look down upon Yiddish, which was the bastardized language used in the Diaspora. The Germans thought this language was beneath them. But at the same temple, the same synagogue, you would have Germans and Russians.

"My wife is Catholic and we were married in the Unitarian church. It's sort of like where you sign peace treaties in a neutral territory.

"The yarmulke, that's really linked more with the Israelis. Most of the things that are worn are worn after the bar mitzvah. I was doing all the things that Orthodox do – the phylacteries and all of that, but when I came to California all of that was knocked out of me. It gradually got knocked out of me in the new environment because there was no support. My father was a cantor at a synagogue in Bellflower, but people in California were not very orthodox. He would only go on the high holidays.

"Jeanne was a Baptist. We would go to church. I think Jeanne was a little more loyal to her church than he was to his, in the sense of actually being religious, but I didn't see anything of the Salvation Army in Jeanne.

"My father was rather sensitive about the approval of his father in Chicago. His father, who had helped raise me, had conveyed to my father that he should not do anything to destroy my faith. The grandfather, being very orthodox, was very concerned."

[You had an adopted stepsister named Mary who was a Catholic, you had Jeanne who was Protestant and yourself who was Jewish. You had the whole Catholic/Jewish/Protestant thing in one household.] "Mary was probably the most religious in the house."

[It is interesting how Ted flew jet airplanes in Korea, and your father was in the aircraft industry, too.] "I don't think I would have made all the connections that you are implying. My awareness of the world was not sufficient at the time; I'm trying to make up for it. My father didn't talk that way. It's funny. He didn't seem to be that proud of his work. It may be that, as a quality controller, he didn't feel that he was doing the building.

"I called her Jeanne. She was a good sort. Definitely. She had issues with my dad. Well, you can imagine my dad wasn't the easiest guy to get along with. With five marriages, he had an over-sized libido.

"She was a real person. I call her 'real people.' I liked her. The one that followed, I sure didn't like. And number 3... she just seemed strange to me. I only saw her a little bit."

[Did you keep in touch with Jeanne after they divorced?] "A little bit. Not much. It sort of petered out. I was so busy with my own work."

[Did Jeanne have any pictures of Ted Williams up on her wall, for instance?] "No. There may have been a photograph in an album, but nothing on the wall. There weren't family pictures displayed on the wall. There wasn't much of that in our family at all. It didn't come up a lot. What would be the basis? What would be the context? Jeanne and Sooky weren't excited about baseball. They didn't seem to have any interest in baseball. I was the one who listened to the radio and listened to the ballgames. I was a Cubs and White Sox fan. I would listen to these re-creations of games. That was my interest in baseball, very vicarious. I seemed to be the only family member that was interested in baseball at all. When I heard that I was somehow related to Ted, that was of interest to me. But the baseball part of it wasn't of interest to anybody. Sure I'd heard of him! Oh, sure! You knew about him or you were an idiot."[183]

Judaism was a new element in the family, Mary explained. "We had a very unusual household. Abby and I did not even know about the Jewish religion, until Howard moved in with us. Then he thought that I was just too nosy and asked too many questions regarding his religion. But I just wanted to know more, in the meantime I have read more on that subject."[184]

Jeanne's alcoholism presented some serious problems, and by the time she personally reformed, it was apparently too late to spare her children the curse. Manuel remembers, "Jeanne was drunk every time we visited and Pop always had a bottle of whiskey to honor the occasion. My sister and I often sat at Aunt Jeanne's beauty shop while Sarah got her hair done and that was a long wasted evening for us kids, especially with Jeanne and Pop drunk!"[185]

"Natalia Venzor was the quiet hero and leader of the family. No one dare abuse me or my sister in her sight, but when she died the protection was gone and the uncles and aunts were very abusive to us. Saul was the worst, he lived to be 60 years old but looked like 90 when he died. I hated him because he made my young life very unhappy and miserable just like Bruno. Paul was rude when he was drunk and if he didn't drink he kept to himself. Aunt Jeanne or Jennie as Ted called her, was an out and out drunk. She could really put the booze away and had no shame. Her two kids hated her and how she acted! Abby had no contact with her mother at all and Joseph is in a rest home where he is an alcoholic and is suffering from brain damage which he got while in a fight. He nearly died, but he is still alive and has no idea who he is or where he is at. A sad situation and life. His kids are heavy drug addicts, heroin and cocaine. A sad ending. Aunt Jeanne did clean up her life, but the impression she put in my mind has never changed."[186]

A sad situation, for sure. One interesting reward for me in doing my research into the Venzor family has been the ability to prompt a few reunions. Howard Winet and Mary Redding had not been in touch with each other for nearly half a century. When I interviewed Howard in November 2002, I learned that he hadn't been in contact with Mary for many years. Having previously interviewed Mary two and a half years earlier, I gave each of them the other's e-mail addresses. In the summer of 2003, Howard and his wife Carol took a trip from Los Angeles and met Mary again in person. He dropped me this note later in the year: "I'd like to thank you most deeply for getting Mary and me together after 48 years. Carol and I drove to Laurel, Montana last summer and visited with her and her husband Bob. The conversations were nonstop, and tears often blurred sight. I learned much that was hidden from me in the 50s and uncovered much I had hidden from myself since."[187]

Young Danny Williams in front of 4121 Utah Street.

Daniel Arthur Williams
(July 20, 1920 – March 28, 1960)

Having learned something about each of Ted's maternal uncles and aunts, let's try to learn more about his brother Danny, and just a bit about Danny's children.

As indicated above, Danny Williams has come down to us in the accounts as a one-dimensional, even distasteful character – a troublemaker who was a source of anguish and bother to his big brother Ted, and a trial to his mother as well.

Is this all Danny Williams was?

Reading about Ted's younger brother Danny, one gets the impression that he was a bad egg, a ne'er-do-well, or worse. Ed Linn introduced readers to Danny Williams very succinctly as "a juvenile delinquent, a small-time thief, a jailbird, a bum."[188]

A chapter later, we're told, "Danny ran with the bad kids. He stole. He packed a gun. He was thrown out of five or six schools." We're told that Ted brought home his first car, a brand-new 1938 Buick, and he soon found the car up on cement blocks. "Danny had stripped all the tires and sold them." After the 1941 season, Ted paid for the renovation of May Williams' home on Utah Street, but "Danny promptly backed a truck up to the house, moved out all the new furniture, including a washing machine and a sewing machine, and sold it." Linn tells us that May finally quit trying to get Danny out of trouble with the authorities and "had him arrested. He spent some time in San Quentin – not that it seemed to do any good."[189]

The San Diego Police Department supposedly termed Danny "the city's most incorrigible youth" and someone the United States Army once arrested as a deserter.[190] There are stories upon stories of Danny's escapades and scrapes with the law. He comes across as someone with no redeeming qualities whatsoever. A surly kid who stewed in spiteful envy of his talented older brother, Ted Williams, who found fame and fortune and left his less-gifted younger brother in a dark shadow. It's a vivid yet tragic portrait; Danny Williams comes across as a pretty one-dimensional character, someone we could all enjoy kicking around.

Was this a fair portrayal? Was he really as uni-dimensional as we've been led to believe? Later in Linn's book, he grants that Danny "straightened himself out... found work as a contract painter and interior decorator. He had married, he had a couple of kids, and he had reconciled with his older brother."[191]

Ted himself had relatively little to say about his kid brother. What he did write was more sympathetic than accusatory. Ted faults his mother and father for Danny turning out differently. Ted felt he himself was very lucky to have families like the Cassies and men like Rod Luscomb encouraging him, and welcoming him into their homes. The lack of a close-knit family home, though, hurt Danny. "I know Danny suffered because of it," he wrote. "I have to think poor Danny had a tormented life. He wasn't an athlete. He threw an orange at somebody one time and just throwing the orange broke his arm. They found out he had leukemia in the bone marrow and with any kind of violent movement, snap, a bone would go. Danny was always more interested in cars and other things, the kind of guy who wanted a motorcycle and never got it. He hung out with an altogether different bunch, and I suppose a lot of people thought he was surly and mean, but I have to think he was just terribly tormented.

"I know he was a thorn in my mother's side, always getting into scrapes. Nothing really serious, but one jam after another – piling up traffic tickets, maybe stealing a bicycle, or owing money on a truck and trying to clear out without paying. Rod Luscomb took a loaded revolver away from him one time."[192]

Ted recognized that "some guys have absolutely no respect for authority, and Danny was one of them." He then proceeded to indicate sympathy for Danny. "There wasn't the closeness between us there should have been. I regret that. After I left for pro ball, I never saw much of him. He used to use my name for things, and I'd have to bail him out, which was unpleasant for both of us. My being in the public eye probably made it tougher for him. He never had too many advantages. He never had the outlets for expression I did. His life was just an existence. He died tough. I got his little pistol. I always thought he would shoot himself because he suffered so much."[193]

Danny died at age 39. He's gone down in history with a bad rap. Surely, it didn't come from nowhere, and much of it was well-deserved, but it can't have been easy living a sometimes sickly life in the shadow of a great athlete, feeling short-changed by life. Who among us would find that a burden we could handle with equanimity?

There really are some fascinating stories about Danny's run-ins with the law, or his running away from trouble. Right near the house, at the University Heights (North Park) playground, there is a large water tower. Any young boy would be intrigued with the possibilities. Danny decided to climb the tower. "Danny was so different from Ted," explained Sarah Diaz. "Danny felt very inferior. He wanted to play ball; he couldn't. He wanted to do what Ted could do; he couldn't. But to attract attention, he did a lot of very odd things. Close to his home on Utah Street, 4121 Utah Street, that's where the park was where Ted used to practice, right there by the school. There was a big water tank, way up on stilts, wooden, and Danny climbed way up the top of that tower and then he couldn't get down. So somebody had to go and look for May. She was out selling *War Crys*. When they found her, they told her and so she had to come home. She had to call the fire department to get him down. But he wasn't anything

The water tower at the North Park playground.

like Ted. He was a little scoundrel. He used to do the darnedest things just to attract attention, because Ted was getting all the fame and doing all the good things that he couldn't do."[194]

The way Manuel tells it, it wasn't just that he couldn't get down – he didn't want to come down! "'Tell them to get the cops! I ain't coming down until they get the cops! Bring the fire department, too!' Attention. He wanted attention. He caused a scene."[195]

That was a time he wanted the cops to come. There were times he was trying to flee them. One of his cousins, Teresa Cordero Contreras, remembers one of those times, around 1936. Danny turned 16 that year. "He was a crazy guy. He tried to sell anything. One time when I was about 7 or 8, my mother sent me up there to help Aunt May because Ted had started playing for the Padres. He was going to remodel her kitchen, make it bigger. My mom sent me up there to help. Danny was there all the time. He was a character. We were going to go to the store and he had an old car. My Uncle Samuel, he was a jail inspector and I guess Danny figured he could just do anything he wanted to. We went to the store and then all of a sudden he went past a stop sign. Then here's a cop, right behind him. We raced through San Diego in his old Model A, you know, without the hood - you know, how they used to strip them. We went through all the streets and alleys, and then all of a sudden we went into somebody's garage, and the police went by! I was so scared, and my Aunt May was just furious. She just couldn't get over how dumb he was to do such a thing. I guess he figured his dad could fix it up. I don't know, I was only 7."[196]

Madeline Cordero Flores.

Danny wasn't the only family figure who was a little wild. Teresa's sister Madeline Cordero was quite a character herself. "My fighting Aunt Madeline," Manuel Herrera called her. Sarah Diaz had told Manny, "Your Aunt Madeline is one tough gal. She has fighting ability and could beat any girl around, not to mention her brothers." "I got my first taste of her capabilities when I was walking my brother Paul back to his house on the East Side. There were Mexican bars on Haley Street and a fight was part of the evening. We were talking and heading east to his house when we passed the El Poche. Suddenly a short Mexican national was flying out the entrance, and soon there was another, flying by the neck and seat of his pants. It was my Aunt Madeline tossing this guy out of the bar. She was pissed, to put it mildly. 'Don't you Mexicans know how to treat a lady?' Hell, them guys were running down the street the minute they could get up off the ground. My fighting Aunt Madeline then looked right at my brother and me as we were laughing and she said, 'What are you doing here? Get your asses home!' as she returned to the bar.

"The next fight was across from my friend's restaurant. I was at Joe's Cafe enjoying a meal and five cop cars pulled up and they headed into Sammy's Bar and Grill across the street. The cops had my cousin Sooky handcuffed in the police car. He was just trying to help Aunt Madeline whip ole Big Betty. Sooky wasn't really needed for support; Aunt Madeline had Big Betty against the wall and was throwing body shots into Betty. I sure was happy to know that my aunt had the situation well under control. Madeline knocked off the toughest gal in town with no trouble; she was the champ of Santa Barbara. The cops finally stopped the fight and cuffed both gals and hauled them off to jail. I later heard she got six months. Since she had plenty of time and could knit very well, she knitted Captain Sheriff Ross a sweater and got off three months early for good behavior. Sheriff Ross was a friend of the family and gave her a break, but he did like the sweater."[197] Sooky Moreno "should have been an actor, playing a Pachuco or a tough Mexican James Dean, because he was a real character and loved attention. He drove a Harley hog and had the road rash to prove it. I liked him, but he was always in and out of jail."[198]

When Madeline and Danny teamed up, well, it was something special. "Old Danny liked to get her riled up and that was something he could easily do. Danny and Madeline went down to a local bar to have a few beers. As the story goes, Danny began to get Madeline going, [taunting her, saying that] she couldn't fight. Aunt Madeline told Danny she could and made a wager with him that she could take on anyone in the bar. Just about that time, two cops walked in, and Danny suggested to Madeline that she take on those cops. Well, Aunt Madeline was stirred up and she was out to prove her worth, so she walked up to the first cop and dropped him like a sack of potatoes. Then the next cop went down like struck lightning. My aunt made it to the door and ran out of the place like a track star!

"Danny sat on his bar stool and laughed his butt off as Madeline ran out of the bar. The guys at the bar wanted to know who was that lady, but Danny wouldn't give out any clues. Danny had the ability to get Madeline worked up, and he enjoyed the results as well! I think the word that describes Danny is 'antagonize.' He loved to taunt people. Danny had the ability to get anyone antagonized and Ted was no exception. Teddy paid many a bill that Danny charged, up in Santa Barbara. The word was, 'Ted is my brother, I'm Danny Williams and Ted will pay this bill.' I heard it was done many a time."[199] Manuel added: "You must realize Aunt Madeline was raised with some tough brothers and fought often. She was built like a Mack truck and learned to use her mitts at a young age. Her hands were very big like mine, extra large, and she drove a truck at an early age. My grandfather owned a trucking business and she loaded and hauled hay just like her brothers. She could trade punches with the best in town. The Cordero family liked Danny much more than Teddy. Ted was serious, but Danny was out for a good time."

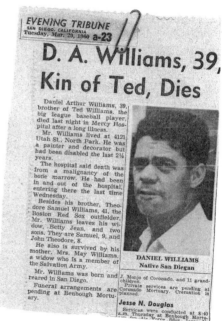

EVENING TRIBUNE
SAN DIEGO, CALIFORNIA
Tuesday, Mar. 29, 1960 a-23

D. A. Williams, 39, Kin of Ted, Dies

Daniel Arthur Williams, 39, brother of Ted Williams, the big league baseball player, died last night in Mercy Hospital after a long illness.

Mr. Williams lived at 4121 Utah St., North Park. He was a painter and decorator but had been disabled the last 2½ years.

The hospital said death was from a malignancy of the bone marrow. He had been in and out of the hospital, entering there the last time Wednesday.

Besides his brother, Theodore Samuel Williams, 41, Boston Red Sox outfielder, Mr. Williams leaves his widow, Betty Jean, and two sons. They are Samuel, 9, and John Theodore, 8.

He also is survived by his mother, Mrs. May Williams, a widow who is a member of the Salvation Army.

Mr. Williams was born and reared in San Diego.

Funeral arrangements are pending at Benbough Mortuary.

DANIEL WILLIAMS
Native San Diegan

J. Monjo of Coronado, and 11 grandchildren.

Private services are pending at Coronado Mortuary. Cremation is planned.

Jesse N. Douglas
Services were conducted at 8:40 a.m. Thursday at Benbough Mortu-

The police got their hands on Danny more than a few times, though. Even as young as the age of 12, Danny spent considerable time at the Anthony Home, located on Texas Street. It was a home for juveniles under 16. "He used to spend half his time down there," said Joe Villarino.[200] Joe told Tom Larwin that he knows Danny was caught at least once selling stolen tires. When he'd hocked all his mom's furniture in early 1942, he was 21 and he was reportedly arrested, but in the end May refused to sign a complaint. "Employing the technicality that with all the furniture gone from the Williams' home it therefore became uninhabitable, the cops jailed Danny as a vagrant. The latter pleaded guilty, got the top misdemeanor rap – 180 days and a $500 fine – but sentence was suspended when Danny agreed to leave town."[201] When he left town, it may have been to join the Army. He enlisted on February 16, 1942.

If the police once termed Danny "the city's most incorrigible youth," it was a characterization picked up by others as well. Leonard Bell was a teammate of Ted's at Hoover High. He later became Fire Chief for the City of San Diego. Bell told about a time he'd come across Danny on the roadside. "Danny Williams was kind of incorrigible. He was hitchhiking down Pershing Drive. So I picked him up and said, 'Where you going, Danny?' He said, 'I'm supposed to be in court, but the hell with it; I'm just going to ignore them.' I think he was one of the reasons Ted never came back to San Diego off season."[202]

Danny was born on July 20, 1920 in San Diego and he died March 28, 1960 at Mercy Hospital in San Diego, and is buried at Memorial Gardens in San Diego. He was living at 4121 Utah Street at the time of his death, but had entered the hospital seven days before his final passing. He was listed in his obituary as a decorator and painter, but it was noted that he had been disabled for 2 1/2 years. The hospital reported that the cause of death was a malignancy of the bone marrow.

He left a widow, the former Betty Jean Klein, and three sons. Two sons, Sam and Ted, were referred to in passing in one or two of the books about Ted Williams. It turns out there was also a son by an earlier marriage, Danny Jr., who had never been mentioned in other writings.

Danny Williams with his boys from his second marriage, Sam and Ted, in Chicago about 1953.

I knew Danny had two sons, Ted and Sam. As indicated above, I met them at the Fenway Park remembrance ceremony for Ted Williams in July 2002. I've kept in close touch with Ted ever since, with a couple of visits to his house in Oakland and with several hundred e-mails back and forth. Ted and his wife Sue have a young son Noah, who's off to a pretty good start in baseball himself at the age of 11. Like his grandfather, Ted also is an accomplished photographer. He has the largest collection of Venzor family photographs and papers I've come across – sadly, most of it fits in one box. Ted is also a talented graphic artist and is the designer of *The Kid: Ted Williams in San Diego*.

Danny's son Samuel Stuart Williams was born in San Diego on May 7, 1950. John Theodore Williams was born in Fort Worth, Texas on October 21, 1951. John Theodore was always called "Ted" - the "John" came from his maternal grandfather, John Earl Calvin Klein (who was himself known as Earl – not Calvin Klein)! Earl was a Chevrolet mechanic who had his own garage, but the family was a very poor one and had seen rough times.

Danny's son Ted told me, "The Kleins are from Germany. They were just German; they weren't Jewish. They came from Pennsylvania, I believe, in 1870 to Texas. My grandfather never had anything except two wifes and ten children. My mother said that during the Depression they lived under a bridge in old abandoned cars. Basically it was flour and water gravy for meals.

"But her aunt had farmed. They had a lot of fresh produce and vegetables, although my mother hated it. I don't know why. When we were kids, she always loved canned peaches, canned corn. Everything was canned because she never had that. She loved canned stuff. Then she'd boil it for about an hour or so (laughs.) She never made a fresh vegetable. Maybe asparagus.

"Her famous story was that here they were living under the bridge in these car bodies, and my grandfather just had it one time. So he said, 'I can't stand seeing my kids hungry any more' and he went and stole a cow, from his sister, my mom's aunt, who had this farm. He slaughtered it to feed them. She arrested him and threw him in jail. Ever since, they were bitter enemies."[203]

Danny's wife Jean Klein lost a brother in World War II. Vance Klein, 19, was killed in the Mediterranean theater in 1943.

What about this other son, Danny's first-born? Neither Sam nor Ted remembered ever meeting him, but they'd heard about him, and Ted had a sympathy card in with some old

Earl Klein with a couple of his buckaroo grandsons, Texas.

photographs May Williams had saved, signed "Mr. and Mrs. Daniel Williams Jr." Ted wrote me in August, 2002: "So maybe the other son had the same name?" It had never been a secret. "We knew about it, but we never knew where he was or who he was or how to contact him."[204]

It intrigued me that Ted and Sam might have a half-brother out there, but they didn't know if he were living or deceased. They had had no contact. As late as December, 2002, they weren't really sure if there was still a Danny Jr. out there. I decided to try to find out.

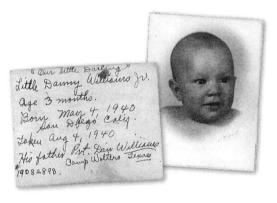

A photograph of Dan Jr. carried by his father, Danny Williams when he was in the army.

If he were a true "junior," then his name would be Daniel Arthur Williams, Jr. There were hundreds upon hundreds of listings for Daniel Williams in the state of California, and many telephone listings don't permit searches by middle name. There was, though, a site www.ussearch.com, which does accept middle names to help narrow searches of their data bases. They also permit you to search by approximate age. Entering "Daniel A. Williams," I came up with 61 names in California. Only one seemed to be around the right age - a 63 year old man living in Arcadia, California. He didn't have a listed telephone. The only way to find his address was to pay U.S. Search.com a fee of $9.95 (it's how they make their money). I did, and received an address (but no phone number) by return mail. I promptly mailed off a letter introducing myself and explaining that I was researching Ted Williams and his brother Danny, and if this were one of Danny's sons, could he please write back and let me know if I could speak with him? I heard nothing.

After a couple of months, when Ted and I were talking, I told him I'd written but had no response, and then suggested that Ted write him. I hunted up where I had the address, and sent it to Ted. He wrote and, not too long afterward, heard back. First contact was made on January 7, 2003. "Well, I talked to him," Ted e-mailed me. "[He] seemed really glad to hear from me, no hard feelings, in fact didn't know Danny much at all." Danny Jr. did exist. He'd come to his father's funeral in 1960, but of course Ted was only 8-years-old and he'd just lost his father and his mother was distraught, and it wasn't a memory that took. Danny Jr. was alive and living in southern California. Interestingly, he, too, had become involved in the graphics industry as a printer.

In March, 2003, Dan and Ted first really met, at the daylong event honoring Ted Williams at the San Diego Hall of Champions. This event offered the opportunity for the two half-brothers to meet, really for the first time. When Ted met Dan and his wife Jan outside the doors of the Hall of Champions before the day's program began, it was the reunion of two brothers who had effectively never met. Their father, Danny, had met Helen Hansen at San Diego High. It was a very short-lived marriage, but in some ways an intense one. "He didn't leave. She divorced him," Dan told me, after informing me that he had been born in 1940, on May 4. His father stuck around for three years, but he was raised by his mother and grandmother. Dan's wife Jan (they were married in 1971) told me that she'd heard that Helen had taken out a restraining order against Danny. "I don't know what that was all about. He was very young."[205]

Danny had joined the army early in 1942, but it seems that he found it very difficult to be away from his wife and young son. So he'd take off and go see them. With or without permission. "My mother told me Danny was dishonorably discharged from the Army for constantly going AWOL to go see his son."[206]

Later in 2003, Ted filed a request for information with the Army, but was only able to learn the dates of Daniel Williams' service, February 16, 1942 to August 18, 1943, that he had held the rank of private, and that his separation from the Army was with an "other than honorable discharge."

There was a war going on, and a soldier who would show no respect for rules and regulations was not going to be a productive soldier. Sarah Diaz told Manuel that the MPs had thrown Pvt. Williams in the brig but he'd broken the toilets and flooded the facility, and escaped while they were trying to deal with the damage. The MPs showed up at 1008 Chino Street, hot on his trail, but he wasn't hiding there.[207] They may have been glad to see the last of him.

By August 1943, too, the marriage had broken up. Helen Hansen found a place in public housing, and eventually remarried. Dan Jr. does recall his dad visiting one time and bringing an electric train. What Danny Williams did for the next few years is unclear. Sometime around 1947, though, he met Betty Jean Klein, when she was 15. He was 10 or more years older. Perhaps she couldn't wait to escape the poverty in Fort Worth, where she was raised with nine brothers and sisters.

Neither Ted nor Sam really know the story, and whenever they've asked one of their aunts in Texas, they get nowhere. It's a taboo subject. No one wants to talk about Danny. "One of the things I find is that when you ask questions about Danny, a lot of the time people clam up."[208] There were apparently a couple of miscarriages, but Sam was born in 1950, three months prematurely.

Danny and Jean married and began to raise a family. With two children and a pretty young wife, Danny may have begun to settle down some. That didn't mean that life became easy. He worked, and worked hard, as did Jean. "When we were in Chicago," Ted told me, "both he and my mom worked. We would go to school and when we came from school we would stay with a neighbor that lived in the apartment below... some retired people... until they got home. She was working in a restaurant – a fairly famous restaurant in Chicago. She was a waitress."

Danny had talents and found pleasures in working with his talents. "He liked painting. I think he was artistic. When we were in Chicago, he painted this huge mural of the city of Chicago across the living room wall. I'm sure the building hated him for it, but he was just obsessed. He would do that kind of stuff. It was not easy. It was huge. He did a few paintings on canvas. My brother has one, of a bullfighter. I don't know if he was a great artist, but it excited him. He liked doing it. It was probably that busy-ness, too. He needed to do something all the time. He puttered with his truck. You saw that picture. That was a truck he bought. He had a red one that was just like that, that I think he bought in Chicago that we drove from Chicago – or that he drove from Chicago; we took the train. But it was not that long after that it disappeared; I think it got repossessed. So he got that used one. In that picture he was in the process of fixing it up. He was painting the inside with a brush. He spent all his time doing that kind of stuff, fixing up cars. He loved his car.

Danny Williams painting the inside of his truck with a brush, in the driveway at 4121 Utah Street, about 1958.

"I remember him building stuff. Making shelves. He was always doing that kind of stuff. Even in Chicago, he made Sam and I each these kind of wall-hanging things – panels that we could hang our clothes on, they had little drawers. They were complicated little things. He made us each one so we could put our stuff away in our bedroom. He framed pictures. He had pictures of the jets Ted used to fly. We had those around on the walls. He liked to read. He had a fair number of books. He liked picture books."

"We bounced around a lot for some reason. I don't know why. Well, again, I think Danny was probably dodging his bills. Texas for a while. And Chicago. San Diego. And back. And back, and back. That was kind of our triangle."[209]

Danny and Jean liked to go out when they could, to dinner and dancing. "They would like to go out at night and sometimes they would just leave us alone at night and just go out. We'd cause lots of trouble when they were gone. [laughs] It's a wonder we didn't die, the things we did. We didn't go out, but one time they left us alone in that apartment building. We were on the sixth floor. We were playing... there was a little bathroom, and we were playing and we got in there and somehow the doorknob came apart and fell on the floor, so we couldn't get out the door. We were locked in the bathroom. We realized we could climb out the window and crawl along the ledge that was right out the window to get to the next window and hop back into the living room, which we did. And then since we had no supervision and no controls, we realized, hey, I guess that ledge goes all the way around the building! So we crawled all the way around the building. On the sixth floor. On this little concrete ledge.

"Another night they went out at night and we were left at home. They stayed out pretty late and we were doing something and we spilled some water on the kitchen floor, on the linoleum. We realized that this made a great slip and slide, so then we just started getting buckets of water and poured it on the floor and we played that for a long time. I remember that as one of the most fun times we ever had! My brother says we got beat pretty bad. It sure was fun. I'm not surprised if people below didn't come up because we probably flooded their place, too. Sam and I talked about that when we were in Boston. That was really fun."[210]

Danny's business card, after he returned to San Diego and his mother's home, suffering from leukemia.

All in all, though, it seemed like Danny was trying to be a decent family man. He'd often take little Ted with him when he went on jobs. He'd paint some big apartment buildings in Chicago, painting interiors all day long, all by himself. He'd tell Ted not to bother him, and Ted would wander off and explore the building. The only fun part of it, though, was when they went to lunch together. "We usually went to lunch in a bar, so he could have a beer. I thought it was really fun to sit at the counter of the bar with everyone drinking."[211]

Danny never drank much, maybe one beer at lunch. Neither Danny or Jean were drinkers. It's very refreshing to hear Ted and Sam talk about life when they were young children, because it leaves us with a picture of Danny Williams as someone who was complex and human, not simply the image we've been given of someone "incorrigible" and maybe even evil.

Danny did eventually move the family back to San Diego to stay. They moved in with May Williams, and it was a nice time for the kids, innocent as they were of much that went on around them. "San Diego was actually a wonderful time. The weather was beautiful. We were out all the time. It was a time when kids just ran. We rode our bikes clear to Balboa Park, however far that was. We were at the playground all the time. There were all kinds of kids on the street. My best friend was across the street. We were just always out playing. We went to school. We played. We might clean up the yard a little bit sometimes, but we didn't have a lot of responsibilities."[212]

Nephews Ted, left, and Sam Williams, right, playing baseball for the North Park Little League, about 1959.

There could have even been another ballplayer in the family. Sam Williams played Little League in San Diego for a year or two. Outfield. His eyes were never good. "I think my biggest problem was concentration, though," he laughs. University Heights (North Park) was "a wonderful playground. It was all dirt when we were kids. We used to play there. That's all we did. Played baseball. It was so close and the weather was so good.

The fence sure seemed a long way away." Sam played ball more than his younger brother Ted. "One of the things that probably turned him off to sports was how competitive I was. I don't have any doubt that I probably would have tried to pursue baseball if my eyes were better. It was a liability."[213]

Moving back to Utah Street placed Danny and family back in his childhood home, and with his mother May. Both Ted and Danny were concerned about their mother, and – regardless of all the vitriol that Manuel noticed – the two brothers did have a relationship. Danny found May's place a little chaotic. She may have been turning a bit senile. He took some photographs of the back yard to send brother Ted, to provide Ted a sense of how things were.

May was apparently a packrat. She kept everything. "When we moved into her house, she had every room stacked with stuff almost to the ceiling, and she just had little trails to get through the rooms. Newspapers... she saved everything on Ted Williams, and I'm sorry we lost it all, because she used to have these huge scrapbooks of everything. But she would also just save every daily paper. She was not very discriminating. Then, unfortunately, to make room for all the unimportant stuff she was saving in the house, all the Ted Williams stuff she put out in the garage where the roof was leaking. It was just all destroyed by water. I just remember boxes and boxes. Books and... I don't know. Maybe old clothes. Even in the living room. The dining room. She had moved out all the furniture. I think towards the end of her life she was going a little senile and maybe some [little] things became equally important with other things that she did."[214]

She also had the habit of writing thoughts down, even just the briefest of little notes to herself, like how much she loved her precious boys or moments of prayer, such as "Oh! Dear Lord, stand by me." She would write out their birth dates (she always wrote August 30 for Ted's), sometimes many times on many pieces of paper. Her grandson Ted has saved some of the papers and we can sense that her writing was what today we would call obsessive-compulsive. You'd find her writings on everything, Ted told me. "You'd find it on everything. Scraps of paper, the margins of magazines, receipts, on the edges of newspapers. It was on everything."[215]

She always called her sons "Precious." Ted never recalls her uttering a negative word about either child. "From her writings, I can see they were equally precious to her. That's one thing about the Venzor family that I felt, even about going to see Sarah and stuff – even though Ted was this superstar, they didn't distinguish between family members. They all loved each other equally... I never felt like I was secondary because I was Danny's kid and not Ted's. I felt very loved and wanted and desired and appreciated by any family members that I came across."[216]

Ted remembers that Danny was far from uniformly negative or hostile toward his brother. Danny urged his kids to get into sports, as a good way to make a living. Young Ted may have been shielded a bit – in which case we need to give his father credit for that – but he was able to tell me in 2002, "I don't recall him ever saying anything negative about Ted. He was very proud of him. He was very... there was love there. I never had the feeling [that he tried to badmouth Ted]. He loved to tell stories about Ted. He loved to say things that Ted had said. Little comments, biting comments. He had photographs of the jets Ted flew. He was proud of that stuff. I have so many pictures of Bobby-Jo because Ted'd send them to May and he'd send them to Danny. [Danny] liked Ted. I don't think there was any negative feeling. He might have been embarrassed by some of his behavior, some of his taking advantage of Ted – if he had those feelings, but I don't know if that was true."[217]

He knew that Danny was angry, that he was upset, that he felt slighted in life, that maybe he somehow was even owed something. Certainly some of that came from his brother being so successful, and him not. "I think that was the source of Danny's anger. I think that was more his personal tribulation, though, than something he attributed as Ted's fault. He spoke about him [Ted] very lovingly. He was proud of him, not just his accomplishments but as a brother, as family, as a companion."[218]

At the same time, the superstar ballplayer wasn't that adept at relationships. Ted didn't come home all that often, and sometimes it probably just seemed easier to him to throw money at a problem than to grapple with it personally. Ted the nephew knew that there were times that Danny abused the relationship and Ted the brother had to bail him out. It was a subject of some sensitivity. All in all, though, matters were just not as "black and white" as they have been portrayed in print.

It's not as though Danny ever became angelic. He carried a pistol – which he may have acquired when doing some non-union work in Chicago. Manuel Herrera said there was one time that May didn't want to get into the car with her son one time in Santa Barbara. "He was trying to get May in the Packard Clipper he owned and she was talking too long, so old Danny had enough of that and fired off a round. He carried a pistol, a .32 special and fired it at the hill where we lived when Aunt May wouldn't get into the car. I was there when he pulled the trigger on his .32 stubbie, then he looked at me and laughed. My poor Aunt May thought Danny was going to kill her and she pleaded, 'Danny, don't shoot me. I'll get in the car, just don't shoot.' I can hear her saying that right now."[219]

When Danny got sick with cancer, things got worse. It's hard to judge another person, unless you have been in that person's shoes. Facing death – and leukemia almost inevitably led to death in the late 1950s – it is hard to judge the behavior of another. We can try to understand. Here was Ted Williams, on the one hand. Ted had enjoyed a tremendously successful career, winning batting titles in 1957 and 1958. He was the highest paid player in baseball. He'd also earned additional glory as a decorated fighter pilot in Korea. And here was Danny Williams, on the other hand, struggling to get by financially, laboring hard at work, and he gets hit with cancer of the bone marrow. There's no question he still had the short end of the stick, and his grip was weakening.

He knew he was dying, and he knew that one of the only hopes he had was to get the best medical treatment available. Who paid for that treatment? His super-successful big brother. All the old envy and jealousy resurfaced. No one likes to be fully dependent on another, and yet here was Danny living back at 4121 Utah Street with an aging mother, dependent on Ted to cover the bills (and the air ambulance flights to Salt Lake City for treatment by the leading specialist of the day). He was dependent on Jean for the morphine injections that addressed his pain. Near the end, with Danny wasting away, Jean even had to light his cigarettes for him. Is it any wonder that the bitterness and spite resurfaced? It had probably never been that deeply buried, in any event.

"He looked frail, like a Jewish prisoner of war," remembered Manuel Herrera.[220] Danny was of different stature than Ted. A temporary drivers license issued in San Diego on 9/23/59 has him listed as 5'11" and 140 pounds. He'd already lost considerable weight by that time, but by no means did he have the 6' 4" frame of his famous brother. But he was angry, and he had a hateful streak. Danny visited Santa Barbara at one time when Manuel was in eighth or ninth grade. "He was awfully ill at the time. He sat right down next to me while I was doing my homework and for four days, he didn't have a good thing to say about his brother. It broke my heart. It confused me as a young kid. I have never met a person who hated his brother more than Danny Williams. He didn't have one good word about his brother!"[221]

Ted had him brought to see Dr. Winthrop at St. Mary's in Salt Lake City and to the Mayo Clinic in Rochester, Minnesota, even to a cancer hospital in Tijuana. "He told me, 'I know my brother's paying for whatever. I hope it cost him a bundle. I'll take him for every cent he's got.' I said, 'Danny, he's trying to help.' He said, 'I don't give a damn,' and he went on and on. I just shut down."[222]

Manuel understood, though. "I could see that he was really a good guy but he was trying to get acceptance and attention. He knew he was dying and his family would be without him. He laughed things off, but I could see that he was hurting inside."[223]

There are other perspectives, though. It's possible that Danny was talking tough to Manuel, more or less for what we might call "public consumption." In private, things may have been different. Danny's son Ted said, "I'm sure Danny gave him a lot of grief, but I saw Ted being very warm and compassionate to Danny. He literally did everything he could, and it was mostly money but he cared immensely in his own way, too. I remember Danny telling us over and over when we were kids, 'Don't bother your uncle. He hates being bothered, and whatever you do, don't ask him for any money."[224] Through it all, though, Ted was taking financial care of his mother, and his brother, and his brother's family.

"It was really hard for my mom, loving him, knowing she was losing him, taking care of him, worrying about him, us, money, taking his abuse, which turned verbal when he could no longer be physical. He was literally bedridden the last year or so, she had to do everything for him, feed him, wash him, give him morphine injections, light his cigarettes. She never complained."[225]

In the end, Danny found peace at last. He left this world with at least one gesture of good will, apologizing to Jean for all she'd had to go through. "She told me once that when he died, he told her he was sorry for being so mean."[226]

How is Danny remembered now? A bit of an enigma, says his son Ted. He had some demons. Maybe he got some of those from his father Samuel. But he worked hard. He tried, in his own way. And he suffered. In the end, one can feel for him, the burdens he bore.

OTHER FAMILY MEMBERS

There are, of course, other Venzors out there. Not to mention Hernandezes, Rubios and others. I called a few. In January 2003, I spoke to Lionel Venzor of El Paso. He wasn't sure of his background, but knew that his mother came from the Rubio side of the family. His grandmother was a Carbajal, and Lionel said he was named after his Uncle Lionel Carbajal of Santa Barbara. Both sides of the family came from Chihuahua. He'd once tried to trace down Venzors in Madrid and Sevilla, but with no luck. He thinks the Venzors were connected to the Morga family in some fashion. He'd never heard of any Ted Williams connection, though. If a researcher had enough time, there are certainly deeper family connections that could be explored.

I felt good that I was able to bring Ted Williams and Dan Williams, Jr. together. At the same SABR/Hall of Champions event, Dan also met Karma Barber, who had grown up with Ted and Sam, after Danny's widow had married Dave Barber. All told, the event in San Diego drew at least 33 family members together for the day of discussion about their Hall of Fame relative (actually, Ted is in 10 Halls of Fame, at last count.) For many, it was the first time they had ever met others in the family. As indicated above, some of the reunions still continue, as Howard Winet drove to Montana to meet Mary Redding. There will no doubt be others in the days to come.

And I do hope, someday, to learn more of significance about Ted's father's side of the family – maybe from that elusive niece or nephew who may or may not have ever been born.

There has been some other baseball played in the family as well.

OTHER FAMILY MEMBERS WHO PLAYED BASEBALL

Aside from Ted Williams and some of the *tios* Venzor, there have been a few other family members who have played baseball. Of course, the one who received the most attention in recent years was Ted's own son, John-Henry Williams. John-Henry tried out for the college team at Bates College, but didn't make the first cut. Had he ever made the majors, however, he would by no means have been the first ballplayer who'd been cut by his college team. John-Henry transferred to the University of Maine at Orono, and showed some initial interest but never truly tried out for the team. Born in 1968, John-Henry's first serious attempt at baseball came in 2002 when he was 33 years old; he signed with the Gulf Coast Red Sox in late June. The club was an affiliate of the Boston Red Sox and most observers assumed that the only reason John-Henry was signed was out of respect for his father, the greatest Red Sox player of all time. He never did get a hit for the Gold Coast team and, in just the second game he played, John-Henry broke a rib chasing a foul ball that fell in the seats. Give him credit for effort. Eight days later, Ted Williams died.

Whatever others might say, Ted himself was proud of his son and glad that he decided to take a shot at baseball. Even in the last weeks of Ted's life, a friend of John-Henry's reported that Ted "was lying in his bed talking to a member of his nursing staff. He had a big Ted Williams smile on his face. The nurse asked him what he was smiling about. Ted told the nurse, "You know I'm really proud of John Henry (sic) playing pro baseball. I never pushed him toward it, but I'm real glad he's doing it now.""[227]

The following year, John-Henry enlisted the help of a full-time hitting instructor and worked out with expensive equipment. Ted's son gave it all he had and hooked on with a couple of independent league teams in 2003, the Selma Cloverleafs in Alabama (a team that had no home park and consequently played all its games on the road) and the Baton Rouge River Bats in Louisiana. Though no one felt a player just starting out at such an advanced age had much of a future, John-Henry hit .190 for the River Bats as a first baseman and DH. Wearing #30, the 6'5" 220-pound Williams' stats read:

	AVG	G	AB	R	H	2B	3B	HR	RBI	BB	SO	SB	CS	SLG	OBP
Williams, John, DH	.273	13	33	3	9	2	0	0	1	4	13	0	1	.333	.400
Williams, John, 1B	.153	26	72	3	11	3	0	0	2	9	33	0	2	.194	.274

The River Bats, interestingly, are owned by a retired United States Marine Corps colonel, Gilda Jackson, an African-American woman. The San Diego Padres invited three of the River Bats to the Arizona Fall League in 2003.

The River Bats won the 2003 South Eastern Professional Baseball League playoffs, but by the time they entered post-season competition, John-Henry was no longer with them. Something was wrong. He was becoming too fatigued. Come October, he was diagnosed with acute myelogenous leukemia, a particularly deadly form of the cancer. Less than six months after diagnosis, despite a bone marrow transplant from his sister Claudia, John-Henry Williams succumbed to cancer.

A parenthetic note might be nice to include at this point. Though John-Henry indeed did attract a great deal of negative ink and comment, many who knew Ted Williams saw how he could light up with pleasure seeing his son enter a room. A father may sometimes be blind to a son's faults, but there is little doubt that this father very much loved this son. It was not a relationship without difficulty, but Ted really loved John-Henry. Ted hadn't made much time for John-Henry in the first couple of decades of his son's life, but he welcomed John-Henry in his latter years. One of Ted's friends, Steve Brown, even found Ted counseling him on healing within the Brown family. "I got to witness John-Henry coming back in Ted's life. A lot of people don't realize that, but when John-Henry came back, Ted was the happiest man on the face of the earth. Even when John-Henry would disappoint him, it was a short-lived thing and Ted would be over it. A lot of people never got to see that side of him, but that was the parent John-Henry never had before."

Brown saw a parallel to Ted's relationship with his brother Danny. "Ted loved his brother despite what he did. He had the same kind of love for him he did John-Henry. He never saw the dark side. He knew it existed. He would even confront it as far as talking about it, but since he was not personally involved in their actions, he forgave them."

Ted even prompted a reconciliation within Brown's family. "Ted was responsible for myself and my son patching up our differences. He made me... Ted made me... he made me call my son. I was a hard-head like him, but he told me he was my son and I was my father. He had met my son Steve and he liked him, and so he physically called me on the carpet about it. He grilled me. Ted made me address [the problem between us] and get it out of the way. I thank him to this day because it was the best thing I could have done."[228]

Back to baseball.

Ted's uncles Saul, Paul and Bruno all played semi-pro baseball, as we have seen. Bruno's son Danny was on the championship Santa Barbara High School team and might have gone farther had he not had to take out a couple of years for the Korean War. The player in the next generation with the most talent, though, was Sal Herrera Jr.

Sal is Manuel Herrera's older brother, taken in by Rayo Hernandez after Sal Sr. had orphaned his children. Sal was scouted by a number of organizations and signed by the same scout who signed Eddie Mathews to the Braves. By all accounts, Sal had the tools. The problem was, he had a temper to match. Manuel explained, "Sal should have been a Hall of Famer – not because he was my brother, [but because] he had the tools. He had a temper and it caused him some big-time problems in baseball. You can not scream at the fans and run after them with a bat into the stands. He was built like Mickey Mantle but bigger and almost as fast as the Mick. He was so talented and strong, but he was tough as they come on others as well as himself. I got to see him play football in high school and no one on the opposing team could bring him down. He was a fullback and ran over people like an out-of-control freight train! I saw him drag three guys 15 yards before he was taken down – many times. I was only 11 years old, but how can a person forget his brother running over people as he did! The guy should have played pro football. He was offered a tryout with the Cleveland Browns, but was signed by Johnny Moore of the [Milwaukee] Braves shortly after the football offer." Sal bought a 1953 Mercury with the $1000.00 bonus money he got for signing with the Braves.[229]

ARELLANES, HERRERA GET TRYOUTS

Bill Arellanes and Sal Herrera, two former Santa Barbara High School baseball stars, currently are working out at the Brooklyn Dodgers' training camp at Vero Beach, Fla., before being optioned out to two of the Bums' farm clubs for regular-season play.

Arellanes, an 18-year-old infielder who held down third base for Dons coach Chuck Sylvester last

SAL HERRERA
—At Vero Beach

• • •

season, probably will play with Bakersfield in the Class C California League this year and thus will make several appearances here in his home town.

He was signed by the Dodgers last June after leading the Dons in hitting last season. He is the son of Mr. and Mrs. Bill Arellanes, 434 Dibblee Ave., Santa Barbara.

Herrera was an all-CIF outfielder on the 1953 Dons line. He was signed after graduation by the Milwaukee Braves and played last year for both Modesto in the California League and in the Pioneer loop.

The Braves released him after last season and he then signed with the Dodgers. He will probably play this year with Ashville, N.C., in the Class B Tri-State League.

Sal Herrera.

Manuel explained more. "Sal came to live with us at about the 8th grade, the Venzor family and me and my twin sister Natalie. He was on his last leg before juvenile hall. He was in the 8th grade as I remember. Sal never spoke about the Rayo household or his school atmosphere. He was a great athlete, but his own worst enemy. Eddie Mathews and he played American Legion and high school ball together. Eddie said, he 'wished he had Sal's power' – but that ol' attitude cut deep into his career. Sal played centerfield at Santa Barbara High School and was All-CIF first team. He came in second for player of the year which was won by Marty Keough, who was from the Claremont area and later played first base for the Cincinnati Reds. Sal was the MVP of the Pomona Tournament and the scouts pored over the house to sign him before he graduated from school." This was the same tournament that Ted Williams had starred in and Sal won the same honor Ted had: a CIF player of the year.

"'A waste of a complete baseball player' – those were the words of many a baseball player who played with or against Sal Herrera. I know because I asked about Sal's talent on the diamond. He was married at the age of 18 and left for baseball the day after. He was a scared kid when he left for baseball, but said playing in the major leagues was so easy that he couldn't believe it! He beat out Hank Aaron and then beat himself out!"[230]

After baseball Sal got a job in the glass business where he graduated from an apprentice to journeyman and later served as a mechanic glazier. He was a supervisor for a large glass company and help build the MGM Grand Hotel, McCarran Airport, Brentwood Towers and many other high rises.

Gene Bowman confirms Manuel's story. Bowman was a pitcher, also signed by Johnny Moore. "Sal had all the talent in the world. Big, fast kid. Could run. Boy, he had the tools. I played with him in Boise. He was just always in trouble, though, fighting with the fans and everything else. He was a talent, but Johnny Moore finally just said he'd had enough. He was maybe four years or so younger than I was. One time he went down to Cabrillo Park in Santa Barbara and wanted Eddie [Mathews] to help him with his hitting. He was having trouble, so he got down there and Ed tried to help him but he turned to Eddie and said, 'Hey, I know more than that.' So Ed said, 'Well, so just stick with it.' He just wouldn't listen to anybody. Ed was nice to him. He said, 'OK, well, good luck to you.'"[231] Sal played some in Boise, some in Evansville, but never rose much higher than B ball.

Gabriel Arellanes signed with the Brooklyn Dodgers around the same time, and played for about five years in the Dodgers system – Texas League, California League, and the Midwest, Southern and Eastern leagues. Arellanes was signed out of Santa Barbara High, too. He had tied Ted Williams' record in the Pomona tournament, hitting four home runs one year. He remembers Sal well: "Sal signed with the Braves a couple of years ahead of me. He got kicked out of the Braves chain – he punched the coach. Then the word was out, 'Hands off of Sal.' He had too much of a temper. He was a pretty tough hombre. We were all raised kind of tough. We all fought and boxed and everything else."[232]

Saul Venzor's grandson, Chaz's boy Greg, knew that he was related to Ted Williams. "We knew in elementary school," he told this author in February 2004. "We would tell our friends and they would just laugh at us." Who was going to believe that little Greg Venzor was related to the Hall of Fame baseball player? The family connection had never been publicized. Greg didn't even play baseball when he went through school, but for the last few years has served as head baseball coach for the junior varsity at Bishop Diego High School in Santa Barbara, and more recently at the city's Dos Pueblos High School. He's also assistant coach for the varsity baseball team.[233]

Greg himself has two sons Joshua and Jacob – Saul Venzor's great-grandsons – who both played middle infield and pitched a bit as well. Josh played at both schools, but did not play in college. Jacob currently plays at Dos Pueblos, and has some aspirations of trying to play college ball. Time will tell.

Ruth Gonzales, one of Ted's cousins, said, about Ted, "He didn't claim any relatives" (meaning that he kept his relatives at arm's length.) I asked about Ted's aunt Sarah Diaz, and she said that Sarah was the exception: "She was the only one that Ted wanted to see. Ted would tell Sarah, 'Don't tell anybody. If you do, I will never come and visit you again.' Some of her cousins, when May died, wanted to go, to see Ted Williams. He [arranged] a private funeral. They didn't say anything much about May; they just wanted to see Ted Williams."

Ruth Gonzales's son David Gonzales played a little bit in high school, but David's son Davey Gonzalez actually starred when he was in high school. Davey says he was about 12 or 13 when he first found that there was a family tie to Ted Williams. He wrote Ted in Islamorada and explained how he was related through his grandmother. He got back a nice note and a personalized photograph, which he has saved. Davey played third base for Downey High School and was team MVP in 1985, and a first-team C.I.F. All-Star selection – the same C.I.F. in which Ted had starred back in the mid-1930s. Davey played for the Norwalk Birds in 1986; the team entered and won the Connie Mack World Series in Farmington, New Mexico. At least one Williams relative was on a team what won a World Series! Davey went to USC and made the JV squad, but he gave priority to his studies and didn't keep at baseball.[234]

Ted's nephews Sam and Ted both played some Little League ball, but neither pursued the game. Ted's grand-nephew Noah Williams (11-year-old son of nephew Ted and Sue Stein) shows an interest in the game. Noah has played since T ball, really enjoys it, and loves playing first base. In 2002, he told this author that he wanted to be "the greatest hitter who ever lived." Must have heard that somewhere. Noah lives in Oakland, California and was fortunate to be drafted on the local Red Sox for the 2004 season, where he'll stay until he moves to the next level... but as his father says, "Ted Williams was a pretty special talent and it may not extend to the rest of us!"

There's a Tom Venzor living in Schuyler, Nebraska. No known relation, but he's a Venzor, son of Armando Venzor, and in July 2003, he pitched the second game of a doubleheader between the towns of York and Schuyler. Unfortunately, he didn't win. We'll keep our ears peeled for more word of Tom Venzor.

Noah Williams, son of nephew Ted, plays first base in the North Oakland/South Oakland Little League. Coincidentally, he was drafted onto the Red Sox, 2004, where he'll play until he moves to the next level.

Lastly, there is a Venzor long associated with base-ball who lives in the Mexican state of Chihuahua, the state from which May Venzor's parents emigrated to the U.S. Señor Jesus Manuel Ruiz Venzor is in his late 60s as of this writing, a baseball announcer very well known throughout Chihuahua. In 2002, the area's top amateur championship was named in his honor.

Was Ted Williams reluctant to talk about his Hispanic heritage?

Was Ted Williams reluctant to talk about his Hispanic heritage? He didn't hesitate to touch on it in talking with John Underwood, but it only produced a line in passing. Nonetheless, Ted recognized that he "would have run into problems in those days" due to "the prejudices people had in Southern California." It may have been something he deliberately concealed during his playing days, and only felt comfortable acknowledging in later years.

It's a fair guess, of course, that his awareness of discrimination led to his welcoming of black players like Larry Doby, the first African-American in the American League, and to his ground-breaking induction speech at the Hall of Fame, calling for the inclusion of the great players from the Negro Leagues. On that occasion in 1966, Ted said, "Baseball gives every American boy a chance to excel. This is the nature of man and the name of the game. I hope that someday Satchel Paige and Josh Gibson will be voted into the Hall of Fame as symbols of the great Negro players who are not here only because they weren't given the chance."

Five years later, on accepting a Brotherhood Award at Howard University, Ted said, "As I look back on my career, I'm thankful that I was given the chance to play baseball; it's about the only thing I could do – and I've thought many a time, what would have happened to me if I hadn't had the chance. A chill goes up my back when I think I might have been denied this if I had been black."[235]

As a youth, Ted was clearly sensitive about his image. He was embarrassed by his mother being "out in the middle of the damn street all the time," about the fact that other kids had better clothing, about how skinny he was, about the house being "dirty all the time." When Eddie Collins came to visit, he was embarrassed that the family had to cover the hole in his chair "with a five-cent towel." Add the prejudice of others to the mix, and it wouldn't be surprising if Ted felt an inclination to distance himself from his mother's family's ethnicity.

Mary Herrera Redding knew the feeling: "At that time Spanish wasn't cool. Like the Indians here in Montana, they were punished for speaking their language and practicing their heritage."[236] As a youngster, Mary proactively tried to lighten her coloring so that she might be perceived a little more like the more favored Anglos around her. Raised by May's sister Jeanne, Mary was a sort of step-sister to Howard Winet. Dr. Winet remembered, "Mary might have had a little Aztec in her. She and Abby [Moreno] – this is something that used to fascinate me as a kid – they used to spend a lot of time peroxiding their arms. This is something that was done by a lot of Latinos, because they wanted to look like gringos. The dark hair would give them away. They thought it was heavy dark hair on their arms – I didn't think it was heavy, but they did – and they were busy at least once a week peroxiding their arms. I was fascinated by it.[237]

Connie Matthews reflected, "Ted... it seems to me now Ted did not like to associate with part of the family, the Hernandez family. He didn't want to be associated with the dark part of the family, which was part of the Hernandezes, Manuel especially. I think he married a very dark woman and most of the kids are dark. Right away you know that they are part Indian or whatever. They're dark. And I know that Ted always... 'Don't bring any [of them around.]'"[238]

Skin color was, rather typically for the era, a topic of some conversation. Connie remembers Sarah Diaz being "kind of catty" about one of the Venzors, asking, "How come this Venzor, he was so dark?" Connie's sister Ruth agrees: "He didn't want to associate with his relatives, and I don't blame him. He didn't like any of us relatives. Partly, he didn't want anyone to know that he was of Mexican descent."[239]

Ted was angry about one thing that happened when he was waiting for an offer from one of the teams who had scouted him. Ted's cousin Madeline Cordero and his Aunt Sarah Diaz were both staying at the Utah Street house, and they knew that May didn't want Ted to get signed. He was too young, she felt, and she didn't want him to be heading East to play baseball, so she asked them to hide the mail. "Ted's waiting for that letter. A few days go by, a week goes by. Ted's getting impatient. Asks the mailman. Turns out Madeline hid the letter because May didn't want Ted to go. When Ted found out, he shouted, 'You damn Indian, go back to the reservation!'"[240]

Maybe there were good days and there were bad days. Matters of race and ethnicity have always been charged. David Ronquillo recounts a story told him recently by Priscilla Wade, another relative. "Priscilla describes this large group of family that goes to meet him at the train station. Here's this unsuspecting 19-year-old kid – maybe 20 – he's been told by the Red Sox, don't let anyone know you're Hispanic. Time and place. Being Hispanic at that time was not something that you want to embrace. There was a lot of discrimination. He doesn't look Hispanic. He's got the last name Williams. Who's going to know he's Hispanic?

"So he sees this whole family coming toward him. He doesn't know what to do. He panics and does a U-turn! Does a 180. Walks away from them. It was as though it happened yesterday. Priscilla was telling us about it and she's saying, "I am STILL mad at him for doing that!"

"The guy didn't know what to do. He was panic-stricken."[241]

He was aware that if he'd been seen as Hispanic, it could have caused difficulties for him? "There's no question about it. That's what I think. That was a very significant crossroads in his life.

"This is speculative on my part but I think it's pretty reasonable speculation. Ted was, I think, embarrassed about his mom's connection with the Salvation Army. But I think he was also somewhat embarrassed by his Hispanic roots. Here you have this guy who's 6'4". He doesn't look in the least bit Hispanic. He has the name Williams so no one's ever going to suspect that he's Hispanic. May was a very attractive woman. I don't know how Hispanic she looked. I've seen many, many photographs, and I saw her, but I don't have a recollection of her looking Hispanic."[242]

Manuel Herrera adds that when they cleaned out the Utah Street home, Ted destroyed all the pictures at home. "Ted was ashamed and tore up the damn pictures, then he laughed it off."[243]

Ronquillo understood the impulse: "If it's not popular to be Hispanic today, my goodness, at that time it was a death knell."[244]

Throughout the extended family, English was the language of those of both May's and Ted's generations. In El Paso, Ruth Gonzales and her family spoke both languages in the home, "but mostly English. Micaela [May Williams], the same. She would speak Spanish to her mother and my mother, but to her kids and sisters and her brothers, she would speak English.[245] There may simply not have been as much self-awareness or self-consciousness about ethnicity in those days. Ruth's niece – Ernest Ponce's daughter – Maureen Surratt comments, "There were no hyphenating Americans when I grew up."[246]

Danny told his sons that Ted called the Santa Barbara family, "the Mexicans." Danny wasn't raised Hispanic, either. "My father never took on the Hispanic lifestyle, never made mention of it. I think he was happy to have come from an English father. I realize in retrospect he totally looks Mexican.

I'm sure for Ted it was a bit of an embarrassment. It was maybe considered lower class, or working class, or peasant. Certainly they were peasant-type people. Not that there's anything negative in that; it was just their life. They were pretty much immigrants. I think that's the exciting part of the story."[247] May, though, was probably not herself viewed as Hispanic. "When I lived with May, you never got the sense that they were Hispanic, or that there were any of those influences. It just seemed pretty everyday and normal. In Santa Barbara, though, they ate tortillas and beans, and cooked food like that. I think May maybe moved more out of it than the others did, maybe because she didn't stay with them.'"[248]

In Santa Barbara, of course, there was a lot of Spanish spoken. Teresa Cordero Contreras talks about her grandmother Natalia Venzor. "She spoke a little bit of English. She'd answer the phone, "Jeannie no here" or "Sarah no here." She understood. I didn't speak any Spanish and when I went over to Grandma's, I'd just say, "Hi Grandma" and give her a great old big hug and a kiss, and outside I went. My dad spoke a lot of English, and my mom, too. The only time I ever heard them speak Spanish is when they didn't want us to know. Then you try to learn but it's hard."[249]

Ted probably heard a lot of Spanish around him, but being a young boy, simply tuned out. And May's ministry was in the Salvation Army in San Diego, and it was not an Hispanic ministry. The Salvation Army photographs we see of her often show her posed with figures of the Anglo establishment. As we have noted as well, Sarah Diaz and other family members emphasized that the family roots were European, not Mexican.

"Mexicans can truly be more discriminatory toward darker-skinned people than we are in this country toward black people," David Ronquillo interjected. "It's not even close. It's incredible. In Mexico, one of the reasons that men began wearing mustaches is to distinguish themselves as not being of Indian blood. People in Mexico who had Spanish heritage, as do I from my father's side, it was like a real premium to have, for example, light-colored eyes, or light-colored hair and particularly light-colored skin."

David illustrates with a modest personal experience from the time he spent living as a student in Mexico. "One day we're out... this is mid-Sixties in Mexico. We go out and buy these sandals from a vendor on the street, the kind with tire treads. There were three of us students who lived with a family, and the woman was highly offended that we bought them because it reflected something that the Indians wore. Sarah would have said this, because my grandmother – who was May and Sarah's aunt – used to wear dark dresses with a white blouse. The Basque look. My grandmother was very light-complected, as was my mother. A lot of Mexican people say, 'I'm from Spain' because they want to distance themselves from the Indian part of the Mexican culture as much as they can."[250]

As it happens the family ethnicity was quite mixed. There were *indios* in the family, and most of the family understood the primary roots to be Basque, but more than one relative spoke of Russian background. Esther Slagle talked of it (see above, in a footnote) and so did Ruth Ponce Gonzales: "My sister tells me that they had Russian blood in there somewhere. Santiago and Eduviges were blond and blue-eyed. They looked Russian. [Natalia Venzor] had golden honey brown hair. My dad's ancestors were probably from France. It was all a mixture. On my mother's side, they had some Russian ancestors. My mother was very white but she had brown hair and brown eyes. All the others were blond *gueros*. My sister was a blonde. I was a brunette.'"[251]

Did Ted Williams truly turn his back on his Hispanic heritage, or was it mostly irrelevant to him? Is it something we focus on more today than people would have in his years of growing up? Probably some of each. Joe Villarino, Ted's schoolboy friend and Hoover High teammate, had a Mexican father and a Spanish mother, and he knew Ted from third grade on. This is how Joe put it: it was "not that he didn't want to be known as a Mexican, but it just wasn't part of his life."[252] Leigh Montville, researching Ted's life for his biography Ted Williams, spoke with Ted's second wife, Lee Howard, at some length. She said "he never ever talked about it when they were married."[253] He truly may not have seen it that important a part of his life. As Ted recognized, having the last name Williams and being raised largely in an Anglo environment no doubt facilitated his acceptance in organized baseball in the 1930s. This lack of focus on his Hispanic heritage may have been convenient, but it may not have been so calculated.

Joe Villarino's perception may have hit the nail on the head – Ted was raised an Anglo and grew up almost entirely in Anglo environments. There are very few seemingly Latino surnames in his high school yearbook. Frank Cushing, who used to shag balls at Hoover, came to know Ted later in life as a fellow Marine. Of Ted's mother, he said, "You would have never known May had any Mexican [blood.] I didn't know it until years later. [Ted] didn't talk about it very much, but he wasn't ashamed of it. He would remark a little about it – why he liked guacamole or so forth. "I guess it's the Mexican in me," or some remark like that. He didn't try to hide it."[254] It is undeniable, though, that he quietly welcomed Larry Doby with dignity; Doby was the first African-American in the American League. He went out of his way to welcome Pumpsie Green, the first Red Sox African-American, choosing him as his partner for tossing the ball on the side while warming up before the game. He made no pronouncement on the subject. Again, he made his point with quiet, even elegant, dignity. Ted did have a feeling for those at a disadvantage – be they kids who got cancer or those who suffered discrimination.

Ted not only crusaded for Negro League players to be brought into the Hall of Fame. He also spoke up for Native Americans, a few years earlier, in December 1962. Reacting to a *New York Times* editorial, Williams angrily wrote in his syndicated weekly column, "The Indians in this country, as usual, are getting the shaft... They're still treated here as the scum of the earth as if they're being punished for being here when all of us first came over. I would think that after all these years, with all the assimilation that has taken place between all our people, that the Indians certainly should have their place in society. But we look the other way. The only good Indian is a dead Indian, still seems to be the motto." He went on to argue that we're spending millions in foreign aid, and CARE sends packages to other lands, but maybe it was time that the Peace Corps did something for American Indians who "can't even belong to a country which they once owned."[255]

Ted returned to the theme in February 1964 with a column headlined "Lo, the Poor Indian Off the Diamond" in the February 16, 1964 *Houston Post*. Both columns complained that only the Cleveland Indians, Milwaukee Braves and Washington Redskins were treated as first-class citizens, but not the American Indian. "I know that there are many people who feel as keenly as I do about the terrible treatment of our people and the word 'our' should be underlined... And it's about time we start making amends to our own people." Ted noted that the average American Indian life span was 42 years, not the 62 years of other Americans, and that the average education was only through eighth grade. "If you're a real American, you should be angry, insulted that this kind of treatment has been allowed for so many years... Why don't we all really begin acting like sports and start off by giving back to the American Indian their dignity and place in the human race? It belongs to them the same way it belongs to us. It's our shame when it should be our glory."

These two columns, which appeared nationally years before his famous Hall of Fame speech, have never attracted attention but, in retrospect, foreshadow Ted Williams' willingness to speak out on the issue of prejudice and fair treatment. Knowing a favored uncle who was directly descended from the Chumash Indians may have infused his words with additional passion. And growing up in a family of diverse backgrounds may have sensitized Ted to the issue in general.

A TRULY AMERICAN FAMILY

Although his family roots are many and diverse, Ted Williams' family was truly an American family. Almost all of us are of immigrant background. Many of us are of mixed roots and many of us truly do not know the full story of our own heritage, even going back just three or four generations. Ted Williams was born and raised in a fascinating, lively, vital family with no shortage of personalities. With family roots in Wales and England, and in Mexico and the Basque country, Ted came from a truly American family which covered the gamut, as we noted at the start: cavalrymen and cowboys, longshoremen and photographers, evangelists and mariachi musicians, cement truck drivers, and more. And from this context was produced a man the likes of whom we may never see again – a crusader against cancer in children, a world-class fisherman, a United States Marines jet pilot, and the man who many feel was the greatest hitter who ever lived.

Venzor and Hernandez family gathering, August, 1928.

FOOTNOTES

1) *Interview with Ernest "Joe" Villarino, May 9, 1997*

2) *Communication from John Underwood, December 12, 2002*

3) *Ed Linn,* Hitter *(New York: Harcourt & Brace, 1993), p. 74*

4) *Ernest Ponce obituary,* El Paso Times, *March 17, 2002*

5) *Bill Nowlin, "Ted and Cuba,"* Ted Williams Magazine, *February 2004*

6) *Interview with Elden Auker, April 6, 1997*

7) *Linn, op. cit., p. 121*

8) *Ted Williams with John Underwood,* My Turn At Bat *(New York: Fireside edition, 1988), p. 30*

9) *Leigh Montville,* Ted Williams *(New York: Doubleday, 2004), p. 19*

10) Boston Globe, *April 7, 1954*

11) My Turn At Bat, *op. cit., p. 30*

12) *Communication from Peter Morris, April 9, 2004*

13) Boston Transcript, *April 12, 1939. Presumably, Sam Williams' friend was named Ted.*

14) *K. Bruce Galloway,* West Point: America's Power Fraternity *(NY: Simon & Schuster, 1973)*

15) My Turn At Bat, *p. 30*

16) *Communication from Kimberly Mack, Salvation Army Museum of the West, December 3, 2002. How did May end up so far north in Petaluma?*

17) *Interview with Manuel Herrera, May 29, 1999. Manuel himself was raised as a Salvationist and remains deeply impressed to his day with May's commitment to the cause.*

18) Boston Globe, *August 29, 1961*

19) *Communication from Kimberly Mack, December 3, 2002*

20) *Interview with Sarah V. Diaz, May 1999*

21) Hitter, *op. cit, p. 30;* My Turn At Bat, *op. cit., p. 19*

22) *Communication from Manuel Herrera, July 19, 2004*

23) *Interview with Edward Donovan, April 7, 2001*

24) Hitter, *op. cit., p. 34*

25) *Williams' position was confirmed by a librarian in the California State Library's Government Publications Section who checked the State telephone directories for 1937 and 1939 and found him listed as jail inspector in the Department of Social Welfare. Communication from Catherine Hanson-Tracy, California State Library, December 23, 2003.*

26) *Interview with Teresa Cordero Contreras, May 28, 2000. Manuel Herrera recalled Samuel driving an old Essex. After the divorce, May would come to Santa Barbara on the Southern Pacific.*

27) *Interview with Sarah V. Diaz, May 31, 1999*

28) Hitter, *op. cit., p. 34*

29) Hitter, *op. cit., p. 72. Mickie Frank, a member of Minnie's church recalls the house as "real sweet, very tiny. I would say modest." Interview with Mickie Frank, January 5, 2003*

30) My Turn At Bat, *op. cit., p. 29*

31) *"Solon Economy Puts State Jail Inspector Out of Job," press clipping bureau excerpt from the* Fresno Bee & Republican, *July 12, 1939*

32) *Samuel S. Williams, "Report on Proceedings, Sixty-Eighth Annual Congress of the American Prison Association," October 14, 1938*

33) Fresno Bee & Republican, *July 12, 1939*

34) *Interview with Alice Psaute, March 1, 2003*

35) My Turn At Bat, *op. cit., p. 29*

36) *Interview with Manuel Herrera, May 29, 1999*

37) *Ibidem*

38) *Interview with Alice Psaute, March 1, 2003*

39) My Turn At Bat, *op. cit., p. 28*

40) *Ibid., pp. 29, 33*

41) Hitter, *op. cit., p. 73*

42) My Turn At Bat, *op. cit., p. 28*

43) Hitter, *op. cit., p. 29*

44) My Turn At Bat, *op. cit., p. 32*

45) *"'Army' Recruiting Station? Perhaps – To Assist Police,"* San Diego Sun, *February 3, 1936*

46) San Diego Union, *February 2, 1936*

47) *"Handling Transients," editorial,* San Diego Sun, *February 1936*

48) *Communication from Ted Williams, October 25, 2002*

49) San Diego Union, *July 7, 1980*

50) *Interview with Alice Psaute, March 1, 2003*

51) *Clippings placed in scrapbook maintained by Alice Fries King, in possession of Alice Psaute.*

52) *Interviews with Mickie Frank and Larry Frank, January 5, 2003*

53) *Communication from Manuel Herrera, June 16, 2002*

54) *Communication from Manuel Herrera, May 1, 2000*

55) *Interview with Mary Ponce, April 26, 2000*

56) *Communication from Manuel Herrera, May 2, 2000 and interview with Ruth Gonzales, February 28, 2003*

57) *Interviews with Connie Matthews, November 26 and December 10, 2002*

58) *Interview with Connie Matthews, December 10, 2002*

59) *Interview with Ernest and Mary Ponce, November 8, 2000. Mary says that they never really saw May.*

60) *Interview with Mary Ponce, April 26, 2002*

61) *Interview with Sarah Diaz, May 31, 1999*

62) *Interviews with David Ronquillo, October 23 and November 24, 2003*

63) *Communication from Manuel Herrera, May 31, 1999*

64) *Interview with Geno Lucero, September 4, 2003*

65) *Interview with Esther Slagle, October 21, 2003*

66) *Interview with Connie Matthews, November 26, 2002*

67) *Communication from Manuel Herrera, May 20, 2000*

68) *Ibidem*

69) *Interview with Ruth Gonzales, February 28, 2003*

70) *Communication from Manuel Herrera, May 16, 2000*

71) *Interview with Sarah Diaz, May 31, 1999*

72) *Stephen Lawton,* Santa Barbara's Flying A Studio, *(Santa Barbara: Fithian Press), 1997, p. 45*

73) *Interview with Sarah Diaz, May 31, 1999*

74) *Communication from Manuel Herrera, May 16, 2000*

75) *Communication from Manuel Herrera, January 23, 2002*

76)   *Communication from Manuel Herrera, September 3, 2001*

77)   *Communication from Manuel Herrera, December 27, 2000*

78)   *Interview with Manuel Herrera, May 29, 1999*

79)   *Communication from Manuel Herrera, May 20, 2000.*
Danny Venzor confirms the story. Similarly named for their Uncle Daniel, Bruno's son Danny remembers that Danny Williams and the "young gal" actually stayed on the living room couch at his house, 1006 Chino – a house Danny still owns today as a rental. "Come to find out that she was underage. He picked her up someplace down south, and they were going to charge him with statutory rape." Interview with Danny Venzor, December 28, 2003

80)   *Communication from Manuel Herrera, January 24, 2002*

81)   *Communication from Kathleen Osowski, May 20, 2000*

82)   *Communication from Manuel Herrera, June 15, 2002*

83)   *Interview with Manuel Herrera, May 29, 1999*

84)   *Ibidem*

85)   *Communication from Manuel Herrera, June 15, 2002*

86)   *Interview with Manuel Herrera, May 29, 1999*

87)   *Frank Cushing to Ed Linn, from the Ed Linn papers made available to author by Hildy Linn Angius*

88)   *Ibidem*

89)   *Both Ballinger and Cushing quotes are from notes in the Ed Linn papers.*

90)   *Communication from Manuel Herrera, September 3, 2001*

91)   *Barry Lorge, San Diego Union, July 7, 1991*

92)   *Undated Don Freeman column from* San Diego Union *found in San Diego Hall of Champions archives.*

93)   *Interview with Joe Villarino, May 9, 1997*

94)   *Communication from Manuel Herrera, May 20, 2000.*
The notion of May Williams as a Mother Teresa figure comes from Manuel. In an October 1, 2000 note, he wrote, "May never got the credit for raising her family alone and much more in a country full of Depression! She did more with a Bible than Ted with baseball. If the country accepted women preaching the streets in the 1910's, 20's, 30's, 40's or even the 50's, then she would have been a Mother Teresa to America. May Williams was just too early for public praise or the advertising media of today! I feel very strongly about Aunt May and her quest to deliver the Word of God in the Depths of Sin. Believe me, there were many whom May Williams led to the promises of Jesus. Her goal: Salvation and your name written in the Book of Life. Ted was ashamed of his mother; I wish I had a mother who cared for me!"

95)   *Communications from Manuel Herrera, February 25, 2000 and September 3, 2001*

96)   *Information from conversation with several Venzor relatives at Dee Allen's house, March 2003*

97)   *Communication from Manuel Herrera, November 4, 2002*

98)   *Communication from Manuel Herrera, February 16, 2000*

99)   *Interview with Manuel Herrera, May 29, 1999*

100) *Communication from Manuel Herrera, May 25, 1999*

101) *Interview with Ted Williams, November 23, 2002*

102) *Communications from Ted Williams, December 27, 2003 and Sam Williams on July 23, 2004.*
May's son Ted attended his brother's funeral, but May herself moved to Santa Barbara several months before Danny died. Sam Williams wrote, "As his health worsened, the family was concerned how she would react to his death. She never knew my dad had died."

103) *Interview with Sarah Diaz, May 31, 1999*

104) *Communication from Manuel Herrera, April 30, 2000. Manuel clearly had Ted in mind.*

105) *Interview with Sarah Diaz, May 31, 1999, and communication from Manuel Herrera, June 2, 1999*

106) *Communication from Manuel Herrera, April 30, 2000*

107) *Ibidem*

108)   Communication from Manuel Herrera, October 23, 2000

109)   Interview with Sarah Diaz, May 31, 1999.
       Sarah's reference to the Japanese attack reminds us that there were two Japanese attacks on the continental United States during the Second World War. There was a February 28, 1942 shelling by a submarine near the Bankline Refinery oil field at Goleta and two airborne attempts to drop incendiary bombs in Oregon forests on September 9 and 10, 1942. Ron Kurtus says that the Goleta attack may have been a personal mission for the sub commander, who had been a ship captain who docked at Santa Barbara in the late 1930s and suffered a real loss of face. He was given a tour of the area, and "as the captain was admiring some scenery on a hillside, he backed up and lost his footing. He fell backwards into a bed of cactus! His guests burst into laughter at his misfortune. The captain did not understand the American sense of humor and felt that he was being ridiculed by these people. He vowed to get revenge on Americans and on Santa Barbara." Returning as commander of a submarine, he shelled the pier and also the nearby oil field, but no one was injured and virtually no damage was done. However, the captain did gain a measure of revenge. Ron Kurtus, "When the Japanese Attacked Santa Barbara," found on the Internet at www.school-for-champions.com/history/sbattack.htm.]

110)   Communication from Manuel Herrera, May 29, 1999

111)   Interview with Teresa Cordero Contreras, May 28, 2000

112)   Interview with Teresa Cordero Contreras, December 29, 2003

113)   Interview with Mary Redding, May 16, 2000

114)   Interview with Teresa Cordero Contreras, May 28, 2000

115)   Ibidem

116)   Communication from Manuel Herrera, August 22, 2000

117)   Interview with Teresa Cordero Contreras, December 29, 2003

118)   Communication from Manuel Herrera, June 7, 2000

119)   Communication from Manuel Herrera, December 27, 2000

120)   Interview with Teresa Cordero Contreras, December 29, 2003

121)   Communication from Manuel Herrera, June 7, 2000

122)   Communication from Mary Redding, November 26, 2002

123)   Communication from Manuel Herrera, October 13, 2001

124)   Interviews with Frank Venzor, May 15 and 18, 2000

125)   Communication from Manuel Herrera, October 11, 2000

126)   Ibidem

127)   Communication from Manuel Herrera, June 7, 2002

128)   Interview with Ruth Gonzales, February 28, 2003

129)   Communication from Manuel Herrera, June 9, 1999

130)   Communication from Manuel Herrera, May 31, 1999

131)   Communication from Manuel Herrera, June 9, 1999

132)   Saul C. Venzor obituary, Santa Barbara News-Press, August 16, 1963

133)   Interview with Danny Venzor, December 28, 2003. Sarah's memory comes from the May, 31, 1999 interview.

134)   Communications from Manuel Herrera, May 7 and May 19, 2000

135)   Ibidem

136)   Interview with Frank Venzor, May 19, 2000

137)   Interview with Rosalie Larson, March 2, 2003

138)   Communication from Manuel Herrera, April 3, 2003.
       Attempts to confirm that Saul Venzor faced Babe Ruth at any time have so far proven fruitless.

139)   Interview with Frank Venzor, May 19, 2000

140)   John Zant, Santa Barbara News-Press, July 6, 2002

141)   Ibidem

142) *Interview with Dee Allen, December 29, 2003*

143) *Ibidem*

144) *Communications from Manuel Herrera, May 4, 2000 and January 26, 2002.*
Danny Venzor scoffs at the story that Saul gave up a chance to play baseball for love. "Oh, that's bullshit! Not in my opinion. If a young guy like that has a chance, he's going to go. And coming from a poor Mexican family, to have a chance like that... there's going to be more than that to stop a guy from going." Interview with Danny Venzor, December 28, 2003

145) *Interviews with Frank Venzor, May 15 and May 18, 2000*

146) *Communications from Manuel Herrera, June 9, 1999 and December 27, 2000*

147) *Interview with Dee Allen, December 29, 2003*

148) *Communication from Manuel Herrera, May 19, 2000*

149) *Communication from Manuel Herrera, June 16, 2002*

150) *John Zant, Santa Barbara News-Press, op. cit. The stranger "poked his head in the door while we were having breakfast, saying he was looking for the elevator. He was looking to check out. He had gotten off on the wrong floor." Interview with Danny Venzor, op. cit.]*

151) *Ibidem*

152) *Communications from Manuel Herrera, May 16 and 17, 2002*

153) *Interview with Charles Venzor, April 17, 2002.*
Chaz grew up with his mother, after his parents divorced, and never played baseball other than a bit at school. But Dee played some. She was a third baseman on a number of softball teams that she joined after she'd graduated school. She allowed as how she was a good runner, but she also had some of that hand-eye coordination. "I was the leadoff hitter because I could usually hit the ball." Dee played for a few years against teams from Oxnard and Ventura and other communities until about age 25 or so. "Did you ever imagine yourself as Ted Williams?" "Oh, no!" There was no such fantasy at play. Paul Venzor's daughter Rozie used to play some, too, and thinks she maybe played against Dee at one point. Like her famous uncle, Rozie played left field. "I really can't say I was that good," she laughed. "But it was fun." Ted's name was invoked, though. Rozie reports that once or twice Aunt Madeline used to yell out at her while she was up at the plate, "Do a Ted Williams!!" Conversation with Dee Allen and Rosalie Larson in Santa Barbara, March 2, 2003.

154) *Interview with Sarah Diaz, May 31, 1999*

155) *Interview with Sam Williams, August 14, 2002*

156) *Sarah makes it sound as though May received a commission on each copy of the magazine she sold. I am assured that Salvation Army soldiers do not.*

157) *Interview with Sarah Diaz, May 31, 1999.*
Ruth Gonzalez says that when Ted first started playing with the San Diego Padres, May mailed newspaper writeups to the Ponce family in El Paso.

158) *Forrest Warren, "I'd Ruther Be Ruth," Boston Globe, September 8, 1946.*
One hopes that May didn't click off her radio after the first home run; Ted went 4-for-4 with two home runs.

159) *Interview with Sarah Diaz, May 31, 1999*

160) *Communication from Manuel Herrera, June 6, 1999*

161) *Communication from Manuel Herrera, June 7, 2002*

162) *Interview with Teresa Cordero Contreras, December 29, 2003*

163) *Interviews with Frank Venzor, May 15 & 18, 2000*

164) *Communication from Rosalie Larson, December 13, 2003*

165) *Ibidem*

166) *Communication from Manuel Herrera, May 19, 2000*

167) *Communication from Manuel Herrera, June 7, 2002*

168) *Interviews with Frank Venzor, May 15 & 18, 2000*

169) *Communication from Manuel Herrera, July 26, 2002*

170) *Communication from Manuel Herrera, May 31, 1999*

171) *Communication from Ted Williams, March 2003*

172) *Communication from Manuel Herrera, June 7, 2000*

173) *Interview with Danny Venzor, May 7, 2000*

174) *Ibidem*

175) *Interviews with Danny Venzor, May 7, 2000 and December 28, 2003.*
       It wasn't that Bruno expected his son to become the next Ted Williams. "But he wanted me to play some ball.
       Professional. Just make the Coast League. A good living."

176) *Communication from Manuel Herrera, June 3, 1999*

177) *Communication from Manuel Herrera, May 19, 2000*

178) *Interview with Danny Venzor, May 7, 2000. There is a stretch of roadway near San Diego named the Ted Williams Freeway.*

179) *Leigh Montville,* Ted Williams, *op. cit., p. 18*

180) *Communication from Manuel Herrera, May 12, 2000*

181) *Interview with Dr. Howard Winet, November 23, 2002*

182) *Ibidem*

183) *Ibidem*

184) *Communication from Mary Redding, November 26, 2002*

185) *Communication from Manuel Herrera, October 12, 2001*

186) *Communication from Manuel Herrera, May 2, 2000*

187) *Communication from Dr. Howard Winet, December 5, 2003*

188) Hitter, *pp. 17, 18*

189) *Ibid., pp. 32-33.*
       Later, on page 72, Linn termed him a "rotten brother." Even with the assistance of California corrections officials, it has
       been impossible to confirm that Danny Williams ever served time in San Quentin.

190) *Steve Corey, "Why Ted Williams Plays It Cool,"* Uncensored, *August 1961*

191) Hitter, *op. cit., pp. 324-5*

192) My Turn At Bat, *op. cit., pp. 31-32*

193) *Ibid., p. 32.*
       Manuel Herrera believed that Danny had taken his own life with that pistol, but the fact that he'd been in the hospital
       for seven days prior to his death would suggest otherwise. His son Sam states for a fact that Danny died in the hospital.

194) *Interview with Sarah Diaz, May 31, 1999*

195) *Interview with Manuel Herrera, May 29, 1999*

196) *Interview with Teresa Cordero Contreras, May 30, 2000*

197) *Communication from Manuel Herrera, June 2, 2000*

198) *Communication from Manuel Herrera, June 13, 2000*

199) *Communication from Manuel Herrera, May 3, 2000*

200) *Interview with Joe Villarino, May 9, 1997*

201) *Steve Corey,* Uncensored, *op. cit.*

202) *Interview with Leonard Bell, September 19, 2003*

203) *Interview with Ted Williams, November 23, 2002*

204) *Ibidem*

205) *Interview with Jan Williams, February 2003*

206) *Interview with Ted Williams, November 23, 2003.*
       One is reminded, of course, that Danny's father's military record reflected "no unauthorized absence of record."

207) *Communications from Manuel Herrera, May 3, 2000 and July 21, 2002*

208) *Interview with Sam Williams, August 14, 2002*

209) *Interview with Ted Williams, November 23, 2002*

210) *Ibidem.*
Sam added a note while editing this piece in May 2004: "Yeah – that was really fun."

211) *Ibidem*

212) *Ibidem*

213) *Interview with Sam Williams, August 14, 2002.*
There may be a Williams in baseball's future, though. Ted's son Noah Williams played first base in youth baseball during the summer of 2003. He was having a little trouble catching up with the fastball, but with another season or two under his belt, who knows…?

214) *Interview with Ted Williams, November 23, 2002*

215) *Ibidem*

216) *Ibidem*

217) *Ibidem*

218) *Ibidem*

219) *Communication from Manuel Herrera, May 3, 2000.*
If the pistol was for protection against union partisans, he may have overcome the need. He and Jean lived for some time at 716 West Grace Street in Chicago, and Danny was initiated into the Brotherhood of Painters, Decorators and Paperhangers I.U. 147 on September 9, 1957, per a union book in his son's possession. "He liked guns and books about guns," Ted recalls. "I remember him strapping his pistol on the steering column of the car whenever we traveled some distance, and him getting busted for it once." Communication from Ted Williams, August 24, 2002.

220) *Communication from Manuel Herrera, July 2, 2000*

221) *Interview with Manuel Herrera, May 29, 1999 and communication dated July 2, 2000*

222) *Ibidem*

223) *Communication from Manuel Herrera, July 3, 2000*

224) *Communication from Ted Williams, September 8, 2003*

225) *Communication from Ted Williams, August 24, 2002*

226) *Ibidem*

227) *Steve Connolly, "Time with son made Kid happy" Boston Herald, July 14, 2002*

228) *Interview with Steve Brown, July 19, 2004*

229) *Communications from Manuel Herrera, May 31, 1999 and January 12, 2004*

230) *Communication from Manuel Herrera, May 2, 2000*

231) *Interview with Gene Bowman, January 19, 2004*

232) *Interview with Gabriel Arellanes, January 19, 2004*

233) *Interview with Greg Venzor, February 19, 2004*

234) *Interviews with Davey Gonzalez and Ruth Gonzalez, February 19, 2004*

235) *Anthony J. Conner, Baseball for the Love Of It (NY: Simon & Shuster, 1982)*

236) *Interview with Mary Redding, May 16, 2000*

237) *Interview with Dr. Howard Winet, November 23, 2002.*
As we have seen, Dr. Winet's family had changed their name from Winetski, because of another form of prejudice.

238) *Interviews with Connie Matthews, November 26 and December 10, 2002.*

239) *Interview with Ruth Gonzales, February 28, 2003*

240) *Frank Venzor, in conversation at Dee Allen's house in Santa Barbara, March 2003.*
Manuel Herrera told essentially the same story in communications on May 3 and June 2, 2000. Madeline's sister Teresa confirmed the story and Ted's words. Asked if she thought Ted's outburst reflected some embarrassment to be associated with Hispanic or Indian people, she said, "I don't think so. He was so upset with her. I don't think he was prejudiced. He never appeared to me like he was. He loved my dad, and my dad, well, he was Indian. He was Indian and Spanish. Ted would come over and they'd talk. My mom would shoo us out. 'Little kids, get out of here' and they would speak. I can't see him being unrespectful or anything." Interview with Teresa Cordero Contreras, December 29, 2003. I also spoke to Ruth Gonzales on February 19, 2004 and she said, about Ted, "He didn't claim any relatives" (meaning that he kept his relatives at arm's length.) I asked about Sarah Diaz, and she said Sarah was the exception. "She was the only one that Ted wanted to see. Ted would tell Sarah, 'Don't tell anybody. If you do, I will never come and visit you again.' Some of her cousins, when May died, wanted to go see Ted Williams. He had a private funeral. They didn't say anything much about May; they just wanted to see Ted Williams."

241) *Interview with David Ronquillo, October 23, 2003.*
There is no evidence that the Red Sox did offer such advice to young Williams.

242) *Ibidem*

243) *Communication from Manuel Herrera, April 30, 2000*

244) *Interview with David Ronquillo, November 24, 2003.*
David found some papers his own mother had written, telling about experiences of discrimination she had experienced. "When my mother first went into the missionary field, she was severely discriminated against. As a result, she convinced my dad – who was very Hispanic and very proud of his Hispanic heritage – to move into a kind of Anglo environment. My mother, I think, was very conscious of all this. I'm just speculating that May may have been in the same situation. When I began school, I couldn't speak English. My grandmother lived with us, who would have been May Williams' aunt, I believe. My dad was more comfortable speaking Spanish, more comfortable than speaking English. My mother was fully bilingual. But I realize by reading my mother's memoirs that she really went through a period of time when she was severely discriminated against and I think she really wanted to see her children integrated into the Anglo environment so that they didn't have to go through that." David adds his observation that there are "far more people in our family from my generation that don't speak any Spanish than there are those that speak Spanish. From what I'm gathering, May spoke English very well, and my guess was that that was the only language spoken at home for Ted."

245) *Interview with Ruth Gonzales, February 28, 2003.*
Ruth herself was a bilingual instructional aide at Los Cerritos Grammar School in the City of Paramount for 20 years, so she was attuned to questions of the use of language.

246) *Interview with Maureen Surratt, January 5, 2004.*
Maureen and her husband farm near El Paso today, working a field just a block away from the Rio Grande. Ernest Ponce was the first Hispanic elected to the El Paso City Council, where he served from 1951 to 1957. He died March 15, 2002.

247) *Interview with Ted Williams, November 23, 2002*

248) *Ibidem*

249) *Interview with Teresa Cordero Contreras, May 28, 2000*

250) *Interview with David Ronquillo, November 24, 2003.*
Times have changed. David is proud of his heritage, and Ted's nephew Ted wrote me, "According to Danny, Ted liked to call the rest of the family 'the Mexicans,' though I think it was more jokingly than serious. May always said they were Spanish, not Mexican, of course. I always liked the idea of being part Mexican: seemed very romantic!" Communication from Ted Williams, October 29, 2002

251) *Interview with Ruth Gonzales, February 23, 2003*

252) *Interviews with Joe Villarino, May 9 and July 5, 1997*

253) *Communication from Leigh Montville, February 26, 2004*

254) *Interview with Frank Cushing, January 24, 2004*

255) *Syndicated column by Ted Williams, written December 13, 1962*

WHAT IF TED HAD STAYED AT HOME?
by Carlos Bauer

When the hot days of May turned into the even hotter days of June, the only thing that even remotely kept me glued to my grammar school seat was the thought that I might being sitting in the very same chair that Ted Williams did all those years before. I went to the same grammar school as Ted Williams, Garfield Elementary – or Garbagefield as it was then commonly called by us kids, perhaps the same as it was called in Ted's time. Some twenty years after going east, Ted Williams still remained a big presence in the neighborhood. We hit baseballs on the same fields he had hit them on, and every time we stood there at bat we knew that Ted Williams had stood there on that same spot. We used to ride our bicycles over to Ted's house to occasionally catch a glimpse of his mother. Why, I don't know. We just did it to, maybe, get close to Ted, as he was the only person in the neighborhood who really made it big. Boston was a long way away, so we worshiped him from afar.

As so, too, were the major leagues. Our baseball consisted of baseball in the Pacific Coast League – or Coast League, as most called it out here. The Coast League Padres was our team, the team with which Ted Williams began his O. B. [organized baseball – ed.] career. But being a Coast League fan meant having to lose heroes all too soon. Either by sale or by call up to the majors. I don't think I was alone in wondering what the Padres would have done if we had Rocky Colavito for a whole season, or Mudcat Grant for another season. From there, it didn't take much to wonder what Colavito would have hit in a full season, or what would Mudcat Grant's 10-win season in the majors have been for the Padres.

It was these last two cases of players leaving San Diego for the majors that got me thinking about what Ted Williams' record might have been like had he remained at home in San Diego, and played his whole career with the minor league Padres. I really never thought I'd ever be able to do much more than just speculate on what his career might have turned out to be. But in the 1980s, Bill James first came up with his theory of major league equivalencies. At the time they didn't seem to be completely fleshed out, but it got me thinking about Ted Williams playing for the Padres again. I thought that James was probably onto something, but believed he'd have to take them through a number of refinements, as he did his other tools, before major league equivalencies could be used with any great deal of exactitude, and quickly forgot about it.

Everything changed, however, when I stumbled upon a small note by John Dewan in the *STATS 1994 Minor League Handbook* that preceded the "Major League Equivalencies" section: "This year we spent many, many hours of research on the MLE system. We were expecting that with all the additional information that we've gathered over the years since Bill developed the system we'd be able to improve on the system. Bill's initial development has withstood the test of time."

That, of course, sent me scurrying back to the 1992 *Minor League Handbook*, where James' Major League Equivalencies was first presented systematically, and where I came across the following: "The 'normal' M2M [majors-to-minors productivity ratio] was .82. What does that mean? That means that the average hitter was 82 percent as productive in the major league season as he had been in the minor league season which came immediately before or after the major league season — or, stated the other way, the normal shrinkage of production is about 18%." And further on, James concludes, "Obviously, not all of the M2M figures were at .82; there were some at .58 and some at .99. But they were not all over the board; they tended to cluster right around .82."

While I still have some reservations about using Bill James' assumptions about major-minor equivalencies, especially in regard to the old Coast League, I felt much better about using it after the STATS crew did their massive study.

CALCULATING A CAREER TO KILL FOR:

Calculating Ted Williams' theoretical PCL career is a two-step process. In the first step, I calculated what percentage of games Ted Williams played for Boston, and, additionally, calculated how many plate appearances per game he made for each season, which I would keep as a constant throughout the calculations. (Note: I used a modified PA that only included at bats plus walks.) From there I calculated the number of games Williams would have played if he had played the same percentage of games for the Padres as he did for Boston. If we take the 1942 season for an example, we have Ted playing 150 of the 152 games Boston played that season, or some 98.7 percent of the Red Sox games. The San Diego Padres played 178 games that season, so Williams would have appeared in 98.7 percent of those games, or 175.7 games. (From 1939 through 1957, the San Diego Padres played anywhere from 167 games in a season up to 201 games in a single season.) Next I calculated a proportional increase for all the statistics, meaning that 175.7 games was an increase of 117.1 percent over 150 games played, and I used that to increase hits (from his actual total of 186 to 217.8) doubles (from 34 to 39.8), home runs (from 36 to 42.4), RBI (from 137 to 160.4), etc., while maintaining the same batting average, etc. (I should note that I did not round off any number until calculating the final numbers.)

Beginning in 1958, the Pacific Coast League adopted a 154 game schedule, so in 1958, for instance, Ted's number of games would be less than he actually played for Boston because the Padres played only 153 games that season while the Red Sox played 155 games.

THE INFLATOR:

In the second part, I simply used the Bill James' deflator as an inflator, with a slight modification. During Williams' career there were only 16 major league teams, so the talent pool in the minors was comparatively better then than it is today. Also, one has to take into consideration the fact that major league players many times returned to the minors to end their careers, arguably making the minors even better. I don't know how much better the high minors were than today, especially in the earlier years of Williams' career, but it's conceivable that it might have been 5 percent better than today. And maybe it was no better than today by the time Ted Williams retired. What I decide to do was split the difference between 0 percent and 5 percent, and reduced the James' deflator by a purely arbitrary 2 1/2 percent, which gave me 84 1/2 percent for the PCL rather than James' 82 percent. (I made the arbitrary decision of assuming the PCL 2 1/2 percent better than the American Association.)

To get our final numbers I multiplied the revised stats by 118.432 percent (18.432 percent rather than 15 1/2 percent when used to go from 100 percent down to 84 1/2 percent) to yield the final numbers: hits, 257.8; doubles, 47.1; home runs, 49.9; RBI, 189.9, etc. At that point, I simply rounded off the numbers, subtracted the final, rounded off base-on-balls, and subtracted that from PA to get at bats.

As a point of comparison, Bill James' stat line for 1942 would read:

G	AB	R	H	2B	3B	HR	RBI	K	BB	SB	AVG
176	574	201	266	49	7	51	196	73	207	4	.463

SOME RESOLVED & UNRESOLVED ISSUES:

Ballpark effects: Let's look at the home parks for Ted Williams. Williams would be going from Fenway Park to Lane Field, and then on to Westgate Park for his last three seasons. As we have learned from other James' studies in the *Baseball Abstract*, Fenway Park tended to favor left-handed power hitters somewhat. Lane Field in San Diego had a slight prevailing wind off the bay out to right field, favoring Williams also. Some have also speculated that the right field fence at Lane Field was even a tad shorter than the stated 325 feet. So for those years (through 1957), Williams would probably have gone from a friendly park to a slightly friendlier park, so one could argue that his home run totals should be increased at Lane Field over the ones generated in this study. Additionally, there was no comparable American League park to Wrigley Field in Los Angeles. Though not a home park, Wrigley Field was a real launching pad, and would have been an ideal place for Ted Williams to add to his HR totals. The one year that Wrigley Field was used as an American League Park (1962), some 248 home runs were hit there, and the short power alley in right was ideally suited to Ted Williams home-run swing. Playing there up to 14 games a season would have had to added more than a few home runs to his totals. On the other hand, playing at Seals Stadium in San Francisco would have cut down on his home runs totals there.

In his last three years, Williams would have played at Westgate Park in Mission Valley, a park that had a slight prevailing cross wind, aiding for left-handed hitters slightly. The fences also were further away, but, in general, Westgate Park appeared to be a neutral park for batters, in all other aspects, so I decided to make no corrections to the generated numbers.

Minneapolis' Nicollet Park was where Ted played in 1938, with its exceedingly short fence in right. According to John Holway, in his book *The Last .400 Hitter*, Williams hit 24 HR at Nicollet Park, and another 19 homers on the road. In 1937, Williams hit 17 at Lane Field and 6 HR on the road. Williams' home-run distribution, at least for that one season (1938), seems to be right in line with Lane Field a year earlier, so I decided to make no changes other than those of playing a longer schedule in the Coast League, and giving the Coast League a 2 1/2 percent advantage.

The Anomaly of the 1946 PCL Season

That season the PCL – I'm convinced – used the same ball as the National League, or one just as bad. Each team in the PCL scored 4.59 runs per game in 1945; it then dropped to 3.77 in 1946; and jumped back up to 4.56 in 1947. Batting averages for those years were .278, .254 and .273. The numbers for the NL in those years were 4.54, down to 3.96 and then back up to 4.57, with corresponding BA's of .265, .256 and .265. A corresponding drop did not occur in the American League in 1946; therefore, my numbers no doubt overstate Ted Williams' record that season by some 8 to 10 percent.

In reviewing Ted Williams' theoretical career, the thing that strikes me – and others – most is how plausible the numbers seem. While we will never know what the real numbers would have been, they just feel right. A lifetime record of 774 home runs and a .416 lifetime batting average seem incredible at first blush. Yet I find it hard to argue that his career could have yielded much lower totals. After all, just ask yourself what a lifetime .344 hitter in the majors would hit in the minors, or what does 521 lifetime home runs translate to in Triple A?

But the final judgment I'll leave to the readers.

TED WILLIAMS
Theoretical Coast League Career

Year	Team	League	G	AB	R	H	1B	2B	3B	HR	RBI	K	BB	SB	AVG
1936	San Diego	PCL	42	107	18	29	19	8	2	0	11			2	.271
1937	San Diego	PCL	138	454	66	132	83	24	2	23	98			1	.291
1938	San Diego	PCL	173	623	149	221	128	34	10	49	162	86	130	1	.355
1939	San Diego	PCL	173	631	180	254	137	60	15	42	199	88	147	3	.405
1940	San Diego	PCL	167	632	184	265	155	59	19	32	155	74	132	6	.419
1941	San Diego	PCL	152	487	181	249	151	44	4	50	161	36	195	3	.511
1942	San Diego	PCL	176	580	195	258	154	47	7	50	190	71	201	4	.445
1943-45	In Military Service														
1946	San Diego	PCL	179	579	200	248	131	52	11	54	174	62	220	0	.428
1947	San Diego	PCL	189	603	179	259	143	57	13	46	163	67	232	0	.430
1948	San Diego	PCL	167	592	179	271	168	63	4	36	183	59	182	6	.458
1949	San Diego	PCL	189	654	216	280	158	56	4	62	229	69	234	1	.428
1950	San Diego	PCL	116	416	127	164	82	37	2	43	150	32	127	5	.394
1951	San Diego	PCL	160	547	140	217	138	36	5	38	162	58	185	1	.397
1952	San Diego	PCL	7	11	3	6	4	0	1	1	4	3	3	0	.545
1953	San Diego	PCL	44	103	24	52	26	8	0	18	47	14	26	0	.505
1954	San Diego	PCL	127	392	119	171	104	29	1	37	114	41	174	0	.436
1955	San Diego	PCL	109	339	102	151	82	28	4	37	110	32	120	3	.445
1956	San Diego	PCL	147	413	91	177	107	36	3	31	105	50	131	0	.429
1957	San Diego	PCL	144	434	124	210	124	36	1	49	112	56	154	0	.484
1958	San Diego	PCL	127	388	95	158	99	27	2	30	99	57	114	1	.407
1959	San Diego	PCL	103	262	38	82	52	18	0	12	51	32	62	0	.313
1960	San Diego	PCL	112	292	65	114	62	18	0	34	84	48	88	1	.390
Coast League totals			**2941**	**9539**	**2675**	**3968**	**2307**	**777**	**110**	**774**	**2763**	**1035**	**2857**	**37**	**.41598**

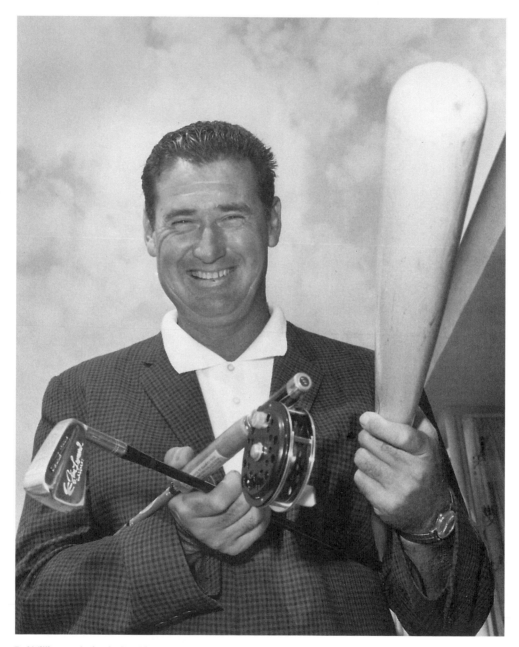

Ted Williams, relaxing in San Diego, August 27, 1965.

"I NEVER MET A SPORTSWRITER I DIDN'T LIKE"
by Bill Nowlin

When the San Diego Padres officially joined the National League, preparing for their first season of play in 1969, what better choice for manager was there than the Padres' Coast League veteran Ted Williams? The Kid from San Diego's final season as a player for the Padres had been in 1960 – and he'd gone out in style, hitting a home run in his last at-bat in the Pacific Coast League. It was homer #774 for "The Splendid Splinter" – a solo shot into the Padres' bullpen out in right field, RBI number 2763.

As Ted himself wrote afterwards, "I'm glad it's over. Before anything else, understand that I am glad it's over." It really was time. After the close of the 1960 season, Ted relaxed in his offshore home in Coronado, enjoying his privacy and the fishing it offered him. This was a man who was 42 years old, and he'd been playing baseball before hometown crowds since 1934 at Hoover High School (and on city playgrounds before that.) A giant of a man, immensely popular with the people and the press in San Diego, it was time for a break.

Ted had taken off a few years after his 22 years as a Padre, even traveling a bit to places like Boston and Florida. "I don't know why, but I have long wanted to visit Boston," he told reporters after he returned from a weeklong visit in 1963. "I was glad to see Johnny Pesky, the manager of the Red Sox. I'd known Johnny back when he was the clubhouse kid up in Portland back in '36 and '37. What a great city. The people there were friendly, and the newspapermen I met were all as helpful as could be." In one of his rare forays to the East Coast, Ted spent a month in Florida, staying with friends in Islamorada, and had a chance to fish in the Keys. "Next year, I'm going to head up to Canada. I hear they've got some great salmon fishing up in New Brunswick on the Miramachi." Williams is known, of course, for his long history of fishing for Pacific coho salmon in the Northwestern United States, British Columbia and the Yukon with old Padres teammate Bobby Doerr. His outspoken and consistent conservation efforts resulted in Ted's induction into the Pacific Salmon Fishing Hall of Fame.

Ted always came back to his hometown, though. In San Diego, where Ted enjoyed hosting his annual "Salute to Sportswriters" dinner – attracting the best of America's sportswriters each year – Ted's popularity was unrivaled. Known by the honorific "Don Ted" in the local Hispanic community, he remained a fixture in the city, and some were already touting him for Mayor of San Diego while still in his final years with the ballclub.

His later successful tenure as Mayor, Congressman and Governor of California (handily beating former baseball broadcaster Ronald Reagan for the Republican nomination) are, of course, well-known. Williams' reform of the Selective Service System and overhaul of military recruitment policies as a freshman Congressman effectively re-tooled the armed services at a time of crisis during the short-lived conflict in Vietnam. Many believe that Williams' counsel helped prevent the initial brushfire there from escalating into a war that could have killed hundreds of American GI's.

Ted and family were known for their charitable good works. Ted's own work raising money for kids with cancer grew into one of the more successful grass-roots fundraising efforts in southern California. His brother Danny followed in the footsteps of his father Samuel and was an active crusader for prison reform, founding and heading up the California Corrections Council. Though he never met his grandmother May, Ted's son John-Henry was inspired deeply by her example. He dedicated himself to selfless service with the Salvation Army.

Though Ted spent eight years in Hollywood making films alongside John Wayne and Robert Ryan, he never forgot the town where it all began and he was a frequent visitor to the area, or to Santa Barbara where many of his mother's relatives lived and where many Western films were shot on the Flying A Studios lot or at the Tecolote Ranch (managed by his uncle Pete Venzor.)

Some felt that the lure of the limelight came a year too soon. There were many who hoped that Ted would have gone for 800 home runs, but after the disappointing 1959 season when he only hit 12, Ted was content to go out with 34 home runs and at least a respectable return to form. He was, after all, 42 years old.

Ted Williams lost most of five baseball seasons while in military service during World War II and Korea, and fans of the San Diego star debated long hours about the records Ted might have set had he not lost so much prime time. There's no doubt that he was the greatest hitter that ever lived. A lifetime average of .416. Thirteen seasons hitting .400 or better, and the only .500 season in history. Sixteen batting titles. Ten times, he led the league in homers and a full fourteen times in runs batted in. Williams won the Triple Crown an unprecedented eight times. It would be a dramatic understatement to say that pitchers feared him. Four times he finished the season with over 200 walks, including a record 234 times in 1949.

If he'd had five more seasons, who knows what he might have accomplished? Barring serious injury, he might have hit 1000 homers, over 4500 hits and over 3500 RBI. Using any simple weighted projection – the lost years were prime years - he would have sported a higher lifetime average, with an on-base percentage through the roof and an equally stratospheric slugging percentage. Because the PCL did not maintain accurate figures for walks and strikeouts in Ted's first two years, it is not possible to correctly project what his figures might have been in 1943-1945. Looking at his next three seasons, however, one sees that he averaged 135 walks per season. He only broke in late in June, 1936 and didn't play full-time in 1937, either. Based on his 561 at bats in the two years combined, it's a fair bet that he would have walked maybe 100 times - even allowing for pitchers not being as wary of Williams' bat as they soon became. Add 100 walks to his career total of 2857. Leave out hit by pitch, which figures we do not have at all. Hits plus walks = 6925. At-bats plus walks = 12496. Divide the two, and Ted totaled a .554 lifetime on-base percentage. No one else was even close.

Slugging average? Total bases (7287) divided by at-bats (9539) = .764 lifetime, a full 74 points above Babe Ruth's lifetime .690.

Not bad for a guy who, through baseball diplomacy as a United States Marine pilot, ended the Korean War and brought unity and peace to the Korean peninsula.

As manager of the Padres, Williams molded a class of great hitters and led San Diego to two straight pennants, losing to the Boston Red Sox once and then beating them the following year, 1972. Ted retired from baseball after that championship '72 season, but stayed on as a Padre elder and special assignment instructor. He particularly enjoyed working with younger players during

Cactus League Spring Training and his frequent appearances in Old Timers Games. The team he launched went on to win three more World Series in the next ten years, equaled only by the three apiece won by the Red Sox and the Chicago Cubs.

Ted Williams almost ended up on the New York Yankees, and there were whispers that even the Red Sox had been interested at one point. After Bill Starr purchased the Padres from Bill Lane, prior to the 1945 season, a new era in Padres baseball began. Starr wanted to make the Pacific Coast League into a third major league and held a number of meetings with AL and NL clubs to that effect. In the interim he sought a working agreement with the Yankees and met with Yankees owner Del Webb. Word has it that late one night, Webb and Starr had been drinking and talking and actually shook hands on a blockbuster trade: the Padres' Ted Williams for Yankees star Joe DiMaggio.

Thankfully, that rumored trade was called off when daylight (and good sense) came to Padres owner Starr the following morning. Otherwise, The Splendid San Diego Splinter might never have become the stalwart of the San Diego sports scene.

As his favorite reporter, Dave Deegan – "the Admiral" – always proclaimed, "The Kid is our kid, and we love him no matter what. No writer in this town would ever write a bad word about good old Teddy Ballgame." Williams, as always, tipped his cap in response, with his trademark phrase, "I never met a sportswriter I didn't like."

TED WILLIAMS

Theoretical Coast League Career without Military Service

Year	Team	League	G	AB	R	H	1B	2B	3B	HR	RBI	K	BB	SB	AVG
1936	San Diego	PCL	42	107	18	29	19	8	2	0	11			2	.271
1937	San Diego	PCL	138	454	66	132	83	24	2	23	98			1	.291
1938	San Diego	PCL	173	623	149	221	128	34	10	49	162	86	130	1	.355
1939	San Diego	PCL	173	631	180	254	137	60	15	42	199	88	147	3	.403
1940	San Diego	PCL	167	632	184	265	155	59	19	32	155	74	132	6	.419
1941	San Diego	PCL	152	487	181	249	151	44	4	50	161	36	195	3	.511
1942	San Diego	PCL	176	580	195	258	154	47	7	50	190	71	201	4	.445
1943	San Diego	PCL	164	533	188	253	153	45	5	50	175	53	198	3	.475
1944	San Diego	PCL	177	579	197	253	143	49	9	52	182	66	210	2	.437
1945	San Diego	PCL	184	591	189	253	137	54	12	50	168	64	226	0	.428
1946	San Diego	PCL	179	579	200	248	131	52	11	54	174	62	220	0	.428
1947	San Diego	PCL	189	603	179	259	143	57	13	46	163	67	232	0	.430
1948	San Diego	PCL	167	592	179	271	168	63	4	36	183	59	182	6	.458
1949	San Diego	PCL	189	654	216	280	158	56	4	62	229	69	234	1	.428
1950	San Diego	PCL	116	416	127	164	82	37	2	43	150	32	127	5	.394
1951	San Diego	PCL	160	547	140	217	138	36	5	38	162	58	185	1	.397
1952	San Diego	PCL	143	469	129	196	123	31	4	38	139	51	178	0	.418
1953	San Diego	PCL	144	470	120	195	115	32	3	45	149	50	159	0	.415
1954	San Diego	PCL	127	392	119	171	104	29	1	37	114	41	174	0	.436
1955	San Diego	PCL	109	339	102	151	82	28	4	37	110	32	120	3	.445
1956	San Diego	PCL	147	413	91	177	107	36	3	31	105	50	131	0	.429
1957	San Diego	PCL	144	434	124	210	124	36	1	49	112	56	154	0	.484
1958	San Diego	PCL	127	388	95	158	99	27	2	30	99	57	114	1	.407
1959	San Diego	PCL	103	262	38	82	52	18	0	12	51	32	62	0	.313
1960	San Diego	PCL	112	292	65	114	62	18	0	34	84	48	88	1	.390
Coast League Totals			**3702**	**12067**	**3471**	**5060**	**2948**	**980**	**142**	**990**	**3525**	**1302**	**3799**	**42**	**.419**

WHAT MIGHT HAVE BEEN

How might Ted Williams have done had he never served in the military and played out his full career with the Padres? This requires doing projections on top of projections. Carlos Bauer was busy, so I tried this myself with the help of SABR's Bill Deane. To come up with stats for each of the World War II years, I averaged stats from the two closest years. For 1943, thus, I averaged 1941 and 1942. For 1944, I averaged 1942 and 1946. For 1945, I averaged 1946 and 1947. For 1952 and 1952, in both cases I averaged 1951 and 1954, but following Bill's suggestion, we can't disregard what Ted actually did accomplish in those two seasons during limited playing time. It's also not right to just absorb them into the projections. So I subtracted 11 at bats from 1952 and 103 from 1953, pro-rating the rest of the stats downward (i.e., multiplying '52 stats times 536/547, or .97989, and '53 stats times 289/392, or .73724.)

Taking the results, one then has to add the actual stats back in. We find that Ted's totals topped out at a .419 lifetime average, over 5000 hits, over 3500 runs batted in and a staggering 990 homers. How could Ted have stopped at 990? That 1000 figure would have proven so tantalizing that, having hit 34 homers in 1960, all he'd need to have done is come back for part of a season to reach the millennium mark in home runs.

TED WILLIAMS
Actual Career

Year	Team	League	G	AB	R	H	1B	2B	3B	HR	RBI	K	BB	SB	AVG
1936	San Diego	PCL	42	107	18	29	19	8	2	0	11			2	.271
1937	San Diego	PCL	138	454	66	132	83	24	2	23	98			1	.291
1938	Minneapolis	AA	148	528	**130**	193	111	30	9	**43**	**142**	75	**114**	1	.366
1939	Boston	AL	149	565	131	185	99	44	11	31	145	64	107	2	.327
1940	Boston	AL	144	561	**134**	193	113	43	14	23	113	54	96	4	.344
1941	Boston	AL	143	456	**135**	185	112	33	3	37	120	27	**145**	2	**.406**
1942	Boston	AL	150	522	**141**	186	111	34	5	36	137	51	**145**	3	**.356**
1943-45	In Military Service														
1946	Boston	AL	150	514	**142**	176	93	37	8	38	123	44	**156**	0	.342
1947	Boston	AL	156	528	**125**	181	100	40	9	**32**	**114**	47	**162**	0	.343
1948	Boston	AL	137	509	124	188	116	**44**	3	25	127	41	**126**	4	**.369**
1949	Boston	AL	155	566	**150**	194	109	**39**	3	**43**	**159**	48	**162**	1	.343
1950	Boston	AL	89	334	82	106	53	24	1	28	97	21	82	3	.317
1951	Boston	AL	148	531	109	169	107	28	4	30	126	45	**144**	1	.318
1952	Boston	AL	6	10	2	4	2	0	1	1	3	2	2	0	.400
1953	Boston	AL	37	91	17	37	18	6	0	13	34	10	19	0	.407
1954	Boston	AL	117	386	93	133	80	23	1	29	89	32	**136**	0	.345
1955	Boston	AL	98	320	77	114	62	21	3	28	83	24	91	2	.356
1956	Boston	AL	136	400	71	138	84	28	2	24	82	39	102	0	.345
1957	Boston	AL	132	420	96	163	96	28	1	38	87	43	119	0	**.388**
1958	Boston	AL	129	411	81	135	84	23	2	26	85	49	98	1	**.328**
1959	Boston	AL	103	272	32	69	44	15	0	10	43	27	52	0	.254
1960	Boston	AL	113	310	56	98	54	15	0	29	72	41	75	1	.316
	Minor League Totals		**328**	**1089**	**214**	**354**	**213**	**62**	**13**	**66**	**251**	**75**	**114**	**4**	**.325**
	Major League Totals		**2292**	**7706**	**1798**	**2654**	**1537**	**525**	**71**	**521**	**1839**	**709**	**2019**	**24**	**.344**

Bold numbers indicate league leadership

Ted Williams arrives at Boston's Back Bay Station, April 1939.

CONTRIBUTORS

CARLOS BAUER *is the publisher of Baseball Press Books. He is also the author of* The Historical Register, The Coast League Cyclopedia *and* The All-time Japanese Register.

DAN BOYLE *grew up in the Bronx and hates the Yankees. He is a consultant for public transit agencies, no doubt a result of all those weekend subway rides he made his parents go on with him as a kid. Despite his grandfather's admonition that "anything west of the Hudson is just camping out," he is very happy to be living in San Diego.*

TOM LARWIN *grew up on Chicago's south side as a die-hard Cubs fan, but after 28 years in San Diego he now shares his allegiance with the Padres. He has written on the San Diego's 1907 Pacific Coast Championship, and is working on a book on the 1936 PCL Padres. Taking advantage of the fact that there are no term limits, Tom has headed up SABR's Ted Williams Chapter for nearly 10 years.*

JOE B. NAIMAN *began following baseball in 1972 and has been a Padres fan ever since. He joined SABR in 1990 and is a freelance writer. Joe is a co-author of* The San Diego Padres Encyclopedia *published in 2002.*

BILL NOWLIN *editor, is the author of ten books related to Ted Williams or the Boston Red Sox. He has served for the last five-plus years as editor of publications for the Ted Williams Museum, and was elected in 2004 as Vice President of the Society for American Baseball Research. He is currently completing* Ted Williams At War, *a companion volume to this work, which will detail Ted Williams' years of military service.*

JAMES D. SMITH III *has been a SABR member since 1982. Born and raised in San Diego, he spent 18 years (with wife Linda and children Ben, Andy and Rebecca) living in Minnesota and Massachusetts. With a doctorate in church history from Harvard University, today he teaches at Bethel Seminary San Diego and the University of San Diego, while serving on the pastoral staff of College Avenue Baptist Church.*

BILL SWANK *is the author of* Echoes from Lane Field *and* Baseball in San Diego: From the Padres to Petco (1936-2004). *He is currently working on* Baseball in San Diego: From the Plaza to the Padres (1871-1936). *His scale model of Lane Field is on display at the San Diego Hall of Champions.*

STEW THORNLEY *is the author of more than 35 books on sports. His first book,* On to Nicollet, *was a history of the Minneapolis Millers, the team Ted Williams played for in 1938. Thornley enjoys visiting the graves of notable people and has been to every grave of members of the Baseball Hall of Fame, a quest that has taken him across the United States as well as to Cuba.*

JAY WALKER *a native New Englander, currently resides in San Diego, a mere 3 or 4 homerun shots from Teddy Ballgame's boyhood home.*

The authors see the study of Ted Williams as part of an ongoing process to document the life of this extraordinary man. We are hopeful that readers of this volume will be able to offer additional information. If you have memories or photographs of Ted Williams, or if you know of others who do, please contact Bill Nowlin via e-mail (billn@rounder.com) or regular mail in care of Rounder Books. Thank you.

Please visit the Rounder Books website for additional information and other photographs, as these become available. **www.rounderbooks.com**

PICTURE SOURCES

Dee V. Allen; 257, 283, 285, 301, 326

Ron Amidon; 216, 235 (bottom), 252, 254, 259, 270, 273, 275, 276, 282

Ron Andreassi; 37

Alice Cooper; 253

Bobby Doerr; 83, 121

Hoover High School; 13, 45, 46, 55, 63, 68, 71, 72, 78, 80, 81, 97

Ruth Gonzales; 44, 256

Alan and Linda Goodwin - 205

Manuel Herrera; 218, 219 (top), 277, 308

Brian Interland; 346

Paul Iverson; 221

Autumn Durst Keltner; 190

Rosalie Larson; 294

Tom and Kathy Larwin; 211, 213, 214, 307

Brian Luscomb; 40

Bill Nowlin; 28, 77, 91, 92, 100, 132, 138, 152, 159, 162, 208, 238

San Diego Evening Tribune; 17, 21, 22, 23

San Diego Hall of Champions; 11, 27, 31, 41, 50, 52, 53, 61, 120, 125, 127, 137, 212

San Diego Historical Society; 18, 24, 30, 183, 191, 192, 193, 194, 195, 202, 203, 242, 336

Maureen Surratt; 219 (bottom), 220, 292

Bill Swank; 88, 122, 123, 131, 134, 135, 139, 140, 143, 148, 185

Daniel Venzor; 295, 296, 297

Claudia Williams; 270

Ted Williams Museum; 129

Transcendental Graphics; 133, 160

Wilbert Wylie; 38

Daniel A. Williams, Jr. and Jan Williams; 311

May Williams; cover photographs, 8, 26, 29, 34, 36, 70, 84, 128, 161, 163, 164, 181, 182, 189, 222, 224, 226, 228, 229, 230, 232, 235 (top), 236, 239, 245, 246, 251, 261, 266, 263, 265, 266, 267, 268, 273, 280, 281, 288, 291, 292, 306, 310, 311 (top), 313, 314

Ted Williams (nephew); 79, 95, 204, 231, 234, 237, 311, 321, 327

Color Insert

All photographs in the insert are from May Williams except:

Photograph inscribed to Hoover High School is courtesy of Hoover High School.

Padres programs courtesy of Bill Swank.

Ted under Lane Field girders courtesy of the San Diego Historical Society.

October 5, 1941 photographs by Heber Epperson, courtesy of Autumn Durst Keltner.

Samuel Williams Inspector badge photo by Sam Williams (nephew).

Photograph of May Williams and Natalia Venzor courtesy Ron Amidon.

Caterina Hernandez and grandchild courtesy Alice Cooper.

Photograph of Paul Venzor, courtesy of Rozie Larson.

Photograph of Ted and Paul Herrera courtesy of Manuel Herrera.

Photographs of 1008 Chino Street, Hoover Field, Ted Williams Field, 33 relatives of Ted Williams, and Ted Williams 2002 are courtesy of Bill Nowlin.

Family gathering photographs courtesy Dee Allen.

Photograph of Ted and lifelong friends, 1991, courtesy of G. Jay Walker.

Photographs of display items at Hall of Champions courtesy of the San Diego Hall of Champions.

INDEX

This index does not attempt to include all the various
amateur or semi-pro teams for which Ted Williams played,
or which he opposed, nor to name all of the high schools
and high school teams which are included in the articles
in question.

Ted Williams

August 30, 1918 – July 5, 2002